keep,

ECONOMIC AND SOCIAL HISTORY OF BRITAIN

BRITAIN AND IRELAND 105

ECONOMIC AND SOCIAL HISTORY OF BRITAIN

General Editor: Martin Daunton

NOW AVAILABLE

Britain and Ireland 1050–1530: Economy and Society
Richard Britnell

Progress and Poverty: An Economic and Social History of Britain, 1700–1850
Martin Daunton

FORTHCOMING

Britain and Ireland 1500–1700: An Economic and Social History
Richard Hoyle

Wealth and Welfare: An Economic and Social History of Britain 1851–1951
Martin Daunton

An Economic and Social History of Britain since 1939
Stephen Tolliday

ECONOMIC AND SOCIAL HISTORY OF BRITAIN

Britain and Ireland 1050–1530

ECONOMY AND SOCIETY

Richard Britnell

OXFORD
UNIVERSITY PRESS

OXFORD

UNIVERSITY PRESS

Great Clarendon Street, Oxford OX2 6DP

Oxford University Press is a department of the University of Oxford.
It furthers the University's objective of excellence in research, scholarship,
and education by publishing worldwide in

Oxford New York

Auckland Bangkok Buenos Aires Cape Town Chennai
Dar es Salaam Delhi Hong Kong Istanbul Karachi Kolkata
Kuala Lumpur Madrid Melbourne Mexico City Mumbai Nairobi
São Paulo Shanghai Taipei Tokyo Toronto

Oxford is a registered trade mark of Oxford University Press
in the UK and in certain other countries

Published in the United States
by Oxford University Press Inc., New York

© Richard Britnell 2004

British Library Cataloguing in Publication Data
Data applied for

Library of Congress Cataloging in Publication Data
ISBN 0-19-873145-0

10 9 8 7 6 5 4 3 2 1

Typeset by RefineCatch Limited, Bungay, Suffolk
Printed in Great Britain on acid-free paper by
Ashford Colour Press Ltd, Gosport, Hampshire

GENERAL EDITOR'S PREFACE

The five volumes of the Economic and Social History of Britain series cover the millennium between the Norman Conquest and the opening of the twenty-first century. This was a period of immense change in Britain's economy and society, of central importance to wider transformations in the history of the world. Until the late eighteenth century, the balance between natural resources and population was finely drawn, with the limits of sustainability reached first in the early fourteenth and again in the early seventeenth centuries. But by the end of the eighteenth century, the population at last exceeded its earlier peak without a collapse into misery and death—and from the mid-nineteenth century both population and welfare moved to new levels. Britain pioneered a fundamental transformation of economic and social life, surpassing by the eighteenth century the levels of urbanization found in other European countries, shifting workers from the land in unprecedented numbers, and developing a highly sophisticated commercial society. Britain was also central to the emergence of a global economy, culminating in the free trade, liberal empire of the second half of the nineteenth century. This was followed by deglobalization in the 1920s and 1930s, and a tentative reconstruction of a global economy after 1945 under American leadership, before the resurgence of globalization in the last quarter of the twentieth century. The economic and social history of Britain is about much more than the insular history of a small European island.

The focus of the series is the development of the economy. The authors use the tools of economists in order to measure the performance of the economy, but they also turn to social, political and cultural history in order to understand how choice was actually driven, how and why collective action was achieved, and how population and resources were balanced. Economic history should work with cultural and social history in helping us to understand the meaning of economic relations. How, for example, were trust and reputation constructed to mitigate the risks of market exchange? Similarly, economic history should work with political history to appreciate the role of political action in distributing scarce resources and limiting the self-defeating pursuit of self-interest. And economic history should ally with intellectual history in order to elucidate the shifting understandings of political thinkers, social critics, and economists about market exchange and its implications for human relations.

Martin Daunton
June 2004

CONTENTS

CONCLUSION

LIST OF FIGURES

LIST OF TABLES

ACKNOWLEDGEMENTS

Parishes and townships of eastern Durham. By permission of Dr Helen Dunsford, University of Northumbria.

The cost of carrying wheat to London. From B. M. S. Campbell, J. A. Galloway, D. Keene and M. Murphy, *A Medieval Capital and its Grain Supply* (London, 1993), 61. Reproduced by permission of the authors.

England: presence of woodland, c. 730–1086. By permission of Professor Brian K. Roberts, University of Durham.

England: aspects of field systems. By permission of Professor Brian K. Roberts, University of Durham.

England: nucleations in the mid-nineteenth century. By permission of Professor Brian K. Roberts, University of Durham.

The fields of Clopton. From D. Hooke (ed.), *Anglo-Saxon Settlements* (Blackwell, 1988), 110. By permission of Blackwell Publishers.

Clerical taxes per square mile, 1291–2. From *Atlas of Scottish History to 1707* (Edinburgh, 1966), 300–1. By permission of the Scottish Medievalists and Department of Geography, University of Edinburgh.

A schematic representation of a multiple estate. From M. Aston, *Interpreting the Landscape: Landscape Archaeology and Local History* (London, 1985), 35. By permission of the author.

The shire of 'Cathermothel' in Perthshire. From G. W. S. Barrow, *The Kingdom of the Scots: Government, Church and Society from the Eleventh to the Fourteenth Century* (London, 1973), 48. By permission of the author.

The commote of Dindaethwy. From A. D. Carr, *Medieval Anglesey* (Llangefni, 1982), 157. By permission of the author.

Estimates of the English currency, 1158–1470. From M. A. Allen, 'The Volume of the English Currency, 1158–1470', *Economic History Review* 54 (2001), 608. By permission of the Economic History Society.

Hundred-penny fines and acquittances at Taunton. By permission of Dr Christopher Thornton, University of Essex.

The number of males aged twelve and over in High Easter and Great Waltham.
1250–1530. From L. R. Poos, 'The Rural Population of Essex in the Later Middle
Ages', *Economic History Review*, 2nd ser. 38 (1985), 522. By permission of the
Economic History Society.

An Index of Mill Numbers in the West Midlands, 1086–1500. From J. Langdon,
'Water-Mills and Windmills in the West Midlands, 1086–1500', *Economic
History Review* 44 (1991), 431. By permission of the Economic History
Society.

Long-term population trends, 1086–1525. From J. Hatcher, *Plague, Population and the
English Economy*, 1348–1530 (London, 1977), 71. By permission of the Economic
History Society.

Towns in Britain and Ireland, c.1100. From B. Harvey (ed.), *The Twelfth and Thirteenth
Centuries* (Oxford, 2001), 294–5.

Scottish burghs in existence by 1300. From *Atlas of Scottish History to 1707*
(Edinburgh, 1966), 198. By permission of the Scottish Medievalists and
Department of Geography, University of Edinburgh.

Grants of markets in England, 1200–1516. From S. Letters, 'Markets and Fairs in
Medieval England: A New Resource', in M. Prestwich, R. Britnell, and R. Frame
(eds.), *Thirteenth Century England IX* (Woodbridge, 2003), 216. By permission of the
author.

Grants of fairs in England, 1200–1516. From S. Letters, 'Markets and Fairs in
Medieval England: A New Resource', in M. Prestwich, R. Britnell, and R. Frame
(eds.), *Thirteenth Century England IX* (Woodbridge, 2003), 217. By permission of the
author.

The proliferation of English markets, 1000–1300. By permission of Dr Emilia
Jamroziak, Univesity of Edinburgh.

County Durham: distribution of common wastes in about 1600. From H. M.
Dunsford and S. J. Harris, 'Colonisation of the Wasteland in County Durham,
1100–1400', *Economic History Review* 56 (2003), 42. By permission of the
Economic History Society.

Landscape and settlement in Akeley. From R. Jones and M. Page, 'Medieval
Settlements and Landscapes in the Whittlewood Area: Interim Report, 2001–2',
Medieval Settlement Research Group: Annual Report, 16 (2001), 17–19. By permission of
the authors.

Scottish wool-producing monasteries. From *Atlas of Scottish History to 1707*
(Edinburgh, 1966), 237. By permission of the Scottish Medievalists and Department
of Geography, University of Edinburgh.

Harvests and prices, 1300–1330. From D. L. Farmer, 'Some Grain Price Movements in Thirteenth-Century England', *Economic History Review*, 2nd ser. 10 (1957), 217. By permission of the Economic History Review.

Decennial mean prices of wheat and oxen, 1160/1–1355/6. From D. L. Farmer, 'Prices and Wages', in H. E. Hallam (ed.), *The Agrarian History of England and Wales, vol. II: 1042–1350* (Cambridge, 1988), 719. By permission of Cambridge University Press.

Rates of duty on wool exports from England after 1275. From E. M. Carus-Wilson and O. Coleman, *England's Export Trade* (Oxford, 1963), 196.

English and Scottish wool exports, 1280–1600. By permission of Dr Martin Rorke.

English and Scottish woollen cloth exports, 1348–1600. By permission of Dr Martin Rorke.

English towns, 1377–1525: rates of population change. From A. Dyer, "Urban Decline" in England, 1377–1525', in T. R. Slater (ed.), *Towns in Decline* 283 (Aldershot, 2000). By permission of Dr Alan Dyer.

Seven-year moving averages of oxen, wheat, and labour prices. From D. L. Farmer, 'Prices and Wages, 1350–1500', in E. Miller (ed.), *The Agrarian History of England and Wales, vol. III: 1348–1500* (Cambridge, 1991), 437. By permission of Cambridge University Press.

An index of cereals output from Durham Priory parishes. By permission of Dr Benjamin Dodds, University of Durham.

'The comparative weight in silver of Scottish and English pounds, 1260–1500'. From A. Grant, *Independence and Nationhood, 1306–1469* (London, 1984), 240. By permission of the author.

Taxes on English lay property, 1207–1485. European State Finance Database, http://www.le.ac.uk/hi/bon/ESFDB/dir.html, Professor W. M. Ormrod, European State Finance Database, \orm\engg009

Taxes on English clerical property, 1272–1485. European State Finance Database, http://www.le.ac.uk/hi/bon/ESFDB/dir.html, Professor W. M. Ormrod, European State Finance Database, \orm\engg044

Taxes on English overseas trade, 1276–1485. European State Finance Database, http://www.le.ac.uk/hi/bon/ESFDB/dir.html, Professor W. M. Ormrod, European State Finance Database, \orm\engg049

Suppliers of King's Hall, Cambridge, 1450–1500. From J. S. Lee, 'The Trade of Fifteenth-Century Cambridge and its Region', in M. Hicks (ed.), *Revolution and Consumption in Late Medieval England* (Woodbridge, 2001), 133. By permission of the author.

Statistics in the various Tables presented in support of my arguments illustrate some of the huge advances in historical understanding of the last hundred years. The earliest, from the pioneering work of Frances Davenport, are nearly a century old (21.1 and 21.3). I owe data in other Tables to Mark Bailey (21.2), Anthony Bridbury (20.2), Bruce Campbell (9.2, 19.4 and 19.6), Bruce Campbell, James Galloway, Derek Keene and Margaret Murphy (1.1), Bruce Campbell and Mark Overton (19.5), Clifford Darby (11.1), Alan Dyer (6.1), Christopher Dyer (9.4 and 19.2), David Farmer (9.1), Eugene Kosminsky (8.2 and 9.3), Michael Lynch and Alexander Stevenson (20.3), Ambrose Raftis (206), Zvi Razi (4.2 and 8.3), Stuart Rigold (4.1), Martin Stephenson (20.1), and Keith Williams-Jones (10.2). I am also indebted to others for most of the maps and graphs supporting the text.

INTRODUCTION

In this study, I have two main objectives. One is to supply an introductory survey of British economic and social history between 1050 and 1530, registering the principal achievements of the last fifty years in improving our data and refining its analysis through discussion and debate. I hope that my treatment will be sufficiently approachable to interest students and other readers in finding out more about the topics covered in the book, sometimes all too briefly. The reading lists have been designed to enable readers to carry some topics much further than an introductory text like this can take them, and include numerous important items not referenced in the main text. I have also supplied, in the bibliographies for Chapters 13 and 23, details of original source material available in English. I hope that this will enable students interested in the period to find suitable topics for dissertations; the problem of finding translated source material has, in my experience, often driven students to later periods against their stronger inclinations.

My other objective is to integrate some of the main aspects of the economic and social history of Britain and Ireland between 1050 and 1530 into a more closely worked comparative analysis than anyone has so far attempted. This is not as straightforward as it sounds, since English, Welsh, Scottish, and Irish history have been generally treated as isolated topics with only intermittent dialogue between different national schools. There is also a great disparity in the amount of surviving evidence between these different countries. Documentation from Wales, Scotland, and Ireland can contribute relatively little to the quantification of population change or productivity that has been a major focus of English work over the past fifty years or more. The still ongoing precision with which we can understand events in Hampshire or Norfolk rides unevenly beside our almost total ignorance of circumstances in Sutherland and Donegal. Even descriptive aspects of the subject present problems, since many aspects of rural and urban institutional development are much less well understood for Scotland and Ireland, in particular, than for England.

Admittedly the best-documented parts of Britain and Ireland were the most heavily populated. Yet one of the purposes of linking the various parts of Britain in a single study ought to be to discuss how different regions with different resources and population levels related together, and whether there was any change in the integration of exchanges between them in the course of time. This exercise requires good evidence from different regions, and is severely hampered by the one-sided nature of our documentation. Because the disparity of archival material is such a prominent obstacle it deserves examination as a distinct historical problem, and I have tackled it head on in Chapters 13 and 23.

Despite problems of source material, the achievements of historians of the separate parts of Britain in developing the study of economic change have nevertheless been great. Economic and social history is, in general, a more specialized activity in England than elsewhere because of the abundance of sources, but a good deal of well-rounded and perceptive writing is to be found in the context of general histories and studies, such as the work of Geoffrey Barrow, Archie Duncan, Sandy Grant on Scotland, or Rees Davies on Wales. There is plenty of other good secondary material to work with in the economic history of these territories, even if some topics (such as urban development) have tended to be overworked relative to other important ones (such as rural development). Trying to put everything together has been a rewarding challenge. Looking over the fence is often a frustrating experience, but can be an exhilarating one.

I have tried to maintain a balanced view by holding back on English detail and using information from elsewhere generously. One way of maintaining this balance has been to concentrate on topics that can be discussed, to some extent, for all parts of Britain and Ireland. There are many aspects of economic change, such as landlord–tenant relations, the growth of towns, the use of money, the composition of overseas trade, that historians have discussed for all parts of Britain and Ireland, and on which a substantial literature exists; these are the obvious topics of comparative and interrelational history, at least at a first go. This approach implies resisting the appeal of some aspects of social and economic change that have generated recent research but that cannot be substantiated outside relatively restricted areas of England. I have nevertheless felt obliged to discuss some topics for which I have not found a way of developing a comparative approach, and in these passages I fear an English perspective is bound to be dominant. The final result is inevitably a compromise. I hope historians of Wales, Scotland, and Ireland will interpret my efforts as an honest attempt to enter into new discussion rather than as yet another English invasion of their territory.

Some explanation is perhaps required for the way I have constructed the exposition of economic and social development in each section of the book, starting with international trade and towns, and then moving towards rural affairs. International trade accounted for only a small part of the incomes of Britain and Ireland, and townsmen were a minority of the population, in most areas a small minority. To give them pride of place is, in this respect, to put the cart before the horse. However, my exposition is strongly geared (after the first three chapters) to examining what changed between 1050 and 1530 rather than what remained the same, and from this point of view the growth of towns and trade is the least ambiguous part of the overall picture. The examination of towns and trade illustrates some of the most interesting contrasts between different parts of Britain and Ireland. It helps, too, to understand some of the ways in which social and economic relations in the countryside were changing. My ordering of the material does not imply any wish to exaggerate the importance of commercialization, except insofar as this approach leads to a more dynamic interpretation of the economic achievements of the period 1050–1530 than the alternatives. It does not imply a wish to minimize the importance of population history or the dynamic of rural class relations as interrelated causes of change.

Reading from cover to cover is perhaps not the best way to approach a book of this kind. Chapters 1–4 are designed to provide a short course. Though more diffuse than later chapters, they contain many of the ideas developed later. Another way to introduce the subject would be through Chapters 4, 5, 15, and 25, a chronological overview followed by three separate period studies. Alternatively Chapters 4, 14, and 24 would make a chronologically orientated trio. For readers primarily interested in social history I should recommend Chapters 4, 7, 8, 17, and 18 as a way through, with 11 and 21 as the most appropriate supplementary reading. As the structure suggests, Chapters 5–14 and 15–24 can treated as separate studies for readers with interests particularly before or after 1300, but in all cases I'd suggest reading Chapter 4 first, because later chapters assume that the reader is aware of information it contains.

I owe many thanks to all those who have allowed me to include unpublished or recently published information from their unpublished researches, especially Ben Dodds, Emilia Jamroziak, Martin Rorke, and Christopher Thornton. I am also most grateful, too, to Martin Daunton and Sandy Grant, both of whom read an entire draft of the book and gave me extensive help with it. It is much better than it would have been without them. I am also pleased to take this opportunity to thank Durham University for awarding me a Christopherson fellowship in 1999–2000, a year during which I undertook basic library work and wrote an initial draft, to Clare Hall, Cambridge, for accommodating me for two terms of that year, and to the Arts and Humanities Research Board for an additional sabbatical term in 2003 in which to finish the project.

Preliminaries

....

CHAPTER I

Material Resources and Economic Constraints

Implicit in the concept of an economy is an awareness that constraints of resources, time, and knowledge limit the potential of human groups for happiness and prosperity. In the course of history certain of those constraints have been eased—and that is what constitutes economic development—but they are never removed, and often new ones are created in the process of change. That being so, it is important, before embarking on a discussion of Britain's economy between the eleventh and the sixteenth centuries, to survey the material restrictions on its potential for development. Economies before 1530 contrast with those of the present day in the much lower level of energy inputs available for productive use; they lacked the means for converting mineral fuels such as coal and oil into generating power mechanically. Apart from the solar energy required to ripen crops, an eleventh-century farmer, like Summerled of Bungay (Suffolk), with 40 acres of land in 1066, depended heavily on human labour for all productive tasks; he had the labour of four tenants and a slave to call upon besides his own exertions. The only other energy sources available to him were oxpower or horsepower for traction and water power for grinding his grain into flour; Summerled had his own plough team and a quarter share in a nearby mill.[1] Because animals required feeding their power was a further charge on agricultural resources, rather than something independently available, like coal. Because some of the constraints operating in the mid-eleventh century were modified over the following centuries, the period 1050–1530 can be described as one of modest economic development, and the evidence for this conclusion will need discussion and appreciation in due course. Yet because large parts of the framework within which development took place were already in place in 1050, and because much of it remained long afterwards, it will be helpful from the outset to consider this period in the long term. That implies pondering aspects of the past that changed slowly, even imperceptibly, but which defined the context in which more rapid change could occur.

The principal constraints on development may be separated for ease of exposition into three groups, though these are interconnected in complex ways. One, to be discussed in this chapter, includes the natural resources available to the inhabitants of Britain, together with their knowledge of how to exploit them productively. A second, to be discussed separately in Chapter 2, covers the range of social values and practices that regulated economic activities. A third group, reserved for Chapter 3, concerns the distribution of power and property. Some aspects of the more rapid course of change will be surveyed in Chapter 4.

Climate and Elevation

Of all the environmental influences on economic activity, the climate was the least susceptible to modification by human investment. That is not to say that it was unchanging; climatic fluctuations may help to explain aspects of agrarian development between 1050 and 1530.[2] Underlying them, though, was considerable continuity in the options open to English agriculture. The range of cultivated cereals was narrow even in drier parts of Britain. It included wheat and rye (both generally sown in October and November for harvesting the following August and September), with barley and oats (both generally sown in February and March for harvesting alongside the wheat and rye). Though writers and accountants made consistent distinctions between these cereals, and between the frequent mixtures that occurred when two cereals were sown together, they showed little discrimination between different strains of each grain. This was not because all the plants of a given cereal type were genetically identical. On the contrary, specimens surviving in medieval thatch imply that farmers sowed together a range of variants which they had no incentive to separate. Since different characteristics responded to different growing conditions, this amount of variation was probably advantageous to crop yields, though it meant that farmers had little choice just which strains of cereal to grow.[3] The favourite bread grain, for those who had access to it, was wheat, which was used to make the finest and more expensive types of bread. Throughout southern, midland, and eastern England, wheat cultivation often accounted for 40–50 per cent of the cropped acreage.

Minor climatic variations across Britain could nevertheless have major implications for agricultural productivity. The wetter climate of west-coast regions disadvantaged cereals farming because it increased the risk of crops being washed out of the ground. Wetness also complicated the tasks of handling cereals after they had been harvested. Even some very small settlements in Scotland had kilns for drying grain before it could be stored.[4] The growing season, too, was shorter in northern Britain; the chances of wheat ripening satisfactorily were poorer, so farmers either depended upon it less or did not attempt it. For these reasons, wheat was less suitable as a staple cereal in western and northern parts of Britain and Ireland than in the south and east. The Welsh consumed a lot of oats; in four commotes of North Wales assessed for the subsidy of 1292–3, taxation fell on 1,370 crannocks of oats as against only 443½ of wheat and 137 of barley.[5] Although Ireland was noted for its warmth, oats were the principal cereal in western parts most heavily soaked by rain from the Atlantic.[6] Oats were also the staple crop in Cumberland and Westmorland, though wheat and barley cultivation may have been relatively more practicable in the Eden Valley.[7] There was wheat in southern Scotland, but oats and barley (commonly the species of barley known as bere) were more important even there, and wheat cultivation became increasingly difficult north of the River Tay.[8] This meant that a traveller going from the English Midlands through to northern Scotland, or west into Wales and Ireland, found farmers sowing a narrower range of crops, employing more restricted crop rotations, and depending more on barley and oats for food. During the thirteenth century some new cropping schemes were devised, chiefly to incorporate the growing of peas, beans, and vetches as field crops,[9] but these developments, too, favoured farmers towards the south and east.

The climate determined that ale, made from malted oats or barley, was at all times the predominant home-produced beverage. But cider, now associated with south-western England, was made much more widely than today throughout southern Britain. The estates of Bec Abbey sold cider from as far north as Atherstone (Warwickshire), Bledlow (Buckinghamshire), and Weedon Beck (Northamptonshire). The earls of Cornwall in 1296–7 sold it from their manors of Watlington (Oxfordshire), Princes Risborough (Buckinghamshire), and Isleworth (Middlesex). It was widely produced on the bishop of Winchester's manors in Somerset, Hampshire, and Wiltshire, but also at Wargrave and Brightwell (Berkshire) and West Wycombe (Buckinghamshire).[10] Although some wine was made by some estate owners of south-eastern England in the eleventh and twelfth centuries, by the 1180s it was normally imported to all parts of Britain and Ireland from vineyards in warmer parts of western Europe.[11]

Because of the absence of vineyards and olive groves, the range of agrarian options, even in the richest parts of Britain, was narrower than in southern Europe. The unsuitability of the climate for olives meant that as elsewhere in northern Europe the main source of fats was of animal origin, whether butter, suet, or lard. Dairy farming was to be found throughout Britain, especially in hilly areas. But climate also favoured the quality of British wools, whose fineness depended partly on the coldness and wetness of the uplands to which native breeds had adapted. The early periods of British wool export are poorly documented, but from the early twelfth century there is evidence of its purchase for the textiles industry of northern France.[12] Wool exports remained a leading feature of British trade across the North Sea for over 300 years, supplemented in the thirteenth century, if not earlier, by additional exports from Ireland.[13]

Climatic contrasts were complemented by those of physical relief. The differences between the upland and lowland regions of Britain strongly influenced patterns of land use, since the poorer and more exposed soils of hills and mountains made extensive arable cultivation risky or impossible. Higher land that had either never been wooded, or had been cleared of woodland in prehistoric times, was usually heath, moor, or grassland that could be used for grazing livestock, or as a source of fuel. One of the early Viking earls of Orkney was called Turf-Einar because he was allegedly the first man to cut peat for fuel, either on the islands themselves or on the mainland at Tarbat Ness between Dornoch Firth and Moray Firth. His innovation is attributed to scarcity of firewood on the Orkneys.[14] There were large areas of natural heath and grassland even in southern and eastern uplands, as on Salisbury Plain, the Marlborough Downs, the Cotswolds, and the Chilterns, which were among the most important regions of England for commercial sheep farming. In much of Cumberland and Westmorland the moors were so vast that they dominated the landscape; settlements were characteristically separated from each other by hundreds of acres of rough grazing.[15] The most extensive pastoral parts of the country were in Scotland and Wales, especially on the many wide moorlands that have never allowed much arable husbandry during recorded history.

The north and the west depended on pasture farming both for subsistence and exchange. Gerald of Wales had observed that the Welsh population 'lives almost altogether from their herds, and on oats, milk, cheese and butter. They are used to abundant meat but not so much to bread.' Similarly, he observed that Ireland was 'more fertile in pastures than crops, in grass than grain', the balance of advantage there, too, being with cattle.[16] Milk and milk products—whey, soured milk, curds, butter, and both soft and hard cheese—were an essential component of everyday diet during the summer months, much more important than in the diet of English families.[17] The same could be said for much of Scotland. The chronicler John Fordun, writing in about the 1380s, described upland Scotland as being 'pastoral, with grazing for herds, and fine pasture along streams through the glens. The region,' he said, 'abounds in woolly sheep and horses; and its soil is grassy, feeds flocks and wild beasts, is rich in milk and wool.'[18] Cattle served as a standard measure of individual wealth, and because of their exceptional mobility cattle raiding was at all times one of the principal forms of conflict between rival kinship groups in Wales, Scotland, and Ireland, and in cross-border conflicts with the English.[19] In such regions livestock and pastoral produce was used to pay rents and taxes to kings, princes, and landlords, and so furnished kings themselves with a means of offering patronage and tribute. In 1169 Ruadrí Ua Conchobair, king of Connaught, endowed the cathedral school of Armagh with ten cows a year in perpetuity for teaching students of Ireland and Scotland. Six years later, under the Treaty of Windsor of 1175 with Henry II of England, he promised an annual tribute from his own land and that of others of a hide of merchantable quality from every tenth animal.[20]

Because of the harsh quality of much of the land, a smaller proportion of land is given up to arable farming in western and northern Britain and Ireland. In Scotland, for example, though the area of the kingdom was about half that of England and Wales, the area of arable land in the year 2000 was only about an eighth as large. The difference may have been even greater before the drainage operations of the eighteenth and nineteenth centuries.[21] These differences not only had implications for the daily life of the inhabitants, but also affected their number. Pasture farming employed many fewer people than arable farming on each acre of land. A lower proportion of the land under crops placed a lower ceiling on the number of families the land could feed, so that on average the upland and more pastoral regions had fewer inhabitants to the square mile than those with richer arable resources. Populations densities approaching 500 to the square mile are recorded from exceptionally fertile land in eastern Norfolk around 1300, and even the less fertile lands of central Essex could support 275–300 inhabitants to the square mile.[22] By contrast, five large and predominantly low-lying parishes in eastern Durham, whose boundaries now include the new town of Peterlee, are unlikely ever to have averaged more than 50 inhabitants to the square mile before the sixteenth century.[23] The population of Merioneth is unlikely ever to have exceeded 20 to the square mile.[24] On the outer edge of the world, pasture farming was of secondary importance to hunting and gathering, and numbers were correspondingly even more sparse. The *Chronicle of the Kings of Man and the Isles* compiled in the thirteenth century commented on Lewis that it was 'larger than the other islands, but it is occupied by few people because it is mountainous and rocky and almost all unfit for tillage. The inhabitants live mostly by hunting and fishing.'[25]

The wetter and higher parts of Britain are amongst the most weakly documented, and their archaeological record is too impoverished for fine analysis. People who lived there had practically nothing durable for an archaeologist to recover, and their houses were flimsy. Even the pottery record fails for cultures that used wooden utensils, like many in Wales, western Scotland, and Ireland before the thirteenth century. Poor evidence means that these regions receive less than their share of attention from historians charting the course of economic and social change. Though these western and northern economies supported lower densities of population than the more cereal-based agrarian regimes of southern Britain, their total population was considerable, and their economies developed in response to change elsewhere. They were affected to varying degrees by the commercial development of Europe because of their potential for supplying meat and dairy produce to more urbanized populations. Cattle, hides, and dairy produce became a primary medium for trade between northern and western Britain and lands further to the south and east. At the point where Scottish customs records begin, in the years 1327–32 the kingdom exported 35,100 hides a year.[26] Ireland, too, exported increasing volumes of hides and dairy produce to British ports from the twelfth century. The composition of the livestock farming changed over time with the growing impact of commerce. The importance of large-scale wool production in much of Wales and Scotland in recent centuries cannot be confidently pushed very far back; the emphasis of such early records as we possess is on cattle farming rather than sheep. Aberdeen was the most northerly port to export wool; virtually none left Inverness, Elgin, or Banff at any time before 1530.[27] But with the growth of long-distance trade between 1050 and 1300, sheep farming became a more attractive option in many more southerly pastoral regions, and during the twelfth and thirteenth centuries became an increasingly widespread feature of commercial development.[28]

Historians of Wales, Scotland, and Ireland have rightly resisted an exaggerated emphasis upon pastoral farming, just as, by contrast, English agrarian historians rightly resist an exaggerated emphasis on arable.[29] The populations of these wetter and higher regions depended for their daily nourishment upon cereals crops, and because they could not rely on long-distance trade for their supplies they grew locally what was needed. Most peasant farmers anywhere spent much of their time cultivating the land for grain. Nor was southern and midland England the only region to benefit from commercial cereals husbandry. During the thirteenth century eastern and southern Ireland, which had the best soils and was heavily occupied by the English, was also developed for commercial grain cultivation.[30] But recognizing the widespread importance of arable in daily life does not conflict with the notion of a real difference in the balance of farming types across Britain.

Of such differences in land use there can be no doubt. The proportion devoted to cereals showed a marked increase towards the east and south of Britain, where in many parishes over three-quarters of the land surface was designated ploughland. The jagged boundaries of many English parishes show that at the time they were determined the boundary had to be accommodated to existing ploughland (Figure 1.1). In northern and upland regions, by contrast, most townships had no more than a few hundred acres under regular cultivation attached to them, and the proportion of the land under crops was small in proportion to pasture and moor. A landscape of this kind could be seen in the Palatinate of Durham at any time between the eleventh and the sixteenth century, even around the eastern settlements from which moorland has now totally vanished (Figure 1.2).[31] It is

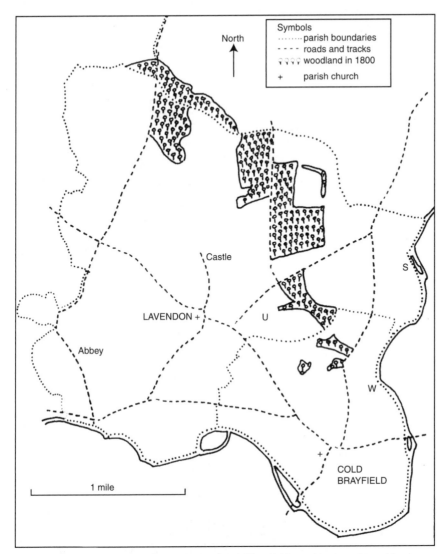

FIG. 1.1. The parish bounds of Lavendon and Cold Brayfield (Buckinghamshire). These two parishes are a wooded region, and the smooth lines of their bounds, partly following the River Ouse, owed much to the fact that they ran through wood and across untilled land. However the jagged line of the boundary between Lavendon and Cold Brayfield south of Lavendon church shows that when the parish division was made (perhaps in the twelfth century) it was drawn round the edge of furlongs in the adjoining open fields of the two parishes. This was a region of multiple manorial centres including Snelson (S), Uphoe (U), and Waterhall (W). Lavendon Castle was the head manor of the barony of Lavendon, whose lord founded the small Praemontratensian abbey nearby sometime in the later 1150s.

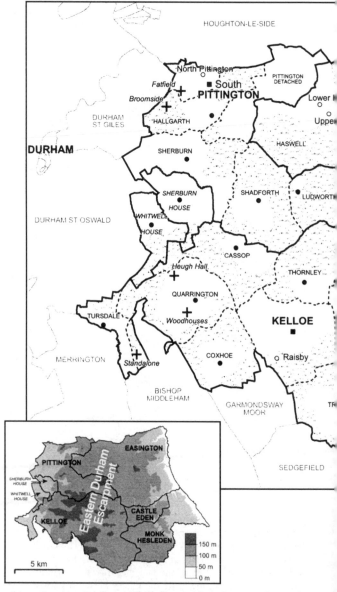

FIG. 1.2. Parishes and townships of eastern Durham. Of the five parishes shown, only Castle Eden corresponded to a single township; it had probably been separated off from Monk Hesledon parish at the instance of a member of the Brus family during the mid-twelfth century. Parish churches were much further apart than in the more densely populated parts of southern and midland England. The moorlands in this region remained extensive into

DALTON-LE-DALE

HAWTHORN

THORPE, LITTLE
DETACHED

*High
allowfield*

EASINGTON

Pesspool

THORPE, LITTLE

bisfield

*Horden
Hall*   HORDEN

Flemingfield

SHOTTON

Edder Acres

atley

Fulwell   Hardwick

MONK
HESLEDEN

CASTLE EDEN

North
Sea

HULAM

HUTTON
HENRY

HART

Hurwick

SHERATON

Sheraton
'Grange

Reddings

5 km

	PARISH TOWN	Reconstructed limits of waste - *c.* 1625
	TOWNSHIP VILL	
	Lost Township Vill	Parish Boundary
	Isolated Freehold	Mid 19th Century Township Boundary

modern times, but they were reduced between 1050 and the early fourteenth century, both
by the extension of township fields and by the creation of new farms, the isolated freeholds
shown on the map.

Source: Helen Dunsford (University of Northumbria).

unlikely that the cropped acreage of the Scottish Highlands in the thirteenth century was greater than in the eighteenth century, when cattle and sheep were preponderant even where every scrap of potential arable had been dug up to provide food for a growing population. In such areas the boundaries between townships were frequently defined by natural features of the landscape, such as rivers, streams, and watersheds, as characteristically in much of Scotland. Where boundaries ran through woodlands or across areas of open moorland they were often defined only loosely until modern times.

Location

The fact that Britain and Ireland are a collection of islands was significant for their economic fortunes insofar as the sea permitted cheap travel by ship and so encouraged particular lines of exchange over longer distances. Table 1.1 illustrates the cost of transporting bulky commodities by land, river, and sea in the London region around 1300, calculated from evidence relating to the carriage of wheat, but excluding handling charges. These comparisons suggest that it was over ten times more expensive to carry grain by land than by sea, and that the difference between land and river transport was almost as great. Waterways accordingly stimulated trade around the shores of Britain and into the interior along the major rivers. They enhanced not only the possibility of exporting produce and manufactures, but also the scope for more local, domestic trade. One consequence of this was the high concentration of urban populations in coastal areas and on principal estuaries, especially along the east and south coasts, rather than in the centre, where towns

TABLE 1.1. *Transport costs in the London region, c.1300* (pence)

	Per ton-mile	Per tonne-kilometre
By land		
In Essex and Hertfordshire	1.85	1.14
In other parts of the London region	1.27	0.78
By river		
Upstream (Faversham to London)	0.16	0.10
Downstream (Abingdon to London)	0.17	0.10
Downstream (Henley to London)	0.13	0.08
By sea	0.10	0.06

Source: Bruce M. S. Campbell, James A. Galloway, Derek Keene, and Margaret Murphy, *A Medieval Capital and its Grain Supply: Agrarian Production and Distribution in the London Region c.1300* (London, 1993), 196.

rarely grew to more than modest size. Figure 1.3 shows how coastal and river systems shaped the cost of feeding London around 1300, showing that it was cheaper to supply grain from Great Yarmouth than it was from parts of Surrey and Hertfordshire. Edinburgh, Dublin, Norwich, and York, though all near rich agricultural land, were also located on or near navigable rivers that contributed much to their development. The costs of transport affected how much trade was profitable, and this in turn affected the extent to which local economies became integrated into wider systems of specialization and interdependence.

The opportunities for trade around the shores of Britain and Ireland varied greatly, despite the advantages of an extended coastline. Indeed, their location on the western seaboard of Europe added another layer of geographical determinism to the structure of internal diversity, to patterns of trade, and consequently to the range of economic opportunities. Flanders and northern France were amongst Europe's most urbanized and highly monetized regions, and consequently important markets for exports, but the resulting opportunities for mercantile enterprise were unevenly distributed because of differential transport costs. Foreign trade benefited regions nearest the Continent, so that England south and east of a line from Exeter to York remained much more urbanized than the rest of Britain, even though there were many new developments beyond that line. At the high point of England's commercial development around 1300, London was the only city in Britain that could compare with the great trading centres of northern Italy and northern France. York and Edinburgh did not reach the size that their considerable environmental assets would have permitted in a more favourable context.

By 1200 there was a string of seaports along the eastern and southern coasts of Britain from Aberdeen in the north-east to Plymouth in the south-west. Britain's peripheral situation worked strongly against urban growth in the west and north. Apart from Bristol, Chester, and Dublin, which handled trade across the Irish Sea, as well as some trade with France and southern Europe, there were no major ports on the west side of Britain until the seventeenth century. In 1367 the leading three out of thirty-four Scottish burghs, to judge from their tax assessments, were Edinburgh, Aberdeen, and Perth, all on the east coast. The wealthiest burgh on the west coast, Irvine, ranked twelfth.[32] Before the development of transatlantic trade, Ireland and the west coast of Britain were on the very edge of Eurasian trade routes, and this affected their capacity for mercantile development despite the possibilities for local specialization around the Irish Sea.

This aspect of geographical location complemented the agrarian advantages of southern and eastern England, and was an additional reason for the greater commercial development of the southern and eastern parts of Britain. Quite apart from markets overseas, urban growth meant that there was more economic

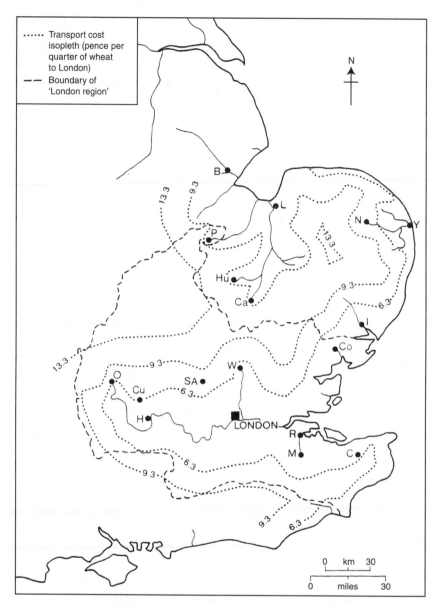

FIG. 1.3. The cost of carrying wheat to London from within southern and eastern England, c.1300. The cost in pence, by the cheapest available means, is represented by isopleth lines. So, for example, from Cuxham it would cost 6.3 pence, and from Henley on Thames, within that isopleth line, it would cost less. The evidence illustrates how lower transaction costs favoured trade by sea or river transport. The letters represent the following places: B, Boston; C, Canterbury; Co, Colchester; Cu, Cuxham; H, Henley-on-Thames; Hu, Huntingdon; I, Ipswich; L, Lynn; M, Maidstone; N, Norwich; O, Oxford; P, Peterborough; R, Rochester; SA, St Albans; W, Ware; Y, Yarmouth.

Source: B. M. S. Campbell, J. A. Galloway, D. Keene and M. Murphy, *A Medieval Capital and its Grain Supply* (1993), 61.

interdependence between towns and villages in south-eastern England than there could be in Wales or Ireland. The most advanced regions of English agriculture by 1300 were all near the east coast—Holderness in Yorkshire, eastern Norfolk, eastern Kent. Although this owes something to the local qualities of their soils, the unique advantage of these regions lay in the relative cheapness with which they could supply a large number of different markets. The more commercial wool-growing regions were widely scattered, and included parts of Wales, the Lake District, and the Scottish borders. Even so, the wool trade mostly benefited the Cotswolds, Lincolnshire, Berwickshire, and the Lothians. Ireland was able to expand its trade in pastoral products to Britain, but chiefly from east-coast regions. Britain's marginal location is relevant for interpreting the distribution of income and wealth at any time between 1050 and 1530.

Natural Endowments and Inherited Structures

British and Irish writers were generally complacent in comparing their resources with those of their neighbours on all sides. Reliable statistical comparisons were, and remain, difficult, so that any comments on this subject were inevitably based on selected indicators with a strong admixture of prejudice. The *litterati* who composed these set pieces followed older writers to a degree that casts doubt on their authors' perceptiveness. The enthusiastic description of Britain by Henry of Huntingdon, writing in the 1120s, following closely that of Bede four centuries earlier, refers to rich resources of arable, woodland, pasture, water, fish and other wildlife, and also mentions mineral deposits of iron, tin, lead, and silver.[33] Geoffrey of Monmouth, whose inventive *History of the Kings of Britain* was probably completed in 1138, followed an even earlier author, Gildas, to much the same effect.[34] Literary conservatism, however, was justified by continuities in real experience. These borrowed lists would have been just as appropriate for the early sixteenth century, and represent very long-term perceptions of Britain's assets. Some resources noted by these authors, such as deposits of coal (particularly those on north-eastern England), and of tin (particularly those of Devon and Cornwall), were little exploited commercially in the eleventh century but were to become important sources of employment and income later on. Increased fishing, especially from the sea, helped to sustain food supplies as population increased through the twelfth and thirteenth centuries. Nor was high fertility uniquely claimed for lands in more commercialized regions. Gerald of Wales commented on the rich pastures of Snowdonia and the fertile soils of Anglesey, though he praised the superior charm of the plains and coastlands of Dyfed.[35] Fordun, while recognizing the wildness of much of Scotland, commented that the coastal lands were fertile and suited to the cultivation of wheat, barley, beans, and peas, as well as having lush pastures.

Even the uplands, suitable only for sowing oats and barley, abounded with cattle, sheep, and horses. He quoted Herodotus (as he thought) to the effect that Scotland's fertility and pleasantness were not inferior to that of Britain (by which he meant England).[36] At an early date Ireland, too, attracted attention for its fertility. Messengers returning from Ireland to King Magnus of Norway in 1103 'told him of the geography of Ireland and its beauty, of the abundance of its crops and of its healthy climate'.[37] Gerald of Wales was similarly alert to the fertility of Irish soils, despite his comments on the adverse climatic conditions that favoured pasture farming.[38] It was for this richness, and the economic potential it implied, that outsiders were so resolute in invading Ireland and settling there after 1169.

Britain's natural endowments of land, climate, and location, were of lasting significance for the shaping of agriculture, trade, and urban life. When we come to look more closely at the way the land was occupied, however, it is a tricky matter to separate these natural endowments from the legacy left by the island's past inhabitants. The landscape had been shaped by human settlement for at least 5,000 years before the beginning of our period, ever since the first farmers began clearing away the forest cover, and there had been times in the past—notably in the second century AD—when many parts of the land had supported as many inhabitants as in 1050.[39] Few parts of Britain could then be thought of as virgin territory. By that time England was no more wooded than modern France, and the rest of Britain and Ireland had been stripped of much of the forest they had once possessed.[40] In Scotland, following extensive deforestation in prehistoric times, Anglo-Saxon settlers had further cleared large areas of the deciduous forests of Berwickshire, Roxburghshire, Dumfriesshire, and the Lothians.[41] Ireland had probably no more forest cover than England; although arable cultivation expanded rapidly there between 1170 and 1300 there is little evidence of extensive deforestation.[42] Woodland was accordingly a valued asset, and little of what survived was really waste, especially in the more populous areas; Domesday Book makes it plain that English woods were used for grazing, and that must have altered their wildwood character and composition. Woodland was also valued for timber (to make beams and planks) and for wood and underwood (for making poles and rods, and for fuel), and this encouraged active forestry on the part of landlords to protect trees from damage and to ensure that the right kinds of material remained available.

Any consideration of Britain's geographical endowments has therefore to take account of the many centuries of past history through which they had been moulded. In some cases past exploitation of the land had worked irreparable damage to natural resources by allowing soils to erode. Prehistoric farming methods had denuded territories that were never subsequently capable of depending upon arable husbandry, as on parts of Dartmoor, or in the East Anglian Brecklands, which had been heavily populated by early farming communities of the Neolithic period. However, the legacy from the past does not deserve to be left with a negative assessment. The labour of former generations had cleared forest land for cultivation, constructed boundaries, pioneered systems of cultivation and cropping, and discovered some of the more easily worked mineral resources. This legacy was most deep-rooted in areas of densest settlement, most extensive arable husbandry, and most complex property divisions, where some boundaries and other surface features of the landscape preserved the forms of prehistoric occupation of the land. From at least the Bronze Age, farmers had made divisions with banks and ditches, and modern observation has amply demonstrated the capacity of such features to survive through time. Long, winding field boundaries originating in the Bronze Age are identifiable in parts of both Devon and Suffolk.[43] To this day it is possible to find fields bisected by Roman roads in such a way as to suggest that their boundaries were already there when the road was first laid.[44] The roads constructed by the Romans were of particular importance as lasting assets, waiting to be revived as busy thoroughfares in the twelfth and thirteenth centuries. Many of Scotland's highways capable of supporting wagons and carts had originated long before England and Scotland could be described as separate realms; they, too, were partly of Roman origin.[45]

In regions of lighter population, on uplands, away from the more commercially active parts of Britain, changes brought about in recent times have often been barely perceptible. The best chance of seeing scenery that has changed little in the past thousand years is on the open moors of Wales, Scotland, and south-western and northern England. This continuity is strikingly attested on the Lizard peninsula in Cornwall, where the boundary marks of a tenth-century charter depend for their usefulness on the visibility that open moorland still offers.[46] Any clearing of woods in regions such as these was prehistoric and catastrophic; the character of the land had been permanently altered and its range of future possibilities drastically circumscribed. Although some such landscapes produce evidence of later cultivation, their more characteristic use has been as rough grazing.

There are many areas of more diversified land use, greater tenurial complexity, and less historical continuity where the legacy of past settlement nevertheless remains visible in archaic patterns of fields and small, scattered settlements, often interspersed with above-average acreages of wood and pasture. They are mostly regions where the available arable was broken up by ancient woodlands, heaths, or hill country (Figures 1.4 and 1.6). Such patterns of settlement are characteristic of Cornwall and Devon, Wales and Scotland. Some of these complex regions, like Essex, or northern and western Worcestershire, were distinctive for large numbers of enclosed fields from the time of our earliest records concerning them.[47] Even in quite densely wooded parts of Britain there are regions of light settlement that

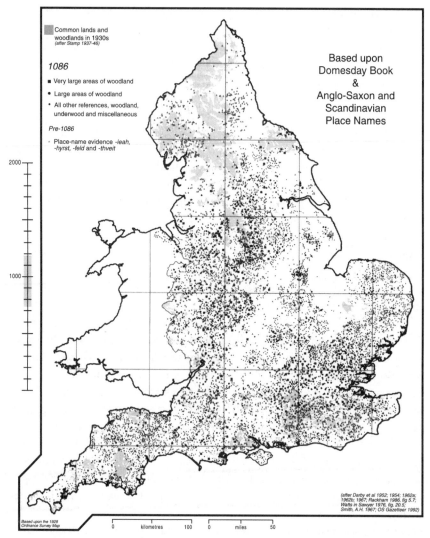

Common lands and
woodlands in 1930s
(after Stamp 1937-46)

1086

■ Very large areas of woodland

● Large areas of woodland

· All other references, woodland,
underwood and miscellaneous

Pre-1086

· Place-name evidence *-leah,*
-hyrst, -feld and *-thveit*

Based upon
Domesday Book
&
Anglo-Saxon and
Scandinavian
Place Names

(after Darby et al 1952; 1954; 1962a;
1962b; 1967; Rackham 1986. fig 5.7;
Watts in Sawyer 1976, fig. 20.5;
Smith, A.H. 1967; OS Gazetteer 1992)

Based upon the 1928
Ordnance Survey Map

0   kilometres   100   0   miles   50

FIG. 1.4. England: presence of woodland, c.730–1086. The evidence of Domesday Book (1086) is here supplemented with place-name and other evidence. Britain was more heavily wooded in the eleventh century than in modern times, though heavy clearances in previous centuries had considerably reduced the wooded area in many parts. High concentrations of nucleated settlement corresponded closely to areas of ancient forest clearance. Woodlands were a valuable resource of pasture, but lands to the west of the midland belt were characteristically more heavily pastoral than the more mixed farming regimes to the east.

Source: B. K. Roberts, 'Of *Æcertyning*', *Durham Archaeological Journal*, 14–15 (1999), 94.

have retained some of their ancient character, with small settlements and scattered farms.[48] These features are widespread in parts of rural East Anglia, Essex, and Kent, whose landscapes, though much altered in detail, are more likely than areas of large nucleated settlement to preserve traces of ancient field patterns.

Past practices inevitably affected current possibilities. Nevertheless, this study opens towards the end of a period of major importance in the recreation of rural landscapes when in many parts older settlement patterns were being vigorously transformed, even if the precise features of the transition, and its chronology, are difficult to perceive from what evidence survives. The main features of this reconstruction demanded greater cooperation between families than in the past, and so had implications for the direction of social change. The landscapes still undergoing the most radical transformation in the eleventh century were those in a belt stretching north-eastwards from Dorset to the East Riding of Yorkshire on the western side (Figure 1.5). This is the region that Oliver Rackham describes as 'planned countryside'.[49] Already by 1050 this central area of England was less wooded than the lands to either side, and the arable area was here less broken up with trees and hedges than any other part of Britain. These characteristics were reinforced from the late Saxon period onwards by two parallel features of change. The inhabitants here showed a stronger tendency than elsewhere in Britain to build their houses and cottages in central nucleated settlements, and so to create a landscape of villages rather than of scattered farms and hamlets—a feature of the region still prominent in the mid-nineteenth century (Figure 1.6). At the same time they also showed a greater propensity to cooperate in the management of their fields to secure a mutually advantageous system of common rights over extensive tracts of arable land. The reasons for this distinct development are obscure. It was not, to judge from the evidence of Domesday Book, that this part of Britain was more crowded than elsewhere, since many of the highest population densities were outside it in East Anglia, Kent, and Somerset. It seems, rather, that the generally poorer provision of woods, heaths, and grasslands inherited from earlier times was creating exceptionally severe problems in the management of livestock as population increased. Great upheaval was involved in these changes—as great as that caused by the enclosure movement of the eighteenth and nineteenth centuries. The fact that there are hardly any echoes of this development in surviving charters (which are exceedingly numerous from the twelfth century onwards) implies that it had passed its peak by 1100.

Although most clearly marked in this central region of England, agrarian organization in other populous parts of Britain and Ireland frequently moved in the same direction, even if restrained by greater abundance of pasture, or alternative ways of combining arable and livestock husbandry. No hard and fast distinction is possible between 'open' and 'enclosed' or 'forest' regions'. Nucleated villages

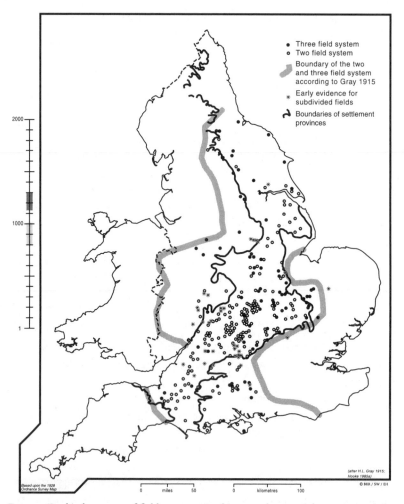

Fig. 1.5. England: aspects of field systems. In this map the area where two- and three-field systems prevailed is compared with the area of highly nucleated settlement patterns (for which see Figure 1.6). It demonstrates that this common-field region excludes some of the most densely populated parts of England to the east as well as some of the least densely populated and more pastoral regions to the west.

Source: B. K. Roberts and S. Wrathmell, *Region and Place: A Study of English Rural Settlement* (2002), 124.

and large unenclosed fields became numerous throughout much of Britain and Ireland outside the English Midlands, and there was widespread shift towards more cooperative patterns of field management. In northern England and Scotland south of the River Forth there is abundant evidence of the development of nucleated

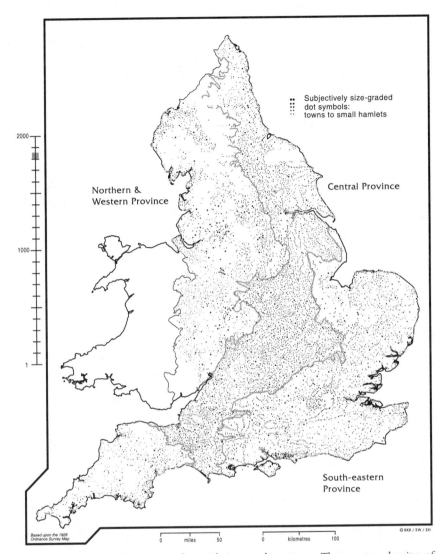

Fig. 1.6. England: nucleations in the mid-nineteenth century. The greater density of nucleated villages in a central belt of England stretching from Dorset in the south to Northumberland in the north is a long-standing feature of settlement patterns. Deserted villages are also more numerous in this belt, which corresponds partly, though not exactly, with the region of two-and three-field systems shown in Figure 1.5.

Source: B. K. Roberts and S. Wrathmell, *Region and Place: A Study of English Rural Settlement* (2002), 5.

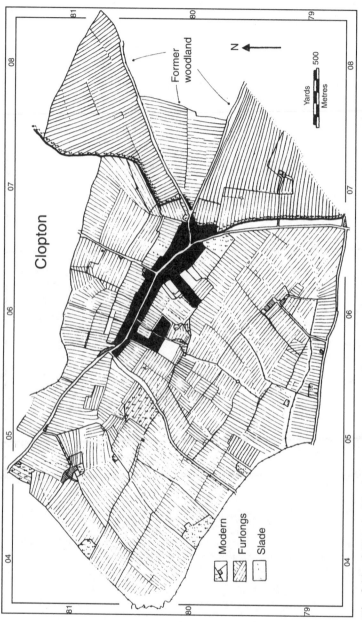

Fig. 1.7. The fields of Clopton (Northamptonshire). Strips of demesne and tenant lands were interspersed in the separate furlongs in the village fields. The oldest arable lay north, south, and east of the village. The land to the west, structured in longer strips, and with less definite furlongs, was assarted from the forest, probably by the late eleventh century.

Source: D. Hall, 'The Late Saxon Countryside: Villages and their Fields', in D. Hooke (ed.), *Anglo-Saxon Settlements* (Oxford, 1988), 110.

settlement continuing well after 1050, and these settlements, too, often had large open tracts of arable land in which individual holdings were intermixed.[50] In Wales and Ireland the extension of Anglo-Norman lordship was often associated with the transformation of settlements in similar ways.[51] Even in regions away from the midlands open-field pattern there was often commoning between villagers. In East Anglia there were nucleated settlements without common fields of the midland type; instead of a single common field they devised various ways of commoning on smaller units of land.[52] In none of these alternative systems was the rotation of crops, and the integration of pasturing on fallow land, so closely regulated as in the midland system. Some of them, in fact, had the advantage of a flexibility that the midlands lacked. The midland common-field belt was not conspicuous as a region of high productivity, and in the course of time institutional rigidity there may have hampered investment and productivity growth.[53]

Britain and Ireland shared in many respects the cultural traditions of their continental neighbours, so that economic and social development between 1050 and 1530 corresponded to parallel changes elsewhere in Europe as details in a broader picture. The growth of trade networks, in particular, inevitably implied co-operation in many ways with merchants and governments in Scandinavia, the Baltic, the Low Countries, France, and Spain, and affected the way commercial institutions evolved. Nevertheless, Britain and Ireland had their own particular resource constraints that shaped what their role in that broader context would be. For this reason, geographical endowments, as modified by many past generations, will figure prominently in the chapters that follow.

NOTES

1. Domesday Book, ii, fo. 300[v].
2. See below (Ch. 4).
3. J. Letts, 'Living under a Medieval Field', *British Archaeology*, 58 (2001), 12.
4. A. Gibson, 'Medieval Corn-Drying Kilns at Capo, Kincardineshire, and Abercairny, Perthshire', *Proceedings of the Society of Antiquaries of Scotland*, 118 (1989), 219–29; D. Pollock, 'The Lunan Valley Project: Medieval Rural Settlement in Angus', ibid., 115 (1985), 363–8; P. A. Yeoman, 'Medieval Rural Settlement: The Invisible Centuries', in W. S. Hanson and E. A. Slater (eds.), *Scottish Archaeology: New Perceptions* (Aberdeen, 1991), 118.
5. *The Merioneth Lay Subsidy Roll, 1292–3*, ed. K. Williams-Jones (Cardiff, 1976), cxiv. The crannock in this case was equivalent to four standard London bushels (i.e. about 146 litres): ibid., xiv (note).
6. A. T. Lucas, 'Irish Food before the Potato', *Gwerin*, 3/2 (1960), 9.
7. E. Miller, 'Farming Practice and Techniques: The Northern Border', in id. (ed.), *The Agrarian History of England and Wales*, iii: *1348–1500* (Cambridge, 1991), 177.
8. A. A. M. Duncan, *Scotland: The Making of the Kingdom* (Edinburgh, 1989), 322–3.

9. B. M. S. Campbell, 'Agricultural Progress in Medieval England: Some Evidence from Eastern Norfolk', *Economic History Review*, 2nd ser. 36 (1983), 31–3; id., 'The Diffusion of Vetches in Medieval England', *Economic History Review*, 2nd ser. 41 (1988), 193–208. See below (Ch. 9).

10. 'Computus Rolls of the English Lands of the Abbey of Bec', ed. M. Chibnall, in *Camden Miscellany XXIX*, Camden 4th ser. 34 (1987), 19, 34, 67, 99; *Ministers' Accounts of the Earldom of Cornwall, 1296–1297*, ed. L. M. Midgley, 2 vols., Camden Society, 3rd ser. 66, 67 (1942–5), i. 2, 40, 85; *The Pipe Roll of the Bishopric of Winchester, 1301–2*, ed. and trans. M. Page (Winchester, 1996), 161, 168, 174, 181, 193, 196, 200.

11. For vineyards in 1086, see H. C. Darby, *Domesday England* (Cambridge, 1977), 275–7. For wine imports to Ireland, see Gerald of Wales, 'Topographica Hibernica', I. vi: *Giraldi Cambrensis Opera*, ed. J. S. Brewer and J. F. Dimock, 8 vols., Rolls Ser. 21 (1861–91), v. 28.

12. E. Power, *The Wool Trade in English Medieval History* (1941), 52–3.

13. W. Childs and T. O'Neill, 'Overseas Trade', in A. Cosgrove (ed.), *A New History of Ireland*, ii: *Medieval Ireland, 1169–1534* (Oxford, 1987), 498–500.

14. *Heimskringla: History of the Kings of Norway*, trans. L. M. Hollander (Austin, 1964), 82; *Orkneyinga Saga: The History of the Earls of Norway*, trans. H. Pálsson and P. Edwards (Harmondsworth, 1981), 29.

15. A. J. L. Winchester, *Landscape and Society in Medieval Cumbria* (Edinburgh, 1987), 81–92.

16. Gerald of Wales, 'Descriptio Kambriae', I. viii, and 'Topographica Hibernica', I. v: *Opera*, v. 26; vi. 179–80; R. E. Glasscock, 'Land and People, c.1300', in Cosgrove (ed), *New History of Ireland*, ii. 205–6.

17. Lucas, 'Irish Food', 19–30.

18. *Johannis de Fordun Chronica Gentis Scotorum*, ed. W. F. Skene (Edinburgh, 1871), 41.

19. e.g. B. Smith, *Colonisation and Conquest in Medieval Ireland: The English in Louth, 1170–1330* (Cambridge, 1999), 54, 81, 85–6, 99, 123, 147–8; G. W. S. Barrow, *Robert Bruce and the Community of the Realm of Scotland*, 2nd edn. (Edinburgh, 1976), 282, 337.

20. *Early Sources of Scottish History, A.D. 500 to 1286*, ed. A. O. Anderson, 2 vols., new edn. (Stamford, 1990), i. 267; M. T. Flanagan, *Irish Society, Anglo-Norman Settlers, Angevin Kingship: Interactions in Ireland in the Late Twelfth Century* (Oxford, 1989), 212, 235, 240–1; Smith, *Colonisation and Conquest*, 54, 83.

21. A. Grant, *Independence and Nationhood: Scotland, 1306–1469* (1984), 62.

22. B. M. S. Campbell, 'Population Pressure, Inheritance and the Land Market in a Peasant Community', in R. M. Smith (ed.), *Land, Kinship and Life Cycle* (Cambridge, 1984), 92; R. M. Smith, 'Human Resources', in G. Astill and A. Grant (eds.), *The Countryside of Medieval England* (Oxford, 1988), 198.

23. R. H. Britnell, 'Fields, Farms and Sun-Division in a Moorland Region, 1100–1400', *Agricultural History Review*, 52 (2004), 23–4.

24. *Merioneth Lay Subsidy Roll*, xli–xlii.

25. *Cronica Regum Mannie et Insularum*, ed. and trans. G. Broderick, 2nd edn. (Douglas, 1995), fo. 41ᵛ.

26. Grant, *Independence and Nationhood*, 236.

27. P. G. B. McNeill and H. L. MacQueen (eds.), *Atlas of Scottish History to 1707* (Edinburgh, 1996), 251–2.

28. See below (Ch. 10).

29. Lucas, 'Irish Food', 9–11.

30. H. Jäger, 'Land Use in Medieval Ireland: A Review of the Documentary Evidence', *Irish Economic and Social History*, 10 (1983), 64.

31. H. M. Dunsford and S. J. Harris, 'Colonization of the Wasteland in County Durham, 1100–1400', *Economic History Review*, 56 (2003), 34–48.

32. T. M. Devine and G. Jackson, *Glasgow*, i: *Beginnings to 1830* (Manchester, 1995), 28.

33. Henry of Huntingdon, *Historia Anglorum*, ed. and trans. D. Greenway (Oxford, 1996), 10–11.

34. *The Historia Regum Britannie of Geoffrey of Monmouth*, i: *Bern, Burgerbibliothek, MS 568*, ed. N. Wright (Cambridge, 1984), pp xvi, 2.

35. Gerald of Wales, 'Descriptio Kambriae', I. v, vi: *Opera*, vi. 170, 176–7.

36. *Johannis de Fordun Chronica*, 41. See pp. 35–7 for the distinction between Scotland and Britain.

37. *Cronica Regum Mannie et Insularum*, fo. 35^r.

38. Gerald of Wales, 'Topographica Hibernica', I. v: *Opera*, v. 26.

39. A recent estimate puts the population of Roman Britain at 3.665 million: M. Millett, *The Romanization of Britain: An Essay in Archaeological Interpretation* (Cambridge, 1990), 185.

40. O. Rackham, *Trees and Woodland in the British Landscape: The Complete History of Britain's Trees, Woods and Hedgerows*, rev. edn. (1990), 28–38, 53–4.

41. M. L. Anderson, *A History of Scottish Forestry*, ed. C. J. Taylor, 2 vols. (1967), i. 82–3.

42. Gerald of Wales, 'Topographica Hibernica', I. iv: *Opera*, v. 26; Glasscock, 'Land and People', 209; Rackham, *Trees and Woodland*, 88; O. Rackham, *The History of the Countryside*, 2nd edn. (1997), 112–13.

43. Rackham, *History of the Countryside*, 72, 156–61; id., *Trees and Woodland*, 35, 45, 48–50.

44. S. Oosthuizen, 'Prehistoric Fields into Medieval Furlongs? Evidence from Caxton, Cambridgeshire', *Proceedings of the Cambridge Antiquarian Society*, 86 (1997), 145–42.

45. G. W. S. Barrow, 'Land Routes', in id., *Scotland and its Neighbours in the Middle Ages* (London, 1992), 207–8.

46. Rackham, *History of the Countryside*, 309–10.

47. C. Dyer, *Lords and Peasants in a Changing Society: The Estates of the Bishopric of Worcester, 680–1540* (Cambridge, 1980), 26; R. H. Britnell, 'Agriculture in a Region of Ancient Enclosure, 1185–1500', *Nottingham Medieval Studies*, 27 (1983), 37–55.

48. F. W. Maitland, *Domesday Book and Beyond* (Cambridge, 1897), 15.

49. Rackham, *History of the Countryside*, 3.

50. G. W. S. Barrow, 'Rural Settlement in Central and Eastern Scotland: The Medieval Evidence', *Scottish Studies*, 6 (1962), 124–6; B. K. Roberts, *The Green Villages of County Durham* (Durham, 1977).

51. M. Davies, 'Field Systems of South Wales', in A. R. H. Baker and R. A. Butlin (eds.), *Studies in Field Systems in the British Isles* (Cambridge, 1973), 480–529; J. Otway-Ruthven, 'The Organization of Anglo-Irish Agriculture in the Middle Ages', *Journal of the Royal Society of Antiquaries of Ireland*, 81 (1951), 1–9.

52. R. H. Britnell, 'Farming Practice and Techniques: Eastern England', in Miller (ed.), *Agrarian History*, iii. 200–2.

53. R. L. Hopcroft, 'The Social Origins of Agrarian Change in Late Medieval England', *American Journal of Sociology*, 99 (1994), 1559–95.

FURTHER READING

Aalen, F. H. A., Whelan, K., and Stout, M., *Atlas of the Irish Rural Landscape* (Cork, 1997).

Anderson, M. L., *A History of Scottish Forestry*, ed. C. J. Taylor, 2 vols. (1967).

Ashley, W., *The Bread of our Forefathers: An Inquiry in Economic History* (Oxford, 1928).

Astill, G., and Grant, A. (eds.), *The Countryside of Medieval England* (Oxford, 1988).

Aston, A., *Interpreting the Landscape: Landscape Archaeology and Local History* (1985).

—— and Lewis, C. (eds.), *The Medieval Landscape of Wessex* (Oxford, 1994).

Atherden, M. A., and Butlin, R. A. (eds.), *Woodland in the Landscape: Past and Future Perspectives* (Leeds, 1999).

Baker, A. R. H., and Butlin, R. A. (eds.), *Studies of Field Systems in the British Isles* (Cambridge, 1973).

Bailey, M., 'The Concept of the Margin in Medieval English Economy', *Economic History Review*, 2nd ser., 42 (1989).

Barrow, G. W. S., 'Rural Settlement in Central and Eastern Scotland: The Medieval Evidence', *Scottish Studies*, 6 (1962).

Campbell, B. M. S., 'England: Land and People', in S. H. Rigby (ed.), *A Companion to Britain in the Later Middle Ages* (Oxford, 2003).

—— Galloway, J. A., Keene, D., and Murphy, M., *A Medieval Capital and its Grain Supply: Agrarian Production and Distribution in the London Region c.1300* (London, 1993).

Chibnall, A. C., *Sherington: Fiefs and Fields of a Buckinghamshire Village* (Cambridge, 1965).

Coones, P., and Patten, J., *The Penguin Guide to the Landscape of England and Wales* (Harmondsworth, 1986).

Cosgrove, A. (ed.), *A New History of Ireland*, ii: *Medieval Ireland, 1169–1534* (Oxford, 1987).

Darby, H. C., *Domesday England* (Cambridge, 1977).

Dodgshon, R. A., *Land and Society in Early Scotland* (Oxford, 1981).

—— *The Origin of British Fields Systems: An Interpretation* (1980).

—— and Butlin, R. A. (eds.), *An Historical Geography of England and Wales*, 2nd edn. (1990).

Duncan, A. A. M., *Scotland: The Making of the Kingdom* (Edinburgh, 1989).

Edwards, N. (ed.), *Landscape and Settlement in Medieval Wales* (Oxford, 1997).

Flanagan, M. T., *Irish Society, Anglo-Norman Settlers, Angevin Kingship: Interactions in Ireland in the Late Twelfth Century* (Oxford, 1989).

Fox, H. S. A., 'Approaches to the Adoption of the Midland System', in T. Rowley (ed.), *The Origins of Open Field Agriculture* (1981).

Gelling, M., and Cole, A., *The Landscape of Place-Names* (Stamford, 2000).

Grant, A., *Independence and Nationhood: Scotland, 1306–1469* (1984).

Gray, H. L., *English Field Systems* (Cambridge, Mass., 1915).

Hamerow, H. F., 'Settlement and the "Middle Saxon Shift": Rural Settlement and Settlement Patterns in Anglo-Saxon England', *Anglo-Saxon England*, 20 (1991).

Hopcroft, R. L., 'The Social Origins of Agrarian Change in Late Medieval England', *American Journal of Sociology*, 99 (1994).

Jäger, H., 'Land Use in Medieval Ireland: A Review of the Documentary Evidence', *Irish Economic and Social History*, 10 (1983).

Jones, E. T., 'River Navigation in Medieval England', *Journal of Historical Geography*, 26 (2000).

Le Roy Ladurie, E., *Histoire du climat depuis l'an mil*, 2 vols. (Paris, 1983).

Letts, J., 'Living under a Medieval Field', *British Archaeology*, 58 (2001).

Lucas, A. T., 'Irish Food before the Potato', *Gwerin*, 3/2 (1960).

McCloskey, D. N., 'English Open Fields as Behavior towards Risk', in P. Uselding (ed.), *Research in Economic History: A Research Annual*, i (Greenwich, Conn., 1976).

Maitland, F. W., *Domesday Book and Beyond* (Cambridge, 1897).

Miller, E. (ed.), *Agrarian History of England and Wales*, iii: *1348–1500* (Cambridge, 1991).

Parry, M., and Slater, T. R. (eds.), *The Making of the Scottish Countryside* (1980).

Power, E., *The Wool Trade in English Medieval History* (1941).

Rackham, O., *The History of the Countryside*, 2nd edn. (1997).

—— *Trees and Woodland in the British Landscape: The Complete History of Britain's Trees, Woods and Hedgerows*, rev. edn. (1990).

Rippon, S., *The Severn Estuary: Landscape Evolution and Wetland Reclamation* (1997).

Roberts, B. K., *Rural Settlements in Britain* (Folkstone, 1977).

—— and Wrathmell, S., *Region and Place: A Study of English Rural Settlement* (2002).

Room, A., *The Penguin Dictionary of British Place Names* (2003).

Smith, B., *Colonisation and Conquest in Medieval Ireland: The English in Louth, 1170–1330* (Cambridge, 1999).

Taylor, C., *Village and Farmstead: A History of Rural Settlement in England* (1983).

Witney, K. P., *The Jutish Forest: A Study of the Weald of Kent from 450 to 1380 AD* (1976).

....

CHAPTER 2

Culture and Economic Constraints

*E*ven if rational economic calculation, in some sense, is common to all men, there have been contrasts both between and within societies concerning what is worth doing. There have been differences in the extent to which people quantify the results of their activity and learn from the past. In different societies, too, there have been variations in the extent to which social institutions have encouraged or inhibited change. These differences have coincided to some extent with those of religion and education, social status, and ethnic identity. The beliefs and allegiances of the period 1050–1530 were sufficiently unlike those of our own day to deserve some discussion from this point of view.

Religion

Of all the cultural traditions relevant to economic and social activity, none was more characteristic of this period than the complex of religious practices and beliefs that made up Latin Christianity. The inhabitants of Britain and Ireland belonged to one of the most tightly organized religious structures, for its size, that the world has ever known. And whereas today economic activity depends on businessmen who maximize profits as the primary goal of their daily activity, even seeing this as a public duty, Catholic Europe lacked professional groups with this distinctive ethic. Even within the wealthiest social ranks, private beliefs and public institutions tended rather to curb the pursuit of profits, and to some extent inhibited the accumulation of property. The most relevant of private beliefs in this context related to the rewards and punishments that a Christian could expect after death. Because giving property to the Church counted as a good deed, a larger proportion of total wealth was committed to pious causes before 1500 than since. During the eleventh and twelfth centuries individual donations as large as whole manors, or whole townships, were made both to the older Benedictine monasteries and to new orders such as those of the Augustinian and Premonstratensian canons and Cistercian monks. To take a Scottish example, Margaret of Hungary, Malcolm III's queen, began a monastic revival with a Benedictine abbey at Dunfermline in about 1070, and vast acreages were transferred to newer orders during the following century. King David I (1124–53) advanced the status and wealth of Dunfermline Abbey and, both as king and earlier, benefited several religious orders as the founder of abbeys at Cambuskenneth, Holm Cultram, Holyrood, Jedburgh, Kinloss, Melrose, Newbattle, and Selkirk (later moved to Kelso), as well as priories at Lesmahagow and St Andrews.[1] Numerous other patrons also endowed Scottish religious houses, and their many donations of land transformed patterns of landownership in some regions, such as the Tweed Valley.[2] Many similar examples could be supplied from the history of the endowment of Cistercian and Premonstratensian abbeys in England, Wales, and Ireland during the twelfth century. From the later twelfth century large gifts became less common, but an increasing number of less wealthy donors made small gifts of land, property, or annual income.

From the twelfth century the Church formulated more precisely the doctrine of Purgatory, a place where the penalty due for sin might be expiated by suffering after death. Release of the souls of the dead from the pains of Purgatory was believed to be expedited by the prayers of the living.[3] This doctrine, once generally adopted, encouraged investment in payments for prayers for the dead even amongst quite ordinary townsmen and villagers. To the extent that planning for heaven crowded out or deterred the accumulation of earthly treasures, it operated to inhibit the sort of economic progress associated with capitalism and modern economic growth.

Another matter of possible significance for economic development is the victimization and suppression of minority religions. There have been two principal ways of explaining the association of Protestant doctrine with business success in more recent times. Some sociologists, Max Weber for example, have emphasized the 'work ethic' associated with certain Protestant and post-Protestant beliefs. Another line of thought emphasizes the sociological consequences of belonging to a tolerated but self-supporting minority religious group. Jews constituted the only group that could approximate to these latter circumstances in the period 1050–1500. They were admitted to English towns by William I in the late eleventh century, though they never established communities in Wales, Scotland, or Ireland, and they prospered particularly in the twelfth century, benefiting commercially from their alien status and royal protection. Alien status was, however, a mixed blessing. Eventually they were so ruthlessly exploited by thirteenth-century monarchs that their business was ruined, and they were eventually expelled from England in 1290.[4] No other minority religious group was ever tolerated; the nearest equivalent would have been the ethic of an ascetic and well-structured religious order, such as the Cistercians.

Between 1050 and 1530 a new economic morality was derived from, and contributed to, the regulation of public markets. It was assumed that there was a clash of interests between private 'greed' and the interests of local or national communities. In this spirit markets were regulated, weights and measures checked, and quality standards imposed. The relationship between these measures and comparable modern regulations is complex. Some were clearly beneficial, but others were of more questionable value. For example, local officers almost everywhere in fourteenth- and fifteenth-century Britain were expected to punish would-be monopolists who bought up food on its way to market 'thirsting for evil profit', an offence known as forestalling.[5] This legislation was criticized in 1776 by the Scottish economist Adam Smith as the basis for prejudices comparable to 'the popular terrors and suspicions of witchcraft'.[6] It is far from obvious that the problem with this legislation was the principles it represented, rather than the manner in which it was enforced. The extent of such legal intervention in the period before 1530 was tiny in comparison with the bulk of modern legislation relating to fair trade, which rests on the same assumption that market exchange requires a legally structured context. The arbitrariness with which these laws were applied may, nevertheless, have inhibited commercial enterprise in some circumstances.

However, the extent to which the absence of a positive capitalist ethic hampered worldly accumulation is difficult to assess, and this very fact argues against leaning upon it heavily. There was no universal set of behavioural norms. Nor did beliefs and practices preclude the avid pursuit of commercial gain or the accumulation of wealth. There was plenty of debate concerning the implications of Christianity for economic activity. Observation of the way people actually behaved reveals the same contrasts between ascetic, altruistic, and acquisitive ethics, or between anti-capitalist and capitalist values, as we are used to in our own society. We also have to reckon with the commonplace observation that in economic matters peoples' actions may be at variance with their formal values. Bishop Wulfstan II of Worcester (1062–95) built a new cathedral for his diocese, but wept over the worldly vanity and loss of spiritual values that it expressed.[7] Conflicts between ideals and reality are implied in sermons, chronicles, tales, and in many a lawsuit. They are commonly found in criticisms of worldly churchmen, as in William of Malmesbury's extended obituary of Roger, bishop of Salisbury, though William also comments on the hypocrisy of some who envied his prosperity.[8] The effect of Christian ethics on individual economic behaviour was selective rather than universal, so that the range of acquisitive and non-acquisitive mentalities was a wide one. The fact that modern business ethics were less ostentatiously promoted and less prevalent in the past does not imply any clean break in the values by which individuals conduct their affairs from day to day. The accumulation of money and property is, after all, intrinsically suspect among many groups in modern societies.

The urge to accumulate is not a distinctively modern one, nor even one particularly associated with commercialization. Gerald of Wales thought that greed for
the possession of land was a particular vice of the Welsh.[9] The secular estates of
established families were more affected by successes and failures of political judge-
ment than ecclesiastical ones, and purchases and sales were generally of secondary
importance, but amongst those rising in status acquisitive instincts were rife. Some
of the most successful accumulators of the fourteenth and fifteenth centuries were
lawyers, like Thomas Tropenell (d. 1488), who accumulated properties in Wiltshire
and Gloucester.[10] There is ample evidence, too, of the pursuit of wealth in the
service of God. Monasteries not only induced landed families to donate property
but also used their savings to buy land. The twelfth-century abbots of Battle Abbey
bought land at Bodiam and built up the new manor of Barnhorn through a
combination of purchases and land reclamation.[11] If religious values did not
inhibit laymen or churchmen from accumulating property, it is difficult to see why
they should have inhibited them from investments that would have promoted
productivity growth and economic development. If investment levels were
characteristically low, it is not obvious that religion is to blame.

The period 1050–1530, in fact, was one in which a merchant culture emerged
in British towns, as elsewhere in Europe. The development of mercantile norms
in the sixteenth and seventeenth centuries modified a way of life and a set of
practices already created during the preceding three or four centuries. Assessing
risks and calculating income had many implications for the development of formal
rationality in everyday life.[12] The leading merchants, at least, had to keep regular
reckonings of their business affairs, and had to be alert to rapid changes in the
market. 'The reckoning will be better now every day', wrote George Cely to his
father on 23 November 1478, 'for money is amended in Flanders 2s. 6d. in an
pound.'[13] Despite the prohibition of usury, which was a characteristic of commercial ethics, there were many developments in credit institutions between
the twelfth and the sixteenth centuries.[14] Much of the credit visible in twelfth and
thirteenth-century records involved Jewish lenders, many of whose records are
preserved in the English royal archive. But by no means all lenders were Jews. In the
thirteenth century landowners were selling wool on credit to Italian merchants and
borrowing large sums to advance their building programmes.[15] Commercial credit
mechanisms depend on trust, which in turn depends upon a certain regularity of
operations. The necessary conditions for merchants to develop a credit system with
formal documentation and procedures for the recovery of unpaid debts matured
from the later thirteenth century. From that time lending and borrowing were a
normal and necessary feature of commerce, even if interest in its modern form was
avoided.[16] The ledgers of Gilbert Maghfield, a London merchant who imported
iron, dyestuffs, wine, and fish, and exported cloth, show that in the early 1390s

over three-quarters of his merchandise was sold on credit rather than for cash, and that he himself regularly bought on credit.[17] Some merchants at all periods, like Godric of Finchale in the early twelfth century, abandoned trade in their later years and adopted a more contemplative lifestyle, but this was not altogether different from modern retirement, even if differently interpreted. William of Malmesbury was willing enough to welcome Sæwulf, a pious merchant, who became a monk only when he was too old and ill to do much else.[18]

Credit relations were not confined to urban contexts. By 1300 it was common for villagers to be borrowing from neighbours if they were sufficiently creditworthy. Some historians of rural society have stressed the role of credit simply as a means whereby the poor could get by in hard times, when work was hard to get, for example, and food was dear. It is doubtful, however, to what extent the poor could borrow except on the security of their very meagre property. More characteristically, borrowers were people who had capital. In normal circumstances lenders and borrowers came from the same groups within village society. Villagers borrowed money in order to improve their position in various ways—to buy land or livestock, for example. Characteristically, and especially in difficult times for the poor, wealthier peasants would borrow to buy land from their less fortunate neighbours. Some land transfers at Hinderclay (Suffolk) in the 1290s were apparently made in settlement of debts.[19]

As this implies, suspicion of acquisitiveness did not promote egalitarian restraint. On the contrary, wealth was even less equally distributed than it is today. It was administered primarily in the interests of private institutions or individuals. Every church, every monastery had its own endowment, and monasteries often sued each other over property rights, just like their secular neighbours. The property of ordinary villagers, too, was held privately, and there were great differences in wealth between cottagers and the landlords or wealthier peasants who employed them as agricultural labourers.[20] Even the use of common lands was defined by individual rights. Status distinctions were everywhere apparent, even within village society, in housing, dress, and diet. Great lords all through the period were ostentatious with their wealth.[21] It is worth stressing this point only because some writers have supposed that contemporary ethics compelled rich men to feel guilty. Nothing could be further from the truth.

Status

Another aspect of culture that affected the goals of economic activity was the cultural tradition of elite families owning large properties, who had the greatest potential for investment in economic development. Neither the epic tales to which people of this background were attracted in the eleventh and early twelfth centuries, nor the romances that came into vogue from then on, inspire confidence in the economic rationality of the culture that produced them. The ideals of the landed elite had many elements militating against saving and investment. Their menfolk were trained for military activity, which carried financial as well as physical risks. As late as the sixteenth century the nobility supplied military leadership, even though the days were long passed when knights were expected to perform military service merely as a condition of their tenure. King James IV personally led his army into war against England in 1513, and he and half the Scottish nobility perished at the disastrous battle of Flodden. Henry VIII's invasion of France in 1523 was led by his brother-in-law, the duke of Suffolk. In addition, maintaining a high social status could undermine financial prudence, since dress, display, and the demands of hospitality were all matters for close observation. Many a landlord was compelled to mortgage property or to sell it to more fortunate contemporaries, often to a religious house, in order to maintain his status. Waltham Abbey acquired the manor of Stanstead in the early 1180s, when the heir, Michael de Wanchy, could not redeem it from a mortgage his father had contracted with a London Jew.[22] Wealthy men were ever the prey of moneylenders and lawyers.

The records they have left nevertheless demonstrate that many property owners of all kinds administered their estates with a high degree of rational deliberation, either personally or through a team of councillors and estate officers. Nothing in the culture of thirteenth-century landlords debarred them from commercial activity. Knights and gentry in south-western England even described themselves as merchants during the 1330s, when they engaged in trade under the stimulus of debt.[23] Military values could be combined with the painstaking accumulation and administration of property. Sir John Fastolf, who made a career in the war in France under Henry V and Henry VI, was an assiduous purchaser of property back home in England, and was outstanding for the way he developed his estates to yield high incomes. He also owned ships with which he traded directly both along the east coast and between England and France.[24] Shipowning was quite common amongst both secular and ecclesiastical nobility; among the largest ships to dock at Sluis in Burgundy in 1464 was a Scottish vessel of 500 tons belonging to the bishop of St Andrews.[25]

Landlords wanting to maintain a lifestyle befitting their dignity needed cash. They therefore did their best to establish an adequate monetary circulation, particularly in regions where coinage was hard to obtain. Much of the enterprise relevant to economic development was undertaken for these reasons. Landlords founded new towns all over Britain between the eleventh and thirteenth centuries, often in association with their manors and castles.[26] When English lords like Theobald Walter acquired Irish estates they reconstructed them in order to exploit their commercial potential, often taking steps to provide settlements for immigrants from England and Wales.[27] The development of Wales involved similar active policies of estate improvement; 'an economy of plunder was being replaced by an economy of profiteering'.[28] Scottish lords introduced English and Flemish settlers in the process of creating new villages, some of which are called Ingleston ('English settlement'); there are examples in Midlothian and Forfar as well as in the south-west.[29] Lords also built water mills, and pioneered the introduction of wind-mills from the late twelfth century. By 1300 there were perhaps 10,000 mills in England, mostly attached to the portion of their estates that lords administered directly. The frequency with which Scottish lords had established mills by this time is attested by the numbers that are mentioned in charters.[30] Again, from the thirteenth century onwards, lords also built fulling mills for the needs of the cloth industry. Especially after the fall off in grain milling after the Black Death, they often converted mills to this new purpose.[31]

Emphasis on the conservative implications of the cultural values of the landed elite also undervalues the activities of men and women from other social ranks. In the day-to-day management of property landlords were responsible for only a subordinate part of total output. Even in midland England less than a third of the land was demesne land subject to direct seigniorial control in the 1270s.[32] In individual townships elsewhere the proportion might be as high or higher—in Coldingham Abbey's township of Old Cambus (Clackmannan), 35 per cent of the arable was in the direct control of the monks[33]—but the share in peasant hands was usually larger.[34] And though landlords supervised the way their property was managed, detailed decisions about what to produce, how to produce it, and how to dispose of it were taken by lessees or estate officials, who were often from peasant backgrounds. Though landlords were responsible for founding and managing towns, they were rarely responsible for any decisions concerning manu-facturing output, technique, or trade. At Castle Combe (Wiltshire) the flourishing textile industry of the early fifteenth century was nurtured by Sir John Fastolf's wartime purchases, and his renewal of the market charter, but the coordination of cloth production and the construction of fulling mills were the responsibility of clothiers and fullers.[35] Even around 1300, less than a quarter of annual British output of goods and services was directly controlled by landlords.

Custom

The power of custom was undoubtedly one of the principal obstacles to economic individualism in earlier periods of development. It was the simplest means of administering property in a relatively non-commercial and preliterate age. The distinction between different grades of tenant status is a very complex matter, to which we shall return, but in a great number of instances there were elements of traditional restraint on what landlords and peasants could expect as rights and obligations. Tenants who held land without contract or charter, such as the thirteenth-century 'rustics' (*rustici*) or 'natives' (*nativi*) of England, Wales, and Scotland, or the 'betaghs' of Ireland, were governed by tradition subject to wide local variation, rather than by common law or written contract.[36] The extent to which custom approximated to law, and gave the tenant positive rights, varied over time and place; in fifteenth-century England it was stronger than it had been in the eleventh century, though it affected a smaller proportion of tenants. It was always, it seems, appreciably stronger in England than in Scotland, where tenures were generally more precarious. The strength of peasant rights in England can be regarded as one of the most distinctive features of rural society, one of the principal sources of English individualism in later centuries.[37] Nevertheless, even some Scottish tenants without formal rights, who held by 'kindly tenure', could in practice expect some customary recognition of their status.[38]

Custom ran strongly counter to the modern ethic of change for change's sake, but it was not, in fact, a fixed body of regulations. It changed in different directions in different parts of Britain and Ireland, and for different reasons. In Wales and Ireland local customs were heavily modified, amongst other things, by conquest and the imposition of new populations governed by new practices. In England and Scotland there was no such external challenge, but custom took a different direction in each. In Scotland lords retained a greater control over their lands, and increasingly, so it seems, replaced older forms of tenure by leasehold. In England custom became more entrenched and better defended in the course of time. In neither kingdom was the situation static. The tendency for custom to change can be illustrated best from England. The procedures involved in its enforcement were continuously modified in parallel with procedural changes in the king's courts.[39] In addition, customary terms of tenure were liable to change. For example, comparison of records from different years shows that when land was scarce landlords were able to increase the amount of 'customary' labour services owed to them.[40] By contrast, when lords were no longer able to exert their former control over the land market after 1349, labour services generally diminished.[41] In practice custom was often an obstacle to the power of landlords as well as on the independence of their tenants. Because of the protection custom offered, for example, most English customary tenants were paying rents below the equivalent of a full commercial rent at a time when land was most scarce in the later thirteenth century.[42]

Custom constrained social change in many ways. For example, it determined aspects of land use. Common pastures, a widespread feature of British farming even in the most commercialized parts, could only be ploughed or developed in other ways with the agreement of those concerned; they were a frequent source of conflict between neighbours.[43] Even among the freemen of towns there were customary constraints on the use of resources such as commons, woods, and waterways. In such ways, custom could hamper the ability of institutions to respond to changing circumstances in the short term.

As this implies, where it operated custom supplied an ethic that resisted change, favoured a conservative attitude to many economic institutions, and acted to slow down the possibilities of innovation. Although a matter of degree rather than of absolute contrast, it was undoubtedly a more powerful force than in the modern world. On the other hand, as we have seen, the evidence shows clearly that there was no time when it was not shifting and evolving.

Ethnic Identity

Anglo-Saxon and English culture, especially as modified by the Norman Conquest of 1066, has been represented as innovative, individualistic, and alert to commercial opportunity. Celtic populations, by contrast, have often been characterized—not least by their own historians—as traditional in their attachment to family, community, and other non-individualistic and non-commercial values. Gerald of Wales described the Irish as committed only to leisure and pleasure.[44] The primary criterion for identifying the different cultures in question is linguistic, but since the relationship between language divisions and other institutional and geographical divisions was a complex one throughout our period of enquiry, it requires some care to identify the unities they are intended to define and the reality of the barriers they represented.

The linguistic divide between regions of Celtic and English speech in the mid-eleventh century can be approximately known from the distribution of place names recorded in early sources. Languages of the Celtic group prevailed through a very large part of Britain and throughout Ireland, though the different branches had evolved so independently that they were not mutually intelligible. The biggest gulf was between the Brittonic and Goidelic Celts, of which the former prevailed in Cornwall and Wales and the latter in Ireland. Scotland was divided between the two branches; although Gaelic Scotland represents invasions of Goidelic Celts from the west, a large part of underlying Scottish culture derived from the Picts, who were probably Brittonic Celts. In Scotland the distribution of common indicative place-name elements such as *baile* (meaning village or hamlet, as in Balbeg, Balgown, and Balfour) or *achadh* (meaning field, as in Auchairn, Auchmore, and Auchintoul), imply that in the eleventh century much of the kingdom was Gaelic speaking. However, there were also predominantly English-speaking populations in the south-east, between the Firth of Forth and the Tweed.[45] In England (except Cornwall) the dominant speech was the group of dialects known as Anglo-Saxon or Old English. Characteristic and universal English place-name elements were *tun* and *ham*, both of which have a wide range of significance but imply a small rural settlement of some kind.

A subordinate linguistic tradition, from the late eighth century onwards, derived from the Norse impact on Orkney, Shetland, most of Caithness, the Hebrides, and much of the western and north-western coast of Scotland. Norse migrants had also been responsible for the earliest development of town life in Ireland. By the later eleventh century, however, Celtic and Norse cultures were merging in a distinctively violent manner of conducting their affairs in the region of the Irish Sea and western Scotland. In England, too, but in a more peaceful context, the culture of the Norse population was by this time becoming integrated with that of their neighbours, though it left a lasting mark on local dialects and rural institutions.

Patterns of conquest and settlement between 1050 and 1300 modified and complicated this division between Celtic and Germanic language groups both by shifts in linguistic boundaries (resulting from migration) and through linguistic interpenetration and bilingualism. The movement of settlers from England into Scotland, Wales, and Ireland brought about an extensive enlargement of anglo-phone territory between the late eleventh and thirteenth centuries. As in eastern Germany in the same period, when Germanic institutions were imposed upon those of the native Slav population, linguistic change stands in a complex relation-ship to social and economic development. Migration into and within Scotland had been a feature of linguistic change long before 1050, but the following 450 years saw greatly extended migrations of this kind northwards and westwards, step by step pushing the frontiers of Gaelic towards the Highland line. English place names began appearing in the south-western counties, the central belt, and the east-coast margin by the later twelfth century, and in some instances Gaelic place names were replaced by English ones.[46] In Ireland, though the great majority of place names remained Gaelic, these were interspersed with some new names of English origin, often ending in 'town', like Thomastown (Kilkenny), Roachtown (Meath), and Laurencetown (Galway).[47]

A further change in cultural tradition occurred in the century after 1066 with the establishment in Britain of a small but politically dominant French-speaking population. The Norman Conquest represents a case of linguistic penetration without a linguistic boundary shift. Parts of Britain acquired a French-speaking aristocracy, but unlike the earlier Viking settlement, and unlike English expansion northwards and westwards, the Normans were not followed by large numbers of peasant migrants. French language and tradition were long cultivated amongst elite social groups and their impact on language and high culture was a major one. The French, too, had some impact on place names, mostly through the imposition of proprietorial family surnames, as in Newton Longville or Newton Blossomville (Buckinghamshire), Newton Ferrers and Newton Tracey (Devon), but such names are much less common outside England. Few changes were as deliberate as that of an estate in eastern Essex from the English Fulepet ('dirty hole') to the French Beaumont ('fair hill').[48] Even new towns and villages were rarely named in French. But in any case, during the twelfth century insular and Norman cultural traditions became so fused at the highest level of society that it became impossible to separate them. For this reason it is feasible to proceed in terms of a single, socially stratified tradition, with reference where necessary to the ways in which practices were modified by Normans.

Lands with Celtic traditions were far from uniform in their laws and customs. In Wales the control and distribution of land was the chief aspect of lordship, whereas in Ireland lordship over freemen worked usually through grants of cattle by the lord and reciprocal annual tributes of livestock from the tenant.[49] However, there were undoubtedly some distinctive features of Celtic tradition, especially affecting families and family rights. Welsh inheritance customs required that on the death of a freeman without a son the family tree was scanned back as far as his great-grandfather, and that the third cousins of the deceased had a right to inherit if there was no closer heir. Kinsmen as far away as agnatic third cousins could also veto the alienation of land belonging to the kindred. In the commote of Cymeirch, as late as 1334, it was the custom that a son paid his lord a fine of 10s. on inheriting a free tenement, that a brother or nephew paid £1, and that 'beyond the third degree they have no claims to inherit, but the land is an escheat at the lord's will'.[50] There were similar provisions in early Irish law, and probably there was once a similar custom among the elite of Gaelic Scotland. The customs of Ireland, Wales, and Scotland had evolved differently, but they stemmed from a common tradition, and there were real points of contrast between Celtic and English cultural tradition.[51]

Concern with the rights of male kin was closely associated with other features of Celtic tradition that operated to restrict the legal claims of women. Wales, Ireland, and perhaps Gaelic Scotland retained customs relating to sexual union, marriage, and the legitimacy of children that were being transformed elsewhere in western Europe in accordance with ecclesiastical law. Men had considerably more discretion than the Church allowed elsewhere, much to the scandal of severely critical arch-bishops of Canterbury. Divorce was relatively easy. Amongst the wealthier elites concubinage was socially accepted, and in Wales men were able to legitimize the children of irregular liaisons by a practice known as cynnwys. These freer customs relating to legitimacy were associated with a more restrictive attitude to the inheritance of property by women.[52] Women in England, and in most of Scotland, were unambiguously able to claim property as heiresses, or by right of marriage, or as the recipient of gifts, but in Wales, Ireland, and Gaelic Scotland women were only rarely allowed to be landowners.

In most respects, however, cultural explanations of differences between English and Celtic economies cannot hold out against environmental ones. Gerald of Wales asserted that the Welsh neglected trade, ships, and industry, and that they did not live in towns and villages but lived in isolated woodlands. He presents this as a matter of habit and preference.[53] Yet a more obvious interpretation of the sparseness of settlement in Wales in the twelfth century (a characteristic it shared with northern England at that time) is the unsuitability of most of its soils for supporting a dense population and its distance from major trade routes. Since the boroughs had been built by Anglo-Norman invaders partly as a way of building up the non-Welsh population, it is hardly surprising that Welsh burgesses were not predominant.

Another ethnic explanation of doubtful validity concerns settlement patterns and field systems. At one time historians assigned to Celtic tradition a landscape of hamlets, and other forms of dispersed settlement, with a distinctive pattern of small enclosed fields. By contrast, areas of Anglo-Saxon settlement were held to be characterized by compact villages with extensive open fields. Settlers from northern Germany in the fifth and sixth centuries were said to have founded compact villages (often named after themselves), in the process replacing older Celtic fields with new common fields of a type they had known back home. As Chapter 1 has explained, however, nucleated villages multiplied long after the original Anglo-Saxon settlement for essentially utilitarian reasons. In fact, similar changes were taking place in lands of Celtic speech, even if the final outcome was different in detail. Systems of intermixed holdings, known in Scotland as runrig and in Ireland as rundale, are to be explained by the same agrarian principle that account for subdivided fields in England or elsewhere in Europe.[54] The first documented rigs in Scottish fields can be traced back only as far as 1200, and were created presumably through the remodelling of older holdings.[55] Ancient boundaries to be observed in the western Highlands, as at the former settlements of Soriby on the island of Ulva and Kendram on Skye, show runrig, perhaps of the thirteenth century, superimposed upon earlier enclosed fields.[56] The contrast in the scale between midland field systems and these Celtic parallels is satisfactorily explained by a different disposition of arable and pasture resources, and consequently the different size of settlements, rather than by differences of cultural inheritance.

The pastoral traditions of the Celts are similarly inseparable from the landscape they inhabited, much of which was better suited to pasture than to arable. The English conquest of Ireland in 1169–72 was indeed associated with the rapid expansion of commercial grain husbandry over the following century. By contrast, during the fourteenth century the recovery of Gaelic lordship in Ireland at the expense of English royal authority was associated with an expansion of pasture farming, and even an extension of nomadic herding. Yet throughout western Europe in the same period arable farming was being expanded in the twelfth and thirteenth centuries and reduced during the fourteenth, so there is nothing in this swing that cannot be explained better by economic change rather than cultural differences, though those changes were accelerated by military events.[57] A parallel instance would be the expansion and contraction of arable husbandry in southern Italy, for reasons that can have nothing to do with a clash of rival ethnic cultures.[58] Ireland would probably have experienced the same sorts of change even if the English had not invaded in 1169, and even if English rule had not weakened during the fourteenth century.

Those with the means to invest most heavily in economic change, whether in opening up new lands, founding towns and markets, or modifying tenures, were open to new ideas wherever they came from. It was increasingly common from the eleventh century for landowners to have property in different linguistic regions and to mix in multilingual groups. In Lowland Scotland, even the most powerful Gaelic-speaking families adapted to anglophone courts as fully integrated noblemen and courtiers.[59] Such flexibility on the part of ruling groups is apparent in other aspects of cultural diffusion. Legal devices like feudal tenure, building types like castles, abbeys, and cathedrals, and commercial institutions like markets, boroughs, and fairs were innovated throughout Britain by knowledgeable landlords. Cultural differences were permeable wherever there was economic advantage to be gained from imitation.

Conclusions

The common weakness of cultural explanations of economic development before the Reformation is that they have no clear idea of what they are trying to explain. Some are premissed on the supposition that economies in that period did not change, and that this stagnation requires the historian to identify relevant constraints. Cultural constraints on growth there no doubt were, but economies were transformed between 1050 and 1530 at a rate that was rapid by all earlier historical standards except those of the Roman epoch, and sometimes in directions that defied the prevailing value system. This was because millions of men and women at all social levels were encouraged to make changes in the ways they did things for practical reasons—to avoid starvation, bankruptcy, or disgrace, to establish their families more securely, or to fund favoured projects. Ad hoc changes do not require major intellectual upheavals. The accumulation of minute variations of practice was accompanied by parallel ethical adjustments to the requirements of new circumstances. Even the most formal economic morality of the period was becoming more sharply defined by lawyers and theologians as a result of economic change.[60] All the while, those value systems that acted as constraints on economic activity varied, as today, between different social groups.

Differences between businessmen in the course of time have less to do with differences of motivation and more to do with accumulating changes in the infrastructure of institutions, knowledge, and techniques that have gradually evolved across the centuries, and could only evolve gradually. Without those institutions, ideas, and techniques, the costs of business activity—especially those deriving from risk—rule out enterprises that later generations can take in their stride. The period 1050–1530 was not one of stagnation, but one in which vital foundations for later development were laid; sixteenth-century capitalism was a continuing modification of what had gone before, not a new birth. Some essential features of a commercial society—the widespread use of money, the keeping of accounts, the formation of business partnerships, trading on credit, the social regulation of trade—became part of everyday culture. Within Christian tradition, theologians and canon lawyers learned to accommodate many of the needs of merchants. The Protestant shift described by Weber, insofar as it developed an affinity with mercantile activity, was no more than a further innovation of this kind. For all their distinctive cultural traditions, ecclesiastical landlords and noble landlords shared in a changing culture, and were often in the forefront of its development. This implies that rather than trying to define some critical cultural difference between their society and ours it is more to the point to study how people then as now, with different technical, institutional, and cultural legacies from the past, adapted to economic opportunities, often in ways of long-term significance for the future.

NOTES

1. A. A. M. Duncan, *Scotland: The Making of the Kingdom* (Edinburgh, 1989), 123, 145–51.

2. J. Gilbert, 'The Monastic Record of a Border Landscape 1136 to 1236', *Scottish Geographical Magazine*, 99 (1983), 4–15.

3. J. Le Goff, *The Birth of Purgatory*, trans. A Goldhammer (Aldershot, 1991).

4. R. C. Stacey, 'Jewish Lending and the Medieval English Economy', in R. H. Britnell and B. M. S. Campbell (eds.), *A Commercialising Economy: England 1086 to c. 1300* (Manchester, 1995), 78–101.

5. See below (Ch. 7).

6. A. Smith, *An Inquiry into the Nature and Causes of the Wealth of Nations*, ed. R. H. Campbell and A. S. Skinner, 2 vols. (Oxford, 1976), i. 534.

7. *Willelmi Malmesbiriensis Monachi de Gestis Pontificum Anglorum*, ed. N. E. S. A. Hamilton, Rolls Ser. 52 (1870), 283.

8. William of Malmesbury, *Historia Novella*, ed. E. King, trans. K. R. Potter (Oxford, 1998), 64–8.

9. Gerald of Wales, 'Descriptio Kambriae', II.iv: *Giraldi Cambrensis Opera*, ed. J. S. Brewer and J. F. Dimock, 8 vols., Rolls Ser. 21 (1861–91), vi. 211–12.

10. *The Tropenell Cartulary*, ed. J. S. Davies, 2 vols., Wiltshire Archaeological and Natural History Society (Devizes, 1908).

11. E. Searle, *Lordship and Community: Battle Abbey and its Banlieu, 1066–1538* (Toronto, 1974), 38–41.

12. A. Murray, *Reason and Society in the Middle Ages* (Oxford, 1978).

13. *The Cely Letters, 1472–1488*, ed. A. Hanham, Early English Text Society 273 (1975), no. 41, pp. 38–9.

14. M. M. Postan, *Medieval Trade and Finance* (Cambridge, 1973), 28–64.

15. R. W. Kaeuper, *Bankers to the Crown: The Riccardi of Lucca and Edward I* (Princeton, 1973), 27–46, 60–5, 68–9, 224–5, 236; T. H. Lloyd, *Alien Merchants in England in the High Middle Ages* (Brighton, 1982), 196–8.

16. J. Kermode, *Medieval Merchants: York, Beverley and Hull in the Later Middle Ages* (Cambridge, 1998), 226–47.

17. M. K. James, *Studies in the Medieval Wine Trade*, ed. E. M. Veale (Oxford, 1971), 203–4.

18. *Willelmi Malmesbiriensis Monachi de Gestis Pontificum Anglorum*, 286–7.

19. C. Briggs, 'Creditors and Debtors and their Relationships at Oakington, Cottenham and Dry Drayton, 1291–1350', in P. R. Schofield and N. J. Mayhew (eds.), *Credit and Debt in Medieval England, c.1180–c.1350* (Oxford, 2002), 136–8; P. R. Schofield, 'Dearth, Debt and the Local Village Land Market in a Late Thirteenth-Century Village Community', *Agricultural History Review*, 45 (1997), 11–15.

20. See below (Ch. 8).

21. E. M. Tyler, ' "The Eyes of the Beholders were Dazzled": Treasure and Artifice in *Encomium Emmae Reginae*', *Early Medieval Europe*, 8 (1999), 247–70; G. Cavendish, *The Life and Death of Cardinal Wolsey*, ed. R. S. Sylvester, Early English Text Society, 243 (1959), 22–3, 67–73, 98–9.

22. H. G. Richardson, *The English Jewry under Angevin Kings* (1960), 87–9, 244–6.

23. P. Nightingale, 'Knights and Merchants: Trade, Politics and the Gentry in Late Medieval England', *Past and Present*, 169 (2000), 36–62.

24. K. B. McFarlane, 'The Investment of Sir John Fastolf's Profits of War', *Transactions of the Royal Historical Society*, 5th ser. 7 (1957), 91–116.

25. D. Ditchburn, *Scotland and Europe: The Medieval Kingdom and its Contacts with Christendom, 1214–1560*, i: *Religion, Culture and Commerce* (East Linton, 2000), 8.

26. M. W. Beresford, *New Towns of the Middle Ages: Town Plantation in England, Wales and Gascony* (1967), 55–97; G. W. S. Barrow, *Kingship and Unity: Scotland, 1000–1306*, 2nd edn. (Edinburgh, 1989), 87–93.

27. C. A. Empey, 'Conquest and Settlement: Patterns of Anglo-Norman Settlement in North Munster and South Leinster', *Irish Economic and Social History*, 13 (1986), 5–31; id., 'The Anglo-Norman Settlement in the Cantred of Eliogarty', in J. Bradley (ed.), *Settlement and Society in Medieval Ireland: Studies Presented to F. X. Martin, O.S.A.* (Kilkenny, 1988), 207–39.

28. R. R. Davies, *Conquest, Coexistence and Change: Wales, 1063–1415* (Oxford, 1987), 157.

29. Duncan, *Scotland*, 436.

30. Ibid. 351; J. Langdon, *Technology and Economy in the Later Middle Ages: The English Milling Industry, 1300–1540* (forthcoming).

31. R. H. Britnell, *Growth and Decline in Colchester, 1300–1525* (Cambridge, 1986), 76, 157.

32. E. A. Kosminsky, *Studies in the Agrarian History of England in the Thirteenth Century*, ed. R. H. Hilton, trans. R. Kisch (Oxford, 1956), 90–2, 287.

33. Duncan, *Scotland*, 316.

34. See below (Ch. 11).

35. E. M. Carus-Wilson, 'Evidence of Industrial Growth on some Fifteenth-Century Manors', in ead., *Essays in Economic History*, 3 vols. (1954–62), ii. 159–67.

36. See below (Ch. 11).

37. A. Macfarlane, *The Origins of English Individualism* (Oxford, 1978).

38. I. F. Grant, *The Social and Economic Development of Scotland before 1603* (Edinburgh, 1930), 247–52.

39. J. S. Beckerman, 'Procedural Innovation and Institutional Change in Medieval English Manorial Courts', *Law and History Review*, 10 (1992), 197–252.

40. M. M. Postan, *Essays on Medieval Agriculture and General Problems of the Medieval Economy* (Cambridge, 1973), 89–106. See also below (Ch. 11).

41. See below (Ch. 21).

42. J. Hatcher, 'English Serfdom and Villeinage: Towards a Reassessment', in T. H. Aston (ed.), *Landlords, Peasants and Politics in Medieval England* (Cambridge, 1987), 259–65; J. Kanzaka, 'Villein Rents in Thirteenth-Century England: An Analysis of the Hundred Rolls of 1279–80', *Economic History Review*, 55 (2002), 593–618.

43. *A Terrier of Fleet, Lincolnshire*, ed. N. Neilson (1920), xliv–lv; F. M. Page, *The Estates of Crowland Abbey* (Cambridge, 1934), 24–8.

44. Gerald of Wales, 'Topographica Hibernica', III. x: *Opera*, v. 152.

45. D. S. Thomson (ed.), *Companion to Gaelic Scotland* (Glasgow, 1994), 89, 232–3.

46. Barrow, *Kingship and Unity*, 12, 14, 35–6; P. G. B. McNeill and H. L. MacQueen (eds.), *Atlas of Scottish History to 1707* (Edinburgh, 1996), 426–7; S. Taylor, 'Place Names', in Michael Lynch (ed.), *The Oxford Companion to Scottish History* (Oxford, 2001), 479–83.

47. Many names of this type were subsequently lost or Gaelicized. Not all English-sounding names are in fact of English origin, and of those that are a number date from a period later than 1530: A. Room, *A Dictionary of Irish Place-Names*, rev. edn. (Belfast, 1994), 8–9.

48. Domesday Book, ii, fo. 77^v.

49. T. M. Charles-Edwards, *Early Irish and Welsh Kinship* (Oxford, 1993), 460–1.

50. *Survey of the Honour of Denbigh*, ed. P. Vinogradoff and F. Morgan (1914), 47.

51. Charles-Edwards, *Early Irish and Welsh Kinship*, 471–7.

52. Davies, *Conquest, Coexistence and Change*, 125–9; Charles-Edwards, *Early Irish and Welsh Kinship*, 211–15.

53. Gerald of Wales, 'Descriptio Kambriae', I. viii, xvii: *Opera*, vi. 180, 200–1.

54. R. A. Dodgshon, 'Rethinking Highland Field Systems', in S. Foster and T. C. Smout (eds.), *The History of Soils and Field Systems* (Aberdeen, 1994), 53–65.

55. G. W. S. Barrow, 'Rural Settlement in Central and Eastern Scotland: The Medieval Evidence', *Scottish Studies*, 6 (1962), 125.

56. Dodgshon, 'Rethinking Highland Field Systems', 58–9.

57. See below (Ch. 20).

58. D. Abulafia, 'Southern Italy and the Florentine Economy, 1265–1370', *Economic History Review*, 2nd ser. 34 (1981), 385–6.

59. G. W. S. Barrow, 'The Lost Gàidhealachd of Medieval Scotland', in W. Gillies (ed.), *Gaelic and Scotland: Alba agus a' Ghàidhlig* (Edinburgh, 1989), 71–2.

60. D. Wood, *Medieval Economic Thought* (Cambridge, 2002), 181–205.

FURTHER READING

Ault, W. O., *Open-Field Farming in Medieval England* (1972).

Baker, A. R. H., and Butlin, R. A., *Studies of Field Systems in the British Isles* (Cambridge, 1973).

Barrow, G. W. S., 'The Lost Gàidhealtachd of Medieval Scotland', in W. Gillies (ed.), *Gaelic and Scotland: Alba agus a' Ghàidhlig* (Edinburgh, 1989).

—— 'Rural Settlement in Central and Eastern Scotland: The Medieval Evidence', *Scottish Studies*, 6 (1962).

Beckerman, J. S., 'Procedural Innovation and Institutional Change in Medieval English Manorial Courts', *Law and History Review*, 10 (1992).

Campbell, B. M. S., *English Seigniorial Agriculture, 1250–1450* (Cambridge, 2000).

Charles-Edwards, T. M., *Early Irish and Welsh Kinship* (Oxford, 1993).

—— *The Welsh Laws* (n.p., 1989).

Coss, P. R., *Lordship, Knighthood and Locality: A Study in English Society, c.1180–c.1280* (Cambridge, 1991).

Davies, R. R., *Conquest, Coexistence and Change: Wales, 1063–1415* (Oxford, 1987).

Ditchburn, D., *Scotland and Europe: The Medieval Kingdom and its Contacts with Christendom, 1214–1560*, i: *Religion, Culture and Commerce* (East Linton, 2000).

Dodgshon, R. A., *The Origin of British Field Systems: An Interpretation* (1980).

—— 'Rethinking Highland Field Systems', in S. Foster and T. C. Smout (eds.), *The History of Soils and Field Systems* (Aberdeen, 1994).

Driver, J. T., 'A "Perilous, Covetous Man": The Career of Thomas Tropenell, Esq. (c.1405–88), a Wiltshire Lawyer, Parliamentary Burgess and Builder of Great Chalfield', *Wiltshire Archaeology and Natural History Magazine*, 93 (2000).

Grant, I. F., *The Social and Economic Development of Scotland before 1603* (Edinburgh, 1930).

Green, J. A., *The Aristocracy of Norman England* (Cambridge, 1997).

Hagger, M. S., *The Fortunes of a Norman Family: The de Verduns in England, Ireland and Wales, 1066–1316* (Dublin, 2001).

Hanham, A., *The Celys and their World: An English Merchant Family of the Fifteenth Century* (Cambridge, 1985).

Harvey, B., *Westminster Abbey and its Estates in the Middle Ages* (Oxford, 1977).

Hatcher, J., 'English Serfdom and Villeinage: Towards a Reassessment', in T. H. Aston (ed.), *Landlords, Peasants and Politics in Medieval England* (Cambridge, 1987).

Homans, G. C., *English Villagers of the Thirteenth Century* (New York, 1960).

Horrox, R. (ed.), *Fifteenth-Century Attitudes: Perceptions of Society in Late Medieval England* (Cambridge, 1994).

Hutton, R., *The Rise and Fall of Merry England* (Oxford, 1994).

Kanzaka, J., 'Villein Rents in Thirteenth-Century England: An Analysis of the Hundred Rolls of 1279–80', *Economic History Review*, 55 (2002).

Kermode, J., *Medieval Merchants: York, Beverley and Hull in the Later Middle Ages* (Cambridge, 1998).

—— (ed.), *Enterprise and Individuals in Fifteenth-Century England* (Stroud, 1991).

Le Goff, J., *The Birth of Purgatory*, trans. A. Goldhammer (Aldershot, 1991).

Macfarlane, A., *The Origins of English Individualism* (Oxford, 1978).

McFarlane, K. B., 'The Investment of Sir John Fastolf's Profits of War', *Transactions of the Royal Historical Society*, 5th ser. 7 (1957).

Mayer, P. J., 'Calstock and the Bere-Alston Silver-Lead Mines in the First Quarter of the Fourteenth Century', *Cornish Archaeology*, 29 (1990).

Murray, A., *Reason and Society in the Middle Ages* (Oxford, 1978).

Otway-Ruthven, A. J., 'The Organization of Anglo-Irish Agriculture in the Middle Ages', *Journal of the Royal Society of Antiquaries of Ireland*, 81 (1951).

Pierce, T. J., *Medieval Welsh Society: Selected Essays*, ed. J. Beverley Smith (Cardiff, 1972).

Pollock, F., and Maitland, F. W., *The History of English Law before the Time of Edward I*, 2nd edn., 2 vols. (Cambridge, 1898).

Pretty, J. N., 'Sustainable Agriculture in the Middle Ages', *Agricultural History Review*, 38 (1990).

Rubin, M., *Charity and Community in Medieval Cambridge* (Cambridge, 1987).

Schofield, P. R., *Peasants and Community in Medieval England* (Basingstoke, 2003).

—— and Mayhew, N. J. (eds.), *Credit and Debt in Medieval England, c.1180–c.1350* (Oxford, 2002).

Stone, D., 'Medieval Farm Management and Technological Mentalities: Hinderclay before the Black Death', *Economic History Review*, 54 (2001).

Swanson, R. N. (ed. and trans.), *Catholic England: Faith, Religion and Observance before the Reformation* (Manchester, 1993).

—— *Church and Society in Late Medieval England* (Oxford, 1989).

Thrupp, S., *The Merchant Class of Medieval London* (Chicago, 1948).

Tyler, E. M., ' "The Eyes of the Beholders were Dazzled": Treasure and Artifice in *Encomium Emmae Reginae*', *Early Medieval Europe*, 8 (1999).

....

CHAPTER 3

Power and Economic Constraints

Differences in the richness of land, and in cultural inheritance, had many implications for the exercise of power. Rich land, permitting high productivity, together with high concentrations of population, offered exceptional opportunities for those in authority to extract both incomes from agriculture and large sums in tribute, taxes, or rents. These two conditions explain why the king of England was wealthier than the king of Scots and why even the greatest Scottish lords rarely enjoyed incomes above those of a middle-ranking English baron.[1] The assessment of clerical incomes ordered by Pope Nicholas IV in 1290 permits assessments in all parts of Britain to be compared, and they show that the average ranged from £4.0 per square mile in England to £1.3 in Scotland and £0.9 in Wales. This broad comparison, inevitably, understates the range of variation; in the diocese of Canterbury ecclesiastical incomes averaged £8.9 per square mile, but in the diocese of Caithness £0.2, and in that of Sodor (the western Isles of Scotland) only £0.1 (Figure 3.1).[2] Although not a measure of total wealth, and subject to numerous distortions, this evidence is broadly in line with what we should expect for other reasons.

In richer areas, where money circulated, those in power had a wide variety of ways in which to extract their subordinates' income, whether in kind or cash. Quite apart from taxes and fines owing to the crown, churches and secular lords received income from their dependants in the form of ecclesiastical tithe, rent (in produce, labour, or cash), the sort of arbitrary levy known as tallage, judicial fines, mill tolls, and tolls on trade. A representative midland peasant farming 30 acres on a three-field system of cultivation in 1300 might expect to produce annually crops and other goods to the value of about £9 all told, of which 10 per cent would be owed in tithe, perhaps 14 per cent in rent, tallage, mill toll, and other obligations to a landlord, and perhaps 2 per cent in taxation to the king.[3]

The constraints of terrain and facility of transport discussed in Chapter 1 affected how much income could be extracted by kings and lords, the forms in which it could be levied, and the formality of legal claims. In the richer lands of southern and midland England or lowland Scotland a greater weight of financial impositions was possible because of the higher productivity of the land; properties often owed rents to more than one superior as well as paying taxes or other dues to the crown. The interlocking of rival interests encouraged the evolution of strongly defined legal rights. In such regions great wealth could be amassed without signifi-cant territorial control, through ownership of scattered estates. By contrast, wide stretches of poor country characteristic of much of northern and central Wales, south-western and northern England, and highland Scotland offered little prospect of a surplus of any kind, and could support powerful lordship only for a magnate who extended his authority over a wide territory, and had the force and organiza-tion to exact tribute, often in the form of produce, from numerous scattered farms. There was little scope for any complex hierarchies of lordship; a single parish rector and a lord exacting what he could in the name of custom was as much as the slim prosperity of such regions could afford. Lordship of this kind was less likely to rely on legal institutions for its support; it depended rather on the forcible control of territory. The difficulty of maintaining such power blocks against jealous neighbours can be demonstrated from the histories of the lordship of the Isles in western Scotland (*c.*1100–1266) or of the principality of Gwynedd (*c.*1216–82). The distribution of power across Britain was not, of course, determined in detail by physical features of the land, but this knowledge has to be called upon to explain why the major kingdoms, with wealthy subordinate lordships and effective legal traditions, centred on southern England and lowland Scotland, and to account for the high concentration of wealthy estates and powerful landlords in the most productive and populous parts of Britain.

Kingdoms

The richer parts of the kingdoms of both England and Scotland constituted a core where royal rights were generally uncontested. Even between 1141 and 1153, when the English monarchy was exceptionally weakened by civil war and divided loyal-ties, King Stephen remained an effective ruler because he continued to draw rev-enues from some of the wealthiest parts of his kingdom in south-eastern England and East Anglia. Domesday Book delineates well the territory that contributed to the finances of the king of the English in 1086; it stretched westwards to include Flint, Cheshire, Shropshire, and Herefordshire, and northwards to Yorkshire and Lancashire. Over this area local officers operated local law courts in the king's name, and in addition the king levied geld. This was a tax that King Æthelred II had first levied in 991 to buy off the Danes, and then regularized as a charge on land from 1012–13 deployed to fund a mercenary fleet.[4] Throughout this core area the

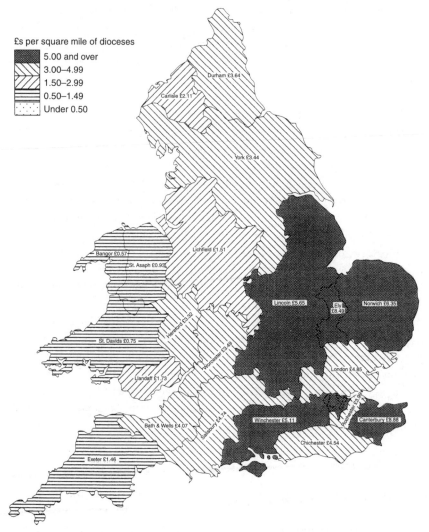

£s per square mile of dioceses

- 5.00 and over
- 3.00–4.99
- 1.50–2.99
- 0.50–1.49
- Under 0.50

Durham £3.64
Carlisle £2.11
York £3.44
Bangor £0.57
St. Asaph £0.93
Lichfield £1.51
Lincoln £5.65
Ely £8.49
Norwich £6.35
Hereford £3.02
St. Davids £0.75
Worcester £3.49
Llandaff £1.73
London £4.85
Salisbury £4.74
Bath & Wells £4.07
Winchester £5.11
Rochester £3.90
Canterbury £8.88
Chichester £4.54
Exeter £1.46

FIG. 3.1. Clerical incomes per square mile, 1291–2. The tax assessments made in 1291–2 for Pope Nicholas IV provide a rare opportunity to compare incomes across Britain as a whole, though the evidence is confined to ecclesiastical revenues. The level of assessment depends in part upon the proportion of the land held by ecclesiastical institutions, which varied considerably. The highest incomes per square mile are from southern and eastern England, but there is another impressive concentration in eastern Scotland. The lowest recorded assessments, not surprisingly, are from the townless region of northern and western Scotland.

Source: P. G. B. McNeill and H. L. MacQueen (eds.), *Atlas of Scottish History to 1707* (Edinburgh, 1966), 300–1.

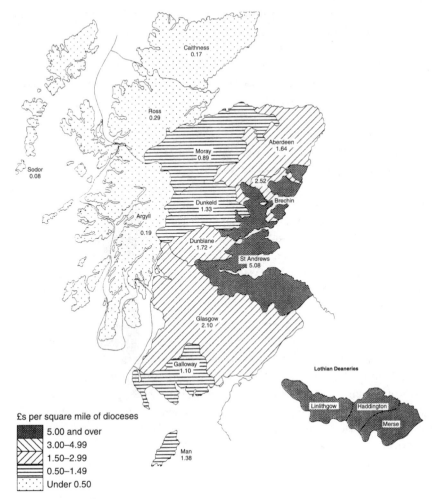

£s per square mile of dioceses

▓	5.00 and over
▨	3.00–4.99
▧	1.50–2.99
▤	0.50–1.49
⋮	Under 0.50

FIG. 3.1.—*continued*

land was assessed for tax in units commonly called hides and virgates (a virgate being a quarter of a hide). At the beginning of our period, under Edward the Confessor, a geld of 2 shillings a hide yielded about £5,000–6,000, allowing for immunities and collection costs, though by 1130 this had reduced to £2,400 because of an increasing number of exemptions.[5] The collecting of gelds was abandoned after 1162. By implication silver currency minted with the authority of the English king circulated wherever geld was levied. The area of royal control was also the area over which royal mints were dispersed; Edward the Confessor had coins struck in about seventy places, of which the most northerly were Chester and York. The king's administration in the provinces, both for the administration of justice and for the collection of geld, was organized through shires, and by subdivisions of the shire known as hundreds or wapentakes. Some texts suggest that there was also an English obligation of military service whose assessment ran parallel to that of geld, though this was probably less systematic than the taxation system and more dependent upon the organizing capacity of individual lords.[6] Domesday Book demonstrates how this exceptionally strong royal grasp rode over an equally impressive powerful class of landlords.

The power of the Scottish crown in the eleventh century did not abut on that of the king of England with any clear frontier, chiefly because of the weakness of royal power in northern England, which was at times close to becoming southern Scotland. The allegiance of an extensive region, roughly corresponding to the later shires of Cumberland, Northumberland, Westmorland, and Durham, was contested between the two monarchies until the later twelfth century. There is no surviving record, like Domesday Book, to define an area of effective Scottish royal fiscal or judicial control in the eleventh century. The core area of Scottish royal authority in the twelfth century was east and south of the Highland line. It was partly defined by the distribution of royal properties and their administrative officers, partly by a number of earldoms which had formerly been ruled by governors called mormaers, stretching in a chain from Lennox on the northern shore of the Clyde estuary to Buchan north of Aberdeen, as well as Fife and Dunbar to the east. Most royal acts were issued from within this sector of Scotland throughout the Middle Ages.[7] Only during the course of the twelfth century were the Scottish kings able to benefit directly from commercial growth by pioneering their own currency (c.1136) and imposing new systems of taxation with the consent of their councillors. A royal levy on land and similar to the English geld, soon known as 'common aid', was applied from the 1170s, and the crown was also able to exact tolls on shipping in Scottish ports from the reign of David I.[8]

The kingdoms of England and Scotland were both expansionist, and frequently came into conflict. The modern Anglo-Scottish border was the end result of rivalry between a Scottish push southwards and the expansion of English royal policy northwards, between them swallowing up the old kingdoms of Northumbria and Strathclyde. However, for both kingdoms the most effective areas for expansion were the more weakly organized lands to the west and north, where political power was differently constructed and kingship had a different meaning. The kings of Norway included the western Isles of Scotland in their dominions until 1266, and the earldom of Orkney until 1469. But in these regions, as elsewhere in western Scotland, power was built up around the heads of powerful family groups and alliances that operated to preserve and enhance the wealth and influence of their members under the leadership of chieftains. The *ceann cineil* or *toiseach cloinne* was the 'head of the kindred', with formal authority over subordinate households within his branch of the family. Similar groupings survived in other lands of Celtic tradition. The authority of the Irish *cenn fine* and the Welsh *pencenedl* was essentially the same. They gave protection and administered justice in return for loyalty and tribute.

Not all such chieftains were equally powerful. The greatest of them called themselves kings, and built up extensive territorial power based on a system of clientage. They sometimes constructed a large network, covering a wide range of different status groups, but with a strong propensity to emphasize the real or supposed blood relationships between its members. Commonly such leaders were aggressive; the more successful an Irish *fine* or Scottish *clann*, the more inclined its head would be to contest territory at the expense of less powerful neighbours. To subjugate them was a difficult task for the wealthier monarchies to the east, because power had to be contested over difficult terrain. Somerled (Somhairle mac Gillebrigte), variously known as 'king of the Isles' or 'lord of the Isles', was able to build up his power in Argyll, the western Isles, and the Isle of Man, from the 1120s until his death in battle in 1164 in the course of an invasion of the Scottish kingdom.[9] His death led to the loss of Man, and the splitting up of his remaining lands into independent lordships. Yet Somerled's death did not end the autonomy of his descendants. Somerled was the progenitor of three major Scottish clans, the MacDougalls, lords of Argyll, the MacDonalds, lords of Islay, and the MacRuaris, lords of Garmoran, named respectively from his son Dugald, and his grandsons Donald and Ruari, sons of Ranald.[10] However, even those parts of the lordship of the Isles previously subject to Norwegian kings were drawn into nominal subjection to the Scottish crown following the Treaty of Perth (1266), by which King Magnus IV of Norway ceded the Isle of Man and the western isles of Scotland to the king of Scots, Alexander III. In north-eastern Scotland, Moray, Ross, and Caithness were subjugated by force. The long-term success of state building, especially between about 1090 and 1290, greatly expanded the area owing effective allegiance to the Scottish crown.

The same is true of the king of England's successes in northern England, Wales, and Ireland during this period. In the north, peaceful relations with Scotland permitted an expansion of Anglo-Norman authority under Henry I (1100–35), and although the rights of the English crown were temporarily thrown into question in the reign of Stephen (1135–54), they were vigorously reasserted by the Angevin kings in the later twelfth and early thirteenth centuries. Increased royal intervention in northern English society explains why northerners were so prominent in the resistance to King John in the events leading up to the sealing of Magna Carta in 1215. Southern and central Wales were subject to invasion by Anglo-Norman families and settlers from the later eleventh century onwards. Ireland, later and more suddenly, experienced invasion and colonization by English settlers from 1169. Both in Wales and in Ireland the English crown insisted on maintaining some level of control. Henry I increased his stake in Wales in the early twelfth century, establishing centres of royal power and extending his control over the Church there. There was a representative of the English crown in Dublin from 1171–2, soon after the conquest.[11]

However, lands newly subject to the English or Scottish crown were often not drawn into the institutional structures normal in the core regions. Kings tolerated districts of relative administrative autonomy under the control of noble families. In south-western Scotland, and northwards beyond the edge of the Highlands, royal authority was mediatized by earls and other lords who exercised power in the king's name but administered their territories with considerable independence of action. Government in Wales was similarly fragmented. From the Norman period parts of the country were divided into franchises conquered by Anglo-Norman noblemen from Welsh rulers and held from the English crown. The lordships of Pembroke, Glamorgan, and Brecon were established, in the face of long and bitter resistance, from the 1090s, and English rule was later extended through subsequent conquests up to the 1280s. The government of these 'marcher lordships', though they were unambiguously attached to the English crown, remained the responsibility of their lords in almost every respect; their courts could impose capital punishment, and their lords were free to impose taxes.[12]

The last major phase of English expansion came in the reign of Edward I (1272–1307), though Edward failed in his ambition, from 1291 onwards, to end the independence of the Scots. His most spectacular success was against the native rulers of Wales. The principality of Gwynedd with its dependencies remained in the hands of native princes until 1282, when Edward I defeated Llywelyn ap Gruffydd and his brother Dafydd, and annexed the principality to the English crown. By that time the Welsh princes had already proceeded further than any western Scottish dynasties in reconstructing their rule on English and Scottish models of kingship. In the 1270s they were able to impose extraordinary taxes similar to English assessed taxes on movable wealth. But their effective control of territory and dependants was precarious, and when their autonomy collapsed their territories passed decisively within the ambit of English royal government. In 1301 Edward I assigned the royal lands in Wales, and the title Prince of Wales, to his teenage son, the future Edward II.[13]

Lordship

This cursory analysis of the territorial structure of kingdoms and the exercise of royal power within them draws attention to the importance of lordship of varying kinds as a distinctive feature of power relationships. The kings of England and

Scotland were themselves lords in several senses. They were the lords of a whole people; the English kings called themselves *rex Anglorum* ('king of the English') and the Scottish kings *rex Scottorum* ('king of Scots'). They were also the superior lords of lesser lords, who held their estates from the crown and rendered some service for them but who also served as representatives of royal authority. In another sense kings were also lords of hundreds of peasants and townsmen who held properties on their personal estates and paid dues to royal officers.

Lordship was not a closely controlled or structured institution. Lords differed very greatly in wealth and power, depending on how they had acquired their estates and where those estates were. Some were sufficiently wealthy to have international profiles and to challenge the power of kings; conflicts between kings and nobles—usually groups of disaffected nobles rather than the nobility as a class—are the stuff of political history, both in England and Scotland, all through the period. Other landlords were very minor figures who nevertheless exercised some measure of control over subordinate tenants. Yet the most striking feature of lordship as a principle of political coordination, at every level, was the transparent fusion of economic power with aspects of political power.

Modern states have established a unique right to levy taxes, to punish crime, and to raise troops, but this is a comparatively recent development with little relevance to the nature of government before 1530. With hindsight, a comparison of financial, judicial, and military institutions demonstrates that the long history of state-formation was well under way between 1050 and 1530. Yet throughout this period royal governments fell short of the criteria that define a modern state. There was no clear distinction between the role of kings and that of their leading subjects in areas of activity that we should regard as essentially public. Kings had certain distinctive prerogatives; for example, in normal circumstances they alone authorized the striking of coinage. But local policing and the exercise of jurisdiction, the authority to levy troops, and the right to levy non-contractual sums of money from dependants, were all widespread features of subordinate lordship. A second feature of the governments of this period was the very limited range of welfare benefits they offered their subjects. They exercised rights—fiscal rights and rights to levy troops—in return for maintaining basic political stability. A third characteristic of these governments was the absence of any concept of citizenship. A small minority had some political role, but for most people it was the Church, and not the State, that offered, through the rite of baptism, a criterion of membership. Even the legal rights of many people were restricted by their subordination to the private authority of lords who claimed jurisdiction over their persons or their land. Finally, a fourth characteristic of these regimes was the variability of the power of kings between different parts of their dominions. It would be impossible to define unambiguously for all parts of Britain what 'the government' might be, given the extent to which in different places power was variously shared, delegated, or contested between kings and magnates.

Throughout Britain, jurisdiction was fragmented. Royal courts expanded the scope of their operations over the centuries, especially in England under Henry II, but never to the total exclusion of rights of private justice by lesser lords. Seigniorial justice was most autonomous in the surviving and newly created territorial jurisdictions, like the marcher lordships of Wales. Within England, the bishop of Durham exercised royal powers within the region that became the later County Durham, and the lordship of Chester was a similarly extensive jurisdiction. Within the core areas of royal power, where royal justice operated at different levels— the king's central courts, county courts, and hundred or wapentake courts—many parts of this system were not managed directly by royal officers. Many hundred courts were in private hands, so that lords other than the king organized their business and used them as sources of authority and revenue. Highworth Hundred in Wiltshire was attached in the thirteenth century to the large manor of Sevenhampton, and its court records from the years 1275–87 survive amongst manorial accounts and court rolls seized by Edward I from Adam de Stratton in 1289.[14] Below the level of the hundred, landlords held courts for their own tenants, though their operation is little documented before the thirteenth century. By that time many such courts had taken over forms of jurisdiction that had originated in public courts. For many English villagers basic police work had passed since 1166 away from the hundred court to the 'leet' courts of larger estates.[15] Even estates that had never been in the hands of kings gave some rights of jurisdiction to their owners, especially over customary tenants and their lands. Manors were the smallest unit of lordship—and their possession was the only claim that minor lords had to lordship of any kind. In areas of English occupation in Wales and Ireland, similar powers of jurisdiction were assumed by even the smallest units of lordship over their tenants, often following English models. The abbey of Llanthony Secunda (Gloucestershire), for example, held courts in its tiny manors of Lougher and Collierstown (Co. Meath), and at Mullingar (Co. Westmeath) it claimed the right to a manor court and a hundred court every three weeks.[16] In Scotland, similarly, many landlords had jurisdiction from the crown. Private jurisdiction on the behalf of the king of Scots became one of the principal characteristics of lay tenure 'in barony'. Birlaw courts exercised jurisdiction for whole Scottish baronies, but since these were usually small they permitted rural communities a great deal of self-help in regulating and policing local activities.[17] It is important to recognize how varied such jurisdictions were, in order to avoid imposing too rigid an ideal type on what was essentially the motley outcome of centuries of unplanned development.

At local level, in much of Britain, jurisdiction was attached to the lordship of multiple estates. These comprised scattered settlements, whether townships, hamlets, or isolated farms, all in a territorial block and owing services at a central hall. The pattern of such estates is ancient; some preserved structures of lordship from Iron Age and Romano-British times. The lord of a multiple estate had lands under his direct control that were themselves often scattered—including specialized home farms such as bartons (where his grain was grown) and wicks (where his animals were pastured). His chief rights as lord, however, were over dependent populations living round about in villages and hamlets (Figure 3.2). Some of the best examples of estates of this kind were in pastoral regions, and their lords often derived much of their power from rights over pasture. Multiple estates also gave their lords rights of jurisdiction over their tenants. In northern England and Scotland some fine examples of multiple estates survived as 'shires', in which the 'shire' element means something quite different from the English shire that was a large unit of royal administration (Figure 3.3). Royal estates of this kind in Scotland were characteristically administered by officers called thanes, and by the late twelfth

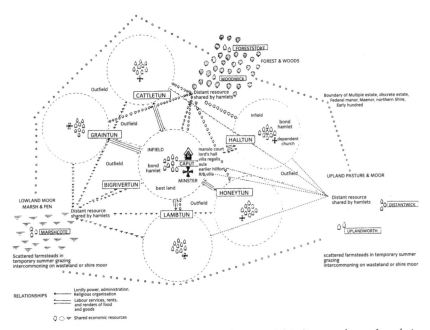

Fig. 3.2. A schematic representation of a multiple estate. This diagram shows the relationship between the head manor, with its church, arable land, and dependent farmworkers, and the surrounding dependent hamlets owing labour services and other dues. It shows a range of specializations that might be found in these dependent settlements, whether in arable or pastoral husbandry. It also indicates the existence of woods, forests, and fenlands shared by all the settlements of the estate. Not all these elements are to be expected in every example.

Source: M. Aston, *Interpreting the Landscape: Landscape Archaeology and Local History* (1985), 35.

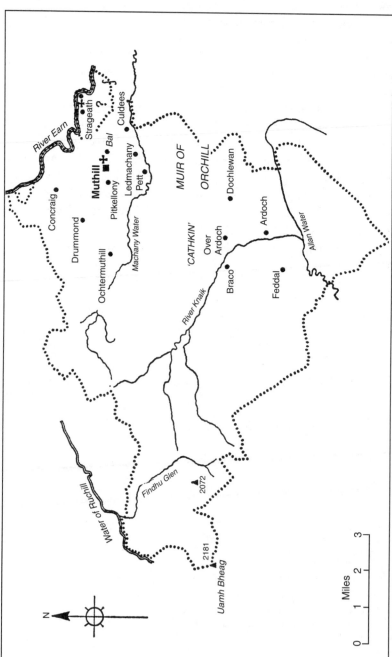

FIG. 3.3. The shire of 'Cathermothel' in Perthshire. This ancient shire, here reconstructed cartographically by Geoffrey Barrow, was centred on the ancient village Muthill, which preserves the second part of its name. The first place-name element seems to be related to the Welsh 'caer', signifying a central place, perhaps a fortified place, or a monastery. Muthill had had an early monastic community of culdees, and remained the ecclesiastical centre of the shire. The map shows the places dependent on Muthill, mostly in the valleys. The Muir of Ochill, otherwise known as 'Cathkin' or 'Cotken' from a Gaelic word meaning 'common', was described in the mid-thirteenth century as 'free and common pasture to all the men dwelling round about it', and may be identified as a shire moor shared with the adjacent shire to the east.

Source: G. W. S. Barrow, The Kingdom of the Scots: Government, Church and Society from the Eleventh to the Fourteenth Century (1)

century were being called thanages.[18] In eastern England an analogous institution was the 'soke', an institution that implied rights of seigniorial jurisdiction over widely diffused groups of people, and sometimes a defined territory, though not always with all the other features of a multiple estate. The 'sokeland' tenures characteristic of these regions had probably been superimposed by the Danes on pre-existing multiple estates.[19]

A system of multiple estates was prevalent in native Wales, where it was a principal feature of royal and ecclesiastical lordship. The equivalent of the shire was here the *cantref* (plural *cantrefi*), meaning 'a hundred farmsteads', which were sometimes divided for convenience into units called commotes—in Welsh, *cwmwd* (plural *cymydau*)—each with a separate administrative centre. Figure 3.4 illustrates the complexities of the commote of Dindaethwy in Anglesey, dependent before Edward I's conquest of Wales on the princely manor of Llan-faes. At the centre of the *cantref*, or of each of the commotes, was a hall from which justice was administered. The lord's own lands were cultivated by bond tenants, many of whom lived in a settlement known as a *maerdref* (plural *maerdrefi*).[20] The judicial importance of Welsh cantrefs and commotes is explicit in the Welsh laws.[21]

Large Anglo-Irish lordships were similarly based on compact territorial units which they designated as cantreds; these were often older units over which Gaelic lords had exercised judicial and other rights. The 'cantreds' of Odorney and Oflannan with Altry structured the lordship of Lixnaw (North Kerry), for which there survives an early rental showing the lords deriving rents and services from fifty-two subordinate property units. Most of these had separate names, and so represent individual farms, hamlets, or townships. Most of these subordinate tenures owed money rents, some owed grain, and some owed suit of court every fortnight, apparently at a court known as the hundred—evidently an import, in some sense, from England.[22]

In much of Britain, lordship was exercised in units more fragmented than the multiple estate, often because larger lordships had been split up. A survey of the estates of the bishops of Durham made in about 1183 captures the final stage of an estate called Quarringtonshire, centred on the bishop's demesne lands at Quarrington, but reduced to the three townships of North Sherburn, Shadforth, and Cassop, with additional rights over the tenants of Tursdale.[23] Bishops had granted parts of the former shire to others, and the integrity of the old unit was consequently lost. Even the townships belonging to Quarringtonshire in the 1180s were subsequently treated as separate units of lordship, so that all reference to the shire disappeared. This process had gone so far in southern England that Domesday Book portrays a patchwork of isolated manors owing no services to a multiple estate. Some tenants, called tenants-in-chief, held manors directly from the king, while others, called mesne lords, had intermediate lords between themselves and

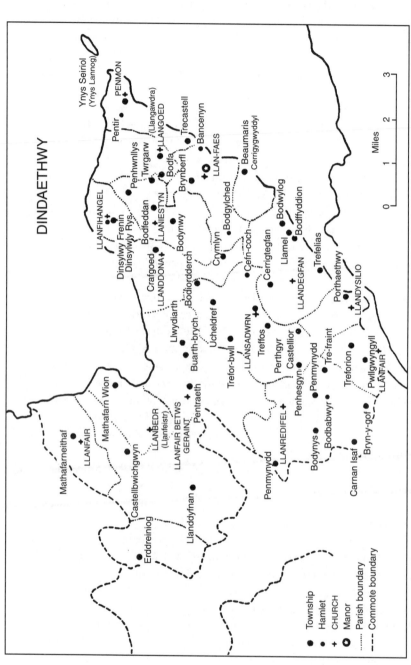

DINDAETHWY

Ynys Seiriol
(Ynys Lannog)

PENMON
Pentir

Penhwnllys
Twrgarw (Llangawdra)
LLANGOED
Trecastell
Bancenyn
Bodfa
Brynberll
LLAN-FAES
Beaumaris
Cerrigrywyddyl

Penwnllys
LLANFIHANGEL
LLANIESTYN
Bodynwy
Bodgylched
Bodwylog
Bodffyddion

Dinsylwy Frenin
Dinsylwy Rhys.
Bodfeddan
Crymlyn
Llamel
Trefelias

Crafgoed
LLANDDONA
Bodiordderch
Cefn-coch
Cerrigtegfan
LLANDEGFAN
Porthaethwy

Llwydiarth
Ucheldref
Treffos
LLANDYSILIO

Buarth-brych
Trefor-bwll
LLANSADWRN
Perthgyr
Penmynydd
Tre-fraint

Castellior
Treforion
Pwllgwyngyll
LLANFAIR

Mathafarneithaf
Mathafarn Wion
LLANBEDR (Llanfeistr)
Pentraeth
Penhesgyn
Penmynydd
LLANFAIR

LLANFAIR
LLANFAIR BETWS GERAINT
LLANREDIFEL
Bodnys
Bodbabwyr
Bryn-y-gof

Castellbwichgwyn
Penmynydd
Carnan Isaf

Erddreiniog
Llanddyfnan

Miles
0   1   2   3

● Township
●●● Hamlet
✝ CHURCH
✚◯ Manor
······· Parish boundary
– – – Commote boundary

FIG. 3.4. The commote of Dindaethwy (Anglesey). Dindaethwy, one of two commotes in the cantred of Rhosyr on Anglesey, was administered from the *maerdref* of Llan-faes, which belonged to the princes of Gwynedd before the Edwardian conquest of 1283. The exceptionally fertile soil supported extensive arable husbandry at Llan-faes, and the Welsh princes had developed it as the commercial centre of Gwynedd with a borough, a Saturday market, and a port. This activity was suppressed from 1295 by Edward I in favour of nearby Beaumaris. The princes held a commote court at Llan-faes that was later redesignated a hundred court. The map shows the range of parishes, townships, and hamlets that owed services to the commote centre.

the crown. Greater lords of the Norman period commonly created new mesne tenancies by granting the hereditary tenancy of manors to favoured supporters in exchange for military or other duties.

Manors were commonly divided into two parts—lands held in demesne (a word deriving from the same root as 'domain', meaning lordship, and usually pronounced the same way) and lands held by hereditary tenants. Demesne lands were those that the lord could dispose of to suit himself; in later centuries they would be known as the 'mains' in Scotland or the 'home farm' in England. A lord could either cultivate a demesne through his servants—often to supply his household, but also as a source of cash from sales of produce—or he could rent it to a suitable tenant. The thousands of English manors recorded in Domesday Book varied in size from as small as a single ploughland (comprising quite a small part of a township) to large enterprises retaining characteristics of a multiple estate. A fine example from this second category was the bishop of Winchester's valuable manor of Taunton (Somerset) in 1086, where there was land for 100 ploughs and extensive meadow, pasture, and woodland as well as a small borough and four sub-manors with their own demesne lands, tenants, and slaves.[24] Where there were tenants, as there usually were, manors were the smallest units of jurisdiction. Manorial courts were held partly as a matter of lordly obligation—some cost more to administer than the revenues they earned—but they could be a source of profit on large manors. They constituted an important facility for the solution of local disputes, for recovering debts, and for the organization of local policing. The idea of a manor was extended to Wales and Ireland in the course of English expansion, but the manors created in conquered territory usually retained native features, and differed in size and organization from English models, varied though those were.

A monopoly of legitimate armed force is one of the defining characteristics of a modern state. But between 1050 and 1530 powers to recruit troops were so far from being monopolized by kings that their military powers always depended upon their ability to work alongside their leading subjects. Like their English predecessors, the Norman kings and their successors expected the defence of their realm to rest on troops raised and led by their magnates. William I provided for the future security of the kingdom by stipulating the number of troops some landlords had to supply, and this system of fixed obligations had become extensive by 1166, when Henry II reviewed it. In order to meet their military obligations to the crown, major English landlords parted with some of their property to create small estates, known as knights' fees (alternatively called fiefs or, in Scots, feus), each of which would notionally support a mounted soldier. Similar tenures were created in Wales after the Anglo-Norman advance of the early twelfth century; Robert fitz Hamo, for example, established knights on land in the Vale of Glamorgan.[25] Fiefs multiplied in Scotland after 1124, sometimes in association with the expansion of settlement on to new land, as an aspect of the Normanization of the kingdom begun by King David I. Some knights' fees were equivalent to traditional territories, often whole townships, particularly in northern England, Scotland, and Ireland. In Scotland they often equated to later baronies.[26] Others, especially in southern and midland England, occupied only part of a township's territories, and were too small even to be considered manors. Many thousands of such varied knights' fees were created across twelfth-century Britain, often with clearly defined terms of tenure, to the point that lawyers came to see them as characterizing the land law, and adapted the Latin word for fief—*feudum*—to describe that law as feudal. It was from this legal usage that historians later extended the term feudal, with a variety of differing senses, as a label for the whole society in which these fiefs existed. However, only a small part of the total land surface of Britain was occupied by tenures of this kind.

This, then, was another widespread aspect of lordship in all parts of Britain and Ireland by the late twelfth century. Military services owed to the crown also implied a continuing bond of service between the king's leading subjects and their subordinates. Personal military ties to noblemen were capable of being weakened if tenants took land from more than one lord. As knight's tenure came to be recognized as hereditary, too, there were periods when fees were in the hands of old men, widows, or children, unable to perform military duties. Yet even in the most powerful kingdoms, members of the nobility had fighting men at their beck and call, and when civil war broke out private armies were rapidly formed. In addition, from the late twelfth century onwards there are examples of noble retinues, independent of tenurial obligations, of the sort that used to be disparaged as forms of 'bastard feudalism'.[27] Such armies did not depend on tenurial obligations; they were funded by money payments, often on a contractual footing.

The levying of taxes and rents also illustrates profound differences from the modern state. The distinction between taxes, due to the state, and rents due to landlords is clear enough both in the law and in the practice of modern states, but it was very imprecise in many past contexts, especially where the surplus available for kings and lords was meagre. Welsh lawbooks compiled in the thirteenth century— *Llyfr Cyfnerth, Llyfr Iorwerth*, and various Latin redactions of the laws—describe a system by which kings derived supplies from the townships of their multiple estates. Free townships owed *gwestfa* (or a cash equivalent), and bond townships owed a twice-yearly gift of food. Both groups were also obliged to support the operations of royal officials.[28] Were these rents or taxes? In Scotland until the twelfth century kings depended upon similar systems of produce renders called conveth (or wayting) and cain.[29]

The rents paid by Scottish peasants were often variable at short notice, and fluctuated according to economic circumstances. Even in England, however, lordship conferred the right to forms of variable income. In particular, tallage was a payment lords could often exact at will. Henry II and his thirteenth-century successors exacted large and irregular tallages on his boroughs and on the tenants of his estates. They also exacted heavy tallages from the Jews, not as assessments on their land but as a charge on their wealth.[30] But the right to tallage was not confined to the king's estates; similar payments were made by private landlords, and were a frequent cause of complaint. Even free tenants might owe tallage at the lord's will.[31] Tallage was evidently neither a rent nor a tax, but an obligation arising from subordinate personal dependence. Such tallages depended on the ability of tenants to acquire ready cash, so were in effect a charge on commercial development, like tolls on trade. They are not recorded from twelfth-century Scotland, presumably because the economy was not yet sufficiently monetized rather than because landlords lacked adequate powers.[32] In England during the course of the period tallages, like other variable dues, were likely to become a fixed sum, and less liable to cause distress. However, at no stage is it safe to treat relations between tenants and lords on the English manor as a simple matter of economic rent, except in circumstances—relatively unusual before the fifteenth century—when villagers held their lands on lease.

As the example of tallage suggests, there were many forms of customary payment due to lords which were defined not as a payment for land but as an obligation arising from personal dependence. Just as the Jewish liability to pay crushing tallages to the crown indicated dependence on royal tolerance for their continuing residence in England, so the tallaging of tenants was a mark of their subordination. The obligation to grind corn at a lord's mill was another custom that could weigh on tenants, and one that could be irksome if the mill was awkwardly sited, poorly maintained, or corruptly managed. Some personal dues were particularly characteristic of tenants whose reduced freedom designated them as villeins, or serfs. The best beast of these tenants was usually owed to their lord as a payment known as a heriot when they died. The obligation of English serfs to make a payment called merchet on the marriage of daughters was evidently a status disability rather than a rent or a punishment. There were similar obligations in Scotland; as late as 1437 Dunfermline Abbey granted lands to Sir David Stewart of Rossyth together with the grain taken in mill toll, the profits of jurisdiction, hergelds (an equivalent of heriots), and merchets, though by this time merchet was so rare in Scotland that this may be merely a legal formula.[33]

Power and Economic Development

The impact of political power on economic development between the eleventh and the sixteenth centuries is a complex one. There was, in effect, competition between kings, princes, and their subordinates for reserves of tenants' wealth. The danger that these rival interests between them might overcharge weaker men to the point that their long-term interests would suffer was a real one. The most striking example of such extortion was the squeezing of Jews by Henry III and Edward I to the point that their wealth was seriously depleted. The difficulty ordinary tenants faced in predicting their liabilities from year to year probably depressed their willingness to accumulate. Arbitrary power creates a severe disincentive to invest on the part of those whose livelihood is threatened, and there are numerous examples from medieval England of individuals of all social ranks whose wealth attracted the rapacity of powerfully connected lords. An example from the higher ranks of English society is the legal chicanery by which between 1266 and 1269 the king's nephew, Henry of Almain, deprived the earl of Derby of his estates.[34] It is not difficult to multiply examples of high-handed lordship and predatory kingship. They were especially likely to occur in crisis situations, when all other considerations were bypassed in financing a dynastic war. During the civil war of Stephen's reign, fear for the security of property no doubt hindered landlords' investment in their estates, though this was a localized and occasional issue rather than a prime cause of low investment in agriculture.

The view that power relations constituted a check on economic development is most at home in structures of thought that define the whole period 1050–1500 as one with traditional and, by implication, unchanging institutions. However, such characterizations of the period deserve to be challenged, because methods of exercising kingship and lordship were far from static. In the pursuit of cash incomes, kings and lords did much to stimulate commercial development. It is difficult to disassociate the growth of town life and local trade from their investment.[35] In colonial contexts, in particular, trade benefited from the requirements of a new, often absentee landlord class, whose models and ideals of power were very different from what had gone before. After the Anglo-Norman invasion of Ireland in 1169, when the island had only five towns, landlords added at least fifty-one new ones by 1300, mostly in the south-eastern half of the island.[36] Landlords' rationality imposed a limit of the extent to which they exploited the cash surpluses of their tenants; their new boroughs and markets could not have flourished otherwise. Local commerce could not have grown as it did unless some of the cash from tenant sales had remained in small households to fund the purchase of marketed goods. Even when royal and seigniorial pressures on their dependants were at their height around 1300 there were signs of real prosperity amongst the higher ranks of peasant society. It was never in the long-term interests of the crown and other landlords to check the course of commercial growth. It was in this context that many obligations which had once been arbitrarily imposed became fixed by agreement between lords and their tenants.[37] Change was not always at the instigation of the powerful. Especially between 1350 and 1470 adaptation was forced on landlords simply by the need to find and retain tenants on their estates.

NOTES

1. N. Mayhew, 'Alexander III—a Silver Age?', in N. H. Reid (ed.), *Scotland in the Reign of Alexander III* (Edinburgh, 1990), 59.

2. P. G. B. McNeill and H. L. MacQueen (eds.), *Atlas of Scottish History* (Edinburgh, 1996), 301.

3. These percentages are derived from Dyer's estimated budget for Robert le Kyng of Bishop's Cleeve, Gloucestershire: C. Dyer, *Standards of Living in the Later Middle Ages: Social Change in Britain, c.1200–1520* (Cambridge, 1989), 110–16.

4. P. Stafford, *Unification and Conquest: A Political and Social History of England in the Tenth and Eleventh Centuries* (1989), 143

5. F. Barlow, *Edward the Confessor*, (1970), 156–7.

6. M. Prestwich, *Armies and Warfare in the Middle Ages: The English Experience* (New Haven, 1996), 59–60

7. G. W. S. Barrow, *Kingship and Unity: Scotland, 1000–1306*, 2nd edn. (Edinburgh, 1989), 49–50; A. Grant, 'Thanes and Thanages', in id. and K. J. Stringer (eds.), *Medieval Scotland: Crown, Lordship and Community. Essays Presented to G. W. S. Barrow* (Edinburgh, 1993), 39–81; McNeill and MacQueen (eds.), *Atlas*, 159–61.

8. A. A. M. Duncan, *Scotland: The Making of the Kingdom* (Edinburgh, 1989), 156, 213.

9. R. A. McDonald, *The Kingdom of the Isles: Scotland's Western Seabord, c.1100–c.1336* (East Linton, 1997), 44–61.

10. Ibid., 70–1, 131, 128–9.

11. R. Frame, *The Political Development of the British Isles, 1100–1400* (Oxford, 1990), 25–6, 85.

12. Barrow, *Kingship and Unity*, 50; McNeill and MacQueen (eds.), *Atlas*, 183–5; Frame, *Political Development*, 50–71; D. Walker, *Medieval Wales* (Cambridge, 1990), 44–66.

13. M. Prestwich, *Edward I* (1988), 226.

14. *The Rolls of Highworth Hundred, 1275–1287*, ed. B. Farr, 2 vols., Wiltshire Archaeological and Natural History Society, 21 and 22 (1966–8); H. M. Cam, 'Manerium cum Hundredo: The Hundred and the Hundredal Manor', in ead., *Liberties and Communities in Medieval England* (Cambridge, 1944), 64–90.

15. *Select Pleas in Manorial Courts*, ed. F. W. Maitland, Selden Society, 2 (1988), xxvii–xxxviii.

16. *The Irish Cartularies of Llanthony Prima and Secunda*, ed. E. St. J. Brooks (Dublin, 1953), 299–301, 304.

17. *Regesta Regum Scottorum*, v: *The Acts of Robert I*, ed. A. A. M. Duncan (Edinburgh, 1988), 42–4; R. A. Dodgshon, *Land and Society in Early Scotland* (Oxford, 1981), 166–8.

18. G. W. S. Barrow, *The Kingdom of the Scots: Government, Church and Society from the Eleventh to the Fourteenth Century* (1973), 7–68; Grant, 'Thanes and Thanages', 39–81.

19. C. Hart, 'Land Tenure in Cambridgeshire on the Eve of the Norman Conquest', *Proceedings of the Cambridgeshire Antiquarian Society*, 84 (1995), 59–90.

20. R. R. Davies, *Conquest, Coexistence and Change: Wales, 1063–1415* (Oxford, 1987), 20–3, 121.

21. *The Latin Texts of the Welsh Laws*, ed. H. D. Emanuel (Cardiff, 1967), 210–11, 257, 349–50, 353, 450, 502, 507.
22. 'An Early Rental of the Lord of Lixnaw', ed. The Marquess of Lansdowne, *Proceedings of the Royal Irish Academy*, 40, section C.1 (1931), 1–18.
23. *Boldon Buke, A Survey of the Possessions of the See of Durham*, ed. W. Greenwell, Surtees Society 25 (1852), 9–11.
24. Domesday Book, i, fo. 87ᵛ.
25. Davies, *Conquest, Coexistence and Change*, 94.
26. Barrow, *Kingdom of the Scots*, 279–314; C. A. Empey, 'Conquest and Settlement: Patterns of Anglo-Norman Settlement in North Munster and South Leinster', *Irish Economic and Social History*, 13 (1986), 12–13.
27. D. Crouch, *William Marshal: Court, Career and Chivalry in the Angevin Empire* (1990), 138, 161–2.
28. D. Stephenson, *The Governance of Gwynedd* (Cardiff, 1984), 64.
29. See below (Ch. 5).
30. H. G. Richardson, *The English Jewry under the Angevin Kings* (1960), 161–75; R. C. Stacey, 'Jewish Lending and the Medieval English Economy', in R. H. Britnell and B. M. S. Campbell, *A Commercialising Economy: England 1086 to c. 1300* (Manchester, 1995), 93–4, 98–9; W. L. Warren, *The Governance of Norman and Angevin England, 1086–1272* (1987), 154–5
31. P. R. Hyams, *Kings, Lords, and Peasants in Medieval England: The Common Law of Villeinage in the Twelfth and Thirteenth Centuries* (Oxford, 1980), 28, 191–2.
32. *Regesta Regum Scottorum*, i: *The Acts of Malcolm IV*, ed. G. W. S. Barrow (Edinburgh, 1960), 54.
33. *Registrum de Dunfermelyn*, ed. C. Innes, Bannatyne Club (1842), no. 407, p. 286; Duncan, *Scotland*, 336–8.
34. N. Denholm-Young, *Richard of Cornwall* (Oxford, 1947), 143–4.
35. See below (Chs. 4, 7).
36. J. Bradley, 'Planned Anglo-Norman Towns in Ireland', in H. B. Clarke and A. Simms (eds.), *The Comparative History of Urban Origins in Non-Roman Europe*, 2 vols. (Oxford, 1985), ii. 411–67.
37. R. H. Britnell, *The Commercialisation of English Society, 1000–1500*, 2nd edn. (Manchester, 1996), 144.

FURTHER READING

Barrow, G. W. S., *Feudal Britain: The Completion of the Medieval Kingdoms, 1066–1314* (1956).
—— *The Kingdom of the Scots: Government, Church and Society from the Eleventh to the Fourteenth Century* (1973).
—— *Kingship and Unity: Scotland, 1000–1306*, 2nd edn. (Edinburgh, 1989).
Cam, H. M., *Liberties and Communities in Medieval England* (Cambridge, 1944).
Carr, A. D., *Medieval Anglesey* (Llangefni, 1982).
Charles-Edwards, T. M., *The Welsh Laws* (Cardiff, 1989).
Cosgrove, A. (ed.), *A New History of Ireland*, ii: *Medieval Ireland, 1169–1534* (Oxford, 1987).

Darby, H. C., *Domesday England* (Cambridge, 1977).

Davies, R. R., *Conquest, Coexistence and Change: Wales, 1063–1415* (Oxford, 1987).

—— *Dominion and Conquest: The Experience of Ireland, Scotland and Wales, 1100–1300* (Cambridge, 1990).

—— *The First English Empire: Power and Identities in the British Isles, 1093–1343* (Oxford, 2000).

—— *Lordship and Society in the March of Wales, 1282–1400* (Oxford, 1978).

Davies, W., *Patterns of Power in Early Wales* (Oxford, 1990).

Ditchburn, D., and Macdonald, A., 'Medieval Scotland, 1100–1560', in R. A. Houston and W. W. J. Knox (eds.), *The New Penguin History of Scotland from the Earliest Times to the Present Day* (2002).

Duncan, A. A. M., *Scotland: The Making of the Kingdom* (Edinburgh, 1989).

Empey, C.A., 'Conquest and Settlement: Patterns of Anglo-Norman Settlement in North Munster and South Leinster', *Irish Economic and Social History*, 13 (1986), 5–31.

—— 'Medieval Knocktopher: A Study in Manorial Settlement', *Old Kilkenny Review*, new ser. 2 (1979–83), 329–42, 441–52.

Faith, R., *The English Peasantry and the Growth of Lordship* (1997).

Frame, R., *The Political Development of the British Isles, 1100–1400* (Oxford, 1990).

Given, J., *State and Society in Medieval Europe: Gwynedd and Languedoc under Outside Rule* (Ithaca, NY, 1990).

Grant, A., *Independence and Nationhood: Scotland 1306–1469* (1984).

—— and Stringer, K. J. (eds.), *Medieval Scotland: Crown, Lordship and Community. Essays Presented to G. W. S. Barrow* (Edinburgh, 1993).

Green, J. A., *The Government of England under Henry I* (Cambridge, 1986).

Griffiths, R. A., *Conquerors and Conquered in Medieval Wales* (New York, 1994).

Hagger, M. S., *The Fortunes of a Norman Family: The de Verduns in England, Ireland and Wales, 1066–1316* (Dublin, 2001).

Hilton, R. H., *Class Conflict and the Crisis of Feudalism* (1985).

—— *A Medieval Society: The West Midlands at the End of the Thirteenth Century*, 2nd edn. (Cambridge, 1983).

Jolliffe, J. A., *The Constitutional History of Medieval England from the English Settlement to 1485*, 4th edn. (1961).

Jones, G. R. J., 'Multiple Estates and Early Settlement', in P. H. Sawyer (ed.), *English Medieval Settlement* (1979).

McDonald, R. A., *The Kingdom of the Isles: Scotland's Western Seabord, c.1100–c.1336* (East Linton, 1997).

Miller, E., *The Abbey and Bishopric of Ely: A Social History of an Ecclesiastical Estate from the Tenth Century to the Early Fourteenth Century* (Cambridge, 1951).

Palliser, D. (ed.), *The Cambridge Urban History of Britain*, i: *600–1540* (Cambridge, 2000).

Pollock, F., and Maitland, F. W., *The History of English Law before the Time of Edward I*, 2nd edn., 2 vols. (Cambridge, 1898).

Prestwich, M., *Armies and Warfare in the Middle Ages: The English Experience* (New Haven, 1996).

Rees, W., *South Wales and the March, 1284–1415* (1924).

Roberts, J. L., *Lost Kingdoms: Celtic Scotland and the Middle Ages* (Edinburgh, 1997).

Smith, B., *Colonization and Conquest in Medieval Ireland: The English in Louth, 1170–1330* (Cambridge, 1999).

Stacey, R., *Politics, Policy and Finance under Henry III, 1216–1245* (Oxford, 1987).

Stafford, P., *Unification and Conquest: A Political and Social History of England in the Tenth and Eleventh Centuries* (1989).

Stenton, F. M., *The First Century of English Feudalism* (Oxford, 1932).

Stephenson, D., *The Governance of Gwynedd* (Cardiff, 1984).

Stringer, K. J., *Earl David of Huntingdon: A Study in Anglo–Scottish History* (Edinburgh, 1985).

Walker, D., *Medieval Wales* (Cambridge, 1990).

Warren, W. L., *The Governance of Norman and Angevin England, 1086–1272* (1987).

Williams, G., *Recovery, Reorientation and Reformation: Wales, c.1415–1642* (Oxford, 1987).

Wolffe, B. P., *The Royal Demesne in English History: The Crown Estate in the Governance of the Realm from the Conquest to 1509* (1971).

....

CHAPTER 4

Contours of Development

*H*istorians broadly agree about the chronology of economic change between 1050 and 1530, even though they disagree about details, and even more about explanations. Later sections of this study will introduce more refinement into the discussion of these matters, but for the moment it will be enough to explain why the discussion in this book has been divided at about the year 1300, to consider some general characteristics of the lengthy periods that fall on either side of that divide, and to categorize some of the grounds for disagreement.

The Course of Economic Development, 1050–1530

The years 1050–1300 were years of considerable, if erratic, economic expansion. As in any period of such length, people had considerable diversities of experience, including times of acute political uncertainty, warfare, and local destruction. Nevertheless, comparisons between Britain in 1050 and 1300 demonstrate many signs of development, particularly during the hundred years between about 1160 and 1260. The number of inhabitants of Britain grew, the use of land for agriculture intensified, as woodland was cleared and marshland drained, the number and size of towns increased, the circulation of money was almost everywhere growing, and writing became extensively used to record contracts, exchanges, and administrative details. These are all signs that the quantity of goods and services being produced in Britain increased. The total output of goods and services grew perhaps by between two and three times between 1050 and 1300.[1]

It is difficult to comment on the implications of these changes for levels of welfare. The greater number of people, especially in towns, and the wide range of new techniques and institutions suggest that productivity gains had been made. Some of the great landowning institutions undoubtedly became richer, and there were by 1300 pockets of mercantile and professional wealth that had not existed in 1050. But a large proportion of the population, no longer able to make a living from the land, was at the mercy of exceedingly volatile market forces, and there is evidence of recurrent distress and chronic poverty around 1300. Standards of living had probably fallen for the poorest sections of the population during the later thirteenth century. Overall, though population and output had increased, average levels of income had probably changed little.[2]

The centuries after 1300 do not share the expansive characteristics of the twelfth and thirteenth centuries, though they are no less interesting as a period of economic development. The fortunes of different decades were varied, and the dangers of assuming continuous trends are as real for these centuries as for earlier ones. Nevertheless, a great deal changed. Between 1300 and 1450 the population of Britain and Ireland declined to no more than half its former level, and it was barely much larger by 1530. The cultivation of the land was less intensive in 1530 than it had been in 1300. Many villages and towns had shrunk. The problem of poverty, on the other hand, was less acute than it had been in 1300. Wage earners could buy more with their wages, and farmers were more likely to have enough land to earn a satisfactory livelihood. Terms of tenure were also more favourable than in 1300. English villeinage in the form in which it had existed in 1300, characterized by the requirement to perform heavy labour services and servile personal obligations, was becoming a thing of the past even if some families still remained technically unfree. Similar changes were reducing the significance of servile tenures through-out Britain and Ireland.[3] These changes cannot be demonstrated with sets of figures produced at the time, but are rather the implication of evidence accumulated in modern times, mostly during the twentieth century. They can be illustrated more precisely with some broader statistical indicators, though further refinements will be offered in the more detailed investigations of later chapters.

Our knowledge of the character and intensity of land use is dependent upon the survival of evidence from particular places. There are no contemporary national surveys, though Domesday Book can be used to estimate the situation through most of England in 1086. Many parts of England were already extensively culti-vated at that time, so in those areas the possibilities for expansion were limited. Local evidence in favour of subsequent agrarian expansion is nevertheless abundant, especially between about 1160 and 1260. Trees were cleared away, as in the Soke of Peterborough and Rockingham Forest (Northamptonshire);[4] moors were converted to farmland, as in the Palatinate of Durham;[5] wetland was drained, as along the Lincolnshire coast and in the fens, in the Severn estuary, and in the Kentish marshes.[6] The total English arable acreage, according to Bruce Campbell's estimates, increased from perhaps 8.0 m. acres in 1086 to 10.5 m. in 1300, an increase of 31 per cent.[7] Though arable cultivation perhaps grew by an even greater percentage in the rest of Britain and Ireland, there is no basis in the evidence for estimating the magnitude of the change. Some of the best northern evidence comes from southern Scottish abbeys, which took in large areas of moorland for arable, like the granges created by Melrose and Dryburgh abbeys in the Tweed Valley and along the coast.[8]

The output of pastoral products also increased, often in specialized farms, both for the home market and to supply overseas demands for wool and hides, though we have no estimates of the magnitude of this increase. Apart from evidence of new land being cleared and drained for pasture, one of the most impressive indications of the expansion of pastoral husbandry was the growth of export trades in wool and hides from all parts of Britain. From barely documented beginnings in the late Saxon period, trade in wool through English ports increased to the level of around 12 m. fleeces in 1304–5.[9] There is no doubt that expanding trade had an impact on the rural economies of Wales, Scotland, and Ireland, especially from the later twelfth century. Monastic flocks steal the limelight, but there were undoubtedly extensive flocks owned by lay landlords and peasants.[10] Ireland's pastoral exports cannot be specified in detail, but at their peak in the 1270s and 1280s the sums received in customs dues would have been equivalent to the export of over 1 m. fleeces a year or 400,000–450,000 hides.[11] Scotland was exporting the wool of about 1.5 m. sheep and 35,000 hides each year in the period 1327–33, after the trade may have already experienced some decline.[12] Quite apart from evidence of expanding acreages at the expense of moorland and marsh, there is also evidence from southern and eastern England that under the stimulus of commercial opportunity, the productivity of the land was being increased in some contexts.[13]

By contrast with the twelfth and thirteenth centuries, between 1300 and the mid-fifteenth century land was used less intensively. Large areas were converted from arable to rough pasture. Between 1300 and 1375 the English crop acreage declined probably by over a third, perhaps from 6.23 m. to 4.01 m. acres, and it declined further up to severe recession of the 1450s.[14] Similar contraction is in evidence in Scotland and Ireland from the early fourteenth century.[15] In the 1520s and 1530s, Tudor governments were so aware of land converted from arable to pasture that they worried about England's depopulation even after the population had in fact started to grow. There is also evidence of declining productivity in some branches of farming where profits were lower than they had been.[16]

The history of urbanization shows a similar contrast between the periods before and after about 1300. Before 1050 there had already been a prolonged expansion of urban life in England since the later ninth century, but that development had largely been restricted to the south and the midlands. By contrast, the urban development of the period 1050–1300, which was most marked between 1160 and about 1260, was widespread, involving the creation of new towns not only in northern England but Wales, Scotland, and Ireland as well. A new town, in this context, is defined as accommodation deliberately constructed for residents not engaged in agriculture, usually in a planned development along one or more streets; residential plots were accompanied by the provision of the facilities tradesmen might need for their livelihood, such as a market and workshops. As many as 600–700 new towns of this type, often described as boroughs (or, in Scotland, burghs) were created in Britain and Ireland between 1050 and 1300, though differing greatly in size and importance.[17] A parallel source of information concerning the expansion of trade is the multiplication of licensed markets and fairs, usually requiring some landlord investment.[18] Not surprisingly, some new markets and fairs were associated with urban growth, but many were small rural affairs that register the growing importance of monetized exchanges in village life.[19] Besides the evidence for new towns and markets, there is widespread evidence for the expansion of older towns, which will be examined in Chapter 7. As a result of these developments urban populations grew in all parts of Britain. In England they probably increased from about 10 per cent of the total in 1086 to 15–20 per cent of a larger population around 1300.[20] Urban proportions were smaller in Wales, Scotland, and Ireland, but they had grown from a lower base in 1050.

Few new towns were founded after 1300, and although some towns were able to grow during parts of the period, chiefly on the strength of industrial enterprise, urban growth was a more restricted phenomenon than earlier. Even in the case of more successful towns, like York and Coventry, growth was often not sustained through the period, and many urban populations were smaller in 1500 than they had been in 1300.[21] Although most of the discussion of these changes has been conducted with respect to English evidence, the contraction of urban populations in Wales and Ireland is well attested, and there are several clear examples from Scotland, notably Roxburgh, a thirteenth-century town abandoned in the fifteenth century.[22] Because urban (like rural) standards of living were generally higher after 1300 than before, historians are reluctant to speak of 'urban decline' without many reservations. Even so, there had been a definite change in momentum. There was nothing akin to the new urban developments of the period 1050–1300 until the eighteenth and nineteenth centuries.

A further contrast before and after 1300, again relating to trade, concerns the size of the money stock. One of the most spectacular indices of the volume of currency is Stuart Rigold's evidence relating to the archaeological recovery of small change lost accidentally, rather than wealth deliberately hoarded. It is not possible, of course, to date precisely when coins were lost, but they can be assigned to the period when they were in circulation, and that is good enough for our present purposes. The changes strongly suggest an increasing amount of small change passing hands between the twelfth and earlier fourteenth centuries, followed by some contraction in this volume. Table 4.1 shows some of this evidence from a hundred different sites classified according to different types of site.

TABLE 4.1. *Site finds of small change from 100 sites dated by the period of minting, and classified by types of site, adjusted to estimate the number of finds from each decade*

	Religious	Castles	Rural	Urban	Total
*c.*973–1053	0.37	0.12	—	1.7	2.25
*c.*1053–*c.*1125	0.15	0.7	0.15	1.4	2.43
*c.*1125–1180	0.5	2.0	—	2.2	4.5
1180–1247	2.25	2.1	0.7	3.0	8.0
1247–1279	2.7	2.7	1.0	6.7	13.0
1279–1351	7.3	9.3	1.7	9.7	28.0
1351–1412	5.5	1.3	0.83	3.8	11.5
1412–1464	2.4	2.5	0.4	2.6	8.0
1464–1544	4.0	1.2	0.12	0.5	6.0

Note: The average total number of finds per decade has been calculated independently and is not arithmetically identical with the sum of the averages from different types of site.

Source: S. E. Rigold, 'Small Change in the Light of Medieval Site-Finds', in N. J. Mayhew (ed.), *Edwardian Monetary Affairs (1279–1344)* (Oxford, 1977), 61, 79.

Estimates of the total volume of currency in circulation, fed mostly by the import of bullion from abroad, confirm this pattern of growth and reversal. The evidence here does not derive from counting the total number of surviving coins—though this might result in a broadly similar conclusion—but from estimates of the number of coins that were minted. For periods before the mid-thirteenth century these volumes have to be derived from a close study of surviving coins to estimate how many different dies were used to strike each issue. The number of dies, coupled with an estimate of how many coins could be struck from each die, gives an approximate indication of how many pieces were struck. After 1247 estimates are based rather on the written records of the mints themselves, though these are not always complete and have problems of their own. These calculations can be used to suggest how much new coin was in existence after each major reminting of the currency, but they cannot show how much of the new coin went into circulation or remained there after hoarding, wear and tear, export abroad, and accidental losses had whittled away its initial volume, so this requires the making of further assumptions. The English money stock was perhaps £25,000 on average in the late Saxon period, perhaps £37,500 on average in the reign of William I, and was in the range £30,000–80,000 in 1158.[23] Figure 4.1 indicates the subsequent expansion of the potential money stock in circulation to around £2 m. in the earlier fourteenth century, and the subsequent reversal of that expansion. A similar account can be

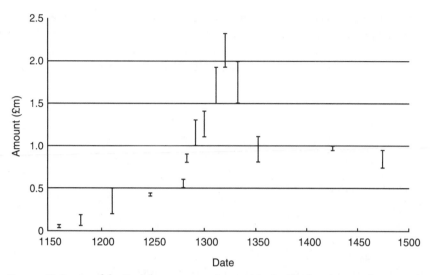

FIG. 4.1. Estimates of the English currency, 1158–1470. Martin Allen's estimates of currency in circulation between 1158 and 1470 demonstrate a process of monetization between 1158 and 1319 (the year of his highest estimate) even more remarkable than our other evidence might imply. It is readily compatible with the evidence of stray finds in Table 4.1. Estimates for the later fourteenth and fifteenth centuries are widely distributed but show the lasting significance of monetary contraction during the early fourteenth century, which for day-to-day purposes was exacerbated by the higher proportion of gold in the estimates from 1351 onwards.

Source: M. A. Allen, 'The Volume of the English Currency, 1158–1470', *Economic History Review*, 54 (2001), 608.

given of the Scottish currency, which is estimated to have increased within little more than a century of its independent existence to about £50,000–60,000 in 1250 and a peak of £130,000–180,000 in 1280. There are no reliable later estimates, though there is evidence for lower mint output and contracted circulation in the fifteenth century.[24] The Irish currency was probably always smaller than that of Scotland, though King John's Irish recoinage of 1204 perhaps put £50,000 into circulation, and a similar sum is possible for the recoinage of 1251–4. It is difficult to convert such figures to estimates of circulation because of the unknown size of outflow. After the 1330s there were no more Anglo-Irish issues of currency until the mid-1420s, and Ireland depended on what could be obtained from England. The subsequent deterioration of the currency in circulation both in quantity and quality is beyond question. Even with the restoration of minting in Ireland between the 1420s and 1505 the chief distinguishing feature of Irish currency was that it was excessively clipped and under-regulated.[25]

These various strands of evidence relating to agricultural output, urban growth, and the money stock constitute the best evidence for what was happening to population. These changes could not have occurred without some corresponding fluctuation both in the size of the labour force and the number of consumers. However, it is more difficult to verify changes in population directly from statistical sources. The figure of tenants recorded in Domesday Book is generally smaller than that recorded in later enumerations of tenants. For example, comparing its evidence with that of the Warwickshire Hundred Rolls shows that recorded tenant population rose between 1086 and 1279 from 1,785 to 2,632 in Kineton Hundred, and from 540 to 1,685 in the more heavily wooded Stoneleigh Hundred where there was greater scope for agricultural expansion.[26] There are some interesting statistical series for parts of the period from individual lordships, mostly relating to a seigniorial poll tax on adult men that was far from universal. Estimates from the bishop of Winchester's large manor of Taunton (Somerset) register an increase in the male population from 612 in 1209 to 900 in 1248 and 1,448 in 1311, implying an annual growth rate of 0.85 per cent (Figure 4.2).[27] Some differently constituted evidence from Halesowen (Worcestershire), derived by analysing the number of men occurring in the court rolls, supports the idea that growth was more characteristic of the period 1270–1315 than later (Table 4.2), and the fact that only 71 tenants are recorded in Domesday Book suggests that population had already grown between 1086 and 1270. There were at least 215 tenants in 1315.

TABLE 4.2. *Estimated number of adult males at Halesowen, 1270–1395*

1271–5	331
1280–2	392
1293–5	435
1301–5	457
1311–15	485
1321–5	412
1331–5	433
1345–9	470
1351–5	270
1361–5	255
1371–5	289
1381–5	275
1391–5	252

Source: Z. Razi, *Life, Marriage and Death in a Medieval Parish: Economy, Society and Demography in Halesowen, 1270–1400* (Cambridge, 1980), 31, 117.

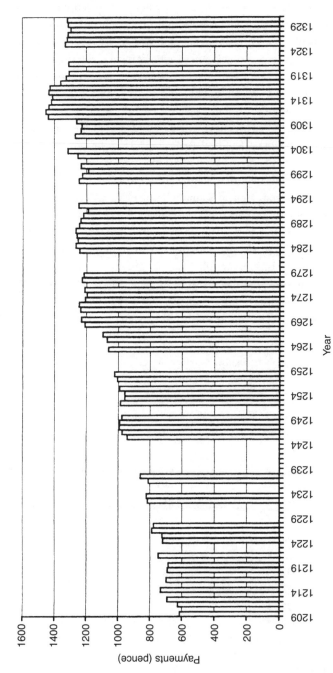

FIG. 4.2. Hundred-penny fines and acquittances at Taunton (Somerset), 1209–1330. The longest series of population data for the thirteenth century is from the bishop of Winchester's manor of Taunton, whose male villeins over the age of 12 had to pay an annual 'hundred-penny' to the bishop. The total receipt, adjusted by those acquitted, indicates a rise of the male population in question from 612 in 1209 to a peak of 1453 in 1311, followed by a dip. The series cannot be continued beyond 1330, when the sum due became fixed. This series does not indicate what happened to the population of Taunton borough, and cannot be taken as representative of rural England as a whole, but it attests a growth of population that historians had already deduced from other sources.

Source: Christopher Thornton (Essex).

For the fourteenth and fifteenth centuries there is more evidence than for the thirteenth, though its quality is debatable. At Halesowen, as at Taunton, population increased through the later thirteenth century and the first decade of the fourteenth; it was knocked back temporarily by famines in 1315–18 and then more permanently by the Black Death of 1348–9. Subsequent recovery to the 1370s was weak and only temporary; the male population of Halesowen in the early 1390s was the lowest on record in the period 1270–1395.[28] Male population on the manors of High Easter and Great Waltham in central Essex changed little in the later thirteenth century. It then fell sharply in the early fourteenth century, recovered slightly for a couple of decades after the Black Death of 1348–9, but then again declined slowly from the later 1370s into the early fifteenth century and showed no sign of recovery for the following 100 years (Figure 4.3).[29] At Writtle (Essex) the male population may have fallen by as much as 56 per cent between 1328 and 1382 and continued to decline into the 1430s, but despite some slight recovery in the mid-fifteenth century numbers then fluctuated before the 1490s, when they leapt ahead for some unknown reason.[30] At Kibworth Harcourt over the same period numbers fell by 40 per cent in the Black Death, recovered to the later 1370s, but then declined again.[31] Comparable evidence from the Aquila honour of Sussex

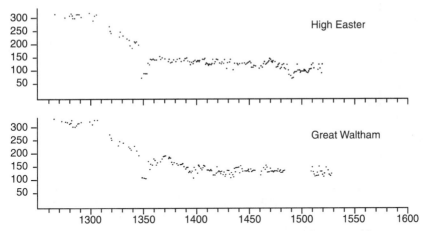

FIG. 4.3. The number of males aged 12 and over in High Easter and Great Waltham (Essex), 1250–1530. The existence of an annual poll tax, tithing-penny, on males over 12 years old in High Easter and Great Waltham (both in Essex) permits an exceptionally continuous indication of population movements in these two villages for 270 years. They cannot be assumed to be typical of Britain as a whole. On the other hand they decisively demonstrate (in a region little affected by local warfare) a tendency for population to contract quite independently of the Black Death—both before 1348 and after 1370.

Source: L. R. Poos, 'The Rural Population of Essex in the Later Middle Ages', *Economic History Review*, 2nd ser. 38 (1985), 522.

registers a continuing drop in population by about a third between 1442–3 and 1485–6 and no unambiguous recovery before the end of the 1520s.[32] All these series are testimony to the great contrast between the demographic experience of the fourteenth and fifteenth centuries and what had gone before. These different trends explain the changing number of mills on 104 sample manors in the midlands, which increases to a peak in the early fourteenth century before declining for over a hundred years, well into the fifteenth century (Figure 4.4). Since mills were needed for the production of flour, their declining number implies a contraction of the demand for bread.

Compared with these local series, evidence for the population of Britain as a whole is both less reliable and less continuous. The three principal benchmarks from which estimates have been attempted for England are Domesday Book of 1086, the poll tax returns of 1377, and the muster returns and subsidy accounts of

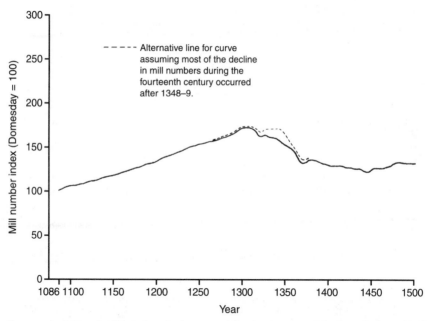

FIG. 4.4. An index of mill numbers in the west midlands, 1086–1500. John Langdon's study of mill numbers on documented manors in the west midlands from the time of Domesday Book (1086) has enabled him to produce this time series to show that their number increased by over 50 per cent by 1300 before falling back to a low point around 1450. This movement is readily explicable by population change, since mills were needed to grind flour for baking; their number was at least partly determined by the local demand for bread, though changes in output per mill could have an independent effect.

Source: J. Langdon, 'Water-Mills and Windmills in the West Midlands, 1086–1500', *Economic History Review*, 44 (1991), 431.

1522–4. These imply English populations of (perhaps) 1.1 m. to 2.5 m. in 1086, 2.2 m. to 3 m. in 1377 and 1.05 m. to 2.92 m. in the 1520s.[33] The large margins of uncertainty in these figures inevitably reduce the use that can be made of them. They are compatible with the hypothesis, well justified by the evidence we have already examined, that population increased after 1086 but then declined again. But the peak of the earlier expansion came not in 1377 but over half a century earlier, before the great famines of 1315–18 and the Black Death of 1348–9. To estimate English population at its peak in 1300 implies either working forwards from 1086, back from 1377, or making estimates on some quite different set of assumptions. Working forward from 1086, and comparing the number of tenants recorded in Domesday Book with those in later estate records, Herbert Hallam suggested that population peaked at a figure between 6.125 m. and 7 m. around 1300.[34] Working backwards from 1377 on the assumption that population was 40–50 per cent lower than at the beginning of the century implies a population of 3.7–6.0 m. in 1300. Bruce Campbell, whose independent figure is based on a calculation of what English resources and technology could support, has opted for 4.25 m.[35] These various estimates define the extremes within which most others lie. No doubt debate will continue, but despite considerable advance in the collection of local statistics, historians are no nearer agreement than they were when John Hatcher defined the range of possibilities in 1977 (Figure 4.5). The population statistics of Wales, Scotland, and Ireland around 1300 are even more a matter for guesswork, but they are likely to be of the order of 300,000 for Wales, 1 m. for Scotland, and 1–2 m. for Ireland,[36] implying a total population of about 7.5–9 m. for Britain and Ireland together. These levels had all fallen by 1520, though the changing order of magnitude is again impossible to assess with any precision.[37] Some estimates have put Scotland's population in the fifteenth century as low as 250,000.[38]

Growth Models of Economic Change, c.1060–1260

Long-term economic and demographic changes are sufficiently complex to require a somewhat abstract explanation. The expansion of the twelfth and thirteenth centuries came about through the decisions of many people in many different contexts over a very long period. Of course, not everybody's decisions were of equal weight. The decision of a king to go to war, to impose taxes, to regulate trade and industry, or to change the currency had implications far more reaching than those any individual peasant farmer was capable of. A single king, nobleman, or churchman, too, could transform the economy of his estates, as in the imposition of heavier services on the tenants of the bishops of Durham following the Norman conquest of northern England, or in the widespread transformation of rural societies that followed the creation of Anglo-Norman lordships in Ireland

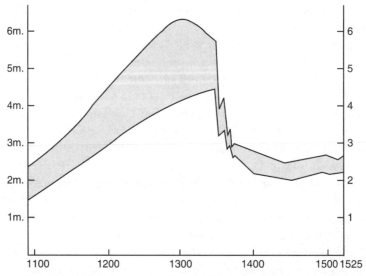

FIG. 4.5. Long-term population trends, 1086–1525. The range of estimates of English population at different times is illustrated in this figure. Estimates are generally closer together,
though still with wide margins of error in 1086 (using Domesday Book), 1377 (using poll
tax data), and 1522–4 (using muster rolls and taxation assessments). They are most
divergent at the peak of medieval population growth around 1300, where various estimates
have been devised on quite different principles.

Source: J. Hatcher, *Plague, Population and the English Economy, 1348–1530* (1977), 71.

after 1169. The desire of these leading and powerful groups to enlarge their estates
and raise their incomes was one of the primary forces for change during the twelfth
and thirteenth centuries. Their investment was largely responsible for the multiplication of towns and markets through which they hoped to raise their status and
their incomes from rents and tolls. They were also active in expanding the area of
cultivated land for the enhancement of their demesne lands or releasing forest and
moorland for settlement by tenants in exchange for money rents. From the late
twelfth century they headed the most considerable commercial enterprises in
Britain, their officers being responsible for the disposal of large quantities of
grain, wool, hides, and other agrarian produce on the most favourable terms. The
founding of new towns and villages, the development of new means of payment
and habits of record keeping, the creation of new systems of administration and
jurisdiction, and the sponsorship of new water-power technologies, transformed
productivity possibilities in almost all parts of Britain and Ireland between 1086
and 1300.

Nevertheless, though their individual decisions made less impact than the individual decisions of the great, small farmers and tradesmen were of enormous

importance both as producers and consumers and as creators of new ideas. Just as landlords were seeking to improve their incomes and raise their way of life, and looking for ways to do so, so were poorer men. Urban growth, the expansion of peasant farming and increasing overseas trade all implied changes in everyday practice, mostly unrecorded, brought about by men and women well below the ranks of kings and nobles.

Various material and economic circumstances can serve as a background explanation to the distinctive surge of creative activity from later Anglo-Saxon times to the thirteenth century. The availability of underutilized land in many parts of Britain must figure in any such list, since it would otherwise have been impossible for agriculture to have expanded as rapidly as it did. Some commentators stress the mildness of the climate during this period. The preponderantly peaceful state of western Europe is also often cited as a reason for economic development, though in the course of numerous civil wars there were phases of local devastation (as in England in 1069–70 or 1138–43). British economies also benefited from the corresponding expansion of population, output, and expenditure across the Channel, which encouraged the growth of exports—particularly wool—and permitted the growth of the money supply. Without any one of these favourable circumstances, economic development must have been slower—more dependent upon intensive rather than extensive agrarian development, less able to maintain or improve agricultural productivity, more inhibited by doubts concerning the future, and more dependent on opportunities for trade within markets internal to Britain. Though the economy grew through the fulfilment of individual ambitions, such ambitions could only be fulfilled when there were no immovable obstacles in their way.

In the long history of economic growth the period 1050–1300 deserves recognition as a period of substantial achievement throughout Britain, since it resulted in the permanent acquisition of new infrastructure (towns, ports, roads, bridges, reclamation), new institutions (law and law courts, modes of taxation, markets, fairs) and new skills (in agriculture, manufacturing, commerce, and administration). To judge from the chronology of urban development and the volume of money in circulation a period of slower growth between 1050 and 1160, was followed by more rapid development during the following hundred or so years. John Langdon, using a theory of economic development devised by the economist Joseph Schumpeter, has recently analysed this period as an upswing of economic activity associated with investment in a distinctive range of institutional and technological innovations, many of which were the product of landlord enterprise, though they required both a response and secondary innovation from other social groups. Amongst the institutional innovations the spread of trading, credit, and legal institutions associated with both new and old marketing centres were exceptionally important, and among technological innovations may be listed the introduction of windmills, fulling mills, and new textile machinery.[39] An interpretation along these lines has the distinctive advantage that it provides an explanation for the accelerated population growth and urban development of the period; population growth was responding, at least initially, to improved opportunities for employment.

The discussion so far leads to no distinctive explanation why urban growth, commercial expansion, and the growth of landlord incomes were arrested in the late thirteenth century or why it was so long before they were resumed. So, having considered some reasons why the economy was able to expand between the eleventh and the thirteenth centuries, it is now time to turn to examine why that phase of development came to an end. This question is a heavily debated one, and no simple answer is satisfactory. Eight different lines of thinking about this phenomenon will be lined up here for convenience; all will need further examination later on. Four of the eight are stagnation models, useful chiefly as explanations for a levelling off of economic development in the late thirteenth century. These will be labelled the investment model, the resources model, the urban-demand model, and the exploitation model. Four others are catastrophe models that aim to explain crises emerging after 1300; these are the climate model, the war-costs models, the Black Death model, and the monetary model. They are summarized, for convenience, in Table 4.3. Since many of these interpretations of the evidence are in some degree compatible with each other—indeed are sometimes complementary—differences between their proponents are often much less profound than they are made to seem.

Stagnation Models of Economic Change, c.1260–1300

The investment model springs directly from the notion that the upswing of the period 1180–1300 was based on a distinctive range of new investment opportunities. The Schumpeterian interpretation of economic development predicts that the profitability of any given collection of investment opportunities will not be capable of indefinite expansion. It is not difficult to see why, after several generations of investment in new towns and markets and new mills, the prospects of continuing development along the same lines were growing poorer. New developments after about 1260 were less profitable because the best locations for new towns, markets, and mills had already been developed, ways of life had accommodated to the new installations, and it was harder for new enterprises to attract custom. The new towns and markets founded after 1260 were minor affairs, and many fewer than in the past were capable of long-term survival. They had less impact on local economies than investments that had gone before, and

TABLE 4.3. *Survey of reasons given for the economic problems of British economies from the later thirteenth century*

	c.1260–1300	c.1300–1348	after 1348
Stagnation models:			
Limited investment opportunities	yes	yes	no
Limited resources of land	yes	yes	no
Limited urban demand	yes	yes	no
Excessive exploitation of the peasantry	yes	yes	no
Catastrophe models:			
Deteriorating climate	?	yes	?
Wartime taxation and destruction	no	yes	no
Epidemic mortality	no	no	yes
Declining money stock	no	yes	yes

Note: 'yes' and 'no' simply signify which arguments have (or have not) been prominent in historians' explanations of the course of events during each of the three time periods. A 'no' does not imply that the argument is wholly irrelevant.

this discouraged further investment along the same lines.[40] No new investment opportunities of comparable potential were available, so the rate of economic development levelled off between 1260 and 1300. This model does not have any strong explanation for the extent to which British economies contracted during the fourteenth and fifteenth centuries.

The resources model springs from the considerations of limited natural resources and limited technical knowledge that were explored in Chapter 1. It postulates that agriculture could no longer expand, and that there was a mounting crisis in the adequacy of peasant livelihoods in the late thirteenth century as a result of intensifying pressure of population on limited resources of land. The argument appeals to declining reserves of available land, the tendency for existing holdings of land to be subdivided, and the small size of the resulting family holdings. To that extent it is a pessimistic model that systematically downplays the significance of innovation and development in the thirteenth-century economy. It relates best to the most commercially developed and heavily settled parts of England and its application is more problematic in more slightly populated regions, where population pressure was less apparent, and land usage less intensive.[41] Its explanatory power is limited to explaining why economic growth based on agrarian expansion might slow down or stop, and to explaining the severity of famine in 1315–18. In the longer term the resources argument fails altogether to explain why the cultivated area and the population supported by agriculture should have suffered a severe and lengthy reduction during the fourteenth and fifteenth centuries. One suggestion has been that over-exploitation of the land during the thirteenth century had undermined the fertility of the soil, and that this prevented a return to former levels of cultivation. Another is that nuptual practices adapted to acute poverty around 1300 in such a way as to inhibit reproduction, probably through later marriages, and that this change became so built into social custom as to inhibit fertility from responding to mortality crises. Unfortunately neither argument is convincingly supported by positive evidence, and neither of them sits very comfortably with such information as we have.

The urban-demand model proposes that the brake on development in the later thirteenth century arose not from the impossibility of increasing or maintaining the supply of food and raw materials (as the resources model implies) but from the weakness of demand. This model includes the high costs of transport to large urban markets as a related consideration. In sharp contrast to the resources model, it lays great store on the importance of the commercial sector, rather than population growth and the subsistence sector, as a force behind the economic expansion of the twelfth and thirteenth centuries. Whereas the resources model argues for limited production possibilities as the principal barrier to development, the urban-demand model takes the restricted level of urban demand as the decisive constraint. The two models are alike in having no explanation for the declining population and output of the fourteenth and fifteenth centuries. It has been suggested that around 1300 towns fell victim to the environmental problems of growth to the extent that poor sanitation and overcrowding raised urban mortality.[42] It is difficult, though, to see why English towns of around 1300 should have been more vulnerable in this respect than the larger and growing towns of the sixteenth century, and the argument is even more awkward when extended to the smaller towns of Wales, Scotland, and Ireland.

The exploitation model derives from the evidence of pressure from kings and lords on the lower ranks of society that was discussed in Chapter 3. Since the types of evidence called upon to support it overlap with that needed for the resources model, the two do not contradict each other, and in practice they are regularly combined. The proponents of this model may argue (contentiously) that large incomes from rents and fines reduced the interest of landlords in investing in their properties or investing in higher productivity. But their most distinctive argument is that the increasing availability of money both encouraged and enabled kings and landlords to inflict unprecedented level of exploitation upon dependent peasants; the argument depends heavily on downplaying the strength of customary constraints on seigniorial rapacity. According to this view, rising levels of exploitation had a limit at the point where, around 1300, exceptional burdens on the peasantry

induced a crisis both in general standards of welfare and in landlord–tenant relations. Around 1300 rents and taxes were undoubtedly high by past standards. A
relatively prosperous tenant like Robert le Kyng of Bishops Cleeve (Gloucestershire), with about 30 acres of land, could expect to raise about £3 12s. 0d. in cash
each year from sales of produce, but would have to pay at least 40–50 per cent of
this sum in rents, in other payments to his landlord, the bishop of Worcester, in
cash tithes to his parish and in taxes to the king.[43] Even among peasants of this
class, such rates of exploitation by their superiors reduced the capacity to maintain
their property, and among poor tenants they undermined the ability of the
population to feed itself and reproduce.[44] The argument can also draw on evidence
that in England the late thirteenth century was a period of exceptionally high and
damaging wartime taxation.[45] In this model unlike the previous one, change was
propelled by the rural rather than the urban economy. The exploitation model is,
again, better at explaining why long-term growth of rents and landlord incomes
slowed around 1300 than at interpreting what happened next. In one version, a
change of course during the fourteenth century was brought about by increasingly
effective tenant resistance. This is a fair observation—as attested, most notably, in
the Peasants' Revolt of 1381—but the model has no intrinsic capacity to explain
why tenant resistance proved successful during the fourteenth and fifteenth century
after having earlier been so seriously ineffective. In this respect the resources model
is needed as a complementary one, since it predicts that landlords would be in a
weaker position as population declined and the demand for land decreased.

Catastrophe Models of Economic Change, c.1300–1460

Of the various explanations for declining population after 1300, the climate model
is the most comprehensive, but also the most problematic. It proposes that what
happened around 1300 was the result of a change in world climate at the end of
a period of warmth. There is indeed widespread evidence for a 'medieval warm
period', that corresponded in various parts of Europe to reduced flooding (as in
eastern Norway), higher tree lines (as on the Kola peninsula in Russia),[46] variations
in ground temperature (Czechoslovakia),[47] or changes in the range of prevalent
fauna and flora (as in the south-western Baltic Sea or the Cairngorms region of the
Scottish Highlands).[48] Unfortunately, the dating of this warm period varies between
the different scientists who have identified it. Amongst recent studies, in eastern
Norway it is estimated to have lasted from 1000 to 1400, on the Kola peninsula from
1000 to 1300, and in Czechoslovakia from 1100 to 1300, but in the south-western
Baltic it was at its peak in 1050 and ended around 1200. A study from western
Norway dates a later warm period from 1330 to 1600.[49] There is growing evidence
from dendrochronology, however, that in many parts of the world temperatures

were low between 1318 and 1353, especially in the 1340s; the reasons remain to be determined, but they may relate to some exceptional movement in the earth's crust.[50] If we concentrate on British documentary evidence, without reference to that from further afield, there is support for the idea that the climate became wetter in the late thirteenth century and was particularly unstable in the early fourteenth; flooding became a particular problem in low-lying areas of the east coast in this period.[51] These various findings, interesting though they may be in the context of current debate about global warming, are at present too imprecise to be used in a general model for any of the changes that concern us, though there is likely to be a valid and useful argument to be built on them should they become more consistent. If the data could be given more precision, they could account both for the end of agrarian expansion and for prolonged decline in arable husbandry in regions where the population-resources model seems inappropriate, as in most of Scotland.[52] At present, though, it is not clear what this climatic evidence can be used to explain.

The war-costs model, a relative newcomer, is again a supply-side argument, this time emphasizing the costs of international trade rather than the costs of agricultural production.[53] It is designed chiefly to explain international problems of the fourteenth-century economy and their impact upon English and Scottish industry and trade. This model draws attention to the fact that the range of commercial opportunities open to merchants was disrupted from the 1290s by major wars that raised transaction costs—in particular the costs of long-distance transport—reduced profits, and lowered expectations. England was at war with both Scotland and France in Edward I's later years, and from 1338 began the long series of conflicts between England and France (often involving Scotland as well) known as the Hundred Years War.[54] As an explanation of the changing course of economic development, this argument has the interesting characteristic that it elevates the international economy to the status of a prime mover, whose fortunes had sufficient impact to affect production levels and welfare throughout rural society. For this reason, it is closely allied to analyses of internal trade that stress the demand of larger towns, and the role of merchants, in the structuring of markets.[55] Many of the implications of this model are yet to be worked out and tested, since it is as yet uncertain whether international trade and urban demand were sufficiently important to British economies to be assigned pride of place in accounting for fundamental changes in trend.

Many of the changes of the later fourteenth and fifteenth centuries need to be explained by the Black Death of 1348–9, a disaster on such a scale, and with such far-reaching implications, that it must figure in any explanation of the course of later events.[56] Although often discussed alongside the effects of high population levels and low living standards in the early fourteenth century, the Black Death was not particularly associated with poor living conditions or overcrowded populations. It made its way readily into monasteries, castles, and manor houses. It was an exogenous cause of social and economic change (one, that is, independent of current social and economic developments) rather than an endogenous one caused by existing problems. The Black Death dominates many discussions of social and economic change, as if it alone was responsible for the trends of the following 150 years. Yet many phenomena once attributed to the Black Death were more apparent thirty years afterwards than in its immediate aftermath.[57] The Black Death, in other words, does nothing to remove the need for theoretical structures to accommodate economic and social change as a complex series of developments rather than single and unique events. The catastrophe of 1348–9 cannot explain the economic contraction that continued into the fifteenth century, but the argument has more long-term implications if subsequent outbreaks of plague are taken into account. There was a serious and widespread epidemic in 1361–2, and numerous repeats through the later fourteenth and fifteenth centuries. Taken in conjunction with other demographic variables, and the presence of other diseases capable of causing crises of high mortality, endemic plague is a necessary part of any explanation of population change between 1349 and 1500.

Finally, the money model proposes that the possibilities for commercial expansion were governed by the availability of money, and of the metals from which money was made. Since coinage is subject to attrition through wear, loss, and export, a steady supply of new metal is required even to maintain it at a given level. The requirements of a growing economy are yet more demanding. Landlord investment, commercial growth, urban growth, agrarian expansion, and population increase could occur only so long as the money base to support such expansion could be increased, and that depended as far as Britain was concerned upon domestic and European reserves of accessible silver and gold. These conditions were met between the eleventh and early fourteenth centuries chiefly by imports of silver obtained through foreign trade, ultimately from mines in Germany and elsewhere in central Europe. These favourable circumstances were not maintained through the fourteenth and fifteenth centuries. The wastage and outflow of silver from England between 1319 and 1351 is estimated to have been about the equivalent of 50–70 per cent of the total money stock at the beginning of the period, and the effect was to depress prices, particularly during the recession of the 1330s. One main reason for the loss of currency in circulation was that at the start of the Hundred Years War silver drained out of England to meet the military and diplomatic needs of King Edward III.[58] In addition, after 1350 Europe's known indigenous sources of silver were becoming exhausted. The mines at Kutná Hora, the principal source, ended their activities in the early fifteenth century.[59] Problems of money supply reversed the expansive role of money in the thirteenth century.

This model has a ready explanation for prolonged economic contraction—reducible to a well-attested secular contraction in the European money supply, much of it explained by events happening outside Britain and affecting the markets for British and Irish exports. But the significance of monetary contraction for overall levels of economic activity relates principally to the period *c.*1390–1460 or later rather than to anything earlier.[60] Up to that point, though there were certainly monetary disturbances affecting economic activity, they were of temporary significance. This suggests that the monetary model is unlikely to be any more self-sufficient as a monocausal explanation of changing trends than the others. It can be combined at will with any of them, since the evidence on which it is based does not contradict them at any point.

These different ways of explaining the break in trend around 1300 are all relevant to different aspects of the complex course of events under review, and they complement each other at many points, though they also explain different things. The desirability of retaining a mixed bag of explanatory devices, rather than settling for a monocausal explanation, is suggested both by the complexity of the events under observation and their very ragged chronology. Even the end of the growth phase is an imprecisely defined moment. The range of explanations depends in part on whether the significant turning point is seen as the slowing down of land clearance and of significant investment in new towns (*c.*1260), the peak volume of wool exports (1304–5), the peak volume of currency in circulation (*c.*1311), the peak of population size (probably in 1314, on the eve of the famines of 1315–18, though earlier in places), the demographic disaster of the Black Death (1348–9), the transformation of manorial structures (mostly after 1380), or bullion famine (after *c.*1390). Because of the complexity of the events in question, willingness to explore the validity of each of the models, and to appreciate where each one may have explanatory force, is preferable to the alternative course of adopting a fixed prejudice in favour of one of them. No attempt will be made in future chapters either to privilege or exclude any one of these various lines of thought.

NOTES

1. N. Mayhew, 'Modelling Medieval Monetisation', in R. H. Britnell and B. M. S. Campbell (eds.), *A Commercialising Economy: England 1086 to c.1300* (Manchester, 1995), 72.
2. Ibid 74; B. M. S. Campbell, *English Seigniorial Agriculture, 1250–1450* (Cambridge, 2000), 409.
3. See below (ch. 21).
4. E. King, *Peterborough Abbey, 1086–110: A Study in the Land Market* (Cambridge, 1973), 70–84.
5. H. M. Dunsford and S. J. Harris, 'Colonization of the Wasteland in County Durham, 1100–1400', *Economic History Review*, 56 (2003), 34–56.

6. H. E. Hallam, *Settlement and Society: A Study of the Early Agrarian History of South Lincolnshire* (Cambridge, 1965), 3–118; S. Rippon, *The Severn Estuary: Landscape Evolution and Wetland Reclamation* (1997), 206–19; R. A. L. Smith, *Canterbury Cathedral Priory: A Study in Monastic Administration* (Cambridge, 1943), 172–89.

7. Campbell, *English Seigniorial Agriculture*, 387, 390.

8. J. Gilbert, 'The Monastic Record of a Border Landscape 1136 to 1236', *Scottish Geographical Magazine*, 99 (1983), 4–15.

9. A sack is reckoned to have contained 260 fleeces. E. M. Carus Wilson and O. Coleman, *England's Export Trade, 1275–1547* (Oxford, 1963), 13, 41.

10. A. A. M. Duncan, *Scotland: The Making of the Kingdom* (Edinburgh, 1989), 426–31; D. H. Williams, *The Welsh Cistercians* (Pontypool, 1970), 67–9; K. Down, 'Colonial Society and Economy in the High Middle Ages', in A. Cosgrove (ed.), *A New History of Ireland*, ii: *Medieval Ireland, 1169–1534* (Oxford, 1987), 477–80.

11. W. Childs and T. O'Neill, 'Overseas Trade', in Cosgrove, ed., *New History of Ireland*, ii. 509–10.

12. P. G. B. McNeill and H. L. MacQueen (eds,), *Atlas of Scottish History to 1707* (Edinburgh, 1996), 241. I have converted 858 tonnes to fleeces at the rate of 1,700 fleeces per tonne: ibid. 251.

13. B. M. S. Campbell, 'Agricultural Productivity in Medieval England: Some Evidence from Eastern Norfolk', *Journal of Economic History*, 43 (1983), 379–404; C. Thornton, 'The Determinants of Land Productivity on the Bishop of Winchester's Demesne of Rimpton, 1208–1403', in B. M. S. Campbell and M. Overton (eds.), *Land, Labour and Livestock: Historical Studies in European Agricultural Productivity* (Manchester, 1991), 183–210.

14. Campbell, *English Seigniorial Agriculture*, 392–5; D. L. Farmer, 'Grain Yields on Winchester Manors in the Later Middle Ages', *Economic History Review*, 2nd ser. 30 (1977), 562.

15. See below, (Chs. 19 and 24).

16. Campbell, *English Seigniorial Agriculture*, 392–5; Thornton, 'Determinants', 201–10.

17. See below (Ch. 7).

18. S. Letters with others, *Gazetteer of Markets and Fairs in England and Wales to 1516*, 2 vols. (2003). This material is on-line, as the Gazetteer of Markets and Fairs in England and Wales to 1516, at **www.history.ac.uk/cmh/gaz/gazweb2.html**.

19. R. H. Britnell, 'The Proliferation of Markets in England, 1200–1349', *Economic History Review*, 2nd ser. 33 (1981), 209–21.

20. R. H. Britnell, *The Commercialization of Medieval Society, 1000–1500* 2nd edn. (Manchester, 1996), 49, 115; C. Dyer, 'How Urbanized was Medieval England', in J.-M. Duvosquel and E. Thoen (eds.), *Peasants and Townsmen in Medieval Europe: Studia in Honorem Adriaan Verhulst* (Ghent, 1995), 172–4, 177.

21. A. Dyer, ' "Urban Decline" in England, 1377–1525', in T. R. Slater (ed.), *Towns in Decline, AD 100–1600* (Aldershot, 2000), 266–88.

22. See below (Ch. 17); D. Ditchburn and A. Macdonald, 'Medieval Scotland, 1100–1560', in R. A. Houston and W. W. J. Knox (eds.), *The New Penguin History of Scotland from the Earliest Times to the Present Day* (2002), 114–15.

23. N. Mayhew, 'Modelling Medieval Monetization', 62; M. Allen, 'The Volume of the English Currency, 1158–1470', *Economic History Review*, 54 (2001), 607.

24. Ditchburn and Macdonald, 'Medieval Scotland', 114; N. Mayhew, 'Alexander III—A Silver Age? An Essay in Scottish Medieval Economic History', in N. H. Reid (ed.), *Scotland in the Reign of Alexander III* (Edinburgh, 1990), 61; E. Gemmill and N. Mayhew, *Changing Values in Medieval Scotland: A Study of Prices, Money, and Weights and Measures* (Cambridge, 1995), 140–1.

25. M. Dolley, 'Coinage to 1534: The Sign of the Times', in Cosgrove (ed.), *New History of Ireland*, ii. 818–26.

26. T. John, 'Population Change in Medieval Warwickshire: Domesday Book to the Hundred Rolls of 1279–1280', *Local Population Studies*, 59 (1997), 41–53.

27. J. Z. Titow, 'Some Evidence of the Thirteenth-Century Population Increase', *Economic History Review*, 2nd ser. 14 (1961–2), 218–24.

28. Z. Razi, *Life, Marriage and Death in a Medieval Parish: Economy, Society and Demography in Halesowen, 1270–1400* (Cambridge, 1980), 28, 39–41, 101–7, 117.

29. L. R. Poos, 'The Rural Population of Essex in the Later Middle Ages', *Economic History Review*, 2nd ser. 38 (1985), 522.

30. K. C. Newton, *The Manor of Writtle* (Chichester, 1970), 79–80.

31. D. Postles, 'Demographic Change in Kibworth Harcourt, Leicestershire, in the Later Middle Ages', *Local Population Studies*, 48 (1992), 41–8.

32. M. Mate, 'The Occupation of the Land: Kent and Sussex', in E. Miller (ed.), *The Agrarian History of England and Wales*, iii: *1348–1500* (Cambridge, 1991), 128.

33. Campbell, *English Seigniorial Agriculture*, 403.

34. H. E. Hallam, 'Population Movements in England, 1086–1350', in id. (ed.), *The Agrarian History of England and Wales*, ii: *1042–1350* (Cambridge, 1988), 512–13.

35. Campbell, *English Seigniorial Agriculture*, 405.

36. Population estimates for 1680, when England's population was about 4.9 m., are 0.4 m. in Wales, 1.1 m. in Scotland, 2.0 m. in Ireland: P. Deane and W. A. Cole, *British Economic Growth, 1688–1959: Trends and Structure* (Cambridge, 1967), 103; R. Schofield, 'British Population Change, 1700–1871', in R. Floud and D. McCloskey (eds.), *The Economic History of Britain since 1700*, i: *1700–1860*, 2nd edn. (Cambridge, 1994), 66. These figures probably need to be scaled down for c.1300 because of the weaker development of west-coast economies.

37. Below (Ch. 25).

38. S. G. E. Lythe, 'Economic Life', in J. M. Brown (ed.), *Scottish Society in the Fifteenth Century* (1977), 66.

39. J. Langdon, 'The Long Thirteenth Century: An Era of Schumpeterian Growth?' (unpublished paper, 2002).

40. Britnell, 'Proliferation of Markets', 219–20.

41. R. A. Dodgshon, *Land and Society in Early Scotland* (Oxford, 1981), 132; Dunsford and Harris, 'Colonization of the Wasteland', 54.

42. G. W. Grantham, 'Espaces privilégés: productivité agraire et zones d'approvisionnement des villes dans l'Europe préindustrielle', *Annales*, 52 (1997), 695–725.

43. C. Dyer, *Standards of Living in the Later Middle Ages: Social Change in England, c.1200–1520* (Cambridge, 1989), 115.

44. R. H. Hilton, *Class Conflict and the Crisis of Feudalism: Essays in Medieval Social History* (1985), 244.

45. J. Maddicott, 'The English Peasantry and the Demands of the Crown, 1294–1341', in T. H. Aston (ed.), *Landlords, Peasants and Politics in Medieval England* (Cambridge, 1987), 285–359.

46. A. Hiller, T. Boettger, and C. Kremenetski, 'Medieval Climatic Warming Recorded by Radiocarbon Dated Alpine Tree-Line Shift on the Kola Peninsula, Russia', *The Holocene*, 11 (2001), 491–7.

47. L. Bodri and V. Cermak, 'Climate Change of the Last Millennium Inferred from Borehole Temperatures: Regional Patterns of Climatic Changes in the Czech Republic, part III', *Global and Planetary Change*, 21 (1999), 225–35.

48. E. Andren, T. Andren, T. and G. Sohlenius, 'The Holocene History of the Southwestern Baltic Sea as Reflected in a Sediment Core from the Bornholm Basin', *Boreas*, 29 (2000), 233–50; S. J. Brooks and H. J. B. Birks, 'Chironomid-Inferred Air Temperatures from Lateglacial and Holocene Sites in North-West Europe: Progress and Problems', *Quaternary Science Reviews* 20 (2001), 1723–41.

49. G. Mikalsen, H. P. Sejrup, and I. Aarseth, 'Late-Holocene Changes in Ocean Circulation and Climate: Foraminiferal and Isotopic Evidence from Sulafjord, Western Norway', *The Holocene*, 11 (2001), 437–46.

50. Campbell, *English Seigniorial Agriculture*, 22.

51. M. Bailey, '*Per Impetum Maris*: Natural Disaster and Economic Decline in Eastern England, 1275–1350', in B. M. S. Campbell (ed.), *Before the Black Death: Studies in the 'Crisis' of the Early Fourteenth Century* (Manchester, 1991), 84–208.

52. Mayhew, 'Alexander III', 58.

53. The argument here takes no account of the impact of taxation of trade, for which see below (Chs. 12, 22).

54. J. Munro, 'Industrial Transformations in the North-West European Textile Trades, c.1290–c.1340: Economic Progress or Economic Crisis?', in Campbell (ed.), *Before the Black Death*, 120–30.

55. J. Masschaele, *Peasants, Merchants and Markets: Inland Trade in Medieval England, 1150–1350* (New York, 1997).

56. See below (Ch. 24).

57. A. R. Bridbury, 'The Black Death', in id. *The English Economy: From Bede to the Reformation* (Woodbridge, 1992), 200–17.

58. Allen, 'Volume of the English Currency', 607; N. J. Mayhew, 'Numismatic Evidence and Falling Prices in the Fourteenth Century', *Economic History Review*, 2nd ser. 27 (1974), 1–15.

59. P. Spufford, *Money and its Use in Medieval Europe* (Cambridge, 1988), 343–4.

60. J. Day, *The Medieval Market Economy* (Oxford, 1987), 1–48.

FURTHER READING

Allen, M., 'The Volume of the English Currency, 1158–1470', *Economic History Review*, 54 (2001).

Bailey, M., 'The Concept of the Margin in the Medieval English Economy', *Economic History Review*, 2nd ser. 14 (1989).

—— 'Peasant Welfare in England, 1290–1348', *Economic History Review*, 51 (1998).

Beresford, M. W., *New Towns of the Middle Ages: Town Plantation in England, Wales and Gascony* (1967).

Bolton, J. L., *The Medieval English Economy, 1150–1500* (1980).

Bradley, J., 'Planned Anglo-Norman Towns in Ireland', in H. Clarke and A. Simms (eds.), *The Comparative History of Urban Origins in Non-Roman Europe* (Oxford, 1985).

Bridbury, A. R., *The English Economy: From Bede to the Reformation* (Woodbridge, 1992).

Britnell, R. H., *The Commercialisation of Medieval Society, 1100–1500*, 2nd edn. (Manchester, 1996).

—— 'The Proliferation of Markets in England, 1200–1349', *Economic History Review*, 2nd ser. 33 (1981).

—— and Hatcher, J. (eds.), *Progress and Problems in Medieval England* (Cambridge, 1996).

Brown, H. P., and Hopkins, S. V., *A Perspective of Wages and Prices* (1981).

Campbell, B. M. S., 'England: Land and People', in S. H. Rigby (ed.), *A Companion to Britain in the Later Middle Ages* (Oxford, 2003).

—— *English Seigniorial Agriculture, 1250–1450* (Cambridge, 2000).

—— (ed.), *Before the Black Death: Studies in the 'Crisis' of the Early Fourteenth Century* (Manchester, 1991).

Challis, G. E. (ed.), *A New History of the Royal Mint* (Cambridge, 1992).

Day, J., *The Medieval Market Economy* (Oxford, 1987).

Ditchburn, D., and Macdonald, A., 'Medieval Scotland, 1100–1560', in R. A. Houston and W. W. J. Knox (eds.), *The New Penguin History of Scotland from the Earliest Times to the Present Day* (2002).

Dobson, R. B., 'Urban Decline in Late Medieval England', *Transactions of the Royal Historical Society*, 27 (1977).

Dyer, A., ' "Urban Decline" in England, 1377–1525', in T. R. Slater (ed.), *Towns in Decline, AD 100–1600* (Aldershot, 2000).

Dyer, C., *Standards of Living in the Later Middle Ages: Social Change in England, c.1200–1520* (Cambridge, 1989).

Farmer, D. L., 'Grain Yields on Winchester Manors in the Later Middle Ages', *Economic History Review*, 2nd ser. 30 (1977), 555–66.

—— 'Prices and Wages', in H. E. Hallam (ed.), *The Agrarian History of England and Wales*, ii: *1042–1350* (Cambridge, 1988).

—— 'Prices and Wages, 1350–1500', in E. Miller (ed.), *The Agrarian History of England and Wales*, iii: *1348–1500* (Cambridge, 1991).

Gemmill, E., and Mayhew, N., *Changing Values in Medieval Scotland: A Study of Prices, Money, and Weights and Measures* (Cambridge, 1995).

Hallam, H. E., 'Population Movements in England, 1086–1350', in id. (ed.), *The Agrarian History of England and Wales*, ii: *1042–1350* (Cambridge, 1988).

Hatcher, J., *Plague, Population and the English Economy, 1348–1530* (1977).

—— and Bailey, M., *Modelling the Middle Ages: The History and Theory of England's Economic Development* (Oxford, 2001).

John, T., 'Population Change in Medieval Warwickshire: Domesday Book to the Hundred Rolls of 1279–1280', *Local Population Studies*, 59 (1997).

Langdon, J., 'Water-Mills and Windmills in the West Midlands, 1086–1500', *Economic History Review*, 44 (1991).

Kershaw, I., 'The Great Famine and Agrarian Crisis in England, 1315–1322', *Past and Present*, 59 (1973), repr. in R. H. Hilton (ed.), *Peasants, Knights and Heretics: Studies in Medieval English Social History* (Cambridge, 1976).

Mayhew, N., 'Alexander III—A Silver Age? An Essay in Scottish Medieval Economic History', in N. H. Reid (ed.), *Scotland in the Reign of Alexander III* (Edinburgh, 1990).

—— 'Modelling Medieval Monetisation', in R. H. Britnell and B. M. S. Campbell (eds.), *A Commercialising Economy: England 1086 to c.1300* (Manchester, 1995).

—— 'Money and Prices in England from Henry II to Edward III', *Agricultural History Review*, 35 (1987).

—— 'Population, Money Supply and the Velocity of Circulation in England', *Economic History Review*, 48 (1995).

Metcalf, D. M. (ed.), *Coinage in Medieval Scotland (1100–1600)* (Oxford, 1977).

Miller, E. (ed.), *The Agrarian History of England and Wales*, iii: *1348–1500* (Cambridge, 1991).

—— 'England in the Twelfth and Thirteenth Centuries: An Economic Contrast?', *Economic History Review*, 2nd ser. 24 (1971).

Poos, L. R., 'The Rural Population of Essex in the Later Middle Ages', *Economic History Review*, 2nd ser. 38 (1985).

Postan, M. M., *The Medieval Economy and Society* (1972).

Postles, D., 'Demographic Change in Kibworth Harcourt, Leicestershire, in the Later Middle Ages', *Local Population Studies*, 48 (1992).

Razi, Z., *Life, Marriage and Death in a Medieval Parish: Economy, Society and Demography in Halesowen, 1270–1400* (Cambridge, 1980).

Rigold, S. E., 'Small Change in the Light of Medieval Site-Finds', in N. J. Mayhew (ed.), *Edwardian Monetary Affairs (1279–1344)* (Oxford, 1977).

Russell, J. C., *British Medieval Population* (Albuquerque, 1948).

Spufford, P., *Money and its Use in Medieval Europe* (Cambridge, 1988).

Titow, J. Z., 'Some Evidence of the Thirteenth-Century Population Increase', *Economic History Review*, 2nd ser. 14 (1961–2).

—— *Winchester Yields: A Study in Medieval Agricultural Productivity* (Cambridge, 1972).

1050–1300

CHAPTER 5

Britain and Ireland in the Later Eleventh Century

All parts of Britain in the later eleventh century had irresistible attractions for the Scandinavian peoples to the north and east, and to their colony further south, in Normandy. Raids from Norway now took the form of occasional royal expeditions to the western seaboard of Scotland, Wales, and Ireland. Snorri Sturluson's *Heimskringla* describes at length a raid of Magnus Barelegs, king of Norway (1093–1103), on the Hebrides, the Isle of Man, and Anglesey in 1098.[1] But the chief threat to these parts was from nearer at hand, since the Viking way of life survived in the Orkneys into the later twelfth century. Svein Asleifarson of Gairsay in Orkney died in a raid on Dublin sometime after 1158. His lifestyle is described in the *Orkneyinga Saga*, of which he is one of the leading actors:

This was how Svein used to live. Winter he would spend at home on Gairsay, where he entertained some eighty men at his own expense. His drinking hall was so big, there was nothing in Orkney to compare with it. In the spring he had more than enough to occupy him, with a great deal of seed to sow which he saw to carefully himself. Then when that job was done, he would go off plundering in the Hebrides and in Ireland on what he called his 'spring trip', then back home just after midsummer, where he stayed till the cornfields had been reaped and the grain was safely in. After that he would go off raiding again, and never came back till the first month of winter was ended. This he used to call his 'autumn trip'.[2]

The wealthiest parts of Britain by far lay in southern and eastern England, whose inhabitants had good reason to regret the attractiveness of their land to Danes and the Normans. The institution of geld, a tax levied for the purpose of buying off Danish aggression, had stripped England of much of her silver in the early part of the eleventh century. Geld payments explain why much of the surviving English coinage from this period is in the museums of Scandinavia; 3,000 Anglo-Saxon pennies have been found in Norway, 4,000 in Denmark, 10,000 in mainland Sweden, and 25,000 in Gotland.[3] The huge levies paid to Danish invaders and Danish kings between 991 and 1051 were not compensated by increased demands for exports.

Such spoliation must temporarily have damaged the commercial opportunities available in England, and hampered the English merchant class in relation to its Flemish competitors. The Norman Conquest of 1066 is again unlikely to have been immediately beneficial for English commerce, given the looting, high taxation, and civil unrest that characterized the Conqueror's reign.[4] England had suffered for its eleventh-century wealth through its openness to external aggression, and its external trade was probably less extensive than it would have been had all external relations been peaceful.

The types of shipping available in the mid-eleventh century had been tested by centuries of trading and raiding in northern waters, chiefly by the Scandinavians. Their contacts with Scotland and Ireland were sustained by oaken, clinker-built ships, propelled by a single sail but also equipped for rowing in calm waters or narrow spaces. In addition to their warships the Vikings had developed a more specialized cargo and transport vessel, the knarr. The streamlined design and shallow draught of these ships enabled them to cover 120 miles or more a day in favourable circumstances, but simultaneously limited their carrying capacity to at most 50 tons, usually less. The ships in use across the North Sea, both by the English and the French, were derived from Viking prototypes. They are best represented by the numerous ships of the Bayeux Tapestry, which was commissioned soon after 1066, though it is not certain to what extent its designer was working from direct observation. They varied in length from about 80 to 140 feet, with the possibility of between 16 and 30 oars on each side, and had a single, centrally positioned, mast and sail. The tapestry demonstrates clearly that in this tradition of shipbuilding rudders were fixed to the sides of ships, not to the keelpost.[5]

Much of Britain was too far away from the main commercial axes of Europe to benefit from long-distance trade in the later eleventh century. The chief exception in the west was the continuing slave trade of Bristol and Dublin, which thrived on the possibility of raiding the undefended shores of Wales.[6] Merchants operating from Dublin exploited Anglesey as a major source of slaves, and actively intervened in the politics of northern Wales to that end. Slaves could be sold from Dublin through the western European ports.[7] Apart from the slave trade, which on the English side came under threat from ecclesiastical and royal disapproval in the late eleventh century, there was little opportunity for long-distance traffic along much of the western coast of Britain. Even the shores facing east and southwards were not all able to take advantage of continental trade. Though the passage from south-eastern England to northern France and the Low Countries was quick and usually safe, the northern parts of Britain were disadvantaged by a much longer and more hazardous crossing. As in most parts of Europe, merchants were reluctant to risk long journeys across open sea. Those from northern England and Scotland had little inducement to cross the North Sea directly, and if they coasted down the eastern flank of England before making their crossing the consequent length of the journey put them at a disadvantage relative to English merchants further south. Except for parts in contact with Norway, there is consequently little sign of overseas trade from Scotland in the mid-eleventh century—little evidence of coastal towns, foreign merchants, or imported products that might have left archaeological remains.[8]

Nevertheless, opportunities for peaceful trade had long been established in parts of Britain nearest the Continent, and were maintained despite all setbacks throughout the eleventh century. Regular exchanges between Scandinavia and eastern England had followed the heavy Scandinavian settlement of the later ninth century, as can be seen from the Coppergate excavations at York, a city much frequented by Danish merchants. From 1016 to 1035 England had been subject to a Danish king, Cnut, who had inherited the kingdom of Denmark from his brother in 1018 or 1019 and conquered the kingdom of Norway in 1028. In his day a large Scandinavian community had grown up in London, particularly in the western and southern suburbs. Anglo-Scandinavian trade perhaps reached its peak during his reign. Five churches in London were dedicated to St Olaf of Norway, and the dedication of St Clement Danes seems to be another legacy of this settlement. The re-establishment of an English royal line after Cnut's death had not removed England from the sphere of Viking trade. It is likely that the dedications to St Olaf, who was killed in battle only in 1030, belong to a period after Cnut's death.[9] The composition of trade between England and Scandinavia cannot be reconstructed in detail, but it included a large proportion of the kingdom's imported furs, together with amber and whetstones. Through connections in the eastern Baltic, this was probably also a route for luxury goods from Asia. In exchange Scandinavian traders probably took wheat and cloth, together with a certain amount of silver coin.[10]

Besides its regular existing contacts with Scandinavia, England also traded with parts of southern Europe, and these links were strengthening in the later eleventh century. The route from London along the Rhine valley and through the Alps to northern Italy, frequented for the importation of gold, silk, and spices, in exchange for silver, was less vigorous after the Norman Conquest than it had been earlier in the century. However, there was an increasing trade with Spain, chiefly in the hands of English merchants who traded English textiles for leather, silk, spices, and gold. Trade with Champagne and the Rhône Valley through northern France was also increasing.[11] Dyestuffs, wine, and oil had long been imported across the Channel. In exchange, England exported cloth, silver, and raw materials. The early growth of the Flemish textile industry probably created a market for English wool, and benefited some eastern ports, though this trade is more a matter of surmise than of record; it was small in comparison with its volume a hundred years later.[12] After 1066, William I encouraged Jewish merchants to migrate from Rouen, probably in order to maintain valued connections with trade routes from Germany and the Mediterranean, but in practice these connections were already served in London.[13]

Scotland's overseas trade was also favourably affected by the development of markets in Flanders, and despite the kingdom's disadvantages relative to England an awakening of trade can be located in the last quarter of the eleventh century. Some part of this was the result of increased spending on luxuries, such as that encouraged by Queen Margaret, the wife of Malcolm III of Scotland. (This was the Malcolm who had defeated and killed Macbeth in 1057.)[14] But the interests involved were wider than those of the court. It was not long before the Scottish kings were deriving income from tolls on shipping; texts relating to these revenues are attributed to David I, though the attribution is unsafe.[15] By analogy with the Scottish estate revenues discussed in Chapter 3, this income was named cain, but unlike the revenue from land it was at least partly paid in money rather than in produce.

Where opportunity and good luck beckoned, there were men willing to take advantage of it. The sparse provision of commercial facilities along the east coast was augmented by the founding of new towns at Newcastle-upon-Tyne (between 1080 and 1130), Boston (between 1086 and 1113), and King's Lynn (between 1086 and 1095). These ports accommodated both trade with the Continent and coastal trade that extended for hundreds of miles. According to the *Orkneyinga Saga*, Norwegian merchants who visited Grimsby in the early twelfth century met men from as far away as the Orkneys and the Hebrides.[16] These routes offered opportunities for newcomers. Godric of Finchale, as he was later known, was born in Walpole (Norfolk) about the time of the Norman Conquest. He engaged in beach-combing to supplement his livelihood, and built up enough capital to operate as a peddlar. Later he pooled his assets with other merchants, and thrived to the point of being able to trade up the east coast as far as St Andrews in Scotland and across the North Sea to Denmark and Flanders. He also went to Italy, and may have been the 'Guderic, a pirate from the kingdom of England' who was in Palestine in 1102. His career is known only because about 1112 he gave up his lucrative but strenuous career to become a hermit, and so became a fitting subject for hagiography.[17]

The importance of overseas trade for the economy as a whole, and for the daily life of most people in Britain, was restricted by low levels of income and high transport costs. Though there were probably many more points of lading and embarkation than we know of, the small number of well-defined ports, and the rareness of references to ships and merchants in our sources, suggests that only a tiny percentage of the population was dependent upon such trade even in southern and eastern England. Nevertheless, through most of England the economy was already benefiting significantly from overseas trade to the extent that it brought into the kingdom silver that could be coined as money. Since the year 968, shortages of silver in Europe had been partly met by a new source from the Harz mountains of

Saxony. From here, silver passed through trade routes to the Rhineland, and then to the Low Countries and northern France. By 1050 German silver, reminted into English coin, was circulating widely through southern and eastern England and the midlands.[18]

At the time when Domesday Book was being drawn up in 1086, there were nevertheless sharp differences between the various parts of Britain in the extent to which people used money. In much of England coinage was relatively abundant by the standards of Europe at that time. There were forty-four mints in operation during the reign of King Harold, on the eve of the Norman Conquest, and their distribution suggests that money circulated easily throughout the southern part of the kingdom. The importance of currency is confirmed by the taxation system of the English monarchy, since geld was universally assessed in cash, and was levied on many peasant households as well as on their superiors. Tenants of 'warland' in late Anglo-Saxon England owed a range of services to the crown amongst which money payments loomed large since they were liable to pay geld. Many of these geldable holdings in East Anglia were small tenures of 5 acres or less, implying that even relatively poor villagers needed to raise cash.[19] In addition to obligations to the crown, peasant farmers often owed cash rents to their lords. A payment called *gafol*, due to kings in the seventh century, had in many instances been transferred to other landlords as a kind of rent.[20] The number of tenants paying money rent, the *censarii* of Domesday Book, was greater than the survey would suggest, as we know from the rentals of Burton Abbey compiled in the following century.[21] This would imply that throughout the area surveyed by Domesday Book peasants were obliged to participate to some extent in market transactions in order to meet their obligations to those above them.

Many manors on the larger estates recorded in Domesday Book were leased out to tenants who paid an annual rent for them. At the end of the record of each manor in Domesday Book the commissioners recorded what it was worth; this *valor* was not a statement of what each property would sell for but of the net annual income from leasing it.[22] Some of the sums in question are impressive. A tenant called Godfrey leased the archbishop of Canterbury's manor of South Malling (Sussex) for £90. Deddington (Oxfordshire) was said to be worth £60 in 1086, and may be the 'Dalintona' that, according to Orderic Vitalis, rendered £80 a year to its owner in 1105.[23] Given the great size and scattered nature of many estates, it is improbable that lords would normally have welcomed the payment of such obligations in the form of produce, and the role of money payments in estate administration must have been extensive.

There were some major exceptions to the monetization of estate administration, since the annual sums paid to large households were not invariably paid in cash. On the royal estates there was an ancient system of food rents whereby each manor was assessed to provide food for a certain number of days. Many large ecclesiastical estates had similar arrangements, notably the monastic cathedrals of Canterbury and Rochester, the dean and canons of St Paul's Cathedral, and the abbeys of Ely, Ramsey, Bury St Edmunds, and St Albans.[24] The requirements of large households such as these were so great that the eleventh-century marketing structure could not be reliably trusted to provide for them. Some enterprising landlords even tried to supply their own wine; the vineyard recorded at Ely in 1086 was one of the most northerly in Europe.[25] But systems of payment in kind were by no means rigid in the late eleventh century, and landlords were able to adopt a more mixed strategy of money as well as produce when it was convenient for them to do so. The frequent absence of the court and other landowning households on the Continent, for example, made regular food farms redundant.[26]

Several regions of Britain, meanwhile, had no established monetary system. Neither Scotland nor Wales had its own currency, and even English coins were used there only infrequently. There are signs that the circulation of money was increasing in south-eastern Wales in the course of the tenth and eleventh centuries, but it was assessed by the weight of silver rather than by its coined value. It is true that the continuing importance of commercial routes between Scandinavia and the Irish Sea through the tenth and eleventh centuries is confirmed by coin finds. There was a mint at Dublin from about 997 and another on the Isle of Man from the 1030s. Of 81 coins of the tenth and eleventh centuries from a hoard at Kirk Michael on Man, only 22 are Anglo-Saxon, and the rest are Norman, Hiberno-Norse, or Hiberno-Manx. The 41 eleventh-century coins from Peel Castle, also on Man, are all Hiberno-Norse.[27] Money and trade had nevertheless not penetrated far into the hinterlands of the Irish Sea region; the circulation of currency was confined to eastern Ireland and a few other coastal regions. Even in Dublin coin finds are rare, and few Irish coins penetrated even as far as Wales and Scotland.[28] Parts of northern Scotland, especially the north and west which had also been drawn within the zone of Viking commerce, used silver bracelets as a form of money, as well as coins (predominantly English), but in view of their high unit value these probably served more as a store of value, and perhaps as the medium for gift giving, than in regular commercial exchange. There was very little coinage as such in Scotland before about 1136.[29] In much of western and northern Britain the rural population was probably self-sufficient for a large part of its needs and dependent on barter for the rest. Only a few peddlars depended on commerce for their livelihood. Where occupational specializations are mentioned they are in agriculture, and represent the availability of employment on large estates rather than dependence upon market exchange. In the absence of money it was impossible to levy taxes in coin, so that lordship was expressed in exactions of services and renders in kind. Given the general absence or shortage of currency in many northern parts of Britain, it was not possible for all kings and princes to operate with money incomes, and least of all with money incomes derived from general taxation. Instead they exacted various forms of direct levy on the labour or the produce of their dependants. Information about these arrangements becomes available only from about the time they were starting to break down in the twelfth and thirteenth centuries, and is rarely precise. This vagueness in itself suggests the long-standing nature of these older arrangements.

It is not surprising that the forms of such payments show similarities across different cultural regions. The range of produce in question was a narrow one—grain or flour, malt or ale, livestock, poultry, eggs—and the range of alternative methods of allocating obligations was limited by practical consideration of the costs of transport and administration. This restricted range of possibilities, combined with legacies of common cultural inheritance, overlaid with patterns of cultural diffusion, meant that there were strong similarities between widely separated parts of Britain. Distinctions between royal income and that of other powerful men were differences of magnitude rather than kind, especially since kings had frequently alienated parts of their revenues to earls, bishops, and abbeys. Such grants of income were made all the more willingly because of their non-monetary nature; courts could consume only limited quantities, especially from outlying royal estates, and it made sense to donate the surplus to the fulfilment of political and religious obligations. Early evidence concerning Scottish royal dues is not easy to interpret; some sources suggest regular payments, while others imply more ad hoc arrangements; recognition of these dues as predictable annual obligations was still imperfect in the twelfth century, especially on estates that were rarely visited.

Ancient categories of royal income are best understood from Wales, thanks to the laws recorded during the thirteenth century, though these texts have an idealizing quality that invites scepticism in detail. The laws for Gwynedd, for example, divide the land into commotes, each commote having fifty townships. These fifty are divided between a royal arable township (*maerdref*), a royal summer-pasture township (*hafod-tir*), eight townships assigned to royal officers, then six free and four bond estates, each estate having four townships. Each township is said to owe standardized dues appropriate to the status of its tenants. Despite this over-prescription of the duties of the Welsh, the laws make some useful distinctions. They define two sources of bond labour—that owed by the bondmen of each *maerdref* on the king's demesne and that owed by the tenants of the sixteen bond townships in each commote. They also define three types of royal income in kind, first the produce of the king's own lands cultivated by his bondmen, secondly the food-gift (*dawnbwyd*) owed by bondmen in the sixteen bond townships in addition to their labour services, and thirdly the food-rent (*gwestfa*) owed by the men of twenty-four free townships in addition to military service.[30]

The Irish kings depended upon an income in kind called coign, from the Old Irish *connmedi*, meaning 'entertainment'. This revenue was paid by each tenant periodically in order to support the king for a fixed period—often a single night. A later source tells how the king of Laeghaire derived *coinnmheadh* from lands at Ardbraccan (Co. Meath). The apparent simplicity of the system was already disturbed before 1050 by new ways of tapping this revenue at source.

A widely recurring term for a seigniorial revenue in kind in Scotland was conveth, a word directly related to the Old Irish *connmedi*. Later medieval Scots records often translate this as 'waiting'. The name signifies an annual debt of hospitality to be paid to a lord by his dependants; the royal conveth was presumably at one time a compulsory personal obligation to accommodate and entertain the king and his household. It seems to be directly equivalent to its Irish namesake. The place name Conveth, of which there are three known examples in Scotland, implies that there were regional centres where the king received this due, and that those who owed him conveth delivered it there.[31] In describing the dues he imposed on shipping as 'cain' David I used an old word in a new sense. Cain in its original sense (from the Gaelic *cáin*, meaning 'rent' or 'tribute' was a payment in kind probably drawn from royal estates all over Scotland, except the Lothians.[32] It was also (unlike conveth) due to the king from earldoms and other lordships, unless it was replaced by military service. These observations imply that cain was thought of as a general levy. Since kings sometimes granted away their cain to others, some details are recorded in monastic charter collections and cartularies. About 1120 Earl David, for example, the king's son, gave his newly founded abbey of Selkirk the tenth of all his cain of cheese from Galloway.[33] In 1133, as King David I, he gave the abbot and brethren of Dunfermline the tithe of his cain 'in flour and cheese and fodder and malt, in pigs and cows', from Fife, 'Fothrif' and Clackmannan,[34] and a few years later he granted the cathedral church of St Kentigern in Glasgow the tithe of his annual cain in beasts and pigs from Strathgryfe, Cunningham, Kyle, and Carrick, except if he went there, stayed, and consumed the produce himself.[35] Cain, like conveth, was collected at particular centres for the king's use, and was probably already customarily delivered to Dunfermline before the making of these last of the grants.[36]

Regional differences in the availability of money were complemented by differences in the distribution of towns and trading institutions. Much of Britain had an urban history that went back many centuries. Many Iron Age communities were easily as large as settlements that would pass for medieval towns, and they must have had some regulated forms of commerce. Roman Britain, too, had known extensive towns. Continuity with these past forms of urban civilization had nevertheless been broken by the social and economic disruption of Anglo-Saxon settlement. Roman towns had become depopulated and ruined, and it was only from the eighth century that it becomes feasible to speak of significant urban revival. In southern England the late Anglo-Saxon period had been one of vigorous urban renewal, sometimes on older urban sites as at London and Winchester, sometimes on sites that were altogether new, as at St Albans. Domesday Book records 112 boroughs and a further 39 places where a market was held. Some of these were described as 'new', having been established or extended by Norman landlords after the Conquest.[37] Difficult though it is to know just how the trade was organized in these places, their number implies an institutional provision for regular exchange. In this part of the world there was continuity between the urban expansion of the ninth, tenth, and eleventh centuries and the growth of the twelfth and thirteenth. The Norman Conquest may, indeed, have seemed a setback to the many towns that had streets and houses cleared away to make room for oppressive Norman castles. Beyond southern and midland England there were already in 1050 towns at Dublin, Wexford, Waterford, Cork, and Limerick on the Irish coast, established by the Vikings as ports at the western termini of their trade routes.

Despite the presence of small towns and monetized trade, it is unlikely that commerce was yet a prime mover of change in peasant society even in southern England. The unit of currency, the penny, was useful in buying and selling livestock, or in local wholesale transactions, but it was too large to be well adapted to the day-to-day requirements of household consumption, so that most small households depended for their normal requirements either on producing for themselves or on barter. For peasant producers, money was required chiefly to pay rents and taxes, and probably figured little in their daily routines. Since commercial transactions were infrequent, they were poorly provided for, by later standards, and transaction costs were high. Though the Anglo-Saxons had built bridges, road transport was hampered by the frequency with which rivers had to be forded. The small ratio of horses to oxen on demesne farms suggests that road haulage was of minor import-ance in the management of estates. Though horses were possibly more numerous amongst the peasantry, there is no very strong reason to suppose they were.[38] The erratic distribution of boroughs and formal markets meant that even some of the most populous parts of the kingdom had only informal trading institutions, such as Sunday gatherings in churchyards, or meetings of local courts of law.[39] The resulting market structure was nevertheless sufficiently mature by the early twelfth century to generate responsive price signals. The Peterborough chronicler tells us of the famine of 1124–5 that the prices of seed corn were high as a result of a simultaneous shortage of grain and debasement of the currency, and Henry of Huntingdon remembered the year 1125 as 'the most expensive of all in our time'.[40]

Only a small part of Britain in 1086 was characterized by recognizable towns. Even in northern England, only York was unambiguously a focus of urban life, though there was perhaps already some urban development at Durham (Figure 5.1). Ireland indeed had a form of commercial institution described as a *margad*, a

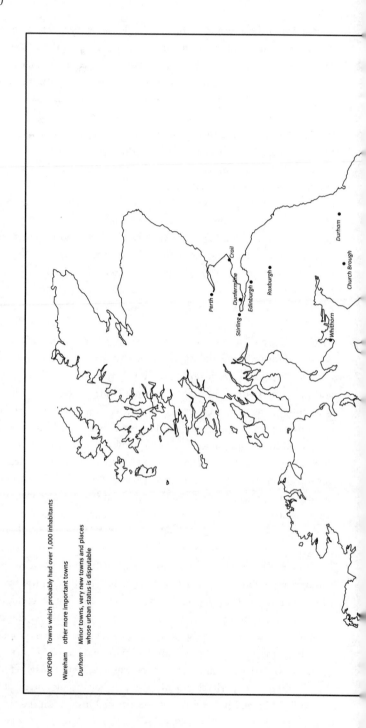

OXFORD Towns which probably had over 1,000 inhabitants

Wareham other more important towns

Durham Minor towns, very new towns and places
whose urban status is disputable

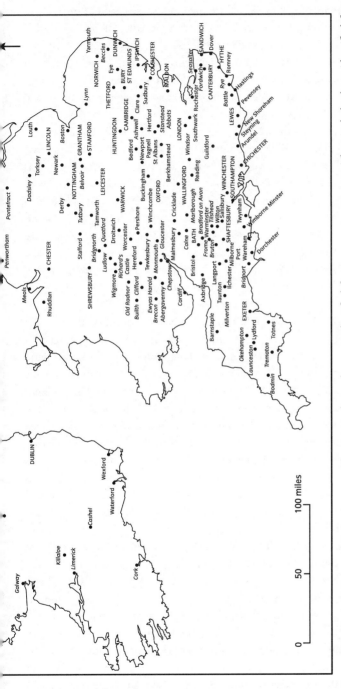

FIG. 5.1. Towns in Britain and Ireland, c.1100. The towns shown here are identified from numerous sources. They include those identified from Domesday Book, new towns of the late eleventh century, the principal Irish ports and a number of likely possible minor urban centres identified by Irish and Scottish historians. The map demonstrates how beyond a line between Exeter and York, towns were sparse, and generally either very small or very new, or both.

Source: B. Harvey (ed.), *The Twelfth and Thirteenth Centuries* (Oxford, 2001), 294–5.

derivative, like the English word market, from the Latin word *mercatus*, or the Late Latin *mercatum*. We know of a *margad* at Limerick in 1108, of one at Cashel (Tipperary), in 1134 and of another of the early twelfth century at Kells (Meath).[41] However, a *margad* was not necessarily held weekly, and may have signified an annual event; the first known occurrence of the English equivalent is in the expression *gearmarket*, equivalent to modern German *Jahrmarkt*, signifying an annual fair. As in England, churches sometimes acted as a minor focus of settlement and exchange. The earliest recorded trading institutions of Ireland are associated with monastic foundations at Kells, Kildare, and Trim.[42] In Scotland, St Andrews, Brechin, Peebles, and Jedburgh are also believed to have had earlier significance as proto-urban trading centres attached to important churches.[43] Caerwent in Wales was another possible monastic trading point of this kind.[44] Notwithstanding such localized developments, except for the Viking ports of the Irish Sea, there are no known Irish or Scottish towns from this era, and the few that existed in Wales were very small and new. So away from southern and midland England, there was less institutional support for local trade and different communities were more weakly integrated into systems of economic interdependence by regular patterns of exchange.

It is unlikely that Britain as a whole had more than 4.5 m. inhabitants in the mid-eleventh century. There have been numerous attempts to estimate England's population in 1086 from the material recorded in Domesday Book. Maitland deduced that England then contained about 1.4 m. people.[45] Later estimates make different assumptions about how the calculation ought to procede. The problem arises because the survey was never intended as a census. Its primary concern was with the value of manors, and the commissioners are unlikely to have been scrupulous in ennumerating smallholders and cottagers. We cannot be sure what allowances to make for omissions. Different estimates, making varying allowances for under-recording, are in the range 1.1–2.5 m. for England as a whole. It is unlikely that the populations of Wales, Scotland, and Ireland together exceeded 1.5–2 m., assuming that their ratio to that of England was no higher than at the start of the eighteenth century.[46]

Population densities were low and the face of the country was rural. Most people lived in villages and hamlets, of which Domesday Book identifies 13,278.[47] Most bear names that are early forms of modern place names, but both historical and archaeological research in recent years has shown that the implied continuity is suspect, and that the eleventh-century world was stranger than at first sight would appear. The townships mentioned in Domesday Book were tax points rather than clearly defined separate communities. Excavations of settlements show that in the early medieval period villages commonly moved about. Brandon in Suffolk, for example, has yielded three early sites. Some villages had already found their present site as population grew in the late Saxon period, but many had not. In parts of the country now associated with nucleated villages, settlement was more characteristically in scattered hamlets, many of which have since disappeared. Estate boundaries were often more permanent features of the landscape than settlement patterns.[48] One conclusion to be drawn from these findings is that the English population in 1086 was even more scattered than Domesday Book suggests.

There was more scope for agrarian expansion in some regions than others, particularly in south-eastern Ireland and southern Scotland. Even within England the intensity with which land was used differed greatly between north and south, and the development of the north was further set back by military events of the later eleventh century. Northern resistance to Norman rule in 1068 and 1069 was suppressed by the systematic destruction of villages and crops, particularly in the Vale of York and the Tyne Valley. The Scots ravaged as far as northern Yorkshire in 1070 under Malcolm Canmore. After a renewed collapse of Norman authority in the north between 1075 and 1079 the king's brother Odo ravaged Northumbria again in 1080.[49] These assaults reduced the population and economic activity of northern England for a generation or more. At the time of the Domesday survey the Yorkshire countryside was still full of deserted villages. Over one-half of the vills of the North Riding and over one-third of those of the East and West Ridings were wholly or partially 'waste', and population densities were low.[50]

In the more populated parts of the south and east the scope for further expansion of the arable area was more limited. When William I commissioned the making of Domesday Book he sought information about 'how much everybody had who was occupying land in England, in land or cattle, and how much money it was worth'.[51] The survey is justly famous for its comprehensiveness and detail, but the measurements it used were not those of a modern surveyor. Land was characteristically measured in 'hides' or 'ploughlands', and there were different but varying ways of measuring pasture and woodland. In 1897 F. W. Maitland calculated that there were more acres of ploughland in 1086 than were ploughed in his own day.[52] A later revised estimate showed that the ploughed acreage in 1086 was only slightly under that for 1914 even if the ploughland was assessed at only 100 acres.[53] There is local evidence, too, to suggest that by 1086 in parts of England the clearance of woods had already proceeded so far that it could go no farther. At Cuxham in Oxfordshire, for example, the four ploughlands of Domesday Book correspond to the fourteenth-century endowment of the manor and at neither period was there any woodland; the process of clearing the land and cultivating it had been completed by 1086.[54]

This extended arable area in the more densely populated parts of Britain has unambiguous implications for agrarian productivity. Though men were few by modern standards the productivity of their working methods was so low that, to modern eyes, their agriculture looks laborious and wasteful of resources. A third or even one-half of the arable land in any one year was lying uncultivated under a fallow course, and, in addition, yields of grain on what was left were low and erratic by modern standards. Crop statistics of the Winchester demesne lands from the period 1325–49 show that the average wheat yield per acre (by volume) was then only one-nineteenth the average level of Great Britain for the five years 1997–2001. The barley yield was a quarter of the modern average and the oats yield one-ninth.[55] The figures for 1086 will not have been significantly different from this. These figures give some idea of how much more land a farmer would have needed in the eleventh century to feed a family than he would with modern levels of productivity.

Even if the area of arable land in much of southern England was as great in 1086 as it was in 1895 or 1914, it does not follow that the pastoral area of the country was also equivalent in area to that of the late nineteenth century. Pasture land in Britain today is more the creation of expertise and investment than it was in the Middle Ages. Modern pastoral husbandry requires large areas of fine enclosed grassland, designated permanent pasture. A large part of the non-arable component of the land in the eleventh century was woodland, heathland, and fenland, much of it unenclosed and subject to common rights. These components of the British landscape in the eleventh century were for the most part lands which attracted little or no investment.

Potentially improvable moor and woodland was still abundant in Scotland and northern England. There were extensive forests north of the Forth and Clyde, but also further south, where there were more people. The forests of Ettrick, Traquhair, and Selkirk, for example, constituted a prominent wooded region around the valleys of the Ettrick, Yarrow, and Tweed, and near Edinburgh the forest of Drumsheugh was still extensive. There was ancient forest near Glasgow (not yet a burgh) on the hills above the Clyde. When Melrose Abbey was founded in 1136, it was given rights in over 17,000 acres of 'waste', probably comprising a mixture of rough open grazing, broken woodland, and wet valley soils.[56] Even in southern England, some areas of surviving woodland were so dense that settlement was thin and scattered. The Weald of Kent was one such region. There were settlements in all parts of the Weald, but nowhere were they frequent, and they became progressively fewer as one went into the heart of the forest. Typically these settlements had only two or three households supported by a few acres of cultivated land. There were nucleated villages only at Tonbridge and Newenden.[57] In southern England the main areas of thick woodland were the Weald of Kent, the clay lands of Essex and Hertfordshire, of which Epping Forest is a remnant, the Chilterns, and the Forest of Arden. In northern England the main wooded areas were on either side of the Pennine ridge. But even outside these outstanding areas the acreage of woods was greater than it is now. Salcey Forest in Buckinghamshire and Rockingham Forest in Northamptonshire are remnants of much larger areas of woodland. Peterborough at this period was 'a small island of habitation between the forest and the fen'.[58]

Wetlands, too, constituted a more prominent feature of coastal and estuarine landscapes than they do today. Hugh White ('Candidus') of Peterborough, writing in the middle of the twelfth century, observed that the fens stretched 60 miles or more eastwards from his abbey, which then stood on an island. He described the fen as 'essential to the people, since there they get wood and straw for fire, hay to provender their beasts, and thatch to roof their houses, along with many other useful necessities; it is teeming with wildfowl and fish'.[59] The rural economy of Lincolnshire, Cambridgeshire, and western Norfolk was powerfully shaped by the distinctive resources of the fens. Similar economies, on a smaller scale, occurred in other areas of badly drained land—the Humber marshes, the Norfolk broadlands, the marshes of the Essex coast especially around the Crouch estuary, Romney Marsh in Kent, the marshlands of the Axe estuary in Somerset between Glaston-bury and the coast. In all these areas the local economy was more dependent on pastoral husbandry and fishing than that of the drier land of the interior.

As these varied observations imply, there was scope for economic development in Britain without recourse to fundamental institutional or technical change. The growth of economies across the North Sea and the Channel was creating new opportunities for trade and specialization, especially in the supply of wool, and exports facilitated the import of silver for conversion into an expanding money supply. Though towns and money had already transformed local economies in southern and midland England, they were still to make an impact on most of Britain and Ireland, but in south Wales, at least, signs of growth were already apparent by 1100.[60] The growth of royal and noble power was to be largely dependent on the growth of local trade and monetization that these developments promised. Meanwhile the resources for supporting an expansion of population and output were there to be found. Notwithstanding the extended ploughlands of southern England, different parts of Britain in the later eleventh century had many more woodlands, heathlands, and wetlands and wastelands than today. There was still scope, in other words, for investment in these lands to allow population to grow and the output of food to be increased even within the limitations of medieval agricultural knowledge.

NOTES

1. *Heimskringla: History of the Kings of Norway*, trans. L. M. Hollander (Austin, 1964), 674–7.
2. *Orkneyinga Saga: The History of the Earls of Norway*, trans. H. Pálsson and P. Edwards (Harmondsworth, 1981), 214–15.

3. P. Spufford, *Money and its Use in Medieval Europe* (Cambridge, 1988), 91 n.

4. P. Nightingale, *A Medieval Mercantile Community: The Grocers' Company of London and the Politics and Trade of London, 1000–1485* (New Haven, 1995), 17–19.

5. *The Bayeux Tapestry*, ed. C. H. Gibbs-Smith (1973), 12–13; *The Bayeux Tapestry*, ed. D. M. Wilson (1985), 226–7.

6. For slavery in Britain, see below (Ch. 11).

7. D. Wyatt, 'Gruffudd ap Cynan and the Hiberno-Norse World', *Welsh History Review*, 19 (1999), 595–617.

8. A. Stevenson, 'Trade with the South, 1070–1513', in M. Lynch, M. Spearman, and G. Stell (eds.), *The Scottish Medieval Town* (Edinburgh, 1988), 180.

9. C. Brooke and G. Keir, *London 800–1216: The Shaping of a City* (1975), 141–2.

10. Brooke and Keir, *London*, 259; J. Campbell (ed.), *The Anglo-Saxons* (1982, repr. 1991), 167, 171; E. Miller and J. Hatcher, *Medieval England: Towns, Commerce and Crafts, 1086–1348* (1995), 14–15; F. M. Stenton, *Anglo-Saxon England*, 2nd edn. (Oxford, 1947), 535.

11. Nightingale, *Medieval Mercantile Community*, 9–19.

12. P. D. A. Harvey, 'The English Trade in Wool and Cloth: 1150–1250: Some Problems and Suggestions', in M. Spallanzani (ed.), *Produzione, commercio e consumo dei panni di lana* (Florence, 1976), 372–3.

13. R. C. Stacey, 'Jewish Lending and the Medieval English Economy', in R. H. Britnell and B. M. S. Campbell (eds.), *A Commercialising Economy: England 1086 to c.1300* (Manchester, 1995), 78–83.

14. *Early Sources of Scottish History, A.D. 500 to 1286*, ed. A. O. Anderson, 2nd edn., 2 vols. (Stamford, 1990), ii. 68–9.

15. 'Supplementum: appendix III: Custuma Portuum', in *The Acts of the Parliaments of Scotland*, ed. T. Thomson and C. Innes, 12 vols. (Edinburgh, 1814–75), i. 671–2; Stevenson, 'Trade', 180.

16. *Orkneyinga Saga*, trans. Pálsson and Edwards, 109.

17. V. Tudor, 'Reginald of Durham and Saint Godric of Finchale: Learning and Religion on a Personal Level', in K. Robbins (ed.), *Religion and Humanism*, Studies in Church History, 17 (1981), 39.

18. I. Blanchard, *Mining, Metallurgy and Minting in the Middle Ages*, 2 vols. (Stuttgart, 2001), i. 529–38; P. H. Sawyer, 'The Wealth of England in the Eleventh Century', *Transactions of the Royal Historical Society*, 5th ser. 15 (1965), 149–53, 160–1.

19. R. Faith, *The English Peasantry and the Growth of Lordship* (1997), 115.

20. Ibid. 105–6.

21. J. F. R. Walmsley, 'The "Censarii" of Burton Abbey and the Domesday Population', *North Staffordshire Journal of Field Studies*, 8 (1968), 74–8.

22. R. Lennard, *Rural England, 1086–1135: A Study of Social and Agrarian Conditions* (Oxford, 1959), 106, 123.

23. Domesday Book, i, fos. 16, 155ᵛ; *The Ecclesiastical History of Orderic Vitalis*, ed. M. Chibnall, 6 vols. (Oxford, 1969–80), vi. 78–9.

24. Lennard, *Rural England*, 130–1.

25. H. C. Darby, *Domesday England* (Cambridge, 1977), 277.

26. Lennard, *Rural England*, 134–41.

27. M. Cubbon, 'A Remarkable Decade of Manx Coin Hoards, 1972–1982', *Proceedings of the Isle of Man Natural History and Antiquarian Society*, 11 (1997–9), 29–50.

28. B. E. Crawford, *Scandinavian Scotland* (Leicester, 1987), 128–30, 134; P. Wallace, 'The Archaeology of Anglo-Norman Dublin', in H. B. Clarke and A. Simms, *The Comparative History of Urban Origins in Non-Roman Europe*, 2 vols. (Oxford, 1985), ii. 399.

29. J. D. Bateson, *Coinage in Scotland* (1997), 35–8; Crawford, *Scandinavian Scotland*, 133–4

30. G. R. J. Jones, 'The Dark Ages', in D. H. Owen (ed.), *Settlement and Society in Wales* (Cardiff, 1989), 177–9.

31. *Regesta Regum Scottorum*, ii: *The Acts of William I*, ed. G. W. S. Barrow (Edinburgh, 1971), 53, and no. 154, p. 224.

32. Ibid., ii. 52.

33. *Early Scottish Charters prior to A.D. 1153*, ed. A. C. Lawrie (Glasgow, 1905), no. 35, pp. 26–8.

34. Ibid., no. 103, pp. 81–2.

35. Ibid., no. 125, pp. 95–6.

36. Cf. ibid., no. 74, pp. 61–3.

37. Darby, *Domesday England*, 364–70.

38. J. Langdon, *Horses, Oxen and Technological Innovation: The Use of Draught Animals in English Farming from 1066–1500* (Cambridge, 1986), 27–38.

39. R. H. Britnell, *The Commercialisation of English Society, 1000–1500*, 2nd edn. (Manchester, 1996), 10.

40. *The Peterborough Chronicle*, ed. C. Clark, 2nd edn. (Oxford, 1970), 45–6; Henry of Huntingdon, *Historia Anglorum*, ed. and trans. D. Greenway (Oxford, 1996), 474–5.

41. C. Doherty, 'Exchange and Trade in Early Medieval Ireland', *Journal of the Royal Society of Antiquaries of Ireland*, 110 (1980), 83; C. Doherty, 'The Monastic Town in Early Medieval Ireland', in Clarke and Simms (eds.), *Comparative History*, i. 67.

42. Doherty, 'Monastic Town', 60–3, 67; B. Graham, 'Anglo-Norman Colonization and the Size and Spread of the Colonial Town in Medieval Ireland', in Clarke and Simms (eds.), *Comparative History*, ii. 361–3, 366.

43. B. Dicks, 'The Scottish Medieval Town: A Search for Origins', in G. Gordon and B. Dicks (eds.), *Scottish Urban History* (Aberdeen, 1983), 42–3.

44. W. Davies, *An Early Welsh Microcosm: Studies in the Llandaff Charters* (London, 1978), 61–2.

45. F. W. Maitland, *Domesday Book and Beyond* (Cambridge, 1897), 437.

46. In 1701 England is estimated to have had 5.439 m., Wales 0.387 m., Scotland 1.040 m., Ireland 2.540 m.: P. Deane and W. A. Cole, *British Economic Growth, 1688–1959: Trends and Structure* (Cambridge, 1967), 6, 103.

47. Darby, *Domesday England*, 15.

48. Christopher Taylor, *Village and Farmstead: A History of Rural Settlement in England* (c. 1983), 123–4.

49. W. E. Kapelle, *The Norman Conquest of the North: The Region and its Transformation, 1000–1135* (1979), 118, 123, 132, 141, 174.

50. Ibid., 161–2.

51. *English Historical Documents*, ii: *1042–1189*, ed. D. C. Douglas and G. W. Greenway, 2nd edn. (1981), 168.

52. Maitland, *Domesday Book and Beyond*, 435–6.

53. Lennard, *Rural England*, 393; Darby, *Domesday England*, 131.

54. P. D. A. Harvey, *A Medieval Oxfordshire Village: Cuxham, 1240 to 1400* (Oxford, 1965), 3.

55. J. Z. Titow, *Winchester Yields: A Study in Medieval Agricultural Productivity* (Cambridge, 1972), 148; '2001 Crop Yields and Production Estimates', Department of Agriculture and Rural Development, press release 16 October 2002.

56. M. L. Anderson, *A History of Scottish Forestry*, ed. C. J. Taylor, 2 vols. (1967), i. 106, 110; J. Gilbert, 'The Monastic Record of a Border Landscape, 1136 to 1236', *Scottish Geographical Magazine*, 99 (1983), 4–5.

57. K. P. Witney: *The Jutish Forest: A Study of the Weald of Kent from 450 to 1380 AD* (1976), 127.

58. E. King, *Peterborough Abbey, 1086–1310: A Study in the Land Market* (Cambridge, 1973), 70.

59. *The Chronicle of Hugh Candidus, A Monk of Peterborough*, ed. W. T. Mellows (1949), 5.

60. See below (Ch. 14).

FURTHER READING

Astill, G. G., 'Towns and Hierarchies in Saxon England', *Oxford Journal of Archaeology*, 10 (1991).

Blanchard, I., *Mining, Metallurgy and Minting in the Middle Ages*, 2 vols. (Stuttgart, 2001).

Bradley, J., 'The Interpretation of Scandinavian Settlement in Ireland', in J. Bradley (ed.), *Settlement and Society in Medieval Ireland: Studies Presented to F. X. Martin, OSA* (Kilkenny, 1988).

Brooke, C., and Keir, G., *London 800–1216: The Shaping of a City* (1975).

Campbell, J. (ed.), *The Anglo-Saxons* (1982, repr. 1991).

Crawford, B. E., *Scandinavian Scotland* (Leicester, 1987).

Darby, H. C., *Domesday England* (Cambridge, 1977).

Doherty, C., 'Exchange and Trade in Early Medieval Ireland', *Journal of the Royal Society of Antiquaries of Ireland*, 110 (1980).

Duncan, A. A. M., *Scotland: The Making of the Kingdom* (Edinburgh, 1989).

Erskine, R. W. H. and Williams, A. (eds.), *The Story of Domesday Book* (Chichester, 2003).

Faith, R., *The English Peasantry and the Growth of Lordship* (1997).

Fleming, R., 'Rural Elites and Urban Communities in Late-Saxon England', *Past and Present*, 141 (1993).

Gillingham, J., 'Thegns and Knights in Eleventh-Century England: Who Was Then the Gentleman?', *Transactions of the Royal Historical Society*, 6th ser. 5 (1995).

Green, J. A., *The Aristocracy of Norman England* (Cambridge, 1997).

Hamerow, H. F., 'Settlement and the "Middle Saxon Shift": Rural Settlement and Settlement Patterns in Anglo-Saxon England', *Anglo-Saxon England*, 20 (1991).

Hart, C., 'Land Tenure in Cambridgeshire on the Eve of the Norman Conquest', *Proceedings of the Cambridgeshire Antiquarian Society*, 84 (1995).

Harvey, S. P. J., 'Domesday England', in H. E. Hallam (ed.), *The Agrarian History of England and Wales*, ii: *1042–1350* (Cambridge, 1988).

—— 'Taxation and the Ploughland in Domesday Book', in P. Sawyer (ed.), *Domesday Book: A Reassessment* (1985).

Holt, J. C. (ed.), *Domesday Studies* (Woodbridge, 1987).

Hooke, D. (ed.), *Anglo-Saxon Settlements* (Oxford, 1988).

Hunt, J., 'Land Tenure and Lordship in Tenth- and Eleventh-Century Staffordshire', *Staffordshire Studies*, 4 (1991–2).

Jones, G. R. J., 'The Dark Ages', in D. H. Owen (ed.), *Settlement and Society in Wales* (Cardiff, 1989).

Kapelle, W. E., *The Norman Conquest of the North: The Region and its Transformation, 1000–1135* (1979).

Lennard, R., *Rural England, 1086–1135: A Study of Social and Agrarian Conditions* (Oxford, 1959).

Lewis, C. P., 'The Domesday Jurors', *Haskins Society Journal*, 5 (1994).

Maitland, F. W., *Domesday Book and Beyond* (Cambridge, 1897).

Miller, E., *The Abbey and Bishopric of Ely: The Social History of an Ecclesiastical Estate from the Tenth Century to the Early Fourteenth Century* (Cambridge, 1951).

—— and Hatcher, J., *Medieval England: Towns, Commerce and Crafts, 1086–1348* (1995).

Nightingale, P., 'The Evolution of Weight-Standards and the Creation of New Monetary and Commercial Links in Northern Europe from the Tenth Century to the Twelfth Century', *Economic History Review*, 2nd ser. 38 (1985).

Palliser, D. M., 'Domesday Book and the "Harrying of the North" ', *Northern History*, 29 (1993).

Pelteret, D. A. E., *Slavery in Early Medieval England* (Woodbridge, 1995).

Reynolds, S., 'Towns in Domesday Book', in J. C. Holt (ed.), *Domesday Studies* (Woodbridge, 1987).

Roffe, D., *Domesday: The Inquest and the Book* (Oxford, 2000).

—— 'Domesday Book and Northern Society: A Reassessment', *English Historical Review*, 105 (1990)

Sawyer, P. (ed.), *Domesday Book: A Reassessment* (1985).

—— 'The Wealth of England in the Eleventh Century', *Transactions of the Royal Historical Society*, 5th ser. 15 (1965).

Spufford, P., *Money and its Use in Medieval Europe* (Cambridge, 1988).

Stafford, P., 'The "Farm of One Night" and the Organization of King Edward's Estates in Domesday', *Economic History Review*, 2nd ser. 33 (1980).

Stenton, F. M., *Preparatory to Anglo-Saxon England, Being the Collected Papers of Frank Merry Stenton*, ed. D. M. Stenton (Oxford, 1970).

Studd, R., 'Recorded "Waste" in the Staffordshire Domesday', *Staffordshire Studies*, 12 (2000).

Tsurushima, H., 'Feudum in Kent, c.1066–1215', *Journal of Medieval History*, 21 (1995).

Valente, M. A., 'Reassessing the Irish "Monastic Town" ', *Irish Historical Studies*, 31 (1998).

Wallace, P., 'The Archaeology of Anglo-Norman Dublin', in H. B. Clarke and A. Simms (eds.), *The Comparative History of Urban Origins in Non-Roman Europe*, 2 vols. (Oxford, 1985).

Walmsley, J. F. R., 'The *Censarii* of Burton Abbey and the Domesday Population', *North Staffordshire Journal of Field Studies*, 8 (1968), 73–80.

Wyatt, D., 'Gruffudd ap Cynan and the Hiberno-Norse World', *Welsh History Review*, 19 (1999).

....

CHAPTER 6

Merchants and their Trade

The development of long-distance, especially seaborne, trade is one of the most demonstrable sources of British urban growth between 1050 and 1300. It was chiefly beneficial to eastern England and Scotland, whose economies it integrated into the expanding North Sea trading area; northern France (including Flanders) and the Rhineland were the principal trading partners. A statistical assessment of the magnitude of change is only possible in part; the evidence of customs accounts becomes available for English ports from 1275, for Welsh ports from the beginning of the fourteenth century,[1] and for Scottish ports from 1327. Comparison between English customs returns of the years 1304–5 with customs dues recorded in a royal exchequer account of 1204 suggests that over that hundred years the value of English overseas trade may have tripled in real terms.[2] For the earlier period the strength of commercial expansion has to be deduced from indirect sources. Fortunately both archaeological and the documentary evidence unambiguously demonstrates commercial growth in the pre-statistical period, even if its magnitude is not ascertainable.

By 1300 exports accounted for perhaps only 4 per cent of England's gross national product, and perhaps an even smaller proportion of incomes in Ireland, Wales and Scotland,[3] but overseas trade does not exhaust the importance of expanding trade over long distances. Besides connecting Britain more closely to the Continent, commercial expansion linked different parts of the island more closely in patterns of economic interdependence, as well as increasing traffic across the Irish Sea, and these internal connections deserve as close attention as the documentary and arch-aeological evidence permits. Within Britain, some commodities like livestock trav-elled better by road than by water, an important consideration given that the west-ern and northern parts had a comparative advantage in pasture farming. Sea routes were nevertheless important in connecting regions too far apart to have communi-cated by road, and, as explained in Chapter 1, their value was enhanced by a number of navigable rivers that gave cheap access to the coast from regions further inland—

notably the Tay, the Forth, the Tweed, the Tyne, the Trent, the Ouse, the Thames, and the Severn. As in overseas trade, transaction costs in dealings between various parts of Britain and Ireland depended on political circumstances, so that good conditions for commercial integration within Britain cannot be taken for granted.

Reducing the Costs of Trade

The growth of long-distance trade encouraged a wide range of institutional and technical developments that reduced the costs of trading, even though these were always subject to momentary increases in times of war. These improvements in turn encouraged further commercial enterprise; such feedback patterns of causation are a normal way in which economic development proceeds. The credit for innovation cannot be narrowly ascribed to any one group. Kings and other landlords established port towns, which inevitably meant setting aside land and investing in a minimum of facilities for residents, as well as creating marketing and port facilities. For example, Hull, originally a port founded in the late twelfth century by the Cistercian Abbey of Meaux, was from 1293 developed as a royal town, Kingston upon Hull.[4] New styles of shipping depended upon an international transfer of ideas amongst the ports of northern Europe. Merchants themselves devised trading structures that enabled them to handle more goods at lower cost, and officers of the law courts developed legal procedures to cope with the hazards of commercial credit. Governments, too, contributed to the growth of mercantile confidence by supporting merchants with high-level commercial justice, and occasionally with diplomatic intervention.

The multiplication and expansion of port towns was the most visible of the innovations that accompanied the growth of maritime trade. Some on the east coast grew particularly rapidly; a number of places that had had no urban character in 1086—Newcastle upon Tyne, Boston, Hull, and King's Lynn—were amongst the wealthiest towns in Britain by 1300. Overseas trade contributed greatly to London's growth in this period, but customs accounts of the late thirteenth century demonstrate that the larger provincial ports carried much of England's overseas trade. During the five years following Michaelmas 1295, 51 per cent of wool exports went through Boston, Hull, Great Yarmouth, and Southampton, as against 41 per cent through London. The two principal ports handling Scotland's wool trade in 1327–33, when we first have the evidence of customs, were Berwick and Aberdeen.[5] There was further development on the east coast in numerous smaller boroughs and trading centres, both old and new. The number and broad spatial distribution of these developments, stretching back in some cases to the eleventh century, attest a general expansion of seafaring long before we have reliable statistical evidence to illustrate its magnitude or degree of continuity. The significance of these developments can be seen from Table 6.1, which shows the ranking of the wealthiest twenty English towns in 1334, as judged by their taxable wealth. The growth of port towns was an added stimulus to the growth of trade in bulk; trade in commodities such as fish and grain was more attractive where a source of demand was at hand at the point of unloading.

Investment in ports was less characteristic of the west coast of Britain, not surprisingly, though the old port towns of Bristol and Chester were evidently thriving. During the later eleventh century and early twelfth—well before the Anglo-Norman conquest of Ireland in 1169–72—there were further signs of commercial expansion around the Irish Sea, and especially along the northern shore of the Severn estuary. Chepstow was founded between 1072 and 1075, Cardiff between 1081 and 1093, and Carmarthen, Kidwelly, Pembroke, and Tenby are all new towns of the first two decades of the twelfth century. Urban development was less apparent in Ireland before the Anglo-Norman conquest of 1169–72, but this does not rule out the probability that a growing trade between Britain and Ireland was a feature of development on the west coast during the previous hundred years. In the early twelfth century there was already a regular trade to Ireland by merchants of Chester and Bristol, to judge from references to its significance in the reign of Henry I of England. According to William of Malmesbury, Henry was able to put effective pressure on Muirchertach Ua Briain, king of Munster

TABLE 6.1. *England's wealthiest twenty towns in 1334 as assessed for taxation*

City	Taxable wealth (£)	City	Taxable wealth (£)
London	11,000	Lynn	770
Bristol	2,200	Coventry	750
York	1,620	Salisbury	750
Newcastle upon Tyne	1,333	Ipswich	650
Boston	1,100	Winchester	625
Yarmouth	1,000	Hereford	600
Lincoln	1,000	Canterbury	599
Norwich	946	Gloucester	540
Shrewsbury	940	Southampton	511
Oxford	914	Beverley	500

Note: These assessments are not to be wholly relied on as an indicator of rank by wealth; some towns were taxed more heavily than others. However, imperfections of this kind are unlikely to affect the list of towns making up the top twenty.

Source: A. Dyer, 'Appendix: Ranking Lists of English Medieval Towns', in D. M. Palliser (ed.), *The Cambridge Urban History of Britain*, i (Cambridge, 2000), 755.

(1086–1119), by threatening an English trade embargo.[6] After 1170, investment in new Irish port towns, as well the multiplication of ports in Wales and on Scotland's west coast, can be attributed at least in part to the development of trading complementarities across the Irish Sea. Ireland contributed to the growth of British trade by at least occasionally supplying agricultural produce to the western towns. Dublin increased in size, stretching laterally along the Liffy and advancing its waterfront by schemes of reclamation; by 1300 the city had at least 10,000 inhabitants. There were numerous other new Irish port towns, notably New Ross and Drogheda. Most of the new ports on the west coast of Britain were of minor importance in the overall statistics of British trade, but some proved of lasting importance for British urbanization, notably Ayr, founded about 1200,[7] and Liverpool, founded in 1207 (Figure 6.1).[8]

The growing number and improving organization of fairs also served to reduce merchants' transaction costs. Although the fair as such was not a novel idea, many standard practices of the late thirteenth century had been innovated since the eleventh. Fairs came in many forms and sizes. At the village level their commercial significance was modest, but the greatest fairs—Boston, Stamford, Lynn, Northampton, St Ives, Bury St Edmunds, Westminster, Winchester—were visited by international traders. Though there were significant regional fairs in Scotland, the one at Roxburgh being the most important, they were of greater significance for the internal livestock market than for foreign trade.[9] The major fairs were all in the most commercially developed part of England. Because of the wide range of imported goods to be obtained there, they were frequented not only by merchants but also by representatives of wealthy lay and ecclesiastical households. The agents of Durham Priory spent £125 11s. 5½d. at Boston fair in 1299, and a further £7 13s. 0d. in transporting their purchases home. The royal wardrobe was also supplied from fairs for much of the twelfth and thirteenth centuries, though in the later thirteenth century it became more usual to buy from dealers in London. The great fairs lost business to urban centres, especially London, from this time on.[10]

The design of ships in which overseas trade was conducted was developed in English, as in other north European ports, to accommodate more bulky produce. The shallow draft of the eleventh-century knarr and its analogues was inadequate for the growing trade in wool, hides, fish, and grain on which much later expansion was built. Ships of newer design were larger; they were also broader and deeper in proportion to their length. The Scandinavian buss was one such development, used in trade across the North Sea to English ports. But the main development in this period was the cog, a vessel up to 30 metres long, with a length-to-breadth ratio of 3 : 1. Not only could such ships carry more than their forerunners, but they required much less manpower. A cog of 200 tons required no more than one man for every ten tons, whereas a 50-ton knarr had required one man for every four. The

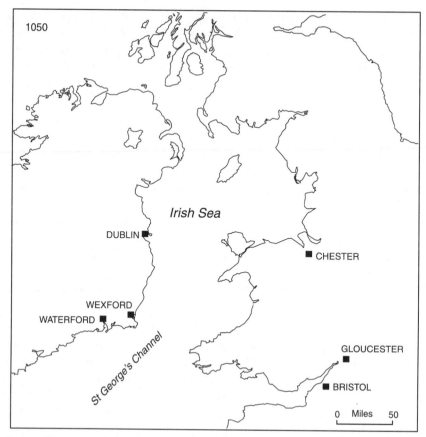

FIG. 6.I. Towns round the Irish Sea, 1050–1307. These three maps illustrate how even in western Britain and Ireland the period 1050–1307 was one of increasing urbanization, even if the towns were mostly very small. Many of these towns had shipping attached to them, and acted as minor ports, even if their waterside facilities were few. The multiplication of southern Welsh towns even before 1170 shows that the expansion of western trade was not dependent upon the English invasion of Ireland, though undoubtedly trade across the Irish Sea was quickened by closer links between British and Irish ports from the later twelfth century.

sail area these ships carried was increased to match their greater bulk, and from the late twelfth century their manoeuvrability was maintained by shifting the rudder from the side to a sternpost. The new forms of shipping improved the mercantile prospects of parts of Britain remote from continental ports. Before their introduction into Scottish trade in the thirteenth century Scottish seafaring had been inhibited by the high costs of sea transport, and merchants had tended to confine their activities to coastal routes. The only point in which the performance

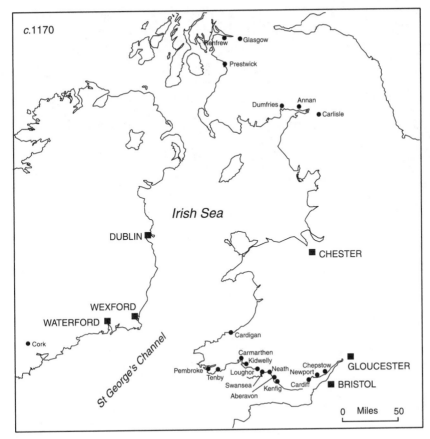

FIG. 6.1.—*continued*

of these newer vessels did not outdo the older ones was in speed. Advances in shipbuilding simultaneously, using improved tools such as the frame saw and the breast auger, meant that ton for ton they were cheaper to construct.[11]

Maritime trade did not always depend upon the existence of elaborate facilities. The shallow vessels of the eleventh century could be beached on the shore without the need for special construction. Commerce had increased for centuries before 1050 along parts of the coast with little institutional provision, at places identifiable only by tell-tale archaeological deposits. Yet with rising volumes of trade, and with the associated change in ship construction, the advantages of greater institutionalization became undeniable. Handling bulky goods from large and round-bellied ships benefited from wooden quays onto which cargoes could be unloaded, and from handling apparatus, such as primitive cranes. Any trade that depended upon warehousing, or the operation of agents over a period of

FIG. 6.1.—*continued*

weeks rather than hours, favoured a built-up urban environment with wharves and inns. To varying degrees, port towns developed technologies and institutions to attract shipping by facilitating trade in these ways, and so reduced the shippers' handling costs. Although most investment along these lines was at seaports, from the late Saxon period there were analogous developments on the waterfronts of riverside towns capable of benefiting from bulk water transport over long distances.[12] The origins of these developments is usually obscure, but from the late twelfth century onwards it is plain that the initiative in developing them passed to the burgesses of the principal trading towns, under the leadership of their mayors or bailiffs.

Other cost-reducing developments in mercantile activity depended more on private organization than on public facilities, as merchants changed the ways they managed their affairs. Information about mercantile organization from the eleventh and twelfth centuries is scarce, though even then there was some pooling of capital amongst merchants, to judge from what we know about Godric of Finchale. Later developments greatly enriched the infrastructure upon which merchants could draw. Later thirteenth-century English customs records, which can be supplemented by details from other sources, demonstrate that merchants no longer normally travelled with their cargoes at sea. Similar developments were facilitating the growth of Scottish contacts abroad. There was a Scottish community in Bruges in the 1290s. The growth of a commercial infrastructure of shippers and mercantile agents—often young men in training to become merchants themselves—allowed principal exporters to stay at home and to play a regular part in the affairs of their home communities. The establishment of regular contacts in foreign ports was an essential part of this development. It was possible for the widows of merchants to remain active in trade without needing to set foot in a ship. In the space of three months in 1292, Isabella of Pandon exported five separate consignments of wool and hides from the port of Newcastle upon Tyne. These developments correspond to a growing prominence of merchants in profiles of urban wealth, and for their rise in status as a group with distinctive interests and abilities. In the course of the twelfth and the thirteenth centuries both English and Scottish kings came to recognize the merchant class as a growing source of wealth.[13]

Exports and Imports

What was the nature of the trade that these developments encouraged? In modern international trade, developed economies characteristically export manufactures and services while developing economies are primary producers, exporting foodstuffs and raw materials. At first sight, the economies of Britain in the twelfth and thirteenth centuries seem to fit into such a scheme as primary-producers, since their exports were for the most part agricultural produce and minerals. Europe's principal urban and industrial centres were elsewhere, notably in northern France, Flanders, and northern Italy. Yet modern analogies are misleading to the extent that differences in levels of technology, capital formation, skills, and wages across Europe in 1300 were much lower than the differences between the richer and poorer countries of the modern world. The difference in per capita GDP between Portugal and Switzerland in 2000 was probably greater than the difference between south-eastern England and the northern Italian states in 1300. It is accordingly misleading to represent Britain at this time as 'underdeveloped' by the standards of the thirteenth century.[14]

For a period it looked as if the parts of Britain nearest Flanders would participate on the fringe of the export textile industry that constituted a strong focus for economic growth in north-western Europe. Up to the mid-thirteenth century

several English towns—York, Beverley, Lincoln, Louth, Stamford, Northampton—
made cloth of merchant quality capable of supplying the English royal court and
the London market. Some English cloth was also marketed abroad, though it
offered no significant challenge to the supremacy of Flemish manufactures. Even
this industry was damaged by rising transactions costs in the later thirteenth
century, however. The high-quality export industries suffered a setback which
had become severe during and after the reign of Edward I.[15] Amongst England's
principal urban clothmaking interests, perhaps the only one to expand was the
London manufacture of 'burel', an inferior and inexpensive cloth made for the
home market rather than for export.[16] The Scots were simultaneously experiencing
an invasion of Flemish cloths in the upper reaches of the market, even though there
is less evidence there of declining native urban industries.[17] At all times up to the
fourteenth century Britain was more conspicuous on the international scene for
the export of its raw wools than for its manufactured cloths.

Wool was a major item in Britain's income from foreign trade. Its export was
growing long before the days of regular customs statistics, chiefly to supply the
growing demand for wool in Flanders. A miracle story from the Abbey of Laon in
northern France implies that merchants were already bringing silver across the
Channel to buy wool in 1119.[18] It seems likely that an accelerated growth of wool
exports after about 1160 made a major contribution to the profits of agriculture and
the stock of bullion available to British mints.[19] These exports were directed chiefly
to the growing textile industry of Flanders, and Flemish merchants remained
dominant in the wool trade up to 1270, though English merchants held a minority
interest.[20] Monasteries secured large contracts with foreign exporters, and some
assumed a middleman function in the local wool trade. In 1262 the people of
Lincoln complained to the king that the Lincolnshire monasteries were buying
wool locally and selling it together with their own to overseas merchants.[21] The
southern borders of Scotland, too, developed a wool export from the early twelfth
century, particularly through the entrepreneurship of the new monasteries that
developed new estates there.[22] As in England, the growth of an export trade to
Flanders is the readiest way to explain the commercial expansion of sheep farming
attested by Scottish royal ordinances.[23]

Later in the century Flemish exporters were eclipsed by Italians through much of
Britain. Flemish trade was interrupted by civil war in England in 1264–5, and the
diplomatic aftermath proved to be a turning point in the trade. There was again a
severe breakdown of Anglo-Flemish relations during the years 1270–5. But, apart
from diplomatic problems, Flemish ascendancy was undermined by the superior
finance and business organization of Italian merchants.[24] Being able to control large
funds, Italians could lend to monasteries on the security of future wool deliveries,
and in that way gained control of wool supplies even before the sheep were

sheared. A surviving letter of 1285 lists twenty monasteries which were committed to supplying wool to the Riccomanni firm, on contracts varying from two years to eleven. Welsh wool producers responded to the same commercial opportunities. Margam Abbey (Glamorganshire) sent its wool to Flanders in 1250, and Dore Abbey (Herefordshire), in the Welsh Marches, had financial dealings with the Sienese as early as 1254. Here too the Italians gained ground; most Welsh Cistercian houses were listed as wool suppliers in Pegolotti's mercantile manual of *c.*1300.[25] Lords with lands in Ireland also benefited from the coming of Italian enterprise. In 1284–5, for example, Richard de Burgh and Nicholas de Segrave undertook to sell 50 sacks of wool to Baroncino Gualteri for the sum of 500 marks (£333 6*s.* 8*d.*).[26] The Italians, like the Flemings, made use of the local enterprise of monasteries willing to act as middlemen in collecting wool from other local producers.[27]

In Scotland, as in England, Flemish merchants were prominent in the wool trade up to the 1270s, and the role of Italians increased rapidly thereafter. The interest of Italian exporters in Scottish wools is well attested by the names of wool-producing monasteries listed by Pegolotti.[28] However, Scotland had no quarrel with the Flemish merchants in the 1270s, and was able to maintain more direct trading relations through the later thirteenth century. As Scottish resistance to Edward I in the Wars of Independence gained support in Flanders, ties between Scotland and Bruges became closer. Italian exporters never gained as strong a hold there as they did elsewhere in Britain.[29]

Until the late thirteenth century Italian merchants supplied wool directly to Flanders, but after that they began also to send it to Italy, where a cloth industry began competing more successfully with that of Flanders. The growth of wool exports to Italy coincided with the development of direct maritime links through the Straits of Gibraltar, a route used only from the 1270s. For twenty years the sea route was chosen only occasionally, but from 1298 onwards Genoese voyages to Flanders became a regular event. It is probably from that point that Italian shipping was regularly to be found in the ports of southern England.[30]

The institution of customs duties on wool, woolfells, and hides in 1275 by Edward I inaugurated the compilation of one of England's major economic statistics for the later Middle Ages—one of the few series which relates to the whole kingdom, and to an important component of total overseas trade. From this point onwards it is possible to chart the movement of English wool exports. It seems likely, on the evidence of the size of sheep flocks, trading contracts, and business organization, that the trade was larger in the last quarter of the thirteenth century than it ever had been before, so that the customs figures start early enough to chart the peak of medieval wool export. Except for a few severe setbacks, the accounts show a generally rising trend between the first surviving figure for 1279–80 (23,957 sacks) and 1304–5 (46,382 sacks). This latter figure was never exceeded throughout the fourteenth and fifteenth centuries. Though there are no surviving Scottish export statistics of comparably early date, there is reason to suppose that the chronology of wool exports there was comparable to that from English ports. Wool exports were already growing during the twelfth century, and by the early fourteenth century the number of fleeces exported from Scottish ports was equivalent to about a fifth to a quarter of England's total.[31]

Wool was Britain's most valuable export commodity in terms of its total annual value, but there were other agricultural commodities which were regularly exported. One of these was hides for the manufacture of leather, which are in evidence in the customs accounts for several ports, notably at Southampton, but also in the east-coast ports of King's Lynn, Hull, Boston, and Newcastle upon Tyne.[32] Exports of hides from Scotland were sufficiently important by the third quarter of the century to be singled out, as in England, for burdening with customs duties. The customs accounts of 1327–33, when Scottish ports exported on average 36,100 a year, show Edinburgh as the leading centre of this trade, though other east-coast ports also participated.[33] Hides were always a major Irish export from at least the twelfth century, when the trade was noted by Gerald of Wales.[34] Grain, too, was sometimes exported to the Continent from east-coast ports, notably Hull and King's Lynn, but this was an irregular matter of exploiting local price differences, and is likely to have occurred only when there were marked regional variations in the quality of the harvest.[35] In some years there was no grain export. A variety of minerals constituted another group of exports. The best documented and most thoroughly researched of these is the English trade in tin, which was used chiefly in the manufacture of pewter. This trade was comparable to that in wool, in that the commodity was a raw material in whose production England had distinct advantages over the rest of Europe, though the benefits of the trade were much more localized because of the concentration of tin deposits in Devon and Cornwall. English tin, the purest as well as the most abundant in Europe, crossed the Continent in all directions, especially southwards to the wealthy centres of tin consumption in the Mediterranean region.[36] The coal trade is less well known, but again England was a source of supply well favoured by its geology and water communications. The customs accounts of Newcastle upon Tyne in the late thirteenth century record many alien ships there, and it is difficult to imagine what they were doing if not collecting coal.[37]

Meanwhile urban development on the coast also responded to the demand for imports. It might be expected, given the prominence of raw materials in exports from Britain, that imports would chiefly comprise manufactured goods from France and the Low Countries. However, this is only in part borne out by the evidence of the customs accounts. Imported linens, silks, and woollen cloths of various kinds were traded by mercers, some destined for families in high-income brackets. Between Michaelmas 1303 and Michaelmas 1309, alien merchants alone imported on average about 12,000 cloths a year into England. The import of Flemish and Italian cloths into Scotland was also satisfying the upper end of the market in Scotland during the thirteenth century, and increased with growing prosperity.[38] Yet most cloth bought in Britain was home produced, as were most other manufactured goods. There was no twelfth- or thirteenth-century equivalent to the science-based manufactures that constitute so much of the exports of leading modern manufacturing economies. Although manufactured goods were prominent in imports into London and Boston, not surprisingly given their status as centres of the luxury trades, they were of secondary importance in other provincial ports like Hull, Lynn, and Southampton.[39] Most British imports in the thirteenth century, and probably earlier, were raw materials, foodstuffs, and agricultural produce, not dissimilar in character from the composition of exports.

One of the bulkiest and most valuable imports was wine, brought principally from Bordeaux, though smaller quantities came from the Rhineland and Spain. In 1300–1 the king of England took a royal prise from 408 wine ships importing a total of about 17,500 tons of wine.[40] Wine was one of the principal imports into the ports of Scotland and Ireland. Smaller quantities were taken into Wales, chiefly by English merchants. English and Irish trade with Gascony was encouraged by the political attachment of the province to the Angevin empire under Henry II and his successors, but the Scots, too, imported much of their wine from Gascony. In 1284 the Scottish royal council had a contract to supply wine with John Mazun, a Bordeaux merchant, who later claimed large debts owed to him by King Alexander III. Both in England and Scotland the royal household was the biggest single consumer.[41]

The supply of some foodstuffs also depended, with varying degrees of frequency, on overseas trade. Preserved fish from the Baltic, mostly herring, was a principal import into English east-coast ports. Even Scotland, which had a surplus of white fish for export, imported salted herring, probably as a re-export from Yarmouth as well as direct from Norway.[42] Salt, which was needed in large quantities as a preservative for fish and meat, was imported into English and Scottish ports, even though both kingdoms had their own centres of manufacture. The principal overseas source was the west coast of France; importers often traded both in salt and wine.[43] Shipments of grain were important, and perhaps a regular necessity, for some Scottish and Welsh towns, especially on the west coast, but because of the distances involved they derived from Ireland and England rather than from the Continent.[44] Grain was also imported into England, but more erratically, and chiefly in years of dearth. Exeter, for example, imported 208 quarters of wheat and rye and 231 quarters of peas and beans in 1295–6, but hardly any during the following four years.[45] By 1300 at least modest grain imports were available from the Baltic; they show up in the evidence of 'new customs' receipts from 1304 onwards.[46]

Another range of imported goods, of great significance for the classification of British overseas trade, comprised raw materials for manufactures. These included imports of woad, unwrought metals (including iron and steel), timber and timber products, pitch, bitumen (for caulking ships), and ashes (used in dyeing). Furs were brought from northern Europe for use in the manufacture of clothing. Some of these commodities figured very prominently in the recorded trade of English provincial ports. Woad constituted 35 per cent of the value of imports by foreign merchants into Hull between July 1304 and August 1309, 21 per cent of alien imports into Lynn between February 1303 and Michaelmas 1307, at least a quarter of alien imports into Ipswich in 1304–5, and 30 per cent of alien imports into Southampton in 1308–9. Woad was also an important import into Scotland, where it was subject to heavy duties.[47] Britain's cloth industry may not have had much impact in foreign markets at this stage, but it was heavily influencing the composition of imports.

Trade across Britain and Ireland

By treating Britain and Ireland as a single entity, this discussion risks overlooking regional differences. As Chapter 1 has explained, different parts of Britain and Ireland participated in long-distance commerce to very varying degrees, and to a large extent those variations were structured according to the distance northwards and westwards from the Thames estuary. Rather than representing Britain and Ireland as homogeneous economies, it is more illuminating to think of south-eastern England as a component of a high-pressure economy focused on Flanders and northern France. Developments in shipping and port organization had progressed further there than elsewhere because of the stimulus of sea trade to the east, and the range of long-distance exchanges was correspondingly wider and more complex. Although the proportion of the population totally dependent upon long-distance trade was minute, in this part of the world a larger part than elsewhere was reliant upon merchants for some part of its daily consumption of food or raw materials. Further north and west the range of long-distance exchanges was narrower and less complex. The trade of Ireland and Wales during the thirteenth century involved supplying a narrow range of foodstuffs (wheat, cattle, dairy produce, and fish) and raw materials (hides, wool), some of which were supplied to English towns. Even in this representation of the British economy as a more commercialized core with a less commercialized periphery it is best to avoid analogies with modern international contrasts, since it is far from established how far these differences in commercial sophistication corresponded to differences in per capita productivity and welfare.

As these comments imply, the development of exchanges between different parts of Britain and Ireland was an important part of economic development in the twelfth and thirteenth centuries, even though it is poorly documented. Overland trade is the most difficult to document, though coin finds from Jedburgh imply that there was road traffic between the Lothians and Northumbria, along the Roman road known as Dere Street, from at least the tenth century.[48] Coastal trade, which benefited from the cheapness of sea transport, was no respecter of national boundaries, except when political restraints were imposed, and there is considerable evidence from an early date of lengthy communications connecting various parts of Britain. Connections between Scotland and east-coast ports of England, already attested in the early twelfth century, were well represented in the subsequent period of commercial expansion. Within a few decades of Dundee's establishment as a borough about the 1190s, Augustine of Dunwich was one of its burgesses. By 1212, merchants of Dundee were trading in London.[49] During the thirteenth century eastern Scotland imported English grain from as far south as East Anglia, through the ports of Dunwich and King's Lynn, by the agency of both English and Scottish merchants.[50]

Although the prospects for overseas trade through Welsh ports were restricted in this period, there was abundant opportunity for trade across the Severn estuary through Bristol. In addition, the eastward movement of commodities in response to the expanding demand in the English market was a stimulus to Welsh commerce, and underpinned Welsh urban growth of the period. Much of the direct contact with English buyers was made through the towns and fairs of the Marcher country. Shrewsbury was a market for Welsh goods throughout the thirteenth century, and Welsh merchants were numbered amongst the members of the merchant guild there. Hereford and Leominster were other ports of call. Welsh merchants sometimes went further afield in search of imported goods; Richard I authorized some of them to go to Boston, Lincoln, and Winchester. In 1232 Henry III allowed the men of Llywelyn the Great to trade in the markets and fairs of Shropshire, Staffordshire, Herefordshire, and Worcester so long as good relations between himself and Llywelyn were maintained, and in 1242 he recognized England and Wales as, in effect, a common market for reciprocal trade. Supplies to England from Wales perhaps included fish, though mountain ponies, cattle and sheep, dairy produce, and wool are more apparent in the records. Welsh wool from the great estates was bought and shipped from English ports by the great bulk exporters. From the twelfth century, at least, Wales became a source of timber for large building projects in southern England. In exchange the Welsh imported salt, wine, iron, and coined silver, and occasionally they needed to buy grain from England. Trade between Wales and England was inevitably threatened by the periodic outbreaks of hostility between Welsh princes and the English crown.[51] The trend towards market integration between England, the Marcher lordships and the principality of Wales was nevertheless unmistakable, and its economic benefits to Wales go far to explaining the capacity of the princes to build up their power base in Gwynedd.

Ireland was drawn into closer trading relations with Britain, especially from 1169. Her contacts with Scandinavia were by that time weakening,[52] and commerce with France was as yet poorly developed. Trade with Ireland contributed to the growth of the Welsh ports of Carmarthen, Cardiff, and Swansea; in 1216, for example, a ship belonging to Cardiff men was reported to be carrying wine and other merchandise on behalf of merchants from Dublin and Drogheda.[53] Ireland's export trade benefited from a rising external demand for agricultural produce; unlike Scotland, Ireland was an exporter of grain, and contributed to food supplies to western British ports as far north as Ayr.[54] In 1212 the steward of Meath sent 120 coombs of wheat (about 60 English quarters) to the king of Man as a pension due to him for his recent submission to King John.[55] By 1230 much of the west coast of England had become partially dependent on Irish grain. In November 1233 Henry III believed Irish supplies were sufficiently important to Llywelyn the Great to justify a ban on exports to Wales, though the bishop of Bangor was subsequently allowed to export Irish grain for sustaining the poor.[56] Edward I, as lord of Ireland, used it in 1257 as a granary to support warfare in Wales.[57] Later in the thirteenth century, Ireland contributed supplies to his troops and garrisons in Gascony, Wales, and Scotland. In the two years from September 1295 to August 1297, Irish ports handled exports of 14,886 quarters of wheat, 4,167 heaped quarters of oats, and 162 quarters of beans on behalf of the government. Similar demands were made of Ireland in subsequent years, though the heavy burdens of purveyance by government officers were resisted, and the amounts that could be supplied declined in the early fourteenth century.[58] Ireland was also a source of supply for hides and wool, though, as we have seen, much of the wool was destined for Flanders rather than for English manufactures.

Falling transactions costs and expanding mercantile activity had brought about an improved integration of commodity markets. This had several distinct aspects. One was that producers were responding to market stimuli over longer distances. The trade in grain and timber between Britain and the Baltic, or in wine between England and Gascony, are prominent examples. The way in which Irish estates responded to market demand in Britain between the 1170s and 1300 is a further good case in point. Secondly, as trade became more regular different localities develop patterns of interdependence based on specialization, since it is to the advantage of trading partners to concentrate on products in which they have a relative cost advantage. A classic case of specialization in response to market opportunity was the concentration of the Bordeaux region in wine production.

And thirdly, price differentials between interrelated markets had narrowed, as merchants increasingly shifted produce from places where it was relatively cheap to places where it was relatively dear. We should not expect too much of market integration in the twelfth and thirteenth centuries. The scope for long-distance trade and specialization was limited by the high costs of overland transport in bulk, and by generally low level of incomes. Price movements were more volatile than they are in modern economies because such a large share of output depended on the weather. Even so, the economy in 1300 was far more dependent on inter-national and interregional trade than in 1050. For that reason it was also more vulnerable to a range of frequent hazards, notably war, international commercial rivalry, and monetary instability.

NOTES

1. E. A. Lewis, 'A Contribution to the Commercial History of Medieval Wales', *Y Cymmrodor*, 24 (1913), 104–5.
2. E. Miller and J. Hatcher, *Medieval England: Towns, Commerce and Crafts, 1086–1348* (1995), 195–6, 210–15.
3. N. Mayhew, 'Modelling Medieval Monetisation', in R. H. Britnell and B. M. S. Campbell (eds.), *A Commercialising Economy: England 1086 to c.1300* (Manchester, 1995), 59.
4. M. W. Beresford, *New Towns of the Middle Ages: Town Plantation in England, Wales and Gascony* (1967), 511–12, 515–16.
5. E. M. Carus-Wilson and O. Coleman, *England's Export Trade, 1275–1547* (Oxford, 1963), 37–8; P. G. B. McNeill and H. L. MacQueen (eds.), *Atlas of Scottish History to 1707* (Edinburgh, 1996), 251.
6. William of Malmesbury, *Gesta Regum Anglorum*, ed. R. M. Thomson, 2 vols. (Oxford, 1998–9), i. 738–9; ii. 371.
7. A. Stevenson, 'Trade with the South, 1070–1513', in M. Lynch, M. Spearman, and G. Stell (eds.), *The Scottish Medieval Town* (Edinburgh, 1988), 183–4.
8. Beresford, *New Towns*, 461.
9. A. A. M. Duncan, *Scotland: The Making of the Kingdom* (Edinburgh, 1989), 511–13.
10. E. W. Moore, *The Fairs of Medieval England: An Introductory Study* (Toronto, 1985), 60–2, 217–22.
11. Stevenson, 'Trade', 184; R. W. Unger, *The Ship in the Medieval Economy, 600–1600* (1980), 136–44.
12. J. Schofield and A. Vince, *Medieval Towns* (London, 1994), 54–9, 67.
13. R. H. Britnell, 'Sedentary Merchants and Long-Distance Trade', in P. R. Coss and S. D. Lloyd, *Thirteenth Century England V* (Woodbridge, 1995), 129–39; Miller and Hatcher, *Medieval England: Towns, Commerce and Crafts*, 25–37; Stevenson, 'Trade', 187.
14. R. H. Britnell, 'England and Northern Italy in the Early Fourteenth Century: The Economic Contrasts', *Transactions of the Royal Historical Society*, 5th ser. 39 (1989), 167–83.
15. A. R. Bridbury, *Medieval English Clothmaking: An Economic Survey* (1982), 30–1; J. Munro,

'The "Industrial Crisis" of the English Textile Towns, c.1290–c.1330', in M. Prestwich, R. Britnell, and R. Frame (eds.), *Thirteenth Century England VII* (Woodbridge, 1999), 103–42.

16. Munro, 'Industrial Crisis', 111–12, 114–15; J. R. Oldman, 'London Clothmaking, c.1270–c.1550' (unpublished Ph.D. thesis, London University, 2003), 30–41.

17. Duncan, *Scotland*, 510.

18. P. H. Sawyer, 'The Wealth of England in the Eleventh Century', *Transactions of the Royal Historical Society*, 5th ser. 15 (1965), 162.

19. P. D. A. Harvey, 'The English Trade in Wool and Cloth: 1150–1250: Some Problems and Suggestions', in M. Spallanzani (ed.), *Produzione, commercio e consumo dei panni di lana* (Florence, 1976), 369–75.

20. T. H. Lloyd, *The English Wool Trade in the Middle Ages* (Cambridge, 1977), 22, 24.

21. E. Power, *The Wool Trade in English Medieval History* (1941), 46.

22. See below (Ch. 12).

23. Duncan, *Scotland*, 513; Stevenson, 'Trade', 183.

24. Lloyd, *English Wool Trade*, 25–7.

25. D. H. Williams, *The Welsh Cistercians: Aspects of their Economic History* (Pontypool, 1970), 68–9.

26. M. D. O'Sullivan, *Italian Merchant Bankers in Ireland in the Thirteenth Century: A Study in the Social and Economic History of Medieval Ireland* (Dublin, 1962), 124–5.

27. N. Denholm-Young, *Seignorial Administration in England* (1937), 55–6.

28. Duncan, *Scotland*, 429–31; McNeill and MacQueen (eds.), *Atlas*, 237; Williams, *Welsh Cistercians*, 68–9.

29. Stevenson, 'Trade', 186–9.

30. E. B. Fryde, 'Italian Maritime Trade with England (c.1270–c.1530)', in id., *Studies in Medieval Trade and Finance* (1983), item xiv, 293–4.

31. See below (Ch. 20).

32. T. H. Lloyd, *Alien Merchants in England in the High Middle Ages* (Brighton, 1982), 211, 214–16, 224.

33. Duncan, *Scotland*, 506, 514, 603–4; A. Grant, *Independence and Nationhood: Scotland, 1306–1469* (1984), 236; McNeill and MacQueen (eds.), *Atlas*, 253.

34. Gerald of Wales, 'Topographica Hibernica', I. vi: *Giraldi Cambrensis Opera*, ed. J. S. Brewer and J. F. Dimock, 8 vols., Rolls Ser. 21 (1861–91), v. 28; W. Childs and T. O'Neill, 'Overseas Trade', in A. Cosgrove (ed.), *A New History of Ireland*, ii: *Medieval Ireland, 1169–1534* (Oxford, 1987), 500.

35. Lloyd, *Alien Merchants*, 44–5, 49.

36. J. Hatcher, *English Tin Production and Trade before 1550* (Oxford, 1973), 2–3, 23–5, 27.

37. Lloyd, *Alien Merchants*, 41.

38. Ibid. 211–26; Duncan, *Scotland*, 510.

39. Lloyd, *Alien Merchants*, 45–6 (Hull), 46–7 (Boston), 49 (Lynn), 54 (London), 58 (Southampton).

40. M. K. James, *Studies in the Medieval Wine Trade*, ed. E. M. Veale (Oxford, 1971), 96.

41. G. W. S. Barrow, *Robert Bruce and the Community of the Realm of Scotland* (Edinburgh, 1976), 78; D. Ditchburn, *Scotland and Europe: The Medieval Kingdom and its Contacts with Christendom, 1214–1560* (East Linton, 2000), 153; K. Down, 'Colonial Society and Economy in the High Middle Ages', in A. Cosgrove (ed.), *A New History of Ireland*, ii: *Medieval Ireland, 1169–1534* (Oxford, 1987), 489; Duncan, *Scotland*, 508–9; James, *Studies in the Medieval Wine Trade*, 96; E. A. Lewis, 'The Development of Industry and Commerce in Wales during the Middle Ages', *Transactions of the Royal Historical Society*, new ser. 17 (1903), 90, 99, 108.

42. Ditchburn, *Scotland and Europe*, 144; Duncan, *Scotland*, 498, 507; T. H. Lloyd, *England and the German Hanse, 1157–1611: A Study of their Trade and Commercial Diplomacy* (Cambridge, 1991), 40–1.

43. A. R. Bridbury, *England and the Salt Trade in the Later Middle Ages* (Oxford, 1955), 41–5; Duncan, *Scotland*, 498, 507.

44. Ditchburn, *Scotland and Europe*, 150–1; Duncan, *Scotland*, 498, 505–7; Stevenson, 'Trade', 184.

45. Lloyd, *Alien Merchants*, 45; M. Kowaleski, 'The Grain Trade in Fourteenth-Century Exeter', in E. B. DeWindt (ed.), *The Salt of Common Life: Individuality and Choice in the Medieval Town, Countryside and Church. Essays Presented to J. Ambrose Raftis* (Kalamazoo, 1995), 12.

46. N. Hybel, 'The Grain Trade in Northern Europe before 1350', *Economic History Review*, 55 (2002), 229–37.

47. Duncan, *Scotland*, 508; Lloyd, *Alien Merchants*, 45, 49, 51, 58.

48. Duncan, *Scotland*, 464.

49. K. J. Stringer, *Earl David of Huntingdon: A Study in Anglo-Scottish History* (Edinburgh, 1985), 75.

50. Duncan, *Scotland*, 505–7.

51. R. R. Davies, *Conquest, Coexistence and Change: Wales, 1063–1415* (Oxford, 1987), 169; Lewis, 'Development of Industry', 130–2, 138–9, 150, 169; Lewis, 'Contribution', 89.

52. B. T. Hudson, 'The Changing Economy of the Irish Sea Province: AD 900–1300', in B. Smith (ed.), *Britain and Ireland 900–1300: Insular Responses to Medieval European Change* (Cambridge, 1999), 63.

53. D. G. Williams, 'Cardiff', in R. A. Griffiths (ed.), *Boroughs of Medieval Wales* (Cardiff, 1978), 127.

54. Duncan, *Scotland*, 505; Hudson, 'Changing Economy', 61.

55. 'The Irish Pipe Roll of 14 John, 1211–1212', ed. O. Davies and D. B. Quinn, *Ulster Journal of Archaeology*, 4, suppl. (1941), 32.

56. *Calendar of Documents Relating to Ireland Preserved in Her Majesty's Public Record Office*, ed. H. S. Sweetman, 5 vols. (1875–86), i, nos. 686, 898, 944, 977, 1040, 1447, 1930, 2073, 2108, pp. 106, 143, 149–50, 159–60, 218–19, 286, 308, 313. A crannock of wheat was about equivalent to an English quarter: see below (Ch. 12).

57. 'Three Exchequer Documents from the Reign of Henry the Third', ed. J. Lydon, *Proceedings of the Royal Irish Academy*, 65, section C.1 (1966), 17–18, 20–7.

58. J. Lydon, 'Ireland in 1297: "At Peace after Its Manner" ', in id. (ed.), *Law and Disorder in*

Thirteenth-Century Ireland: The Dublin Parliament of 1297 (Dublin, 1997), 14–17; id., 'Edward I, Ireland and the War in Scotland, 1303–1304', in id. (ed.), England and Ireland in the Late Middle Ages: Essays in Honour of Jocelyn Otway-Ruthven (Dublin, 1981), 52–4.

FURTHER READING

Blanchard, I., 'Lothian and Beyond: The Economy of the "English Empire" of David I', in R. Britnell and J. Hatcher (eds.), Progress and Problems in Medieval England: Essays in Honour of Edward Miller (Cambridge, 1996).

Bridbury, A. R., Medieval English Clothmaking: An Economic Survey (1982).

Britnell, R. H., 'England and Northern Italy in the Early Fourteenth Century: The Economic Contrasts', Transactions of the Royal Historical Society, 5th ser. 39 (1989).

—— 'Sedentary Merchants and Long-Distance Trade', in P. R. Coss and S. D. Lloyd (eds.), Thirteenth Century England V (Woodbridge, 1995).

Carus-Wilson, E. M., Medieval Merchant Venturers, 2nd edn. (1967).

—— and Coleman, O., England's Export Trade, 1275–1547 (Oxford, 1963).

Childs, W., and O'Neill, T., 'Overseas Trade', in A. Cosgrove (ed.), A New History of Ireland, ii: Medieval Ireland, 1169–1534 (Oxford, 1987).

Chorley, P., 'The Cloth Industry of Flanders and Northern France during the Thirteenth Century: A Luxury Trade?', Economic History Review, 2nd ser. 40 (1987).

—— 'English Cloth Exports during the Thirteenth and Early Fourteenth Centuries: The Continental Evidence', Historical Research (1988).

Davies, J. C., 'Shipping and Trade in Newcastle upon Tyne, 1294–6', Archaeologia Aeliana, 4th ser. 31 (1953).

Ditchburn, D., Scotland and Europe: The Medieval Kingdom and its Contacts with Christendom, 1214–1560 (East Linton, 2000).

Down, K., 'Colonial Society and Economy in the High Middle Ages', in A. Cosgrove (ed.), A New History of Ireland, ii: Medieval Ireland, 1169–1534 (Oxford, 1987).

Duncan, A. A. M., Scotland: The Making of the Kingdom (Edinburgh, 1989).

Fryde, E. B., Studies in Medieval Trade and Finance (1983).

Galloway, J. A., 'One Market or Many? London and the Grain Trade of England', in id. (ed.), Trade, Urban Hinterland and Market Integration, c.1300–1600 (2000).

Harte, N. B., and Ponting, K. G., eds., Cloth and Clothing in Medieval Europe: Essays in Memory of E. M. Carus-Wilson (1983).

Harvey, P. D. A., 'The English Trade in Wool and Cloth: 1150–1250: Some Problems and Suggestions', in M. Spallanzani (ed.), Produzione, commercio e consumo dei panni di lana (Florence, 1976).

Hatcher, J., English Tin Production and Trade before 1550 (Oxford, 1973).

Hudson, B. T., 'The Changing Economy of the Irish Sea Province: AD 900–1300', in B. Smith (ed.), Britain and Ireland 900–1300: Insular Responses to Medieval European Change (Cambridge, 1999).

Hurst, J. G., 'Medieval Pottery Imported into Ireland', in G. Mac Niocaill and P. F. Wallace (eds.), Keimelia: Studies in Medieval Archaeology and History in Memory of Tom Delaney (Galway, 1988).

Hybel, N., 'The Grain Trade in Northern Europe before 1350', *Economic History Review*, 55 (2002).

James, M. K., *Studies in the Medieval Wine Trade*, ed. E. M. Veale (Oxford, 1971).

Lewis, E. A., 'A Contribution to the Commercial History of Medieval Wales', *Y Cymmrodor*, 24 (1913).

—— 'The Development of Industry and Commerce in Wales during the Middle Ages', *Transaction of the Royal Historical Society*, new ser. 17 (1903).

Lloyd, T. H., *Alien Merchants in England in the High Middle Ages* (Brighton, 1982).

—— *England and the German Hanse, 1157–1611: A Study of their Trade and Commercial Diplomacy* (Cambridge, 1991).

—— *The English Wool Trade in the Middle Ages* (Cambridge, 1977).

McNeill, P. G. B., and MacQueen, H. L. (eds.), *Atlas of Scottish History to 1707* (Edinburgh, 1996).

Mayhew, N., 'Modelling Medieval Monetisation', in R. H. Britnell and B. M. S. Campbell (eds.), *A Commercialising Economy: England 1086 to c.1300* (Manchester, 1995).

Miller, E., and Hatcher, J., *Medieval England: Towns, Commerce and Crafts, 1086–1348* (1995).

Moore, E. W., *The Fairs of Medieval England: An Introductory Study* (Toronto, 1985).

Munro, J., 'The "Industrial Crisis" of the English Textile Towns, c.1290–c.1330', in M. Prestwich, R. Britnell, and R. Frame (eds.), *Thirteenth Century England VII* (Woodbridge, 1999).

Nightingale, P., *A Medieval Mercantile Community: The Grocers' Company of London, 1000–1485* (New Haven, 1995).

—— 'The Growth of London in the Medieval English Economy', in R. H. Britnell and J. Hatcher (eds.), *Progress and Problems in Medieval England: Essays in Honour of Edward Miller* (Cambridge, 1996).

O'Brien, F., 'Commercial Relations between Aquitaine and Ireland c.1000 to c.1550', in Jean-Michel Picard (ed.), *Aquitaine and Ireland in the Middle Ages* (Dublin, 1995).

O'Sullivan, M. D., *Italian Merchant Bankers in Ireland in the Thirteenth Century: A Study in the Social and Economic History of Medieval Ireland* (Dublin, 1962).

Palliser, D. M. (ed.), *The Cambridge Urban History of Britain*, i (Cambridge, 2000).

Platt, C., *Medieval Southampton: The Port and Trading Community, A.D. 1000–1600* (1973).

Power, E., *The Wool Trade in English Medieval History* (1941).

Rigby, S. H., *Medieval Grimsby: Growth and Decline* (Hull, 1993).

Ruddock, A. A., *Italian Merchants and Shipping in Southampton, 1270–1600* (Southampton, 1951).

Spufford, P., *The Merchant in Medieval Europe* (2002).

—— *Money and its Use in Medieval Europe* (Cambridge, 1988).

Stevenson, A., 'Trade with the South, 1070–1513', in M. Lynch, M. Spearman, and G. Stell (eds.), *The Scottish Medieval Town* (Edinburgh, 1988).

Sutton, A., 'Mercery through Four Centuries, 1130s–c.1500', *Nottingham Medieval Studies*, 41 (1997).

—— 'Some Aspects of the Linen Trade c.1130s to 1500 and the Part Played by the Mercers of London', *Textile History*, 30 (1999).

Unger, R. W., *The Ship in the Medieval Economy, 600–1600* (1980).

CHAPTER 7

Towns, Industry, and Local Trade

*F*or anyone accompanying Edward I northwards to Galloway in the summer of 1300, Britain was a showcase of different types of town and different degrees of regional urbanization. From Britain's largest city, and the commercially vigorous south-east, a traveller passed through the small towns and village markets of provincial England and the Scottish burghs, into tracts of the Scottish mainland and the western isles that remained as remote from urban experience as any part of Europe, having few institutions of any kind to encourage formal trade. The route passed through regional centres, small towns, and mere villages with markets, and the traveller would observe a continuum in size and institutional complexity from the largest down to the smallest. Very few of these centres of trade would have more than 2,000–3,000 inhabitants, and most would have fewer than 1,000. Britain had many small focal points of market demand but very few large ones.

In 1300, despite a proliferation of towns and markets during the preceding 250 years, there remained significant differences between England, Wales, Scotland, and Ireland in the size of towns and the level of urbanization, for reasons which we examined in Chapter 1. Few towns in Scotland had more than 1,000 inhabitants, which was about the size of Aberdeen.[1] If around 1300 urban populations accounted for 15–20 per cent of the English population, as already suggested, this high proportion was mostly owing to the concentration of towns in the south and east. In Scotland the proportion was lower, but perhaps amounting to 3–4 per cent of the total population. Though there were towns in the east as far north as the Moray Firth, they did not extend westwards into the highlands and islands, so that over a half of Scotland's total land surface was townless.[2] In Wales and Ireland the urban proportion is likely to have been similarly low.[3] These contrasts correspond to significant differences in the urban stimulus to agrarian production, and to different levels of monetization in the broader economy outside towns.

Other variation across Britain arose from differences between the commercial rights of towns in different legal or political contexts. In England even the greatest towns had no great territorial authority; they were not able to insist that the agrarian produce of the surrounding countryside should be brought to a staple market place. Landlords were able to establish new markets on their manors, subject only to the requirement that they should obtain a charter from the king, and with some reservations, after 1200, about not damaging the interests of existing markets.[4] The principal anomaly in England was the Palatinate of Durham, whose lords, the bishops of Durham, were empowered to grant market charters in lieu of the king, but who did so very sparingly. The few new marketing centres in the Palatinate were mostly the bishop's own creations, and were located on the perimeter as far from Durham as possible.[5] Outside England, borough monopolies were more common. Carmarthen acquired virtually a monopoly of trade within a 15-mile radius in the late thirteenth century. Brecon had extensive jurisdiction over surrounding settlements, and in 1308 was authorized to suppress trading in the rising borough of Llywel, over 11 miles away.[6] Similar powers were probably widespread throughout Wales; in the fourteenth century even the tiny borough of Chirkland (chartered in 1324) monopolized transactions of over 4*d.* within the commote of Nanheudwy.[7] In Scotland, from the time of David I the crown adopted a similar policy of granting local territorial monopolies of public trade to royal burghs, the object being to maximize the income from market tolls. David I gave the burgesses of Rutherglen rights and tolls in a territory 'from Nethan to Polmadie, from Garrion to Kelvin, from Loudoun to "Prenteinith" and from Cairn to "Karun" '. Subsequently William I of Scotland, sometime in the 1180s, prohibited anyone from bringing goods to sell within those bounds unless he had first taken them to the burgh of Rutherglen.[8] Territorial privileges of this kind have been described as 'the fundamental burghal privilege' in Scotland. They may be regarded as devices to protect infant commerce in regions where it was being deliberately fostered as a novelty. Such controls meant that Scotland did not experience the proliferation of rural markets that characterized most of England, and the costs of trading for Scottish countrymen were consequently higher.[9] Some such formal territorial rights had been tolerated in England before the rapid increase in the number of markets and fairs from the late twelfth century.[10]

Urban Growth

A good deal of urban development of the period 1050–1300 in southern and midland England was built on earlier foundations. Older cities, boroughs, and market towns grew in dimension, in the range of their institutions and amenities, and in the size of their populations. The city of London is the prime example of an Anglo-Saxon town that expanded. Its population around 1300 was at least

60,000 and may have been as large as 80,000, making it one of the largest cities in Europe.[11] The city had probably doubled in size since the beginning of the thirteenth century and was from four to eight times larger than it had been in the reign of William I. The provincial cities of Anglo-Saxon England similarly grew. Suburban growth, outside the core of an existing town, beyond its walls if it had any, was particularly characteristic of the eleventh and twelfth centuries.[12] For example, the city of Gloucester expanded its trade with the surrounding country-side in the course of this period, benefiting from the growing wealth of its hinter-land and from the expansion of long-distance trade along the River Severn. To the north, houses and shops spread beyond the old North Gate of the walled Roman city along Lower Northgate Street to a region called Newland. Beyond East Gate a suburb developed in what was called Barton Street. Beyond Westgate the suburbs stretched down to the river in part of the town called Home Bridge. In this period the old Saxon churches of the city were rebuilt, and probably mostly enlarged, and four new parish churches were constructed. The population of the town grew from perhaps 2,500–3000 in 1086 to 4,000 in 1300.[13]

Besides the expansion of older towns, a network of new ones was created, extending the spatial incidence of urban communities. An emphasis on the dynamism of the period after 1050 is in no way to deny the vitality of urban life in later Anglo-Saxon and Danish England, nor the widespread trade and use of money through much of England at the time of the Norman Conquest. However, vigorous new towns, like Chelmsford in Essex, were established even in the regions of England that had been most commercialized in the eleventh century, and the transformation of local economies beyond southern England and the midlands was even more extensive. Only in the centuries after 1050 is it possible to ascribe urbanization to the greater part of Britain or Ireland. This period saw a remarkable development north of York, including many new towns of lasting significance, like Newcastle, Sunderland, and Carlisle, and the earliest developments of town life in Wales, Scotland, and most of Ireland. Perhaps in England about 400–500 new enterprises of the period 1050–1300 became sufficiently developed to be considered urban.[14] Maurice Beresford lists a further 75 for Wales. George Pryde identified 62 Scottish burghs chartered in these years (Figure 7.1), and John Bradley has identified 54 new boroughs with definite urban features in Ireland.[15] Most of these towns survived to create a new urban framework of permanent importance for local trade and agrarian development. Even in Scotland, where royal enterprise was particularly conspicuous, many of the new burghs were created by prominent landlords; St Andrews and Glasgow were both founded by their bishops, the former before 1144 and the latter during the 1170s.[16]

Their creation depended upon the investment activity of landlords, who sur-rendered land for the purpose, and usually laid out sums for providing the essential

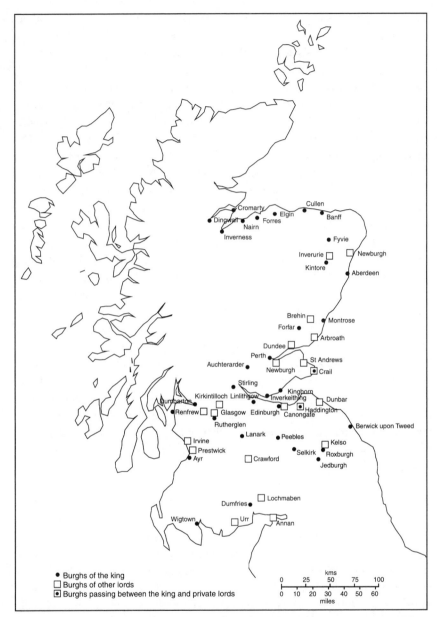

FIG. 7.1. Scottish burghs in existence by 1300. A remarkable increase in the number of burghs between *c*.1120 and 1300 represents the origins of urban life in Scotland. The crown was notably active especially in the earliest phase of this development under David I. Note, though, the absence of town life from much of Scotland, especially the Highlands and most of the west coast.

Source: P. G. B. McNeill and H. L. MacQueen (eds.), *Atlas of Scottish History to 1707* (Edinburgh, 1966), 198.

amenities of the market place. Other investment, whether by landlords or others, was needed to construct streets, houses, or churches. Such activity, though sometimes encouraged by consideration of regional status, depended upon the anticipation of financial returns, and was recognized throughout Europe as a way of raising the value of property and the level of cash income.[17] Some landlords engaged in multiple foundations across their estates, the most remarkable example being David I of Scotland (1124–53), who founded at least fourteen burghs with weekly markets, mostly at ancient centres of royal authority.[18] In the course of developing their estates landlords also worked to increase the accessibility of markets. This might be achieved, as at Chelmsford or Witham in Essex, by shifting trade from older centres onto main road sites. Alternatively it could result from the improvement of communication by road and water; some towns, like Ware, Durham, and Perth were improved by bridges that facilitated access to their streets and markets.[19] A successful borough could make a significant direct contribution to a landlord's income. The sum owed each year by the burgesses of Scarborough to the king increased from £20 in 1163 to £76 in 1201.[20] More indirectly, landlords benefited to the extent that new centres of demand for food and raw materials enlarged marketing opportunities for rural tenants. If tenants could sell their produce with greater ease, this facilitated levying money rents and payments from them. The new market places, with their stalls and weighing apparatus, were less important, both as a source of seigniorial income and as a commercial facility to tenants, than the concentration of new rent-paying burgesses gainfully employed. So the signals that would induce a landlord to found a borough were, on the one hand, indications of good opportunities for local employment in industry and trade, and, on the other, evidence that some particular site—especially if associated with the residence of a big-spending household—was likely to attract resident artisans and tradesmen, if provided with an appropriate institutional infrastructure.

Urban growth depended upon the willingness of men and women to become dependent upon market relationships for their livelihood, exchanging manufactures and services for food and raw materials. Towns that grew did not rely on exceptionally high rates of natural increase, but on their capacity to attract migrants. In general mercantile boroughs exercised a strong pull just because of the employment opportunities they offered. Townward migration was local in the case of smaller ventures, but more successful towns drew families over long distances. From the late twelfth century, Dublin attracted newcomers from many parts of Wales, western England, and the English midlands.[21] In areas without previous urban traditions, townspeople came from afar because landlords made efforts to draw suitable settlers by offering them attractive terms and protection. Though the new Welsh towns were small, urban development was associated with the immigration of English settlers. Even in the late thirteenth century Cardiff was a predominantly English town; all the jurors who provided information for a survey of the town in 1295 were of English origin.[22] Some of Scotland's early burghs were similarly centres of English habitation, according to William of Newburgh, and his view gains support from the evidence of the personal names of early settlers; there were also numerous Flemings.[23]

One of the ways landlords attracted people to towns was by granting them facilities adapted to a non-agrarian way of life. These included a market place for the purchase of food and raw materials; resident townspeople had the right to buy what they needed there free of toll. But urban families also came to expect special terms of tenure to enable them to come and go easily. One of the most fundamental institutions of urban life was a cluster of burgage plots held by burgage tenure. Characteristically these were standardized units of half an acre or so ranged along a road, each with a street frontage. But their tenurial characteristics were equally distinctive. Rents were paid in money, without the burden of labour services that would have hindered a tradesman or artisan from earning a precarious livelihood. In addition, the burgess who held a burgage plot was free in law to sell it and move away at any time, or bequeath it by will. This was one of the freest forms of property ownership, though it differed from freehold in being more normally subject to local customs relating to inheritance or rights of dower.[24] It would be misleading to imply that independent owner-occupation remained universally true of town life. Particularly in the larger towns properties were given to churches, abbeys, guilds, and chantries in large numbers. By the end of the thirteenth century York was dominated by institutional landlords; the cathedral church was the wealthiest of these, but many other Yorkshire abbeys had property in the city.[25] Exactly the same phenomenon is found in Scottish towns; great abbeys had properties in several burghs, and like Arbroath Abbey, for example, used them as bases for trade as well as sources of rent.[26] Increasingly the occupants of properties were leaseholders of dependent status, many of them brought within the jurisdiction of their landlord's courts. Yet this development did not undermine the virtues of burgage tenure for a commercial community, since tenants were still free to surrender properties and move away if that was what their interests dictated.

The occupational structure of towns differed considerably in accordance with their size, location, and territorial assets. Many old towns had extensive agricultural land attached to them, and though in the course of time the ownership of this land might pass to abbeys, colleges, or hospitals, it nevertheless created employment for townspeople. If a town had extensive commons, the freemen were likely to enjoy common rights that allowed them at least to supplement their incomes by keeping livestock. A classic case of this agrarian involvement, drawn to the attention of historians as long ago as 1898, was the city of Cambridge.[27] In Aberdeen the importance of farming was such that some urban occupations were exercised only seasonally.[28] Agrarian employment was also to be found in newer towns that had developed from older settlements, like Thornbury (Gloucs.).[29] However, many new towns, especially those on virgin sites, had been carved out of village territories, sometimes indeed out of heaths, and no agricultural resources were assigned to the urban plots that lined the market place.[30] In these cases agrarian involvement depended upon families with land transferring their residence to the town or, alternatively, on townsmen building up sufficient reserves to be able to buy land.

The size of a town was an important determinant of the range of occupations to be found in it; the larger the town, the larger the range of occupations. A large town depended upon being able to satisfy its requirements for food and raw materials by selling manufactured goods and services in exchange for agricultural produce, and this necessarily required supplying a broad range of different products across an extensive market area. Larger towns accommodated some tradesmen sufficiently committed to a particular trade to acquire dedicated premises. Medieval street names in town centres often indicate which crafts occupied them. An occupational analysis of three major provincial English towns around 1300—Winchester, Norwich, and York—suggests that across the three, 43 per cent of the townsmen associated with particular occupations were traders in food, textiles, hides, or miscellaneous wares, 46 per cent were engaged in manufacturing, especially in textiles, clothing, leatherwork, and metalwork, and 11 per cent were in service occupations, especially transport, building, clerical work, law, and medicine. There were differences of balance, of course; York was the most industrial of the three and the least mercantile; Winchester, with a population in 1300 of 10,000–12,000, was the most mercantile and the least industrial. In none of the towns, though, did trade and manufacturing occupations together amount to less than 83 per cent of the total.[31] The balance of occupations was perhaps little different in many smaller towns. The court rolls of Halesowen give less than half the number of occupations recorded in Winchester for the period 1300–39 (35 against 72), but they split roughly 50 : 50 between manufacturing and trade.[32] The sparse evidence from Wales and Scotland implies occupational structures very similar to those in English towns of comparable size. Thirteenth-century Carmarthen and Aberdeen had a predictable range of crafts and trades in the supply of basic housing, clothing, food, and drink; the earliest Aberdonian identifiable by name was Richard the mason (cementarius) in 1272. The presence of weavers, fullers, and dyers there shows that, as in England, textiles were often produced very locally.[33] Not all townsmen were highly specialized in what they did. Many made a living in more than one way—combining a manufacturing or commercial occupation with farming, for example.[34]

The economic opportunities of female employment were not wasted in medieval towns, though they are less easy to identify than those of male heads of households, partly because a man was legally responsible for his wife's debts and for managing her property. Needless to say, perhaps, there were no administrative or political roles for women either in the government of boroughs, nor in the clerical and legal professions; this is another reason why women are less prominent than men in our records. Most manufacturing activities were also associated with male householders, though no doubt many women assisted with their husband's craft. Some roles, however, were strongly associated with women. Perhaps the most distinguished of these was embroidery, a high art employed for the decoration of ecclesiastical, noble, and royal vestments. Some embroiderers are known by name, such as one employed by Queen Margaret of Scotland, called Heliseuld, whose skills were acclaimed in 1113, or Mabel of Bury St Edmunds, who worked for the English court between 1239 and 1245.[35] Women were also employed for the manufacture of mercers' goods, as in linen weaving. Slave women had probably performed these tasks for wealthier households at the beginning of our period, but by the thirteenth century they had become commercialized. At the lower end of the manufacturing scale, wool spinning was very widespread in a period when clothmaking was carried on in towns large and small all over Britain. At least by 1250 flax spinning, though more localized, must have been a significant source of female employment in Norfolk, notably in the market town of Aylsham and its neighbourhood.[36] Butchery and baking were commonly male occupations, though that is not to say that wives, daughters, and female servants did not become involved. But ale brewing and selling, though unspecialized and often casual, were almost exclusively female activities throughout this period,[37] and women were elsewhere prominent in retailing of food and drink. They may even have dominated urban market places as sellers of dairy produce, poultry, and fish, whether produced on lands around the town or brought in from a greater distance. Women were often prominent amongst those prosecuted for breaking the regulations of these trades. In York in 1304, twenty-seven people were prosecuted for regrating—that is, for buying up produce to resell it against the rules of the market—and eighteen of these were women.[38] Women migrated into towns specially for the opportunities that such trade offered. Prostitution, too, was essentially an urban occupation, and one that was generally tolerated, though under strict conditions. Many towns insisted that prostitutes should live in suburbs outside their walls; London introduced a ruling to that effect in 1276–8, perhaps because their number was growing at the time.[39]

Institutional Innovations and Trade

The multiplication of towns, each with regular market days and predictable facilities for trade, brought the same benefits to local trade as ports and fairs did to commerce over long distances. It reduced the costs of trading both for agricultural producers, who had shorter distances to travel to market their produce, and to craftsmen, who had better institutional facilities and more regular custom than they would have had in smaller rural settlements. Urban courts were often an additional asset to townsmen, since they reduced the costs of securing redress when debtors defaulted or contracts were broken. Some other strands of development, such as innovations in the way trade was conducted, and in the character of market-place facilities, are almost wholly hidden from us for want of early sources. But closer inspection of the information available shows innovations deriving from numerous different quarters—from governments, from landlords, and from the urban inhabitants themselves. One line of development, instigated by the crown, was the closer definition of markets in law, and the partial elimination of insti-tutional forms that did not comply with the legal definition. Royal licensing of markets seems to have been inaugurated in England by William the Conqueror and in Scotland under David I,[40] and the enforcement of this right entailed the build-up of a certain amount of case law. By the end of the thirteenth century the Scottish burghs had a common code, unlike anything in England, known as the 'Burgh Laws' (*Leges Burgorum*), which in its printed version has 119 clauses.[41] England had no equivalent, either, to the arrangement, in evidence in 1295, by which four burgesses each from Berwick, Roxburgh, Edinburgh, and Stirling could formulate common regulations and constitute a court of appeal from the courts of individual burghs; the earliest known meeting of this kind was concerned with rules of inheritance.[42] The Scottish and English crowns continued to follow differ-ent courses in their regulation of towns and trade, but in both cases there was standardization under the aegis of a growing body of law. English kings, who had unified the currency in circulation well before 1050, increasingly standardized weights and measures, and by the thirteenth century regulated the retail prices of basic provisions such as bread and ale.[43] The earliest known attempts by the Scottish crown to control weights and measures, as well as to regulate the prices of bread and ale, are ascribed to David I, though there are no reliable texts dating back so far.[44]

Institutions favouring the development of urban life were not entirely the innovations of kings and landlords. Once towns were in existence, many new ideas originated amongst their inhabitants—especially, of course, the wealthiest inhabitants whose land or commercial capital gave them exceptional influence. Local initiatives, in cooperation with landlords and their advisers, brought about a widespread transformation in the administration of larger towns. Landlords with major borough revenues were often persuaded to set them at lease, whether to an individual lessee, a consortium, or the townsmen as a body. Through this last practice, the larger English royal boroughs had by 1200 begun to enjoy limited powers of self-government authorized by the crown. The king's revenues as landlord were leased to the leading inhabitants of the town, in exchange for a regular sum of money called the borough farm (*firma burgi*). In England, rights of urban self-administration were often spelled out in written grants of liberties. Early in his reign, Richard I of England (1188–99) conceded in perpetuity to the townsmen of Bedford, Colchester, Hereford, Northampton, and Worcester the right to lease the king's revenues.[45] The right to lease these revenues was closely associated with the related right of burgesses to elect their own reeves or bailiffs. From this time onward the administration of the principal English royal boroughs was commonly headed either by an elected mayor or by two elected bailiffs; in either case, these officials were directly answerable to the king for the good state of the borough in their charge. Scottish towns were characteristically administered through one or two reeves, who were perhaps elected.[46] The burgesses of Inverkeithing (Fife), headed by a town reeve, were apparently leasing the royal revenues there in 1170. Several thirteenth-century royal grants out of the revenue of Scottish royal burghs show that they were the responsibility of burgh reeves, and this was general by 1327, though unlike England the sum due each year (the 'ferm') remained a matter for recurrent reassessment.[47] The characteristic composition of urban revenues can be exemplified by those from Dublin, which in 1275–6 totalled £218 2*s*. 6¾*d*. As listed in the Irish pipe roll account of that year, they comprised the rents of urban properties (including 'landgabel'), other rents from market stalls and a mill, the profits of jurisdiction (including 'alewyte' from enforcing the assize of ale), revenue from the sale of fishing rights in the River Liffy, market tolls, receipts from fairs and guilds (English and Irish), and a tax on trade for the upkeep of the city walls.[48]

The existence of such liberties necessarily implied that boroughs should have a definite group of beneficiaries, known as freemen or burgesses. Borough charters usually granted rights to the burgesses of such-and-such a place and their heirs, but in order to maintain their numbers towns admitted suitable newcomers as burgesses on payment of some entry fee to the community chest. Another route into membership of the body of freemen was by apprenticeship to an existing freeman. Only such freemen enjoyed the trading rights, or rights over pastures, fisheries, and wastelands, implied by the borough charter. These burgesses, whether by inheritance or by formal admission, constituted in law the community of the borough—community, in this sense, being a technical term to describe the burgesses as a privileged group.[49]

Some urban institutions were more characteristic of self-governing boroughs than of other towns, both in England and Scotland. One was the merchant guild, whose primary purpose was to secure the control of trade in a town to guild members. Some townsmen pioneered guilds of this kind before the coming of urban self-government; Canterbury and Burford had them around 1100. Merchant guilds became more widespread in the course of the twelfth and thirteenth centuries, often in association with more extensive liberties. They regulated the rights of different groups of merchants and the contractual arrangements between them. For example, the rules of the merchant guild of Dublin, authorized in 1192 by Prince John, stipulated that outside merchants trading in Dublin should buy grain, leather, and wool only from the citizens, not from other outsiders, that no outsider should retail cloth in the city, and that no outside merchant should trade there for more than forty days at a time.[50] Scottish merchant guilds are known from about 1205, when William I recognized one at Perth, though Berwick may have had one earlier.[51] The right of non-guildsmen to trade was circumscribed both by rules and outright prohibitions and by the imposition of market tolls from which guildsmen were exempt. The merchant guild at Berwick was mostly concerned with regulating competition between its members and controlling the manufacturing and trading procedures of craftsmen.[52]

In the twelfth and thirteenth centuries merchant guilds probably pioneered the formal discussion of borough affairs; the guild assembly in England was called the 'mornspeche' or 'morwespeche'. Nevertheless, there was other business to do with responsibilities to the crown, and in English towns other forms of assembly were devised to handle them. In self-governing boroughs such decision taking rarely had much formality before 1300, so that it is difficult to locate its workings through any definite constitutional apparatus. Many towns were small enough for open meetings of burgesses to be feasible, even if in practice only the more socially secure burgesses were expected to attend. However in the course of time most self-governing English towns developed an administrative apparatus independent of the merchant guild, often with a written constitution. Borough councils, whose existence implies some elective system, are to be found in London, Ipswich, and Northampton by the time of King John's death in 1216, and at nine other English towns by 1300. Dublin was Anglicized in this respect about 1229, after its citizens had been granted the right to appoint their own mayor; they also then established a council of twenty-four.[53] These were ideal circumstances for formulating new regulations adapted to local circumstances, either as by-laws, or less formally as the rulings of mayors and bailiffs in the borough court. In the course of time borough councils came to take responsibility for economic regulations that had previously belonged to the merchant guild. Quite often the borough council met in the old guildhall. Merchant guilds survived, but with restricted responsibilities.[54] Scottish urban institutions developed differently. There merchant guilds remained the dominant administrative bodies, representing all burgesses. This difference between England and Scotland is perhaps to be explained by the continuing responsibility of the Scottish king's chamberlain for monitoring burgh reeves closely.[55]

Some 'mesne' boroughs (boroughs on the lands of wealthy churches or lay landowners rather than on the demesnes of the crown) were also permitted by their lords to elect their own senior officers, though it was unusual for such towns to have powers of self-government as extensive as those of royal boroughs. Three well-known examples are the liberties granted to Salford by Ralph, earl of Lincoln (*c.*1230), to Stockport by Robert of Stockport (*c.*1260), and to Manchester by Thomas Grelley (1301). The burgesses of all three were allowed to choose their own borough reeve (*prepositus*), though not to lease their lord's revenues nor to hold courts unless the overlord's steward presided.[56] It was no foregone conclusion that all boroughs should enjoy even this limited degree of independence, and smaller 'seigniorial' boroughs most commonly did not; an estate steward presided over their courts, and estate officials collected judicial fines and tolls. However, there were many other institutions in towns which took decisions on matters of common concern, and some were just as characteristic of seigniorial boroughs as of boroughs with chartered liberties. Town courts were universally one of the principal agencies of local government, and gave authority to local elites even in towns whose courts were presided over by their overlord's estate steward. Policing, in particular, depended upon the panelling of local jurors who would accept responsibility for reporting offenders in everyday matters of law and order under various headings—those who used false weights and measures, those who disregarded market regulations, those who obstructed the highway, and so on. Court business was just as dependent on the cooperation of urban elites in seigniorial boroughs as in those that were self-governing. In this context, seigniorial boroughs, too, could mould regulations to suit local circumstances.

Transport and Urban Supply

Rising urban demand for agricultural produce was doubtless one of several incentives operating during the twelfth and thirteenth centuries to reduce inland transport costs, impossible though it is to ascribe weights to the various causes of improvement. The carts and wagons used as road vehicles, when larger quantities were being marketed, were undergoing long-term progress both in wheel design and in techniques for attaching draught animals to pull them.[57] However, changes in inland transport systems were not all favourable. There was ongoing competition between the requirements of river navigation and developments in water-mill technology, which often obstructed the flow of rivers in order to use water power more effectively. Since individual mill owners were able to thwart the interests of boatmen, the competition was unequal. There was consequently some loss of amenities during the course of the period, though its impact—and the extent of the navigable waterway system—have been the subject of debate.[58] No changes in transport significantly modified the structure of relative costs, which, as we have seen, greatly favoured sea transport, or river transport as second best, over road transport.[59]

The urban stimulus to agriculture was greatest in the London region, if only because London's consumption of food, drink, fuel, and raw materials outstripped that of any other town by three or four times. Here, if anywhere, it should be possible to see traces of the market-orientated pattern of land use modelled by Justin Heinrich von Thünen in 1826. He envisaged that if transport costs over land were the chief determinant of land use, dairying, fruit cultivation, and other branches of agriculture producing perishable foodstuffs intolerant of travel and lengthy marketing times would be concentrated near the city. A second zone close to the city would specialize in producing fuel and timber because the costs of transporting them by road over long distances were prohibitively high relative to their selling price. Cereals, being bulky, would be grown extensively beyond this, and a fourth zone, yet further away, would specialize in livestock husbandry, because it was relatively cheap to move livestock on foot over long distances. Of course, once complicating factors like water transport, differences in soil quality, and the location of lesser towns are admitted into the analysis, von Thünen's model looks excessively artificial. Nevertheless, it explains some features in the pattern of land use around London in 1300. Market gardening and fruit growing is well attested at Holborn and Southwark, in the immediate vicinity of London, in the late thirteenth century. London's demand for fuel did indeed encourage specialization in Middlesex, Kent, and Surrey, from which a large part of the city's supplies derived. Cereals derived chiefly from an outer zone stretching higher up the Thames Valley, as well as to regions approachable from the Thames Estuary. Livestock for fattening often came from even further away—from Lincolnshire or Worcestershire for example.[60]

Supplying a large town like London both attracted mercantile enterprise and encouraged the formation of exceptionally complex institutional arrangements. At least 146 cornmongers operated in London at various times during the period 1288–1315, and of these about 54 are not known to have engaged in trade except in grain. They often had interests in baking and brewing, occupations that depended upon a regular grain supply. Besides a number of specialized grain markets within the city itself, London depended upon satellite grain markets upriver at Henley upon Thames and downriver at Faversham, where grain was brought for shipment to the London market. Londoners also drew on other marketing centres in the home counties, especially those connected by water communications, like Ware and Rochester.[61] It is difficult to generalize from London's experience to that of smaller towns since the city was doubtless exceptionally dependent for grain both on mercantile enterprise and upon subsidiary marketing centres. Other basic supplies for London similarly depended on mercantile enterprise and marketing networks. The London butchers were a sufficiently distinctive group by 1180 to have formed their own guild, and there were already specialist traders in fuel and timber by 1200.[62] To a lesser degree the same pattern may have been important for regional centres, creating a mercantile network of inter-market transfers across much of southern and midland England.[63]

The requirements of smaller towns were less conducive to such development because their demand was more easily satisfied locally, and by less elaborate procedures. The sort of specializing zones to be traced around London are not to be expected around populations of only a few thousand people. Nor were provision merchants so prominent in small towns, which were normally supplied directly by rural producers. Both peasant farmers and the agents of manorial lords sold their produce in urban markets. Manorial accounts of the later thirteenth century frequently refer to sales of grain 'in the market' (*in foro*). It was often the duty of tenants to carry produce to town as one of the conditions of their tenure, sometimes over long distances; the tenants of Lawshall (Suffolk) might have to go as far as Colchester, Ipswich, or Bury St Edmunds. Manors without adequate carriage services of this kind had to depend upon their regular servants, or on carters hired specially for the purpose. On other occasions townsmen themselves bought produce from rural producers and had it transported back at their own cost.[64] The large number of small towns and village markets in Britain by 1300 implies that a large proportion of grain and meat—probably over a third—was marketed over short distances by these very direct exchanges between producers and consumers.[65] There was similarly an extensive local market for meat, dairy produce, hides, and fuel. Even some of Britain's wool was sold in local markets to supply the widespread cloth industry that provided for everyday needs. The proportion of wool sold through mercantile contracts was nevertheless much higher than for most agricultural products, since industry was more concentrated in particular places, and much of what was produced was exported.

Despite the growth of the urban proportion in Britain between 1050 and 1300, particularly in England, the urban impact on the countryside had done little by 1300 to transform rural institutions or agricultural methods. Certainly, as we shall see, there had been local increases in productivity, but these had been far from amounting to a general transformation of agrarian procedures, and in some ways Britain looked archaic by the standards of Flanders or northern Italy.[66] Ultimately this weakness is to be explained by the low productivity, low level of specialization, and consequently low levels of consumption in British towns. Most townsmen were producing standard products for local sale at low levels of return, and buying their materials locally. The scope for agrarian specialization within any particular urban area was correspondingly poor, even in many of the more commercialized parts of England. Ordinary urban families are unrecognizable as 'middle class' or 'bourgeois', especially in Britain's smaller towns, since their income and style of life was much lower than these terms imply; they were not particularly well off by the standards of their peasant neighbours. An income from half an acre of land, and an industrial occupation, perhaps intermittently pursued, did not generate a high or discriminating demand for food or raw materials, even if backed up by burgesses' liberties. Besides drawing in families with resources and initiative, towns also attracted the rural destitute in search of a livelihood, and these were likely to become dependent upon charity, rather than swelling effective demand, especially in years of dearth and low employment. The multiplication of towns had not produced more than a small minority of wealthy townsmen, mostly to be found in the very largest towns.

NOTES

1. G. W. S. Barrow, *Kingship and Unity: Scotland, 1000–1306*, 2nd edn. (Edinburgh, 1989), 94; E. Ewan, 'The Crafts in Thirteenth-Century Aberdeen', in A. Grant and K. J. Stringer (eds.), *Medieval Scotland: Crown, Lordship and Community. Essays Presented to G. W. S. Barrow* (Edinburgh, 1993), 158.

2. The figure is based on an estimate that Scotland had a population of 0.9–1.2 m. (a fifth of the English level) and that the 62 boroughs contained no more than 31,000 inhabitants. This assumes (generously) an average population of no more than 500 inhabitants per burgh.

3. R. E. Glasscock, 'Land and People, c.1300', in A. Cosgrove (ed.), *New History of Ireland*, ii: *Medieval Ireland, 1169–1534* (Oxford, 1987), 212.

4. R. H. Britnell, 'King John's Early Grants of Markets and Fairs', *English Historical Review*, 94 (1979), 90–6.

5. M. H. Dodds, 'The Bishop's Boroughs', *Archaeologia Aeliana*, 3rd ser. 12 (1915), 86–98.

6. R. A. Griffiths, 'Carmarthen', and R. R. Davies, 'Brecon', in R. A. Griffiths (ed.), *Boroughs of Medieval Wales* (Cardiff, 1978), 55–6, 147.

7. *The Extent of Chirkland, 1391–1393*, ed. G. P. Jones (1933), 3.

8. W. M. Mackenzie, *The Scottish Burghs* (Edinburgh, 1949), 66–9; *The Charters of David I*, ed. G. W. S. Barrow (Woodbridge, 1999), no. 271, p. 167; *Regesta Regum Scottorum*, ii: *The Acts of William I*, ed. G. W. S. Barrow (Edinburgh, 1971), no. 244, pp. 281–2.

9. A. Gibb and R. Paddison, 'The Rise and Fall of Burghal Monopolies: The Case of the North East', *Scottish Geographical Magazine*, 99 (1983), 136–7; H. L. MacQueen and W. J. Windram, 'Laws and Courts in the Burghs', in M. Lynch, M. Spearman, and G. Stell (eds.), *The Scottish Medieval Town* (Edinburgh, 1988), 209.

10. R. H. Britnell, 'English Markets and Royal Administration before 1200', *Economic History Review*, 2nd ser. 31 (1978), 194–5.

11. B. M. S. Campbell, J. A. Galloway, D. Keene, and M. Murphy, *A Medieval Capital and its Grain Supply: Agrarian Production and Distribution in the London Region c.1300* (1993), 10.

12. D. Keene, 'Suburban Growth', in M. W. Barley (ed.), *The Plans and Topography of Medieval Towns in England and Wales* (1976), 78.

13. H. C. Darby, *Domesday England* (Cambridge: 1977), 307; N. Herbert, 'Medieval Glouces-
    ter', in id. (ed.), *Victoria County History of Gloucestershire*, iv: *The City of Gloucester*
    (Oxford, 1988), 13, 18; M. D. Lobel and J. Tann, 'Gloucester', in M. D. Lobel (ed.), *Historic
    Towns*, i (1969).

14. This figure is derived by taking an estimate of 500–600 boroughs in 1300 and deducting
    the 112 boroughs recorded in Domesday Book, some of which were new: Darby,
    Domesday England, 364–8; C. Dyer, 'How Urbanized was Medieval England?', in
    J.-M. Duvosquel and E. Thoen (eds.), *Peasants and Townsmen in Medieval Europe: Studia
    in Honorem Adriaan Verhulst* (Ghent, 1995), 176.

15. M. W. Beresford, *New Towns of the Middle Ages: Town Plantation in England, Wales and
    Gascony* (1967), 330, 342; G. S. Pryde, *The Burghs of Scotland: A Critical List* (1965), 3–20,
    37–43; J. Bradley, 'Planned Anglo-Norman Towns in Ireland', in H. Clarke and A. Simms
    (eds.), *The Comparative History of Urban Origins in Non-Roman Europe*, 2 vols. (Oxford,
    1985), ii. 411–67.

16. Pryde, *Burghs*, 37, 39.

17. R. H. Britnell, 'Local Trade, Remote Trade: Institutions, Information and Market
    Integration, 1050–1330', in S. Cavaciocchi (ed.), *Fiere e mercati nella integrazione delle
    economie europee, secc. XIII–XVIII* (Florence, 2001), 185–203.

18. Aberdeen, Berwick, Dunfermline, Edinburgh, Elgin, Forres, Haddington, Linlithgow,
    Peebles, Perth, Renfrew, Roxburgh, Rutherglen, Stirling, and perhaps Montrose and
    Lanark: Pryde, *Burghs*, 3–8.

19. *Victoria History of the County of Hertford*, ed. W. Page, 5 vols. (1902–23), iii. 499; M. Bonney,
    Lordship and the Urban Community: Durham and its Overlords, 1250–1540 (Cambridge, 1990),
    17, 28, 31, 52; Duncan, *Scotland*, 469.

20. *Early Yorkshire Charters*, 12 vols., ed. W. Farrer and C. T. Clay (Edinburgh, 1914–16 and
    Leeds, 1935–65), i. 285.

21. Bradley, 'Planned Anglo-Norman Towns', 421–2.

22. R. A. Griffiths, *Conquerors and Conquered in Medieval Wales* (Stroud, 1994), 344.

23. Barrow, *Kingship and Unity*, 92–3; Mackenzie, *Scottish Burghs*, 36–9.

24. F. Pollock and F. W. Maitland, *The History of English Law before the Time of Edward I*, 2nd
    edn. (Cambridge, 1898), i. 295–6.

25. E. Miller, 'The City of York', in *Victoria History of the County of York: The City of York*,
    ed. P. M. Tillott (Oxford, 1961), 49–50.

26. E. Ewan, *Townlife in Fourteenth-Century Scotland* (Edinburgh, 1990), 96–7.

27. F. W. Maitland, *Township and Borough* (Cambridge, 1898), 54–67.

28. Ewan, 'Crafts', 162.

29. R. H. Hilton, 'Low-Level Urbanization: The Seigneurial Borough of Thornbury in the
    Middle Ages', in Z. Razi and R. Smith (eds.), *Medieval Society and the Manor Court*
    (Oxford, 1996), 496–9.

30. Beresford, *New Towns*, 133–41.

31. D. Keene, *Survey of Medieval Winchester*, 2 vols. (Oxford, 1985), i. 352–65, 367–8; E. Miller
    and J. Hatcher, *Medieval England: Towns, Commerce and Crafts, 1086–1348* (1995), 326.

32. R. H. Hilton, *Class Conflict and the Crisis of Feudalism* (1985), 201.

33. Ewan, 'Crafts', 158–72; Griffiths, 'Carmarthen', 151–2; A. Keith, *A Thousand Years of Aberdeen* (Aberdeen, 1972), 19–20.

34. R. H. Britnell, 'Specialization of Work in England, 1100–1300', *Economic History Review*, 54 (2001), 11–14.

35. A. F. Sutton, 'Mercery through Four Centuries, 1130s–c.1500', *Nottingham Medieval Studies*, 41 (1997), 103, 108–10.

36. Miller and Hatcher, *Medieval England: Towns*, 4, 54–5, 102, 129; A. F. Sutton, 'The Early Linen and Worsted Industry of Norfolk and the Evolution of the London Mercers' Company', *Norfolk Archaeology*, 40 (1989), 202, 210–11.

37. J. M. Bennett, *Ale, Beer and Brewsters in England* (Oxford, 1996), 24–6.

38. H. Swanson, *Medieval Artisans* (Oxford, 1989), 11.

39. M. Carlin, *Medieval Southwark* (1996), 209.

40. R. H. Britnell, 'The Proliferation of Markets in England, 1200–1349', *Economic History Review*, 2nd ser. 33 (1981), 189; *Charters of David I*, ed. Barrow, no. 243, p. 165.

41. *Ancient Laws and Customs of the Burghs of Scotland*, ed. C. Innes and R. Renwick, 2 vols. (Edinburgh, 1868–1910), i. 4–58; Barrow, *Kingship and Unity*, 97–8; Duncan, *Scotland*, 481; Mackenzie, *Scottish Burghs*, 21–30.

42. *Records of the Convention of the Royal Burghs of Scotland, 1295–1597*, ed. J. D. Marwick (Edinburgh, 1870), 501–2; Ewan, *Townlife*, 146–7.

43. R. H. Britnell, *The Commercialisation of English Society, 1000–1500*, 2nd edn. (Manchester, 1997), 90–1, 93–7.

44. E. Gemmill and N. Mayhew, *Changing Values in Medieval Scotland: A Study of Prices, Money, and Weights and Measures* (Cambridge, 1995), 30–1, 48, 85–7.

45. J. Tait, *The Medieval English Borough: Studies on its Origin and Constitutional History* (Manchester, 1936), 178–9.

46. Mackenzie, *Scottish Burghs*, 97–8.

47. *Handlist of the Acts of Alexander II, 1214–1249*, ed. J. M. Scoular (Edinburgh, 1959), nos. 259, 305–6, pp. 44, 50; *Handlist of the Acts of Alexander III, the Guardians, John*, ed. G. G. Simpson (Edinburgh, 1960), nos. 14, 15, 64, pp. 9, 16; *Exchequer Rolls of Scotland*, ed. J. Stuart, G. Burnett, and others, 23 vols. (Edinburgh, 1878–1908), i. 59–74; Duncan, *Scotland*, 483.

48. 'Accounts on the Great Roll of the Pipe of the Irish Exchequer for the Reign of Edward I', *The Thirty-Sixth Report of the Deputy Keeper of the Public Records and Keeper of the State Papers of Ireland* (Dublin, 1904), 29.

49. S. Reynolds, *An Introduction to the History of English Medieval Towns* (Oxford, 1977), 108, 114, 116, 136, 198.

50. C. Gross, *The Gild Merchant*, 2 vols. (Oxford, 1890), ii. 59.

51. *Regesta Regum Scottorum*, ii, ed. Barrow, no. 467, p. 431; Duncan, *Scotland*, 488–9.

52. Duncan, *Scotland*, 498.

53. Gross, *Gild Merchant*, i. 72–6; Tait, *Medieval English Borough*, 223–34, 265–80.

54. Gross, *Gild Merchant*, i. 32, 43–51, 61–76; Keene, *Survey*, i. 80–1; D. M. Palliser, 'The Birth of York's Civic Liberties', in S. Rees Jones (ed.), *The Government of Medieval York* (1997), 96.

55. Mackenzie, *Scottish Burghs*, 99–104.

56. J. Tait, *Medieval Manchester and the Beginnings of Lancashire* (Manchester, 1904), 71–7.

57. J. Langdon, *Horses, Oxen and Technological Innovation: The Use of Draught Animals in English Farming from 1066 to 1500* (Cambridge, 1986), 14–15.

58. E. T. Jones, 'River Navigation in Medieval England', *Journal of Historical Geography* (2000), 26, 60–75; J. Langdon, 'Inland Water Transport in Medieval England—The View from the Mills: A Response to Jones', ibid., 75–82.

59. See above (Ch. 1).

60. J. A. Galloway and M. Murphy, 'Feeding the City: Medieval London and its Agrarian Hinterland', *London Journal*, 16 (1991), 7–12; J. A. Galloway, D. Keene, and M. Murphy, 'Fuelling the City: Production and Distribution of Firewood and Fuel in London's Region, 1290–1400', *Economic History Review*, 49 (1996), 458–60.

61. Campbell and others, *Medieval Capital*, 47–9, 81–7.

62. G. Unwin, *The Gilds and Companies of London* (1908), 48; Galloway and others, 'Fuelling London', 452.

63. J. Masschaele, *Peasants, Merchants and Markets: Inland Trade in Medieval England, 1150–1350* (New York, 1997), 83–91, 165–88.

64. D. L. Farmer, 'Marketing the Produce of the Countryside, 1200–1500', in E. Miller (ed.), *The Agrarian History of England*, iii: *1348–1500* (Cambridge, 1991), 348–51, 360–7.

65. R. H. Britnell, 'Urban Demand in the English Economy, 1300–1600', in J. A. Galloway (ed.), *Trade, Urban Hinterlands and Market Integration c.1300–1600* (2000), 4–5.

66. J. Langdon, 'Was England a Technological Backwater in the Middle Ages', in G. Astill and J. Langdon (eds.), *Medieval Farming and Technology: The Impact of Agricultural Change in Northwest Europe* (Leiden, 1997), 251–74.

FURTHER READING

Adams, I. H., *The Making of Urban Scotland* (1978).

Astill, G. G., 'Towns and Town Hierarchies in Saxon England', *Oxford Journal of Archaeology*, 10 (1991).

Barrow, G. W. S., 'Land Routes', in id., *Scotland and its Neighbours in the Middle Ages* (1992).

Beresford, M. W., *New Towns of the Middle Ages: Town Plantation in England, Wales and Gascony* (1967).

Britnell, R. H., 'Boroughs, Markets and Trade in Northern England, 1000–1216', in id. and J. Hatcher (eds.), *Progress and Problems in Medieval England: Essays in Honour of Edward Miller* (Cambridge, 1996).

—— *The Commercialisation of English Society, 1000–1500*, 2nd edn. (Manchester, 1997).

—— 'Local Trade, Remote Trade: Institutions, Information and Market Integration, 1050–1330', in S. Cavaciocchi (ed.), *Fiere e mercati nella integrazione delle economie europee, secc. XII–VIII* (Florence, 2001).

—— 'The Proliferation of Markets in England, 1200–1349', *Economic History Review*, 2nd ser. 33 (1981).

—— 'Urban Demand in the English Economy, 1300–1600', in J. A. Galloway (ed.), *Trade, Urban Hinterlands and Market Integration c.1300–1600* (2000).

Campbell, B. M. S., Galloway, J. A., Keene, D., and Murphy, M., *A Medieval Capital and its Grain Supply: Agrarian Production and Distribution in the London Region c.1300* (1993).

Carlin, M., *Medieval Southwark* (1996).

Carus-Wilson, E. M., 'The First Half-Century of the Borough of Stratford-upon-Avon', *Economic History Review*, 2nd ser. 18 (1965).

Clarke, H., and Simms, A. (eds.), *The Comparative History of Urban Origins in Non-Roman Europe* (Oxford, 1985).

Dicks, B., 'The Scottish Medieval Town: A Search for Origins', in G. Gordon and B. Dicks (eds.), *Scottish Urban History* (Aberdeen, 1983).

Dobson, R. B., 'The Jews of Medieval Cambridge', *Jewish Historical Studies*, 32 (1990–2).

Dyer, C., 'How Urbanized was Medieval England?', in J.-M. Duvosquel and E. Thoen (eds.), *Peasants and Townsmen in Medieval Europe: Studia in Honorem Adriaan Verhulst* (Ghent, 1995).

Ewan, E., 'The Crafts in Thirteenth-Century Aberdeen', in A. Grant and K. J. Stringer (eds.), *Medieval Scotland: Crown, Lordship and Community. Essays Presented to G. W. S. Barrow* (Edinburgh, 1993).

Farmer, D. L., 'Marketing the Produce of the Countryside, 1200–1500', in E. Miller (ed.), *The Agrarian History of England*, iii: *1348–1500* (Cambridge, 1991).

Fox, R., 'Urban Development, 1100–1700', in G. Whittington and I. D. Whyte (eds.), *An Historical Geography of Scotland* (1983).

Galloway, J. A., and Murphy, M., 'Feeding the City: Medieval London and its Agrarian Hinterland', *London Journal*, 16 (1991).

Graham, B., 'Urbanization in Medieval Ireland, ca. A.D. 900 to ca. A.D. 1300', *Journal of Urban History*, 13 (1987).

Griffiths, R. A. (ed.), *Boroughs of Medieval Wales* (Cardiff, 1978).

—— *Conquerors and Conquered in Medieval Wales* (Stroud, 1994).

Herbert, N., 'Medieval Gloucester', in id. (ed.), *Victoria County History of Gloucestershire*, iv: *The City of Gloucester* (Oxford, 1988).

Hilton, R. H., 'Low-Level Urbanization: The Seigneurial Borough of Thornbury in the Middle Ages', in Z. Razi and R. Smith (eds.), *Medieval Society and the Manor Court* (Oxford, 1996).

Holt, R., and Rosser, G. (eds.), *The Medieval English Town: A Reader in English Urban History* (Harlow, 1990).

Keene, D., 'London in the Early Middle Ages, 600–1300', *London Journal*, 20 (1995).

—— 'Medieval London and its Region', *London Journal*, 14 (1989).

—— 'Suburban Growth', in M. W. Barley (ed.), *The Plans and Topography of Medieval Towns in England and Wales* (1976), and in Holt and Rosser, *Medieval English Town* (above).

—— *Survey of Medieval Winchester*, 2 vols. (Oxford, 1985).

—— 'Wardrobes in the City: Houses of Consumption, Finance and Power', in M. Prestwich, R. H. Britnell, and R. Frame (eds.), *Thirteenth Century England VII* (Woodbridge, 1999).

Kowaleski, M., *Local Markets and Regional Trade in Medieval Exeter* (Cambridge, 1995).

Lynch, M., Spearman, M., and Stell, G. (eds.), *The Scottish Medieval Town* (Edinburgh, 1988).

Mackenzie, W. M., *The Scottish Burghs* (Edinburgh, 1949).

Maitland, F. W., *Township and Borough* (Cambridge, 1898).

Masschaele, J., *Peasants, Merchants and Markets: Inland Trade in Medieval England, 1150–1350* (New York, 1997).

Miller, E., 'The City of York', in *Victoria History of the County of York: The City of York*, ed. P. M. Tillott (Oxford, 1961).

—— and Hatcher, J., *Medieval England: Towns, Commerce and Crafts, 1086–1348* (1995).

Mundill, R. R., 'Lumbard and Son: The Business and Debtors of Two Jewish Moneylenders in Thirteenth-Century England', *Jewish Quarterly Review*, 82 (1992).

Nightingale, P., 'The Growth of London', in R. Britnell and J. Hatcher (eds.), *Progress and Problems in Medieval England: Essays in Honour of Edward Miller* (Cambridge, 1996).

—— *A Medieval Mercantile Community: The Grocers' Company and the Politics and Trade of London, 1000–1485* (New Haven, 1995).

O'Brien, F., 'Medieval Youghal: The Development of an Irish Seaport Trading Town, c.1200 to c.1500', *Peritia*, 5 (1986).

Palliser, D. M. (ed.), *The Cambridge Urban History of Britain*, i: *600–1540* (Cambridge, 2000).

Pryde, G. S., *The Burghs of Scotland: A Critical List* (1965).

—— 'The Origin of the Burgh in Scotland', *Juridical Review*, 47 (1935).

Reynolds, S., *An Introduction to the History of English Medieval Towns* (Oxford, 1977).

Rosser, G., *Medieval Westminster, 1200–1540* (Oxford, 1989).

Smith, R. M., 'A Periodic Market and its Impact on a Manorial Community: Botesdale, Suffolk, and the Manor of Redgrave, 1280–1300', in Z. Razi and R. Smith (eds.), *Medieval Society and the Manor Court* (Oxford, 1996).

Soulsby, I., *The Towns of Medieval Wales: A Study of their History, Archaeology and Early Topography* (Chichester, 1983).

Stacey, R. C., 'Jewish Lending and the Medieval English Economy', in R. H. Britnell and B. M. S. Campbell (eds.), *A Commercialising Economy: England 1086 to c.1300* (Manchester, 1995).

Summerson, H., 'The Place of Carlisle in the Commerce of Northern England in the Thirteenth Century', in P. R. Coss and S. D. Lloyd (eds.), *Thirteenth Century England I* (Woodbridge, 1986).

Swanson, H., *Medieval British Towns* (Basingstoke, 1999).

Veale, E., 'The "Great Twelve": Mistery and Fraternity in Thirteenth-Century London', *History Research*, 64 (1991).

Watt, J. A., 'Dublin in the Thirteenth Century: The Making of a Colonial Capital City', in P. R. Coss and S. D. Lloyd (eds.), *Thirteenth Century England I* (Woodbridge, 1986).

Williams, G. A., *Medieval London: From Commune to Capital*, 2nd edn. (1970).

....

CHAPTER 8

Rural Settlement and Society

Despite the expansion of urban settlement between 1050 and 1300, British population remained overwhelmingly rural. In 1300 at least four-fifths of the population of England lived in settlements with no urban attributes, and the proportion for all Britain and Ireland was higher. Just as the character of towns varied from London at the apex to regional towns and smaller market towns, so did the character of rural settlement, which varied in accordance with regional differences we have already examined. Larger settlements were more characteristic of extensive arable cultivation, and especially numerous in southern and midland England; small hamlets and isolated farms were more usual in the predominantly pastoral landscapes of uplands and areas remote from large urban markets. As in the history of towns, however, the distribution of settlement changed over time, as a result of innumerable separate decisions by landlords and their tenants about how to manage the land. Many of the changes may be regarded as responses to population growth, but feedback effects enabled institutional development to encourage further growth of population.

As in the case of towns, one of the most striking features of economic development, particularly after 1160, was the growing reliance of country dwellers on exchange, whether or not it was monetized. The level of self-sufficiency remained much higher than it is in the modern world, and over Britain as a whole most country dwellers produced most of their own food. However, many of the same sorts of phenomena that occurred in towns were transforming rural life. Settlements were becoming characteristically larger, institutional structures were becoming more formal, more money was in circulation, families were becoming more interdependent, and the class of propertyless or near propertyless families was growing relative to the total population.

Analogies between urban and rural development are most visible in the institutionalization of rural trade. The proliferation of village markets ran parallel to the multiplication of towns discussed in Chapter 7, and in many respects the two phenomena converged. In both cases the estate policies of landlords were a power-ful agent of change. Lords acquired licences from the crown to set up markets for many settlements too small to be classified as towns. In Norfolk, where there were perhaps between 30 and 40 places with markets by 1200, the number included such minor centres as Holt and Wormegay.[1] In England as a whole there were already 600–700 markets held by ancient right, or licensed by the crown before 1200, and the number increased yet further during the thirteenth century. The royal charter rolls and close rolls record licences for 1,146 new markets in England between 1200 and 1299 (as well as 1,286 fairs in the same period).[2] The distinctive importance of the thirteenth century for this activity is well illustrated in Figures 8.1 and 8.2, which represent the number of markets and fairs for which royal permission was obtained. An allowance has to be made for ineffective grants, and many of the grants that were implemented had little impact on the villages they benefited. The distribution of newly chartered markets across the country at different periods is indicated in Figure 8.3. Yet on the evidence that only 500–600 places in England are classifiable as towns, a large number of markets must have been held in rural settlements. Such commercial development in the countryside, sometimes accompanied by the relocation of tofts and houses, contributed significantly to the consolidation of focused village settlements. Little Linton in Cambridgeshire, for example, was depopulated in favour of the growing market centre at Great Linton nearby.[3] Rustic markets, which were best adapted to areas of dense rural population, were less a feature of local trade in Wales and Ireland, where marketing centres were more likely to have urban characteristics, though English kings licensed a few, such as those at Tiscoffin (1245) and Bunratty (1253) in Ireland, Llanarmon Mynydd Mawr (1279) and Llanddewi-Brefi (1281) in Wales.[4] By the end of the thirteenth century the sheriff of Cork recognized 37 markets in his county, and even so his list was incomplete.[5] Village markets were not created in Scotland, partly, no doubt, because older burghs were protected against such competitive developments, but also because there was less call for them. Royal grants of markets and fairs are quite rare, and confined either to old burghs or to newly created ones, as at Dumbarton in 1222 or Newburgh in 1266.[6] Presumably Scottish rural households, like those of Durham, depended more on private trading outside formal market places.

The Expansion of Settlement

Where extensive waste was available for colonization, as in regions of extensive forest or moorland, scattered settlement remained characteristic of the land-scape, and was likely to be enhanced as individual families struck out on their own, sometimes taking up land that had not been cultivated since Iron Age or

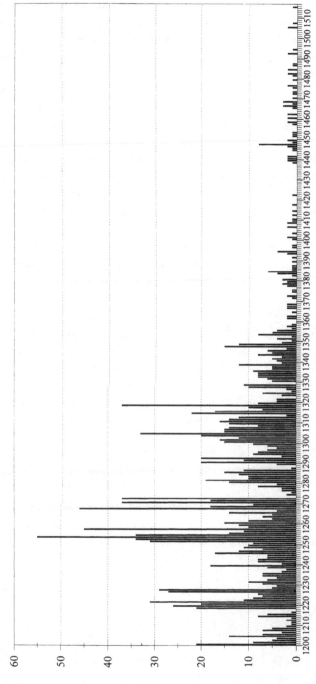

FIG. 8.1. Grants of markets and fairs in England, 1200–1516. Royal authorization of new weekly markets and annual fairs shows no very smooth trend over time, though there was clearly a boom in the 1250s. This activity declined sharply after the mid-fourteenth century, though the number of new fairs did not decline quite as sharply as the founding of markets. Fairs were more adapted to the seasonal sales of pastoral produce and consumer goods that were relatively more in demand in the fourteenth and fifteenth centuries.

Source: S. Letters, 'Markets and Fairs in Medieval England: A New Resource', in M. Prestwich, R. Britnell, and R. Frame (eds.), *Thirteenth Century England IX* (Woodbridge, 2003), 216.

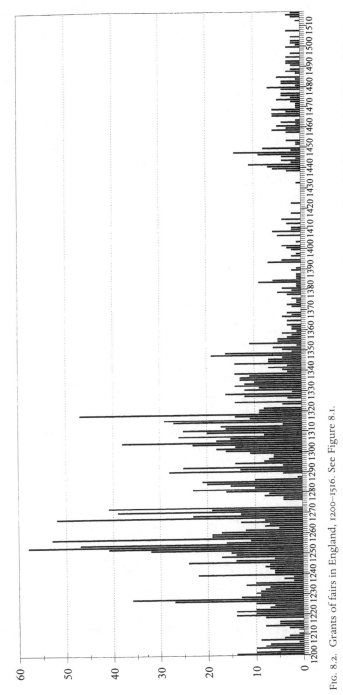

FIG. 8.2. Grants of fairs in England, 1200–1516. See Figure 8.1.

Source: S. Letters, 'Markets and Fairs in Medieval England: A New Resource', in M. Prestwich, R. Britnell, and R. Frame (eds.), *Thirteenth Century England IX* (Woodbridge, 2003), 217.

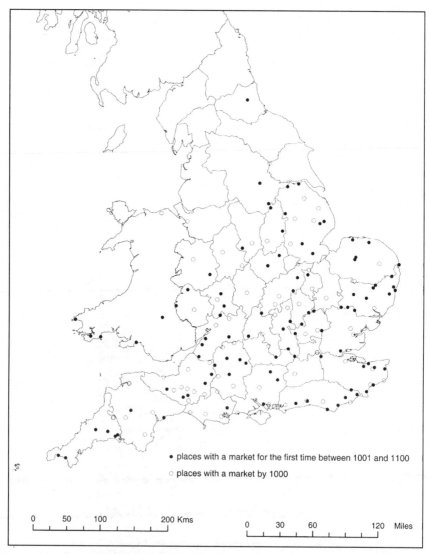

FIG. 8.3(*a*). The proliferation of English markets, 1000–1300. These maps record the first appearance of markets in England and Wales, often in a royal charter authorizing their establishment. The number probably multiplied during the eleventh century, though there is little sign of this in northern England (map *a*). The twelfth century saw a more general spread (map *b*). By the later thirteenth century most newly established markets were of minor importance, but many were established, especially in areas of very mixed employment; by this time new creations are significantly more numerous in East Anglia and the south-west than in the more agrarian counties of Hampshire, Berkshire, and Buckinghamshire (map *d*).

Source: Emilia Jamroziak (University of Edinburgh).

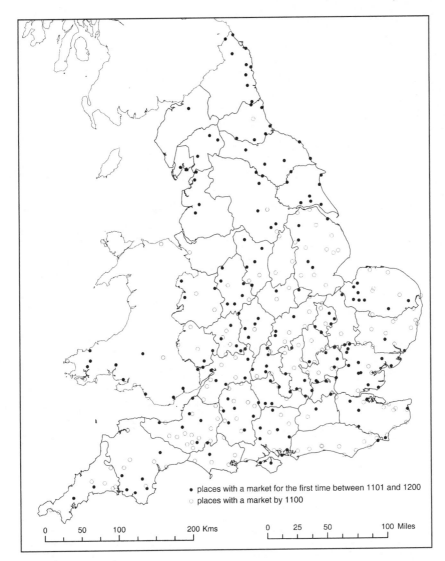

places with a market for the first time between 1101 and 1200
places with a market by 1100

0   50   100   200 Kms   0   25   50   100 Miles

Fig. 8.3(*b*).—*continued*

Romano-British times. Between 1150 and 1250 large numbers of hamlets and farms were founded on the margin of existing settlements in Devon, as a result of which most isolated farms there today were already in existence by the early fourteenth century. Land was taken into cultivation in several different ways. On the moorland slopes of Dartmoor the turf was broken up and burned to fertilize the underlying soil; elsewhere forest land was cleared of tree cover.[7] A similar multiplication of

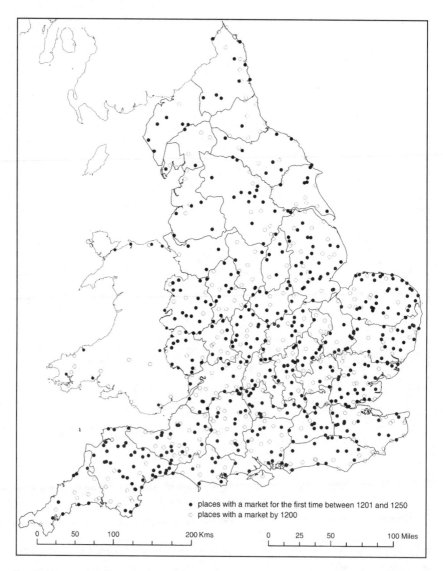

places with a market for the first time between 1201 and 1250
places with a market by 1200

0   50   100   200 Kms   0   25   50   100 Miles

FIG. 8.3(c).—continued

farms and hamlets reduced the moors of northern England (Figure 8.4). The hamlet of Crook in Durham was carved out of the waste in the thirteenth century, together with the two new farms, Beckley and Andrew's House.[8] In Wales, both the granting of formerly bond land to freemen, and the growth in the size of families, encouraged the dispersion of settlements away from older hamlets and townships.

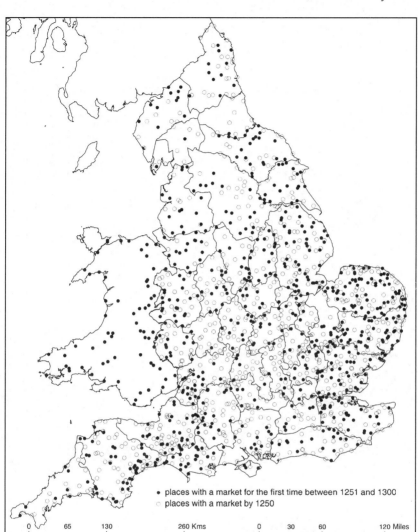

FIG. 8.3(*d*).—*continued*

The creation of new livelihoods was often accompanied by the carving of new lands out of the surrounding waste and the establishment of new settlements away from the *hendref*, the original family settlement, so that it is from this period that some of the most marked features of modern Welsh settlement are to be dated.[9] Especially in pastoral areas, scattered farms continued to proliferate through the thirteenth century. In Trefnant parish (Montgomeryshire) the expansion of

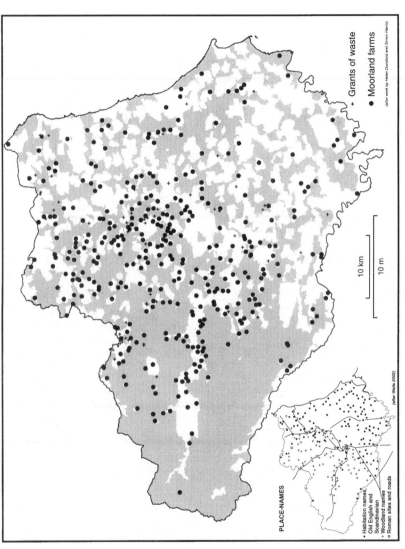

PLACE-NAMES

• Habitation names,
  Old English and
  Scandinavian
+ Woodland names
□ Roman sites and roads

(after Watts 2002)

Grants of waste +
Moorland farms ●

(after work by Helen Dunsford and Simon Harris)

10 km

10 m

Fig. 8.4. County Durham: distribution of common wastes in about 1600, and the location of moorland farms. This map is based partly on a careful assessment of the evidence for moorland in 1600 (the grey areas of the map) and partly on evidence of the creation of new moorland farms outside existing township fields (the black circles), mostly during the period 1150–1315. The two sets of evidence together suggest that there was a great expansion of farmland during the twelfth and thirteenth centuries, but that the landscape remained one of extensive moors. The map does not take into account the extension of township fields, which is less well documented. Most of these will be included in the white areas of the map, which represent all land cleared and retained in cultivation up to the year 1600.

settlement took the form of dispersed houses and outbuildings built on platforms cut into hillsides.[10] Even these scattered farms were drawn in to market relationships, especially if their relative advantage lay in producing livestock and pastoral products.

Many nucleated villages were already in existence in England and lowland Scotland in 1050, especially in southern and midland England, as a result of earlier settlement changes in the late Saxon period. It is difficult to generalize about the later fortunes of such nucleated settlements with any claim to exactness, but there are strong indications that most settlements grew larger between 1050 and 1300. Our numerical evidence of rural population derives from manorial lists of tenants rather than from village censuses, and since the relationship between manors and settlements was highly indeterminate it is not safe to assume that the two things are equivalent. However a growth in the size of settlements is a likely implication of the well-nigh universal tendency for tenant numbers to increase between 1086 and 1300,[11] and this interpretation is supported by such close studies as we have of individual places. The adult population of the two townships of Holywell and Needingworth (Huntingdonshire) was probably about 160 in 1086, when Domesday Book records 32 tenants and a priest, but there are estimated to have been 251 adults living there in 1300.[12] At Cuxham (Oxfordshire) Domesday Book records 15 tenants, implying an adult population of about 75, but there were at least 110 adult inhabitants in January 1349, on the eve of the Black Death.[13] Unfortunately, though population growth in these villages can serve to illustrate a general tendency, neither Holywell and Needingworth nor Cuxham can be assumed to have grown at an average rate, so their experience cannot be used as a guide to the magnitude of the overall increase.

Meanwhile the founding of new villages, drawing together scattered rural populations, was by no means complete by 1050. They are often associated with the acquisition and development of estates by landlords, following a pattern of estate improvement widespread in western Europe, and often contain strong elements of planning. They are particularly in evidence in northern England, Wales, Scotland, and Ireland—regions being subjected to new traditions of lordship and land management as a result of infiltration or conquest from outside.[14] Despite the very widespread occurrence of new villages, the event is rarely well recorded in contemporary documentation, and we depend chiefly on archaeological evidence, topographical deduction, and place names for any account of it. Even in midland England, however, it is sometimes possible to identify examples of late nucleation. In Cambridgeshire, for example, the villages of Toft, Great Eversden, and Comberton overlie earlier medieval fields, and are probably settlements that Norman landlords created by moving tenants from older sites.[15] In northern England a characteristic type of new settlement in the late eleventh and twelfth centuries was the 'green village'—that is, a regular planned settlement around a central green.[16]

The consolidation of settlements was simultaneously as much a part of the history of Wales, Scotland, and Ireland as of England. New planned villages in Pembrokeshire—like Wiston and Tancredston, named after the Flemings Wizo and Tancred who founded them in the early twelfth century—were created following the Norman Conquest by incoming landlords. Tenants were brought in from afar to occupy them. The best example of a planned village in this region, Templeton, was probably created at the end of the eleventh century.[17] Scottish villages occur similarly in twelfth- and thirteenth-century sources as the creation of landlords to whom territory was given for improvement. The lost township of 'Gocelynton', founded on Dere Street between Dalkeith, Cranston, and Cousland, is described in a charter of about 1160 as the township of Gocelin the cook, suggesting a founder who had lived within recent memory.[18] The monks of Newbattle created a cottars' township adjacent to their agrarian and industrial development at Preston Grange.[19] The monks of Kelso were given 3 acres of land on which to build houses—presumably a new village—in the territory of Yetholm on the border between Scotland and England.[20] Two villages called Symington, one in Lanark-shire and one in Ayrshire, both take their name from Simon Lockhart, a twelfth-century knight.[21] The nucleated appearance and structure of such settlements is suggested by details of 'Bemersyde', near Melrose, which was in the lordship of Peter de Haga around 1220, when he gave two bovates of land in his lordship to the canons of Dryburgh. He also gave them a messuage there, 'the fifth to the east', suggesting a row of homesteads standing side by side, together with a garden, with the provision that they should settle only one man and his family. He was allowed to have three cows and twenty sheep on the commons with the men of the township.[22] Some new settlements were on land previously occupied only seasonally, like the township of 'Samson[s]chelis', meaning Samson's shieling, lying between Dere Street and Leader Water. A shieling was a summer pasture;[23] this one takes its name from the Samson whose son Henry gave property there to the canons of Dryburgh in about 1220.[24] 'Panscheles' was another such township, recorded about this time in a charter of the monks of the Isle of May.[25] New nucleated townships were not all very deep-rooted, and could be moved. In the mid-twelfth century the monks of Holyrood in Edinburgh gave their village of Pittendriech to Newbattle Abbey on condition that it should never be moved nearer to Newbattle than it was on the day that Newbattle was founded.[26]

In Ireland some deliberate founding of new villages was a feature of conquest after 1169, and was in large part designed to attract settlers from Wales, England, and Flanders. Landlords sometimes gave special privileges as well as land to new settlers, so creating the 'rural boroughs', often associated with a 'hundred' court, which were another distinguishing feature of the Anglo-Norman Irish landscape.[27] For county Wexford as many as fifty-four new villages have been claimed, of which thirteen survive as settlements.[28] However, the counting of Irish nucleated villages has been overenthusiastic. Archaeological investigation of the supposed site of Newcastle Lyons (Co. Dublin) has failed to find the expected evidence of settlement there, and this has cast doubt on the methodology used to identify others.[29] Even at the end of the period the prevalence of nucleated villages did not compare with midland or eastern England. The extent of this form of seigniorial redevelopment was limited by considerations of defence against attack from the native Irish. Study of County Meath, where the impact of Anglo-Norman occupation was at its greatest, shows that settlements were concentrated east of a barrier of mottes that had been erected following the conquest, and which represented a permanent frontier zone.[30]

Many new settlements were created by the fission of older townships and their territories. This process often leaves traces on modern maps in the juxtaposition of villages of the same name modified by prefixes such as North, South, Upper, and Lower, or by 'surnames', often the names of lordly families that held them in the twelfth or thirteenth centuries. Sometimes the splitting of villages was prompted purely by the family concerns of landowning families, following the subdivision of estates. It seems, for example, that a division between the lost villages of Great and Little Lumsden (Berwickshire) came about in the twelfth century through the division of Lumsden between two owners,[31] and the same is apparent at Beath near Dunfermline, which became divided during the twelfth and thirteenth centuries between Dunfermline Abbey's estate, and the settlements of Beath Waldef, West Beath, and Beath Fleming.[32] Some extensive territories already under cultivation were divided, as perhaps at Kibworth Harcourt and Kibworth Beauchamp in Leicestershire. This form of subdivision was presumably important for the rationalization of open-field systems in parts of the country, since it created an ideal opportunity for redistributing landholding and for planning new schemes for commoning on fallow lands.[33] On other occasions fission was obviously geared to the needs of a rising population. It occurred whenever founding colonies from a parent township were created on lands cleared from woodland or drained from the marshes. The southern Lincolnshire hamlets of Whaplode Drove, Holbeach Drove, Gedney Hill, and Sutton St Edmund, named from the older townships of Whaplode, Holbeach, Gedney, and Sutton, were established following the construction of the Common Dyke in 1241 and the consequent drainage of an extensive area of fenland.[34]

The size of the resulting townships varied according to what the land would support. In much of England and the more fertile parts of southern Scotland villages with forty or fifty households were common by the thirteenth century.

Most of the tenants of Kelso Abbey lived in settlements of this size (Table 8.1). In highland Scotland, by contrast, because the land was less favourable for supporting dense populations, it was unlikely that townships commonly had more than four to eight households, as in later centuries.[35] Settlements in Wales, too, were characteristically small, chiefly because the cultivable land was so broken up with less fertile intrusions. Although large villages were unusual in the more upland parts of Britain, the converse is not true. There were always many small settlements and scattered farms throughout southern and eastern Britain. They are little studied, because there is usually little to say about them, but they emerge clearly from any regional survey of settlement patterns, particularly in wooded or moorland regions less suited to extensive arable farming.

Some forms of communal responsibility were old and well established, especially those that involved dues in money, food, and labour charged on each township. The bond tenants of Welsh *maerdref* often owed such dues even in the late thirteenth century.[36] In eleventh-century England the compilation of Domesday Book was premissed on the assumption that each English township could produce a priest, reeve, and six men as representatives. These reeves perhaps served primarily as estate officers, but in this capacity they might be expected to mediate with manorial lords on behalf of their neighbours. The continuing growth and multiplication of

TABLE 8.1. *Tenants on the estates of Kelso Abbey, c.1290*

Place	Husbandlands	Cottars' lands
Redden in Sprouston	8	19
Sprouston	0	6 (1 with 6 ac., 5 with 1½ ac.)
Mow in Morebattle	0	14
'Faudon'	0	21
Whitmuir in Selkirk	10	8 (7 with 1 ac., 1 with none)
Whitlaw in Galashiels	0	18
Bowden	28	36 (12⅝ ac. between them)
Selkirk	15[a]	16 (10 ac. between them)
Midlam	29	11 (9 ac. between them)
'Clarilaw'	0	21 (2¾ ac. each + common for 2 cows)
Makerstoun	0	12 (½ ac. each + common for 2 cows)
Gordon	0	6 (1½ ac. each + common rights)
'Spertildon' Grange	0	16 or more (no land)

[a] Each of which contained a bovate of land

Source: *Liber S. Marie de Calchou*, ed. C. Innes, 2 vols., Bannatyne Club, 82 (1846), 456–65.

villages up to 1300 implied an enhanced degree of cooperation between neighbours. Larger villages required their inhabitants to agree over the management of arable and pasture resources, especially when, as in the midland common-field region, an agrarian system had been devised to permit a complex interaction between private and common rights. Growing pressure on agricultural resources in the twelfth and thirteenth centuries increased the need for regulation and co-operation; the court rolls of English manors often attest the need to make new by-laws to regulate the management of the fields. There is a lengthy set of regulations from the Buckinghamshire township of Newton Longville in 1290 to restrict gleaning activity, to limit the hours for harvesting and carting, to provide for the maintenance of stiles and access routes, and to control certain pasturing arrangements.[37]

Another development that focused cooperative activity in rural society was the widespread development of parochial organization. By the later eleventh century it had become a common event for landlords to establish churches in centres of rural population and to assign to them an income from tithes (or teinds, in Scots). This development became universal through Britain during the twelfth and thirteenth centuries; all Scotland, even the western highlands and islands, was studded with parish churches by 1300. The standardization of the Welsh Church probably proceeded at a similar pace, though parochial organization may not have been complete until the fourteenth century.[38] In Ireland the multiplication of parish churches began to be organized after the Anglo-Norman conquest of 1169–72.[39] The priests who served these churches derived their income from tithes allocated to them, in the first instance, by their founders. In most of England the principal tithe income was usually derived as 'the tenth sheaf', that is a tenth of all the cereal crops harvested by those owing tithes, though the 'tenth fleece' and the 'tenth lamb' were important in more pastoral areas, and other produce was similarly liable to tithing. During the eleventh and twelfth centuries tithe obligations were rationalized in accordance with canon law and local power politics to the point that each church had the right to tithes from producers within a defined territory, the parish. Once established, parish churches became the focus for a wide range of communal activities, some centring on religious observance and festivities, and some of a charitable nature, though much depended upon the size and population of each parish. Ordinary parishioners incurred some responsibility for the upkeep of the fabric of the church where this was not taken care of by a local lord.

Other pressures towards communal activity in village society derived from developments in lordship and kingship. The increasingly formal organization of manorial justice and record keeping generated regular routines and multiplied the need for responsible officers of the manor or barony. Often tenants were allowed to elect officers to represent their interests and perform regular duties for a manorial lord.[40] Some villages acted as a community in owning or leasing property, as when the men of Hemingford leased the abbot of Ramsey's manor there for seven years from Michaelmas 1280.[41] Some Irish and Welsh tenures were the joint responsibility of the tenants of a township, and the same was probably true in Scotland, as it certainly was in later centuries.[42] Other villagers combined together to resist their lords when they sensed that they were victims of seigniorial injustice.[43] The relationship between lordships and villages was not always such that manorial organization involved a whole village community, but this created its own need for appropriate institutional devices: a village with several lordships was likely to have quite a complex structure of regulations to harmonize their various interests.

Inequalities and Exchange

Increasing interdependence of households in rural society was not solely a matter of institutional structures. As in towns, the multiplication of formal institutions of government, law, and administration was accompanied by increasing economic interdependence between households. Much of this arose from inequalities of wealth. The existence of principles of cooperation and sharing of resources, such as common land, did not imply that rural society was egalitarian. The many surviving tenant lists and tax lists of the twelfth and thirteenth centuries demonstrate profound inequalities of wealth and status between families. Some of the most extensive evidence relating to differences of wealth come from the English Hundred Rolls of 1279, which supply a large body of statistics concerning the distribution of land in the midland counties (Table 8.2). These documents are the product of commissions instructed by the government to establish the rights of the crown and other lords 'so that we may know for future time what belongs to us and should belong to us, and others may know what belongs and should belong to them'.[44] Since the virgate was a customary and imprecise measure, no very fine tuning on these figures is possible, but it is unlikely that a tenant with half a virgate or less (15–20 acres or less) had much surplus grain over the requirements of his household, even in the absence of children. Without additional support, the tenants of these and smaller holdings—accounting for 65 per cent of farming units—were close to the margin of bare subsistence.

Inequalities of wealth amongst the peasantry were not peculiar to the more commercialized parts of Britain. In northern England and Scotland, the contrast to be met with between tenants with husbandlands and cottars is very striking, and the latter seem to have been a numerous group. They are well documented in the Kelso estate rental of about 1290, which records more cottars' lands than husbandlands in many places (Table 8.1). These cottars usually had less than 2 acres of land, and were evidently employed chiefly as a workforce on the lands of others.

TABLE 8.2. *The distribution of landholding (demesne lands and peasant tenures) in some midland hundreds of England, according to the Hundred Rolls*

County and Hundred	demesnes (average acres in brackets)	Over 1 virgate	1 virgate	½ virgate	¼ virgate	Petty holdings
Huntingdonshire						
Normancross	43 (192)	26	288	311	32	674
Cambridgeshire						
Chilford	30 (227)	26	51	125	109	396
Bedfordshire						
Stodden and Willey	56 (144)	27	133	412	374	489
Buckinghamshire						
Bunstow	24 (137)	12	41	134	205	126
Oxfordshire						
Bampton	49 (195)	59	350	362	65	235
Chadlington	38 (384)	67	623	206	44	250
Ploughley	65 (224)	62	611	417	26	196
Warwickshire						
Stoneleigh and Kineton	160 (154)	196	991	920	276	1,127
Total	465 (193)	475	3,088	2,887	1,131	3,493
Percentage	4.0	4.1	26.8	25.0	9.8	30.3

Note: The demesnes of manors in Oxfordshire are stated by Kosminsky in virgates. These are converted to acres here at the rate of 1 virgate = 30 acres.

Source: E. A. Kosminsky, *Studies in the Agrarian History of England in the Thirteenth Century*, ed. R. H. Hilton, trans. R. Kisch (Oxford, 1956), 90–1, 97, 100, 228.

At 'Spertildon' Grange, where the cottagers apparently had no land, they are described as the monks' shepherds. Such cottars existed on lay estates as well. In 1316 Robert I granted John Logan 18 bovates and 4 cottagers' lands in the township of West Linton (Peeblesshire), together with a brewhouse.[45] In Northumberland an inquest of the Umfraville family estates in 1245 records 38 cottagers as against 19 husbandmen on its border properties at Otterburn in Redesdale and Alwinton in Coquetdale. Further south, on Tyneside, there were 66 cottagers to 50 husband-men on properties around the headquarters of the barony at Prudhoe, and their landholdings averaged no more than 1.6 acres each.[46] Large numbers of cottagers also occur on some Irish manors, though as a minority of the tenant population. An extent of the manor of Cloncurry (Co. Kildare) in 1304 lists 42 cottagers, almost all with Irish names. They constituted about 23 per cent of the rural tenant population (that is, not taking into account the unknown number of burgesses on the manor).[47]

Inequalities of landholding within rural society were particularly marked in colonial Ireland as a result of the introduction of a privileged peasant class from outside. Many newly settled farmers had extensive freeholdings, often in the form of compact farms derived from the native Irish townland organization. Over 7,000 acres of land were held by freeholders and burgesses at Swords in 1326.[48] On the Butler manors of the early fourteenth century many tenants, quite apart from those occupied as military tenures, occupied one or more ploughlands, like Gilbert Palmer with a ploughland and 20 acres at Carrig (Co. Kildare), presumably about 140 acres in all.[49] Such large holdings could have contributed substantially to supplying both the export and the domestic market. A tenant called Richard de Wodehouse who died in 1323 on the royal manor of Chapelizod in the Liffey Valley, had 39 crannocks of wheat, 21 crannocks 4 pecks of oats, and 4 crannocks of peas in store, together with 42 acres of wheat growing in the fields.[50] Some individual tenant holdings were expanded in the course of time by purchase, to spread the fixed costs of husbandry over a greater area of land.[51] These large tenures contrasted sharply with the holdings of unfree native tenants,[52] and with those of many cottagers and smallholders who contributed to the labour force in eastern Ireland.

Differences between families in the amount of land they had to cultivate are not the same thing as differences in wealth, and such statistics could lead to misrepresentation in comparisons between midland England and some parts of Britain where wealth was assessed chiefly in sheep and cattle rather than in arable husbandry. Ideally allowance ought to be made, in such an analysis, for the extent of villagers' common rights, which could very materially extend the amount of land at their disposal. Even where animals can be taken into account, however, very unequal distributions of wealth are apparent.[53] A tax assessment of 1292–3 for the commote of Cafflogion, on the Lleyn peninsula, lists eleven taxpayers from the township of Carnuwch; their assessed goods ranged in value from £4 4s. 0d. (belonging to a man called Meilyr) to 3s. 4d. (belonging to Ieuan ap Ieuan). The former was taxed on two horses, four oxen, nine cows, eight ewes, and ten crannocks of flour; the latter was taxable on a single cow. Analysis of taxable wealth in the Welsh March in 1292 shows that in a sample of about 4,891 taxpayers, 5 per cent of that number owned about two-fifths of the total taxable wealth.[54]

Evidence of marked inequalities within English village societies is confirmed by taxation records of the later thirteenth century. Since only the wealthier people in this period were taxed, the distinctions to be observed within the tax schedules greatly understate the differences to be seen in reality. They are nevertheless striking enough, even amongst tenants with apparently equivalent tenures. Assessed values of the taxable goods of ten half-virgaters at Cuxham in 1295 ranged between £3 and 13s. 4d.[55] Differences of wealth are also reflected visibly in the archaeological evidence of peasant housing. In many parts of Britain and Ireland the homes of the poor were flimsy constructions that leave little archaeological evidence behind them. The 'cot' that defined the cottager was a simple one-roomed construction with a central hearth, far removed from our romanticized perception of a 'cottage'. Meanwhile, a common form of house for the wealthier peasantry in much of Britain was the long house, of two or more rooms in a row, of which one was used as a room for sitting and sleeping, while the other was more for preparing food, storage, and in some cases housing livestock. Amongst the wealthier English peasantry standards of housing improved during the course of the twelfth and thirteenth centuries. Exclusively timber houses, which risked rot in posts set into the earth, were superseded in many regions by timber-framed buildings constructed on a stone base. One of the most satisfactory traditions to emerge was the cruck cottage of the midlands, with solid timber frames, of which some examples from around 1300 still stand.[56] This archaeological evidence is one of the best indications we have a widening gap between wealthier peasant and the poorest during the twelfth and thirteenth centuries.

These distinctions of wealth were a feature of fundamental significance for ways of life. Wealth was much more likely than poverty to be associated with positions of authority within the village, and such positions in turn brought secondary economic and social advantages.[57] Differences of wealth also affected the ability to marry. A detailed study of families in Halesowen (Warwickshire) has established that marriage was easier and earlier for the sons and daughters of wealthy families; sons who were given property while their parents were still alive could marry as a result (Table 8.3). Differences in wealth affected the size of households. The characteristic peasant households were small units of parents and children, rather than of large extended families; in the later thirteenth century the average household size was apparently between four and five people. But there were wide differences between wealthier households, which could sustain that number or more, and the households of the poor, whose children were more likely to be sent out as hired workers.[58] This is a pointer to the fact that inequalities of wealth also affected the levels and forms of economic dependence. Managers of demesne lands, and peasants with more land than they could manage with family labour, depended upon employing workers either on an annual contract or for particular seasonal tasks. Villagers without sufficient land to live on were inevitably dependent upon

TABLE 8.3. *Families in Halesowen whose sons obtained land and whose daughters were married while their father was still alive, 1270–1349*

Status	No. of families	No. of families whose sons obtained land and whose daughters married while the father was still alive
Rich	131	99 (76%)
Middling	285	119 (42%)
Poor	304	42 (14%)

Source: Z. Razi, *Life, Marriage and Death in a Medieval Parish: Economy, Society and Demography in Halesowen, 1270–1400* (Cambridge, 1980), 59.

some form of employment that they could not themselves control. Either they had to work for an employer or they had to sell some manufacture or skill.

One of the best options for poorer families, especially after the decline of slavery, was employment on a demesne farm with an annual contract. The contract would not be a written one, but it was understood that a man hired as a ploughman or a carter would receive an annual money wage and an allowance of food through the year. Such employment guaranteed an income for the year, and reduced, even if it did not wholly eliminate, the need to hunt for alternative employments. Demesne farms had teams of such employees, who were usually described in manorial records as *famuli*, a term meaning originally 'members of the household', though in this usage it means little more than 'servants' or 'staff'. On the Oxfordshire manor of Cuxham in the later thirteenth century, for example, there were normally four ploughmen, a carter, a cowman, a dairy assistant and a shepherd.[59] Some wealthier peasant farmers may have created similar employment for *famuli*. The same terminology was employed on the large monastic estates of southern Scotland; the shepherds at Kelso Abbey's 'Spertildon' Grange enumerated above in Table 8.1 were said to be of the abbey's *familia*. One of the consequences of increasing competition for employment was to depress the value of wages, as measured in the goods they would buy, during the later thirteenth century.[60] Despite the pressures in the economy for rising employment and higher prices, many groups of workers became individually worse off. The workers on the bishop of Winchester's estates were so vulnerable around 1300 that the bishop's officers were able to make widespread wage cuts.[61] The annual wage of even the most secure farmworker of the later thirteenth century guaranteed little more than bare subsistence, representing about a half of what an English farmworker could earn around 1750, on the eve of industrialization.[62]

Such security was not available to everyone, and perhaps only to the most skilled.

Though the manor of Cuxham in the 1280s gave regular employment to eight *famuli*, the village contained nine cottagers without land and eight half-virgaters with only 12 acres each, implying that most householders would have wanted to find some form of supplementary income.[63] An additional consequence of an increasingly abundant labour supply during the thirteenth century was greater insecurity of employment, which inevitably increased the precariousness of existence for poor families, who had nothing to fall back on except wealthier relations and meagre institutionalized charity. Many took up seasonal or casual sources of employment, paid by the day or by piece rates, even if skilled. Some poorer families were able to specialize in particular crafts like building or thatching, moving from job to job as work became available, but the more normal experience was probably a string of seasonal and unspecialized activities put together according to what was available. Men with craft names were often amongst the poorest people in the community, implying that specialization in this period was no highroad to high productivity and accumulation. As the number of smallholdings increased during the twelfth and thirteenth centuries, and as the number of village markets and small towns increased, so did the proportion of the rural population that depended on finding at least part of its income in casual employment.[64] The cottars of Prestongrange (East Lothian), to judge from an agreement about tithes made in 1320, engaged in tavern keeping, weaving, trading, and fishing.[65] Even in the absence of large towns, there was scope for occupational diversification in rural areas.

Women and their work figure less prominently in our record sources than their role warrants, partly because women's work was more centred on the home, and partly because a man was legally responsible for his wife's debts. Since a large part of a married woman's working life was likely to be spent either in pregnancy or with responsibilities for small children, and because of the prevailing patriarchal ethos, there was characteristically a fairly clear division between women's work and men's. However, there can be no doubt of the contribution that women made to the welfare and income of rural households. Just how this was achieved would depend upon the wealth and status of the family in question. In the upper ranks of society a woman might exercise considerable authority over household, estate, and servants (particularly, of course, if she were a widow, or had an absent or ailing husband). Among more ordinary village households women were commonly responsible for looking after the house (of course) and caring for cattle and poultry, rather than for heavy field work, and they were often responsible for marketing farm produce, especially dairy produce, eggs, and poultry. They probably had a significant role in finding supplementary food by picking nuts, fruit, and herbs from the wild, and gleaning (after the harvest was brought in). Heavy tasks such as ploughing, carting, threshing, and ditching were generally man's work, though in his war against Scotland in 1302 Edward I employed women ditchers at 1½*d.* a day (as against 2*d.* for men) to strengthen the fortifications at Linlithgow and Dumfries castles. Women would be expected to help with farmwork at peak periods of activity, such as harvesting, however, and were no doubt called in to help at other times. Their chances of acquiring paid employment were less good than a man's, and perhaps deteriorated in the course of the thirteenth century as male under-employment worsened, but some obtained good employment serving demesne farms, or other larger units, as dairy maids, and some were able to obtain seasonal work, particularly as weeders; it is likely that slave women had been allocated these tasks in the eleventh century, and that they represent traditional female roles. Women might also be employed as assistants to some male workers such as that-chers.[66] Like townswomen, country women were often able to increase the house-hold income by selling ale they had brewed at home.[67] They also engaged in some craft activities, either in association with their husbands or on their own account if unmarried or widowed. In Cambridgeshire in 1279 about 7 per cent of villagers whose surnames indicated a craft were women.[68] It is difficult, given the state of our evidence, to point to contrasts across Britain in these respects, but it seems likely that contrasts between income groups were stronger than contrasts between regions.

The resulting relations of interdependence in rural society cannot have depended entirely on the use of money. A silver penny bought decreasingly less during the course of the thirteenth century because of inflation. Even so, it was a large unit of currency in relation to the regular requirements of a market-dependent household. To obtain smaller units of currency, pennies could be cut into two (to make halfpennies) or into four (to make farthings)—though not clipped around the edge, which was a criminal offence. A farthing by the late thirteenth century was relatively adaptable; in southern England it would buy a loaf of bread, whose size varied according to the price of wheat, or 5 eggs, or ¼–½ lb. of butter.[69] But day labourers earned only a penny a day, which would not allow them many purchases for cash even in a week of full employment. Village society was probably dependent upon complicated systems of credit and barter, even if transactions had to be expressed in monetary terms when legal disputes arose. The best evidence we have for the use of payments in kind is that of stipendiary farm servants hired for the year, the greater part of whose remuneration was nearly always paid in grain.[70]

In one way the expansion of economic activity between 1050 and 1300 can be regarded as evidence of economic development, and it was certainly evidence of increasing economic complexity. Yet its implications for welfare in rural society were socially divisive. A countryman with enough grain to feed his family and sell some surplus in ordinary years could build up an adequate buffer against a year of poor crops, or could at least hope to ride out the lean years by borrowing on the security of his land. Meanwhile a smallholder or cottager was likely to go hungry in years of poor harvest, and ran the risk of starving when conditions were really bad. There is abundant evidence of the suffering of the poor in years of bad harvest, especially in the famines of 1315–18 when thousands of people perished from malnutrition.[71]

NOTES

1. Domesday Book, ii, fo. 111^v; *Regesta Regum Anglo-Normannorum*, ed. H. W. C. Davies, C. Johnson, H. A. Cronne, and R. H. C. Davies, 4 vols. (Oxford, 1913–69), iii. 249.

2. S. Letters, 'Markets and Fairs in Medieval England: A New Source', in M. C. Prestwich, R. H. Britnell, and R. F. Frame (eds.), *Thirteenth Century England IX* (Woodbridge, 2003), 215.

3. A. E. Brown and C. C. Taylor, 'Little Linton and the Linton Landscape', *Proceedings of Cambridge Antiquarian Society*, 84 (1995), 91–104.

4. *Calendar of Charter Rolls*, 6 vols. (1903–27), i. 289, 420; ii. 213, 258.

5. A. F. O'Brien, *The Impact of the Anglo-Normans on Munster* (Cork, 1997), 57; id., 'Politics, Economy and Society: The Development of Cork and the Irish South Coast Region, c.1170 to c.1583', in P. O'Flanaghan and C. G. Butler (eds.), *Cork History and Society: Interdisciplinary Essays on the History of an Irish County* (Dublin, 1983), 93–4.

6. *Handlist of the Acts of Alexander II*, ed. J. M. Scoular (Edinburgh, 1959), no. 61, p. 17; *Handlist of the Acts of Alexander III, the Guardians and John*, ed. G. G. Simpson (Edinburgh, 1960), no. 58, p. 15.

7. W. G. Hoskins, 'The Making of the Agrarian Landscape in id. and H. P. R. Finberg, *Devonshire Studies* (1952), 318–24.

8. R. A. Lomas, 'Crookbank, Beckley and Andrew's House and the de Laley Family', *Durham Archaeological Journal*, 13 (1997), 99–102.

9. T. J. Pierce, *Medieval Welsh Society: Selected Essays*, ed. J. B. Smith (Cardiff, 1972), 258–9, 266–9, 333–4.

10. R. J. Silvester, 'The Landscape and Settlement of Trefnant Township', *Montgomery Collections*, 89 (2001), 147–62.

11. H. E. Hallam, 'Population Movements in England, 1086–1350', in id. (ed.), *The Agrarian History of England and Wales*, ii: *1042–1350* (Cambridge, 1988), 508–93.

12. E. B. DeWindt, *Land and People in Holywell-cum-Needingworth: Structures of Tenure and Patterns of Social Organization in an East Midlands Village, 1252–1457* (Toronto, 1971), 9, 169.

13. Domesday Book, i, fo. 159^v; P. D. A. Harvey, *A Medieval Oxfordshire Village: Cuxham, 1240 to 1400* (1965), 135.

14. I. Whyte, 'Pre-Improvement Rural Settlement in Scotland: Progress and Prospects', *Scottish Geographical Magazine*, 114 (1998), 78; B. K. Roberts, *The Green Villages of County Durham* (Durham, 1977), 38, 45.

15. S. Oosthuizen, 'Medieval Settlement Relocation in West Cambridgeshire: Three Case Studies', *Landscape History*, 19 (1997), 43–55.

16. B. K. Roberts, *Rural Settlement in Britain* (Folkstone, 1977), 147–50.

17. J. Kissock, ' "God Made Nature and Men Made Towns': Post-Conquest and Pre-Conquest Villages in Pembrokeshire', in N. Edwards (ed.), *Landscape and Settlement in Medieval Wales* (Oxford, 1997), 123–32.

18. *Registrum S. Marie de Neubotle*, ed. C. Innes, Bannatyne Club, 89 (1849), no. 10, pp. 7–8; *Registrum Honoris de Morton*, ed. T. Thomson, A. Macdonald, and C. Innes, 2 vols., Bannatyne Club, 94 (1853), ii. no.1, pp. 1–2.

19. *Registrum S. Marie de Neubotle*, no. 147, pp. 111–12.

20. *Liber S. Marie de Calchou*, ed. C. Innes, 2 vols., Bannatyne Club, 82 (1846), ii. no. 392, p. 307.

21. J. B. Johnston, *Place-Names of Scotland* (1934), 47–8.

22. *Liber S. Marie de Dryburgh*, ed. W. Fraser, Bannatyne Club, 83 (1847), no. 133, p. 94.

23. See below (Ch. 10).

24. *Liber S. Marie de Dryburgh*, nos. 176–83, pp. 123–30.

25. *Records of the Priory of the Isle of May*, ed. J. Stuart (Edinburgh, 1868), no. 24, pp. 16–17.

26. *Registrum S. Marie de Neubotle*, no. 5, p. 5.

27. J. Otway-Ruthven, 'The Medieval County of Kildare', *Irish Historical Studies*, 11 (1959), 183–4.

28. B. Colford, 'Anglo-Norman Settlement in County Wexford', in K. Whelan and W. Nolan (eds.), *Wexford: History and Society. Interdisciplinary Essays on the History of an Irish County* (Dublin, 1987), 81–2.

29. T. B. Barry, 'Rural Settlement in Medieval Ireland', in id. (ed.), *A History of Settlement in Ireland* (2000), 114, 117.

30. B. J. Graham, 'Anglo-Norman Settlement in County Meath', *Proceedings of the Royal Irish Academy*, 75, section C (1975), 223–48.

31. R. A. Dodgshon, 'Medieval Rural Scotland', in G. Whittington and I. D. Whyte (eds.), *An Historical Geography of Scotland* (1983), 54.

32. *Registrum de Dunfermelyn*, ed. C. Innes, Bannatyne Club, 74 (1842), nos. 1, 86–7, 89, 177–8, 207–10, pp. 3, 52–4, 100–1, 120–1.

33. R. A. Dodgshon, *The Origin of British Field Systems* (1980), 137–49.

34. H. E. Hallam, *The New Lands of Elloe: A Study of Early Reclamation in Lincolnshire* (Leicester, 1954), 37–9.

35. P. A. Yeoman, 'Medieval Rural Settlement: The Invisible Centuries', in W. S. Hanson and E. A. Slater (eds.), *Scottish Archaeology: New Perceptions* (Aberdeen, 1991), 115.

36. F. Seebohm, *The Tribal System in Wales* (1904), appendices, 3–25.

37. W. O. Ault, *Open-Field Farming in Medieval England* (1972), 82–3.

38. P. G. B. McNeill and H. L. MacQueen (eds.), *Atlas of Scottish History to 1707* (Edinburgh, 1996), 347–60; A. D. Carr, *Medieval Anglesey* (Llangefni, 1982), 266–7.

39. R. E. Glasscock, 'Land and People, c.1300', in A. Cosgrove (ed.), *A New History of Ireland*, ii: *Medieval Ireland, 1169–1534* (Oxford, 1987), 221.

40. H. S. Bennett, *Life on the English Manor* (Cambridge, 1937), 170–1.

41. H. M. Cam, 'The Community of the Vill', in ead., *Law-Finders and Law-Makers in Medieval England* (1962), 71–84; G. C. Homans, *The English Villagers of the Thirteenth Century* (New York, 1960), 330–1.

42. See below (Ch. 11).

43. R. H. Hilton, *A Medieval Society: The West Midlands at the End of the Thirteenth Century*, 2nd edn. (Cambridge, 1983), 154–61.

44. E. A. Kosminsky, *Studies in the Agrarian History of England in the Thirteenth Century*, ed. R. H. Hilton, trans. R. Kisch (Oxford, 1956), 13.

45. *Regesta Regum Scottorum*, v: *The Acts of Robert I*, ed. A. A. M. Duncan (Edinburgh, 1988), no. 83, pp. 366–7.

46. *Calendar of Documents Relating to Scotland Preserved in Her Majesty's Public Record Office*, ed. J. Bain, G. G. Simpson, and J. D. Galbraith, 5 vols. (Edinburgh, 1881–1987), i. 305.

47. *The Red Book of Ormond*. ed. N. B. White (Dublin, 1932), 29–34.

48. J. Mills, 'Tenants and Agriculture near Dublin in the Fourteenth Century', *Journal of the Royal Society of Antiquaries of Ireland*, 21 (1890–1), 59; K. D. O'Conor, *The Archaeology of Medieval Rural Settlements in Ireland* (Dublin, 1998), 46, 70; A. Simms, 'The Geography of Irish Manors: The Examples of Duleek and Colp in County Meath', in J. Bradley (ed.), *Settlement and Society in Medieval Ireland: Studies Presented to F. X. Martin, OSA* (Kilkenny, 1988), 315; ead., 'Core and Periphery in Medieval Europe: The Irish Experience in a Wider Context', in W. J. Smyth and K. Whelan (eds.), *Common Ground: Essays on the Historical Geography of Ireland Presented to T. Jones Hughes* (Cork, 1988), 34–5, 37.

49. *The Red Book of Ormond*, 15 (five other examples). Cf. 16 (one example), 17 (three examples), 19 (six examples), 20 (ten examples). An Irish ploughland was 120 acres: A. F. O'Brien, 'Medieval Youghal: The Development of an Irish Seaport Trading Town', *Peritia*, 5 (1986), 350.

50. M. C. Lyons, 'Manorial Administration and the Manorial Economy in Ireland, c.1200–c.1377' (unpublished Ph.D. thesis, Trinity College Dublin, 1984), i. 35.

51. K. Down, 'Colonial Society and Economy in the High Middle Ages', in Cosgrove (ed.), *New History of Ireland*, ii. 460–1.

52. These were the 'betaghs', discussed below (Ch. 11).

53. E. Miller and J. Hatcher, *Medieval England: Rural Society and Economic Change, 1086–1348* (1978), 153.

54. 'A Lleyn Lay Subsidy Account', ed. T. J. Pierce, *Bulletin of the Board of Celtic Studies*, v (1929–31), 57; R. R. Davies, *Lordship and Society in the March of Wales, 1282–1400* (Oxford, 1978), 399–401.

55. P. D. A. Harvey, *A Medieval Oxfordshire Village: Cuxham, 1240 to 1400* (1965), 174.

56. C. Dyer, *Standards of Living in the Later Middle Ages: Social Change in England, c.1200–1520* (Cambridge, 1989), 160–3.

57. J. A. Raftis, 'Social Structures in Five East Midland Villages', *Economic History Review*, 2nd ser. 18 (1965), 84–7.

58. P. R. Schofield, *Peasant and Community in Medieval England, 1200–1500* (Basingstoke, 2003), 83–4.

59. Harvey, *Medieval Oxfordshire Village*, 168–71.

60. D. L. Farmer, 'Prices and Wages', in H. E. Hallam (ed.), *The Agrarian History of England and Wales*, ii: *1042–1350* (Cambridge, 1988), 772–8.

61. M. Page, 'Challenging Custom: The Auditors of the Bishopric of Winchester,

c.1300–c.1310', in M. Prestwich, R. H. Britnell and R. Frame (eds.), *Thirteenth Century England VI* (Woodbridge, 1997), 39–48.

62. This is based on an estimate of incomes as equivalent to 44–64 bushels of barley a year in 1296–7 and 80–120 bushels in 1750: R. H. Britnell, *The Commercialization of English Society, 1000–1500*, 2nd edn. (Manchester, 1996), 106–7; K. Wrightson, *Earthly Necessities: Economic Lives in Early Modern Britain* (New Haven, 2000), 318. Wrightson's figure of £8–12 has been converted to barley at 2s. a bushel. For discussion of this contrast, see G. Clark, 'Labour Productivity in English Agriculture, 1300–1860', in B. M. S. Campbell and M. Overton (eds.), *Land, Labour and Livestock: Historical Studies in European Agricultural Productivity* (Manchester, 1991), 211–35.

63. Harvey, *Medieval Oxfordshire Village*, 119–35.

64. R. H. Britnell, 'Specialisation of Work in England, 1100–1300', *Economic History Review*, 54 (2001), 1–16.

65. *Registrum S. Marie de Neubotle*, no. 147, pp. 111–12.

66. B. A. Hanawalt, *The Ties that Bound: Peasant Families in Medieval England* (New York, 1986), 146–8; H. Swanson, *Medieval British Towns* (Basingstoke, 1999), 50.

67. J. M. Bennett, *Ale, Beer and Brewsters in England* (Oxford, 1996).

68. E. Miller and J. Hatcher, *Medieval England: Towns, Commerce and Crafts, 1086–1348* (1995), 132.

69. The farthing loaf was standard. Prices of eggs and butter are here taken from *Ministers' Accounts of the Earldom of Cornwall, 1296–1297*, ed. L. M. Midgley, 2 vols., Camden Society, 3rd ser. 66, 67 (1942–5), i. 190. 225 (eggs); *The Pipe Roll of the Bishopric of Winchester, 1301–2*, ed. and trans. M. Page (Winchester, 1996), 78. 133, 193, 208, 251, 284, 363 (butter).

70. Miller and Hatcher, *Medieval England: Rural Society*, 51–2.

71. I. Kershaw, 'The Great Famine and Urban Crisis in England, 1315–1322', in R. H. Hilton (ed.), *Peasants, Knights and Heretics: Studies in Medieval English Social History* (Cambridge, 1976), 85–132.

FURTHER READING

Astill, G., and Grant, A. (eds.), *The Countryside of Medieval England* (Oxford, 1988).

Aston, M., Beresford, M., and Dyer, C. (eds.), *The Rural Settlements of Medieval England: Studies Dedicated to Maurice Beresford and John Hurst* (Oxford, 1989).

Ault, W. O., *Open-Field Farming in Medieval England* (1972).

Barrow, G. W. S., 'Rural Settlement in Central and Eastern Scotland: The Medieval Evidence', *Scottish Studies*, 6 (1962).

Barry, T. B., ' "The People of the Country . . . Dwell Scattered": The Pattern of Rural Settlements in Ireland in the Later Middle Ages', in J. Bradley (ed.), *Settlement and Society in Medieval Ireland: Studies Presented to F. X. Martin, OSA* (Kilkenny, 1988).

—— 'Rural Settlement in Medieval Ireland', in id. (ed.), *A History of Settlement in Ireland* (2000).

Bennett, J. M., *Ale, Beer and Brewsters in England* (Oxford, 1996).

Britnell, R. H., 'Specialisation of Work in England, 1100–1300', *Economic History Review*, 54 (2001).

Brown, A. E., and Taylor, C. C., 'Little Linton and the Linton Landscape', *Proceedings of Cambridge Antiquarian Society*, 84 (1995).

Cam, H. M., 'The Community of the Vill', in ead., *Law-Finders and Law-Makers in Medieval England* (1962).

DeWindt, E. B. (ed.), *The Salt of Common Life: Individuality and Choice in the Medieval Town, Countryside and Church. Essays Presented to J. Ambrose Raftis* (Kalamazoo, 1995).

Dodgshon, R. A., *Land and Society in Early Scotland* (Oxford, 1981).

—— 'Medieval Rural Scotland', in G. Whittington and I. D. Whyte (eds.), *An Historical Geography of Scotland* (1983).

—— 'Medieval Settlement and Colonisation', in M. L. Parry and T. R. Slater (eds.), *The Making of the Scottish Countryside* (1980).

Dyer, C., 'Dispersed Settlements in Medieval England: A Case Study of Pendock, Worcestershire', *Medieval Archaeology*, 34 (1990).

—— *Everyday Life in Medieval England* (1994).

—— *Standards of Living in the Later Middle Ages: Social Change in England, c.1200–1520* (Cambridge, 1989).

Hallam, H. E., *Settlement and Society: A Study in the Early Agrarian History of South Lincolnshire* (Cambridge, 1965).

—— (ed.), *The Agrarian History of England and Wales*, ii: *1042–1350* (Cambridge, 1988).

Hanawalt, B. A., *The Ties that Bound: Peasant Families in Medieval England* (New York, 1986).

Harvey, P. D. A., *A Medieval Oxfordshire Village: Cuxham, 1240 to 1400* (1965).

—— (ed.), *The Peasant Land Market in Medieval England* (Oxford, 1984).

Hilton, R. H., *A Medieval Society: The West Midlands at the End of the Thirteenth Century*, 2nd edn. (Cambridge, 1983).

Homans, G. C., *The English Villagers of the Thirteenth Century* (New York, 1960).

Jones, G. R. J., 'The Distribution of Bond Settlements in North-West Wales', *Welsh History Review*, 2 (1964–5).

—— 'The Pattern of Settlement on the Welsh Border', *Agricultural History Review*, 8 (1960).

—— 'Post-Roman Wales', in H. P. R. Finberg (ed.), *The Agrarian History of England and Wales*, i (2), *A.D. 43–1042* (Cambridge, 1972).

—— 'Rural Settlement in Anglesey', in S. R. Eyre and G. R. J. Jones (eds.), *Geography as Human Ecology: Methodology by Example* (1966).

Kosminsky, E. A., *Studies in the Agrarian History of England in the Thirteenth Century*, ed. R. H. Hilton, trans. R. Kisch (Oxford, 1956).

McIntosh, M., *Autonomy and Community: The Royal Manor of Havering, 1200–1500* (Cambridge, 1986).

—— 'Land Tenure and Population in the Royal Manor of Havering, Essex, 1251–1352/3', *Economic History Review*, 2nd ser. 33 (1980).

Miller, E., and Hatcher, J., *Medieval England: Rural Society and Economic Change, 1086–1348* (1978).

Otway-Ruthven, A. J., 'Parochial Development in the Rural Deanery of Skeen', *Journal of the Royal Society of Antiquaries of Ireland*, 94 (1964).

Owen, D. H., 'The Middle Ages', in id. (ed.), *Settlement and Society in Wales* (Cardiff, 1989).

Page, M., 'The Peasant Land Market on the Estates of the Bishopric of Winchester before the Black Death', in R. H. Britnell (ed.), *The Winchester Pipe Rolls and Medieval English Society* (Woodbridge, 2003).

Pierce, T. J., *Medieval Welsh Society: Selected Essays*, ed. J. B. Smith (Cardiff, 1972).

Pollock, D., 'The Lunan Valley Project: Medieval Rural Settlement in Angus', *Proceedings of the Society of Antiquaries of Scotland*, 115 (1985).

Postan, M. M., *The Famulus: The Estate Labourer in the XIIth and XIIIth Centuries*, Economic History Review Supplements, 2 (1954).

Raftis, J. A., 'Social Structures in Five East Midland Villages', *Economic History Review*, 2nd ser. 18 (1965).

Razi, Z., *Life, Marriage and Death in a Medieval Parish: Economy, Society and Demography in Halesowen, 1270–1400* (Cambridge, 1980).

Roberts, B. K., *Rural Settlement in Britain* (Folkstone, 1977).

—— and Wrathmell, S., *Region and Place: A Study of English Rural Settlement* (2002).

Schofield, P. R., 'England: The Family and the Village Community', in S. H. Rigby (ed.), *A Companion to Britain in the Later Middle Ages* (Oxford, 2003).

—— *Peasant and Community in Medieval England, 1200–1500* (Basingstoke, 2003).

Smith, R. M. (ed.), *Land, Kinship and Life-Cycle* (Cambridge, 1984).

Taylor, C., 'Dispersed Settlement in Nucleated Areas', *Landscape History*, 17 (1995).

Titow, J., *English Rural Society, 1200–1350* (1969).

Toorians, L., 'Twelfth-Century Flemish Settlements in Scotland', in G. G. Simpson (ed.), *Scotland and the Low Countries, 1124–1994* (East Linton, 1996).

Whyte, I. D., 'The Evolution of Rural Settlement in Lowland Scotland in Medieval and Early Modern Times: An Exploration', *Scottish Geographical Magazine*, 97 (1981).

Yeoman, P. A., 'Medieval Rural Settlement: The Invisible Centuries', in W. S. Hanson and E. A. Slater (eds.), *Scottish Archaeology: New Perceptions* (Aberdeen, 1991).

....

CHAPTER 9

Arable Husbandry

The growth of population and trade in Britain between the eleventh and the thirteenth century predictably encouraged a considerable increase in the production of food. We cannot measure how great that increase was, nor analyse exactly how it was achieved, and there are unavoidable gaps in our understanding. Yet neither problem precludes agreement on many details, nor eliminates the need for debate about the interpretation of the information we have. Though more abundant in parts of Britain than in others, the evidence, both archaeological and documentary, is sufficiently voluminous and widespread to carry conviction that the twelfth and thirteenth centuries were an age of expanding crop acreages through the reduction of heath, moor, and woodland and the draining of marshes and fens. Beyond that raw evidence of quantitative change, two areas of discussion are particularly fruitful. One concerns the extent to which the enlarged output of cereals by extensive methods (extending the ploughed area at the expense of other forms of land use) was complemented by the adoption and diffusion of intensive methods of cultivation (raising output from existing fields by increased applications of labour, fertilizing agents, or both). The other concerns the extent to which arable farming grew to provide subsistence for producers, or producing institutions, rather than in response to commercial incentives. Both these discussions have a bearing on just how close in character the economic development of these centuries was to that of more recent times.

Extensive or Intensive Growth?

In parts of Britain there had been so much agrarian expansion during the Anglo-Saxon period that there was little scope for continuing expansion. Yet even in southern and midland England there was some clearance of forest, moor, and heath. On the estates of Ramsey Abbey the number of demesne ploughs increased by 20 to 30 per cent between the 1080s and the 1130s, seemingly an extension of arable cultivation.[1] On Ramsey manors there are also incidental references to cleared areas of woodland in the early twelfth century; a description of Cranfield (Bedfordshire) in about 1160 records 350 acres of cleared land held by about 30 tenants. Some of these 'assarts' (woodland clearings) had been won before 1135.[2] Hundreds of acres were cleared in some parts of England. One of King Stephen's charters granted to Peterborough Abbey 240 acres of assarts at Longthorpe, Walton, Castor, and Ailsworth, and the abbey had cleared a further 400 acres of forest in its manor of Oundle by 1189.[3] Figure 9.1 contrasts the heavily wooded landscape of Akeley near Buckingham, in 1100 with the landscape there as it was in 1300. The name ('Achelei' in Domesday Book) means 'oak wood'; this was a settlement in Whittlewood Forest. Its woods remained exceptionally large by the standards of midland England in 1300, but cultivation had greatly expanded at their expense. Extensive reserves of arable land permitted exceptionally rapid population growth. In the more open Feldon region of Warwickshire, recorded tenant numbers grew by 47 per cent between 1086 and 1279, but in the more heavily forested Arden region they grew by 212 per cent.[4]

Land was also reclaimed from marshes and fens, though there was less scope for this in the north and west than in the low-lying valleys and marshy estuaries of eastern and southern England. One of the best-recorded instances, chiefly because of an abundance of charter evidence, is from south Lincolnshire, where land was won on two fronts from both the sea and the fens. The main sea banks in existence in the twelfth century dated from before the Norman Conquest, but from about 1100 at least lords and villagers pushed beyond them. On the landward side, too, drainage of the fens has a pre-conquest history continuing into the period 1086–1180. A considerable intake from the fen, involving the cooperation of a number of different villages in the construction of a channel called Saturday Dyke, was won in about 1160–70.[5] Other examples of coastal reclamation are well attested from the Kent marshes and the Severn estuary.[6]

Away from the more commercialized areas, especially those poorly supplied by cheap transport, there was less incentive to plough up moors and forests even when land was available. Nevertheless the structure of demand could be transformed through the movement of people and institutions into regions of wilderness and sparse settlement, and this was one of the most recurrent features of agrarian expansion away from the pull of urban demand. Attention has long been drawn to the impact of new monasteries in northern England, such as the larger twelfth-century Cistercian houses of the North and West Ridings of Yorkshire—Jervaulx, Byland, Rievaulx, Kirkstall, and (wealthiest of all) Fountains. They did not always occupy virgin territory, and some of their activities involved moving peasant families already settled, but they also took in new land to construct compact farms

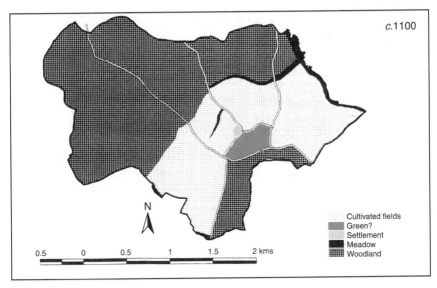

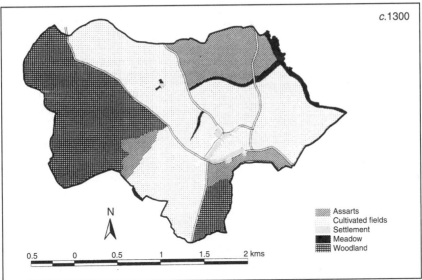

FIG. 9.1. Landscape and settlement in Akeley (Buckinghamshire). These two maps of Akeley two centuries apart, *c.*1100 and *c.*1300, suggest how the woodland had been cut back in the intervening period. The extension of arable lands to the north of the Anglo-Saxon settlement of Akeley was associated with the formation of a new manor of Stockholt, around 1230, but there were numerous other assarts carved from the surrounding woods.

Source: R. Jones and M. Page, 'Medieval Settlements and Landscapes in the Whittlewood Area: Interim report, 2001–2', *Medieval Settlement Research Group: Annual Report*, 16 (2001), 17, 19.

and extend their sheep flocks. In Scotland Melrose Abbey and Dryburgh Abbey established arable granges in the Tweed Valley and along the coast at Blainslie, Kedslie, Sorrowlessfield, Gattonside, and Eildon.[7] Lay magnates and kings in these regions were also significant beneficiaries of colonization of the waste; between 1266 and 1286 there was extensive forest clearance at Wark in Tynedale, bringing in rents of £17 11s. 10d. to the English crown.[8]

In Scotland, where much of the forest cover had been removed in prehistoric times, references to assarts are not numerous in charters of the twelfth and thirteenth centuries. Nevertheless there are direct references to land being carved from waste lands. In the 1160s Malcolm IV of Scotland gave Glasgow Cathedral and one of its tenants rights over pasture in the royal forest at Ashkirk (Selkirkshire). Then in 1179 his successor, William I, authorized the canons to plough up an area within stated bounds.[9] Lands at Quarrelwood, just west of Elgin, were uncultivated when King Alexander II (1214–49) gave the mills of Elgin, Forres, and elsewhere to the prior and monks of St Andrew of Pluscarden (Morayshire), but they were cultivated, and so owed multure at the prior's mill, by the reign of Robert I (1306–29).[10] In 1265 the sheriff of Traquair (Peeblesshire) recorded produce rents from two tenants 'who took waste lands', and in 1266 the sheriff of Kincardine noted an increment of rent 'from a new land by the forest of Cowie'.[11] Grants of waste land are likely to have led to cultivation even where this is not specified.[12] Some evidence of extensive land clearance may be attested, too, in the occurrence of lands measured by the 'ploughgate' in regions north of the River Forth; these were distinct from older lands measured by the 'davoch'.[13] Population pressure probably encouraged the formation of outfields in Scotland, though they are not recorded in our sources. There is an instance from Northumberland, about 1220, in a grant of common rights to Kelso Abbey by Robert of 'Schottun'. He mandated that no one should plough on the east side of Humbledon Hill, near Wooler, or do anything else to heed access by the abbey's sheep. This would not be intelligible if this land was recognized as regular tillage.[14]

Welsh Cistercian abbeys, Tintern, Dore, Basingwerk, Grace Dieu, and Strata Florida, are credited with numerous assarts.[15] Military campaigns in Wales during the twelfth and thirteenth centuries often involved tree felling, an activity that increased greatly in 1277, and for many years later, on the grounds that woodlands served as cover for criminals, as well as to supply timber for castles and other defences. Though many thousands of acres were deforested in this way, it is impossible to know how much of the cleared land was converted to agricultural use.[16] But the spread of settlement must have been associated with enlarged areas under the plough. For example, there was migration into the interior of Anglesey from the old bond settlements to found on the better quality of land. Meanwhile from the earlier twelfth century new settlements, usually on poorer soils, were created by freemen, whose presence as settled inhabitants of the island had been subordinate to that of bondmen. There had been no free townships on Anglesey up to that point. From then on, not only did freemen create new arable fields, but they expanded them onto areas of pasture and waste as families grew. The characteristic free holding, the *gwely*, was inherited on the death of its founder by his sons jointly. This system of inheritance encouraged all the sons to stay on family territory and to take in more land in order to accommodate their growth in numbers as long as there was new land to be had. The old township (*hendref*) of Llysdulas, for example, was originally appropriated by two freemen called Griffri and Carwed about 1170, but their descendants created seven separate *gwelyau*, each with homes and portions of land at the original settlement but with additional patches of land elsewhere. Similar patterns of expansion, but by unfree settlers, are implied by the existence of bond townships whose land was held by *tir gwelyawg* tenure, that is by the rules of partible inheritance normally characteristic of freemen. It has been surmised that bond families were allowed this privileged tenure to encourage them to move from their old lands and cultivate less attractive sites elsewhere. A good deal of expansion was achieved by extending outfields under temporary cultivation rather than any intensified rotation of crops. By the end of the thirteenth century the arable resources of Anglesey were heavily exploited, and the distribution of townships and hamlets was directly related to the distribution of cultivable soils of different qualities.[17]

Expanding the area under crops was also a widespread response to colonial settlement and population growth in Ireland, especially on lands most suitable for tillage in the east and south.[18] This has left only fragmentary evidence, but there are references to clearances in charters and estate records. In 1229 permission was given to clear woodland on the manor of Shankill (Co. Dublin).[19] Sometime in the period 1230–4, Richard Marshal granted his free tenants permission to 'clear, enclose and cultivate' lands within the forests of Ross and Taghmon.[20] Geoffrey de Turville, bishop of Ossory (1244–51), allowed the burgesses of Durrow to pasture their beasts in a nearby grove, but only on the understanding that he might at any time take it back to assart and cultivate it.[21] Marketing opportunities, both to supply towns and export markets, were another stimulus to grain production. Though Irish domestic demand can only be crudely assessed, there is little doubt of its preponderance over exports. A guess of at least 50,000 town dwellers might be hazarded for the whole of Ireland around 1300. Glasscock's suggested urban proportion of 'probably less than five per cent' of a population of a million implies a figure of this order. Assuming an annual average consumption of 1.65 quarters of mixed grain per capita, this would imply a minimum annual urban grain requirement of 84,000 quarters, much of which would have to be secured through purchase.[22] As a result of subsistence and commercial pressures the arable acreage expanded to over 70 per cent of recorded estate acreages in many parts of Ireland, though it is not certain how these estimates relate to the total land surface.[23]

Evidence for extended arable acreages is therefore very widespread between 1050 and 1300; and constitutes the best body of evidence we have for the expansion of crop production in this period. In the Lincolnshire fenlands between a half and three-quarters of the land was under crops around 1300.[24] The proportion was even higher in much of southern and south-eastern England. It is most unlikely, though, that increasing arable acreages alone were sufficient to support the growth of towns and villages in evidence elsewhere in the archaeological and documentary record. An increase in the arable acreage of England of 31 per cent between 1086 and 1300, if we accept Campbell's estimate, is significantly below any plausible estimate of the increase in English population during this period. One of the most conservative estimates suggests an increase of between 64 and 168 per cent (from 1.68 to 2.75 million in 1086 to 4.5 million in 1300).[25] These figures imply an increase in the productivity of the land that contributed at least as much to feeding the population as increases in the area of ploughland. Tracking the sources of this productivity growth is therefore high on the agenda of topics for research in agrarian history. It is inconceivable for many reasons—including the evidence of port accounts—that grain imports could have done more than alleviate occasional shortages.

Intensification of husbandry took many forms. It could be achieved by raising the output of each acre under crops. It could also come about by increasing the proportion of the ploughlands under crops in any one year—that is, by reducing the area normally left fallow. In either case, it was likely that the soil would need increased nutrients to maintain a more intensive cropping regime. One of the most remarkable instances of this second kind of development has been observed in the Orkneys from the West Mainland and from Stronsay, where a deep layer of 'plaggen' soil has been identified as a man-made deposit accumulated between the twelfth century and the nineteenth. It derives from the practice of stripping turfs from the hillsides beyond the dykes surrounding the township land, using them for animal bedding in the byres around the farmsteads, and then casting out the turfs, enriched with animal manure, onto the town fields. In effect the farmers of Marwick, by dint of extra labour in proving both for their livestock and their crops, built up their fields at the expense of the surrounding hillsides. This is an extreme example of the interdependence of livestock and crop husbandry in the intensification of agriculture.[26] The most abundant nutrient that could be added to the soil was animal and human manure, which could be spread either by allowing animals to graze the vegetation on fallowed lands or, more expensively, by collecting dung in a farmyard heap and then spreading it from carts. A similar effect was achieved in many areas of Britain through the ploughing in of marl. Marl is a natural resource of clay mixed with carbonate of lime; it could be dug from marl pits, and because of its crumbly texture could be mixed in the soil to lighten it, modify its acidity, and increase the retention of nitrogen.[27] Both manuring and marling were widespread—especially the first, though the adequacy of manure supplies, and the economy with which they were used, varied very much from place to place. Intensive manuring was a form of investment, and was most widespread in areas, like eastern Norfolk, where landlords had high inducements to increase output per acre. British settlers took some new forms of fertilizer with them to Ireland.[28]

Raising output per acre involved increasing the amount of labour used in crop husbandry, whether in manuring or in other ways. The frequency or care with which the land was tilled, cleared of stones, ploughed, weeded, protected from predators, and reaped, all counted towards the quality of the harvest, and were all susceptible to variation depending on the expected pay-off. Both human and animal labour was involved in these developments. It is not difficult to gauge the motivation of a smallholder with no alternative means of support. Even though at the mercy of the weather from year to year, it might still be worth the while of a family dependent on its land to win the greatest possible crop by conducting its farming operations thoroughly, and the increased number of hands on many such farms during the course of the twelfth and thirteenth centuries made it easier to find the labour required. It is likely—given the large number of families engaged in smallholding—that increases in the productivity of land were frequently won at the expense of decreasing productivity of labour, as people put more and more work into raising the output from their scraps of family land. It has been plausibly argued, on this supposition, that output per acre on peasant holdings may have outstripped what is known from the better-recorded demesne lands.[29] Even some demesnes, however, experienced significant increases in labour inputs per acre. These could be achieved by increases in labour services from a growing body of tenants, by hiring more *famuli*, or by substituting paid labour for labour services. The notion that labour services were grudgingly performed, and less effective than hired labour, is both intrinsically probable and substantiated with statistical evidence.[30]

A major source of improvement, dependent on these increases in labour inputs, was the modification of farming methods to increase the proportion of the arable that was actually cropped each year. In the late eleventh century, as we have seen, as much as a half or a third of the available ploughlands were commonly lying fallow in any one year in order to control weeds and to prevent exhaustion of the land by overcropping. This proportion could be reduced, if agrarian institutions allowed it, through an intensification of work on the land in weeding and manuring. Campbell's estimates suggest that though the total English arable acreage increased by only 31 per cent, the area under crops grew by 89 per cent between 1086 and 1300 (from 3.29 to 6.23 million acres).[31] This implies that the reduction of fallows was much more widespread than our direct evidence demonstrates, but it is difficult to think of a better way of explaining how the growing population of England was fed.

Continuing modification of the common fields of central England in the eleventh and twelfth centuries perhaps contributed to the intensification of land use, difficult though it is to document. Drawing together the lands of different occupiers into a common scheme of crop rotation and fallowing could improve the pasturing of livestock, and so allow land to be cultivated more frequently, and with more manure, without reducing its fertility. Some accounts of agrarian development assign prime importance to this development as the means by which a larger population could be fed. It is unfortunate that evidence for the development of common fields is so weakly linked to evidence relating to productivity; we cannot assess the contribution of agrarian reorganization to increased output of crops, or the extent to which any hypothesized improvement was durable. Yet the common-field areas were not those whose arable productivity increased most. It was once argued that gains in output were achieved by a secondary rationalization of common fields to convert two-field to three-field systems. Some communities, it was suggested, had first organized their lands into two common fields (cultivated and fallowed in alternate years) but then, under pressure of rising demand, switched to a system of three fields that allowed each parcel of land to be sown two years in every three. There are a few known examples of this, as on Winchester Cathedral Priory's demesne at Stockton (Wiltshire) in the early fourteenth century, but evidence for such a switch is so rare that it is most unlikely to have been a frequent event.[32]

As has already been suggested, the midland common-field system locked many villagers into a system of arable farming that was detrimental in the long run to high productivity. The intensity of cultivation was difficult to regulate precisely when individual farmers had little control over how they could use their land. Yields per seed and yields per acre are not altogether reliable indicators of agricultural productivity, since neither measure takes into account all the factors of production needed to produce grain (the labour, the buildings, the livestock, the equipment), nor the frequency with which the soil was cropped, but they constitute a prima facie case for supposing that the midlands was an area of generally modest performance by the best European standards. Table 9.1 shows the yields on the demesnes of the bishopric of Winchester for ten successive years at the end of the thirteenth century. These figures conceal the wide differences in performance between different demesne farms on the estate, but they demonstrate well the variability of harvests from year to year and the considerable inroad that seedcorn made into annual production. Wheat repaid as much as four times the seed only twice in ten years, and barley only once; oats never even reached three times the

TABLE 9.1. *Crop yields per seed on the demesne manors of the bishopric of Winchester, ten consecutive years, 1282/3–1291/2*

	Wheat	Barley	Oats
1282/3	2.79	3.41	2.08
1283/4	3.62	3.60	1.99
1284/5	3.51	3.02	2.10
1285/6	3.51	3.14	1.91
1286/7	4.77	4.00	2.26
1287/8	4.18	3.82	2.34
1288/9	3.48	3.29	2.12
1289/90	3.16	2.90	2.47
1290/1	3.67	2.69	2.16
1291/2	3.65	2.92	1.97

Source: D. L. Farmer, 'Prices and Wages', in H. E. Hallam (ed.), *The Agrarian History of England and Wales*, ii: *1042–1350* (Cambridge, 1988), 796–7.

seed. This meant that to maintain a constant acreage the demesne officials had to set aside over a quarter of the wheat and barley harvest (after tithe) in most years and over a third of the oats. Winchester's performance was in this respect far from impressive, but these figures are representative of much of England, and they are based on the largest statistical sample available in any surviving source. Even some commercially advanced regions, like central Essex, used simple three-course rotations of wheat, oats, fallow, that were likely to lead to impoverishment of the soil in the absence of careful attention to detail.[33]

The regions of highest productivity were outside the common-field belt. The strongest concentration of highly productive farms was in eastern Norfolk. As in the midlands, development here depended upon a heavier commitment to providing the soil with manure, but it was achieved with a more flexible integration of arable and livestock husbandry than that of the midland system. Here the intensification of manuring and reduction of fallowing had already in the late thirteenth century been carried so far that on eleven demesnes for which there is detailed statistical evidence from before 1350 at least three-quarters of the land was under crops each year. This intensity of cultivation was accompanied by distinctive patterns of cropping. The proportion of the sown acreage under peas and beans was as high as 14 per cent, which is significant both because an extended cultivation of fodder crops implies intensified land use and because peas and beans were valuable for the continuing fertility of the soil. Leguminous crops are now known to restore nitrogen that cereal crops remove.[34] Another feature of east Norfolk husbandry was a trade in night soil from the towns, supplementing the manure available from farm animals. This local intensity of land use may be compared with that of the most productive agricultural regions of Europe at the time, in Flanders, the Paris region, and the more densely populated parts of northern Italy, all areas of high urban demand. It was the more remarkable because, despite the exceptional frequency of cropping on Norfolk demesnes, their yields compared very favourably with those from elsewhere in England (Table 9.2).

Norfolk husbandry was so remarkable, even by the standards of some neighbouring counties, that it raises the question why it did not spread more quickly to other parts of Britain, as a later development of Norfolk husbandry did in the eighteenth century. Similar intensity of land use elsewhere in Britain was confined, to the best of our knowledge, to eastern Kent and to the downland and coastal plain of Sussex.[35] Neither ignorance nor institutional conservatism are satisfactory explanations, since landlords who practised the most advanced techniques on their demesnes in eastern Norfolk did not do so elsewhere. Fertile soils, low transport costs, and an exceptionally reliable intensity of demand both regionally and over the North Sea were the chief reasons for the precocity of these advanced regions. It may be that the flexibility of the Norfolk field system should also be considered as an institutional reason for higher productivity, but it is not clear to what extent it was a cause or an effect of the sophistication of Norfolk husbandry.

Without appropriate soils and adequate manure supplies there were severe limits to the extent that productivity per acre could be increased. An inappropriately

TABLE 9.2. *Average gross yields per seed from the demesnes of the bishopric of Winchester (Wi), Westminster Abbey (We), and sample Norfolk manors (N)*

	Wheat			Barley			Oats		
	Wi	We	N	Wi	We	N	Wi	We	N
1225–1249	4.09	—	—	4.69	—	—	2.68	—	—
1250–1274	3.87	—	3.83	4.03	—	3.17	2.52	—	2.37
1275–1299	3.75	3.27	4.57	3.25	3.63	3.06	2.18	2.37	2.40

Source: B. M. S. Campbell, 'Land, Labour, Livestock, and Productivity Trends in English Seignorial Agriculture, 1208–1450', in id. and M. Overton (eds.), *Land, Labour and Livestock: Historical Studies in European Agricultural Productivity* (Manchester, 1991), 161.

intensive rotation could even lead to falling productivity. The increasing commercialization of cereals production could itself be detrimental to productivity if it led to essential nutrients, such as phosphorus, passing into crops and being sold at a distance instead of being recycled in the form of manure.[36] There are examples of land becoming impoverished by over-cropping or under-weeding, though it is uncertain how widespread or how permanent this was.[37] Worn-out soils were unable to sustain even a crop rotation with a year's fallow every two or three years. At Charing (Kent) a field called Oatfield was described in 1268 as having been long out of cultivation, being more suitable for growing broom and ferns than corn.[38]

It is unfortunate that the evidence is so poor relating to cereals output in Ireland, where the rate of growth between 1170 and 1300 was probably higher than in Britain. Traditions of arable cultivation were already well established by 1170. The cultivated area had increased between the sixth and the twelfth centuries to feed a growing population, and some trade in grain is implied by the urban developments of the east coast.[39] The Anglo-Norman expansion of cultivation, in response to internal urban growth and stronger links to external markets, did not depend primarily on changes in farming methods brought by immigrant settlers; on the de Burgh manors of Kilsheelan and Kilfeakle (Co. Tipperary) in 1243 a preponderantly arable economy was associated with a native Irish population.[40] The introduction of horse-ploughing seems to be associated with Anglo-Norman settlement, but its advantages for arable productivity are very uncertain; the switch from the use of oxen to the use of horses that was gradually taking place in Britain is reckoned to have benefited marketing costs rather than arable productivity.[41] Nevertheless, the expanding cultivation of cereals implied a massive restructuring of the use and occupation of land.

Subsistence or Commercial Enterprise?

The discussion of urban growth and commercial development in earlier chapters implies that commercial stimuli account in part for the increasing production of grain. Yet that cannot be the whole of the story. The institutional forms of arable husbandry in the twelfth and thirteenth centuries were by no means all conducive to commercial enterprise. Farming enterprises ranged all the way from tiny peasant holdings that could not even feed the family that occupied them to the vast demesnes of major landlords that could produce surpluses far beyond the needs of those who worked their land. Even in southern England, the land was very imperfectly distributed for highly commercialized cereals production. Demesne lands occupied only about 32 per cent of the arable in those parts of the midlands for which there is evidence in the Hundred Rolls (Table 9.3). Nor was this land cultivated wholly with an eye to the market; demesnes in the London region

TABLE 9.3. *Demesne, villein, and free land in parts of the English midlands, 1279*

	Size of sample (acres)	Demesne (%)	Villein land (%)	Free holdings (%)
Huntingdonshire	94,272	32	47	21
Cambridgeshire	63,728	36	29	33
Bedfordshire	24,102	33	21	46
Buckinghamshire	41,133	35	35	32
Oxfordshire	237,125	31	42	26
Warwickshire	86,696	28	44	27
All six counties	547,057	32	40	28

Source: E. A. Kosminsky, *Studies in the Agrarian History of England in the Thirteenth Century*, ed. R. H. Hilton, trans. R. Kisch (Oxford, 1956), 90–1.

around 1300 sold about 36 per cent, by value, of the grain grown on their lands, net of tithes, to judge from the evidence of surviving manorial accounts.[42] Many of the tenant farmers, who occupied the remaining 68 per cent of the arable, sold some grain. Yet even a relatively well-off tenant with a standard customary holding of 30 acres had to devote much of his produce to household needs and seed corn for the following year, especially in years of bad harvest, or on farms supporting large families. Table 9.4 shows how a Gloucestershire couple occupying a 30-acre virgate

TABLE 9.4. *Hypothetical disposal of crops from a Gloucestershire virgate, 1299–1300 (quarters and bushels)*

	Wheat	Barley	Peas	Oats
Parish tithe	0q. 5b.	2q. 2b.	0q. 1b.	0q. 1b.
Seedcorn	1q. 6b.	5q. 0b.	0q. 6b.	0q. 3b.
Food corn	2q. 2b.	4q. 0b.	0	0q. 3b.
Drink corn	0	3q. 0b.	0	0
Mill toll	0q. 1b.	0q. 2b.	0	0
Sales	1q. 4b.	7q. 6b.	1q. 0b.	0q. 2b.
Total	6q. 2b.	22q. 2b.	1q. 7b.	1q. 1b.

Note: 1 quarter = 8 bushels = 32 pecks = 64 gallons (equivalent to about 3 hectolitres). Grain was measured by volume (not by weight).

Source: C. Dyer, *Standards of Living in the Later Middle Ages: Social Change in England, c.1200–1520* (Cambridge, 1989), 113, with tithe calculated.

with three children might have expected to dispose of the grain they grew in the year 1299–1300 if they farmed according to a three-course rotation of crops. The grain sold would represent about 36 per cent of the total value (net of tithes) at the prices obtaining in 1300. Many tenants would not voluntarily have disposed of such a large proportion of their crop.

This reference to tithes serves as a reminder that in addition to grain that producers sold to raise cash, another major source was the tithecorn that producers surrendered annually to the rector of their parish church. This grain, assessed at a tenth of each producer's output, was normally levied in the fields by the rector's officers before the harvested crops were stowed in barns. Between 1050 and 1300 many rectories, with the right to collect tithes, were transferred into the hands of abbeys, priories, and colleges; these institutions then became liable to appoint parish priests, paying fixed stipends. The way in which tithe grain was used depended very much on the corporate needs of the institution in question. Sometimes it was fed to the owners' household. However, wherever rectories remained unappropriated by religious houses, and wherever rectories were remote from the owners' household, there was a strong probability that most or all of the tithe grain would be marketed. Sometimes this took the form of direct sales by the owner, but on other occasions the owner leased the tithes to a local agent who would sell them to make his profit. It is likely that over half of all grain tithes were marketed and that the crops of small farmers contributed universally to market supply by this involuntary route.

Commercial production of grain was of considerable importance for development in England. Though always absolutely smaller than output for subsistence, it probably increased more rapidly than output for consumption, and in parts of the kingdom influenced decision taking to the point that even the extent of subsistence farming was governed by commercial considerations. Widely scattered estates had to balance the advantages of self-sufficiency against the costs of transporting grain around the countryside, and in many circumstances it was more advantageous to sell the produce of more remote demesnes, even if this meant that the household had to buy supplies from sources nearer at hand.[43] Ramsey Abbey combined a more flexible system of food-rents from its manors with a closer orientation of the demesne farms to production for the market.[44] The monks of Canterbury Cathedral Priory in the last decade of the thirteenth century were willing to allow large sums of grain to be sold from their demesnes even when this meant that the demesnes in question were unable to fulfil their produce quotas.[45] Economic rationality was carried on some estates to the point that market opportunities dominated the whole policy of estate administration. As early as 1208 sales of grain were a major component of the cash income of the bishop of Winchester. In 1300 the bishop sold nearly three-quarters of the wheat grown on his demesnes, two-thirds of the rye, two-fifths of the barley, and even one-third of the oats.[46] Demesne cultivation in England reached its medieval peak between 1240 and 1300, as high profits from grain cultivation encouraged landlords to expand their commercial operations. Some abbeys, like Ramsey, Peterborough, and Thorney, purchased land for the purpose, often from tenants.[47] Individual demesnes were rarely more than a few hundred acres; on Peterborough estates in 1301 the acreage of demesne under crop averaged 234 acres on 21 manors, and the largest demesne had only 560 sown acres.[48] But looked at in terms of ownership and estate management there were some enormous concentrations of enterprise. By 1299 the bishop of Worcester had 6,969 acres of arable land in demesne, so presumably about 4,500 acres under crops in any one year.[49] Peterborough Abbey had about 5,437 acres under crops in 1301.[50] The archbishop of Canterbury had all told nearly 7,000 acres under crops in 1274.[51] By 1322 the monks of Christchurch, Canterbury, had 8,373 acres of demesne land under crops in Kent, Surrey, and Essex, and this is chiefly attributable to the attractions of production for sale, mostly in local markets.[52] This dependence on the market encouraged responsiveness to price changes, and a willingness to vary production plans accordingly.[53] To estimate the proportion of grain sold based on the evidence from the south-eastern counties of England we need to take all these institutional considerations into account. If grain output was proportionate to the share of the arable occupied by different groups, and if the proportion of output sold, net of tithes, was as we have suggested, then perhaps 6–8 per cent of all grain harvested (by value) was sold by rectories, about 12 per cent by demesnes, 12–20 per cent by the wealthier peasants, and some small proportion by smallholders. In total this suggests that 30–40 per cent of all grain harvested in this part of England was sold.[54]

For all England, however, the proportion of grain sold was no doubt smaller than this, since urban demand was higher in the London region than elsewhere. The proportion was smaller still for Britain as a whole. The surviving evidence of Scottish estates is unfortunately too imperfect to assess the extent to which produce was sold. Undoubtedly some of what the Scottish crown received in conveth and cain was marketed. The sheriff of Edinburgh in 1263 sold almost all the grain he received—60 chalders of wheat, 5 chalders of oatmeal, 65 chalders of malt, and 140 chalders of 'provender' (presumably oats).[55] But the slight development of demesne farming, and the smaller number of marketing centres, implies an arable husbandry much more dependent on subsistence. If the urban proportion in Wales, Scotland, and Ireland was appreciably below that of England, the same will be true of the commitment of farmers there to production for the market, and it seems unlikely that more than 5–10 per cent of grain output was sold outside south-eastern England and the English midlands.

In short, then, the commercial production of grain expanded more rapidly than subsistence farming in much of England, where it had wide-ranging implications for decision taking and farming methods throughout the agrarian system. In most of Britain, however, it is doubtful whether such commercialization was under way by 1300. The high proportion of produce that did not reach the market was not the result of non-commercial attitudes amongst grain producers. Rather, it reflected the absence of profit opportunities, given the narrowness of the market and high transport costs. Even in more urbanized regions it was often the result of rational calculations on the part of estate managers, who found it cheaper to use their own grain to feed a large household than to sell from their estates and buy in produce from elsewhere. A high level of self-sufficiency was an inevitable feature of an agrarian structure dominated by minute peasant farms with little surplus to dispose of. It was also attributable in part to agrarian techniques that held grain yields very low and therefore required a large proportion of each year's grain to be retained for seed.

NOTES

1. J. A. Raftis, *The Estates of Ramsey Abbey* (Toronto, 1957), 65–6.

2. *Cartularium Monasterii de Rameseia*, ed. W. H. Hart and P. A. Lyons, 3 vols., Rolls Ser. 79 (1884–93), iii. 301–4; Raftis, *Estates*, 70–2; E. Miller and J. Hatcher, *Medieval England: Rural Society and Economic Change, 1086–1348* (1978), 34.

3. E. King, *Peterborough Abbey, 1086–1310: A Study in the Land Market* (Cambridge, 1973), 72, 81.

4. T. John, 'Population Change in Medieval Warwickshire: Domesday Book to the Hundred Rolls of 1279–1280', *Local Population Studies*, 59 (1997), 41–53.

5. H. E. Hallam, *Settlement and Society: A Study of the Early Agrarian History of South Lincolnshire* (Cambridge, 1965), 7–9, 19–20.

6. S. Rippon, *The Severn Estuary: Landscape Evolution and Wetland Reclamation* (1997), 186–239; R. A. L. Smith, *Canterbury Cathedral Priory: A Study in Monastic Administration* (Cambridge, 1943), 166–89.

7. J. Gilbert, 'The Monastic Record of a Border Landscape 1136 to 1236', *Scottish Geographical Magazine*, 99 (1983), 7, 10–11.

8. N. Mayhew, 'Alexander III—A Silver Age?', in N. H. Reid (ed.), *Scotland in the Reign of Alexander III* (Edinburgh, 1990), 58.

9. *Regesta Regum Scottorum*, i: *The Acts of Malcolm IV*, ed. G. W. S. Barrow (Edinburgh, 1960), no. 284, p. 281; *Regesta Regum Scottorum*, ii: *The Acts of William I*, ed. G. W. S. Barrow (Edinburgh, 1971), no. 215, pp. 263–4.

10. *Registrum Episcopatus Moraviensis*, ed. C. Innes, Bannatyne Club, 58 (Edinburgh, 1837), no. 153, p. 169.

11. *The Exchequer Rolls of Scotland*, ed. J. Stuart, G. Burnett, and others, 23 vols. (Edinburgh, 1878–1908), i. 21, 32.

12. e.g. *Liber S. Marie de Calchou*, ed. C. Innes, 2 vols, Bannatyne Club, 82 (Edinburgh, 1846), i, no. 183, p. 151.

13. A. A. M. Duncan, *Scotland: The Making of the Kingdom* (Edinburgh, 1989), 319–20.

14. *Liber S. Marie de Calchou*, ii, no. 362 (pp. 289–90), confirmed by nos. 361 (pp. 288–9) and 363 (pp. 291–2).

15. D. H. Williams, *The Welsh Cistercians: Aspects of their Economic History* (Pontypool, 1970), 47–51.

16. W. Linnard, *Welsh Woods and Forests: A History* (Llandysul, 2000), 28–33.

17. T. J. Pierce. *Medieval Welsh Society: Selected Essays* (Cardiff, 1972), 88–9; G. R. J. Jones, 'Some Medieval Rural Settlements in North Wales', *Transactions and Papers of the Institute of British Geographers*, 19 (1954 for 1953), 51–64; id., 'The Distribution of Medieval Settlement in Anglesey', *Transactions of Anglesey Antiquarian Society* (1955), 27–96; id., 'Rural Settlement in Anglesey', in S. R. Eyre and G. R. J. Jones (eds.), *Geography as Human Ecology: Methodology by Example* (1966), 203–4; id., 'Post-Roman Wales', in H. P. R. Finberg (ed.), *The Agrarian History of England and Wales*, i(2): *A.D. 43–1042* (Cambridge, 1972), 341, 351.

18. C. A. Empey, 'The Norman Period, 1185–1500', in W. Nolan (ed.), *Tipperary, History and Society: Interdisciplinary Essays on the History of an Irish County* (Dublin, 1985), 80; A. P. Smyth, *Celtic Leinster: Towards a Historical Geography of Early Irish Civilization A.D. 500–1600* (Blackrock, 1982), 104–8.

19. J. Bradley, 'The Medieval Boroughs of County Dublin', in C. Manning (ed.), *Dublin and beyond the Pale: Studies in Honour of Patrick Healy* (Wicklow, 1998), 137–8.

20. B. Colfer, 'Anglo-Norman Settlement in County Wexford', in K. Whelan and W. Nolan (eds.), *Wexford History and Society: Interdisciplinary Essays on the History of an Irish County* (Dublin, c.1987), 79.

21. *Irish Monastic and Episcopal Deeds, A.D. 1200–1600*, ed. N. B. White (Dublin, 1936), 215.

22. R. E. Glasscock, 'Land and People, c.1300', in A. Cosgrove (ed.), *A New History of Ireland*, ii: *Medieval Ireland, 1169–1534* (Oxford, 1987), 212. The multiplier for grain requirements is from B. M. S. Campbell, J. A. Galloway, D. Keene, and M. Murphy, *A Medieval Capital and its Grain Supply: Agrarian Production and Distribution in the London Region c.1300* (1993), 35.

23. A. Simms, 'Core and Periphery in Medieval Europe: The Irish Experience in a Wider Context', in W. J. Smyth and K. Whelan (eds.), *Common Ground: Essays on the Historical Geography of Ireland Presented to T. Jones Hughes* (Cork, 1988), 35; H. Jäger, 'Land-Use in Medieval Ireland', *Irish Economic and Social History*, 10 (1983), 51–65; C. A. Empey, 'Medieval Knocktopher: A Study in Manorial Settlement', *Old Kilkenny Review*, new ser. 2 (1979–83), 218–19; id., 'Norman Period', 80; id., 'The Anglo-Norman Settlement in the Cantred of Eliogarty', in J. Bradley (ed.), *Settlement and Society in Medieval Ireland: Studies Presented to F. X. Martin, OSA* (Kilkenny, 1988), 218–19; M. S. Hagger, *The Fortunes of a Norman Family: The de Verduns in England, Ireland and Wales, 1066–1316* (Dublin, 2001), 150.

24. Hallam, *Settlement and Society*, 194–5.

25. B. M. S. Campbell, *English Seigniorial Agriculture, 1250–1450* (Cambridge, 2000), 400, and see above (Ch. 4).

26. D. A. Davidson and I. A. Simpson, 'Soils and Landscape History: Case Studies from the Northern Isles of Scotland', in S. Foster and T. C. Smout (eds.), *The History of Soils and Field Systems* (Aberdeen, 1994), 68–9.

27. Smith, *Canterbury Cathedral Priory*, 135–8.
28. F. Kelly, *Early Irish Farming* (Dublin, 2000), 230.
29. B. M. S. Campbell, 'Agricultural Progress in Medieval England: Some Evidence from Eastern Norfolk', *Economic History Review*, 2nd ser. 36 (1983), 39–41.
30. D. Stone, 'The Productivity of Hired and Customary Labour: Evidence from Wisbech Barton in the Fourteenth Century', *Economic History Review*, 50 (1997), 640–56.
31. Campbell, *English Seigniorial Agriculture*, 400.
32. H. S. A. Fox, 'The Alleged Transformation from Two-Field to Three-Field Systems in Medieval England', *Economic History Review*, 2nd ser. 39 (1986), 526–48; B. Harrison, 'Field Systems and Demesne Farming on the Wiltshire Estates of Saint Swithun's Priory, Winchester, 1248–1340', *Agricultural History Review*, 43 (1995), 11.
33. R. H. Britnell, 'Agriculture in a Region of Ancient Enclosure, 1185–1500', *Nottingham Medieval Studies*, 27 (1983), 46–9.
34. Campbell, 'Agricultural Progress', 29, 33.
35. P. F. Brandon, 'Farming Techniques: South-Eastern England', in H. E. Hallam (ed.), *The Agrarian History of England and Wales*, ii: *1042–1350* (Cambridge, 1988), 317–23; Campbell and others, *Medieval Capital*, 126, 135–8, 140–1, 179.
36. E. I. Newman and P. D. A. Harvey, 'Did Soil Fertility Decline in Medieval English Farms? Evidence from Cuxham, Oxfordshire', *Agricultural History Review*, 45 (1997), 119–36.
37. Miller and Hatcher, *Medieval England: Rural Society*, 216–17; W. Harwood Long, 'The Low Yields of Corn in Medieval England', *Economic History Review*, 32 (1979), 459–69.
38. Brandon, 'Farming Techniques: South-Eastern England', 312–13.
39. K. Down, 'Colonial Society and Economy in the High Middle Ages', in A. Cosgrove (ed.), *A New History of Ireland*, ii: *Medieval Ireland 1169–1534* (Oxford, 1987), 440–1; V. A. Hall, 'The Documentary and Pollen Analytical Record of the Vegetational History of the Irish Landscape AD 200–1650', *Peritia*, 14 (2000), 354, 368.
40. M. Hennessy, 'Manorial Organisation in Early Thirteenth-Century Tipperary', *Irish Geography*, 29 (1996), 116, 123–4.
41. Duncan, *Scotland*, 310–11; Kelly, *Early Irish Farming*, 95; J. Langdon, *Horses, Oxen and Technological Innovation: The Use of Draught Animals in English Farming from 1066–1500* (Cambridge, 1986), 265–72.
42. Calculated from B. M. S. Campbell, 'Measuring the Commercialisation of Seigneurial Agriculture, c.1300', in R. H. Britnell and B. M. S. Campbell (eds.), *A Commercialising Economy: England 1086 to c.1300* (Manchester, 1995), 158–60.
43. Smith, *Canterbury Cathedral Priory*, 132.
44. Raftis, *Estates*, 114–15, 178–9.
45. Smith, *Canterbury Cathedral Priory*, 132–3.
46. Miller and Hatcher, *Medieval England: Rural Society*, 225.
47. Raftis, *Estates*, 109–12; King, *Peterborough Abbey*, 66–9; S. Raban, *The Estates of Thorney and Crowland: A Study in Medieval Monastic Land Tenure* (Cambridge, 1977), 62.
48. King, *Peterborough Abbey*, 151.
49. C. Dyer, *Lords and Peasants in a Changing Society: The Estates of the Bishopric of Worcester, 680–1540* (Cambridge, 1980), 67.

50. King, *Peterborough Abbey*, 151.

51. Miller and Hatcher, *Medieval England: Rural Society*, 182.

52. Smith, *Canterbury Cathedral Priory*, 132–3, 141–2.

53. D. Stone, 'Medieval Farm Management and Technological Mentalities: Hinderclay before the Black Death', *Economic History Review*, 54 (2001), 612–38.

54. R. H. Britnell, 'Urban Demand in the English Economy, 1300–1600', in J. A. Galloway (ed.), *Trade, Urban Hinterlands and Market Integration c.1300–1600* (2000), 5.

55. *Exchequer Rolls of Scotland*, i. 25.

FURTHER READING

Andrews, D. D. (ed.), *Cressing Temple: A Templar and Hospitaller Manor in Essex* (Chelmsford, 1993).

Astill, G., and Grant, A. (eds.), *The Countryside of Medieval England* (Oxford, 1988).

Ault, W. O., *Open-Field Farming in Medieval England* (1972).

Bailey, M., 'The Concept of the Margin in Medieval English Economy', *Economic History Review*, 2nd ser. 42 (1989).

—— *A Marginal Economy? East Anglian Breckland in the Later Middle Ages* (Cambridge, 1989).

Baker, A. R. H., and Butlin, R. A. (eds.), *Studies of Field Systems in the British Isles* (Cambridge, 1973).

Biddick, K., 'Missing Links: Taxable Wealth, Markets and Stratification among Medieval English Peasants', *Journal of Interdisciplinary History*, 18 (1987).

Campbell, B. M. S., 'Agricultural Progress in Medieval England: Some Evidence from Eastern Norfolk', *Economic History Review*, 2nd ser. 36 (1983).

—— 'The Diffusion of Vetches in Medieval England', *Economic History Review*, 2nd ser. 41 (1988).

—— *English Seigniorial Agriculture, 1250–1450* (Cambridge, 2000).

—— 'Land, Labour, Livestock, and Productivity Trends in English Seigniorial Agriculture, 1208–1450', in id. and M. Overton (eds.), *Land, Labour and Livestock: Historical Studies in European Agricultural Productivity* (Manchester, 1991).

—— 'Measuring the Commercialisation of Seigneurial Agriculture, c.1300', in R. H. Britnell and B. M. S. Campbell (eds.), *A Commercialising Economy: England 1086 to c.1300* (Manchester, 1995).

—— Galloway, J. A., Keene, D., and Murphy, M., *A Medieval Capital and its Grain Supply: Agrarian Production and Distribution in the London Region c.1300* (1993).

Down, K., 'Colonial Society and Economy in the High Middle Ages', in A. Cosgrove (ed.), *A New History of Ireland*, ii: *Medieval Ireland, 1169–1534* (Oxford, 1987).

Duncan, A. A. M, *Scotland: The Making of the Kingdom* (Edinburgh, 1989).

Dyer, C., *Lords and Peasants in a Changing Society: The Estates of the Bishopric of Worcester, 680–1540* (Cambridge, 1980).

Farmer, D. L., 'Grain Yields on Westminster Abbey Manors, 1271–1410', *Canadian Journal of History*, 18 (1983).

—— 'Grain Yields on Winchester Manors in the Later Middle Ages', *Economic History Review*, 2nd ser. 30 (1977).

—— 'Marketing the Produce of the Countryside, 1200–1500', in E. Miller (ed.), *The Agrarian History of England*, iii: *1348–1500* (Cambridge, 1991).

Fox, H. S. A., 'The Alleged Transformation from Two-Field to Three-Field Systems in Medieval England', *Economic History Review*, 2nd ser. 39 (1986).

Glasscock, R. E., 'Land and People, c.1300', in A. Cosgrove (ed.), *A New History of Ireland*, ii: *Medieval Ireland, 1169–1534* (Oxford, 1987).

Hallam, H. E. (ed.), *The Agrarian History of England and Wales*, ii: *1042–1350* (Cambridge, 1988).

—— *Settlement and Society: A Study of the Early Agrarian History of South Lincolnshire* (Cambridge, 1965).

Harrison, B., 'Field Systems and Demesne Farming on the Wiltshire Estates of Saint Swithun's Priory, Winchester, 1248–1340', *Agricultural History Review*, 43 (1995).

Harvey, P. D. A., *A Medieval Oxfordshire Village: Cuxham, 1240 to 1400* (Oxford, 1965).

Harwood Long, W., 'The Low Yields of Corn in Medieval England', *Economic History Review*, 32 (1979).

Kelly, F., *Early Irish Farming* (Dublin, 2000).

Kershaw, I., *Bolton Priory: The Economy of a Northern Monastery, 1286–1325* (1973).

King, E., *Peterborough Abbey, 1086–1310: A Study in the Land Market* (Cambridge, 1973).

Kosminsky, E. A., *Studies in the Agrarian History of England in the Thirteenth Century*, ed. R. H. Hilton, trans. R. Kisch (Oxford, 1956).

Langdon, J., *Horses, Oxen and Technological Innovation: The Use of Draught Animals in English Farming from 1066 to 1500* (Cambridge, 1986).

Mate, M., 'Profit and Productivity on the Estates of Isabella de Forz (1260–92)', *Economic History Review*, 2nd ser. 33 (1980).

Miller, E., 'Farming in Northern England during the Eleventh and Twelfth Centuries', *Northern History*, 11 (1976).

—— and Hatcher, J., *Medieval England: Rural Society and Economic Change, 1086–1348* (1978).

Newman, E. I., and Harvey, P. D. A., 'Did Soil Fertility Decline in Medieval English Farms? Evidence from Cuxham, Oxfordshire', *Agricultural History Review*, 45 (1997).

Otway-Ruthven, A. J., 'The Organization of Anglo-Irish Agriculture in the Middle Ages', *Journal of the Royal Society of Antiquaries of Ireland*, 81 (1951).

Postan, M. M., 'Medieval Agrarian Society in its Prime: England', in id. (ed.), *The Cambridge Economic History of Europe*, i: *The Agrarian Life of the Middle Ages*, 2nd edn. (Cambridge, 1966).

Postles, D., 'Markets for Rural Produce in Oxfordshire, 1086–1350', *Midland History*, 12 (1987).

Raftis, J. A., *The Estates of Ramsey Abbey* (Toronto, 1957).

Roden, D., 'Demesne Farming in the Chiltern Hills', *Agricultural History Review*, 17 (1969).

Smith, R. A. L., *Canterbury Cathedral Priory: A Study in Monastic Administration* (Cambridge, 1943).

Stern, D. V., *A Hertfordshire Demesne: Profits, Productivity and Weather*, ed. C. Thornton (Hatfield, 2000).

Stone, D., 'Medieval Farm Management and Technological Mentalities: Hinderclay before the Black Death', *Economic History Review*, 54 (2001).

Stone, D., 'The Productivity of Hired and Customary Labour: Evidence from Wisbech Barton in the Fourteenth Century', *Economic History Review*, 50 (1997).

Thornton, C., 'The Determinants of Land Productivity on the Bishop of Winchester's Demesne of Rimpton, 1208–1403', in B. M. S. Campbell and M. Overton (eds.), *Land, Labour and Livestock: Historical Studies in European Agricultural Productivity* (Manchester, 1991).

—— 'The Level of Arable Productivity on the Bishop of Winchester's Manor of Taunton, 1283–1348', in R. H. Britnell (ed.), *The Winchester Pipe Rolls and Medieval English Society* (Woodbridge, 2003).

Titow, J. Z., 'Evidence of Weather in the Account Rolls of the Bishopric of Winchester, 1209–1350', *Economic History Review*, 2nd ser. 12 (1960).

—— *Winchester Yields: A Study in Medieval Agricultural Productivity* (Cambridge, 1972).

....

CHAPTER 10

Pasture Husbandry

The history of crop husbandry has long dominated the discussion about agrarian trends in the period 1050–1300, partly because surviving estate records from the thirteenth century onwards are more numerous from predominantly arable regions of Britain. In addition, the history of arable farming is more easily related to concerns about the demand for food and the history of population, and has contributed more to discussions about the relationship between population and resources. In debates about standards of living amongst the peasantry, pasture farming has finished up as a matter of residual interest, on the assumption that providing families with bread came first, and that only resources left over could be applied to supplying meat, dairy produce, or wool. In one influential formulation, the history of the period 1050–1300 was told as the steady encroachment of arable on to pasture lands as the demand for food increased, implying a progressive undermining of Britain's capacity to produce pastoral products. If, as we have seen, many parts of England were already heavily committed to arable husbandry in 1086, with only residual reserves of pasture and woodland, then it is reasonable to argue that further expansion of the ploughland restricted the possibility of expanding pastoral activities.

However, there are many reasons for emphasizing not only the extent but also the growth of pastoral husbandry, particularly in a study of Britain as a whole. A revival of interest in pasture farming in its own right in recent years has accompanied increasing interest in commerce as a source of economic development, and in particular of the ways in which commercial activity could contribute to peasant economies. As soon as commercial inducements are allowed to have been operating, amongst both manorial lords and peasant farmers who had more land than they needed for subsistence, the status of pasture farming becomes more open to question. It is also noteworthy that dairy products were much more prominent in the diet of some parts of Britain than they were in the much-studied counties of south-eastern and midland England, and that they are not irrelevant to the food supply of a growing population.

Extensive or Intensive Growth?

Increases in the number of animals can be directly attested from the records of some larger estates. The sheep flocks of Peterborough Abbey increased from an estimated 1,701 in 1125 to 2,297 in 1211 and 4,480 in 1300–1.[1] Ramsey Abbey manors generally increased their livestock numbers between the twelfth century and the end of the thirteenth: across four manors in the eastern fenlands the number of cows increased by 192 per cent and the number of ewes by 159 per cent (Table 10.1). Even when the demand for cereals was at its peak in the late thirteenth century, efforts were still being made to increase the size of flocks and herds. The abbot of Ely increased livestock numbers in 1277 as a matter of estate policy.[2] Henry of Eastry, prior of Canterbury Cathedral Priory, greatly expanded sheep farming on the priory estates from 1285.[3] These isolated examples must represent a much wider expansive tendency, even if statistical evidence of the magnitude and chronology of change is unavailable. This argument looks inevitable in the case of working beasts, oxen, and horses, which were required to work the enlarged area of arable land. It seems inevitable, too, with the number of sheep. It is difficult to say what was happening to the internal demand for wool, leather, meat, and dairy produce, though some increase in domestic demand surely accompanied the rising number of people requiring to be clothed and fed. The history of the wool trade, meanwhile, implies that the number of fleeces being exported rose through the period, as we saw when discussing British exports in Chapter 6. So far from declining as the arable acreage increased, sheep flocks, like wool exports, peaked in the first decade of the fourteenth century.

Some growth in pastoral farming was undoubtedly achieved, as in the case of arable farming, by extensive means—that is, by using more land. This could mean putting livestock on moorland that had never been stocked before, though in this instance it would be difficult to distinguish between genuinely 'new' areas of natural pasture and areas that had merely been lightly exploited in the past. The most unambiguous examples of extended pastoral land are those of land

TABLE 10.1. *Increasing livestock numbers on Ramsey Abbey's eastern fenland manors*

	Brancaster		Wimbotsham		Hilgay		Ringstead	
	c.1200	1303	c.1200	1303	c.1200	1303	c.1200	1303
Cows	7	16	7	11	6	33	5	13
Ewes	25	88	19	31	11	41	44	96

Source: J. A. Raftis, *The Estates of Ramsey Abbey* (Toronto, 1957), 117.

reclaimed from wetland by draining. Reclamation was often for meadow or pasture rather than for crops. When the men of Moulton, Weston, and Spalding reclaimed their fens about 1076, according to a later writer, 'some of them tilled their portions, some kept them for hay, and others, as before, allowed theirs to lie as privately occupied pasture for their beasts'. As a result of these and later activities there were growing fenland resources for pastoral husbandry.[4] Fenlands that were valued only for fish in 1086 were converted to pasture lands by Ramsey Abbey and its neighbours in the twelfth and thirteenth centuries, and villagers' intercommoning rights there were more intensively used and more vehemently defended or contested.[5] Some moorlands were also developed as improved pasture rather than as arable. Waste north of the Tweed was taken into cultivation by the abbeys of Melrose and Dryburgh to be used partly as arable, but also as pasture for cattle, sheep, horses, and pigs. The monks created specialized dairy farms on higher forest ground at Colmslie, Buckholm, and Whitelee.[6]

For animal, as for arable husbandry, expanding output was also heavily dependent upon the more intensive use of already committed resources. This could take several forms. It might be a case, as on lightly used moorland, of simply increasing the number of beasts that a given area was required to sustain. It might take the form of increasing the number of beasts that grazed on common fields when they lay fallow, or in the period following the taking-in of cereal crops. It might, further, involve more investment in animal care through improved herding and closer attention to techniques of feeding, breeding, and medical care. These different degrees of intensification were regionally variable, depending on the resources of available natural pasture, the social organization of arable fields, and the extent to which profit levels justified high investment in herding and stock management.

The presence of extensive moor or heath, either attached to the territory of a particular township or commoned between several, was pivotal to many local economies. They were a normal feature of agriculture in regions where there is barely a trace of them today, as in Scotland which has no surviving common land. The density of occupation in surrounding arable areas often meant that the use of natural pasture was shared or contested by a number of different settlements with common rights. A common moor, used by families from different settlements, was a normal component of the 'shire' system of lordship in Scotland and northern England. The Shire Moor of Tynemouth (Northumberland) was the moor for the men of Tynemouthshire.[7] About 1150 David I gave May Priory 'common pasture in the shire of Kellie and in the shire of Crail',[8] a grant that would have been unintelligible in the absence of commons belonging to the shire as such. Common rights on the Weald were also a regular feature of the lathes of

Kent.[9] Similar intercommoning rights were to be observed in many parts of England even where no shire system was in evidence, especially where the possibility of arable farming was ruled out by extensive infertile heath or fenland. An early recorded example is the great common pasture at the centre of Colneis Hundred, Suffolk, which according to Domesday Book was common to all the men of the hundred.[10] Tiptree Heath (Essex) was formerly inter-commoned by free tenants of at least eight townships.[11] In the Fenlands of Lincolnshire and western Norfolk such intercommoning between villages was a normal feature of the rural economy.[12] Commons of this sort were available every year, since they were never ploughed. They represented a weak integration of arable and pasture husbandry, since any dung dropped by animals there was wasted as manure for the fields.

It was difficult to control the number of animals placed on such commons, and an increased intensity of use was probably universal. In some instances there was pressure on resources by the thirteenth century. In the course of the commercial expansion of pasture farming the interests of larger producers often collided with those of small farmers when land was in short supply, either because there was competition for pasture resources or because there were disputes about how land should be used. In Scotland, a supposed assize of William I from 1209, but perhaps spurious, required earls, barons, and freeholders to live as 'lords of lands, rents, and farms, and not as husbandmen or shepherds, despoiling their lordships and the country with a multitude of sheep and beasts, and bringing poverty and destruction upon God's people'.[13] There are numerous examples of disputes over such matters. Pressure on pasture sources on the Scottish borders is illustrated by twelfth-century agreements over pasture rights between Melrose Abbey and its neighbours. A dispute over pasture with the men of Wedale in the Valley of Gala Water has been interpreted as a challenge by the abbey to the use of shielings in the hills.[14] Dore Abbey's pasture rights in Cantrefselyf in the Welsh Marches were challenged by the monks of Strata Florida and by the lords neighbouring lay estates, even after a written agreement of 1252.[15] In some instances, especially where the rights of powerful landlords were concerned, the expansion of commercial sheep farming led to the formal partitioning of pastures and the recording of new boundaries between townships or estates. An agreement between Scone Abbey and Coupar Angus Abbey over the boundaries of 'Clenkatyn' and 'Drumyn' (both unidentified) can be interpreted in this way.[16]

In areas where natural pastures were very extensive some form of transhumance was a likely form of flock management, implying the seasonal migration of herdsmen, their families, and their livestock into summer pastures. Scotland and northern England shared a tradition retrospectively described by William Marshall in 1794:

Formerly, it was a practice, common, I believe, to the Central Highlands, to drive cows and other stock to distant SHEELINGS, or hill pastures; where they were kept during six or seven weeks in the summer months. Within the memory of many men now living, the environs of Loch Tay were deserted in that interval.[17]

The widespread Scots and northern English place-name elements shieling, shiel, or shield (from Old English 'scela') and scale (from West Scandinavian 'skali', meaning a hut) show both how general this practice was in the uplands. Such shielings comprised both pasture for the animals and huts where herdsmen and their families would live temporarily. In Scotland the practice of transhumance of this kind is indicated both by place names and by parish boundaries that stretch back into the hills from settlements on lower ground. A good example is the parishes on the southern edge of the Lammermuir Hills. There are also early charter references to this practice. David I of Scotland gave to Walter of Ryedale, probably in the early 1150s, 'the shielings that are to the west of Riccalton' in Oxnam (Roxburghshire), and about the same time he gave the shielings of Fornighty in Ardclach (Nairnshire) to the Benedictine priory of Urquhart.[18] Just north of the English border, a number of grants of shielings were made to Kelso Abbey in the later twelfth century, including some demonstrating that these were properties with demarcated boundaries, some of them subject to the exclusive use of landlords, others assigned to groups of small farmers. 'Bothkillscheles', given to the monks by Cospatrick, earl of Dunbar, dating from before 1159, was described later in the century as having bounds

From the springhead of 'Kaldewelle' down as far as the watercourse into which that spring runs, and from that watercourse until the stream falls into 'Bothkil', and from there until 'Bothkil' falls into 'Witheddre', and afterwards from 'Witheddre' to the highway that goes past 'Sperceldoun', and along that road back to the spring of 'Kaldewelle' and the common pasture between them and the shielings of my men of 'Pinkerdun'.[19]

The seasonal nature of these shielings is sometimes explicit, as when in 1199 Humphrey de Berkeley gave a shieling to Arbroath Abbey, in an upland part of his estates, to be used each year between Easter and the feast of All Saints.[20] In Cumbria, too, a shieling tradition was well established by the mid-thirteenth century. There are documented references to shielings high up in Longsleddale from 1246, and in the area of Martindale from the 1260s and 1270s. Some shielings were closer to the parent settlement, and involved less seasonal displacement of population; these were sometimes converted at an early date to permanent settlements, like Deanscales, which was originally a shieling attached to the Cumberland parish of Dean.[21] The practice of transhumance was common in some form to all the linguistic divisions of Britain, and has no particular ethnic association. In Wales such a summer pasture with its huts was called a *hafod* (plural *hafodydd*), and this occurs frequently as a place-name element.[22] In 1336 a man was fined at Llanaber (Merioneth) because he had continued to keep his animals 'in the common pasture of the old settlement (the *hendref*)' after the community of the township had taken their animals up to the mountains early in May.[23] This demonstrates well the extent to which transhumance could be formally built into a regular annual routine. As in the case of more ordinary commons, there were limits to the extent that shielings could be multiplied, and even in remote areas there was sometimes competition from the requirements of arable farming. It has been suggested, for example, that in south-eastern Scotland the shielings system was in retreat by the thirteenth century.[24]

An early practice of demesne farming in the richer parts of Britain, still in evidence in the eleventh century, was the specialized cattle or sheep unit attached to a large estate. Farms of this kind, analogous to the berwicks devoted to grain production, were often called a herdwick. They were a common element in old multiple estates,[25] but also existed as free-standing enterprises, often newly created during the twelfth and thirteenth centuries. They were especially likely to occur in areas of natural pasture such as coastal or river marshes, or grassy uplands. The cattle farms of Wales, Lancashire, and the Pennines were farms of this sort. The princes of Wales had a number of cattle farms in Snowdonia that passed in 1284 to the custody of Edward I's chamberlain for North Wales.[26] Similar farms are commonly found as a way of managing demesne sheep flocks. By the edge of the Blackwater estuary at Tolleshunt Bourchier (Essex) in the early fourteenth century the three marshland wicks of 'Sywardiswick', 'Crawesprotewyk', and 'Wetherwyk' were all devoted to sheep, and contained both sheepfolds and huts where shepherds could stay. Such, too, were the specialized upland cattle farms of Henry de Lacy, earl of Lincoln, in Lancashire. The moor edges of the forests of Rossendale, Trawdon, Pendle, and Accrington had 28 of these farms by 1295–6, each with about 80 animals managed by a cowherd.[27] Specialized livestock farms permitted a greater input of labour into the care for animals, and to that extent represented a more intensive mode of pasture farming than the grazing of beasts on common heaths, but the integration of pasture and arable might nevertheless be very weak under such a system of farming.

On large estates individual demesnes were often required to specialize in one category of sheep, in an attempt to use pasture resources and perhaps shepherding skills as productively as possible. On the estates of the bishopric of Winchester in 1208–9 a rudimentary division of activities was already operating between groups of manors. The Clere group (High Clere, Woodhay, Ashmansworth, and Itchingswell) in the north-western corner of Hampshire was managed by John of 'Welton' or 'Wolton'. High Clere was the central manor of the group, specializing in ewes and lambs. It received all the surviving lambs from Ashmansworth and Itchingwell, but sent out all the males after about a year to Woodhay and Ashmansworth. Woodhay kept only rams and wethers (castrated males), Itchingswell specialized in ewes for breeding—presumably with Woodhay rams, and Ashmansworth kept only ewes and wethers. All the wool from these flocks was collected at High Clere. A comparable pattern of specialization had been devised between the demesnes of Brightwell and Harwell in north Berkshire. Brightwell had the ewes, and all lambing took place there; Harwell had all the wethers and young sheep, received from Brightwell. The young ewes were returned to Brightwell for lambing in their third year. In this case the manors sold their wool independently.[28] A century later, Peterborough Abbey flocks were divided between an intermanorial flock on demesnes near Peterborough, and to the west, and self-contained flocks on manors further to the north. Manors in the former group annually exchanged sheep to enable them to specialize, so that, for example, Longthorpe specialized in wethers, while Glinton was a breeding manor.[29] On the estates of Crowland Abbey a central-ized system of shepherding embracing all the manors of the estate, and accounting separately from the manorial structure, was perfected in the period 1289–1313.[30] This pattern of sheep farming was also practised in Scotland; the monks of Kelso around 1300, for example, envisaged separate flocks of breeding ewes, sterile ewes, hoggets, wethers, and lambs on their different properties.[31]

Subsistence or Commercial Enterprise?

The peasant farmer with his pig, or the poor widow with her cow and hens, are figures that come readily to mind in contemplating villagers of the past, and there is no question of the importance of livestock to the household economies of the poor. As we have seen, pasture farming in many parts of Britain contributed more to the everyday diet than in the more cereal-based populations of the south and east.[32] In parts of Britain remote from commercial centres, cattle were of more consequence than sheep because they were more useful in such predominantly subsistence economies. In marked contrast with later developments, sheep flocks were small in most of Wales and northern Scotland.[33] Table 10.2 shows the numbers of livestock recorded in subsidy rolls from four commotes in North Wales, and indicates that the number of oxen and cows together almost equalled that of sheep. Given the relative prices of oxen, cattle, and sheep at the time, this implies that the investment in cattle was nearly seven times higher than that in sheep.[34]

Amongst the larger estates whose records have survived, we find many examples of livestock raised primarily as working beasts or to supply large households rather than for sale. Households that derived their sustenance directly from their estate in the form of food renders were likely to be only partially commercial in their orientation, and this was especially characteristic of the earlier part of the period.

TABLE 10.2. *Livestock taxed in four Welsh cantrefi, 1292–1293*

Area	Taxpayers	Oxen	Cows	Horses	Mares	Affers[a]	Sheep
Aberffro	69	136	265	72	36	128	757
Cafflogion	201	278	767	179	0	184	711
Creuddyn	128	127	293	22	37	39	548
Nefyn	93	87	175	48	0	42	205
	491	628	1500	321	73	393	2,221

[a] Affers (*affri*) were beasts of burden, usually draught horses.

Source: *The Merioneth Lay Subsidy Roll, 1292–3*, ed. K. Williams-Jones (Cardiff, 1976), cxiv.

Peterborough Abbey in the early twelfth century used the livestock on its estates more for its own consumption than as a producer for the market.[35] There were strong shifts towards greater market orientation in the course of the period, but even in 1300 large landowners pursued mixed strategies, often using some properties to supply their households and others to supply cash. Large monastic estates, in particular, bypassed the market by transferring livestock around their estates and consuming their own produce. Across all recorded estates in the London region between 1288 and 1315, 40 per cent of all the livestock written off from demesne herds and flocks (other than animals that died of natural causes) were either sent to another manor of the estate, butchered, or sent on the hoof to the household for consumption there.[36]

In general, though, by 1300 the commercial development of livestock farming, especially of sheep farming, was significantly more advanced than that of grain farming, and the proportion of output sold was greater. In the London area sales accounted for a larger proportion of demesne livestock disposed of than of grain— about 56 per cent in aggregate—though the comparison is not exact, since many animals were retained from year to year, whereas almost all grain was disposed of annually. In the case of animal products comparison with grain is more meaningful, and the contrast is stronger: in all about 70 per cent by value of all wool, hides and dairy produce was sold. Even in south-eastern England, therefore, pasture farming was the most commercialized branch of demesne farming.[37] The contribution of livestock and animal products to peasant farming is less easily established. The late thirteenth-century taxation assessments imply it formed an important component of the cash incomes of the wealthier peasantry, who tended to dominate commercial pasture farming in village society. Surviving tax assessments of 1,050 rural Bedfordshire taxpayers in 1297 show that livestock constituted 62.3 per cent of their total taxable wealth—wealth, that is, that was not part of their subsistence needs.

This implies that livestock was an important source of cash entering the rural economy. Cows were the most evenly distributed type of livestock, but sheep and oxen were very unequally distributed. Ten per cent of taxpayers owned 45 per cent of the taxable wealth in sheep, and 10 per cent (not altogether the same 10 per cent) owned about 67 per cent of the taxable wealth in oxen.[38]

In parts of Britain remote from major urban markets, dairy farming was more likely than arable to be developed commercially. The heavy commitment to cattle characteristic of Wales was not simply a matter of peasant subsistence. The Cistercian abbeys of Aberconwy, Valle Crucis, Strata Marcella, Margam, and Tintern all had specialized units for the breeding of cows and oxen for dairy produce and to raise income from the sale of surplus beasts.[39] Henry de Lacy's cattle farms in Lancashire were similarly commercial ventures, each in the charge of a keeper who leased the milk from the cows in his charge. Oxen sold from these farms supplied the local markets of Bolton-le-Moors and Pontefract.[40] Commercial cattle farming of this type was to be found through southern Scotland, as at Whitlaw in Galashiels (Selkirkshire), where around 1290 Kelso Abbey estimated a capacity for 80 cows. At Thirlestane in Lauder (Berwickshire) the canons of Dryburgh had common pasture for 60 cows.[41] Some regions show evidence of specialization that implies a commercial context even where no trade is in evidence. The sheriff of Forfar in 1264 accounted at the Scottish exchequer for deliveries of 37½ cows (evidently slaughtered) and about 46,000 lb of cheese from the conveth of Forfar, Glamis, and elsewhere.[42]

Specialization in cattle raising characterized many small farmers in upland areas, as in the Pennines, where by 1300 the hamlets of upper Swaledale each centred on a fold yard. Cattle and oxen were also the most characteristic branch of Irish pastoral husbandry. In 1211–12 the royal steward of Meath accounted for the custody of 1,927 cows, 906 oxen, 23 other draught animals, 930 sheep, and 393 pigs.[43]

However, the most striking development of pasture farming for the market during the thirteenth century is provided by the history of sheep. The beginnings of commercial sheep farming are obscure, though they belong in Anglo-Saxon England. By the time Domesday Book was compiled in 1086 there were already flocks much larger than any model of subsistence farming could accommodate. In counties where Domesday Book records the numbers of different kinds of livestock, sheep were the most numerous, and the size of many flocks indicates a strong commitment to commerce. Demesne flocks of several hundred occur frequently, and some were much bigger; aggregate tenant flocks were also large enough to be commercially important. There were about 9,000 sheep scattered across the demesnes of Ely Cathedral Priory and over 4,000 more amongst the abbey's tenants.[44] The biggest concentrations of sheep in East Anglia in 1086 were to be found either in regions of coastal or fenland marshes (like the remarkable 2,100 sheep assigned to West Walton in the Norfolk fens) or on dry heath (like the flock of 1,029 at Mildenhall in the Suffolk Breckland). In western England the commercial production of wool was already most pronounced, as it was to remain, on upland pastures, as in the Dorset Hills, the Mendips, and the southern Cotswolds.[45] The name Shepton, meaning 'sheep farm', of which there are at least three separate examples in Somerset, implies specialized sheep farming in that region in Saxon England, and the southern English Shiptons usually have the same derivation (though the Yorkshire Shipton is different). Early developments in commercial sheep farming were not confined to southern Britain, though from other regions we lack many references to sheep as early as the eleventh century. The development of wool production in Scotland attested by thirteenth-century records was already under way before the end of the twelfth century. Sometime before 1165, Philip de Euermele granted the canons of Holyrood pasture for 1,000 sheep and 60 cattle together with a ploughland.[46] When Roger de Quincy gave the monks of Newbattle the land of Preston Grange in about 1180 he accompanied it with the right to pasture 700 sheep as well as their plough beasts on his own land in Tranent.[47] And there is positive evidence of trade in Scottish wool by this time; between 1165 and 1174, the monks of Holmcultram were licensed by William I of Scotland to trade freely in wool and other produce in the Scottish burghs.[48]

By the later thirteenth century sheep farming was big business over a wider area than in 1086, stretching from the Cheviots of southern Scotland southwards to the English Channel, and from south Wales and the Welsh Marches eastwards to East Anglia. The articles of grievance presented to Edward I in 1297, in the name of the whole community of the realm of England, alleged that wool constituted almost half the annual value of all the land—hardly the comment of people to whom it was a residual concern.[49] If pasture farming mattered so much to incomes from land, it is not surprising to find farmers looking for ways of maintaining, or even increasing, their output of pastoral products, so circumventing any fatalist predictions that more grain must mean less wool. Some of the biggest flocks were those of the Cistercian abbeys founded during the twelfth century (Figure 10.1). Cistercians valued lightly settled parts of the country, remote from towns, where they could create new compact estates and derive an income from agriculture rather than rents. This often meant that they were chiefly dependent upon large sheep flocks for their income, since much of what they obtained in endowments was upland pasture. The abbey of Melrose, the largest monastic wool producer in Scotland, is estimated to have had at least 12,000 sheep in the early fourteenth century. The abbeys of Newbattle and Coupar Angus had each at least 7,000, and Dundrennan and Glenluce had at least 3,500.[50] In 1291 large flocks

FIG. 10.1. Scottish wool-producing monasteries. This map (which shows the location of many of Scotland's principal monastic houses) shows the restricted geographical distribution of those whose estates produced wool commercially. Commercial wool production was not as yet a feature of the Highland economy.

Source: P. G. B. McNeill and H. L. MacQueen (eds.), *Atlas of Scottish History to 1707* (Edinburgh, 1966), 237.

of sheep are recorded in Wales for the Cistercian abbeys of Margam (5,285), Neath (4,897), Tintern (3,264), Basingwerk (2,000), Strata Florida (1,327), and Whitland (1,100).[51]

Sheep farming on this scale was in no way peculiar to the Cistercians, however, and other landlords developed their estates in this way when the commercial opportunities beckoned. The Scottish Benedictine houses of Kelso and Arbroath were both large producers, expected to export about 7,700 and 6,250 fleeces respectively through Italian merchants in the early fourteenth century. Kelso could probably supply this number from its own flocks; a survey of c.1290 reported that it had pasture on its manors and granges for 6,530 sheep over a year old, and presumably could accommodate about 3,000 new lambs each year.[52] Numbers on the estates of the Benedictine Canterbury Cathedral Priory rose to a peak of 13,730 in 1322.[53] Some lay estates, too, had a large commitment to sheep and wool. The Holderness estates flocks of Isabella de Forz, Countess of Devon and Aumale, numbered 7,816 sheep and lambs in September 1265.[54]

Commonly the business of sheep farming was taken out of the hands of the officers of individual manors and organized as a separate division of estate management, with its own set of accounts, so that the costs of the whole operation could be wholly or partly centrally supervised and the wool could be disposed of by the most advantageous bulk deal that could be negotiated for the whole estate. Sheep farming on the Holderness estates between 1260 and 1280 was so organized in a single scheme of management, and the wool was sold year by year to the Riccardi of Lucca, a company of Italian merchants.[55] At Canterbury Cathedral Priory the flocks were organized into four 'custodies' of East Kent, the Weald and the Marshes, Surrey and Oxford, and Essex and Suffolk; sales of the wool from the first two of these were centralized at Canterbury from 1288.[56] Peterborough Abbey centralized the management of its flocks in 1307.[57] A similar scheme was operating around 1290 on the demesnes of Kelso Abbey in Scotland, to judge from a description of the pastoral resources of the demesne.[58] These monastic sheep-farming enterprises were exceptionally large, but smaller estates also sold their wool centrally rather than by separate manorial sales. Bolton Abbey built up its flocks in specialized sheep farms on the Yorkshire fells, and assigned their management to a single stockman or master shepherd rather than to local officials.[59]

Wool was the most commercialized of all agricultural products, since few producers kept their own for household use. Throughout most of England and the adjacent parts of Scotland and Wales, many minor landlords and peasant farmers made a considerable contribution to its market supply. Recent work, indeed, has suggested that the bulk of exported wool, both from English and Scottish ports, was peasant produce rather than that of the great estates. Since it required an estimated 260 fleeces to make up a woolsack, few even of the largest estates could produce more than 50 sacks, but by 1301–10 England was exporting an average of 34,493 sacks a year.[60] The wool production of Scottish monasteries, for all its impressive scale, perhaps accounted for no more than a sixth of Scotland's total export around 1330.[61] The activities of smaller producers are inevitably less well recorded than those of large estates, but something of their scope can be recovered from tax assessments. In the East Anglian Brecklands, an assessment of 1283 suggests that though individual peasant taxpayers averaged only 20 sheep each, in many villages, their combined flocks outstripped those on manorial demesnes.[62] There were distinctive marketing systems resulting from the fact that in more remote areas large producers, through their international mercantile contacts, could market wool at much lower unit costs than small ones. This gave them the advantage of being able to operate as intermediaries. Meaux Abbey in the 1280s contracted to supply to exporters 120 sacks of wool over and above the produce of its own demesnes, which implies a very considerable acquisition of wool from lesser estates and tenancies of Yorkshire. Bolton Abbey engaged in the same sort of middleman activity on a smaller scale, but demonstrably at high rates of profit.[63] Sheep farming was probably of more concern to wealthy peasants than to lesser ones, to judge from the very unequal distribution of livestock in village society, but even the wealthiest peasant was at a cost disadvantage in gaining access to international markets.

Evidence from estate accounts concerning the contribution of pasture farming to agrarian cash incomes in the later thirteenth century confirms its considerable weight, even if 'half the value of the land' overstates the value of wool. A computer-assisted analysis of demesnes in south-eastern England has established that animals and animal products there accounted for about a third of gross sales.[64] It was presumably larger on estates in less populated regions. At Bolton Abbey, in the Yorkshire dales, sales of wool, livestock, and hides together accounted for 88 per cent of gross income other than seigniorial income from rents and fines (or 54 per cent net, if purchases of wool and livestock are set against pastoral receipts).[65] The contribution of pastoral activity to peasant sales was also no doubt substantial. Robert le Kyng, the virgater from Bishop's Cleeve in 1299–1300 whose income is modelled by Christopher Dyer, derived perhaps half his cash income from wool, cheese, and young livestock.[66] For the monetization of economies in the more pastoral regions of Britain the significance of wool, hides, and cattle can hardly be exaggerated. All told, the contribution of the pastoral sector both to everyday diets, to local trade, and to the development of long-distance commerce, was so widespread that it needs to be placed near the forefront of our attention, as a defining characteristic of development, rather than relegated to a side issue.

NOTES

1. K. Biddick, *The Other Economy: Pastoral Husbandry on a Medieval Estate* (Berkeley, Calif. 1989), 56, 101.

2. R. Trow-Smith, *A History of British Livestock Husbandry to 1700* (1957), 107.

3. R. A. L. Smith, *Canterbury Cathedral Priory: A Study in Monastic Administration* (Cambridge, 1943), 150, 179–82.

4. e.g. H. E. Hallam, *Settlement and Society: A Study of the Early Agrarian History of South Lincolnshire* (Cambridge, 1965), 35.

5. J. A. Raftis, *The Estates of Ramsey Abbey* (Toronto, 1957), 152–6; Hallam, *Settlement and Society*, 25–6.

6. J. Gilbert, 'The Monastic Record of a Border Landscape 1136 to 1236', *Scottish Geographical Magazine*, 99 (1983), 10–11.

7. G. W. S. Barrow, *The Kingdom of the Scots: Government, Church and Society from the Eleventh to the Fourteenth Century* (1973), 52.

8. *The Charters of David I: The Written Acts of David I King of Scots, 1124–53, and of His Son Henry, Earl of Northumberland, 1139–52*, ed. G. W. S. Barrow (Woodbridge, 1999), no. 165, p. 132.

9. J. E. A. Jolliffe, *Pre-Feudal England: The Jutes* (1933), 49–51; K. P. Witney, *The Jutish Forest: A Study of the Weald of Kent from 430 to 1380 AD* (1976), 31, 49–55.

10. Domesday Book, ii, fo. 339ᵛ.

11. P. Morant, *The History and Antiquities of the County of Essex*, 2 vols. (1748), ii. 141.

12. *A Terrier of Fleet, Lincolnshire*, ed. N. Neilson (London, 1920), xlix–lvi and map following p. 214.

13. 'Assise Regis Willelmi', 60, in *Acts of the Parliaments of Scotland*, ed. T. Thomson and C. Innes, 12 vols. (Edinburgh. 1814–75), i.

14. G. W. S. Barrow, 'Rural Settlement in Central and Eastern Scotland: The Medieval Evidence', *Scottish Studies*, 6 (1962), 127; Gilbert, 'Monastic Record', 11.

15. D. H. Williams, *The Welsh Cistercians: Aspects of their Economic History* (Pontypool, 1970), 67.

16. R. A. Dodgshon, 'Medieval Settlement and Colonisation', in M. L. Parry and T. R. Slater (eds.), *The Making of the Scottish Countryside* (1980), 57.

17. W. Marshall, *General View of the Agriculture of the Central Highlands of Scotland with Observations on the Means of their Improvement* (1794), 45.

18. *Charters of David I*, ed. Barrow, nos. 177, 185, pp. 141, 144–5.

19. *Liber S. Marie de Calchou*, ed. C. Innes, 2 vols, Bannatyne Club, 82 (Edinburgh, 1846), i, no. 72, p. 54.

20. A. A. M. Duncan, *Scotland: The Making of the Kingdom* (Edinburgh, 1989), 415–16.

21. A. J. L. Winchester, *Landscape and Society in Medieval Cumbria* (Edinburgh, 1987), 94–5.

22. Williams, *Welsh Cistercians*, 66.

23. G. R. J. Jones, 'Post-Roman Wales', in H. P. R. Finberg (ed.), *The Agrarian History of England and Wales*, i (2): A.D. 43–1042 (Cambridge, 1972), 298.

24. R. A. Dodgshon, *Land and Society in Early Scotland* (Oxford, 1981), 164.

25. Above (Ch. 3).

26. 'Early Accounts Relating to North Wales Temp. Edward I', ed. J. Griffiths, *Bulletin of the Board of Celtic Studies*, 14 (1950–2), 240–1, 309; 'The Account Roll of the Chamberlain of the Principality of North Wales from Michaelmas 1304 to Michaelmas 1305', ed. E. A. Lewis, ibid., 1 (1921–3), 257.

27. Essex Record Office, D/DK/M.86; M. A. Atkin, 'Land Use and Management in the Upland Demesne of the de Lacy Estate of Blackburnshire, *c.*1300', *Agricultural History Review*, 42 (1994), 1–19.

28. *The Pipe Roll of the Bishopric of Winchester, 1208–1209*, ed. H. Hall and others (1903), 5–16.

29. Biddick, *Other Economy*, 100–9.

30. F. M. Page, ' "Bidentes Hoylandie" (A Medieval Sheep Farm)', *Economic History*, 1 (1926–9), 603–13.

31. *Liber S. Marie de Calchou*, ii. 455–73.

32. Above (Ch. 1).

33. Trow-Smith, *History of British Livestock Husbandry*, 145–6.

34. Taking five-year averages of price around 1292–3, calculated from D. L. Farmer, 'Prices and Wages', in H. E. Hallam (ed.), *The Agrarian History of England and Wales*, ii: *1042–1350* (Cambridge, 1988), 804, i.e. oxen at £11.60, cows at £8.21, sheep at £1.30 (averaging ewe and wether prices).

35. Biddick, *Other Economy*, 48.

36. B. M. S. Campbell, 'Measuring the Commercialisation of Seigneurial Agriculture, *c.*1300', in R. H. Britnell and B. M. Campbell (eds.), *A Commercialising Economy: England 1086 to c.1300* (Manchester, 1995), 170.

37. Ibid. 171, 173. For arable percentages, see above, pp. 195–6.

38. K. Biddick, 'Missing Links: Taxable Wealth, Markets and Stratification among Medieval English Peasants', *Journal of Interdisciplinary History*, 18 (1987), 283, 287.

39. Williams, *Welsh Cistercians*, 64.

40. Atkin, 'Land Use and Management', 1–19.

41. *Liber S. Marie de Calchou*, ii. 461; *Liber S. Marie de Dryburgh*, ed. W. Fraser, Bannatyne Club, 83 (Edinburgh, 1847), no. 124, pp. 88–9.

42. *The Exchequer Rolls of Scotland*, ed. J. Stuart, G. Burnett, and others, 23 vols. (Edinburgh, 1878–1908), i. 6–7. The weight, recorded in a unit called the cogal, has been converted to pounds using information from E. Gemmill and N. Mayhew, *Changing Values in Medieval Scotland: A Study of Prices, Money, and Weights and Measures* (Cambridge, 1995), 291, 391, 405–7.

43. 'The Irish Pipe Roll of 14 John, 1211–12', ed. O. Davies and D. B. Quinn, *Ulster Journal of Archaeology*, 4, suppl. (1941), 36–42.

44. E. Miller, *The Abbey and Bishopric of Ely* (Cambridge, 1951), 41.

45. H. C. Darby, *Domesday England* (Cambridge, 1977), 163, 165–7; R. Lennard, *Rural England, 1086–1135: A Study of Social and Agrarian Conditions* (Oxford, 1959), 260–4.

46. *Liber Cartarum Sancte Crucis*, ed. C. Innes, Bannatyne Club, 70 (1840) appendix II, no. 11, pp. 215–16. This is described as 'mirabilis concessio' in the margin of the transcript in *Registrum S. Marie de Neubotle*, ed. C. Innes, Bannatyne Club, 89 (1849), no. 130, pp. 97–8.

47. *Registrum S. Marie de Neubotle*, no. 64, pp. 51–2.

48. *Regesta Regum Scottorum*, ii: *The Acts of William I*, ed. G. W. S. Barrow (Edinburgh, 1971), no. 87, p. 184.

49. *Documents Illustrating the Crisis of 1297–98 in England*, ed. M. Prestwich, Camden 4th ser. 24 (1980), 117.

50. Duncan, *Scotland*, 429–30.

51. Williams, *Welsh Cistercians*, 64. Slightly different figures are given in *The Merioneth Lay Subsidy Roll, 1292–3*, ed. K. Williams-Jones (Cardiff, 1976), cxv.

52. *Liber S. Marie de Calchou*, ii. 445–73; T. B. Franklin, *History of Scottish Farming* (1952), 80.

53. Smith, *Canterbury Cathedral Priory*, 153.

54. N. Denholm-Young, *Seigneurial Administration in England* (1937), 59 n.

55. Ibid. 58–60.

56. Smith, *Canterbury Cathedral Priory*, 149.

57. Biddick, *Other Economy*, 100.

58. *Liber S. Marie de Calchou*, ii. 455–73.

59. I. Kershaw, *Bolton Priory: The Economy of a Northern Monastery, 1286–1325* (1973), 80–3.

60. A. R. Bridbury, *Medieval English Clothmaking: An Economic Survey* (1982), 3–45, 116; P. G. B. McNeill and H. L. MacQeeen (eds.), *Atlas of Scottish History to 1707* (Edinburgh, 1996), 251.

61. I owe this assessment to Sandy Grant.

62. M. Bailey, *A Marginal Economy? East Anglian Breckland in the Later Middle Ages* (Cambridge, 1989), 121.

63. Kershaw, *Bolton Priory*, 85–8.

64. Campbell, 'Measuring', 144–5.

65. Kershaw, *Bolton Priory*, 163.

66. C. Dyer, *Standards of Living in the Later Middle Ages: Social Change in England, c.1200–1520* (Cambridge, 1989), 114–15.

FURTHER READING

Atkin, M. A., 'Land Use and Management in the Upland Demesne of the de Lacy Estate of Blackburnshire, *c.*1300', *Agricultural History Review*, 42 (1994).

Bailey, M., *A Marginal Economy? East Anglian Breckland in the Later Middle Ages* (Cambridge, 1989).

Biddick, K., *The Other Economy: Pastoral Husbandry on a Medieval Estate* (Berkeley, Calif. 1989).

—— 'Missing Links: Taxable Wealth, Markets and Stratification among Medieval English Peasants', *Journal of Interdisciplinary History*, 18 (1987).

—— 'Pig Husbandry on the Peterborough Abbey Estate from the Twelfth to the Fourteenth century A.D.', in J. Clutton-Brock and C. Grigson (eds.), *Animals and Archaeology*, iv: *Husbandry in Europe*, British Archaeological Reports, International Ser. 227 (Oxford, 1985).

Birrell, J., 'Deer and Deer Farming in Medieval England', *Agricultural History Review*, 40 (1992).

Bischoff, J. P., ' "I Can't Do't without Counters": Fleece Weights and Sheep Breeds in Late Thirteenth and Early Fourteenth Century England', *Agricultural History*, 57 (1983).

Campbell, B. M. S, 'Commercial Dairy Production on Medieval English Demesnes: The Case of Norfolk', *Anthropozoologica*, 16 (1992).

—— *English Seigniorial Agriculture, 1250–1450* (Cambridge, 2000).

—— 'Measuring the Commercialisation of Seigneurial Agriculture, c.1300', in R. H. Britnell and B. M. S. Campbell (eds.), *A Commercialising Economy: England 1086 to c.1300* (Manchester, 1995).

Darby, H. C., *Domesday England* (Cambridge, 1977).

—— *The Medieval Fenland* (Cambridge, 1940).

Denholm-Young, N., *Seignorial Administration in England* (1937).

Duncan, A. A. M., *Scotland: The Making of the Kingdom* (Edinburgh, 1989).

Farmer, D. L., 'Marketing the Produce of the Countryside, 1200–1500', in E. Miller (ed.), *The Agrarian History of England*, iii: *1348–1500* (Cambridge, 1991).

Finberg, H. P. R., 'An Early Reference to the Welsh Cattle Trade', *Agricultural History Review*, 2 (1954).

Fox, H. S. A. (ed.), *Seasonal Settlement* (Leicester, 1996).

Gemmill, E., and Mayhew, N., *Changing Values in Medieval Scotland: A Study of Prices, Money, and Weights and Measures* (Cambridge, 1995).

Gilbert, J., 'The Monastic Record of a Border Landscape 1136 to 1236', *Scottish Geographical Magazine*, 99 (1983).

Grant, A., 'Animal Resources', in G. Astill and A. Grant (eds.), *The Countryside of Medieval England* (Oxford, 1988).

Hallam, H. E. (ed.), *The Agrarian History of England and Wales*, ii: *1042–1350* (Cambridge, 1988).

Kelly, F., *Early Irish Farming* (Dublin, 2000).

Kershaw, I., *Bolton Priory: The Economy of a Northern Monastery, 1286–1325* (1973).

Lloyd, T. H., *The Movement of Wool Prices in Medieval England*, Economic History Review, suppl. 6 (1973).

McDonnell, J. 'The Role of Transhumance in Northern England', *Northern History*, 24 (1988).

—— 'Upland Pennine Hamlets', *Northern History*, 26 (1990).

Miller, E., and Hatcher, J., *Medieval England: Rural Society and Economic Change, 1086–1348* (1978).

Murphy, M., and Galloway, J. A., 'Marketing Animals and Animal Products in London's Hinterland *circa* 1300', *Anthropozoologica*, 16 (1992).

Overton, M., and Campbell, B. M. S., 'Norfolk Livestock Farming, 1250–1740: A Comparative Study of Manorial Accounts and Probate Inventories', *Journal of Historical Geography*, 18 (1992).

Page, F. M., ' "Bidentes Hoylandie" (A Mediaeval Sheep Farm)', *Economic History*, 1 (1926–9).

Page, M., 'The Technology of Medieval Sheep Farming: Some Evidence from Crawley, Hampshire, 1208–1349, *Agricultural History Review*, 51 (2003).

Pierce, T. J., *Medieval Welsh Society: Selected Essays*, ed. J. Beverley Smith (Cardiff, 1972).

Postan, M. M., 'Medieval Agrarian Society in its Prime: England', in id. (ed.), *The Cambridge Economic History of Europe*, i: *The Agrarian Life of the Middle Ages*, 2nd edn. (Cambridge, 1966).

—— 'Village Livestock in the Thirteenth Century', *Economic History Review*, 2nd ser. 15 (1962), and in id., *Essays on Medieval Agriculture and General Problems of the Medieval Economy* (Cambridge, 1973).

Ryder, M. L., 'Medieval Sheep and Wool Types', *Agricultural History Review*, 32 (1984).

Smith, R. A. L., *Canterbury Cathedral Priory: A Study in Monastic Administration* (Cambridge, 1943).

Stephenson, M. J., 'Wool Yields in the Medieval Economy', *Economic History Review*, 41 (1988).

Thomas, C., 'Thirteenth-Century Farm Economies in North Wales', *Agricultural History Review*, 16 (1968).

Thornton, C., 'Efficiency in Medieval Livestock Farming: The Fertility and Mortality of Herds and of Flocks at Rimpton, Somerset, 1208–1349', in P. R. Coss and S. D. Lloyd (eds.), *Thirteenth Century England IV* (Woodbridge, 1992).

Trow-Smith, R., *A History of British Livestock Husbandry to 1700* (1957).

Ward, A., 'Transhumance and Settlement on the Welsh Uplands: A View from the Black Mountain', in N. Edwards (ed.), *Landscape and Settlement in Medieval Wales* (Oxford, 1997).

Williams, D. H., *The Welsh Cistercians: Aspects of their Economic History* (Pontypool, 1970).

Winchester, A. J. L., *Landscape and Society in Medieval Cumbria* (Edinburgh, 1987).

Witney, K. P., 'The Woodland Economy of Kent, 1066–1348', *Agricultural History Review*, 38 (1990).

CHAPTER II

....

Lords and Tenants

Between 1050 and 1300 most of Britain experienced at some time or other an unwelcome change from a native aristocracy to one imposed from outside. In England this occurred under William I following the Norman Conquest of 1066. As a result of rebellions by the English nobility the vast majority of lay estates were transferred to Normans. In Wales the elimination of a native aristocracy was less complete, but there was a heavy infiltration of Norman nobility in the late eleventh and early twelfth centuries, and again during the later thirteenth following Edward I of England's conquest of Gwynedd in 1282–3. The landlord class in much of Ireland was similarly transformed after the Anglo-Norman invasion of 1169–72. Scotland was not subjected to any comparable violent intrusion, but from 1124 onwards, under David I of Scotland and his successors, the introduction of Anglo-Norman and Flemish lords as feudal tenants of the crown alongside native landowners had something of the same effect. The acquisition of estates by landlords strange to local culture was bound to have implications for estate management because it raised distinct administrative problems. Especially in areas not accustomed to the commercial disposal of produce, older styles of management were unsuited to outsiders who did not intend to reside on their new lands. They had a strong inducement to convert customary renders to cash. This is a dominant theme in the development of Britain and Ireland between 1066 and 1300. Establishing markets and boroughs in outlying places, and trying to substitute money rents for services and rents in produce, was a direct response to this concern.

Conquest was not the only, or even the major reason for alterations in estate management in this period. Other changes, sometimes the secondary effects of conquest but sometimes quite independent, resulted from the transfer of land to ecclesiastical landlords.[1] Gifts to the monasteries, in particular, were very numerous before the thirteenth century. Both the older Benedictine monasteries and those of the newer orders gained property all through Britain and Ireland. Ecclesiastical lordships had very distinctive characteristics because their owners were perpetual bodies, not suffering the accidents of dynastic and political fortune that beset lay families. Once formed, the core of a monastic or episcopal estate was likely to change little over centuries, and this sometimes encouraged bureaucratic conservatism. The fact that ecclesiastical lands and rights were regarded as gifts to God by pious benefactors also inhibited churchmen from treating them as negotiable economic assets. Another distinctive feature of monastic estates and colleges, though not so much of bishopric estates, was the fixed centrality of the religious house. However far-flung their properties, the monastic life required most monks to live in stable communities most of the time. This ruled out the migratory pattern of life common among lay households, and so restricted the ways in which estates could be managed.

A further source of change in the structure of lordships, but one with very different implications for estate structure and management, resulted from eleventh- and twelfth-century gifts by greater landlords to loyal dependants, often in exchange for some specified military or other secular service. These gifts were usually small and compact—the knight's fee which was the land supposed to support a knight was normally about 180 acres in Norman England[2]—and, unlike gifts to churches, rarely carried with them large numbers of subtenants. None of the considerations that made for stability or conservatism on monastic estates were relevant here. Unlike monastic estates, knights' fees and analogous tenures were subject to all the vagaries of family life. Like the larger estates of the aristocracy, many of them became combined together or subdivided in the course of time through the operation of the laws of inheritance. They were more likely than ecclesiastical estates to be forfeited for political reasons. Because of the propensity of small landowners to run into debt, they were also liable to be mortgaged or sold, and contributed significantly to the growth of the land market in the twelfth and thirteenth centuries.[3]

The Management of Estates

The changing requirements of estate owners implied by these alterations in the structure of landownership were paralleled by changes in the commercial opportunities opening up in the course of the period. These altered even the way in which landlords could exploit territorial conquests. The Norman invasion of England did not result in any shift towards greater commercial awareness in the management of estates, but the Normanization of Scotland coincided with a period of expanding commercial opportunity. Even more strikingly, the English conquest of Ireland, a century after the Norman conquest of England, was dramatic in its impact because of the intervening growth of long-distance trade and the maturing of economic commercial institutions. Landlords taking up properties in eastern

Ireland rapidly developed them to raise more cash than before through the production and sale of wool or grain.

Where commercial incentives were few the problems of estate management were simple enough. On small estates, with a single property, the owner himself characteristically supervised his lands and the collection of his dues. On larger estates where commercial opportunities were weak, or where household demands were large, manorial demesnes were likely to be managed directly as sources of supply, as on monastic estates in twelfth-century Scotland.[4] On large and scattered estates, even where demesne farming was of subordinate importance or absent, someone had to be responsible for collecting traditional renders of produce from the inhabitants of each dependent settlement and conveying them to where they were required. As long as the tribute due was defined by tradition no great feat of memory was involved, and no written records were required. This system was one that operated through much of Britain and Ireland during the eleventh and twelfth centuries, and its chief characteristics survived at later dates in outlying regions, as on the estate of Aberffro on Anglesey.[5] Another ancient procedure, achieving much the same result, involved various forms of clientage; a king or other lord would grant his client livestock, or perhaps land, in exchange for annual food-rents to be delivered to where the lord needed them.[6] Where renders were traditional the difference between a royal servant and a lessee or a client may be difficult to define. Men of the eleventh and twelfth centuries did not, in any case, operate with modern legal categories.

Leasing is unlikely ever to have been a prevalent practice on small estates, such as those of most twelfth-century knights, since the properties were small enough for their owners to manage personally. On larger English estates, however, it was the prevalent mode of estate management at the beginning of our period. Written leases are already known from the eighth century onwards, notably on the estates of the bishopric of Worcester, but they are unlikely to have been widespread for a long time after that.[7] Though leases were a widespread feature of English estate management in the later eleventh century, we do not know how often they were committed to writing.[8] The twelfth-century canons of St Paul's usually leased their manors for the life of the lessee, backed by a written, but rarely dated, 'agreement'.[9] The character of early leases in other parts of Britain is difficult to document at this early date. The kings of Scotland and their leading subjects were managing at least parts of their estates through 'farmers' (*firmarii*) in the later twelfth century, probably implying some contractual, though not necessarily written, agreement.[10] The circumstances in which formal leases were introduced into estate management are obscure, and they were probably varied. It is surmised that in Scotland they were introduced only in the thirteenth century.[11] Until late in the twelfth century it is unlikely that they required frequent renegotiation in response to changing market conditions; they were more traditional in character than commercial, allowing properties to be managed by local men while reserving to their lord an acceptable income in goods or cash. Nevertheless, some decisions affecting manorial structures must have been taken centrally by lords and their councils, especially in the aftermath of conquests or other changes in lordship.[12]

The management of large estates through lessees had many hazards, especially when lessees had traditional expectations. There was always a danger that landlords would lose control of their estates to the farmers upon whom they depended. If leases were renewed automatically they eventually became difficult to renegotiate. The practicalities of estate management were complicated by legal ambiguities. In Anglo-Norman England, when property law was in flux, and landlords were used to some arbitrariness in the descent of property, the distinction between a lease and a feudal benefice was not always easy to maintain. While families were striving to establish the hereditary status of fiefs, lessees also hoped to establish the hereditary status of leases.[13] Neither in English nor Scottish law was there anything legally irregular in perpetual leases—a tenure known as fee farm or feu farm. Indeed, they were a common form of tenure in thirteenth-century Scotland, especially on ecclesiastical estates. But where established they prevented the landlord from adjusting rents in line with changing prices. Such loss of control, and the tendency for bits of demesne to be hived off and misappropriated, was a recurrent theme throughout the period from the 1080s to the 1180s, even in times of peace.[14] A reduction of demesne lands is in evidence from the estates of the bishopric of Worcester throughout the years between 1086 and c.1170; its timing is not confined to the period of civil war.[15] At Ramsey Abbey the disintegration of demesnes was even more in evidence in the 1160s and 1170s than it had been in Stephen's reign, and it continued to the end of the twelfth century.[16]

The problems of estate management were nevertheless particularly exacerbated by civil disturbance. Sometimes properties were simply seized by aggressive magnates; the Norman invaders of Wales, for example, snatched properties from the bishops of Llandaff and St David's.[17] But large estates also risked losses more surreptitiously through losing control of their lessees. Localized but widespread disruption of the economies of large estates occurred in the mid-twelfth century partly as a result of civil war under Stephen. On the estates of Caen Abbey the demesne of Minchinhampton manor (Gloucestershire) disintegrated and a prominent lessee, Simon of Felsted, carved himself a large holding out of the demesne both here and at Felsted (Essex). Administration of these estates was complicated by the fact that the abbey was in Normandy. The abbey of Bury St Edmund's lost land to lessees in its Suffolk manors during the reign of Stephen and was unable to recover it later. Stephen's reign created especially favourable circumstances for leaseholders who wished to make their tenure permanent. At a time when communications in the kingdom were difficult, they dug themselves in to the point where they were difficult to dislodge once the tradition of reletting had broken down. The reign of Henry II was consequently full of campaigns by major landlords to regain control over their estates either by litigation in the king's courts, or through purchase.[18] Thomas Becket made it his business to assert control over the demesnes of the archbishopric of Canterbury immediately after his consecration in 1162. By turning out lessees and renegotiating the terms on which manors were held he upset the propertied interests of Kent as well as the king and his fellow bishops.[19]

From the late twelfth century there were new developments in the management of larger estates of English landlords, particularly in the more urbanized half of the kingdom, probably because it was difficult for landlords to make the leasehold system flexible enough to respond to new commercial opportunities and rising prices. In some cases magnates needed to defend their incomes against the effects of accumulated debt and losses or alienations of income-bearing property. The system of leasing manors was abandoned on most large English estates, both ecclesiastical and lay. Instead, landlords employed servants or other dependants to manage their demesne lands for them. The manager, variously called a reeve, a bailiff, or simply a servant, received a fixed wage or some other allowance for his services; the lord received what was left.[20] This system did not mean that landlords were personally responsible for agricultural operations, but simply that their income varied from year to year in accordance with the fluctuating proceeds of demesne agriculture. In order to achieve this more effectively, some estates devised systems of middle management between their local agents and their estate head-quarters. Canterbury Cathedral Priory, for example, had already by the 1180s divided its estates into four custodies, each with a warden to supervise the manorial officials. At least as early as 1225 the wardens were monks.[21] Other estates depended upon an itinerant steward or some other high-ranking officer.

A similar change of policy was in place by the later thirteenth century in other parts of Britain where landlords had property they farmed commercially. Numerous surviving bailiffs' accounts demonstrate the direct management of demesnes on the Bigod estates in Ireland and, though less well documented, other landlords also engaged in direct husbandry.[22] On the Butler family estates in Ireland, the bailiff of Dunkerrin manor (Offaly) submitted an account to be audited in 1297, and in 1303 the bailiff of Eliogarty (Co. Tipperary) and 'Elykarwill' (Offaly) ran into trouble when the auditors decided that he owed £98 13s 7½d. on his account.[23] There were comparable estates in northern England and Scotland. Durham Priory directly administered fourteen of its twenty demesnes in 1290.[24] About this same time Kelso Abbey was directly engaged in managing the arable and pastoral husbandry on about half its grange farms, and the sacrist of Coldingham apparently did the same in some of the priory demesnes at least up to 1344.[25] However direct demesne administration was not the norm in northern England and Scotland, where demesnes were smaller and lords, in general, continued to lease them.[26] Perhaps landlords had less to lose from the leasehold system in relatively less commercially orientated parts of Britain. Even so it is likely that even in these regions leases were more frequently negotiated, more carefully recorded, and to that extent significantly more adapted to changeable economic conditions, than the more traditional leases of the eleventh and twelfth centuries. In Scotland, where incomes from demesnes were perhaps universally subordinate to those from tenant rents on large estates, a long-term tendency for demesne land to be converted to short-term peasant leases can be interpreted as a response to commercial incentives.[27]

The problem of superintending the efficiency of local managers, and the perennial problem of preventing them from profiting at the landlord's expense, was in some ways more onerous when demesnes were managed directly than under the system of demesne leasing, since there was no fixed expectation of what income each property would return each year. But at least under direct management landlords had the power to change the personnel responsible for local operations the moment they became discontented with the way their interests were being served.

Relations between Lords and Hereditary Tenants

Tenants who leased whole manors or townships were supposedly bound by some form of contract, and had managerial responsibilities for the collection and payment of estate revenues. Their status was very different from that of the much more numerous subordinate manorial tenants of peasant status whose tenure was rarely contractual and whose obligations were only exceptionally managerial. Most relationships between lords and tenants were defined by custom. Especially on large estates, there was a wide range of tenures of a non-negotiated kind.[28] Landlords, or their agents, dealt with tenants as people who belonged in particular social categories, and occupied particular tenements, to which particular rights and duties were attached. Changes in tenure following the Norman conquest of England, or the later Anglo-Norman expansion into Wales, Scotland, and Ireland, did little to modify this ancient characteristic of rural society. Because rural hierarchies of status, both for men and for land, were products of long and piecemeal adaptation rather than legislative fiat, they were very varied, and it was impossible to predict precisely what any tenant owed his lord without local knowledge. Nevertheless, across Britain the hierarchies of rural society to some degree resembled each other, and a preliminary survey of landlord–tenant relationships may start by examining some of the broadest lines of division.

In the Domesday survey of Buckinghamshire, 17 manors and 4 other lands are recorded as held from the king by Geoffrey, bishop of Coutances in Normandy, one of the leading tenants-in-chief who had about 280 English manors altogether. One of these manors, in Lavendon, was held from the bishop by another Norman, William of Bidon, sometimes called William the steward, presumably because he served the bishop in that capacity. William held other manors at Lathbury (Bucks.), Shelton (Beds.), and Newton Bromswold (Northants), which, together with Lavendon, were later recognized as constituting the barony of Lavendon. Lavendon was the administrative centre where the Bidon family built a castle, constructed a park, and between 1155 and 1158 founded a small monastery. On his manor in Lavendon, we are told that in 1086

William holds from the bishop 4 hides and 2 thirds of a virgate for one manor. The land is [for] 4 ploughs. On the demesne [are] 2 ploughs, and 7 villains with 6 bordars have 2 ploughs. There [are] 3 slaves and 1½ mills rendering 27 shillings and 250 eels. [There is] meadow [for] 4 ploughs [and] woodland [for] 60 pigs. It is worth 60 shillings. . . . This land 8 thegns held [in 1066], and 1 of these, Alli, a man of King Edward, was lord of the others. All could sell their land.[29]

The various categories of men recorded here may be divided roughly between three ranks. The lowest in status were the three slaves, who were by definition unfree; they were the lord's chattels, like his plough teams and his pigs. The highest-ranking recorded tenants, though no longer part of the scene, were the Anglo-Saxon thegns who had been able to sell their land. These men had been unambiguously free. The villeins and bordars were of intermediate status; later they would be called customary tenants. They were not the lord's chattels, and they could claim customary rights, but custom also restricted their liberty to use their land as they wished. This threefold classification was of widespread relevance to British and Irish society in the later eleventh century, even though local conditions varied considerably and boundaries between the three groups were inevitably fuzzy. Tenants elsewhere in England described as sokemen, for example, varied considerably in their degree of personal independence and were often not very significantly freer than villeins. Table 11.1 classifies the rural tenants given in the Domesday survey for all the recorded counties. It suggests that the intermediate groups—the villeins, bordars, and cottagers—were a very numerous class, making up between them about 74 per cent of the recorded rural population. The fortunes of these three categories altered significantly between 1050 and 1300.

Slaves

Domesday Book was compiled just in time to catch the last vestiges of slavery in England. Excluding those in what later became Wales, it enumerates 29,627 slaves,

TABLE 11.1. *Classes of population recorded in 1086 (000s)*

More free	
Freemen	13.6
Sokemen	23.3
Less free	
Villeins	109.0
Bordars	81.6
Cottars and coscets	6.9
Least free	
Slaves	28.1
Unclassified	
Others	5.8
Total	268.3

Note: The terms cottar and coscet in Domesday Book are both used to describe customary small holders, but the distinction between them was slight.

Source: H. C. Darby, *Domesday England* (Cambridge, 1977), 63.

oxmen, and maids, 15.7 per cent of the total recorded population, though they were very unequally distributed, with a strong concentration in the west midlands.[30] Slaves of various kinds were numerous throughout Britain in the eleventh century, but nowhere survived long afterwards, partly because of the rising problems of replacing them. In England a decline in their number already under way since the tenth century was accelerated by the Norman Conquest. Landlords came to prefer geld-paying tenants to dependent slaves, so that many slaves were liberated from the late eleventh century onwards, formally or informally.[31] By 1150 their numbers were everywhere so few as to render them barely visible, even if their descendants can sometimes be identified amongst tenants of low status. In the eleventh century the main value of slaves to their lord was that he commanded their labour sufficiently to employ them as full-time farmworkers responsible for animals and equipment, often as ploughmen.[32] Slaves were therefore particularly numerous on estates that had a heavy commitment to demesne farming, such as those of Earl Roger of Montgomery in 1086.[33] Domesday Book also demonstrates the existence of slavery in north-west Wales, where 17 per cent of the recorded population were slaves or oxmen. Slavery was not a Norman import to Wales; the servile status of the *caeth* was recognized in the native Welsh laws. However, the institution had died out long before the English conquest of Gwynedd in 1282–3, so we have little direct evidence of its characteristics.[34] In

Gaelic Ireland the institution survived at least into the twelfth century. Latterly it seems to have depended upon slaves imported from abroad. Gerald of Wales tells a tale, which may not be true, that at the time of the Conquest English slaves in Ireland were ordered to be liberated at an ecclesiastical council held at Armagh in 1170. True or not, slavery was by then a vanishing institution, as elsewhere.[35] There were undoubtedly differences between slave and slave in the degree of dependence. Some twelfth-century slaves had their own smallholdings to maintain them, while others lived in the farm buildings where they worked or in some communal hut provided for them. But in terms of personal freedom they all rank at the bottom.

Slavery in Scotland has a shadowy existence, even though the word *servus* was commonly used of the lower ranks of rural tenants into the thirteenth century. It is strongly implied by the raiding for slaves in northern England by Malcolm III (1058–93). 'Five times', says Symeon of Durham, 'he had harried [Northumbria] with savage devastation, and carried off the wretched inhabitants as captives, to reduce them to slavery'.[36] Not all Scottish slaves had English names, however, so servitude was evidently an indigenous institution. The existence of slaves perhaps explains some recorded sales of men with their progeny without any reference to land. When William I of Scotland gave Gillandrea mac Futhen and his children to Dunfermline Abbey, the monks headed their record of this gift in the abbey's register with the words 'concerning slaves' (*de seruis*).[37] Some 'scallags' who worked for Dunfermline Abbey can have been little better than slaves since the abbey took the trouble to record their genealogies. Though the priory's notes record where some were buried, they makes no reference to land, implying that their role was that of a landless workforce rather than a group of tenants.[38] It is likely that in Scotland and northern England, too, slave numbers declined to the point that their status as mere chattels had been modified by 1200.[39] Many Scottish and English natives (*nativi*), of the twelfth century and later, sometimes called *cumerlaches* in the Scottish sources, had land but were not free to leave their tenancies, and were presumably descendants of former slaves, still regarded as part of the estate's assets.[40]

Customary Tenants

A different status attached to middle-ranking tenants who had a hereditary claim to land and held it on customary terms. Often lords were not able to command the full-time services of such tenants, most of whom had a family holding of between 12 and 40 acres of land which had to be worked. However, one of the characteristic features of these tenants was that directly (in the form of labour services) or indirectly (in the form of tribute in goods) they worked for their lord as a condition of tenure. All the populations of Britain had tenures of this kind, though they varied in detail. In England it was common for tenants to owe assistance on the lord's demesne lands at key periods of the agrarian year when labour might otherwise be hard to get—at ploughing, at weeding, and at harvesting. Particularly in southern England, it was also common for tenants to owe a certain number of days' work every week. Domesday Book does not go into details such as these, but twelfth-century surveys from the estates of Caen Abbey, Glastonbury Abbey, and Peterborough Abbey show heavy labour services in different parts of the kingdom. Such services characterized the customary English form of tenurial dependency generally known as villeinage. Each of the forty villeins at Kettering, for example, was obliged in the 1120s to fallow-plough 4 acres of the lord's demesne during the summer, to contribute seven times in the year to supplying 22 ploughs for the lord's use, and to work for the lord three days a week; this was in addition to his money rent of 2s. 1½d. and his contribution towards supplying 50 hens and 640 eggs.[41] A number of sources of the twelfth century show unambiguously that the performance of labour services was considered to make a man less free than a tenant who had fewer labour services. In the course of the twelfth and thirteenth centuries in England they came to define a tenant as unfree, in the sense that the king's courts would not defend his title to his property against his lord.[42]

The dependent nature of ordinary village life went farther than these regular payments of rents and services. English villeins were commonly subject to personal impositions of a humiliating kind. Their lords had the right to tallage them at will, a power that was sometimes rationalized by the principle that villeins' personal possessions were the property of their lord.[43] Villeins suffered further personal humiliating interference by landlords in their matrimonial arrangements since a fine called 'merchet' was due when their daughters married. This was a custom that became widespread only from the late twelfth century,[44] though perhaps as a substitute for less specifically servile dues of a much earlier date.[45] A further disability is generalized in the archaizing *Leis Willelmi*, an English compilation of the third quarter of the twelfth century, in the principle that 'villeins may not depart from their lands . . . If, however, one of them should depart, none may receive him or his chattels nor retain him; but he should be made to return to his own lord with all his possessions. If other landlords do not compel errant villeins to return to cultivate their lands, the justices will do so.'[46] Formal gifts of villeins 'and their offspring', together with their land, were not uncommon. From the later twelfth century villeins were commonly called natives (*nativi*), a disparaging term, implying that the tenant's legal standing was determined by his birth. In this respect they had, or had acquired, some of the characteristics of former slaves.

In northern England and southern Scotland the prevalent form of dependent tenure, equivalent to villeinage further south, was 'bondage' (*bondagium*). The bishop of Durham's tenants in bondage were described simply as villeins (*villani*) in Boldon Book, a survey of the episcopal estate made about 1183. Such a tenant, usually called a 'bond' or 'husband' (*bondus* or *husbandus*), terms that will be translated here as 'bondsman' and 'husbandman', owed services that were no more standardized than those of villeins, and there are fewer detailed accounts of their terms of tenure. A husbandman on Kelso Abbey's lands at Redden, in Sprouston (Roxburghshire) about 1290 was described as owing the following services:

Each week in summer one carrying service with one horse to Berwick [22 miles away] and the horse will carry three bolls of grain or two bolls of salt or a boll and a half of coal, and in winter they will do the same carrying service except that the horse will carry only two bolls of grain, one and a half bolls of salt or a boll and a 'ferloth' of coal. And each week of the year in which they go to Berwick each land will perform a day's work as instructed. But any week in which they do not go to Berwick they will work for two days. And at harvest time when they do not go to Berwick they will perform three days' work.[47]

This was a limited range of obligations by the standard of southern villeins, and such a difference was generally true of northern customary tenants, though the bishop of Durham's bondsmen were more heavily burdened after the Norman Conquest.[48] There were other common obligations not included in the Redden account, such as the duty to mill at the lord's mill and pay toll to his miller, an obligation more often emphasized in northern records than in southern ones. Bondsmen, like villeins, were also subject to their lord's jurisdiction. This was implicit in Scottish baronial tenure, which submitted all a barony's inhabitants to the baron court, but it is sometimes made explicit. When the abbot of Scone leased the land of 'Belgarvi' (unidentified) in 1312 he stipulated that the husbandmen there should attend the law court for all the abbot's pleas in the barony of Scone, and that major disputes between them should be subject to his jurisdiction, while giving the lessees jurisdiction over minor disputes.[49] As with England villeins, bondsmen, and their offspring could be transferred to other lords without their status being affected. Richard de Moreville, constable of Scotland between 1162 and 1189 or 1190, sold to Henry of St Clare for 3 marks two brothers, Edmund and Gillemichel, sons of Bonde, with all their progeny, on condition that if in future Henry allowed them to leave his service they should revert to Richard rather than any other lord.[50]

Scottish bondsmen were less successful than English villeins and northern English bondsmen in establishing hereditary rights to their land; they usually occupied their lands on insecure tenures. The Scottish bondsman therefore lacked anything comparable to the English villein's right to defend a hereditary title to land in his lord's court. There is also evidence, including the abbot of Scone's lease of 1312, to suggest that bondsmen continued to be ejected from their holdings with little ceremony. When Richard, bishop of Moray, sometime in the period 1187–1203, gave a lifetime lease of lands to Duncan, earl of Fife, he distinguished between those tenants he was moving off the land 'to wherever he chose', and those who were 'native' to the land, and would remain to occupy it as tenants of the earl.[51] This presumably represents the distinction between bondsmen of non-servile origin, in effect treated as tenants at will, and neifs, bondsmen of servile origin, who were in effect part of the estate chattels. On the estates of the bishopric of Durham neifs were treated, at least from the twelfth century, as a subgroup of bondsmen; they comprised about 10–20 per cent of the total number in the later fourteenth century.[52]

Even granted the greater vulnerability of Scottish husbandmen to eviction, it is hazardous to deduce that peasant tenures were already normally characterized by short lettings, as they commonly were in the fifteenth century.[53] The best example of short-term leases is from the crown estates in 1305. In that year some peasants who leased their lands by the year petitioned Edward I for more secure tenures of the English kind.[54] It is impossible, though, to say what proportion of Scottish peasant tenures this represents. The two surviving Scottish estate surveys of the late thirteenth century (of the estates of Kelso Abbey and Coldingham Priory) show quite a different structure of rents, and one more likely to be ancient. On the Coldingham Priory estates—suffering badly at the time from the effects of war—lessees are recorded in only three townships. At Fishwick (Berwickshire), where there were five, they are distinguished from sixteen husbandmen and six cottars owing heavier labour services. No lessees are recorded on the Kelso estates, though the record is specifically a record of 'ancient' rents and obligations.[55]

The Welsh equivalent of the villein was the unfree taeog or bilain. Like English villeins they could be referred to as 'natives'. Their status was strictly hereditary, and they were defined as not having true Welsh blood. Such tenants constituted a large part of the population in the eleventh and twelfth centuries. Their responsibilities were similar to those of the northern bonds though their status and terms of tenure were very different.[56] They lived in particular types of settlement, where they were jointly responsible with their neighbours for the performance of labour services, as well as the payment of dues in kind and cash. Unlike English villeins or bondsmen they had no hereditary right to their tenements. In this they resembled Scottish bondsmen, though the principles on which land was allocated to them were different. They held tircyfrif ('reckoned land'), whose tenure involved the occasional redistribution of land between families. They were nevertheless tied to the land.[57] Any account of unfreedom in Wales, as in England, risks excessive schematization, since not only did its incidence vary considerably from region to region but so did its character. Although it imposed a clear distinction between free and unfree, Welsh custom also recognized gradations in status as in wealth between different classes of the unfree. In the marcher lordships these differences were even more complicated than elsewhere because of differences of ethnic origin, since many of the unfree were immigrants from England.[58] In general, however, their obligations were defined more by reference to payments in cash and kind than in labour.[59] In 1284, for example, the nine remaining villeins at Aberffro in Anglesey owed labour services that were lighter than those of most English villeins, in that they did not owe week work through the year, though their produce rents were very heavy.[60]

The ranks within Irish rural society between 1050 and 1200 are very imperfectly recorded. The uncertainties are such that a grant by Dermot MacMurrough in 1166 of Melisu Mac Feilecan and his sons and grandsons to a monastery in Dublin has been variously interpreted as a grant of serfs and a grant of rights over a freeman.[61] Early Irish law recognized a type of dependant called a *senchléithe*, who could not leave his land but was not a slave, but it is uncertain to what extent such a class survived until the twelfth century.[62] From the time of the Anglo-Norman conquest, the characteristic unfree tenant there was the betagh, whose status in legal thinking was often assimilated to English villeinage, though in fact there were significant differences. Betaghs were in some respects like Welsh tenants holding *tircyfrif*. Their duties were comparatively lighter than those of English villeins, since, like many northern English bonds, they did not owe week work and it seems that landlords either did not try to exact it from them or failed in the attempt.[63] The records of thirteenth- and fourteenth-century Irish manors rarely list betaghs individually. Instead they group them together, with a statement of the land held between them and the rent they owe all together, and it is generally supposed that they occupied small townships separate from the rest of the tenantry, and perhaps held their land in interspersed strips or blocks.[64] At the manor of Cloncurry (Co. Kildare) in 1304, 63 betaghs together held 341½ ploughlands for a rent of 1s. 8d. an acre, implying an average of 5.4 acres a head and an individual responsibility for a rent of 8s. 1½d.[65] A later rental for Swords (Co. Dublin) implies an average 16.7 acres a head and an average rent of about 13s. 7½d. (Table 11.2). Betaghs were at least sometimes individually responsible for different rents, as at Maynooth in 1328–9, which implies that they held separate plots of land even if each was obliged to guarantee the rent payment of the others.[66] The betagh's average resources of land, as stated in acres, were smaller than those of the English villein, but the significantly larger size of Irish acres exaggerates the difference.[67] Individual betaghs, like English villeins, could be relatively well off. When Clement 'Ocathyll', a royal betagh, was killed in 1303, he was found to possess three horses and an ox, four cows, four calves, thirty sheep, a piglet, five crannocks of oats, a bushel of wheat, two bushels of beans, a similar quantity of barley, and a stack of turf.[68]

During the period 1050–1300 the relations between landlords and customary tenants were changing in response to the growing commercial opportunities of

TABLE 11.2. *Betagh holdings on the manor of Swords (Co. Dublin), 14 March 1326*

Township	No. of betaghs	Acres	Acres per head	Rent per acre
'Baligyghe'	8	102	12.75	10d.
'Werue'	6	100	16.67	8d.
Gillenston	3	66.5	11.08	12d.
Ballycannon	6	115	19.17	10d.
Total	23	383.5	16.7[a]	9.8d.[a]

[a]Average.

Source: *Calendar of Archbishop Alen's Register, c.1172–1534*, ed. C. McNeill (Dublin, 1950), 176.

the age, which allowed landlords to insist on payments in money, where it suited them, rather than in labour or produce. In twelfth-century England the number of cash payers—molmen as they were often called—increased to accommodate the need of lords for extra funds in cash. When in the thirteenth century English lawyers came to define labour services as a characteristic of villein status, landlords were more concerned to retain their rights to labour services even if in practice they took money in lieu. They 'sold' the labour services year by year rather than commuting them permanently for an annual money rent. This accounts for the somewhat contradictory evidence relating to labour services on English manors during the thirteenth century. On the one hand the number of labour services tended to increase as a result of the subdivision of holdings—which landlords used as an opportunity to increase the total burden of work due.[69] On the other hand, particularly towards the end of the thirteenth century, estate surveys increasingly attest the practice of valuing labour services at money sums, and manorial accounts record receipts for 'works sold', these sales being at the will of the landlord, and not a matter of tenant right. In Scotland the lord's best interests were served by multiplying the number of short leases in tenants' hands, and that, as we have seen, was apparently a way in which rural tenures were being developed by 1300.

The power of lords to please themselves in this way was possible because the increasing volume of currency in circulation in rural societies was accompanied by a rising demand for land. Though custom restricted what landlords could do with hereditary tenant land, there were many ways in which they could raise their money incomes. Many obligations owed by tenants—such as judicial fines, or the 'entry fines' that tenants paid when they entered into new tenancies—were not fixed. Landlords increasingly demanded money instead of rents that had formerly been paid in kind. It is far from certain that this increased demand for money was generally neutral in its implications for tenants' welfare. Replacing produce renders with cash payments transferred to tenants the costs of marketing, without necessarily any compensating advantage. In thirteenth-century circumstances families, with more labour than they needed to work their family landholdings would have done better to pay their rents in labour rather than sacrificing their resources of produce or cash. In southern and midland England the Hundred Rolls of 1279 demonstrate unambiguously that money rents were more important than labour and produce rents. Similar changes were taking place throughout Britain and Ireland. Money rents started to replace produce labour and rents in southern Scotland from about 1140, especially south of the River Tay.[70] In south-eastern Wales, rents formerly paid in flour and cheese had been converted to cash by the early thirteenth century.[71] Bishop Anselm of St David's (1231–c.1247) fixed a money rent for his tenants at Tre-fin in Penfro (Pembrokeshire), though the arrangement was 'at the bishop's will'; presumably the tenants had hitherto owed produce.[72]

Money rents were being demanded from some Irish betaghs early in the twelfth century, and the practice had become common by 1300. Those of 'Othee' in the Vale of Dublin were paying £12 in money rents in 1212, and the Irish pipe roll of sixteen years later lists rents of £14 3s. 4d. from the betaghs of 'Othee', £11 4s. 0d. from those of 'Obrun', and £8 10s. 4d. from those of 'Okelli'.[73] The rents from Lucan (Co. Dublin) included £9 11s. 10d. from betaghs in 1274.[74] On the extensive Butler estates the obligations of native betaghs were recorded as cash sums by the early fourteenth century.[75] There are various indications that the rents recorded in manorial extents were actually paid in cash. The cash receipts recorded in the annual account of 1283–4 from the Bigod manor of Fennagh (Co. Carlow) record betaghs' rents of £25 6s. 6½d. received half at Easter and half at Michaelmas, together with an increment of 3s. 5d. received at Michaelmas.[76] On Thomas de Clare's manor of Youghal (Co. Cork) in 1288, 44 betaghs owed no works because they paid rent.[77] Some customary labour services owed by betaghs on the Butler estates were said in 1304 to be of no value because the betaghs paid cash in lieu.[78] Such statements would not occur had the services in question in fact been performed.

One consequence of the partial commercialization of customary tenures was a gradual erosion of many aspects of local custom, though this phenomenon became much more marked in the fourteenth and fifteenth centuries. It is true that many landlords were cautious in the extent to which they allowed custom to be super-seded. Nevertheless relations between lords and tenants were very different in 1300 from what they had been 250 years earlier. The transformation was greatest in Wales, perhaps because of the exceptional rapidity with which the economy was converted from non-monetized institutions dependent upon transfers of produce and labour to one in which monetized relationships were commonplace.

Tircyfrif townships were allowed to convert to hereditary tenures, and the number of demesne manors (*maerdrefi*) dependent on labour services declined.[79] This resulted in the formation of groups of hereditary tenants owing labour services, whose status was more akin to contemporary English villeins than that of the traditional *teog*. They remained unlike English villeins insofar as they often occupied settlements separate from those of free families, though there were also some mixed townships.[80]

One of the biggest sources of change, and evidence of a willingness of landlords to allow considerations of cash to trump attachment to custom, was the operation of the peasant land market. From the later twelfth century there is considerable evidence of the buying and selling of free land among peasants, particularly in eastern England. During the thirteenth century even customary holdings—the traditional 'tenements' of East Anglia or virgates of southern and midland England—were being allowed to fragment through the alienation of parcels to others. It was common for the eleventh-century virgates to have been broken up into fractions of virgates or irregular numbers of acres. Lords were willing to allow this because they could make the splitting of tenements an opportunity to raise rents and charge additional fees.[81]

Free Tenants

Table 11.1 shows that freemen, though no longer present on William of Bidon's manor of Lavendon, constituted an important category in 1086. They made up 14 per cent of the recorded population of England and were especially numerous in Lincolnshire, East Anglia and parts of Nottinghamshire and Leicestershire. These were categories of tenant who were not necessarily richer in lands than others, but whose obligations to lords were significantly lighter, and were unlikely to include heavy labour services. In the short term, free tenants suffered a loss of status, like the rest of the population, from the effects of conquest. In England many of them lost a measure of independence after 1066; they were attached to manors and subjected to new forms of lordship. Some, like the eight thegns on William of Bidon's manor at Lavendon, disappeared in obscure circumstances. In Ireland at the time of the conquest many freemen undoubtedly lost their land to incoming land-lords, and according to some accounts, surviving freemen were reduced in status to join the thirteenth-century class of betaghs.[82] As in similar arguments about the effects of the Norman Conquest in England, argument is hampered by the poverty of our information concerning the pre-conquest period.

The period as a whole, however, favoured the multiplication of free tenures and free families. In England knights' fees and serjeanties (held in return for military service below the status of a knight, or for some other form of service) constituted an important category of new freeholdings that reshaped the structure of many rural settlements; they were carved sometimes from existing demesne lands, some-times from the holdings of former customary tenants and sometimes from waste-land. In England, where the possibility of quantification exists, there were perhaps 7,525 knights' fees in existence in 1166, mostly created by 1135.[83] However, knights' fees and serjeanties were exceptionally large by the standards of most new free-holdings; other categories were both more numerous and, as a rule, much smaller. In many villages of eastern England the freeholders constituted a population of paupers. Free rents multiplied as towns grew, since lords were everywhere conscious of the opportunity to attract burgesses and increase cash income as a direct benefit of increasing monetized trade. The main share of seigniorial exactions from towns was always in the forms of money rents and money tolls. Burgage tenure was a free tenure in English law, which meant that a burgage holding could be freely bought and sold, but also that it paid a money rent to the lord.[84] A third reason for the multiplication of English free tenures was the expansion of cultivation into new lands. The more recently colonized lands on the estates of St Paul's of London in 1222 were listed separately from the customary tenures on each manor, and were held in small parcels for money rents, though sometimes with boon works and sometimes slight rents in kind. On the estates of the bishops of Durham, lands taken into cultivation after the compilation of Boldon Book in 1183—more numerous on the hilly western manors of the estate than on the lower-lying lands towards the coast—were classified as exchequer lands because they paid a simple money rent to the bishop's exchequer on Palace Green.[85] The relative freedom of these late-colonized lands affected the balance between free rents and money rents on the bishop's estate as a whole. In the west midlands the Hundred Rolls permit us to compare the Warwickshire hundreds of Kineton and Stoneleigh, the former already a well-settled arable region in the twelfth century, the latter a forest region whose population grew rapidly between 1086 and 1279. In 1279 free tenants comprised 30 per cent of the recorded tenants in Kineton Hundred but 50 per cent of the tenants in Stoneleigh Hundred.[86] An increasing number of free tenures in England was particularly encouraged by the growth of population and the reclamation of land in the eastern counties. On the estates of the bishopric of Ely the number of new free and semi-free tenants of the twelfth and thirteenth centuries probably exceeded the number of older free tenants in this region. Large areas of reclaimed Fenland were settled by money-paying tenants, as at Wiggenhall and Wisbech.[87]

A similar expansion of free tenure has been observed in Wales and Ireland, and for many of the same reasons. Knights' fees were created, boroughs founded, and new cultivation claimed from the moors. Even in rural areas of Wales freedom increased from about 1100. Anglesey, like much of the principality of Gwynedd, was slow to change relative to most of Wales, but even there lightly occupied tracts of land in the interior of the island were made over to relatives and courtiers of the ruling princes and some lands were formally converted from bond to free tenure. By the end of the thirteenth century the island had 43 free townships as well as 95 bond townships.[88] In Ireland the creation of new fiefs, the multiplication of boroughs, and the settling of migrants from Britain and elsewhere resulted in the establishment of very many free tenures, but comparisons with previous conditions are here too greatly inhibited by the disruption caused by the Anglo-Norman conquest and the poverty of evidence relating to pre-conquest conditions. As in England the multiplication of free tenures was largely associated with an increase in monetary obligations. In an early example, in about 1174 Richard FitzGilbert of Clare gave land at 'Censale' to Hamund son of Torkill for an annual rent of two marks payable to the canons of Holy Trinity, Dublin.[89]

There are differences in terminology between different parts of Britain that complicate the discussion of free tenure. In regions subject to English law by 1300 only baronies, knights' fees, and serjeanties are counted by legal historians as 'feudal' tenures, but there were other types of free hereditary tenure, such as burgage and socage, in English common law during the twelfth and thirteenth centuries. In England by 1300 socage had become a catch-all legal term to describe most free tenures that did not owe military services. Scotland's different legal system lacked a concept of free tenure other than either feudal or burghal tenure. The difference is chiefly accountable to the way in which the twelfth-century English legal system had created a chasm between free tenures that had access to the king's courts and unfree tenures that did not. Free tenants in Scotland were more restricted in the courts they could go to than in England because of the more restricted role of royal justice and the dominant role of baronial justice. These differences need bearing in mind in any generalizations about freedom across Britain. However, even in the Scots' own terms the multiplication of free tenures resulting from the creation of feus and the multiplication of burghs was a distinguishing feature from the reign of David I onwards, and urban growth continued into the thirteenth. Hereditary and freely alienable burgage tenure became a normal feature of the new burghs created during the twelfth and thirteenth centuries. Indeed, townsmen are credited with pioneering a new commercialism to property ownership in the Scottish kingdom.[90]

The welfare implications of an expansion of free tenure were very limited in the short term. Most of the new free tenures were small, and because they were subject to fragmentation they often became smaller in the course of time. Many accommodated families at lower standards of living than the customary tenants of old with their virgates and semi-virgates. However, they represent a shift that is often overlooked towards the breakdown of the legal gulf between free and unfree. In Wales bondmen had been a majority of the population in 1100, but by 1300 they were already a minority. In England by 1279, not only had slavery disappeared but the proportion of customary tenants had fallen. In 1086 slaves and customary tenants (as defined in Table 11.1) together represented about 98 per cent of the recorded population of the counties of Bedfordshire, Buckinghamshire, Cambridgeshire, Huntingdonshire, and Oxfordshire. In 1279, by contrast, villeins and other customary tenants made up only 58 per cent of the tenant households in the portions of these counties analysed by Kosminsky from the Hundred Rolls.[91]

NOTES

1. Above (Ch. 2).
2. S. Harvey, 'The Knight and the Knight's Fee in England', in R. H. Hilton (ed.), *Peasants, Knights and Heretics: Studies in Medieval English Social History* (Cambridge, 1976), 145.
3. H. M. Thomas, 'Subinfeudation and Alienation of Land: Economic Development and the Wealth of Nobles in the Honour of Richmond, 1066 to 1300', *Albion*, 26 (1994), 397–417.
4. R. A. Dodgshon, *Land and Society in Early Scotland* (Oxford, 1981), 122, 124.
5. A. D. Carr, *Medieval Anglesey* (Llangefni, 1982), 97–100.
6. F. Kelly, *A Guide to Early Irish Law* (Dublin, 1988), 29–33.
7. C. Dyer, *Lords and Peasants in a Changing Society: The Estates of the Bishopric of Worcester, 680–1540* (Cambridge, 1980), 17–18.
8. R. Lennard, *Rural England, 1086–1135: A Study of Social and Agrarian Conditions* (Oxford, 1959), 105–212.
9. *The Domesday of St. Paul's of the Year M.CC.XII*, ed. W. H. Hale, Camden Society, old ser. 69 (1858), 122–39.
10. *Regesta Regum Scottorum*, i: *The Acts of Malcolm IV*, ed. G. W. S. Barrow (Edinburgh, 1960), 52–3; *Regesta Regum Scottorum*, ii: *The Acts of William I*, ed. G. W. S. Barrow (Edinburgh, 1971), 51–2; K. J. Stringer, *Earl David of Huntingdon: A Study in Anglo-Scottish History* (Edinburgh, 1985), 77–8.
11. Dodgshon, *Land and Society*, 122–3.
12. E. Miller, 'Farming of Manors and Direct Management', *Economic History Review*, 2nd ser. 26 (1973), 139–40.
13. Lennard, *Rural England*, 111–13.
14. E. Miller and J. Hatcher, *Medieval England: Rural Society and Economic Change, 1086–1348* (1978), 208–10.
15. Dyer, *Lords and Peasants*, 62.
16. J. A. Raftis, *The Estates of Ramsey Abbey: A Study in Economic Growth and Organization* (Toronto, 1957), 86–9.
17. R. R. Davies, *Conquest, Coexistence and Change: Wales, 1063–1415* (Oxford, 1987), 180.
18. *Charters and Custumals of the Abbey of Holy Trinity, Caen*, ed. M. Chibnall (1982), xlix–li; ead., *Anglo-Norman England, 1066–1166* (Oxford, 1986), 146–7.
19. F. Barlow, *Thomas Becket* (1986), 83–4.

20. P. D. A. Harvey, 'The English Inflation of 1180–1220', in Hilton (ed.), *Peasants, Knights and Heretics*, 59; E. Miller, 'England in the Twelfth and Thirteenth Centuries: An Economic Contrast?', *Economic History Review*, 2nd ser. 24 (1971), 7–12.

21. R. A. L. Smith, *Canterbury Cathedral Priory: A Study in Monastic Administration* (Cambridge, 1943), 100–1.

22. K. Down, 'Colonial Society and Economy in the High Middle Ages', in A. Cosgrove (ed.), *A New History of Ireland, ii: Medieval Ireland, 1169–1534* (Oxford, 1987), 459–61.

23. *The Red Book of Ormond*, ed. N. B. White (Dublin, 1932), 91–2, 95–6.

24. R. Lomas, *North-East England in the Middle Ages* (Edinburgh, 1992), 189.

25. *Liber S. Marie de Calchou*, ed. C. Innes, 2 vols., Bannatyne Club, 82 (1846), ii. 455–73; *The Correspondence, Inventories, Account Rolls and Law Proceedings of the Priory of Coldingham*, ed. J. Raine, Surtees Society, 12 (1841), appendix, i, cv–cvii (cf. lxxxv–civ); Dodgshon, *Land and Society*, 123, 125.

26. N. Mayhew, 'Alexander III—A Silver Age? An Essay in Scottish Medieval Economic History', in N. H. Reid (ed.), *Scotland in the Reign of Alexander III* (Edinburgh, 1990), 59.

27. A. A. M. Duncan, *Scotland: The Making of the Kingdom* (Edinburgh, 1989), 424.

28. Chapter 3 above.

29. Domesday Book, i, fo. 145$^\text{v}$.

30. H. C. Darby, *Domesday England* (Cambridge, 1977), 76–7; D. A. E. Pelteret, *Slavery in Early Medieval England* (Woodbridge, 1995), 192–3.

31. Pelteret, *Slavery*, 234–5, 251–5.

32. M. M. Postan, *The Famulus: The Estate Labourer in the XIIth and XIIIth Centuries*, Economic History Review Supplements, 2 (1954), 7–11.

33. S. Harvey, 'The Extent and Profitability of Demesne Agriculture in England in the Later Eleventh Century', in T. H. Aston, P. R. Coss, C. Dyer, and J. Thirsk (eds.), *Social Relations and Ideas: Essays in Honour of R. H. Hilton* (Cambridge, 1983), 56.

34. T. M. Charles-Edwards, *Early Irish and Welsh Kinship* (Oxford, 1993), 409.

35. Gerald of Wales, 'Expugnatio Hibernica', I. xviii, in id., *Expugnatio Hibernica: The Conquest of Ireland*, ed. and trans. A. B. Scott and F. X. Martin (Dublin, 1978), 68–71; F. Kelly, *Early Irish Farming* (Dublin, 2000), 439–40.

36. *Scottish Annals from English Chroniclers, A.D. 500 to 1286*, ed. A. O. Anderson (1908), 112–13.

37. *Registrum de Dunfermelyn*, ed. C. Innes, Bannatyne Club, 74 (1842), no. 64, p. 36.

38. *Registrum de Dunfermelyn*, nos. 325–31, pp. 220–2; cf. *Liber de Attachiamentis*, in *Acts of the Parliaments of Scotland*, ed. T. Thompson and C. Innes, 12 vols. (Edinburgh, 1814–75), i. 655; W. F. Skene, *Celtic Scotland*, 3 vols. (Edinburgh, 1876–80), iii. 222.

39. Duncan, *Scotland*, 329.

40. *Regesta Regum Scottorum*, ii. 71.

41. *Charters and Custumals of the Abbey of Holy Trinity, Caen*, 33–137; *Chronicon Petroburgense*, ed. T. Stapleton, Camden Society, old ser. 47 (London, 1849), 157–83; *Surveys of the Estates of Glastonbury Abbey, c.1135–1201*, ed. N. E. Stacy (2001).

42. P. Vinogradoff, *Villeinage in England* (Oxford, 1892), 215–16.

43. P. R. Hyams, *Kings, Lords and Peasants in Medieval England: The Common Law of Villeinage in the Twelfth and Thirteenth Centuries* (Oxford, 1980), 192.

44. R. H. Hilton, 'Freedom and Villeinage in England', in id. (ed.), *Peasants, Knights and Heretics*, 181.

45. J. Scammell, 'Freedom and Marriage in Medieval England', *Economic History Review*, 2nd ser. 27 (1974), 523–37.

46. H. G. Richardson and G. O. Sayles, *Law and Legislation: From Aethelberht to Magna Carta* (Edinburgh, 1966), 141–2.

47. *Liber S. Marie de Calchou*, ii. 456.

48. W. E. Kapelle, *The Norman Conquest of the North: The Region and its Transformation, 1000–1135* (1979), 183–6.

49. *Liber Ecclesie de Scon*, ed. C. Innes, Bannatyne Club, 78 (1843), no. 144, pp. 104–5.

50. *Acts of the Parliaments of Scotland*, i. 94.

51. *Registrum Episcopatus Moraviensis*, ed. C. Innes, Bannatyne Club, 58 (1837), no. 16, p. 12.

52. P. Larson, 'Local Law Courts in Late Medieval Durham', in C. D. Liddy and R. H. Britnell (eds.), *North-East England in the Later Middle Ages* (forthcoming).

53. This is argued by I. F. Grant, *Social and Economic Development in Scotland before 1603* (Edinburgh, 1930), 84–92.

54. A. Grant, *Independence and Nationhood: Scotland, 1306–1469* (1984), 66.

55. *Liber S. Marie de Calchou*, ii. 455–73; *Correspondence, Inventories, Account Rolls and Law Proceedings of the Priory of Coldingham*, appendix, lxxxv–civ.

56. Kapelle, *Norman Conquest*, 56–7.

57. T. J. Pierce, *Medieval Welsh Society: Selected Essays*, ed. J. B. Smith (Cardiff, 1972), 43, 276, 316, 343.

58. R. R. Davies, *Lordship and Society in the March of Wales, 1282–1400* (Oxford, 1978), 378–91.

59. For some detailed comments, see W. Rees, *South Wales and the March, 1284–1415* (1924), 157–73.

60. Davies, *Conquest, Coexistence and Change*, 119–20; F. Seebohm, *The Tribal System in Wales* (1904), appendix A(a), 3–25. For the date of the extent of Anglesey printed by Seebohm, see D. Stephenson, *The Governance of Gwynedd* (Cardiff, 1984), 235–6.

61. 'Rental of the Manor of Lisronagh, 1333, and Notes on "Betagh" Tenure in Medieval Ireland', *Proceedings of the Royal Irish Academy*, 43, Section C (1935–7), 64; K. Nicholls, 'Gaelic Society and Economy in the High Middle Ages', in A. Cosgrove (ed.), *A New History of Ireland*, ii: *Medieval Ireland, 1169–1534* (Oxford, 1987), 431.

62. Kelly, *Guide*, 35–6.

63. C. A. Empey, 'Medieval Knocktopher: A Study in Manorial Settlement', *Old Kilkenny Review*, new ser. 2 (1979–83) 341; A. J. Otway-Ruthven, 'The Organization of Anglo-Irish Agriculture in the Middle Ages', *Journal of the Royal Society of Antiquaries of Ireland*, 81 (1951), 9–10.

64. Empey, 'Medieval Knocktopher', 340; V. B. Proudfoot, 'Clachans in Ireland', *Gwerin*, 2 (1958–9), 112–15.

65. *Red Book of Ormond*, 32.

66. *The Red Book of the Earls of Kildare*, ed. G. Mac Niocaill (Dublin, 1964), 99–100.

67. Early fourteenth-century information in the *Red Book of Ormond* implies averages of

10.1 acres at 'Colabrenan', 7.5 acres at 'Kilmactethe', 7.3 acres at Bray, Co. Wicklow, 5.6 acres at 'Lanath' and 'Grag Dermot', 5.4 acres at 'Tathcony', 5.4 acres at Cloncurry, Co. Kildare, 4.2 acres at Brun, Co. Wicklow (pp. 23, 25, 32, 49, 151).

68. P. Connolly, 'The Irish Memoranda Rolls: Some Unexplored Aspects', *Irish Economic and Social History*, 3 (1976), 73.

69. M. M. Postan, *Essays on Medieval Agriculture and General Problems of the Medieval Economy* (Cambridge, 1973), 100–3, 105; E. Miller, *The Abbey and Bishopric of Ely: A Social History of an Ecclesiastical Estate from the Tenth Century to the Early Fourteenth Century* (Cambridge, 1951), 101–2.

70. Duncan, *Scotland*, 394–5; W. W. Scott, 'The Use of Money in Scotland, 1124–1230', *Scottish Historical Review*, 58 (1979), 112–19, 123.

71. Davies, *Conquest, Coexistence and Change*, 163.

72. *St David's Episcopal Acta, 1085–1280*, ed. J. Barrow (Cardiff, 1998), no. 112, p. 130.

73. 'The Irish Pipe Roll of 14 John, 1211–1212', ed. O. Davies and D. B. Quinn, *Ulster Journal of Archaeology*, 4, suppl. (1941), 10; 'Accounts on the Great Roll of the Pipe of the Irish Exchequer from the Reign of Henry III', in *The Thirty-Fifth Report of the Deputy Keeper of the Public Records and Keeper of the State Papers in Ireland* (Dublin, 1903), 29.

74. J. Mills, 'The Norman Settlement in Leinster: The Cantreds near Dublin', *Journal of the Royal Society of Antiquaries of Ireland*, 24 (1894), 161–75.

75. *Red Book of Ormond*, 9, 14, 23, 32, 49–50, 54, 149, 150, 157; C. A. Empey, 'The Anglo-Norman Settlement in the Cantred of Eliogarty', in J. Bradley (ed.), *Settlement and Society in Medieval Ireland: Studies Presented to F. X. Martin, OSA* (Kilkenny, 1988), 220.

76. The National Archive, Public Record Office, SC6/1237/34ʳ.

77. *Calendar of Documents Relating to Ireland, 1171–1307*, ed. H. S. Sweetman and G. F. Hand-cock, 5 vols. (1875–86), iii, no. 459, p. 202; cf. the evaluation of works on two other properties on pp. 205–6.

78. *Red Book of Ormond*, 49–50.

79. Davies, *Conquest, Coexistence and change*, 120–1; G. R. J. Jones, 'The Tribal System in Wales: A Re-Assessment in the Light of Settlement Studies', *Welsh History Review*, 1 (1960–3), 124–31.

80. *Survey of the Honour of Denbigh, 1334*, ed. P. Vinogradoff and F. Morgan (1914), lxxxvii; Pierce, *Medieval Welsh Society*, 317–18.

81. Miller, *Abbey and Bishopric*, 102, 144; Postan, *Essays*, 102.

82. G. Mac Niocaill, 'The Origins of the Betagh', *Irish Jurist*, new ser. 1 (1966), 292–8.

83. P. Coss, *The Knight in Medieval England, 1000–1400* (Stroud, 1993), 24.

84. M. de W. Hemmeon, *Burgage Tenure in Medieval England* (Cambridge, Mass, 1914), 61–153.

85. *Bishop Hatfield's Survey*, ed. W. Greenwell, Surtees Society 32 (1857), 5–6, 12–14, 16–17, etc.

86. J. B. Harley, 'Population Trends and Agricultural Development from the Warwickshire Hundred Rolls of 1279', *Economic History Review*, 2nd ser. 11 (1958), 14.

87. Miller, *Abbey and Bishopric of Ely*, 119–20, 129.

88. Pierce, *Medieval Welsh Society*, 266–9, 285–6, 316, 322, 401.

89. *Twentieth Report of the Deputy Keeper of the Public Records in Ireland* (Dublin, 1888), 36.

90. E. Ewan, *Town Life in Fourteenth-Century Scotland* (Edinburgh, 1990), 92–111.

91. Darby, *Domesday England*, 338–4; E. A. Kosminsky, *Studies in the Agrarian History of England in the Thirteenth Century*, ed. R. H. Hilton, trans. R. Kisch (Oxford, 1956), 205–6.

FURTHER READING

Aston, M., Austin, D., and Dyer, C., *The Rural Settlements of Medieval England: Studies Dedicated to Maurice Beresford and John Hurst* (Oxford, 1989).

Britnell, R. H., 'Social Bonds and Economic Change', in B. Harvey (ed.), *The Twelfth and Thirteenth Centuries* (Oxford, 2001).

—— *The Commercialisation of English Society, 1100–1500*, 2nd edn. (Manchester, 1996).

Carpenter, D., 'English Peasants in Politics, 1258–1267', *Past and Present*, 136 (1992).

Carr, A. D., *Medieval Anglesey* (Llangefni, 1982).

Darby, H. C., *Domesday England* (Cambridge, 1977).

Davies, R. R., *Conquest, Coexistence and Change: Wales, 1063–1415* (Oxford, 1987).

DeWindt, E. B., *Land and People in Holywell-cum-Needingworth: Structures of Tenure and Patterns of Social Organization in an East Midlands Village, 1252–1457* (Toronto, 1972).

Dodgshon, R. A., *Land and Society in Early Scotland* (Oxford, 1981).

Down, K., 'Colonial Society and Economy in the High Middle Ages', in A. Cosgrove (ed.), *A New History of Ireland*, ii: *Medieval Ireland, 1169–1534* (Oxford, 1987).

Duncan, A. A. M., *Scotland: The Making of the Kingdom* (Edinburgh, 1989).

Dyer, C., *Lords and Peasants in a Changing Society: The Estates of the Bishopric of Worcester, 680–1540* (Cambridge, 1980).

Empey, C. A., 'The Anglo-Norman Settlement in the Cantred of Eliogarty', in J. Bradley (ed.), *Settlement and Society in Medieval Ireland; Studies Presented to F. X. Martin, OSA* (Kilkenny, 1988).

—— 'Medieval Knocktopher: A Study in Manorial Settlement', *Old Kilkenny Review*, new ser. 2 (1979–83).

Faith, R., 'Demesne Resources and Labour Rent on the Manors of St. Paul's Cathedral, 1066–1222', *Economic History Review*, 47 (1994).

—— *The English Peasantry and the Growth of Lordship* (1997).

Green, J. A., *The Aristocracy of Norman England* (Cambridge, 1997).

Hallam, H. E. (ed.), *The Agrarian History of England and Wales*, ii: *1042–1350* (Cambridge, 1988).

Harley, J. B., 'Population Trends and Agricultural Development from the Warwickshire Hundred Rolls of 1279', *Economic History Review*, 2nd ser. 11 (1958).

Harvey, P. D. A., *A Medieval Oxfordshire Village: Cuxham, 1240 to 1400* (1965).

Hatcher, J., 'English Serfdom and Villeinage: Towards a Reassessment', *Past and Present*, 90 (1981), and in T. H. Aston (ed.), *Landlords, Peasants and Politics in Medieval England* (Cambridge, 1987).

Hennessy, M., 'Manorial Organisation in Early Thirteenth-Century Tipperary', *Irish Geography*, 29 (1996).

Hilton, R. H., *Class Conflict and the Crisis of Feudalism* (1985).

—— *The Decline of Serfdom in Medieval England* (1969).

—— *A Medieval Society: The West Midlands at the End of the Thirteenth Century*, 2nd edn. (Cambridge, 1983).

Hilton, R. H., 'Why Was There So Little Champart Rent in Medieval England', *Journal of Peasant Studies*, 17 (1989–90).

Holland, P., 'The Anglo-Norman Landscape in County Galway: Landholdings, Castles and Settlements', *Journal of Galway Archaeology and History*, 49 (1997).

Hyams, P. R., *King, Lords and Peasants in Medieval England: The Common Law of Villeinage in the Twelfth and Thirteenth Centuries* (Oxford, 1980).

Jones, G. R. J., 'The Tribal System in Wales: A Re-Assessment in the Light of Settlement Studies', *Welsh History Review*, 1 (1960–3).

Kanzaka, J., 'Villein Rents in Thirteenth-Century England: An Analysis of the Hundred Rolls of 1279–80', *English Historical Review*, 55 (2002).

Kapelle, W. E., *The Norman Conquest of the North: The Region and its Transformation, 1100–1135* (1979).

Kelly, F., *A Guide to Early Irish Law* (Dublin, 1988).

King, E., *Peterborough Abbey: A Study in the Land Market* (Cambridge, 1973).

Kosminsky, E. A., *Studies in the Agrarian History of England in the Thirteenth Century* ed. R. H. Hilton, trans. R. Kisch (Oxford, 1956).

Lennard, R., *Rural England, 1086–1135: A Study of Social and Agrarian Conditions* (Oxford, 1959).

McIntosh, M. K. *Autonomy and Community: The Royal Manor of Havering, 1200–1500* (Cambridge, 1986).

Miller, E., *The Abbey and Bishopric of Ely: A Social History of an Ecclesiastical Estate from the Tenth Century to the Early Fourteenth Century* (Cambridge, 1951).

—— and Hatcher, J., *Medieval England: Rural Society and Economic Change, 1086–1348* (1978).

Otway-Ruthven, A. J., 'The Character of Norman Settlement in Ireland', *Historical Studies*, 5 (1965).

—— 'The Organization of Anglo-Irish Agriculture in the Middle Ages', *Journal of the Royal Society of Antiquaries of Ireland*, 81 (1951).

Owen, D. D., 'The English of Denbigh: An English Colony in Medieval Wales', *Transactions of the Honourable Society of Cymmrodorion* (1974–5).

Page, F. M., *The Estates of Crowland Abbey* (Cambridge, 1934).

Pelteret, D. A. E., *Slavery in Early Medieval England* (Woodbridge, 1995).

Pierce, T. J., *Medieval Welsh Society: Selected Essays*, ed. J. B. Smith (Cardiff, 1972).

Pollock, F., and Maitland, F. W., *The History of English Law before the Time of Edward I*, 2nd edn., 2 vols. (Cambridge, 1898).

Postan, M. M., *Essays on Medieval Agriculture and General Problems of the Medieval Economy* (Cambridge, 1973).

—— 'Medieval Agrarian Society in its Prime: England', in id. (ed.), *The Cambridge Economic History of Europe,* i: *The Agrarian Life of the Middle Ages*, 2nd edn. (Cambridge, 1966).

Raban, S., 'Landlord Return on Villein Rent in North Huntingdonshire in the Thirteenth Century', *Historical Research*, 66 (1993).

Raftis, J. A., *The Estates of Ramsey Abbey: A Study in Economic Growth and Organization* (Toronto, 1957).

Razi, Z., and Smith, R. (eds.), *Medieval Society and the Manor Court* (Oxford, 1996).

Rees, W., *South Wales and the March, 1284–1415* (1924).

Schofield, P. R., *Peasant and Community in Medieval England, 1200–1500* (Basingstoke, 2003).

Stephenson, D., *The Governance of Gwynedd* (Cardiff, 1984).

Thomas, H. M., 'Subinfeudation and Alienation of Land: Economic Development and the Wealth of Nobles in the Honour of Richmond, 1066 to 1300', *Albion*, 26 (1994).

....

CHAPTER 12

Government

Although governments had no concept of an economic policy designed to facilitate economic growth, there can be no doubt that their activities affected the economy in various ways. Many measures both in war and peace affected transaction costs, and so had a bearing on levels of profit that traders could expect. Other activities, notably through taxation, directly affected the level and distribution of incomes. These two aspects of the impact of government deserve separate consideration to determine how rulers responded to commercial development between 1050 and 1300, and also to assess how they enhanced or dampened productive and commercial incentives.

Government and Transaction Costs

Royal diplomacy and warfare affected the development of trade for good or ill, especially over long distances, if only because they influenced the risk of loss. For the fortunes of internal trade, weak government was generally more dangerous than aggressive government, since it increased the chance of civil war or invasion. The most favourable conditions for internal trade were under an effective, law-enforcing government in times of peace. Such governments could also benefit external trade, by encouraging good international relations. War, by contrast, could damage foreign trade and affected internal trade through the impact of higher taxation on incomes, a point to be examined in the next section.

The security of urban life is one of the best indicators of internal stability. Twelfth-century warfare was 'castle-based warfare'.[1] In England this is particularly apparent from the anarchy of Stephen's reign, which has been described as a 'chess-like war of castles and sieges'. But castles were frequently attached to towns, either to subjugate urban populations, as in the many urban castles built in England under William I or as centres of baronial power, as in Wales and Ireland in the course of English expansion. This meant that in the wars of Stephen's reign urban castles were at the centre of many an engagement and townsmen suffered—notably at Lincoln in 1141 and the following year at Oxford. Similarly in the north, David I of Scotland launched his invasion of Stephen's kingdom by taking Newcastle and Carlisle and besieging Durham.[2] The horrors of civil warfare for townspeople were experienced at Selby (Yorkshire), when Henry de Lacy's castle building, perhaps shortly after 1143, incited an attack on the town by Earl William of Aumale.[3] Jordan Fantosme's account of the war in the north of 1173–4 shows that though castles did not halt the Scottish advance they defined the pattern of the military campaign; William the Lion besieged the king's castles of Wark and Carlisle.[4] The civil war that followed King John's repudiation of Magna Carta in 1216 was again fought as a war of sieges, in Rochester, Colchester, Windsor, Barnard Castle, Durham, Lincoln, and Dover. English experience had shown, long before 1169, that when landlords established new towns by their castles the amount of protection they could offer was definitely limited. Towns in parts of Ireland also continued to be victims of internal disorder throughout the period. In eastern Connacht, Aed O'Connor destroyed castles and towns after defeating an English army in 1269. Roscommon and Athlone were attacked in 1272, and Roscommon again in 1277. In Scotland, after a long period of internal stability, towns were exposed to the hazards of war with England after 1296, the year in which Berwick's castle surrendered to English troops and the burgh's inhabitants were indiscriminately massacred.

During the thirteenth century, however, castles largely gradually dropped out of the picture as serious military installations through most of Britain, except in border territories, and most towns virtually ceased to have any military role other than supplying troops. The fall of Rochester Castle to King John in 1215 is sometimes regarded as a turning point. After Bedford Castle was demolished in 1224 it was never rebuilt, and many other castles were abandoned and fell into disrepair during the thirteenth century. Those that survived, like the the Tower of London, Kenilworth, or Durham, had roles additional to the purely military. The reasons for the retreat of the defensive castle are debated and complex, and they partly have to do with the invention of the trebuchet, which made only the most strongly built castles worth defending. However the contrast between southern and midland England and other parts of Britain suggests that the strength of the crown, and the rarity of internal warfare, was a major reason for the increased security of town life. As a very broad generalization, it may be said that, despite several temporary disturbances, over the period 1050–1300 the development of the England and Scottish kingdoms favoured the growth of internal trade by reducing the incidence of civil war and invasion. Even in Ireland and Wales the impact of English rule was favourable to internal law and order and the growth of trade. That said, however, it is evident that in much of Britain and Ireland these gains were fragile, and towards the end of the period there were ominous signs of reversion to lower expectations.

The weakness of the Scottish crown after the death of the young Queen Margaret in 1290 was followed by internal divisions and by Edward I's aggressive intervention in Scottish affairs in campaigns between 1296 and his death in 1307. The continuing vulnerability of towns to military action in northern England, Wales, Scotland, and Ireland contributed to the problems created by demographic and economic change in the fourteenth and fifteenth centuries.

Both as consumers and as recipients of tolls, taxes, and loans, kings and lords had a strong interest in encouraging overseas trade. A wide range of commercial interests stood to benefit, though royal favour could prove very fickle. In practice kings often favoured particular groups of merchants at the expense of others. Given the relatively immature state of the British merchant classes throughout period, governments turned to foreign merchants for commercial and financial services. William I encouraged Jewish traders from Rouen to settle in England. Henry II dealt with William Cade the Fleming. Richard I and John borrowed from Flemings and Italians.[5] The interdependence between royal interests and those of such merchants is well illustrated by the instructions that Henry III issued to his treasurer on 15 June 1245. Merchants of Siena, Cahors, Florence, and elsewhere, except subjects of the king of France, were to be summoned to attend a meeting at Westminster. The king hoped for a loan of 6,000 marks in return for the great advantages that these merchants gained from their business transactions and loans in England.[6] As this shows, the encouragement kings gave to merchants was governed by narrowly fiscal considerations, and was always liable to sudden changes of direction. Edward I depended heavily on Italian merchant companies, who gained a strong hold over wool exports during his reign. He borrowed heavily from them in 1277, 1282–3, 1287, 1294, and 1297–1300, but he inflicted heavy losses on the Riccardi company in 1294, when he stopped their activities and seized their assets on the grounds that it owed him money.[7] The favour Edward had shown to Spanish merchants since his accession was suddenly withdrawn in 1294 when Sancho IV, king of Castile, supported the French against the English in the conflict over Gascony.[8]

The decision to go to war, though completely outside the control of the merchant community, could seriously affect commercial interests. The twelfth and thirteenth centuries were comparatively peaceful, in this respect; the principal wars affecting relations between Britain and the mainland of Europe were limited conflicts between the king of England and the king of France over Normandy in 1090–2, 1104–6, 1194–9, 1202–4, and 1214, and the French intervention in English civil war in 1216–17. But the war between Edward I of England and Philip IV of France over Gascony in 1294–1303 was the beginning of a more belligerent phase of English history. Commerce was also affected by wars in which no British interests were involved. English kings relied so heavily on customs revenues that they could not afford to ignore the interests of foreign trade for very long. However, wars had periodic adverse consequences, especially as overseas trade became more significant to incomes in Britain. The war with France that broke out in 1294 disturbed England's wool exports because of the decreased opportunities for trade, the higher cost of protecting wool shipments, and because Edward I interfered with the trade as a source of wartime revenue. He raised the export tax on a woolsack to £2 between November 1294 and November 1297. Both in 1294 and, more seriously in 1297, commercial confidence was undermined by royal proposals to seize wool stocks as a forced loan. It is difficult to show that any group of merchants benefited from the war, and in the early years of conflict normal commercial links were severely disrupted.[9]

Though both English and Scottish crowns had fitful bursts of ambition to extend the borders of their realms, the construction and reconstruction of power blocs outside the core of the two ancient realms were not altogether a result of government activity and did not always advance the power and revenues of their kings. The expansion of Anglo-Norman settlement in Wales during the late eleventh century was largely effected by individual magnates like Hugh of Avranches and Robert of Rhuddlan in the north or Robert Fitz Hamon and Roger of Montgomery, earl of Shrewsbury in the south. Although subject to the king of England, these lordships retained significantly greater independence than those in England itself. The invasion of Ireland in 1169–70 was similarly spearheaded by Anglo-Norman lords, Robert Fitz Stephen, Maurice Fitz Gerald, and Richard FitzGilbert of Clare, earl of Striguil and Pembroke (alias 'Strongbow') in alliance with Dermot McMurrough, the deposed king of Leinster. In this case Henry II's support for the conquest from 1170 onwards ensured that he acquired a permanent extension of territory and authority for the crown and for English law.[10] In Scotland the construction of new power blocs was pioneered by nobles, not only independently of the crown but sometimes in opposition to royal interests. Somerled created an extensive lordship over much of the west and western isles of Scotland between about 1140 and 1160 independently of the kings of both Scotland and Norway. In the early thirteenth century the Stewarts acquired lordships and built castles on the Argyll coast and the inner Hebrides.[11] The lords of Galloway, too, were sufficiently independent of the Scottish crown to be a problem until after the extinction of the male line in 1234, and the suppression of a Gallovidian rebellion by Alexander II in 1235. Only gradually, and sometimes very much later, were some of these noble lordships fully integrated into the institutions of royal government. Despite the ruthlessness of the Edwardian conquest of the principality of North Wales in 1282–3, and the final extinguishing of Welsh independence, the full integration of Wales into English forms of administration waited till the sixteenth century. Alexander III of Scotland finally eliminated the interest of the Norwegian crown in Man and the western isles by the Treaty of Perth in 1266, and thereby secured both and extension of the rights of the crown and a greater possibility for control, but the highlands of Scotland remained administratively and politically distinctive until the eighteenth century. In Ireland the royal gains of the twelfth and thirteenth centuries were to be significantly reduced thereafter by failure to check the independence of local Anglo-Irish and Gaelic lordship.

The welfare gains and losses resulting from such English invasions of Wales and Ireland, and the Scots 'winning of the west', are incommensurable, but examined strictly by reference to their effects on trade there can be little doubt that trade followed the invaders' banners. To the extent that the occupying lords and their dependants developed their new properties commercially they accelerated the growth of trade that would otherwise have occurred more slowly. Edward I's royal acquisitions in North Wales were placed under the custody of a chamberlain, who from 1284 accounted at the exchequer for the revenues of the principality and its new boroughs.[12] To the extent that linguistic, legal, and other cultural norms followed the invaders, transactions could be ventured with less risk and at lower cost. Some of the commercial expansion discussed in Chapter 6 can reasonably be attributed to the increased security of trading operations around the western shores of Britain, though its impact was limited to the coast south of the Clyde estuary.

The more peaceful arts of statecraft were also relevant to economic expansion, and in many ways favourable. The standardization of coinage, weights, and measures, though achieved only imperfectly, became a consistent goal of policy for the English and Scottish kings in this period, and not without appreciable success. These were not novel government objectives. In the late eighth century, Charlemagne had attempted to establish standard measures of capacity and weight, as well as to create a uniform currency, though his success was probably very limited and certainly ephemeral. Anglo-Saxon kings had followed suit; King Edgar (959–75) had legislated to regulate weights and measures by the standard of Winchester. An early eleventh-century work called *Episcopus* ('The Bishop') regarded it as the duty of each priest to ensure that just measures were used. From the later twelfth century there is repeated evidence not only of the English crown's concern to standardize weights and measures, but also of active enforcement of this requirement through local authorities, special commissions, and officers of the king's court. As the king's court perambulated, the clerk of the market held courts at which local measures were tested.[13] By 1300 there was probably a fair degree of uniformity throughout southern and midland England as a result of these measures. Throughout this region, manorial records use the same measures of volume (the quarter of eight bushels, the bushel of four pecks, and the peck) and in recording sales and transfers of grain they very rarely made allowance for differences between measures. That this standardization was limited, however, is suggested by the employment of different volumetric systems in more remote areas. In north-eastern England, for example, grain was also measured by the chalder, usually equivalent to four quarters; the standard English quarter was a quarter of a measure that survived only in the north.[14] Another northern measure was the *rasa* (variably a third or a quarter of a quarter).[15] The English measures did not apply to much of English-occupied Wales and Ireland, where up to the end of the fourteenth century they used a measurement of volume called the crannock, which was not effectively standardized, and varied in different contexts and for different cereals. For purposes of tax assessment in 1292–3 the Welsh crannock was required to contain four English bushels,[16] but there was considerable variation around this. The Irish crannock from about this time is reported to have been twice this volume for the measurement of wheat, and so about the equivalent of an English quarter, but for the measurement of oats it could be as large as 16 bushels.[17] Attempts were nevertheless made to impose some uniformity of measures. A fine for false measures is recorded from Ireland in 1212.[18] Henry III ordered all Ireland to adopt the measures of Dublin 'if they be such as can be followed', but in 1253 it was reported that even Dublin measures were not standardized.[19] Attempts continued to be made through Edward I's reign to enforce these requirements, as in Tipperary in 1303–4,[20] but it is unlikely that any success was more than localized.

In Scotland attempts by the crown to police weights and measures were even less effective, so that the study of Scottish units is fraught with difficulty. From at least the earlier twelfth century the standard measure for large quantities of grain was the chalder, as in northern England. Smaller quantities were measured by the boll, another variable measure, but roughly equivalent to a sixteenth of a chalder or to two English bushels.[21] The earliest attempts at standardization are attributed to King David I.[22] Central oversight of local measures was assigned, at least by the mid-fourteenth century, to the chamberlain of the king's court, whose position in this respect was analogous to the English clerk of the market.[23] Control of measures was more effective town by town rather than across the kingdom as a whole; some urban charters explicitly include weights and measures in a generalized list of liberties.[24] The 'Laws of the Burghs' required burgesses' measures of volume, length, and weight to be sealed by their burgh seal.[25] National standardization was not achieved until modern times,[26] but the authority of towns over the trade of surrounding rural districts probably resulted in at least regional standardization of some significance.

In their control of coinage, British kings before 1300 were as near exemplary as any governments in Europe. Many minting authorities on the Continent had succumbed to the temptation to debase the coinage—that is to reduce the number of pennies that were struck from a pound of silver brought to the mint—to the point that there was hardly any precious metal left in units of currency that had once contained pure silver. The English kings, and following them the kings of Scotland, maintained a stable quality of coinage that gave sterling a high reputation throughout western Europe. The very name sterling, whose earliest appearance (in the Latin form *sterilensis*) is from *c.*1078, seems to derive from an Old English word *ster* meaning 'strong', with reference to its stability.[27] Although Edward the Confessor minted some heavier issues, the standard penny between 1050 and 1080 weighed 21.5 grains (1.39 grams). In 1080 the standard weight was raised to 22.5 grains (1.46 grams), and it remained stable at this level for 200 years until Edward I's recoinage of 1279–80, when it was reduced to 22.25 grains (1.44 grams). The proportion of silver in the coin metal normally exceeded 92.5 per cent. Many individual coins in circulation diverged from these standards because of the imprecision of minting techniques, as well as through the wear coins suffered in circulation, but by the standards of most of Europe the stability and quality of the English coinage were remarkable. The Scottish currency, from its inception in *c.*1136, was based on the sterling standard of weight and fineness, from which it only very occasionally diverged.[28] Sterling circulated widely in Scotland, as in Wales and Ireland; less than a tenth of Scotland's currency in the thirteenth century was actually Scottish.[29] A stable currency minimized price instability and reduced the mercantile risks associated with monetary uncertainty. In the late thirteenth century, too, governments showed more concern than ever before with the problem of negotiating small transactions. Both English and Scottish mints began to produce halfpence and farthings after 1279–80; up to that time fractions of a penny had been created by cutting pennies into halves or quarters.

Price controls were restricted, in normal times, to attempts to limit the profits of traders in a few basic commodities. Bakers and brewers were checked by regulations that linked the weight of standard loaves and the price of ale to the fluctuating price of grain, and retailing vintners were controlled by reference to the basic import price of wine. In Scotland assizes of ale, bread, and wine are attributed to David I (1124–53), but their attestation is late and such an early date is unlikely; another assize of ale is attributed to Scotland's William I (1165–1214).[30] Whatever the date of the existing texts, the existence of assises of bread and ale in Scotland was taken for granted in the 'Laws of the Burghs'.[31] In England such regulations, after some shadowy local and private household regulations, became a matter of royal concern from the 1190s.[32] By at least the reign of Edward I there is evidence of the enforcement of these assizes in Welsh and Irish towns, presumably following English models.[33]

Governments were also constructive in supplying trusted institutional means for the settlement of disputes. Much of this activity was the business of local courts, particularly borough and burgh courts, which in England were managed in accordance with the precepts of common law and in Scotland were guided by the 'Laws of the Burghs'. These courts had the advantage of cheapness and convenience, and were likely to be particularly effective in the resolution of local disputes; often they were used simply to put pressure on a creditor to settle out of court. They were less effective in bringing to book creditors who lived beyond the jurisdiction of the local court, which would be the case with many debts between merchants. As late as the 1270s it had still been in order for English borough courts to regard the burgesses of a town as jointly responsible for each others' debts. If a merchant sued for a debt in the home town of the debtor and failed he could then renew his plea in some other court, the court attached to a fair, for example, by seeking to distrain the goods of the debtor's fellow townsmen. This led to much rough justice as the volume of commercial debt increased. In 1275 Edward I's First Statute of Westminster made it illegal to distrain the goods of a native merchant unless he was the principal debtor or an acknowledged surety for the debt.[34] The Statute of Acton Burnell (1283) and Statute of Merchants (1285) made litigation for debt easier by allowing debts to be officially registered in the records of stated towns. A debt officially registered in this way could then more easily be recovered by litigation because the court had already established the validity of the claim.

It is difficult to assign values to these various unifying and facilitating measures on the part of British governments. On the one hand they make England appear as a precocious example of the state building that is held to have facilitated European economic development in the fourteenth and fifteenth centuries. They presumably exercised some beneficial influence on the growth of internal trade. On the other hand, economic development in Europe between 1050 and 1300 was most pronounced in parts of the continent that lacked such extensive unification—notably in northern Italy, where in 1300 there were about forty different currencies circulating in an area not much larger than England. There were other transaction costs, such as those of transport, and securing market information, on which government activity had little or no impact, and which were cumulatively important enough to subordinate any advantages derived from such measures of unification as existed. In this period nowhere in Britain had an insurance system to reduce the risks of commercial losses.

Government and the Distribution of Incomes

By the late eleventh century systems of tribute in kind such as those of Scotland and Wales had already been broken down in England, partly because of the greater fragmentation of estates, and partly because of the greater availability of cash. Numerous features of rural society preserved relics of an older unmonetized economy, but England differed decisively from Scotland in 1050 in having already in place a system of money taxation covering all except the four northernmost counties, whose attachment to either England or Scotland was still a matter of dispute, and where there was in any case little money to be had. From 991 English kings had frequently levied geld from their subjects across England as far north as Lancashire and Yorkshire, initially as a way of buying off Danish raids, but between 1021 and 1051 as a peacetime tax. As we have seen in Chapter 3, land was assessed for geld according to units normally called hides. The great monument to geld collection is Domesday Book, which systematically records the number of hides for which each manor was assessed, as well as including information that would permit a revision of those assessments. One of the chief weaknesses of the geld as a general tax was the difficulty of imposing assessments on towns, where land was only a subordinate form of wealth. In 1086 the task of surveying England's largest towns, London and Winchester, defeated the Domesday commissioners. As towns grew during the twelfth century a taxed based on agrarian units became increasingly anomalous. In addition the value of the tax to the king was severely undermined by the multiplication of exemptions and reductions granted over the years as favours to particular individuals and institutions.[35] Geld was last levied in 1162, after which English kings made do with a variety of sources of income that tapped different areas of activity.[36]

Elsewhere during the twelfth and thirteenth centuries, royal dependence upon payment in produce was modified by the impact of commercial opportunities, though the older forms of income were not abandoned. In Scotland by the later twelfth century, though there is plenty of evidence of continuing payment in kind, the obligations of both cain and conveth were sometimes being acquitted with a money payment.[37] Already by the reign of Malcolm IV it is possible to identify a range of sources of money income available to the king of Scots, all dependent upon relatively recent developments in the Scottish kingdom. One was the income to be derived from burghs, a direct indication of the dependence of urban economic life on monetized trade. Some feudal dues were also levied in cash and so were the profits of justice. The best evidence for these dues in the twelfth century is from charters by which kings gave them away to abbeys; in 1144 David I and his son jointly gave the newly founded priory of St, Andrews 13s. 4d. a year out of his income from the burgh of Perth as well as £2 from the cain of ships there.[38]

Although in more recent times customs duties have frequently been used as a form of government policy for ends other than fund-raising, there was no such subtlety in the thirteenth century. Customs duties had no role in any sort of planning for economic growth, and their increasing prominence seems merely to reflect the growing awareness of governments that here was a source of income not taxed in any other way. Already in 1200 both England and Scotland had some income from overseas trade. In England there were various levies on local trade from at least the mid-twelfth century, but they were often granted to towns and other beneficiaries, and made little contribution to royal income. King John collected a fifteenth of the value of imports and exports for a few years following 1203, and a similar levy was imposed by Henry III for a few years from 1266. In Scotland, at least from the time of David I, kings took cain from ships unloading in Scottish port towns.[39] In both kingdoms the major new development of the thirteenth century was the heavy taxation of wool exports, which was introduced in both kingdoms about the same time. The magnitude of the wool trade resulting from England's unchallengeable position as a supplier of fine wools to continental industries had not been lost on Edward I. In 1275, when seeking to establish a working relationship with the Riccardi Company, he instituted a tax of 6s. 8d. a sack on all exports of wool, 6s. 8d. for every 300 woolfells, and 6s. 8d. for every 100 hides. The tax was to be levied in Welsh and Irish ports as well as those of England.[40] By 1282 Alexander III of Scotland had introduced similar duties on exports of wool and hides; they are recorded in that year as being owed on exports through Berwick.[41] In England, the *Carta Mercatoria* of 1303 supplemented the customs duty from all merchants with an additional levy of 3s. 4d. a sack from foreign merchants, so that English merchants ('denizens') paid 6s. 8d. a sack and foreigners ('aliens') paid 10s. 0d. It also imposed on foreign merchants a duty of 3d. in the £1, or 1.25 per cent, of the value of all goods exported or imported. From 1275 the taxation of wool exports rapidly became the main element in the medieval English customs system. Edward I temporarily, between 1294 and 1297, made the tax very much steeper when he persuaded merchants to accept his 'maltote' of 40s. 0d. a sack.[42] England's commercial development had supplied the crown with a major new source of income from taxation, all the more valuable because its level could be negotiated with the merchants separately from other taxpaying groups.

Increasing commercialization affected English royal income from England, Wales, and Ireland in other ways that had no direct equivalent in Scotland, the most important of these being the development of an assessed tax on the movable goods of the king's subjects, which had originated in crusading levies of 1166, 1188, and 1201 and an emergency levy to pay for Richard I's ransom in 1193–4. John had raised two such levies in 1203 and 1207 to pay for wars with France, and Henry III levied four, in 1225, 1232, 1237, 1269. Edward I levied three in the first eighteen years of his reign (1275, 1283, 1290), but the frequency and burden increased with the onset of major wars in his latter years; six paid in the fifteen years from 1294 to 1306 (1294, 1295, 1296, 1297, 1301, 1306) obtained in all £292,146, implying an average annual total of about £19,476 raised in this way.[43] Such taxes were based on the assessed value of each taxpayer's movable goods (goods, that is, excluding land, buildings, and other fixed property). The assessors then calculated a proportion of that value which the taxpayer was bound to pay to the king's collectors. If, for example, a man's movable goods were valued at 5*s*. 0*d*. (60 pence), and if the collectors were instructed to levy a tenth, then the man would have to pay 6*d*. Edward's taxation of the shires was at variable rates—a fifteenth in 1290, a tenth in 1294, an eleventh in 1295, a twelfth in 1296, a ninth in 1297, a fifteenth in 1301, and a thirtieth in 1306. Towns were sometimes taxed at rates even higher than these—a sixth in 1294, a seventh in 1295, an eighth in 1296. These repeated taxes shifted the costs of warfare more on to the peasantry and townsmen than they had been in the twelfth and earlier thirteenth centuries.[44] By 1300 they were considered to depend upon a grant by the English parliament, in the case of levies in England and Wales, and on the Dublin parliament in the case of levies in Ireland.

The taxation of Edward I struck way down the social scale in rural society. It was not only the rich who were taxed. The poor were supposed to be exempt, and indeed the very poorest, labourers and beggars, were. But the Exchequer's orders defined as poor a man with less than 10*s*. worth of movable goods beyond his subsistence requirements, the value of a single cow, or of two quarters of wheat. Taxation struck just at the group in village society with a small surplus for sale who were on the margin of commercial farming, and ensured that the surpluses available should be sold for the king's interest rather than that of the individual. Moreover, quite apart from the money that reached the king, the collectors themselves expected to gain from their activities. The collecting of taxes on movables subjected the population to a whole new range of corrupt local officialdom. In 1332 a sub-taxer responsible for assessments at Hemingford Abbots (Huntingdonshire) was said to have got his position by bribing the chief taxers for the county. As this case implies, the chief taxers in turn expected to profit from their office. One common device was to refuse to accept the accounts of the village sub-taxers unless they were accompanied by a gift of a shilling or two.[45]

A further way in which English royal rapacity responded to the greater commercialization of England and Ireland was through the practice of purveyance; in wartime the king commissioned the sheriffs of certain counties to supply him with the grain, livestock, hay, and other supplies necessary to maintain his armies. Counties on the east coast of both England and Ireland were the most affected after Scotland became a theatre of war during Edward I's reign. The system was arbitrary by its very nature; the provisions in question were simply seized by the purveying officers in return, if the owner was lucky, for a wooden tally. In principle goods were supposed to be paid for at market prices, but at best payment was in arrears, and in practice it was often costly for the owner of the purveyed goods to get his money back. The wealthier landlords in each county usually managed to exempt themselves from purveyance either by purchasing exemption or by bribing the sheriff's officials, so that much of the burden of purveyance fell upon the peasantry.[46]

Ireland suffered particularly heavily from the royal right of purveyance, which was being exercised there at least from the 1240s.[47] Yet earlier interventions were minor in comparison with the impact of Edward I's wars from the autumn of 1294. During the two years following September 1295, 14,886 quarters of wheat, 4,167½ of oats, and 162 of beans were shipped from Ireland to Gascony, and some supplies were also sent to Welsh castles. Royal demands were more modest in 1297–8, but just before Christmas 1298 the Irish officials were mandated to supply for the war in Scotland 8,000 quarters of wheat (6,000 as bolted flour, 2,000 as grain), 10,000 of oats, 2,000 of malt, 500 carcasses of salt beef, 1,000 fat pigs, and 20,000 dried fish to be sent to Skinburness on the Solway Firth.[48] Proportionately to her size and wealth, Ireland was burdened more heavily than England in these years. In 1300 the justiciar, chancellor, and treasurer of Ireland were instructed to supply 3,000 quarters of wheat and 2,000 of oats for the war in Scotland, which was equivalent to 30 per cent of the grain requested from the whole of England.[49] Up to the 1280s at least, agrarian activity in Ireland was to some extent able to expand to meet such demands. Handling these large consignments of produce on behalf of the king stimulated the trade of Dublin, where supplies were normally collected and shipped, and brought prosperity to its merchants. But though Ireland was expected to be able to produce large surpluses, these demands were not met easily, nor without causing unrest.[50] Heavy demands continued to be made on Ireland all through the wars of Edward I into the reign of his successor, and even after the Bruce invasion, Edward II diverted large quantities of grain to his Scottish armies, in 1322–3.[51]

The burden of royal taxation and purveyance was undoubtedly creating some poverty in the English and Irish countryside, and by the end of Edward I's reign it had given rise to a literary protest. In the vernacular Song of the Husbandman (*c.*1300) the author laments that 'to seek silver for the king I sold my seed, wherefore my land lies fallow and learns to sleep'. The picture is no doubt drawn for maximum effect, but in a number of documented instances land was abandoned or left uncultivated on account of poverty attributed to the king's taxes.[52]

Concluding Remarks

The impact of central governments on economy and society had extended in many ways between 1050 and 1300, and not always to the benefit of their subjects. The impact of warfare on society may not have increased, since for much of Britain the eleventh century was more disturbed than the thirteenth in this respect, but the character of warfare and the ways in which it was resourced had been transformed. Edward I's military ambitions in the last thirteen years of his reign were detrimental to the welfare of British and Irish populations in many ways. In peacetime government, some forms of royal intervention, such as the willingness to pander to urban trading interests, or to patronize select coteries of merchants, were probably more harmful than beneficial to the growth of output and trade. Nor was the role of government extensive enough to be assigned any guiding or driving role in the development process. In comparison with any modern state, even in 1300 the inactivity of the medieval British kingdoms in matters of social and economic regulation is much more striking than either their positive or their negative contributions to development. Apart from measures to improve royal estates, which did not differ from forms of investment by other landlords, there was no government investment in the economy. In this respect British kings were far less active than some of the precocious urban governments of northern Italy.

Nevertheless, through much of Britain the expanded scope of government had permitted long periods of domestic peace and stability, without which it is difficult to envisage economic development of the rapidity that occurred, particularly in the hundred years after 1160. The core areas of English and Scottish royal power were specially favoured from this point of view. In particular, the resource advantages of southern and midland England discussed in Chapter 1 were enhanced by the security offered by relatively effective government. Even areas where authority was more contested, such as eastern Ireland, had long periods of stability in which estates could be developed, towns could grow, and the circulation of money could increase. The maintenance of internal peace, and the light burden of external wars through most of the period, brought more benefits than any specific measures of unification or regulation that governments attempted, and they deserve to be positively assessed amongst the conditions that allowed development to proceed during these centuries.

NOTES

1. R. Bartlett, *England under the Norman and Angevin Kings, 1075–1225* (Oxford, 2000), 283.
2. A. A. M. Duncan, *Scotland: The Making of the Kingdom* (Edinburgh, 1989), 219–20.
3. Bartlett, *England under the Norman and Angevin Kings*, 284; W. E. Wightman, *The Lacy Family in England and Normandy, 1066–1194* (Oxford, 1966), 76.
4. W. L. Warren, *Henry II* (1973), 132–5.
5. A. L. Poole, *From Domesday Book to Magna Carta, 1087–1216*, 2nd edn. (Oxford, 1955), 423.
6. *Close Rolls of the Reign of Henry III*, Public Record Office, 14 vols. (1902–38), v: 1242–7, 314–15.
7. T. H. Lloyd, *Alien Merchants in England in the High Middle Ages* (Brighton, 1982), 175–6, 185–92.
8. W. R. Childs, *Anglo-Castilian Trade in the Later Middle Ages* (Manchester, 1978), 14–15.
9. T. H. Lloyd, *The English Wool Trade in the Middle Ages* (Cambridge, 1977), 75–98.
10. R. Frame, *The Political Development of the British Isles, 1100–1400* (Oxford, 1990), 85–9.

11. G. W. S. Barrow, *Kingship and Unity: Scotland, 1000–1306*, 2nd edn. (Edinburgh, 1989), 105–21.

12. 'The Account Roll of the Chamberlain of the Principality of North Wales from Michaelmas 1304 to Michaelmas 1305', ed. E. A. Lewis, *Bulletin of the Board of Celtic Studies*, 1 (1921–3), 256–75.

13. R. H. Britnell, *The Commercialisation of English Society, 1100–1500*, 2nd edn. (Manchester, 1997), 90–1, 96.

14. The word chalder derives from the same root as 'cauldron' (a large cooking pot), and ultimately from the Latin *caldaria* or *caldarium* (a hot bath).

15. *Bishop Hatfield's Survey*, ed. W. Greenwell, Surtees Society, 32 (1857), 278, 283.

16. Above (Ch. 1).

17. *Account Roll of the Priory of the Holy Trinity, Dublin, 1337–1346*, ed. J. Mills (Dublin, 1891), 212.

18. 'The Irish Pipe Roll of 14 John, 1211–12', ed. O. Davies and D. B. Quinn, *Ulster Journal of Archaeology*, 4, suppl. (1941), 14.

19. *Calendar of Documents Relating to Ireland, 1171–1307*, ed. H. S. Sweetman and G. F. Handcock, 5 vols. (1875–86), i, no. 2713, p. 404; ii, no. 222, p. 34; *Historic and Municipal Documents Relating to Ireland, A.D. 1172–1320 from the Archives of the City of Dublin*, ed. J. T. Gilbert (1870), no. 33, p. 102.

20. 'Accounts of the Great Roll of the Pipe of the Irish Exchequer for the Reign of Edward I', *Thirty-Eighth Report of the Deputy Keeper of the Public Records and Keeper of the State Papers in Ireland* (Dublin, 1906), 91–2.

21. *The Charters of David I: The Written Acts of David I King of Scots, 1124–53, and of his Son Henry, Earl of Northumberland, 1139–52*, ed. G. W. S. Barrow (Woodbridge, 1999), nos. 147, 183, pp. 124, 143; E. Gemmill and N. Mayhew, *Changing Values in Medieval Scotland: A Study of Prices, Money, and Weights and Measures* (Cambridge, 1995), 388–91.

22. 'Assise Regis David' and 'Assisa Regis David de Mensuris et Ponderibus', in *The Acts of the Parliaments of Scotland*, ed. T. Thomson and C. Innes, 12 vols. (Edinburgh, 1814–75), i. 324, 673–4.

23. *Regesta Regum Scottorum*, vi: *The Acts of David II*, ed. B. Webster (Edinburgh, 1982), no. 85, p. 123.

24. *Regesta Regum Scottorum*, v: *The Acts of Robert I*, ed. A. A. M. Duncan (Edinburgh, 1988), nos. 158 (Aberdeen), 163 (Berwick), pp. 430, 438.

25. *Ancient Laws and Customs of the Burghs of Scotland*, ed. C. Innes and R. Renwick, 2 vols. (Edinburgh, 1868–1910), i. 33–4.

26. R. E. Zupko, 'The Weights and Measures of Scotland before the Union', *Scottish Historical Review*, 56 (1977), 119–38.

27. P. Grierson, 'Sterling', in R. H. M. Dolley (ed.), *Anglo-Saxon Coins: Studies Presented to F. M. Stenton on the Occasion of His Seventieth Birthday* (1961), 266–83.

28. D. M. Metcalf, 'The Quality of Scottish Sterling Silver, 1136–1280', in id. (ed.), *Coinage in Medieval Scotland (1100–1600)* (Oxford, 1977), 73–84.

29. N. J. Mayhew, 'Money in Scotland in the Thirteenth Century', in Metcalf (ed.), *Coinage in Medieval Scotland*, 90.

30. *Acts of the Parliaments of Scotland*, i. 675–9.

31. *Ancient Laws and Customs*, i. 10.

32. Britnell, *Commercialisation*, 94–6.

33. e.g. *Historic and Municipal Documents*, no. 47(2), 140–1; *The Welsh Assize Roll, 1277–84 (Assize Roll No. 1147)*, ed. J. C. Davies (Cardiff, 1940), 272; *The Court Rolls of the Lordship of Ruthin or Dyffryn-Clwydd of the Reign of King Edward the First*, ed. R. A. Roberts, Cymmrodorion Record Ser. 2 (1893), 21.

34. Lloyd, *Alien Merchants*, 15–17.

35. J. A. Green, *The Government of England under Henry I* (Cambridge, 1986), 69–74.

36. Warren, *Henry II*, 377–8.

37. *Regesta Regum Scottorum*, ii. 53 and no. 514, pp. 465–6.

38. *Charters of David I*, no. 126, pp. 114–15.

39. See above (Ch. 5).

40. Duncan, *Scotland*, 156–7; N. S. B. Gras, *The Early English Customs System* (Cambridge, Mass., 1918), 27–58, 223–4.

41. Duncan, *Scotland*, 603–4.

42. E. M. Carus-Wilson and O. Coleman, *England's Export Trade, 1275–1547* (Oxford, 1963), 194; Lloyd, *English Wool Trade*, 76.

43. M. Ormrod, 'England in the Middle Ages', in R. Bonney (ed.), *The Rise of the Fiscal State in Europe, c.1200–1815* (Oxford, 1999), 29–31; M. Prestwich, *War, Politics and Finance under Edward I* (1972), 179; J. F. Willard, *Parliamentary Taxes on Personal Property, 1290 to 1334: A Study in Medieval English Financial Administration* (Cambridge, Mass., 1934), 3.

44. J. R. Maddicott, 'The English Peasantry and the Demands of the Crown, 1294–1341', in T. H. Aston (ed.), *Landlords, Peasants and Politics in Medieval England* (Cambridge, 1987), 2, 6; Willard, *Parliamentary Taxes*, 9.

45. Maddicott, 'English Peasantry', 10–11.

46. J. F. Lydon, *The Lordship of Ireland in the Middle Ages* (Dublin, 1972), 127–36; Maddicott, 'English Peasantry', 17, 19–22, 26–7, 30.

47. *Calendar of Documents Relating to Ireland*, i, nos. 1055, 2531, 2768, 2803, pp. 162, 377, 413, 418; cf. no. 2831, p. 423.

48. Ibid., iv, nos. 345, 346, 565, 570, pp. 159, 165–6, 269–71; *Irish Exchequer Payments, 1270–1446*, ed. P. Connolly (Dublin, 1998), 132, 135; M. D. O'Sullivan, *Italian Merchant Bankers in Ireland in the Thirteenth Century: A Study in the Social and Economic History of Medieval Ireland* (Dublin, 1962), 119; A. F. O'Brien, 'Commercial Relations between Aquitaine and Ireland c.1000 to c.1550', in J.-M. Picard (ed.), *Aquitaine and Ireland in the Middle Ages* (Dublin, 1995), 67.

49. M. J. McEnery, 'The State of Agriculture and the Standard of Living in Ireland in the Years 1240–1330', *Journal of the Royal Society of Antiquaries of Ireland*, 50 (1920), 11; Prestwich, *War, Politics and Finance*, 122.

50. J. F. Lydon, 'The Dublin Purveyors and the Wars in Scotland, 1296–1324', in G. Mac Niocaill and P. F. Wallace (eds.), *Keimelia: Studies in Medieval Archaeology and History in Memory of Tom Delaney* (Galway, 1988), 435, 440, 444–6; M. C. Lyons, 'Manorial Administration and the Manorial Economy in Ireland, c.1200–c.1377' (unpublished Ph.D.

thesis, Trinity College Dublin, 1984), i. 57–75; ii. 18–24; B. Smith, *Colonisation and Conquest in Medieval Ireland: The English in Louth, 1170–1330* (Cambridge, 1999), 152.

51. *Irish Exchequer Payments*, 167, 170, 178, 188, 196, 199, 202, 206–7, 212, 215, 221, 224–5, 230–1, 237, 244, 285, 288, 294; J. Lydon, 'The Impact of the Bruce Invasion, 1315–27', in Cosgrove (ed.), New History of Ireland, ii. 125; O'Sullivan, *Italian Merchant Bankers*, 122.

52. Maddicott, 'English Peasantry', 4, 13, 62–4, 69–71.

FURTHER READING

Amt, E., *The Accession of Henry II in England: Royal Government Restored, 1149–1159* (Woodbridge, 1993).

Barrow, G. W. S., *Kingship and Unity: Scotland, 1000–1306*, 2nd edn. (Edinburgh, 1989).

—— *Feudal Britain: The Completion of the Medieval Kingdom, 1066–1314* (1956).

—— 'Frontier and Settlement: Which Influenced Which? England and Scotland, 1100–1300', in R. Bartlett and A. Mackay (eds.), *Medieval Frontier Societies* (Oxford, 1989).

Bartlett, R., *England under the Norman and Angevin Kings, 1075–1225* (Oxford, 2000).

—— 'The Celtic Lands of the British Isles', in D. Abulafia (ed.), *The New Cambridge Medieval History*, v: *c.1198–c.1300* (Cambridge, 1999).

Bateson, J. D., *Coinage in Scotland* (1997).

Biddick, K., 'Power in Early English Development', *Comparative Studies in Society and History*, 32 (1990).

Blakely, R. M., 'The Scottish Bruses and the English Crown', in M. Prestwich, R. H. Britnell, and R. Frame (eds.), *Thirteenth Century England IX* (Woodbridge, 2003).

Blanchard, I., 'Lothian and Beyond; The Economy of the "English Empire" of David I', in R. Britnell and J. Hatcher (eds.), *Progress and Problems in Medieval England: Essays in Honour of Edward Miller* (Cambridge, 1996).

Carpenter, D., 'English Peasants in Politics, 1258–1267', *Past and Present*, 136 (1992).

—— 'The Plantagenet Kings', in D. Abulafia (ed.), *The New Cambridge Medieval History*, v: *c.1198–c.1300* (Cambridge, 1999).

Challis, C. E. (ed.), *A New History of the Royal Mint* (Cambridge, 1992).

Church, S. D. (ed.), *King John: New Interpretations* (Woodbridge, 1999).

Cosgrove, A. (ed.), *A New History of Ireland*, ii: *Medieval Ireland, 1169–1534* (Oxford, 1987).

Crump, J. J., 'The Mortimer Family and the Making of the March', in M. C. Prestwich, R. H. Britnell, and R. F. Frame (eds.), *Thirteenth Century England VI* (Woodbridge, 1997).

Davies, R. R., *Conquest, Coexistence and Change: Wales, 1063–1415* (Oxford, 1987).

—— *Domination and Conquest: The Experience of Ireland, Scotland and Wales, 1100–1300* (Cambridge, 1990).

—— *The First English Empire: Power and Identities in the British Isles, 1093–1343* (Oxford, 2000).

Duncan, A. A. M., *Scotland: The Making of the Kingdom* (Edinburgh, 1989).

Frame, R., *The Political Development of the British Isles, 1100–1400* (Oxford, 1990).

Fryde, E. B., and Fryde, M. M., 'Public Credit with Special Reference to North-Western Europe', in M. M. Postan and E. E. Rich (eds.), *The Cambridge Economic History of Europe*, iii: *Economic Organization and Policies in the Middle Ages* (Cambridge, 1963).

Gemmill, E., and Mayhew, N., *Changing Values in Medieval Scotland: A Study of Prices, Money, and Weights and Measures* (Cambridge, 1995).

Given, J., *State and Society in Medieval Europe: Gwynedd and Languedoc under Outside Rule* (Ithaca, NY, 1990).

Gras, N. S. B., *The Early English Customs System* (Cambridge, Mass., 1918).

Green, J. A., *The Government of England under Henry I* (Cambridge, 1986).

Grierson, P., 'Sterling', in R. H. M. Dolley (ed.), *Anglo-Saxon Coins: Studies Presented to F. M. Stenton on the Occasion of His Seventieth Birthday* (1961).

Harriss, G. L., *King, Parliament and Public Finance in Medieval England to 1369* (Oxford, 1975).

Harvey, B. (ed.), *The Twelfth and Thirteenth Centuries* (Oxford, 2001).

Holt, J., *Magna Carta*, rev. edn. (Cambridge, 1992).

—— *The Northerners: A Study in the Reign of King John* (Oxford, 1961).

Jenks, S., 'The Lay Subsidies and the State of the English Economy (1275–1334)', *Vierteljahrschrift für Sozial- und Wirtschaftsgeschichte*, 85 (1998).

Jones, R., 'Changing Ideologies of Medieval State Formation: A Growing Exploitation of Land in Gwynedd, c.1100–c.1400', *Journal of Historical Geography*, 26 (2000).

Lloyd, T. H., *Alien Merchants in England in the High Middle Ages* (Brighton, 1982).

—— *The English Wool Trade in the Middle Ages* (Cambridge, 1977).

Lydon, J. F., 'The Dublin Purveyors and the Wars in Scotland, 1296–1324', in G. Mac Niocaill and P. F. Wallace (eds.), *Keimelia: Studies in Medieval Archaeology and History in Memory of Tom Delaney* (Galway, 1988).

—— *The Lordship of Ireland in the Middle Ages* (Dublin, 1972).

McDonald, R. A., *The Kingdom of the Isles: Scotland's Western Seaboard, c.1100–c.1336* (East Linton, 1997).

Maddicott, J. R., 'The English Peasantry and the Demands of the Crown, 1294–1341', in T. H. Aston (ed.), *Landlords, Peasants and Politics in Medieval England* (Cambridge, 1987).

Metcalf, D. M., (ed.), *Coinage in Medieval Scotland (1100–1600)* (Oxford, 1977).

Miller, E., 'War, Taxation and the English Economy in the Late Thirteenth and Early Fourteenth Century', in J. M. Winter (ed.), *War and Economic Development* (Cambridge, 1975).

Mitchell, S. K., *Taxation in Medieval England* (New Haven, 1951).

Mundill, R. R., *England's Jewish Solution: Experiment and Expulsion, 1262–1290* (Cambridge, 1998).

Ormrod, W. O., 'England in the Middle Ages', in R. Bonney (ed.), *The Rise of the Fiscal State in Europe, c.1200–1815* (Oxford, 1999).

—— 'Royal Finance in Thirteenth-Century England', in P. R. Coss and S. D. Lloyd (eds.), *Thirteenth Century England V* (Woodbridge, 1995).

Otway-Ruthven, A. J., *A History of Medieval Ireland*, 2nd edn. (New York, 1980).

Prestwich, M., *War, Politics and Finance under Edward I* (1972).

Richardson, H. G., *The English Jewry under Angevin Kings* (1960).

Stacey, R., *Politics, Policy and Finance under Henry III, 1216–1245* (Oxford, 1987).

Stringer, K. J., *Earl David of Huntingdon: A Study in Anglo-Scottish History* (Edinburgh, 1985).

Stringer, K. J., 'Periphery and Core in Thirteenth-Century Scotland: Alan Son of Roland, Lord of Galloway and Constable of Scotland', in A. Grant and K. J. Stringer (eds.), *Medieval Scotland: Crown, Lordship and Community. Essays Presented to G. W. S. Barrow* (Edinburgh, 1998).

Stephenson, D., *The Governance of Gwynedd* (Cardiff, 1984).

Willard, J. F., *Parliamentary Taxes on Personal Property, 1290 to 1334: A Study in Medieval English Financial Administration* (Cambridge, Mass., 1934).

....

CHAPTER 13

Procedural Routines and the Uses of Literacy

Opportunities for studying the economic and social history of Britain between 1050 and 1300 become progressively more favourable because of a huge increase in the number of written records during the course of the period. Archaeological evidence also improves; more structures were built and more material remains were deposited with the growth of total population and wealth. But for the first time in British history, from the eleventh century written records begin to outstrip archaeological evidence as a source for economic and social history, supplying new sorts both of quantitative and qualitative evidence. They also supply an increasingly precise chronology of change, though the study of timbers by dendrochronologists is now also permitting the fine dating of some types of unwritten evidence. This transformation of our source material has implications for the character of economic and social change, but its analysis requires care. The volume of surviving records is not always a good guide to the number that once existed. Roman Britain, for example, was heavily administered both publicly and privately, yet little written evidence survives apart from literary works, monumental and funerary inscriptions, the legends on coins, and a few fragmentary handwritten texts preserved in exceptional contexts such as those at Vindolanda. All the administrative archives relating to the government of the Roman province are lost, together with the archives of those who had land or trade there. There have been similar catastrophic losses of records from medieval Asia, whose civilizations included states at least as literate and heavily governed as those of western Europe. These considerations are relevant to a survey of the increase in record keeping in Britain between 1050 and 1300 since not only is there a strong contrast between the beginning and end of the period, but also an equally strong contrast between different parts of Britain. It is a delicate matter to judge the significance of these chronological and spatial differences, but they are so very striking that the attempt needs to be made.

Even if we were sure that the surviving written evidence from the period

1030–1300 fairly reflects the original situation, care is needed in translating this into economic and social realities. In many circumstances complex economic institutions and patterns of exchange have existed without the use of written records; written records substituted for forms of memorization that lost their importance as writing things down became the norm.

Pragmatic Literacy: An Archival Revolution

Charters

Already from the late Anglo-Saxon and Norman periods we have appreciably more documentation than ever before in the form of charters recording transfers of land and other fixed property. All told about 1,850 charters and charter texts survive from Anglo-Saxon England (many of them not authentic).[1] Though the surviving texts of early charters from Wales, Ireland, and Scotland are almost always a lot later than the supposed original, there is enough material to postulate a Celtic tradition of charter writing. It is in evidence in Wales from at least the mid-ninth century, and may have been practised equally early in Ireland.[2] The examples of 'Celtic' charters are fewer than 200 all told, however, and of these 149 derive from the problematic *Book of Landaff* put together by Bishop Urban between 1119 and 1134 to defend the rights of his church in the course of a dispute with the bishops of St David's and Hereford.[3]

Whatever the strength of earlier traditions, in sheer quantity and range the twelfth and thirteenth centuries were revolutionary. For the period 1100–1530 there are over 10,000 charters in the archives of Durham Cathedral Priory alone, most of them authentic. The forms of charters were radically transformed as their use became more widespread; there was a real break in tradition between the Celtic and Anglo-Saxon charter styles and the models used later. In Wales and Ireland the adoption of Latin as the language for such documents and the abandonment of traditional vernacular scripts created a radical break with the past.[4] Everywhere, the characteristics of such documents became both more diverse and more formalized during the course of the period. The social range of written testimony broadened to include charters in the names of peasants and townsmen. From Holkham (Norfolk) at least 130 peasant transactions are attested by charters between 1250 and 1350.[5] Charters were normally written on quite small pieces of parchment, recorded details of a property transaction, listed the names of people who had witnessed it, and were then authenticated with at least one wax seal.

The increase in written evidence over the twelfth century can be illustrated from the evidence of English royal charters, whose texts have been systematically collected for their importance for the history of government and administration. Table 13.1 records the number of known royal charters from each reign up to King Henry II. Though there are no known authentic Latin charters from Scotland before 1094, they became more numerous and more a matter of routine during the twelfth century.[6] The three known royal charters and other *acta* of Alexander I (1107–24), 219 of David I (1124–53), 213 of Malcolm IV (1153–65), and 597 of William I (1165–1214) represent respectively an average of 0.2, 7.6, 17.8, and 12.2 texts a year for the four consecutive reigns. William I of Scotland is credited with assuming the right to punish those who forged charters, whether royal or private.[7] The surviving charters of Welsh rulers imply an increasing resort to writing. Of the 282 known from the period 1132–1283; many are only approximately datable, but at most 87 (31 per cent of the total) are from 1132–1200 (45 per cent of the time period).[8]

Alongside the growth in the number of royal and princely charters, there was also a vast increase in the number of surviving private charters for the conveyance of free land, both lay and ecclesiastical. The increase continued vigorously into the thirteenth century. Thousands survive in their original state, but many more are known from copies written into manuscript registers, or occasionally rolls, known as cartularies. The earliest cartularies date from the twelfth century; they were themselves a remarkable example of the record-keeping urge characteristic of the estate bureaucracies of the period. Another, less common, source of evidence relating to deeds and other documents is the record kept by those issuing them. Whereas a cartulary records charters received, and is consequently most useful for

TABLE 13.1. *The number of surviving royal* acta, *1066–1189*

	No. of *acta*	No. per year
William I (1066–87)	353	17
William II (1087–1100)	191	15
Henry I (1100–35)	1369	39
Stephen (1135–54)	720 (+27)	39
Henry II (1154–88)	(about 4,000)	115

Note: This calculation includes only *acta* issued by kings themselves.

Source: Regesta Regum Anglo-Normannorum, ed. H. W. C. Davies, C. Johnson, H. A. Cronne, and R. H. C. Davies, 4 vols. (Oxford, 1913–69); Regesta Regum Anglo-Normannorum: The Acta of William I, ed. D. Bates (Oxford, 1998); N. Vincent, 'New Charters of King Stephen with some Reflections upon the Royal Forests during the Anarchy', English Historical Review, 114 (1999), 899–928; M. T. Clanchy, From Memory to Written Record, 2nd edn. (Oxford, 1993), 58–9.

showing how an estate was built up, a record of documents issued is most useful for studying the administrative practices of the issuing authority. By far the most important examples of this latter type of record are the series of enrolments of royal charters maintained by the English kings from the reign of King John onwards. Up to that point no systematic attempt had been made, so far as we know, to retain a record of what the king had granted to others. From the beginning of King John's reign in 1199 royal charters were enrolled, perhaps to assist the facilitate the work of the justices in verifying the status of royal instruments presented in court.[9] From that time we have a much fuller record of them than for earlier reigns, despite some archival losses.

The increasing availability of private charters and charter collections is not a uniquely English phenomenon. The issuing of charters by the Scottish nobility had become a matter of common course by the late twelfth century. There are ninety surviving deeds for Earl David of Huntingdon between 1172 and 1228, of which twenty-seven relate to his property and rights in Scotland.[10] It became normal for Scottish magnates to have a seal, to employ a clerk or two as a regular part of their households, and to keep a documents chest. Some Scottish bishoprics and monasteries were keeping cartularies from the earlier thirteenth century.[11] Even Scottish peasants and townsmen occasionally issued charters.[12] There remains ample testimony to this increase, though the survival of early Scottish private charters was perhaps affected adversely by the English occupation of Scottish castles during the War of Independence following Edward I's invasion of 1296. The *Book of Llandaff*, with all its problems, is testimony to the rising importance of documentation in legal disputes in Wales even in the earlier twelfth century. In Glamorganshire genuine charters by Welsh and English donors other than lay and ecclesiastical magnates start to become numerous from the 1180s.[13] Although private deeds are less numerous from northern Wales and from western and northern Scotland, there are many examples. There are seven extant charters of Alan of Galloway between 1210 and *c*.1225, of which five relate to property in the modern Kirkcudbrightshire and Ayrshire.[14] In Ireland the making of private charters to record property transactions became more common, along with so many more Anglo-Norman practices, after the conquest of 1169, though it was some while before charters become numerous.[15]

Alongside charters new forms of legal record proliferated in the course of the twelfth and thirteenth centuries, too numerous to detail here. Land transactions often involved more than a single charter, as written records were adopted to terminate the claims of third parties. New instruments of credit were devised to record the terms of borrowing; some of the earliest were the Jewish 'stars', which survive in quite large numbers.[16] Written receipts and contracts became more numerous. Administrators also increasingly resorted to various sorts of written letters to convey their instructions. The writ system of the Anglo-Saxon kings was vastly expanded with the extension of royal justice under Henry II of England and his successors. The Scottish kings adopted a similar system of 'legal brieves'. Different types of lawsuit each had their own form of writ and legal procedure.[17] In addition, kings sent out letters of a non-judicial character. At the beginning of King John's reign, in addition to the enrolment of royal charters, the king's chancery inaugurated the regular enrolment of royal letters. One set of rolls recorded all the king's formal open letters (letters patent) and another recorded the more private sort of letter that was folded over and sealed (letters close).[18] Needless to say, these enrolments constitute some of the most frequently used sources of English history from the beginning of the thirteenth century onwards. Bishops, too, began in this period to record important mandates, and other notes, in official registers. The earliest, the *Liber Antiquus* of Hugh Wells, bishop of Lincoln, begun about 1216, is mostly concerned with the provision of vicarages in accordance with the decrees of the third Lateran Council of the Church in 1215.[19]

Administrative Records

The evidence of charters and other legal instruments and written mandates deserves special attention in this context because such records were drawn up all through the period, and their numbers provide an impressively coherent testimony to the growth of record keeping. In the course of time, however, large numbers of additional types of record began to be kept as a normal part of administrative routines, particularly in England, both by governments and by private individuals. Major categories of material, of outstanding importance for our understanding of the economy and society of the time, are surveys of property and landlord rights, financial accounts, and records of jurisdiction.[20]

Domesday Book (1086) is one of the earliest, as well as one of the most astonishing, surveys of property. Later royal administrations had surveys made of the estates of principal tenants of the crown whenever one of them died; each of these records, known as inquisitions *post mortem*, was a little echo of Domesday Book, and served much the same purpose of enabling the king to check up on his rights and exercise them. Later fact-finding ventures by kings of England include the Hundred Rolls of 1274–5 and 1279–80, which have already been cited for their evidence of landholding and estate structures in the English midlands.[21] Edward I's reign was a peak period for the systematic collection of data by the English crown; besides the Hundred Roll inquiries, the Quo Warranto proceedings between 1278 and 1294 added to the government's information about the powers landlords were exercising in the shires. In Wales, too, Edward also initiated fact-finding exercises in 1280–1, 1284–5, and 1290 to clarify his rights and the state of local government there.[22]

As late as the eleventh century, landlords seem not to have kept detailed records of which tenants owed rent and services nor of what rents and services they owed. The complex structure of obligations on which the agrarian system depended could be remembered because it changed only slowly. From the twelfth century, however, lords began to survey their estates in order to establish the value or to record what their tenants owed. When the first surveys and custumals were compiled to record the names of tenants and their obligations, landlords obtained the information they needed by summoning a panel of villager jurors to give oral testimony.[23] The same practices were used and retained for centuries where there was uncertainty about boundaries. Twelfth-century surveys survive from the abbeys of Glastonbury, Peterborough, Ramsey, and Burton, for the English estates of the Norman abbey of Caen, and from the bishopric estates of Durham, and they enable us to describe tenant rents and services much more accurately than Domesday Book, which does not record such detail.

The earliest annually audited English royal accounts date from 1130, and they become a regular series from 1155 onwards. These are the pipe rolls, whose value for economic and social history has been proved in numerous different enquiries, but most notably in the history of prices, estate management, and taxation. They are complemented by ancillary records relating to the collection of royal income later in the thirteenth century, such as sheriffs' accounts and the accounts of those charged with the custody of royal estates. At the centre of the financial system, the various exchequer rolls were supplemented by account books of the king's wardrobe, which became a major spending department of the government under Henry III and Edward I. These various forms of account open up vast new opportunities for historians. Records of English lay taxation make it possible to examine the distribution of wealth between different towns and townships, though the most comprehensively preserved series date from after 1300.[24] The course of English overseas trade can be charted in part from the records of customs receipts following the inauguration of export duties on wool in 1275. Another major development in the uses of literacy for routines of government affected legal procedures. Records of litigation and procedure in the courts of the king of England are of major significance for the history of English law, but also contain evidence concerning the incidence of crime, institutions of credit and patterns of indebtedness, social conflict between landlords and tenants, and many other features of the thirteenth century that it would be difficult to capture elsewhere. These records start in a fairly small way in the late twelfth century with the *curia regis* rolls, the rolls of itinerant justices, and the so-called 'feet of fines' that record settlements of property disputes in the king's courts, building up to an enormous bulk of plea rolls by the reign of Edward I. The practices of the English administration were transferred quite early on to the administration of Ireland, which had its own series of chancery enrolments, plea rolls, statute rolls, and exchequer rolls. The earliest known Irish pipe roll was from 1211–12.[25]

Royal administrative records from Scotland from this period also increased appreciably in bulk but unfortunately they have suffered much severer losses than those from England. Some enrolled sheriffs' and bailiffs' accounts of Alexander III's reign from 1263 to 1266, and from the Interregnum of 1288–90, survived long enough to be seen and very imperfectly transcribed in the seventeenth century.[26] Unfortunately, though, no original royal administrative documentation from before 1300 is known to be still extant. Responsibility for these losses is at least partly attributable to Edward I, who removed the Scottish royal archives and either destroyed them or failed to secure their preservation. The riches that once existed in Scotland may be judged from the indenture recording the archive sent from Edinburgh Castle in 1292 in two coffers. Into them were packed hundreds of rolls and other documents—the accounts of sheriffs, bailiffs, lessees, thanes and borough officers, customs collectors, moneyers, together with records of inquests, perambulations and extents, plea rolls, memoranda rolls, enrolled royal charters, and original letters, charters, feet of fines, and other instruments. Subsequent consignments of archival material from Edinburgh and elsewhere included sheriffs' accounts going back to at least 1204 and further sets of rolls containing extents of royal manors and sheriffs' accounts from northern Scotland.[27] The Scottish royal archive, though doubtless smaller than that of the contemporary English kingdom, was evidently closely analogous, even to the extent of sharing the taste for rolls rather than books as the preferred form of record keeping.

Evidence for the administrative archives of the Welsh princes is thinner than for the Scottish crown. Given the small size and relative poverty of the principality, its thirteenth-century records are unlikely to have been bulkier than those of an English magnate's estate. The centralizing policy of Llywelyn ap Iorwerth, David ap Llywelyn, and Llywelyn ap Gruffydd, and their success in raising unprecedented amounts of cash, make it likely that archival activity increased, as elsewhere in Britain. The Welsh princes are known to have had a chancellor and a chamberlain, but nothing is known about the size of the establishments under them. One indication that there were financial records is that between 1266 and 1279 two clerks— Richard of Mold and David ap Ithel—were involved in some capacity in financial administration. We have no explicit contemporary statement that Edward I removed Welsh records as he did those of the Scottish crown, but his policy was probably identical. A record of some of the princely archive may be represented in the so-called 'Welsh Letters' (*Littere Wallie*), an important source for the life of Llywelyn ap Gruffydd, the last native prince of Wales. They are known from a register of transcripts made in the late thirteenth century from original records deposited in the exchequer at Westminster, but since lost.[28] The Treasury of Receipt at Westminster also held an unintelligible quire beginning 'Edmygaw douit duyrmyd diuas' and a collection of material relating to Wales including 'various quires and rolls in the Welsh language very foreign to the English language', which sound like material removed from Wales.[29] Some at least of the archive of the Welsh princes was last seen at Westminster, but it is impossible to gauge what it contained.[30] The problems of documenting the princely administration of Wales before its conquest by Edward I in 1284 have been compared with those of discussing the English royal administration before its takeover by William I in 1066.[31] With Edward I's annexation of the former principality of Wales in 1282, however, the newly acquired royal assets there were subjected to standard account-ability that has left abundant documentary survivals both as audited enrolments in the exchequer pipe rolls and, from 1304–5, in the form of original accounts.[32]

In the course of time many thirteenth-century English landlords similarly began to require records from their estate officers. The practice of keeping accounts had no known antecedents before the thirteenth century; the earliest surviving estate accounts are those from Canterbury Cathedral Priory (1207–8) and the bishopric of Winchester (1208–9). Such accounts record cash receipts and expenses in detail at each manor of an estate, supply an inventory of grain and livestock available at the beginning of the accounting period, and comment on how and why stocks changed.[33] Detailed annual accounts of this kind gradually become more common through the thirteenth century to reach a peak in the early fourteenth, and they allow unprecedented insights into agricultural practices and productivity.[34] Although the earliest examples are from ecclesiastical estates, lay lords were having them compiled by the 1250s: an example survives from 1257–8 for the Segrave manor of Caludon in Warwickshire.[35] Even some very minor lords kept manorial accounts by the 1280s, like Henry le Cat at Hevingham in Norfolk.[36] Accounting of this nature was advantageous to landlords once they had switched into adminis-tering manors directly, rather than farming them out to leaseholders,[37] but there was a long time lag between the general assumption of direct control of manors (c.1180–1220) and the widespread adoption of accounting practices (c.1240–80). This implies there was more to the introduction of estate accounts than mere organizational necessity. Exactly the same period saw the formalizing and multipli-cation of other sorts of account—such as those of monastic obedientiaries, and the office holders in lay households—which had nothing to do with forms of estate administration. There was, in other words, a more general cultural shift towards using written records to impose greater discipline. A subordinate who has to render an account, even if he gets away with unseen perks of office, is someone whose performance is being watched.

Like their kings, English private landlords also learned to keep a written record of their judicial activity, though this was later in starting. These practices carried judicial recording into the heart of rural society. The bishops of Winchester were precocious in recording the fines they levied in their courts as early as 1209,[38] but the practice was widespread in England by the late thirteenth century. For the insight they offer into the structures and practices of village life these local legal records—especially manor court rolls—are unmatched, and they are the source of most of what we know about family composition, inheritance rules, social hierarchy, and rural credit. Because many landlords exercised minor policing responsibilities, manorial court records are also a substantial source of information about some commercial activities that were regulated by law, such as brewing and milling. The practices that landlords had implemented on their English estates in the late thirteenth century were, not surprisingly, extended to Irish and Welsh properties, so that there too there is a proliferation of local detail from this period. The important series of accounts for the Bigod family's Irish manors between 1279 and 1304 is a major, if one-sided source of information about agriculture in Edward I's reign.[39] There are similar estate accounts from Wales.[40] The earliest Welsh court records are from 1262/3, and the long and important series from the lordship of Dyffryn-Clwydd begins in 1294.[41] By the last decades of the thirteenth century not only most landlords but also many self-governing boroughs were keeping regular series of judicial records. The same impetus was experienced in some Scottish burghs about this time. The earliest court roll from Aberdeen dates from 1317, but it was probably not the first.[42]

These increases in documentation represent a real increase in dependence upon the written word, and a real increase in the number of records that were written. What has survived can only be a small proportion of what existed, but the pattern of survival is inconsistent with a heavy and systematic bias towards later periods across all types of archival material. It is true that there is some evidence of the destruction of Anglo-Saxon records by the increasingly Norman royal administration of the late eleventh and early twelfth centuries, but this observation cannot reasonably be extended very far. If the management of Anglo-Saxon properties had depended heavily on administrative records, we should expect the production from at least the 1070s onward of large numbers of equivalent records in Latin or French. The absence of any records of private estate administration other than surveys throughout the twelfth century speaks against there having been any major discontinuity in this respect until later, and suggests that the series of accounts and court records that survive from the thirteenth century were an innovation. Many of the known charters (or copies of their wording) survive in the private archives of abbeys that had everything to gain from preserving their early muniments. It would be difficult to explain a systematic bias to later records in the charter collections and cartularies of institutions that were so alert to the need to preserve ancient legal evidence. In the twelfth century monks were more likely to be forging charters they thought they needed than to be destroying ones they actually possessed.[43] It would similarly be difficult to explain the infrequency of references in existing charters, surveys, accounts, and legal records to ancient records if these had existed. Such cross-referencing as occurs to older records is wholly consistent with the idea that royal and private archives alike were much slimmer in the eleventh century than in the thirteenth.

Why did record keeping become so much part of administrative routines? It is, of course, possible to suggest a different administrative reason for each type of record separately—title deeds were a safeguard against legal challenge, estate surveys and court rolls facilitated the exaction of landlords' rights, accounts were a check on the honesty of administrative officials, and so on. But such piecemeal explaining misses the full force of the phenomenon, which seems to represent rather a broad culture shift in favour of recording and preserving detailed information of a legal and financial nature. Keeping records can be a self-driven phenomenon, to the extent that keeping one set of records makes it irrational not to keep another set, and a third set, and to account for things that nobody previously thought it necessary to account for. Record keeping, like monetized trade, was a large cluster of innovations interrelated in complex ways.

The availability of clerks, which was essential to the archival revolution, was not a problem for the larger institutions, especially royal and ecclesiastical institutions, with numerous literate men to hand, though the new procedures required training. Yet the increase in the number of documents written for peasants and minor land-lords implies that outside such institutions there were men who were sufficiently educated to compile legal instruments and administrative records for a fee. The difficulty of compiling charters, surveys, accounts, and court rolls of all kinds was compounded by the fact that they were rarely composed in anything other than Latin. Though the Latin required for these purposes was fairly standardized, the vocabulary and grammar required were far from negligible, since the usefulness of the records hinged on their clarity and fluency of expression. They often, too, had to be written in haste. The expansion of clerical career prospects explains the multiplication of grammar schools which has been observed as one of the features of England in this period. Evidence for the existence of local freelance clerks, some of them laymen, has been found in a number of different contexts.[44] In turn, the increased supply of clerks encouraged employers to expand their record keeping to plug administrative loopholes.

Regional Variation

Though the growth in record keeping was so widespread, there are great differences in the quantity of surviving documentary evidence between southern

England and the rest of Britain and Ireland, a difference that greatly complicates the task of writing a history of Britain before 1300, and continues to be problematic for a long time afterwards. The differences are least marked for charters and legal instruments, since there are numerous monastic cartularies from all over Britain. As this implies, there is a strong bias in all private archival material throughout Britain towards ecclesiastical collections, but even so it is striking how few charters survive for north-western Scotland, western Ireland, north Wales, and Cornwall. But the differing availability of administrative records across Britain and Ireland is much sharper.

Even within southern and eastern England the amount of surviving documentation varies for reasons that have not wholly been explained. A lot depends upon the distribution of manors on particular well-documented estates; Hampshire benefits enormously from the fine archive of the bishopric of Winchester, Huntingdonshire from that of Ramsey Abbey, and Kent from that of Canterbury Cathedral Priory.[45] Some counties, like Lincolnshire, appear unaccountably badly off. In total, however, the availability of estate archives from southern and midland English estate administrations by the later thirteenth century is remarkable. These types of record are to some extent matched in northern monastic centres. Bolton Abbey in Yorkshire has a fine series of estate accounts for the late thirteenth and early fourteenth centuries.[46] Durham Priory, in addition to a large charter collection, has central bursars' accounts from 1278, some incomplete series of manorial accounts from 1277, and local court rolls from about 1295. But such archives are rarer in northwestern England, Wales, and Ireland, and if they were kept in Scotland none survives. Even lists of tenants rents and customs, which had become quite a normal part of the administration of large monastic estates in twelfth-century England, seem to have been unusual in Scotland; only two survive, both from around 1300, and both perhaps the result of wartime disturbance rather than normal administrative routine.[47] Differing archival survivals explain why we know so much more about agriculture and rural society in southern and midland England than we do about most parts of Britain.

Despite the evidence for an independent Celtic tradition of charter composition, native rulers of Ireland and western Britain neither developed it significantly nor adopted the Anglo-Norman tradition with any enthusiasm. The scarcity of their written deeds from before 1300 would be difficult to account for if they were once numerous. The earliest native Irish Latin charter, of the sort familiar elsewhere in Britain, is one of 1156–7 by the high king of Ireland granted to Newry Abbey.[48] The same lack of concern for bureaucracy extended to other everyday business. No administrative archives survive from Ireland before the Anglo-Norman conquest, and it is not at all certain how far Irish forms of government would have depended upon them. The Anglo-Norman conquest undoubtedly caused severe administrative discontinuity, and its impact was especially catastrophic in the areas where native Irish administrators were most likely to have used written records. On balance, however, the disinclination on the part of Irish rulers to use written *acta* makes it unlikely that writing was very much required for other forms of administration. Well-developed memories were still a valid alternative. It is similarly unlikely that the destruction of records by Edward I and the English wholly accounts for the contrasts between northern Wales and the English midlands. Though the Welsh princes, as we have seen, had some administrative archive by the later thirteenth century, it can only have been a small one given the size of their clerical staff and the small number of surviving charters and other written instruments.

The only plausible explanation for systematic differences across Britain and Ireland is that the increasing use of literacy for pragmatic purposes both started earlier in southern England, and developed further. It is true that some of the least documented parts of Britain were amongst the most politically unstable, and that some record losses might be explained by that consideration. Yet on the wider canvas of medieval Europe some of the most politically disturbed regions—like northern Italy or Flanders—have exceptionally rich archival collections from this period. Highly literate societies whose medieval archives are lost, like Sung and Yuan China, have left other materials attesting their extensive use of written archives; such evidence is not to be found to counter the absence of materials from much of Britain and Ireland. Enormous differences in the quantity and range of private records are in this respect more significant than differences between government archives, since widely dispersed collections might be expected to have left more evidence than politically targeted ones.

The differing use of literacy across Britain implies that there were equally strong differences between the practices of rulers and landowners. It would nevertheless be fallacious to suppose that these divisions were shaped by ancient traditions. The contrasts under discussion were not deep-rooted in the history of culture; there had been times when the uses of literacy were at least as advanced in Celtic and northern societies as they had been in southern and midland England. Differences in the volume of surviving archival material are not neatly associated with any linguistic or cultural barrier. Since the archival revolution was almost wholly based on Latin literacy rather than the vernacular there was no reason for the speakers of Celtic languages to be disadvantaged.

Exploring these differences helps to explain the cultural shift that pragmatic literacy involved. As in the case of different patterns of urbanization and land use,[49] the differing use of records as an administrative device can be related to more material and practical considerations affecting governors and governed alike. The overall European pattern of archival preservation corresponds much more to the varying distribution of commercial activity than to the distribution of political stability. This suggests the principal explanation why there are these contrasts across Britain; they correspond to differences in the level of urbanization, population density, and commercial involvement on the part of local populations. There was, it would seem, some functional or cultural affinity between commercial development and the multiplication of records, even if the latter cannot be given any particular utilitarian explanation. This phenomenon can be observed on a world scale,[50] but it is here equally manifest in the interregional contrasts within Britain that we have already observed. It remains to explain why record keeping and commercial development should be so closely allied.

Organizational complexity is not, by itself, enough to explain an increasing resort to written records. The estate organizations of the Anglo-Saxon kings, or the twelfth-century kings of Scotland, were doubtless complicated if they were able to supply royal households week in and week out, but it is unlikely that the details were written down. Similarly the manorial customs that estate administrations recorded for their own convenience from the twelfth century onwards were frequently highly complex even at the level of a single village; different tenants had differing status, and owed different combinations of labour, produce, and money rents. The unwritten tenant customs of the late eleventh century were characteristically more complex, in fact, than the written rents of the late fifteenth. It is easy to underestimate the capacity of memory to retain elaborate detail, especially when livelihood and status depend upon it. Memory serves well if obligations are truly customary, and remain much the same from generation to generation. It becomes much less satisfactory if obligations are liable to change, since any alteration increases the hazard that different people will remember differently.

Three features of commercial development are particularly important in explaining the increasing predilection for written detail. One, and probably the most important, was the increasing propensity for social relations of all kinds to be modified in response to new pressures and commercial opportunities. The commercialization of social relationships between 1050 and 1300 implied numerous departures from tradition even in the most customary of contexts. The obligations of customary tenants, English villeins for example, were transformed by the subdivision of older tenements, and the increasing requirement that services and rents should be capable of being acquitted by money payments. The recording of manorial customs by twelfth and thirteenth-century landlords, though it may have had some residual benefit for tenants in defining the limits of seigniorial pressure, was primarily in the interests of estate administrators who required an authoritative statement of what tenants owed. Initially, of course, such records depended upon the sworn testimony of villagers reporting from memory,[51] but once a custumal had been compiled oral testimony was never again the sole available resource. In addition, custumals preserved agreements made with tenants, individually or collectively, and so admitted an element of contract and modification into relations between lords and their tenants despite their supposedly customary basis.[52] In these ways literacy was an instrument used by lords in the process of establishing, contesting, and renegotiating their relations with their tenants and servants. A case in point was the refusal to allow customary tenants any written title to their holdings, which was a legal characteristic of English villein tenure. A customary holding could not be conveyed by charter, but only by a ritual in the lord's court by which the property was first surrendered to the lord and then regranted to the new tenant. Lords had an interest in preventing their villeins from using written documents and seals in transferring customary land, and punished those who did so.[53]

A second relevant feature of commercial development was the increasing amount of legal and administrative activity, often of a complex and technical nature, associated with large institutions in a developing economy. Like the modification of custom, new administrative procedures placed a strain on traditional forms of memorization. The increasing activity of large institutions was partly the result of population growth, but it had much more to do with new demands on legal institutions and new opportunities for raising cash. Increased commercial activity encouraged commercial regulation, which in turn increased the need for new types of police work. The implementation of the assizes of bread and ale, for example, became a widespread feature of local government in both urban and rural courts from the early thirteenth century.[54] The volume of litigation coming before law courts of all kinds responded directly to the increase in the number of debts and commercial contracts. The greater possibilities for raising cash by taxes, fines, and rents encouraged the recording of the various sources from which it was to be collected.

A third relevant aspect of commercial development was the increasing dependence of incomes on unpredictable transactions governed by economic variables such as prices and profit opportunities. Such challenges to the power of memory affected many ranks of society in which the pattern of trading followed opportunistic rather than traditional and predictable patterns. Quantities, prices, and customers changed from year to year, and could not be securely remembered, but this information was important both as a check on the efficiency of agents such as manorial officers and, often, as security against bad debts. The keeping of manorial accounts was in part, at least, the result of the interest lords had in following what had been sold from their demesnes, at what prices and, in some instances, to whom. We know little about the form of merchant records in this period, but at least the leading merchants kept some record of their transactions, and even quite modest ones had from time to time to look after recorded obligations of debt, bonds, and other financial instruments.[55] A large amount of trade was conducted without such written evidence, depending still on the testimony of witnesses in case of disagreement between the contracting parties, but urban clerks could find work in drawing up a widening range of ephemeral documents, and many townsmen kept seals with which to authenticate them, like John the glovemaker of Newcastle upon Tyne, whose seal design bore the representation of a glove.[56] In this way, too, literacy and economic development were closely allied, and the alliance explains much of the differing distribution of written records in Britain and Ireland.

NOTES

1. P. H. Sawyer, *Anglo-Saxon Charters: An Annotated List and Bibliography* (1968).

2. W. Davies, 'The Latin Charter-Tradition in Western Britain, Brittany and Ireland in the Early-Medieval Period', in D. Whitelock, R. McKitterick, and D. Dumville (eds.), *Ireland in Early Medieval Europe: Studies in Memory of Kathleen Hughes* (Cambridge, 1982), 258–80; ead., 'Charter-Writing and its Uses in Medieval Celtic Societies', in H. Pryce (ed.), *Literacy in Medieval Celtic Societies* (Cambridge, 1998), 109.

3. J. R. Davies, '*Liber Landavensis*: Its Date and History', *Cambrian Medieval Celtic Studies*, 35 (1998), 1–11; id., 'The Book of Llandaff: A Twelfth-Century Perspective', *Anglo-Norman Studies*, 21 (1998), 31–46; K. L. Maund, 'Fact and Narrative Fiction in the Llandaff Charters', *Studia Celtica*, 31 (1997), 173–93.

4. M. T. Flanagan, 'The Context and Uses of the Charter in Twelfth-Century Ireland', in Pryce (ed.), *Literacy*, 117.

5. D. Postles, 'Country Clerici and the Composition of English Twelfth- and Thirteenth-Century Private Charters', in K. Heidecker (ed.), *Charters and the Use of the Written Word in Medieval Society* (Turnhout, 2000), 33.

6. A. A. Duncan, 'The Earliest Scottish Charters', *Scottish Historical Review*, 37 (1958), 103–35; id., 'Yes, the Earliest Scottish Charters', ibid., 78 (1999), 1–38; G. W. S. Barrow, 'The Pattern of Non-Literary Manuscript Production and Survival in Scotland, 1250–1330', in R. H. Britnell (ed.), *Pragmatic Literacy, East and West, 1200–1330* (Woodbridge, 1997), 132.

7. *The Acts of the Parliaments of Scotland*, ed. T. Thomson and C. Innes, 12 vols. (Edinburgh, 1814–75), i. 373.

8. *Handlist of the Acts of Native Welsh Rulers, 1132–1283*, ed. K. L. Maund (Cardiff, 1996), 2–83.

9. V. H. Galbraith, *Studies in the Public Records* (1948), 69.

10. K. J. Stringer, *Earl David of Huntingdon: A Study in Anglo-Scottish History* (Edinburgh, 1985), 220–70.

11. G. R. C. Davis, *Medieval Cartularies of Great Britain: A Short Catalogue* (1958), no. 1150, p. 133 (see of Glasgow); no. 1164, p. 134 (Lindores).

12. *Registrum S. Marie de Neubotle*, ed. C. Innes, Bannatyne Club, 89 (1849), nos. 176–7, 191, pp. 143–5, 154; *Charters of the Abbey of Inchcolm*, ed. D. E. Easson and A. Macdonald, Scottish History Society, 3rd ser. 32 (1938), nos. 8, 31, pp. 8, 30–1; Barrow, 'Pattern of Non-Literary Manuscript Production', 136.

13. *Cartae et Alia Munimenta quae ad Dominium de Glamorgancia Pertinent*, ed. G. L. Clark, 6 vols. (Cardiff, 1910), i, nos. 159–66, 168, 173–80, pp. 159–85.

14. K. J. Stringer, 'Periphery and Core in Thirteenth-Century Scotland: Alan Son of Roland, Lord of Galloway and Constable of Scotland', in A. Grant and K. J. Stringer (eds.), *Medieval Scotland: Crown, Lordship and Community. Essays Presented to G. W. S. Barrow* (Edinburgh, 1993), 103–12.

15. For early examples, see *Calendar of Archbishop Alen's Register, c.1172–1534*, ed. C. McNeill (Dublin, 1950), 2, 8–9, 11, 13–14, 17, 20; *Calendar of Ormond Deeds*, ed. E. Curtis, 6 vols. (Dublin, 1932–43), i. nos. 1–5, pp. 1–3; 'Calendar of Christ Church Deeds', *Twentieth Report of the Deputy Keeper of the Public Records in Ireland* (Dublin, 1888), 36–41, and *Twenty-Third Report . . .* (Dublin, 1891), 75–8.

16. Many are edited with commentary, texts, and photographs in *Starrs and Jewish Charters Preserved in the British Museum*, ed. I. Abrahams, H. P. Stokes, and H. Loewe, 3 vols. (Cambridge, 1930–2).

17. *Regesta Regum Scottorum*, ii: *The Acts of William I*, ed. G. W. S. Barrow (Edinburgh, 1971), 71–4; Galbraith, *Studies in the Public Records*, 57–61; F. W. Maitland, *The Forms of Action at Common Law*, ed. A. H. Chaytor and W. J. Whittaker (Cambridge, 1936), 20–40.

18. Galbraith, *Studies in the Public Records*, 72–4.

19. *Liber Antiquus de Ordinationibis Vicariarum Tempore Hugonis Wells, Lincolniensis Episcopi, 1209–1235* (Lincoln, 1888); M. T. Clanchy, *From Memory to Written Record*, 2nd edn. (Oxford, 1993), 74–5.

20. For examples of different types of estate records in translation, see M. Bailey, *The English Manor, c.1200–c.1500* (Manchester, 2002).

21. Above (Ch. 8).

22. S. Raban, 'Edward I's Other Inquiries', in M. C. Prestwich, R. H. Britnell, and R. F. Frame (eds.), *Thirteenth Century England IX* (Woodbridge, 2003), 43–57.

23. *Cartularium Monasterii de Rameseia*, ed. W. H. Hart and P. A. Lyons, 3 vols., Rolls Ser. 79 (1884–93), iii. 241 (Hemmingford Abbots), 246 (Graveley), 248 (Elsworth), etc.; *Charters and Custumals of the Abbey of Holy Trinity, Caen*, ed. M. Chibnall (1982), 46, 48, 51, 63; *Surveys of the Estates of Glastonbury Abbey, c.1135–1201*, ed. N. Stacy (2001), 90, 102–3, 114, 120, etc.

24. M. Jurkowski, C. L. Smith, and D. Crook, *Lay Taxes in England and Wales, 1188–1688* (1998), xxvi–xxxi.

25. These collections were already depleted by the time of their final destruction in 1922, but what survived up to that date can be surveyed in Herbert Wood, *A Guide to the Records Deposited in the Public Record Office of Ireland* (Dublin, 1919). For legal records, see *Calendar of the Justiciary Rolls or Proceedings in the Court of the Justiciar of Ireland*, ed. J. Mills and M. Griffith, 3 vols. (Dublin, 1905, 1956).

26. M. Livingstone, *A Guide to the Public Records of Scotland Deposited in H. M. General Register House, Edinburgh* (Edinburgh, 1905), 33. The extracts are printed in *The Exchequer Rolls of Scotland*, ed. J. Stuart, G. Burnett, and others, 23 vols. (Edinburgh, 1878–1908), i. 1–51.

27. 'Instrumenta et Acta de Munimentis Regni Scotie', 7–11, in *Acts of the Parliaments of Scotland*, ed. T. Thomson and C. Innes, 12 vols. (Edinburgh, 1814–75), i. 113–18.

28. *Littere Wallie Preserved in Liber A in the Public Record Office*, ed. J. G. Edwards (Cardiff, 1940), xxviii–xxix.

29. *The Antient Kalendars and Inventories of the Treasury of His Majesty's Exchequer*, ed. F. Palgrave, 3 vols. (1836), i. 106, 113–21.

30. R. I. Jack, *Medieval Wales* (1972), 53–7.

31. D. Stephenson, *The Governance of Gwynedd* (Cardiff, 1984), xxxvi.

32. 'Early Accounts Relating to North Wales, Temp. Edward I', ed. J. Griffiths, *Bulletin of the Board of Celtic Studies*, 14 (1950–2), 235–41, 302–12; 15 (1952–4), 126–56; 16 (1954–6), 109–33; 'The Account Roll of the Chamberlain of the Principality of North Wales from Michaelmas 1304 to Michaelmas 1305', ed. E. A. Lewis, ibid., 1 (1921–3), 256–75; *Ministers' Accounts from West Wales, 1277 to 1306*, ed. M. Rhys, Cymmrodorion Record Series, 13 (1936).

33. For a later example in translation, see *The Pipe Roll of the Bishopric of Winchester, 1301–2*, ed. and trans. M. Page (Winchester, 1996).

34. P. D. A. Harvey, *Manorial Records*, rev. edn. (1999), 25–37.

35. P. R. Coss, *Lordship, Kinship and Locality: A Study in English Society, c.1180–c.1280* (Cambridge, 1991), 99–102.

36. B. M. S. Campbell, 'The Complexity of Manorial Structure in Medieval Norfolk: A Case Study', *Norfolk Archaeology*, 39 (1986), 241–2.

37. See above (Ch. 11).

38. K. Stocks, 'Payments to Manorial Courts in the Early Winchester Accounts', in R. H. Britnell (ed.), *The Winchester Pipe Rolls and Medieval English Society* (Woodbridge, 2003), 45–59.

39. P. Connolly, *Medieval Record Sources* (Dublin, 2002), 52.

40. H. Watt, *Welsh Manors and their Records* (Aberystwyth, 2000), 98. For examples, see *Cartae et Alia Munimenta de Glamorgan*, iii, nos. 743–9, pp. 813–48.

41. Watt, *Welsh Manors*, 58; *The Court Rolls of the Lordship of Ruthin or Dyffryn-Clwydd of the Reign of King Edward the First*, ed. R. A. Roberts, Cymmrodorion Record Series, 2 (1983).

42. *Early Records of the Burgh of Aberdeen, 1317, 1398–1407*, ed. W. C. Dickinson, Scottish History Society, 3rd ser., 49 (1957), 3–17.

43. Clanchy, *From Memory*, 148–9; D. Bates, 'The Forged Charters of William the Conqueror and Bishop William of St Calais', in D. Rollason, M. Harvey, and M. Prestwich (eds.), *Anglo-Norman Durham, 1093–1193* (Woodbridge, 1994), 111–24.

44. *Manorial Records of Cuxham, Oxfordshire, c.1200–1359*, ed. P. D. A. Harvey (1976), 36–42; Postles, 'Country Clerici', 27–42.

45. B. M. S. Campbell, 'A Unique Estate and a Unique Source: The Winchester Pipe Rolls in Perspective', in R. H. Britnell (ed.) *The Winchester Pipe Rolls and Medieval English Society* (Woodbridge, 2003), 29–39; *Kentish Demesne Accounts up to 1350: A Catalogue*, ed. James A. Galloway, M. Murphy, and O. Myhill (1993).

46. *The Bolton Priory Compotus, 1286–1325, together with a Priory Account Roll for 1377–78*, ed. I. Kershaw and D. M. Smith, Yorkshire Archaeological Society Record Series, 154 (2000).

47. *Liber S. Marie de Calchou*, ed. C. Innes, 2 vols., Bannatyne Club, 82 (1846), ii. 455–73; *The Correspondence, Inventories, Account Rolls and Law Proceedings of the Priory of Coldingham*, ed. J. Raine, Surtees Society, 12 (1841), appendix, lxxxv–civ.

48. Flanagan, 'Context and Uses of the Charter', 113–14.

49. See above (esp. Chs. 1 and 7).

50. R. H. Britnell, 'Pragmatic Literacy beyond Latin Christendom', in id. (ed.), *Pragmatic Literacy*, 181.

51. Clanchy, *From Memory*, 295–6.

52. e.g. *Select Documents of the English Lands of the Abbey of Bec*, ed. M. Chibnall, Camden 3rd ser. (1951), 49, 57, 83, 108, 123.

53. P. R. Hyams, *King, Lords and Peasants in Medieval England: The Common Law of Villeinage in the Twelfth and Thirteenth Centuries* (Oxford, 1980), 39, 43–8.

54. R. H. Britnell, *The Commercialisation of English Society, 1000–1500*, 2nd edn. (Manchester, 1996), 94–6.

55. T. F. T. Plucknett, *The Legislation of Edward I* (Oxford, 1949), 138–46.

56. P. D. A. Harvey and A. McGuinness, *A Guide to British Medieval Seals* (1996), 80.

FURTHER READING

Britnell, R. H. (ed.), *Pragmatic Literacy, East and West, 1200–1330* (Woodbridge, 1997).

—— (ed.), *The Winchester Pipe Rolls and Medieval English Society* (Woodbridge, 2003).

Clanchy, M. T., *From Memory to Written Record*, 2nd edn. (Oxford, 1993).

Chrimes, S. B., *An Introduction to the Administrative History of Medieval England* (Oxford, 1959).

Connolly, P., *Medieval Record Sources* (Dublin, 2002).

Davies, J. R., 'The Book of Llandaff: A Twelfth-Century Perspective', *Anglo-Norman Studies*, 21 (1998).

—— '*Liber Landavensis*: Its Date and History', *Cambrian Medieval Celtic Studies*, 35 (1998).

Davies, W., 'The Latin Charter-Tradition in Western Britain, Brittany and Ireland in the Early-Medieval Period', in D. Whitelock, R. McKitterick, and D. Dumville (eds.), *Ireland in Early Medieval Europe: Studies in Memory of Kathleen Hughes* (Cambridge, 1982).

Davis, G. R. C., *Medieval Cartularies of Great Britain: A Short Catalogue* (1958).

Denholm-Young, N., *Seignorial Administration in England* (1937).

Drew, J. S., 'Manorial Accounts of St Swithun's Priory, Winchester', *English Historical Review*, 62 (1947), and in E. M. Carus-Wilson (ed.), *Essays in Economic History*, 3 vols. (1954–62), ii.

Duncan, A. A., 'The Earliest Scottish Charters', *Scottish Historical Review*, 37 (1958).

—— 'Yes, the Earliest Scottish Charters', *Scottish Historical Review*, 78 (1999).

Galbraith, V. H., *Studies in the Public Records* (1948).

Gervers, M. (ed.), *Dating Undated Medieval Charters* (Woodbridge, 2000).

Harvey, B., 'Introduction' in ead., *The Obedientiaries of Westminster Abbey and their Financial Records, c.1275–1540* (Woodbridge, 2002).

Harvey, P. D. A., 'Introduction', in *Manorial Records of Cuxham, Oxfordshire, c.1200–1359*, ed. P. D. A. Harvey (London, 1976).

—— *Manorial Records*, rev. edn. (1999).

—— and McGuinness, A., *A Guide to British Medieval Seals* (1996).

Heidecker, K. (ed.), *Charters and the Use of the Written Word in Medieval Society* (Turnhout, 2000).

Hone, N. J., *The Manor and Manorial Records* (1906).

Jack, R. I., *Medieval Wales* (1972).

Maitland, F. W., *The Forms of Action at Common Law*, ed. A. H. Chaytor and W. J. Whittaker (Cambridge, 1936).

Martin, G. H., 'The English Borough in the Thirteenth Century', *Transaction of the Royal Historical Society*, 5th ser. 13 (1963), and in R. Holt and G. Rosser (eds.), *The Medieval English Town: A Reader in English Urban History* (Harlow, 1990).

Page, M., *The Medieval Bishops of Winchester: Estate, Archive and Administration* (Winchester, 2002).

Patterson, R. B., *The Scriptorium of Margam Abbey and the Scribes of Early Angevin Glamorgan: Secretarial Administration in a Welsh Marcher Barony, c.1150–c.1225* (Woodbridge, 2002).

Piper, A. J., 'Evidence of Accounting and Local Estate Services at Durham, c.1240', *Archives*, 20 (1992).

Postles, D., 'Country Clerici and the Composition of English Twelfth- and Thirteenth-Century Private Charters', in Heidecker (ed.), *Charters and the Use of the Written Word*.

Pryce, H. (ed.), *Literacy in Medieval Celtic Societies* (Cambridge, 1998).

Raban, S., 'Edward I's Other Enquiries', in M. C. Prestwich, R. H. Britnell, and R. F. Frame (eds.), *Thirteenth Century England IX* (Woodbridge, 2003).

Razi, Z., and Smith, R. (eds.), *Medieval Society and the Manor Court* (Oxford, 1996).

Roffe, D., *Domesday: The Inquest and the Book* (Oxford, 2000).

Sawyer, P. (ed.), *Domesday Book: A Reassessment* (1985).

Scales, L. E., 'The Cambridgeshire Ragman Rolls', *English Historical Review*, 113 (1998).

Stacey, R., 'Agricultural Investment and the Management of the Royal Demesne Manors, 1236–1240', *Journal of Economic History*, 46 (1986).

Stephenson, D., *The Governance of Gwynedd* (Cardiff, 1984).

Vincent, N. 'The Origins of the Winchester Pipe Rolls', *Archives*, 21 (1994).

Watt, H., *Welsh Manors and their Records* (Aberystwyth, 2000).

Webster, B., *Scotland from the Eleventh Century to 1603* (Ithaca, NY, 1975).

Woolgar, C. M., 'Introduction', in *Household Accounts from Medieval England*, 2 vols. (1992).

Primary Sources for Economic and Social History in Modern English

Calendar of Letter Books of the City of London, i: *Letter Book A*, ed. R. R. Sharpe (1899).

Calendar of Archbishop Alen's Register, c.1172–1534, ed. C. McNeill (Dublin, 1950).

Calendar of Documents Relating to Ireland, 1171–1307, ed. H. S. Sweetman and G. F. Handcock, 5 vols. (London, 1875–86).

Calendar of Early Mayor's Court Rolls, A.D. 1298–1307, ed. A. H. Thomas (Cambridge, 1924).

The Cartularies of Southwick Priory, ed. K. A. Hanna, Hampshire Record Ser. 9 (1988).

The Cartulary of Canonsleigh Abbey: A Calendar, ed. V.C.M. London, Devon and Cornwall Record Society, new ser, 8 (1965).

Cartulary of Holy Trinity, Aldgate, ed. G. A. J. Hodgett, London Record Society, 7 (1971).

Court Roll of Chalgrave Manor, 1278–1313, ed. M. K. Dale, Bedfordshire Historical Record Society, 28 (1950).

'Documents', in J. Z. Titow, *English Rural Society, 1200–1350* (1969).

Domesday Book: A Complete Translation, ed. A. Williams and G. H. Martin (2002).

The Early Records of Medieval Coventry, ed. P. R. Coss (1986).

The English Manor, c.1200–c.1500, ed. M. Bailey (Manchester, 2002).

Flint Pleas, 1283–1285, ed. J. G. Edwards, Flintshire Historical Society Publications, 8 (1921).

The Havener's Accounts of the Earldom and Duchy of Cornwall, 1287–1356, ed. M. Kowaleski, Devon and Cornwall Record Society, new ser. 44 (2001).

The Ipswich Recognizance Rolls, 1294–1327: A Calendar, ed. G. H. Martin, Suffolk Records Society, 16 (1973).

Irish Exchequer Payments, 1270–1446, ed. P. Connolly (Dublin, 1998).

The Laws of the Kings of England from Edmund to Henry I, ed. A. J. Robertson (Cambridge, 1925; Lampeter, 2000).

Leges Henrici Primi, ed. L. J. Downer (Oxford, 1972).

Local Customs Accounts of the Port of Exeter, 1266–1321, ed. M. Kowaleski, Devon and Cornwall Record Society, new ser. 6 (1993).

The Northumberland Lay Subsidy Roll of 1296, ed. C. M. Fraser, Society of Antiquaries of Newcastle upon Tyne (1968).

The Pipe Roll of the Bishopric of Winchester, 1301–2, ed. M. Page, Hampshire Record Ser. 14 (1996).

Select Pleas in Manorial Courts, i, ed. F. W. Maitland, Selden Society, 2 (1888).

Stamford in the Thirteenth Century: Two Inquisitions from the Reign of Edward I, ed. D. Roffe (Stamford, 1994).

Yorkshire Hundred and Quo Warranto Rolls, 1274–1294, ed. B. English, Yorkshire Archaeological Society, Record Ser. 151 (1996).

....

CHAPTER 14

Stability and Crisis

Although the course of economic development between 1050 and 1300 is perceptible in broad outline, we can have little confidence, as we have seen, in measuring the perceived changes, and there is room for major difference of opinion concerning its welfare implications. For most of this period, none of our sources supplies the sort of continuous statistical data that are necessary to define economic trends. Some of the principal documentation used for this purpose in discussions of the fourteenth and fifteenth centuries—estate accounts, customs records—becomes abundant only from the 1270s. The chronological analysis of economic change for the twelfth and earlier thirteenth centuries can barely rise above the level of a sketch, and in this respect the period is less well understood than later centuries. In the absence of any finer analysis it is tempting to assume that development between 1050 and 1300 proceeded unchecked, and to contrast a twelfth- and thirteenth-century golden age with the troubles of later times. This complacency is justifiable to the extent that there were favourable background circumstances that permitted population, output, and commerce to increase over this long period. However, closer analysis shows that the course of development was very far from smooth. This chapter will first define some causes of severe economic and social disruption in the period of growth, and will then discuss how it can be subdivided into shorter periods, each with a distinct character of its own.

Causes of Economic Instability

In modern economies, though output fluctuates from year to year—and indeed fluctuations can be assessed over even shorter periods—instability of this kind is very minor compared with the normal experience of the period 1050–1300. The chief reason for this, though not the only one, is that most modern production is independent of variations in the weather. The largest sector of the economy, whose performance strongly affected the general price level and the value of wages, was cereals cultivation, whose output was governed from year to year by circumstances affecting the germination, growth, and ripening of crops. Chapter 9 has already shown the extent to which crop yields varied from year to year during the 1280s, when wheat yields on the Winchester manors varied from 2.79 to 4.77 times the seed sown. Such variations strongly affected the price of basic food from year to year, as Figure 14.1 shows. Because people had to have food before thinking of most other commodities, a bad harvest meant that spending was diverted into food away from clothing, utensils, furnishings, and repairs to property, so affecting the demand for goods in the manufacturing and service sectors of the economy. Fluctuations in employment and welfare from year to year were accordingly much more stark than anything normally experienced in a modern industrial economy.

At the worst, bad weather could create shortages of food so severe that people died of starvation. Famine conditions can be prevented, even in the absence of international trade in cereals, to the extent that grain is stored to allow the surpluses of one year to make up the deficits of another. However, the storage of grain presented many problems because it was so prone to deterioration in damp conditions, or to the ravages of vermin, and it required more investment than most people could have afforded. Because the effects of bad weather on the size of harvests depended upon how much grain had been sown, rather than on how much land was available for sowing, there could be famine conditions even in periods when there was no particular population pressure on resources. Historians are so used to discussing high food prices and recurrent shortages of the late thirteenth and early fourteenth centuries as evidence of an ecological imbalance that the incidence of earlier famines tends to be neglected. However, widespread famine, with accompanying disease and a high mortality of men and animals, is reported at a time when there was still plenty of potential arable land available for cultivation, in 1087[1] and again in 1111[2] and 1124–5. Symeon of Durham tells us that in 1124 throughout England dead bodies lay unburied in both town and countryside.[3] The Holyrood chronicler records a 'very great famine' in Scotland in 1154.[4] William of Newburgh records severe famine and prolonged pestilence in 1196, causing such high mortality that normal burial customs had to be waived.[5]

The implications of famine conditions for mortality depended very much upon the distribution of land and the structure of employment. In a village of substantial peasant proprietors there would be less food than usual in a poor year, but safety margins were likely to be high. Farmworkers who received a subsistence food allowance as their traditional wage were likely to survive relatively unscathed. By contrast, in a manufacturing community, when individual families had to buy food at famine prices, at a time when the demand for their goods and services was depressed, a bad harvest could be devastating. Economic development between 1050 and 1300 increased the proportion of smallholders, casual workers, and

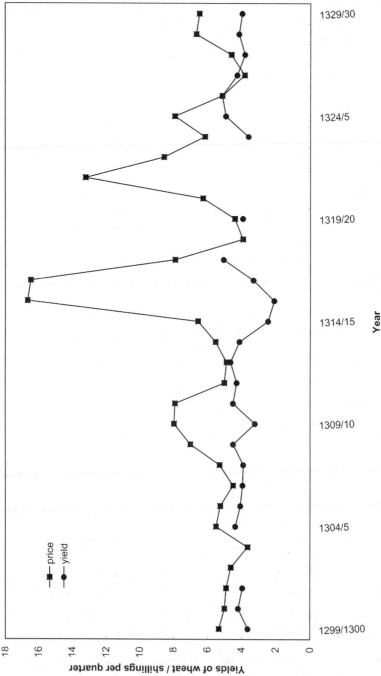

Year

Yields of wheat / shillings per quarter

Fig. 14.1. Harvests and prices, 1300–1330. Yields of wheat on the bishop of Winchester's estates and the price of wheat in shillings per quarter. A poor harvest, and especially a run of poor harvests, could have a devastating effect on cereals prices, as demonstrated here. One of the time series shown here is the price of wheat, which reached a peak of 16.67 shillings between Michaelmas (29 September) 1315 and Michaelmas 1316, and 16.48 shillings in the following twelve-month period. These famine prices are explained by the other times series, which shows that on average (here measured on the bishop's estates) wheat had returned only 2.47 times the seed sown at the harvest of 1314, 2.11 times in 1315, and 3.33 times in 1316.

Sources: D. L. Farmer, 'Prices and Wages', in H. E. Hallam (ed.), The Agrarian History of England and Wales, ii: 1042–1350 (Cambridge, 1988), 794–5;

townspeople in the total population, so that incomes for many families were precarious. There was also a long-term tendency for prices to increase during the thirteenth century, as demand increased with the underpinning of an increasing money supply (Figure 14.2). This would imply that dearth and famine caused by bad weather was more likely to have adverse long-term consequences around 1300 than around 1050. However, it is unfortunately impossible to test this hypothesis. The vulnerability of peasant welfare to harvest fluctuations in the late thirteenth century is well attested[6] but we have no comparable means of demonstrating the severity of the crises of the eleventh and twelfth centuries.

By the later thirteenth century the vulnerability of peasant economies to poor harvests can be illustrated from manorial records, which show that the social context of dearth and famine allowed many responses not available in 1050. Though we cannot demonstrate that the consequence of a given harvest shortfall for mortality was more severe around 1300 than earlier, we can at least be confident

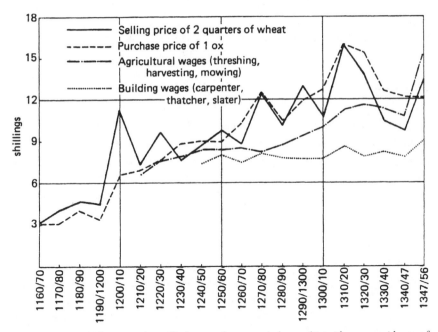

FIG. 14.2. Decennial mean prices of wheat and oxen, 1160/1–1355/6, with some evidence of average wages. The time series here demonstrate the peak of inflation in 1198–1206 and the generally higher prices, accentuated in recurrent years of crisis, in the late thirteenth and early fourteenth centuries. They also suggest the tendency for wage rates to lag behind prices, at least after about 1260.

Source: D. L. Farmer, 'Prices and Wages', in H. E. Hallam (ed.), *The Agrarian History of England and Wales*, ii: *1042–1350* (Cambridge, 1988), 719.

that the way peasants responded was different. The growth of monetized relationships during these centuries had created a whole range of options for survival,
including the increased possibility of borrowing money and the improved possibility of disposing of assets. In the Norfolk village of Coltishall during the 1280s and
1290s there was a direct relationship between the price of grain and the amount of
land that was bought and sold. Low prices following the harvests of 1287 and 1299
were associated with low levels of activity in the land market, but harvest failures in
1293, 1294, and 1297 brought about an appreciable increase. This was presumably
because in years of high prices some tenants were driven to selling or mortgaging
land in order to buy food.[7] In some instances the transfer of land was a second
resort, since some tenants were able to fend off hunger by mortgaging property,
only to find that they were unable to redeem it.[8]

Even if we could analyse long-term changes in the significance of harvest
fluctuations for welfare, we should nevertheless have to reckon with other sources
of instability whose effects could be just as damaging. One of these was the scourge
of epidemic diseases, which could take a heavy toll in the absence of any means
to combat them. Epidemics could be severe even in regions of relatively low
population density, and there are numerous examples of raised mortality from
this cause in the less well-populated parts of Britain, as well as in the southern
counties. There was an epidemic in Ireland in 1095 so severe that 'the number of
the people whom it killed could not be counted'. The Melrose chronicler records
a coughing epidemic that killed many people in 1173.[9] Some of these epidemics
are said to have been very widespread. Welsh chroniclers report a pestilence
that caused high mortality throughout Britain and France in 1197.[10] We have no
means of assessing the effects of these epidemics upon either local economies or
that of Britain as a whole. In view of the capacity of later epidemics to cause
severe crises, we are obliged to leave open the possibility that some of them
destabilized normal social and economic relationships and had extended
consequences, though none of these crises was remotely as dreadful as the Black
Death of 1348–9.[11]

Military activity, too, was often disruptive; its object was all too often to cause
devastation to civilian populations. Although, as was argued in Chapter 12, the
economy normally benefited from internal peace, war, when it occurred, could
seriously interrupt normal activity. The invasions of England by the Normans, and
of Wales, Ireland, and Scotland by the English, are well-known periods of destructive disturbance, but there were many others. Two episodes of conflict on British
soil have particularly attracted the attention of historians for the brutality recorded
by contemporary chroniclers. One is the ravaging in northern England by Norman
troops in 1169–70, and the other is the devastation wrought at various places and
times by contending armies between 1140 and 1153 in the civil war of Stephen's

reign. Other examples that might be noted are the plundering of lands around the Irish Sea by King Magnus of Norway in 1098 and 1102–3, the pillaging of Northumberland by the Scots in 1079, 1135, and 1173, and the local devastation wrought by both parties to the English civil war of 1215–17. The damage caused by warfare was often confined to very specific locations, but widespread local damage of this kind could amount to a severe shock to an economic system in which the security of communications and reliability of the money supply mattered in everyday life.

Closely allied to the impact of warfare as a source of instability was that of taxation, which, as explained in Chapter 12, resulted either in heavier taxes and tallages or in novel and uncustomary exactions. Here it is necessary simply to repeat that warfare inevitably diverted expenditure into different channels from those they normally took, and especially if kings spent their income abroad the effects upon internal demand would be destabilizing. Chapter 10 commented on the adverse consequences of Edward I's wartime taxation from 1294 onwards. However, high wartime taxation was no novelty, and some earlier phases of high taxation, when the money stock was appreciably smaller than in the 1290s, may have had more devastating implications for internal trade. It is salutary to recall the crippling gelds said to have been imposed on England in the early eleventh century—sums so large, indeed, that it is doubtful how far we should believe what the chroniclers tell us. The Anglo-Saxon Chronicle gives figures for nine levies between 991 and 1041, ranging from £10,000 in the first of these years to as much as £83,000 in 1018.[12] The taxes imposed on England by William the Conqueror were onerous because of their frequency rather than the rate at which they were levied, though in 1083 he imposed a geld of three times the normal weight. However, his taxes came on top of the widespread damage caused by the suppression of native rebellions, and their effects were the more detrimental to the economy because much of the resulting revenue was diverted abroad to Normandy.[13] Even if only half of Richard I's ransom of £666,667 (100,000 marks) was levied in England in 1193–5, that represented at least 17.5 per cent of the estimated coin in circulation at the time, and the proportion may have been over twice as high.[14] When the level of King John's revenues from England rose to an average of about £58,000 in the years 1210–14, almost half the money collected was locked away in royal treasuries as a war chest, to the point that by October 1213 the king had taken perhaps a third of England's current coin out of circulation.[15] Since one of the most interesting features of English politics in the thirteenth century was the growing ability of magnates to organize consorted resistance to inordinately high taxes, we should surely be prepared to accept that some early levies had been sufficiently high to disrupt normal income flows and depress economic expectations. Scotland, meanwhile, with its less burdensome tradition of taxation, had probably escaped the worst destabilizing consequences of royal military activity.

Finally, the money supply itself deserves comment as an independent source of economic crises. Monetary phenomena were in part the direct result of variations in royal taxation and expenditure, which could significantly affect the volume of currency in circulation, but there were also independent sources of monetary crisis. Panics over coinage of poor quality could cause sudden increases in the general price level, such as those in 1198–1206, shortly to be discussed, as well as in the famine of 1124–5. These disorders explain the savage penalties inflicted by Henry I on his moneyers in 1126: 'he had almost all the moneyers throughout England castrated and their right hands cut off for secretly debasing the coinage'.[16] The low quality of the imported imitation sterling pennies known as 'crockards and pollards' perhaps contributed to high prices in the 1290s.[17]

In all these ways, the developing economy of the period 1050–1300 was subject to shocks that retarded or redirected growth in particular places or at particular times. We are extremely badly informed of their effects in detail, in particular concerning the duration of their impact, and though doubtless there is much to be learned from ongoing research it is very doubtful whether the evidence to be collected can ever be good enough even to identify economic fluctuations reliably, let alone to assign magnitudes to them or to attribute causes definitively. It must be enough to be aware that economic development in this period was an exceedingly bumpy ride, far from being a matter of universal experience in all regions at all times. It was much more obscured by setbacks and stalling than it has been in more recent centuries, which explains why contemporary writers will discuss ephemeral disasters—famines, epidemics, wars, rebellions, high taxes—without observing long-term economic and social change. The economic and social development of the period is a construct of historians.

Periodization

In spite of this cautionary conclusion, current historiography suggests that a case can be made for splitting up the period 1050–1300 into separate phases, even if the distinctions between them remain blurred and consequently controversial. Four subperiods will be proposed here. The first, from 1050 to 1139, embraces the end of the Anglo-Saxon monarchy and the establishment of a Norman ruling elite in England, with all its implications for economic and social change. The second, brief period, 1139–54, is a distinctive one of very mixed experience. In England it comprises the years of political uncertainty and civil war under Stephen, but the

Scottish experience was very different, partly because of the discomfiture of their southern neighbours. The third, 1154–1260, is a most remarkable, prolonged phase of general economic expansion, corresponding to the Schumpeterian long-wave that was discussed in Chapter 4. Finally, 1260–1300 can be regarded as a period when the earlier possibilities for growth were being exhausted, and when other pressures damped down the possibility of welfare gains.

Despite destruction of property in both town and country in the aftermath of the Norman Conquest, perhaps the primary stimulus to development in the period 1050–1138 was the entrepreneurial activity of landlords wishing to improve the value of their properties. The fact of conquest not only implied a break in continuity with past traditions of landlordship, but also allowed incoming Norman landlords to rule with a firmer hand than their predecessors in reorganizing their properties. The count of Eu, for example, disregarded existing structures of lordship to settle knights in thinly populated territory near Hastings.[18] In the absence of estate accounts from this period, we are dependent on hearsay, but there are several examples of deliberate estate improvement. The estates of Ely Abbey were said to have been improved in value to the extent of £54 under Abbot Symeon (1081–93), and those of Abbot Ralph of Battle Abbey (1107–15) by about £20. Amongst laymen the best-attested example is Ernulf of Hesdin, whom William of Malmesbury described as an agricultural expert.[19] Our earliest surviving estate surveys—from Burton Abbey, Peterborough Abbey, and from the English estates of Bec Abbey—are from this period, and we know that there were others made for Ramsey Abbey and Glastonbury Abbey, though it is uncertain to what extent these may have had earlier precedents.[20] The new boroughs and markets founded by landlords, a phenomenon discussed more generally in Chapter 8, give further testimony to a desire to promote the commercial development of estates between 1050 and 1138. In Huntingdonshire, for example, Ramsey Abbey founded St Ives and St Neots Priory founded St Neots in this period. This policy was carried northwards and westwards in the wake of Norman settlement in northern England, Wales, and Cornwall. All told, Maurice Beresford assigns about forty new towns in England and eighteen in Wales to the period 1066–1140.[21] In Scotland, Berwick, Roxburgh, Dunfermline, Edinburgh, Perth, and Stirling were all defined as royal burghs before 1127, and so probably were Elgin and Linlithgow.[22] The extent to which population gains exceeded losses in these years is not calculable, but there are some indications of increase. The arable acreage was probably enlarged. The Domesday survey of 1086 noted examples where the number of plough teams might be increased,[23] and increases are in evidence on most of Ramsey Abbey manors by 1135.[24] There was probably forest clearance on the lands of the monks of Peterborough, who were granted the right to 200 acres of assarts in the Soke of Peterborough early in King Stephen's reign.[25]

A further source of development in this period was a stimulus to overseas trade, chiefly through the improving trade connections with Flanders and Normandy. William I's admission of Jews into England introduced a dynamic new entre- preneurial group of traders. By 1138 they were a wealthy group, probably through the profits to be made by trading in precious metals, usually worked into plate or foreign currencies, as well as in moneylending.[26] Some new fairs of international significance facilitated trade between import merchants and native consumers and distributors. St Giles fair at Winchester was licensed by William II in 1096 and extended by Henry I in 1110; St Ives fair was licensed by Henry I in 1110.[27] Though we have no commercial statistics, the founding of major new ports implies that new opportunities for overseas trade were opening up in many parts of Britain. On the east coast the urban and commercial characteristics of Berwick, Newcastle, Boston, and King's Lynn originated in this period.[28] The introduction of tolls on shipping implies that the late eleventh century was a period of growing overseas trade from Scotland.[29] The Irish Sea region also displayed signs of exceptional dynamism in this period, during which new port towns were established on the southern Welsh coast at Chepstow, Cardiff, Swansea, Tenby, and Carmarthen.[30] These west-coast ports of Britain in this period may have been concerned chiefly with servicing local coastal trade.

The period of political uncertainty and civil war in England, between 1139 and the end of Stephen's reign in 1154, is likely to have experienced setbacks to economic development, though these were far from being universal. Contem- porary chroniclers record the destruction of property that resulted from the sacking of towns and the devastation of rural areas. English currency, too, was in disarray as a result of loss of control by the king and the production of numerous local issues of substandard weight.[31] The earliest surviving royal exchequer account of Henry I's reign, from 1155/6, records the loss of income to the extent of £1,241 6s. 3d. through 'waste', especially from the midlands, and though the meaning of this expression has been debated, it is likely to refer in part to the devastating effect of warfare, or to economic hardship inflicted on areas that had suffered from exceptionally high wartime demands for cash from the warring parties.[32] Not all the misfortunes that befell the crown and other landlords in this period were necessarily deleterious to economic development. The reduction of demesne lands recorded on some estates[33] did not necessarily imply a reduction in the cultivated area. Nor did the usurpation of rights by manorial lessees necessarily imply a reduction of activity. Simon of Felsted, though he diverted income the abbey of Bec should have received from its manor of Felsted in Essex, nevertheless developed the estate through the clearing of woodland and the multiplication of tenancies.[34] A major inquest into forest offences in 1155 implied that Stephen's loss of control had resulted in forest clearances in many parts of England.[35] However, the troubles of the period probably depressed both landlord incomes and their investment in mills, markets, and new towns. Beresford's chronology of new urban foundations in England assigns fewer to the 1140s than to any other decade of the twelfth century.[36] Unless magnates had thought themselves to be disadvantaged by the political crises of Stephen's reign it is difficult to explain the success of the peace movement of November 1153 or the subsequent success of Henry II in reconstructing a monarchy more authoritative than ever. The extent to which long-distance trade was disrupted by the troubles of Stephen's reign has been the subject of some disagreement, but there is inadequate evidence for any reasoned conclusion to be drawn.[37]

The negative features of Stephen's reign have nevertheless to be balanced by other considerations. The economy of twelfth-century Britain was not so well integrated that the misfortunes of the midlands had universal implications. Stephen's reign corresponds to an expansive phase of Scottish history, partly because David I was able to annex territory in Cumberland, Westmorland, Northumberland, and Durham and to turn their assets to the advantage of the northern economies. A principle attraction of these regions was the silver that had recently begun to be extracted from the Silverbeck-Minerdale mines of Cumberland. The period 1133–54 was one of heightened mining activity that directly benefited Carlisle, which passed under Scottish administration in 1136. David I's inauguration of a Scottish silver currency shortly afterwards was followed by a creative period of royal government that stimulated both urban development and agriculture.[38] The development of new burghs probably continued vigorously into this period; Scotland had about twenty-two burghs by 1153, though it is uncertain just at what point in David I's long reign most of them had been founded.[39] Even in eastern England, it is likely that forest clearance continued into the troubled years of Stephen's reign on the estates of Peterborough Abbey and Ramsey Abbey.[40] With such divergences of experience within Britain it is tempting to dismiss the problems of King Stephen's rule as a local and ephemeral problem. For much of Britain, however, the degree of disruption and change was sufficiently high for this to be regarded as a distinct period, even if its characteristics were not universally the same.

With the restoration of internal peace in England under Henry II, the possibilities for economic development became less ambiguous, and probably more universal. It has become traditional to define the 1180s as marking the beginnings of the long thirteenth-century phase of expansion, and it is true that some features of development, such as deforestation and the ploughing up of moorlands, are more in evidence after 1180 than before. However, this is at least in part the result of an increasing volume of documentation, and the distinction between the last two decades of the twelfth century and the previous twenty-five years is far from clear-cut. The period 1155–80 was one of recovery and development. Royal, ecclesiastical, and baronial administrations were restored and began to innovate. Some valuable estate surveys of high quality—those of Ramsey Abbey (c.1160) and a second series from Bec Abbey (c.1170)—are from this period. Economic development was unambiguously continuing in many parts of Britain. References to lands won from the sea, and from the edge of the fens, multiply in Lincolnshire charters, and in some drainage schemes can be dated before 1180 with a high probability. The Saturday Dyke, built by cooperating families from several villages of south Lincolnshire in order to claim hundreds of acres of land from the fens, was constructed about 1160–70.[41] References to expansion into woodland also multiply from the mid-twelfth century. The general royal forest eyres held in 1166–7, 1175, and 1179, by which Henry II raised fines for offences against forest law, uncovered a good deal of illegal assarting as well as other offences. Peterborough Abbey was reported to be clearing woodland in Oundle (Northamptonshire) in the eyre of 1166–7, and indeed in an earlier local eyre of 1163; by 1189 it had won 400 acres.[42] Expanding trade is suggested by the number of new towns founded throughout England from Hartlepool in the north to Poole in the south; Beresford estimates that twenty-one new English towns and four Welsh ones were founded between 1151 and 1180. The optimism of the age is well expressed in the name Baldock (Hertfordshire), named after the great oriental city of Baghdad, which was known as 'Baldac' in western Europe; the borough was established with a licensed market in Henry II's reign, sometime before 1185.[43] In Scotland, too, there were important new foundations, notably Glasgow, Inverkeithing, Kinghorn, Crail, Arbroath, Brechin and probably Jedburgh and Lanark.[44] Perth, founded as a burgh in the 1120s, developed as a town and port both under David I and his successors.[45] Any setback that England's international trade had suffered under Stephen was made good under his successor, and the export of wool expanded vigorously from the 1150s in response to Flemish demand.[46] The currency in circulation in England perhaps doubled between 1158 and 1180.[47] These various expansive features of the period suggest that population was growing, even though there is no independent statistical evidence for it.

It used to be argued that the economy was distinguished from the 1180s by the beginnings of a secular price rise associated with a growth in the money supply, but recent research has modified this view and weakened the significance of the 1180s in this respect. The money supply was already growing before 1180, but no unambiguous price rise can be attributed to it because much of the increase was hoarded. A sharp price rise of lasting significance came only in 1198–1206, and it is attributable to a general panic about the prevalence of underweight coins and loss of confidence in money as a store of value.[48] The decision of landlords to manage their estates directly through their servants, rather than through lessees, was also more apparent from the 1180s than earlier, but since this was more an institutional response to economic change than an initiating cause of growth it is not enough to define the beginnings of an economic trend. If our chief concern is with economic expansion, it now seems advisable to take the analysis back before 1180.

The economic development of the period 1155–1260 was underpinned by rising domestic and foreign demand. Many aspects of the development of this long period have been examined in earlier chapters. Population and consumption expanded in all parts of Britain. Imports of commodities and silver bullion from Ireland and from the European continent were balanced by a growing volume of exports, particularly of wool and hides. Besides a continuing expansion of agriculture, and the founding of new towns and markets, growth was facilitated by numerous technical and institutional innovations of lasting significance. Windmills are first recorded in Britain in 1185, and soon became widespread. Fulling mills, for the finishing of woollen cloth, were innovated in Britain about the same time; the earliest definitely known are also from 1185, though there are some possibly to be dated a few decades earlier.[49] The fulling mill was also widely diffused. The first Welsh fulling mill is recorded from 1275 at Rhuddlan, but twenty-four others are recorded in Wales from before 1300, mostly in Glamorgan and Monmouth.[50] Fulling mills were not numerous in Ireland, but there was more than one in Wexford in 1298.[51] The spinning wheel began to replace spinning by hand in the thirteenth century, though its use was retarded by the fact that the early machines produced an inferior thread.[52] Some recognized technical developments, such as improvements in loom design, are hard to date, and there were no doubt innumerable minor modifications of agrarian and industrial technique that have left no documentary or pictorial evidence. Many institutional innovations, facilitating credit and regulating the environment in which commercial growth could occur, are attested by the massive increase in documentation discussed in Chapter 13.

A more subtle chronological analysis of the period 1155–1260 may one day allow historians to define periods of faster and slower development within these 105 years. It is possible, for example, that King John's heavy taxation had deflationary consequences in England, and may have retarded development, but it is difficult at present to substantiate this, and some indices—such as the number of new towns and markets founded in his reign—would seem to argue against it. It may be that the 1250s was a period of particularly rapid development, to judge from the peak of market founding in that decade, but the willingness of the crown to grant licences may have been related to political circumstances independently of economic trends.[53] At present it is best to leave such refinements of the analysis to be resolved by future research and debate.

The identification of a new phase of development after about 1260 derives not so much from any indices of overall economic performance as from a change in the characteristics of development. The expansion of agrarian resources, and the multiplication of towns, that had been such a marked feature of development through the period 1155–1260, both became much less characteristic of local developments in the late thirteenth century. Although the intake of new land for cultivation continued into the fourteenth century in outlying parts of England, like the Palatinate of Durham, it is much less in evidence after about 1260 than in earlier decades in the core areas of settlement; available resources of colonizable woodland and marshland had become harder to find. The foundation of new market towns of any significance was a rare event after the third quarter of the thirteenth century, chiefly because the most appropriate sites had already been occupied, and the infrastructure of towns was adequate for the needs of local trade.[54] The drying up of these investment opportunities did not in itself prevent continuing development, though it probably had adverse implications for welfare. Continuing population growth after the third quarter of the thirteenth century was less adequately matched by the investment needed to support it, so that landlessness and unemployment became more serious problems than in earlier decades. The wage levels of English craftsmen and farmworkers deteriorated from this time rather than earlier.[55] Edward I's use of the possibilities of economic development to raise levels of taxation and resort to warfare in Wales and Scotland had a depressing effect on welfare throughout Britain and Ireland by the 1290s, and the war itself had a destructive effect on the Scottish economy.[56] It seems likely, nevertheless, that rising exports and continuing local innovation permitted further expansion of aggregate output and population. Here again there are many questions to be answered, since the quality and characteristics of Britain's economic development from 1260 into the early fourteenth century are far from clearly understood.

NOTES

1. *The Chronicle of John of Worcester*, ed. and trans. R. R. Darlington and P. McGurk, 3 vols. (Oxford, 1995–8), iii. 44; *The Peterborough Chronicle*, ed. C. Clark, 2nd edn. (Oxford, 1970), 10.

2. *Chronicle of John of Worcester*, iii. 126. The Waverley annalist records a heavy mortality amongst livestock in 1111: *Annales Monastici*, ed. H. R. Luard, 5 vols., Rolls Ser. 36 (1864–5), ii. 214.

3. *Peterborough Chronicle*, ed. Clark, 45–6; Henry of Huntingdon, *Historia Anglorum*, ed. and trans. D. Greenway (Oxford, 1996), 474–5; Symeon of Durham, 'Historia Regum', in *Symeonis Monachi Opera Omnia*, ed. T. Arnold, 2 vols., Rolls Ser. 75 (1882–5), ii. 275.

4. *Early Sources of Scottish History, A.D. 500 to 1286*, ed. A. O. Anderson, 2nd edn., 2 vols. (Stamford, 1990), ii. 224.

5. *Chronicles of the Reigns of Stephen, Henry II, and Richard I*, ed. R. Howlett, 4 vols., Rolls Ser. 82 (1884–9), ii. 484–5.

6. C. Dyer, 'Did the Peasants Really Starve in Medieval England?', in M. Carlin and J. L. Rosenthal (eds.), *Food and Eating in Medieval Europe* (1998), 53–71; M. M. Postan and J. Z. Titow, 'Heriots and Prices on Winchester Manors', *Economic History Review*, 2nd ser. 11 (1959), 383–411; Z. Razi, *Life, Marriage and Death in a Medieval Parish: Economy, Society and Demography in Halesowen, 1270–1400* (Cambridge, 1980), 34–50; P. Schofield, 'Dearth, Debt and the Local Land Market in a Late Thirteenth-Century Village Community', *Agricultural History Review*, 45 (1997).

7. B. M. S. Campbell, 'Population Pressure, Inheritance and the Land Market in a Fourteenth-Century Peasant Community', in R. M. Smith (ed.), *Land, Kinship and Life-Cycle* (Cambridge, 1984), 113, 115–16.

8. P. R. Schofield, *Peasant and Community in Medieval England, 1200–1500* (Basingstoke, 2003), 146.

9. *Early Sources*, ed. Anderson, ii. 94–5, 279.

10. *Brut y Trwysogion, or the Chronicle of the Princes*, ed. T. Jones (Cardiff, 1952), 76.

11. See below (Ch. 24).

12. J. Gillingham, ' "The Most Precious Jewel in the English Crown": Danegeld and Heregeld in the Early Eleventh Century', *English Historical Review*, 104 (1989), 373–4.

13. D. C. Douglas, *William the Conqueror* (1969), 302–4, 372–3; S. P. J. Harvey, 'Taxation and the Economy', in J. C. Holt (ed.), *Domesday Studies* (Woodbridge, 1987), 262–4.

14. W. M. Ormrod, 'Royal Finance in Thirteenth-Century England', in P. R. Coss and S. D. Lloyd (eds.), *Thirteenth Century England V* (Woodbridge, 1995), 150; M. Allen, 'The Volume of the English Currency, 1158–1470', *Economic History Review*, 54 (2001), 607.

15. J. L. Bolton, 'The English Economy in the Early Thirteenth Century', and N. Barratt, 'The Revenues of John and Philip Augustus Revisited', in S. D. Church (ed.), *King John: New Interpretations* (Woodbridge, 1999), 33–4, 88.

16. Henry of Huntingdon, *Historia Anglorum*, ed. Greenway, 474–5.

17. N. J. Mayhew, 'Money and Prices in England from Henry II to Edward III', *Agricultural History Review*, 35 (1987), 128.

18. E. Searle: *Lordship and Community: Battle Abbey and its Banlieu, 1066–1538* (Toronto, 1974), 53–4.

19. R. Lennard, *Rural England, 1086–1135: A Study of Social and Agrarian Conditions* (Oxford, 1959), 208–12.

20. E. King, 'Economic Development in the Early Twelfth Century', in R. Britnell and J. Hatcher (eds.), *Progress and Problems in Medieval England* (Cambridge, 1996), 2–4.

21. M. W. Beresford, *New Towns of the Middle Ages: Town Plantation in England, Wales and Gascony* (1967), 330, 342, 456; J. A. Green, *The Aristocracy of Norman England* (Cambridge, 1997), 156–60.

22. G. S. Pryde, *The Burghs of Scotland: A Critical List* (1965), 3–5, 7.

23. S. P. J. Harvey, 'Taxation and the Ploughland in Domesday Book', in P. Sawyer (ed.), *Domesday Book: A Reassessment* (1985), 88, 93, 97–8.

24. J. A. Raftis, *The Estates of Ramsey Abbey: A Study in Economic Growth and Organization* (Toronto, 1957), 65–6.

25. E. King, *Peterborough Abbey, 1086–1310: A Study in the Land Market* (Cambridge, 1973), 72.

26. R. C. Stacey, 'Jewish Lending and the Medieval English Economy', in R. H. Britnell and B. M. S. Campbell (eds.), *A Commercialising Economy: England 1086 to c.1300* (Manchester, 1995), 83.

27. E. W. Moore, *The Fairs of Medieval England: An Introductory Study* (Toronto, 1985), 13, 17–18.

28. Beresford, *New Towns*, 463–5, 467–8, 473–4; Pryde, *Burghs*, 3.

29. Above (Ch. 5).

30. Beresford, *New Towns*, 539, 553–4, 556–7, 559, 569–70,

31. M. Blackburn, 'Coinage and Currency', in E. King (ed.), *The Anarchy of Stephen's Reign* (Oxford, 1994), 169–73.

32. E. Amt, 'The Meaning of Waste in the Early Pipe Rolls of Henry II', *Economic History Review*, 44 (1991), 240–8; ead., *The Accession of Henry II in England: Royal Government Restored, 1149–1159* (Woodbridge, 1993), 32, 133–43.

33. Raftis, *Estates of Ramsey Abbey*, 85–9.

34. *Charters and Custumals of the Abbey of Holy Trinity, Caen*, ed. M. Chibnall (1982), xl–xlii, 39–40.

35. E. M. Amt, 'The Forest Regard of 1155', *Haskins Society Journal*, 2 (1990), 189–95.

36. Beresford, *New Towns*, 330.

37. Amt, *Accession of Henry II*, 91–2.

38. I. Blanchard, 'Lothian and beyond: The Economy of the "English Empire" of David I', in Britnell and Hatcher (eds.), *Progress and Problems*, 23–45.

39. Pryde, *Burghs*, 1–10, 37–8.

40. King, *Peterborough Abbey*, 72; Raftis, *Estates of Ramsey Abbey*, 71–3.

41. H. E. Hallam, *Settlement and Society: A Study of the Early Agrarian History of South Lincolnshire* (Cambridge, 1965), 7–10, 19–21, 83–4, 87, 94, 110.

42. King, *Peterborough Abbey*, 81.

43. Beresford, *New Towns*, 452.

44. Pryde, *Burghs*, 9–12, 38–9.

45. A. A. M. Duncan, *Scotland: The Making of the Kingdom* (Edinburgh, 1989), 467–9.

46. T. H. Lloyd, *The English Wool Trade in the Middle Ages*, (Cambridge, 1977), 6.

47. Allen, 'The Volume of the English Currency', 606.

48. P. Latimer, 'Early Thirteenth-Century Prices', in Church (ed.), *King John: New Interpretations*, 41–73; id., 'The English Inflation of 1180–1220 Reconsidered', *Past and Present*, 171 (2001), 3–29.

49. R. Holt, *The Mills of Medieval England* (Oxford, 1988), 20, 153.

50. I. R. Jack, 'The Cloth Industry in Medieval Wales', *Welsh History Review*, 10 (1980–1), 447–9; id., 'Fulling Mills in Wales and the March before 1547', *Archaeologia Cambrensis*, 130 (1981), 120.

51. 'Accounts on the Great Rolls of the Pipe of the Irish Exchequer for the Reign of Edward I', *Thirty-Seventh Report of the Deputy Keeper of the Public Records and Keeper of the State Papers in Ireland* (Dublin, 1905), 42. The supposed fulling mill at Clones in 1212, mentioned in some accounts of Irish textile technology, rests on a misreading of the pipe roll of 1211–12.

52. J. L. Bolton, *The Medieval English Economy, 1150–1500* (1980), 154; J. H. Munro, 'Textile Technology in the Middle Ages', item 9, in id., *Textiles, Towns and Trade: Essays in the Economic History of Late-Medieval England and the Low Countries* (Aldershot, 1994).

53. Information kindly supplied by Dr Emilia Jamroziak.

54. R. H. Britnell, 'The Proliferation of Markets in England, 1200–1349', *Economic History Review*, 2nd ser. 33 (1981), 218–19.

55. D. L. Farmer, 'Prices and Wages', in H. E. Hallam (ed.), *The Agrarian History of England and Wales*, ii: *1042–1350* (Cambridge, 1988), 775–8.

56. J. R. Maddicott, 'The English Peasantry and the Demands of the Crown, 1294–1341', in T. H. Aston (ed.), *Landlords, Peasants and Politics in Medieval England* (Cambridge, 1987), 285–359.

FURTHER READING

Allen, M., 'The Volume of the English Currency, 1158–1470', *Economic History Review*, 54 (2001).

Amt, E., 'The Meaning of Waste in the Early Pipe Rolls of Henry II', *Economic History Review*, 44 (1991).

Bailey, M., 'Peasant Welfare in England, 1290–1348', *Economic History Review*, 51 (1998).

Beresford, M. W., *New Towns of the Middle Ages: Town Plantation in England, Wales and Gascony* (1967).

Bolton, J. L., 'The English Economy in the Early Thirteenth Century', in S. D. Church (ed.), *King John: New Interpretations* (Woodbridge, 1999).

—— 'Inflation, Economics and Politics in Thirteenth-Century England', in P. R. Coss and S. D. Lloyd (eds.), *Thirteenth Century England IV* (Woodbridge, 1992).

Britnell, R. H., 'The Proliferation of Markets in England, 1200–1349', *Economic History Review*, 2nd ser. 33 (1981).

Campbell, B. M. S., 'Population Pressure, Inheritance and the Land Market in a Fourteenth-Century Peasant Community', in R. M. Smith (ed.), *Land, Kinship and Life-Cycle* (Cambridge, 1984).

Cosgrove, A. (ed.), *A New History of Ireland*, ii: *Medieval Ireland, 1169–1534* (Oxford, 1987).

Dyer, C., 'Did the Peasants Really Starve in Medieval England?', in M. Carlin and J. L. Rosenthal (eds.), *Food and Eating in Medieval Europe* (1998).

Farmer, D. L., 'Prices and Wages', in H. E. Hallam (ed.), *The Agrarian History of England and Wales*, ii: *1042–1350* (Cambridge, 1988).

Gemmill, E., and Mayhew, N., *Changing Values in Medieval Scotland: A Study of Prices, Money, and Weights and Measures* (Cambridge, 1995).

Gillingham, J., ' "The Most Precious Jewel in the English Crown": Danegeld and Heregeld in the Early Eleventh Century', *English Historical Review*, 104 (1989).

Harvey, P. D. A., 'The English Inflation of 1180–1220', *Past and Present*, 61 (1973).

Harvey, S. P. J., 'Taxation and the Economy', in J. C. Holt (ed.), *Domesday Studies* (Woodbridge, 1987).

King, E., 'Economic Development in the Early Twelfth Century', in R. Britnell and J. Hatcher (eds.), *Progress and Problems in Medieval England: Essays in Honour of Edward Miller* (Cambridge, 1996).

King, E., *Peterborough Abbey, 1086–1310: A Study in the Land Market* (Cambridge, 1973).

—— (ed.), *The Anarchy of Stephen's Reign* (Oxford, 1994).

Latimer, P., 'Early Thirteenth-Century Prices', in S. D. Church (ed.), *King John: New Interpretations* (Woodbridge, 1999).

—— 'The English Inflation of 1180–1220 Reconsidered', *Past and Present*, 171 (2001).

—— 'Wages in Late Twelfth- and Early Thirteenth-Century England', *Haskins Society Journal*, 9 (2001 for 1997).

Lock, R., 'The Black Death in Walsham-le-Willows', *Proceedings of the Suffolk Institute of Archaeology and History*, 37 (1992).

McNamee, C. J., 'William Wallace's Invasion of Northern England in 1297', *Northern History*, 26 (1990).

Maddicott, J. R., 'The English Peasantry and the Demands of the Crown, 1294–1341', in T. H. Aston (ed.), *Landlords, Peasants and Politics in Medieval England* (Cambridge, 1987).

Miller, E., 'England in the Twelfth and Thirteenth Centuries: An Economic Contrast?', *Economic History Review*, 2nd ser. 24 (1971).

—— 'War, Taxation and the English Economy in the Late Thirteenth and Early Fourteenth Century', in J. M. Winter (ed.), *War and Economic Development* (Cambridge, 1975).

Ormrod, W. O., 'England in the Middle Ages', in R. Bonney (ed.), *The Rise of the Fiscal State in Europe, c.1200–1815* (Oxford, 1999).

Postan, M. M., and Titow, J. Z., 'Heriots and Prices on Winchester Manors', *Economic History Review*, 2nd ser. 11 (1959).

Razi, Z., *Life, Marriage and Death in a Medieval Parish: Economy, Society and Demography in Halesowen, 1270–1400* (Cambridge, 1980).

Rigold, S. E., 'Small Change in the Light of Medieval Site-Finds', in N. J. Mayhew (ed.), *Edwardian Monetary Affairs (1279–1344)*, British Archaeological Reports, 36 (Oxford, 1977).

Schofield, P., 'Dearth, Debt and the Local Land Market in a Late Thirteenth-Century Village Community', *Agricultural History Review*, 45 (1997).

Stone, D., 'Medieval Farm Management and Technological Mentalities: Hinderclay before the Black Death', *Economic History Review*, 54 (2002).

Titow, J. Z., 'Evidence of Weather in the Pipe Rolls of the Bishopric of Winchester, 1209–1350', *Economic History Review*, 2nd ser. 12 (1960).

1300–1530

....

CHAPTER 15

Britain and Ireland in the Early Fourteenth Century

The economic development achieved in Britain and Ireland between 1050 and 1300 represented a lasting achievement in many respects. It is true that the levels of trade and population reached then were not maintained. Yet many of the innovations that had made population growth possible during these 250 years made a lasting contribution to the technical and institutional resources of later generations, benefiting their levels of productivity, their standards of living, and the quality of their collective culture in a wide variety of ways. It is impossible to envisage life in the fourteenth and fifteenth centuries without ethical norms, administrative and political institutions, systems of money and credit, levels of literacy, and industrial and agrarian technologies, that had been absent in 1050. These achievements were shared to varying extents with much of the Eurasian land mass, and indeed partly depended upon innovations from abroad in France, the Low Countries, and Italy. In pausing to assess the progress that had been made, and to examine the costs incurred and the resulting problems, it will therefore be appropriate to comment briefly on Britain's place in the world, and to make some comparisons with neighbouring economies.

Britain and Ireland in Comparative Perspective

The demarcation of 'economies' for international comparisons in the modern world usually uses states as the relevant units. There are two principal ways in which such units can be compared. One is by measuring their size in terms of total output, or some other aggregate indicator relevant to the particular problem in hand, such as population. The other is by measuring average output per head of the population, which supplies a rough indicator of international differences in productivity and welfare. A very small economy may have a high average income, and a very large economy may have a very low average income. It is difficult to apply these methods of comparing economies to evidence for the period 1050–1500, partly because the statistical data is poor, but also because the concept of a national economy is anachronistic. One of the chief reasons for using national economies as economic units in the modern world is simply that statistics are usually collected by separate states. However, states are not necessarily the best units for the purpose of examining economic change. In comparing small and large economies one is not comparing like with like, and this obscures the way in which past economic development has occurred. The same objection would have to be raised against using state-bounded statistics for the early fourteenth century; there would be little point in comparing the whole of England with the Venetian republic, given the much greater variety of economic resources and structures in the former. The absence of national income data is accordingly less of a handicap than it may at first sight appear.

We are compelled to decide for ourselves what to compare on the strength of the available data. Many studies of modern economic development have made their point by comparing development regions rather than aggregate economies, and this is an approach to which earlier data lends itself quite well. From what has already been said, particularly in the first three chapters of this study, it is plain that different parts of Britain were strongly contrasted in almost every aspect of their economic development. The same would be true of any large region of Europe that included mountainous areas and swampy marshes as well as fertile plains and navigable waterways. The most useful form of comparison is perhaps one that compares the achievements of Britain's most commercialized and populous regions with those of similarly developed regions of continental Europe. This implies comparing southern and eastern England with Flanders and northern France, on the one hand, and northern Italy on the other.

Four principal comparisons are suggested by such information as we have: levels of urbanization (which indicate the capacity of agriculture and trade to support non-agrarian activities), levels of technical knowledge, the extent to which economic institutions were capable of flexibility to meet changing economic opportunities, and, finally, the extent to which the existence of core regions of urban and commercial development affected standards of living. These four indices together may be taken as indicating degrees of commercialization, and to some extent they may also be regarded as substitutes for comparative measures of labour productivity and per capita income.

Levels of urbanization deserve a prominent place in this analysis because there are differences between even the most advanced areas of Britain and the most commercialized parts of the Continent. In Britain, London was the only large city. By contrast, northern Italy, and the north-west European commercial region embracing Paris, Ghent, and Cologne, had a higher density of cities whose combined effect on regional market structures was more powerful.[1] It is true that high recent estimates of English urban population, at 15–20 per cent of the total, have to some extent narrowed international differences that used to be asserted more confidently.[2] Nevertheless the English proportion has been raised chiefly through the inclusion of large numbers of small towns whose impact upon marketing organization, employment structure, commercial incentives, and urban culture was far less than that of larger towns grouped together. Contrasts are more striking if only large towns are taken into account. In Italy north of the kingdom of Naples at least 16 per cent of the population lived in cities of over 10,000 inhabitants, but in England the proportion of the population in such towns is unlikely to have exceeded 6 per cent.[3] A constellation of towns, because it placed more pressure upon local agrarian resources, gave a greater stimulus to agrarian specialization and productivity than a scattering of small ones that could be supplied within a short radius. The populations of large towns were also differently composed; they included a larger proportion of long-distance merchants, lawyers, and other feed professionals than equivalent numbers in small towns. Exceptional opportunities for mercantile trade and professional activity had been one of the circumstances that had enabled towns to grow large in the first place.[4] For these reasons, London excepted, England was not in the forefront of development of mercantile or industrial institutions, and historians seeking the early roots of modern company organization, banking, capitalist industrial structures, and formal secular education, have rightly looked to Italy and Flanders rather than to England. Though an infrastructure of mercantile activity developed in Britain to accommodate the sedentary merchant, as we saw in Chapter 6, large international companies with branches in England, like the Frescobaldi and the Bardi, were the product of Italian enterprise.[5] A large share of English overseas trade was in the hands of continental merchants. In 1304–5, when wool exports reached their highest recorded level of 46,382 sacks, alien merchants accounted for 53 per cent of the trade, although that proportion declined over the following five years with the end of the boom in wool exports.[6]

International comparisons of technology and productivity are notoriously tricky to interpret, chiefly because it is not always possible to distinguish those differences that are economically rational (corresponding to real differences in profit opportunities) from those that are economically irrational (an indicator of failure to seize profit opportunities through ignorance or want of motivation). To take an extreme case, it would be absurd to blame English merchants for want of enterprise in not developing an international trade in spices and silks, since Italians and other Mediterranean merchants had a distinct locational advantage in these trades, but the English may be more open to criticism in not making more of native iron deposits.

A preliminary generalization to be made with some confidence concerns the resources of knowledge available for raising productivity through technical change. As observed in Chapter 2, technical information passed easily both into Britain from overseas and internally, either through the connections of the landowning elite or through the numerous long-distance contacts of British merchants. The windmill became so rapidly diffused in north-western Europe around the 1180s that it is uncertain whether it was innovated in England, France, or Flanders, so we can be confident that by 1200 there was nothing secret about windmill technology through most of western Europe. In Ireland no windmills are known before one recorded in 1281 at Kilscanlan (Co. Wexford).[7] If this indicates a real lag, rather than a defect of the documentary and archaeological evidence, it is one that cannot be attributed to ignorance, given the origins and interests of the Irish landowning class after 1179. The same circumstances, incidentally, argue against this being the result of differences in attitudes to profit. The explanation must rather be that Ireland had sufficient resources of water power to supply the needs of her population.

In agriculture, similarly, advanced agricultural practices in Flanders or northern France had close equivalents in Britain. If there were long-standing regional differences of cropping, manuring, marling, and rotation between manorial demesnes within Britain, it is unlikely to mean that some landlords were better informed than others. The use of horses as draught animals also varied considerably, being most advanced on light soils, which included some regions of more intensive husbandry near the eastern coast of England.[8] As in the case of the windmill, it is unreasonable to explain these as the result of variations in levels of knowledge, especially given the extensive interregional scattering of properties on large estates. Different manors on large estates show strikingly varied agrarian regimes and levels of productivity.[9] If agrarian techniques were more intensive in Holderness, eastern Norfolk, and eastern Kent, this can hardly be ascribed to the failure of knowledge to travel to other parts of Britain and Ireland.[10] The constraint on development would seem rather to be one of perceived marketing opportunity. It has been observed that these regions of advanced cropping in England, unlike those in Flanders, were less orientated to domestic urban markets than to those overseas. Even London's demand had not shaped agrarian practices in the south-eastern counties to the extent that large cities had transformed Flemish agriculture.[11] This implies that the differences of urban development between Britain and the more commercialized parts of the Continent had implications for the progress of agriculture.

British institutions, though often influenced by continental models, show divergences that might suggest a slower response to commercial incentives. The decision of major English landlords to administer their estates directly from the 1180s into the fourteenth century is variously interpreted in this respect. In other contexts an aristocracy and gentry willing to engage in commercial risk taking might be seen as evidence of exceptionally entrepreneurial social values. If we were to follow Karl Marx in identifying large wage-paying institutions as harbingers of capitalism, or Max Weber in recognizing the development of accounting as a capitalist characteristic, we should be obliged to see England's large estates as some of the most advanced units of production in medieval Europe. If, on the other hand, we assume that operations managed for the nobility and gentry are, either by definition or by likelihood, irredeemably 'feudal', pre-capitalist, and doomed to be superseded, then the English scene in the early fourteenth century looks less impressive. Historians respond differently to this issue for reasons that are not usually very apparent. However, in one respect at least many English landlords appear laggard in comparison with their continental equivalents, and that is in their preservation of customary relationships with tenants. Although, as Chapter 11 shows, custom was a significantly less important element in landlord–tenant relations in 1300 than in 1050, contract still played a smaller role in English tenancy arrangements than in Flanders or northern Italy. Landlords were inclined to cling to their right to customary labour services even if in practice they frequently took cash instead. They were also often inclined to allow customary peasant tenements to be split up into precarious smallholdings, rather than move in the opposite direction to increase the number of commercially viable farms. It is difficult to explain this by any weakness of commercial incentives, since custom flourished in regions of intensive and commercially responsive agriculture.[12] In part English practice can be explained by reference to a legal system that allowed lords powers over customary tenants that they could not exercise over free tenants, and so gave them an inducement to preserve the distinction, even if they managed to find some ways of evading the low-productivity straitjacket that customary relations implied. However, since lords often derived less revenue from customary tenures than they would have done from the same holdings on contractual rents,[13] it remains likely that traditionalist attitudes preserved inefficiencies that would have been eliminated by a more ruthless disrespect for custom.

Contrasts in technology and organization are most marked with regions that were exceptionally commercialized and urbanized, like Flanders, Lombardy, and Tuscany. Yet these differences did not translate into widely divergent levels of productivity and welfare. High levels of urbanization implied burdens of administrative expense, enhanced by corruption, that were lighter in England. Wealthy cities attracted predatory ambitions on the part of kings and noblemen that entailed heavy military expenditures. Because no English cities had significant territorial controls, they were less involved in conflict with their neighbours than those of Flanders and Italy. English cities were consequently freer of both internal and external conflict than their Flemish or northern Italian counterparts, and the weight of taxation was almost certainly lower, despite Edward I's best efforts, especially since under England's system of assessing movable goods many families were too poor to pay taxes.[14] Though the urban middle class was undoubtedly larger and wealthier in Flanders, France, or northern Italy than in Britain, it is not evident that this difference implied greatly divergent aggregate levels of per capita income and welfare, since even in those regions international merchants, lawyers, and other professionals constituted only a few per cent of the total population. The Italian middle class 'was still, though probably larger than the European average, a small, and in growth or consumer terms, insufficient minority'.[15] In modern economies differences in employment opportunities between wealthier and poorer economies have generated irresistible flows of migration, even across oceans and continents, by those in search of a better life. There is no reason to doubt that such flows would have occurred in early fourteenth-century Europe, had there been significant differentials in standards of welfare. There is no evidence that they did, however, and no evidence to suggest that they should have done. The only significant migrations of artisans across the Channel in the fourteenth century were from Flanders into Britain rather than the other way round.[16] As for the labouring and manufacturing population, chronic poverty and unemployment were as much a feature of Flemish and Italian cities as they were of London. In terms of what they would buy, wage levels were probably equally low in southern England and northern Italy.[17]

Problems

Impressive though the performance of the early fourteenth-century economy was in many respects, economic development had created problems whose solution depended upon more than short-term expedients. The more urbanized parts of Britain shared these problems with the other commercially advanced parts of Europe—another point of similarity rather than contrast. Some of these problems can be expressed in the somewhat abstract terms of the various models discussed in Chapter 4: there was tension between population and the land and technology available to support it in foodstuffs, and tension relating to the way in which income was distributed between town and country, between landlords and tenants. Ultimately these problems mattered to the extent that they had direct implications for the welfare and security of familes, so it is important not to lose sight of the realities of everyday life in considering what they amounted to.

In spite of the potential for growth in Britain during the twelfth and early thirteenth centuries, there were limits to what development was possible. One limit was set by the available land suitable for producing food of all kinds. Because bread and ale were so fundamental to the diet in southern and eastern Britain, the limits to arable cultivation were often the most restrictive. Expansion of arable cultivation could not proceed indefinitely, because sooner or later reserves of woodland and waste would run out. This limit was reached sooner in the medieval economy than in later periods of expansion; the area of woodland, heath, and moorland was undoubtedly more extensive in the early fourteenth century than today, but it needed to be so because of uses for which later generations found substitutes. These lands could not be written off as waste even if they were sometimes described as such (*vastum*). There was often a fine balance of advantages between cutting woodland down for new crops or alternatively managing it for recreational use (hunting), or for producing raw materials and other resources for which demand grew along with population and aggregate consumption. The balance sometimes swung against arable where the profits in pasture farming were judged to be higher; this seems to explain why from 1250 Ramsey Abbey reduced the sown acreages on its demesnes, especially of oats.[18] Woods and heaths were a main source of pasture for village communities. The significance of their diminution varied greatly from place to place, depending on the extent of reserves, but in some communities a loss of pasture threatened to reduce the numbers of animals the villagers could maintain and led to conflict, especially where rights of ownership were indistinct. This is implied by one of the items of legislation approved at a meeting of the king's great council on 23 January 1236; in future manorial lords were entitled to appropriate any woodland or common pasture over and above what their tenants needed.[19] In addition to their use as pasture, woods and heaths were a main source of fuel, the only source for some households, both for heating buildings and for cooking. The textile industry was not in this period a great consumer of fuel, but the metal industries were. Woodlands were also the source of timber, the main construction material for buildings and vehicles. The destruction of woodland gradually reduced the stock of building materials and other sylvan products to the point where, in the fourteenth century, parts of Britain became dependent upon imports from Scandinavia.[20] There was inevitably a limit how far the process of agricultural expansion could go without causing grave ecological problems.

Marshy regions, like the forests, contained resources whose value increased as population expanded. They comprised two main zones in which differing levels of wetness determined the use of the land. The really wet lands were a source of freshwater fish, eels, and wildfowl. Ely takes its name from two Old English words meaning 'eel district', and in the eleventh and twelfth centuries eels were so important in these parts that they were used in the payment of rents and the settlement of debts.[21] The wet lands were also a source of reeds and rushes for basket work and for covering floors. Along the coast, marshlands which were permeated by seawater were a main source of salt. In the less wet zone on the edges of marshlands, a more obviously agricultural economy was possible, but one which did not depend upon cereals. Essentially these were pastoral regions where hay was grown and livestock raised. This is why some of the main regions of commercial pasture farming in medieval England were the edges of the Humber marshes, the Lincolnshire Fens, and the region of the Norfolk Broads in East Anglia.[22]

Besides economic constraints upon expansion there were also technical limits. Some soils which could be profitably cultivated with modern fertilizers and crop rotations were inaccessible to the much more limited farming methods of the thirteenth century. The reclamation of new lands was hampered, too, by limited experience of drainage techniques. The methods known to medieval landlords and peasants were modest even by the standards of the sixteenth century; they did not use windmills for pumping water, and had to depend on gravity to move water from one point to another. This limited what it was possible to achieve; even at the end of the thirteenth century the coastline of Britain was very different from what it is today in low-lying regions.[23]

In most parts of England, and certainly in most parts of southern England, the limit to feasible expansion from forest and moorland was already being approached by the mid-thirteenth century. At the time when Domesday Book had been compiled Devon had had several hundreds of thousands of acres of wastelands. New settlers moved in, creating large numbers of freehold hamlets and isolated farms on the margin of existing settlements, but this activity was at its height between 1150 and 1250. Most modern Devon farms were already in existence by the early fourteenth century.[24] In other regions of England there was a similar exhaustion of opportunities. The main areas of clearance in southern England, besides Devon, were the Forest of Arden in the west Midlands, Rockingham Forest and Salcey Forest in the east Midlands, the Forest of Essex and the Weald of Kent in the south-east, and in all of these there is evidence of declining activity after about 1250. The main phase of Peterborough Abbey's woodland clearances in the Soke of Peterborough, and also in its forested manors on the edge of Rockingham Forest at Oundle, Cottingham, and Great Easton, was over by 1250.[25] In Salcey Forest the peak of assarting came in the 1230s and 1240s, and after a phase of more localized activity in the 1240s and 1250s assarting came to an end.[26] On the estates of the bishopric of Winchester, the most heavily wooded manors of the estate, Wargrave (Berkshire) and Witney (Oxfordshire), saw more deforestation in the first half of the century than in the second half even though the number of tenants was growing.[27] Even in some parts of northern England the clearing of woodlands was past its peak by 1300. The canons of Bolton Priory had carved out new farms for themselves in the late twelfth or early thirteenth century, but there is no sign of deforestation or drainage in the voluminous estate accounts of the years between 1286 and 1325.[28] Much of southern Scotland, too, had reached its full potential for agrarian expansion by 1300. There may have been room for continuing expansion in the border counties, but the central belt was heavily occupied. Clydesdale had few reserves of acceptable farmland. The Stewart family's forests in Renfrew were mostly under cultivation by the mid-thirteenth century. What remained here as forest, moor, or marsh was characteristically on acid soils, or incapable of being drained at sufficiently low cost. The prospects for further Scottish population growth were poor.[29]

Drainage from marshland and saltmarshes was also at its peak before 1250 rather than later. An area of about 50 square miles was drained in south Lincolnshire in several stages between 1086 and 1241. In this region, too, the mid-thirteenth century was the end of the phase of extensive new cultivation because by then colonists were coming up against deeper fens against which their drainage techniques were to no avail. In southern Lincolnshire the last of a long series of cooperative ventures between villages to drive back the fenlands was the construction of the Common Dyke, which divided the deep inland fens from the drained land to the north.[30] In the Romney Marsh and Welland Marsh in Kent drainage perhaps reach its technical limits later. Expensive schemes between 1285 and 1331 are known from the records of the estates of Canterbury Cathedral Priory. Even so, much of the Canterbury evidence from this period relates to defensive operations against floods rather than to new gains, and it is likely that as in the Fenlands the main period of expansion came earlier in the thirteenth century.[31]

It is difficult to assess to what extent other investment opportunities were constrained by the prospects of agrarian expansion. To some extent the possibilities of specialization over long distances permitted urban development independent of local agricultural prosperity; London's expansion is a case in point. The multiplication of small towns was meanwhile subject to its own constraints, determined by transport costs. Once the number of viable urban centres had attained a certain density in any given region there was less likely to be much profit in increasing their number; for that reason, economic geographers work on the assumption that the probable distribution of marketing centres can be mathematically modelled.[32] Population density and local levels of consumer demand are other determinants that have to be fed into the premises of any such model. Since the expansion of settlement and growth of consumer demand are intrinsic to any explanation of urban growth in the eleventh and twelfth centuries, the cessation of that expansive phase is likely to have some bearing on the simultaneous dwindling of opportunities for new urban foundations in the later thirteenth century. A similar argument will serve for other types of investment, such as mills, which are indeed subject to particular constraints on development—the availability of suitable sites— but which also, nevertheless, respond to the distribution and volume of demand.[33] The resources model and the investment model that we discussed in Chapter 4 are not altogether independent.

That said, it is far from evident that reserves of colonizable land and other investment opportunities were exhausted simultaneously all over Britain, and it would be nothing short of astounding if that had been the case. Northern England and Wales had been relatively lightly settled in the eleventh century, and there were reserves of forest and moorland to enable colonization to continue longer than in southern England. Assarting continued in the forest of Macclesfield well into the fourteenth century.[34] Durham experienced a major flurry of moorland clearance to create new farms in the time of Bishop Kellawe (1311–16).[35] There was scope for continuing investment and increasing productivity in the lordship of Chirk from the 1330s until the 1370s.[36] It is true that new resources available in the north were often of poor quality and inconveniently located with reference to centres of market demand. They were not quantitatively or qualitatively sufficient to sustain aggregate economic development during the later thirteenth and early fourteenth centuries. Yet these deficiencies cannot explain why the fourteenth century brought a reversal even sharper there than that in the south.[37]

The circumstances of Ireland were also dramatically different from those of southern and eastern England, since the possibilities of arable expansion there were very much greater between the English conquests of 1169–72 and the later thirteenth century. Units of peasant farming around 1300 were characteristically larger and less constrained by communal traditions than in England. Population densities were lighter.[38] Yet the chronology of change was much the same as in England; agrarian output reached a peak in the late thirteenth century and then contracted during the fourteenth. On the Bigod manors in Ireland some retreat from the expanded arable of the 1280s was already apparent by 1307.[39] Arable farming around Dublin was in retreat by 1326.[40] At Carrick-on-Suir (Co. Tipperary) in 1338 only 20 out of 216 acres were cultivated.[41] Declining estate revenues are widely reported. From 1316 onwards the lands of the de Verdun family at Duleek, Dundalk, and elsewhere in Ireland rendered only three-fifths of the income they had done within recorded memory.[42] It takes some credulity to suppose that balance between population and resources in Ireland and in England just happened to reach a critical relationship at the same time. Explanations other than population–resource balance are needed. The chronology of expansion in Wales is less well attested than in Ireland, but declining profitability has been suspected in the early fourteenth century on demesnes in the lordships of Glamorgan and Chirk.[43] If, as seems likely, expansion was interrupted in Scotland in the early fourteenth century, or even earlier, this again is unlikely to have been wholly the result of the exhaustion of reserves. Either we need to emphasize local conditions other than population pressure on resources (such as weather, warfare, and disease), or we need to postulate some externally induced cause, such as a cessation of exports. This would depend on identifying northern England, Wales, Scotland, and Ireland as peripheral economies and southern Britain as a core economy. In some contexts both arguments may be simultaneously relevant. In either case the argument from depleted resources needs to be modified as a general explanation.

These conclusions have wider implications for British development in the Middle

Ages. They indicate that the exhaustion of possibilities for agrarian expansion and investment in southern and midland England cannot be the whole explanation for the problems of growth in the early fourteenth century. Had that been the case, we should find a continuing expansion of agrarian economies to the north and west to new levels of production, as they attracted immigrants from outside and multiplied their commercial links with southern and midland England and continental Europe. That was the pattern of their development between the seventeenth and nineteenth centuries, but not in the century after 1260. In Chapter 4 a distinction was made between those models that explain a slowing down of development in the thirteenth century (stagnation models) and those that explain falling population and contracting trade in the fourteenth (catastrophe models). In much of southern England the two need to be kept separate because of evidence of two distinct phases, even if their chronology was imperfectly synchronized between different regions. In parts of Britain where the possibilities for continuing expansion were less constrained, notably the north and the west, stagnation models are much less relevant to an understanding of their history in the early fourteenth century. Perhaps the clearest exemplar of this case is the Palatinate of Durham, where agrarian expansion continued into the second decade of the fourteenth century, to be rapidly succeeded by a rapid downturn following the collapse of border defences in 1314 and the disastrous famine and depopulation of 1315–18.[44]

Britain in the early fourteenth century was poised on the brink of a new phase of development in which, after responding vigorously to a series of disasters, economic development was no longer driven by population growth and agrarian expansion. It shared this experience with much of the known world. In many ways, despite a few insular peculiarities, Britain's fortunes mirrored those of her neighbours. Levels of technical knowledge and commercial know-how had the same limitations, and cultural norms were hardly very distinctive. If in some respects even south-eastern England was at a disadvantage relative to merchants from Flanders or northern Italy, the same disabilities were to be found in many other parts of Europe. The varied experience within Britain, which contained some of the most lonely as well as some of the most densely populated regions of Europe, was itself mirrored elsewhere in Europe, even in Italy. Many of Britain's problems in the fourteenth century were shared with much of western and southern Europe. One of those was an increasing prevalence of warfare, which disrupted long-distance trade routes and so raised transaction costs. However, British governments, and notably the English, must bear their share of the blame for this particular fourteenth-century problem. Between 1294 and 1450 England was one of Europe's most belligerent nations, and almost all her neighbours were victims at some time or other.

NOTES

1. J. C. Russell, *Medieval Regions and their Cities* (Newton Abbot, 1972), 112–45.
2. Above (Ch. 4).
3. R. H. Britnell, 'England and Northern Italy in the Early Fourteenth Century: The Economic Contrasts', *Transactions of the Royal Historical Society*, 5th ser. 39 (1989), 168. The percentage for England cited there has been raised to accommodate revised estimates of the size of English towns, for which see B. M. S. Campbell, J. A. Galloway, D. Keene, and M. Murphy, *A Medieval Capital and its Grain Supply: Agrarian Production and Distribution in the London Region c.1300* (1993), 9–11.
4. R. H. Britnell, 'The Towns of England and Northern Italy in the Early Fourteenth Century', *Economic History Review*, 2nd ser. 44 (1991), 28–9.
5. M. Prestwich, 'Italian Merchants in Late Thirteenth Century and Early Fourteenth Century England', in Centre for Medieval and Renaissance Studies, University of California, Los Angeles, *The Dawn of Modern Banking* (New Haven, 1979), 77–104.
6. E. M. Carus-Wilson and O. Coleman, *England's Export Trade, 1275–1547* (Oxford, 1963), 41.
7. C. Rynne, *Technological Change in Anglo-Norman Munster* (Carrigtwohill, 1998), 79.
8. J. Langdon, *Horses, Oxen and Technological Innovation: The Use of Draught Animals in English Farming from 1066 to 1500* (Cambridge, 1986), 100–3.
9. B. M. S. Campbell, *English Seigniorial Agriculture, 1250–1450* (Cambridge, 2000), 324.
10. See above (Ch. 9).
11. J. Langdon, 'Was England a Technological Backwater in the Middle Ages?', in G. Astill and J. Langdon (eds.), *Medieval Farming and Technology: The Impact of Agricultural Change in Northwest Europe* (Leiden, 1997).
12. F. G. Davenport, *The Economic Development of a Norfolk Manor, 1086–1565* (Cambridge, 1906), 62–9. For Forncett's status as a high-productivity manor, see Campbell, *English Seigniorial Agriculture*, 324–5.
13. Above (Ch. 11).
14. D. Nicholas, *Medieval Flanders* (1992), 180–208.
15. P. Jones, *The Italian City-State: From Commune to Signoria* (Oxford, 1997), 234.
16. E. Lipson, *The Economic History of England*, i: *The Middle Ages*, 12th edn. (1959), 452–3.
17. Britnell, 'England and Northern Italy', 180–1.
18. J. A. Raftis, *The Estates of Ramsey Abbey: A Study in Economic Growth and Organization* (Toronto, 1957), 161–3.
19. F. M. Powicke, *King Henry III and the Lord Edward: The Community of the Realm in the Thirteenth Century*, 2 vols. (Oxford, 1947), i. 149–50.
20. T. H. Lloyd, *Alien Merchants in England in the High Middle Ages* (Brighton, 1982), 45, 148–9.
21. H. C. Darby, *The Medieval Fenland* (Cambridge, 1940), 28–32.
22. O. Rackham, *The History of the Countryside* (1985), 358–9.
23. M. Aston, *Interpreting the Landscape: Landscape Archaeology and Local History* (1985), 94–7.
24. W. G. Hoskins, 'The Making of the Agrarian Landscape', in id. and H. P. R. Finberg, *Devonshire Studies* (1952), 318–24.
25. E. King, *Peterborough Abbey, 1086–1310: A Study in the Land Market* (Cambridge, 1973), 81, 83.

26. J. A. Raftis, *Assart Data and Land Values: Two Studies in the East Midlands, 1200–1350* (Toronto, 1974), 102, 119.

27. J. Z. Titow, 'Some Differences between Manors and their Effects on the Condition of the Peasant in the Thirteenth Century', *Agricultural History Review*, 10 (1962), 8; E. Miller and J. Hatcher, *Medieval England: Rural Society and Economic Change, 1086–1348* (1978), 34.

28. I. Kershaw, *Bolton Priory: The Economy of a Northern Monastery, 1286–1325* (1973), 32, 128–9.

29. I owe these comments to Sandy Grant.

30. H. E. Hallam, *Settlement and Society: A Study of the Early Agrarian History of South Lincolnshire* (Cambridge, 1965), 31–2, 39.

31. R. A. L. Smith, *Canterbury Cathedral Priory: A Study in Monastic Administration* (Cambridge, 1943), 172–89; H. E. Hallam, *Rural England, 1066–1348* (Glasgow, 1981), 77.

32. W. Christaller, *Central Places in Southern Germany*, trans. C. W. Baskin (Englewood Cliffs, 1966).

33. J. Langdon, *Technology and Economy in the Later Middle Ages: The English Milling Industry, 1300–1540* (forthcoming).

34. A. M. Tonkinson, *Macclesfield in the Later Fourteenth Century: Communities of Town and Forest*, Chetham Society, 4th ser. 42 (1999), 4–5, 10.

35. H. M. Dunsford and S. J. Harris, 'Colonization of the Wasteland in County Durham, 1100–1400', *Economic History Review*, 56 (2003), 48.

36. L. B. Smith, 'Seignorial Income in the Fourteenth Century: The Arundels in Chirk', *Bulletin of the Board of Celtic Studies*, 28 (1979), 443–57.

37. R. Lomas, *North-East England in the Middle Ages* (Edinburgh, 1992), 112–14.

38. Above (Ch. 8).

39. M. C. Lyons, 'Manorial Administration and the Manorial Economy in Ireland, c.1200–c.1377', 2 vols. (unpublished Ph.D. thesis, Trinity College Dublin, 1984), i. 95, 179–80.

40. Ibid., i. 36–7; H. Jäger, 'Land-Use in Medieval Ireland', *Irish Economic and Social History*, 10 (1983), 56, 64–5.

41. C. A. Empey, 'The Manor of Carrick-on-Suir in the Middle Ages', *Journal of the Butler Society*, 2 (1982), 208.

42. M. S. Hagger, *The Fortunes of a Norman Family: The de Verduns in England, Ireland and Wales, 1066–1316* (Dublin, 2001), 136.

43. D. H. Owen, 'The Middle Ages', in id. (ed.), *Settlement and Society in Wales* (Cardiff, 1989), 206.

44. C. M. Fraser, *A History of Anthony Bek, Bishop of Durham, 1283–1311* (Oxford, 1957), 116–17.

FURTHER READING

Allen, M., 'The Volume of the English Currency, 1158–1470', *Economic History Review*, 54 (2001).

Bailey, M., 'The Concept of the Margin in the Medieval English Economy', *Economic History Review*, 2nd ser. 14 (1989).

—— 'Peasant Welfare in England, 1290–1348', *Economic History Review*, 51 (1998).

Bridbury, A. R., 'Before the Black Death', *Economic History Review*, 2nd ser. 30 (1977), and in id., *The English Economy from Bede to the Reformation* (Woodbridge, 1992).

Briggs, C., 'Creditors and Debtors and their Relationships at Oakington, Cottenham and Dry Drayton, 1291–1350', in P. R. Schofield and N. J. Mayhew (eds.), *Credit and Debt in Medieval England* (Oxford, 2002).

Britnell, R. H., 'England and Northern Italy in the Early Fourteenth Century: The Economic Contrasts', *Transactions of the Royal Historical Society*, 5th ser. 39 (1989).

—— 'The Towns of England and Northern Italy in the Early Fourteenth Century', *Economic History Review*, 2nd ser. 44 (1991).

Campbell, B. M. S. (ed.), *Before the Black Death: Studies in the 'Crisis' of the Early Fourteenth Century* (Manchester, 1991).

—— *English Seigniorial Agriculture, 1250–1450* (Cambridge, 2000).

—— 'Progressiveness and Backwardness in Thirteenth- and Early Fourteenth-Century English Agriculture: The Verdict of Recent Research', in J.-M. Duvosquel and E. Thoen (eds.), *Peasants and Townsmen in Medieval Europe: Studia in Honorem Adriaan Verhulst* (Ghent, 1995).

—— Galloway, J. A., Keene, D., and Murphy, M., *A Medieval Capital and its Grain Supply: Agrarian Production and Distribution in the London Region c.1300* (1993).

Chorley, P., 'English Cloth Exports during the Thirteenth and Early Fourteenth Centuries: The Continental Evidence', *Historical Research* (1988).

Down, K., 'Colonial Society and Economy in the High Middle Ages', in A. Cosgrove (ed.), *A New History of Ireland*, ii: *Medieval Ireland, 1169–1534* (Oxford, 1987).

Duncan, A. A. M, *Scotland: The Making of the Kingdom* (Edinburgh, 1989).

Dunsford, H. M., and Harris, S. J., 'Colonization of the Wasteland in County Durham, 1100–1400', *Economic History Review*, 56 (2003).

Ecclestone, M., 'Mortality and Rural Landless Men before the Black Death: The Glastonbury Head-Tax Lists', *Local Population Studies*, 63 (1999).

Evans, R., 'Merton College's Control of its Tenants at Thorncroft, 1270–1349', in Z. Razi and R. Smith (eds.), *Medieval Society and the Manor Court* (Oxford, 1996).

Galloway, J. A., 'One Market or Many: London and the Grain Trade of England', in id. (ed.), *Trade, Urban Hinterlands and Market Integration, c.1300–c.1600* (2000).

Harvey, B., 'The Population Trend in England between 1300 and 1348', *Transactions of the Royal Historical Society*, 5th ser. 16 (1966).

Harvey, P. D. A., *A Medieval Oxfordshire Village: Cuxham, 1240 to 1400* (1965).

Jäger, H., 'Land-Use in Medieval Ireland', *Irish Economic and Social History*, 10 (1983).

Jordan, W. C., *The Great Famine: Northern Europe in the Early Fourteenth Century* (Princeton, 1996).

Kershaw, I., *Bolton Priory: The Economy of a Northern Monastery, 1286–1325* (1973).

—— 'The Great Famine and Agrarian Crisis in England, 1315–1322', *Past and Present*, 59 (1973), repr. in R. H. Hilton (ed.), *Peasants, Knights and Heretics: Studies in Medieval English Social History* (Cambridge, 1976).

Langdon, J., 'Lordship and Peasant Consumerism in the Milling Industry of Early Four-teenth-Century England', *Past and Present*, 145 (1994).

—— 'Was England a Technological Backwater in the Middle Ages?', in G. Astill and J. Langdon (eds.), *Medieval Farming and Technology: The Impact of Agricultural Change in Northwest Europe* (Leiden, 1997).

Lloyd, T. H., *Alien Merchants in England in the High Middle Ages* (Brighton, 1982).

Lomas, R. A., 'The Impact of Border Warfare: The Scots and South Tweedside, c.1290–c.1520', *Scottish Historical Review*, 75 (1990).

Maddicott, J. R., 'The English Peasantry and the Demands of the Crown, 1294–1341', in T. H. Aston (ed.), *Landlords, Peasants and Politics in Medieval England* (Cambridge, 1987).

Mate, M., 'High Prices in Early Fourteenth-Century England: Causes and Consequences', *Economic History Review*, 2nd ser. 28 (1975).

Mayer, P. J., 'Calstock and the Bere Alston Silver Mines in the First Quarter of the Fourteenth Century', *Cornish Archaeology*, 29 (1990).

Miller, E., 'War, Taxation and the English Economy in the Late Thirteenth and Early Fourteenth Century', in J. M. Winter (ed.), *War and Economic Development* (Cambridge, 1975).

Munro, J., 'The "Industrial Crisis" of the English Textile Towns, c.1290–c.1330', in M. C. Prestwich, R. H. Britnell, and R. F. Frame (eds.), *Thirteenth Century England VII* (Woodbridge, 1999).

Postan, M. M., 'Medieval Agrarian Society in its Prime: England', in id. (ed.), *The Cambridge Economic History of Europe*, i: *The Agrarian Life of the Middle Ages*, 2nd edn. (Cambridge, 1966).

—— and Titow, J. Z., 'Heriots and Prices on Winchester Manors', *Economic History Review*, 2nd ser. 11 (1955), repr. in M. M. Postan, *Essays on Medieval Agriculture and General Problems of the Medieval Economy* (Cambridge, 1973).

Pounds, N., *An Historical Geography of Europe, 450 BC–AD 1330* (Cambridge, 1973).

Prestwich, M., 'Currency and the Economy of Early Fourteenth-Century England', in N. J. Mayhew (ed.), *Edwardian Monetary Affairs (1279–1344)* (Oxford, 1977).

—— 'Italian Merchants in Late Thirteenth Century and Early Fourteenth Century England', in Centre for Medieval and Renaissance Studies, University of California, Los Angeles, *The Dawn of Modern Banking* (New Haven, 1979).

Raban, S., *England under Edward I and Edward II, 1259–1327* (Oxford, 2000).

Razi, Z., *Life, Marriage and Death in a Medieval Parish: Economy, Society and Demography in Halesowen, 1270–1400* (Cambridge, 1980).

Russell, J. C., *Medieval Regions and their Cities* (Newton Abbot, 1972).

Rutledge, E., 'Immigration and Population Growth in Early Fourteenth-Century Norwich: Evidence from the Tithing Roll', *Urban History Yearbook*, 1988.

—— 'Landlords and Tenants: Housing and the Rented Property Market in Early Fourteenth-Century Norwich', *Urban History*, 22 (1995).

Schofield, P. R., 'Access to Credit in the Early Fourteenth-Century English Countryside', in id. and N. J. Mayhew (eds.), *Credit and Debt in Medieval England* (Oxford, 2002).

Titow, J. Z., *English Rural Society, 1200–1350* (1969).

—— 'Some Differences between Manors and their Effects on the Condition of the Peasant in the Thirteenth Century', *Agricultural History Review*, 10 (1962).

....

CHAPTER 16

Merchants and their Trade

The long-distance trade that had grown up before 1300 was important to a wide range of people and contributed a sufficiently large amount to incomes across Britain to be a matter of political significance. Any landlord who sold wool, any merchant who handled it, any shipman who shipped it, and the king himself who taxed it, felt the effects of fluctuations in international markets or the breakdown of normal relations. So did townsmen who depended upon imported goods for a livelihood—the clothmakers who needed imported dyes, the furriers, the mercers who sold linen, the vintners who imported wines and sold them both whole-sale and retail. By 1300 foreign trade was sufficiently valuable to affect landlords' incomes, and to a lesser extent the volume of employment, in most parts of Britain, as Edward I's critics appreciated when they criticized the tax he imposed on wool exports.[1] Fluctuations and crises in international trade were inevitably of greater moment from the thirteenth century onwards than they had been before commerce overseas had attained such significance. They became gradually more important for urban employment from the 1350s as a result of the growth of cloth-exporting industries, whose crises made textile workers idle and discontented. It seems likely that exports counted for a higher proportion of British aggregated incomes in 1500 than in 1300 because of this switch into woollen cloth rather than raw wool as the primary source of overseas earnings. However, this achievement was won erratically, with many setbacks. Neither supply nor demand conditions were as favourable to the overall expansion of foreign trade as they had been through the twelfth and thirteenth centuries.

Before 1300, as we have seen, the growth of long-distance commerce had been sustained by a growth of demand in western Europe which the British and Irish economies had been able to benefit from, particularly through the supply of raw materials such as wool, hides, and minerals. What happened to international demand after 1300 is a matter for some dispute; we can neither compare the total value of trade in Europe in 1300 and in 1530, nor identify any single trend throughout the period. However, the combination of demographic decline and monetary contraction, especially between 1350 and 1460, were plainly not conducive to an expansion of international trade comparable to that of the period before 1300. This in itself gives the period a distinct character, which is enhanced by the consequent competition in international markets for such trade as there was. This, of course, set at a disadvantage those economies, or sectors of economies, that were particularly hampered by rising costs or vulnerable to commercial aggression.

Two periods stand out as particularly affected by the failure of export demand affecting Britain, both corresponding to international recessions that lowered the demand for British products in foreign markets.[2] Between about 1390 and 1415 Europe experienced a major international crisis of liquidity, or bullion famine, associated in both the north-western and Mediterranean trading areas with declining monetary circulation and reduced mint output. English cloths exported, as registered in the customs accounts, declined suddenly after 1402 from an annual average of 36,842 (1390–4) and 40,404 (1398–1402) to 27,183 in the trough of the recession (1411–15), while the number of sacks of wool exported declined from 19,691 (1390–4) to 13,593 (1411–15).[3] Scottish wool exports declined catastrophically from an annual average export of 4,760 sacks (1390–4) to a trough of 1,840 (1400–5), recovering to still only 2,950 sacks in 1410–14. The second more prolonged depression, the mid-fifteenth-century slump or second bullion famine, lasted from about 1445 to 1465. The average annual export of cloths declined from 56,456 (1441–5) to 29,002 in the years 1461–5, and wool exports fell from 8,029 sacks a year to 6,695 sacks over the same twenty-year period.[4] Scottish wool exports had already collapsed during the 1430s to an annual average of only 1,580 sacks (1441–5), and they were less affected by the recession of the mid-fifteenth century.[5] English cloth exports in 1464–5 were lower than in any other year of the fifteenth century, and this year corresponds to the blackest months of the continental recession; the Strozzi bank in Florence failed in 1464.[6] This recession, as far as cloth exports were concerned, was chiefly caused by falling demand across Europe, exacerbated by a ban on imports of English cloth imposed by the Burgundians in 1447 in retaliation for English bullionist regulations. Textile workers, whose livelihood depended more than most on the level of export trade, were among the most clearly defined dissident groups of the period; they were prominent in Cade's Rebellion of 1450 and in other manifestations of popular discontent.[7]

In the later fifteenth century, British economies benefited to some extent from the fact that economic revival in several parts of Europe was running ahead of revival in Britain. Most of the bright spots in the economy in the period 1450–1530 were indebted to the stimulus of overseas markets. The expansion of the textile industry in the last decades of the fifteenth century was export led. Between the early 1450s and the early 1540s English textile exports grew at an average annual rate of 1.3 per cent, and it is difficult to identify anything else so dynamic in that period. The Mediterranean and Iberian economies increased their demand for imports at the same time; Castile, which had no very commercial textile manufacture of its own, increased its consumption of English cloth during the 1480s and 1490s, to the point that by the early years of Henry VII's reign, between 1485 and 1487, over 10 per cent of English exports were destined for Spain.[8] But the major support of English textile expansion was the growth of Antwerp and its trade, which accounted for the lion's share of textile exports. The improved trade with Burgundy was helped by a trade agreement from 1496—the so-called *Intercursus Magnus*, negotiated between Henry VII of England and Philip, duke of Burgundy—but trade through the Low Countries, especially through Antwerp, had been growing before this, despite a period of hostile diplomatic relations following the accession of Henry Tudor in 1485.

Though fluctuations in overseas demand were important, they are not the whole story. This chapter will also examine how trade was also affected adversely by the movement of transactions costs. It will examine the impact of these conditions on the overall level and composition of trade and examine how and why in these troubled times British merchants benefited in competition with merchants from abroad, bearing in mind the high profile of foreign merchants in overseas trade in 1300. Finally it will argue that the integration of the internal British market, which has earlier been discussed as a feature of the period 1050–1300, suffered setbacks in the following two centuries as a result of these same changes in demand and supply conditions.

Transaction Costs

The impact of warfare on economic activity was bound to increase as international trade figured more prominently in the way livelihoods were won. The fragile international trading structure built up over the twelfth and thirteenth centuries was to suffer severe damage from around 1290 from the activities of rulers prepared to put claims of family honour or legal entitlement above the welfare of their subjects. Warfare was not a distinctly north-European phenomenon; it affected the Mediterranean economies as much as those of the North Sea. But British rulers, and especially the kings of England, played a prominent role in destabilizing normal trade. The Scottish economy was one of the early sufferers in this new phase of belligerence. Losses of income resulting from warfare imposed a check on what kings could hope to achieve, but they frequently operated in the fallible belief that what was destroyed by war could be restored by treaty. Recurrent warfare was the bane of international trade, obstructing its development and preventing its advantages from being realized.[9] The author of the *Libelle of Englyshe Polycye* (1436) pleaded for the stalwart defence of the 'narrow sea' between England and the Continent in order to protect English trade, but his ultimate desired result was peace. If England protected her interests adequately, he argued, foreign governments would be compelled to sue for peace.

> And thus should every land, one with another,
> Intercommon as brother with his brother
> And live together warless in unity,
> Without rancour, in very charity.[10]

In reality, merchants suffered particularly from the dependence of their trade on precarious travel by sea at a time when the costs of overland travel in Europe were falling.[11] These hazards affected not only the principal ports on the east and south coasts of Britain but also the Welsh and Irish ports.[12] Piracy, itself a predictable consequence of the growth of maritime trade through the twelfth and thirteenth centuries, became all the more prevalent when it was legitimized by war. This was not a problem confined to English shipping; the Scots' reputation for piracy in the late Middle Ages has obscured the extent to which they too were vulnerable.[13] The dangers, even in peacetime, are well illustrated by the misfortunes of the *George* of Beverley in 1464. This ship, crossing from Zeeland to Hull with a mixed cargo valued at £553 9s. 8d., finished up on the coast of Norway, where either it was blown off course or it was seized by a Danish pirate—the stories differed. In either case, its cargo, or what was left of it, was seized in Norway by two German merchants who claimed they had a legal right to it because they had won it from a known pirate.[14] Merchants not only had to pay to defend their cargoes from attack, but stood to lose large sums if that protection failed. In addition, their ships were liable to be commandeered for naval purposes by the king. Navies in this period were made up not of specialized vessels, but of ordinary ships temporarily diverted from mercantile activity.[15] Rising transaction costs resulting from warfare and piracy account, in large measure, for the declining international trade in cheaper textiles during the fourteenth century.[16]

A rising incidence of warfare and economic rivalry, though particularly damaging in the early fourteenth century, was accompanied by increases in other costs. Rising wages during the later fourteenth century pushed up the cost of mariners' labour. In 1390 the heavier demands of mariners were a matter for complaint in a parliamentary petition, and wages recorded in the Cely letters in the final quarter of the fifteenth century show a clear increase over those specified in the Inquisition of Queenborough in 1375.[17] Wages were probably a significant cost in many of the short journeys in small ships that were normal for much of British overseas trade; on a simple return trip to Zeeland in 1487 by the Celys' ship the *Margaret*, which was of about 60 tons, the labour costs were £9 0s. 5d. out of a total outlay of £31 4s. 11d., or 29 per cent of the total.[18] Rising labour costs seem not to have been offset by changes in ship design, important though those were. Where ships had formerly made do with a single mast, during the fifteenth century ships with two, three, or four masts and an increased area of sail were appearing in northern European waters, and larger ships were being employed on more distant trade routes.[19] During the first half of the fifteenth century the average cargo of wine brought into Bristol increased from 88 to 150 tons.[20] However, the peacetime cost of transporting a ton of wine from Bordeaux to London increased from around 8s. 0d. to 10s. in the 1320s and 10s. in the 1390s to around £1 in the 1480s.[21] While not all this increase can be attributed to wage costs, it is likely that they contributed to it.

The institutional structures that supported mercantile activity showed less development between 1300 and 1530 than during the two previous centuries, but the role of fairs in mercantile operations was restructured. International fairs remained significant occasions for overseas merchants, but those within Britain itself declined during the fourteenth century. At the end of the thirteenth century officers of the king's wardrobe still bought cloth, wax, and skins at the fairs of Stamford, St Ives, Boston, Winchester, and Bury St Edmunds, and even in the 1320s they were buying heavily at Boston and St Ives. However, these fairs were already in decline during the thirteenth century, as trade in imported goods shifted to larger towns, especially London. By the 1320s London had captured a large share of the internal market in cloth, furs, wine, and spices and was by far the most important port for wool exports, with 45 per cent of the recorded English total between 1320–1 and 1329–30. The trade of the fairs became increasingly localized.[22] The major fairs of the fourteenth and fifteenth centuries were chiefly important for the distribution of goods within Britain in response to the changing pattern of consumer demand after the Black Death. Stourbridge fair, just outside Cambridge, increased in importance from the later fourteenth century to become the greatest British fair of the sixteenth century.[23] It is not obvious that this restructuring of fair activity represented a net gain in the facilities for mercantile activity. For merchants in large towns it was in part the result of cost-reducing procedures that allowed trade to be carried on throughout the year without the expense of travelling into the provinces. The London market for cloth, for example, was eventually formalized in 1395–6 when the city acquired Blackwell Hall to serve as a market for both English and foreign cloth.[24]

The decline of the international fairs in the early fourteenth century can also be seen as a direct consequence of wartime disruption. They had depended for much of their trade on foreign merchants coming to England for wool. As this trade responded to the effects of conflicts with Flanders (1270–7, 1294–1303, 1307–22), and, from 1337, to higher taxes on wool exports and the imposition of a staple, the export of wool was increasingly handled by English merchants travelling abroad. Merchants who had lost interest in fairs at home nevertheless continued to frequent those overseas, and contributed to the rise of international fairs in Brabant in the late fifteenth century. The Celys, during the 1470s and 1480s, traded at the Easter and winter fairs at Bergen-op-Zoom, and the Antwerp fairs at the feasts of Whitson and St Bavo.[25] The fairs of Antwerp, Bergen-op-Zoom, and Middelburg were a principal destination for Scottish merchants; this was one of the routes by which Scottish wools reached their markets in the Netherlands.[26] There was no revival of British international fairs in the late fifteenth century comparable to that on the Continent because the Brabant fairs were serving well enough, though this was not an optimal solution for British merchants because the risks were inevitably higher than trade at home would have been.[27]

Trade benefited both from the further development of credit systems devised in the thirteenth century and from the introduction of a gold currency that facilitated large payments, but these advantages were not able to offset all the problems merchants faced in making necessary payments. International payments were complicated both by recurrent debasements that reduced the status of sterling as an international currency, and in the increasing obstacles to the international movement of bullion imposed by governments in an attempt to maintain a satisfactory level of monetary circulation.[28] In the fifteenth century, as in the eighteenth, deficiencies of small change affected employers as well as their employees. In addition, the trade recessions of the fifteenth century, which were partly the result of defects in the monetary system, encouraged hoarding, the contraction of credit, and higher interest rates.[29]

Increases in domestic transaction costs were a secondary effect of other economic changes. There is little information about changes in the state of the roads during this period, but there is little reason to suppose that there was any improvement in transport along navigable waterways. Already before 1300 the extent of inland navigation had become more restricted by the multiplication of water control systems to accommodate the requirements of watermills. That particular trend did not continue after 1300 because the number of mills declined. Yet this probably had little significance for ease of communications, and some inland waterways continued to deteriorate simply for want of investment in their maintenance.[30] Around 1300, for example, Henley was the normal upriver limit of navigation on the River Thames, but the stretch between Henley and Oxford could still be used. However, this last stretch, which was more difficult because of the number of flashlocks along it, was completely abandoned in the depths of the mid-fifteenth-century recession and became unnavigable for several generations.[31]

The Dimensions and Composition of Overseas Trade

Because of these adverse conditions affecting Britain's trade, the total value of trade from all parts of Britain and Ireland, and probably its contribution to incomes, fell over lengthy periods. In the years 1301–10, the decade in which English wool exports were at their peak, their total value was probably at least £210,000 a year; other exports such as hides and tin, though of lesser importance, will have raised that figure to over £220,000.[32] Yet for the ten years 1421/2–1430/1 the average total annual value of English exports has been estimated at only £166,687. Wool and cloth exports together in this latter period were worth no more than about £154,370 a year.[33] The real decline in the volume of exports was less severe than this comparison suggests, since prices had also fallen: average wool prices, for example, had fallen by 27 per cent between 1301–10 and 1421–30.[34] Even so, considering that at the latter date about 47 per cent of exports were made up of manufactured cloth rather than raw wool, the contrast is striking. The current value of England's exports was to fall even further during the slump of the mid-fifteenth century, to an average of only £157,256 between 1442/3 and 1451/2, and perhaps to as low as £114,839 between 1452/3 and 1460/1.[35] Scotland's exports recovered from the adverse effects of the War of Independence and the recession of the late 1330s and earlier 1340s to reach a peak in the third quarter of the century. But these heights were never recovered. No estimate of Scotland's total trade is available, but the decline in exports of wool and hides is in line with indications of a more general contraction. A falling number of ships were leaving Scottish ports between the 1370s and the earlier fifteenth century.[36] Irish trade also suffered from the contraction of overseas demand, and the revenues from port towns declined.[37] Finds of pottery from south-western France and Spain are rarer in Ireland after 1330 than before.[38]

From the low point of the 1450s and 1460s English overseas trade expanded more rapidly than that of other parts of Britain, chiefly because of the expansion of cloth exports. Overseas markets constituted by far the most dynamic source of expenditure on English goods in the late fifteenth and early sixteenth century, and the consequent increase in customs revenues gave powerful support to the English crown during Edward IV's second reign (1471–83) and subsequently under the early Tudors. By 1546 the combined value of cloth, tin, and lead exports alone was perhaps about £335,000 a year,[39] and though allowance has to be made for an increase in the price level by perhaps 75 per cent between the 1450s and the 1540s the growth in the value of exports was plainly a matter of real advantage. The benefits of commercial expansion were more apparent in south-eastern England in this period than in other parts of Britain and Ireland. Irish trade, in particular, languished until the later sixteenth century without the distinguishing specialization that might have attracted more merchants from France or Spain.[40]

Both England and Scotland suffered a severe contraction of their wool trade over the course of the fourteenth and fifteenth centuries, though there was no constant trend, and the performance of the two kingdoms differed. Exports recorded in the English customs accounts fell from a peak of 38,658 sacks a year on average between 1302/3 and 1306/7, and recovered to similar levels during the boom years between 1354 and 1362, but subsequently declined to only 3,698 between 1527/8 and 1531/2.[41] Scottish wool exports rose to surpass their level of 1327–32 (about 5,700 sacks a year) after 1365; they averaged perhaps 7,360 sacks a year in the years 1370–4 but had declined to only 759 sacks by the 1520s.[42]

Wool exports from both kingdoms benefited after 1350 from a drop in prices that ran counter to the general price level, no doubt because of heavy investment in sheep in the aftermath of the Black Death.[43] English trade also benefited from the fact that the textile industry of Flanders, in order to survive increasing transactions costs in international trade, was shifting its emphasis into higher qualities of cloth that depended upon a high quality of wool.[44] The boom wool exports after the Black Death proved short-lived as falling output of textiles reduced demand for wool in the Low Countries in the late fourteenth century.[45] Exports declined to significantly lower levels; they never again reached the levels of the early fourteenth century. This was not altogether the result either of social crises in overseas manufacturing, falling incomes, or increased transactions costs resulting from wartime disruption and rising wages. It also derived from the high taxes on wool exports imposed by the governments of Edward III in England and David II in Scotland. These had not been sufficiently high to eliminate the favourable circumstances of the third quarter of the fourteenth century, though they presumably dampened their impact, but from the 1370s onwards they contributed to a decline in the demand for British wools. In order to finance his war with France, Edward III in 1336 secured the agreement of an assembly of merchants at Nottingham to raise the basic export duty payable by English exporters on a sack of wool from 6s. 8d. to £1 6s. 8d., subsequently raised in March 1338 to £2. It remained at that level, with occasional fluctuations, into the sixteenth century.[46] Foreign merchants, meanwhile, were required first to increase the duty they paid from the 10s. they had owed since 1303, to £1 10s., and then £2 3s. 4d. in March 1338. Figure 16.1 shows the subsequent course of increases in duty on English exports; they resulted in alien merchants paying £3 16s. 8d. a sack by the end of the fifteenth century. Scotland, of course, was subject to a different tariff regime, but there too duties on a sack of wool were raised from 6s. 8d. to 13s. 4d. in 1358, to £1 in 1359, and reached a peak of £1 6s. 8d. in 1368.[47] These rates were lower than that of England, but so too was the average value of Scottish wool. Some northern English wools, which were

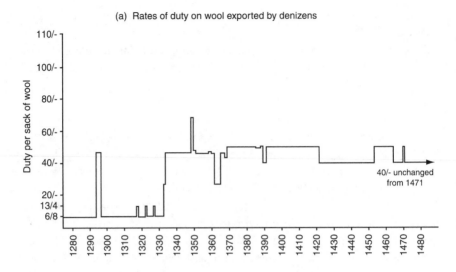

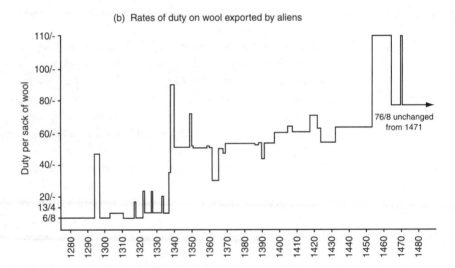

FIG. 16.1. Rates of duty on wool exports from England after 1275. Though there were many minor fluctuations in export duties on wool, the greatest discontinuity came in 1337–8 in anticipation of war with France. Comparison between the two time series shows the increasing disadvantages of 'alien' merchants (who did not include German merchants of the Hanseatic League) during the fifteenth century.

Source: E. M. Carus-Wilson and O. Coleman, *England's Export Trade* (Oxford, 1963), 196.

comparable to those of Scotland, were illegally exported through Scotland to evade the higher English duties; the volume of such smuggling is estimated at over 1,600 sacks in 1373–4, at the height of the Scottish export boom.[48] As a percentage of average wool prices English duties were normally above 33 per cent even on denizen exports, and on alien exports from the 1390s they were over 50 per cent.[49] They could to some extent be passed on to Flemish buyers, who were afraid that they would be unable to maintain the reputation of their cloth if they substituted cheaper and inferior wool.[50] Even so in the long run they discouraged the export of wool, while simultaneously giving advantages to English clothmakers, as we shall see. Northern English and Scottish wools and hides were of a relatively low value on international markets, so that increases in transaction costs affected their exports particularly badly. In addition, during the 1330s and subsequently Scottish wool suffered the indignity of being excluded from the manufactures of Bruges and other principal Flemish cloth towns, at a time when their industry was moving into cloths of higher quality. Nevertheless the Scots showed enterprise in establishing new markets, especially in the Netherlands.[51] Over the period as a whole, despite the differences in the general quality of their wool and the differences of their tariff history, the volume of Scottish exports remained consistently at about one-fifth the level of those from England (Figure 16.2).[52]

Tariff duties, despite their adverse effects on the wool trade, gave a measure of protection to textile manufacturers, who were able to acquire wool significantly more cheaply than their foreign competitors.[53] The decline of the wool trade from the 1350s was accordingly partly compensated by the growth of cloth exports, which had the advantage of generating more employment in the clothmaking regions. England was the principal beneficiary of this shift simply because of the high quality of her wool. We have no relevant English statistics before 1347/8, when 4,422 cloths were exported. After some lower figures immediately following the Black Death, exports rapidly recovered to an annual average of 9,961 during the five years from 1356/7 to 1360/1, and rose over ninefold to 90,745 by the years between 1527/8 and 1531/2. It does not follow, however, that the growth of cloth exports is a mirror image of the decline in wool exports. As we have seen, there were prolonged periods of recession when they both declined together. During the 1460s the number of fleeces exported in the form of raw wool and manufactured cloth together amounted to only 41 per cent of the raw wool exported in the years between 1302/3 and 1306/7, though after that the growth of cloth exports brought the ratio up to 66 per cent of the early fourteenth-century peak by the 1520s.[54] Irish and Welsh textile industries also benefited from the English tariff regime to some extent, and, as at Ruthin,[55] there were local developments equivalent to some of the more rural English centres both in the later fourteenth and again in the later fifteenth centuries. However, distance from major markets, and the poorer quality

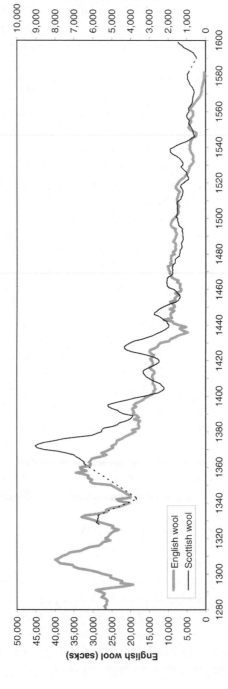

Fig. 16.2. English and Scottish wool exports, 1280–1600. This graph demonstrates that the course of wool exports from England and Scotland was very different in the 1370s but that from then on they shared a similar tendency to decline, Scottish exports being about a fifth of the English.

Source: Martin Rorke (University of Edinburgh).

of local wools, hampered the emergence of industrial concentrations comparable to those of England. Irish textiles, which also benefited from the tariffs on wool exports, sometimes reached continental markets, but they were characteristically of low unit value.[56] The cloth known as 'Welsh cloth' was a cheap fabric used for the clothing of the poor.[57]

In Scotland, too, though higher export duties on wool encouraged a shift from exports of raw wool to exports of cloth, both to the Baltic and to France and England, textiles manufacture did not benefit from tariff protection to the same extent as in England. The lower quality of Scottish wools precluded entrepreneurs from making middling and superior grades of cloth equivalent to those for which England became known abroad in the later fourteenth century and later (Figure 16.3).[58] English textiles exports in the 1520s had recovered to 2.7 times higher than the depression levels of the 1460s; Scottish cloth exports only 1.1 times higher.[59] Scottish sheep farmers were correspondingly more affected in the long run than their English counterparts by declining exports.

The switch from trade in raw materials to trade in manufactures that occurred in the English wool and woollen trades was an exceptional development. For the most part Britain and Ireland continued to be known abroad, if at all, for raw materials. Hides were exported from all parts to northern France, the Low Countries, and the Baltic. The recorded export of hides from Scotland peaked at an annual average of 56,400 during the years 1380–4, but remained throughout the fifteenth and sixteenth centuries at a lower level; the poorest decades, with exports at 16,000 a year or less, were the 1460s and the 1480s.[60] Hides were sufficiently important both in England and Scotland to attract heavier customs duties during the fourteenth century, for the same reasons that led kings to raise the duties on wool. Fish exports were characteristic of numerous coastal regions, but it is difficult to define fluctuations with any reliability from the data at our disposal. Ireland, too, exported fish, especially salmon and hake, much of it to western England rather than further afield.[61] Scottish exports of salmon, herring, and cod all seem to have increased from the 1450s onwards, though with no sustained trend.[62] Tin exports to both the Mediterranean and to Flanders were a regional interest of south-western England. Export statistics for tin are poor before 1478/9, but what is known about the level of production suggests that they increased in the early fourteenth century to *c.*1330–45, and again in the period *c.*1390–1415, but then suffered prolonged periods of recession in the fifteenth century before growing rapidly after about 1475.[63]

The variety of products imported into Britain and Ireland in return was, as ever, much wider than that of exports, though inevitably subject to fluctuations and changes in composition. On the whole our information about imports is less coherent than that for exports, but some developments, such as the decline in wine imports into English ports from Gascony, are clear enough from the customs

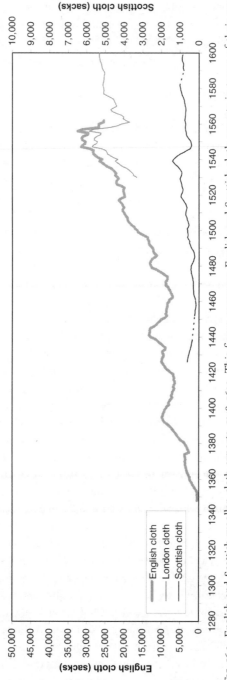

FIG. 16.3. English and Scottish woollen cloth exports, 1348–1600. This figure compares English and Scottish cloth exports in terms of their wool content. Of course, there was considerable value added in converting wool to cloth, but the comparison shown here has the advantage of demonstrating directly the implication of cloth exports for sheep farmers. Scotland's inability to export rising quantities was to the disadvantage of her wool producers from the 1370s. Cloth exports, meanwhile, made up some of the ground that English farmers lost through contracting exports of raw wool. At present it is not possible to compare the value of cloth exports through time.

Source: Martin Rorke (University of Edinburgh).

records. Even in the period 1495/6–1499/1500, imports of non-sweet wines, mostly from Gascony, still amounted to an annual average of at least 9,155 tuns, worth about £35,000–45,000. Ireland, too, imported direct from Gascony, Spain, and Portugal, though the Scots derived much of theirs indirectly from the Low Countries. Various spices from the eastern Mediterranean continued to be part of the festive diet of large households, together with dried fruit and other exotica from the Iberian peninsula. Most of these were brought to British ports by foreign merchants or acquired through entrepôts in the Low Countries; the Scots derived most of their spices, together with their wine, from the Netherlands.[64] Other goods for consumption included mercery, especially a quantity of linens from Holland, Brabant, northern France, Westphalia, Saxony, Prussia, Ireland, and elsewhere which increased over the period 1380–1480. By the late fifteenth century linen imports into England were worth some £5,000–10,000.[65] In addition the British economies relied heavily upon overseas sources for some of their basic raw materials and foodstuffs. Dyestuffs for the textile industry were a regular import, whose volume responded to the industry's various phases of growth. Iron was a basic requirement for the well-equipped farms and workshops of the fourteenth and fifteenth centuries. From about 1,000 tons a year in the late fourteenth and earlier fifteenth centuries, imports into England from the mines of Biscay and Guipúzcoa in Spain above all, but also from Sweden, and indirectly through Flanders, rose by 1500 to probably over 3,500 tons, worth about £14,000–21,000; most of the increase came after 1470. Scotland also imported iron from the same sources, which presumably explains the occasional presence of Spanish merchants in Scottish ports, though much of Scotland's requirement was re-exported from England or the Low Countries. Irish iron was also mainly from Spain.[66] England was mostly self-sufficient in foodstuffs, but imported small quantities of vegetables, beer, and grain. In addition to the supplies of fish from native fishermen there were regular imports of herring, cod, and other sea fish from the Baltic and the Low Countries. At Hull this trade was worth around £1,000 a year in the early fourteenth century, but declined severely during the following two centuries.[67] Salt for preserving meat and fish was imported into England, Scotland, and Ireland from France. Scotland was also an exporter of salt, and included English east-coast ports amongst its markets, especially Hull, though its contribution to England's total requirements was minor.[68]

The Merchants

A striking feature of change in eastern England and Scotland was the reduction of trade routes to a narrower range of alternatives, the tightening of mercantile networks to accommodate merchants on those routes, and the freezing out of those who were not able to share them. In England the narrowing of markets was more a feature of the fifteenth century than of the fourteenth. The commercial expansion of the later fourteenth century corresponded to the growth of enterprise through provincial ports to a variety of continental markets stretching from Prussia to Spain. Even Colchester, not generally reckoned as an international port, benefited from its cloth exports to the extent of expanding wharfing facilities at Hythe on the River Colne, and the city treasury derived increasing revenues from tolls and handling charges.[69] However, especially from the 1450s trade concentrated more on the route between London and the Low Countries, notably Antwerp, and was more dominated by the port of London. Eastern port towns, notably Hull and Grimsby, lost population and trade in recession years and never recovered.[70] The proportion of cloth exports going through London increased from 42 per cent in the years 1440/1–1444/5, just before the mid-century slump, to 68 per cent in the years 1528/9–1532/3. A similar process of concentration occurred in Scotland, whose merchants became increasingly dependent on trade through Bruges and Middelburg, though the destination of Scottish exports remained more varied than that of England. In the 1470s over half of Scotland's overseas trade passed through Leith, the port serving Edinburgh, and that proportion had risen to over two-thirds by the 1530s.[71] Irish trade with England, which mostly passed through Bristol and Chester, showed less propensity to channel through a single Irish town; most of Chester's contacts were with Dublin and the more northerly ports, and most of Bristol's with Waterford and the more southern ones. Dublin's trade in fact lost ground to Howth and Malahide in the north and to Cork, Waterford, and Wexford in the south.[72]

These changes were perhaps encouraged by the depth of the mid-century recession, which gave well-connected merchants groups a long-sustained chance to survive at the expense of those less well connected, though throughout the second quarter of the fifteenth century London's falling share of overseas trade had suggested no such competitive edge.[73] From the 1450s, provincial merchant networks developed in earlier phases of expansion struggled to survive the competition of London and Edinburgh. In London's case, however, there were institutional and political causes, deriving both from the increased importance of foreign trade as a source of government income and from the strategic importance of diplomatic relations with Burgundy. The focus of London privilege was a Merchant Adventurers' organization that drew support from a number of London companies but was dominated by the Mercers. Apart from the advantages of close group coordination, they received political patronage from Edward IV, who in 1462 confirmed their right to appoint their own governor in the Low Countries, and valued their cooperation in his diplomacy. In 1478 the London Merchant Adventurers were criticized by the merchants of York, who had their own formally constituted fraternity of merchants, as a dangerously powerful and privileged body, but northerners could make no headway in this dispute. In 1486 the London Merchant

Venturers received official recognition in London as a 'fellowship'.[74] Lower costs, strong credit arrangements, and exceptional privileges made the London merchant network irresistibly powerful, which helps to explain why the proportion of exports going through London rose.

Amongst all branches of English commerce, the wool trade was exceptional in the degree to which it became dominated by English merchants. Royal dependence on the export tax on wool encouraged kings to yield to the monopolistic ambitions of the English wool-exporting interest. At the opening of the fourteenth century the biggest English merchants already concerted their sales abroad to sell through a single port (the staple port) in order to reap the advantages of a quasi-monopoly. Subsequently the crown maintained a wool staple to police the wool trade. The location of the staple shifted, but from 1399 it was fixed at Calais—a compromise between various conflicting interests.[75] English merchants dominated the export of wool through the fifteenth century and into the sixteenth,[76] but as this was a declining trade their ascendancy did nothing to increase the size or the prosperity of a native merchant class. Such dominance was not achieved in other trades. In the export of cloth English merchants were competing with German and Italian interests, and the Germans in particular enjoyed the considerable trade privileges granted by English kings to their powerful organization, the Hanse.[77] Estimates for 1452–61 suggests that English merchants then accounted for 62 per cent of imports and 60 per cent of all exports. The subsequent expansion of cloth exports benefited foreign merchants almost as much as English ones; the English share of cloth exports was 46 per cent in 1452–61 and 56 per cent in 1522–31.[78] The entrepreneurial achievements of English merchants in the later fourteenth and fifteenth centuries need, therefore, to be described in guarded terms. There was little new in the trade routes they frequented and they were successfully challenged by other mercantile groups both on the more northerly trade routes to the Baltic and Scandinavia and on the southern routes to the Mediterranean. The main English trades of the east coast were simple bilateral exchanges with the Low Countries. In the Baltic the Dutch were already by 1500 showing greater acumen than the English. Of all English provincial merchants, those of Bristol and the south-west were the most adventurous; almost alone in the fifteenth century they anticipated the voyages of discovery that were to transform the context of international trade after 1500.[79]

No other group of merchants faced such competition from continental merchants as the English. Irish merchants shared the commerce of the Irish Sea chiefly with English merchants, especially those from Bristol and Chester, who remained prominent in the business of Irish and Welsh ports. Though 100 or more Irish ships were plying to Bristol, Bridgwater, and Chester in the 1480s, their number seems even to have declined relative to that of English merchants during the fourteenth and fifteenth centuries. The most adventurous of the Irish ports was Galway, in a Gaelic-speaking area of the west coast, which grew vigorously and independently after 1350 as a centre of trade with Spain and Portugal.[80] Scotland's overseas trade, meanwhile, was dominated by Scots. There were few resident alien traders, even in Edinburgh or Leith, and the proportion of foreign shipping in Scottish ports was minute. Of 300 consignments of goods exported through Dundee in 1527 fewer than 7 per cent were traded by recognizably foreign merchants.[81] Scottish trade had operated a mixed strategy. From the early fourteenth century, trade with the Low Countries operated through a staple policy that, unlike England's, was not restricted to wool. The staple shifted in accordance with current advantage, chiefly between Bruges and Middelburg, but in 1508 it was fixed by James IV at Veere, where it remained till the seventeenth century. Meanwhile Scottish merchants maintained direct contact with France and were more successful than the English in keeping a foothold in the ports of the Baltic.[82]

Internal Trade

Changes in the use of resources and trade mechanisms complicate generalizations about interregional interdependence between 1300 and 1530. It is unlikely that any such developments were as significant as those of the preceding 250 years, but there may nonetheless have been gains. It will help to start from some relevant propositions likely to command general assent. First, the market for basic foodstuffs and low-quality manufactures contracted relative to the market for goods of better quality as standards of living rose in the later fourteenth century. Secondly, the activities of London and Edinburgh merchants expanded relative to those of provincial towns during the course of the fifteenth. The first of these propositions suggests that interregional interdependence declined in some commodities while it increased in others. The second proposition implies that interregional trade became more dependent upon metropolitan networks of credit and enterprise than in the past. These suggestions help to explain why thirteenth-century patterns of inter-regional interdependence and local specialization, based on problems of food supply, were weakened during the following centuries, while new structures emerged to supply manufactures and raw materials.

The principal doubt whether any great strides were made in the economic inte-gration of England and Scotland in this period derives not from a priori reasoning about changes in demand and supply but from the demonstrable obstacles to trade created by warfare and political disruption. For many years from the commence-ment of war between the two kingdoms in 1296, trade between them was curtailed, and the borders remained a region of lawlessness and potential hazard during much of the following two centuries. Both southern Scottish and north-eastern English ports had been affected by warfare by the 1330s, in the course of which Berwick passed into English hands in 1333 following a destructive siege and permanent loss of trade, even if Linlithgow and Dundee benefited from the troubles of ports further south.[83] Later on, it is true, trading connections between England and Scotland were maintained whenever the diplomatic context made that possible. The Scots exported fish, salt, wool, hides, and coal, together with some cheap textiles, in exchange for cloth, other manufactures such as soap and glass, occasionally grain, and re-exported goods.[84] The cross-border connections between Scotland and some more northerly east-coast ports, such as Newcastle and Hull, were quite frequent, though mostly small-scale. In some years around 1500, Scottish boats from Leith, Dysart, and other small Fifeshire ports made up a fifth of all shipping in and out of Hull.[85] Prices of grain were characteristically higher in Scotland than in England, so cross-border sales were frequent.[86] In the wake of trade connections, or in search of employment, Scots migrated into England, mostly from east-coast regions, particularly from 1480; some reached as far as East Anglia and the south-eastern counties.[87] But though it is hazardous to make simple generalizations about a period as long as 230 years, especially in the absence of reliable statistics, it is difficult to identify new features of interdependence between the Scottish economy and any part of England, and it is likely, given the increased hostility between the two kingdoms, the rising costs of trade, and the decline of the east-coast ports, that no great progress was made in this direction. It is surely significant that having maintained their currency on a par with that of England for over two centuries, the kings of Scotland abandoned it from 1367, as we have seen, and so added a further impediment to the ease of exchange between the two kingdoms.[88]

The evidence for Ireland, partly recoverable from surviving customs statistics, suggests strongly that trade with England developed no new components and stagnated rather than increased during this period.[89] Already by the 1330s in eastern Ireland the blight of warfare had been a severe setback to commercial agriculture, and there is little hint of subsequent recovery.[90] Migration across the Irish Sea was slight; there were perhaps 1,000 settled adult Irishmen resident in England in 1440, together with an unknown number of itinerant workers. Bristol, Chester, and London were towns of obvious interest to Irish traders, and all had Irish communities.[91] Some of the older trading links were occasionally revived. In 1403 and 1404 surpluses from Ireland were still available to provision coastal Welsh towns and forts during Glyn Dŵr's rebellion.[92] In the later fifteenth century, shortages of grain in Dublin were blamed, tendentiously no doubt, on exports to England, Scotland, and Wales.[93] The range of Irish trade nevertheless narrowed in the fourteenth and fifteenth centuries. Fish was Ireland's major export by 1500, but wool exports were minor, and Ireland's function as a granary for western Britain and for England's wartime needs was for the most part ended. Between 1477 and 1482, imports from Ireland accounted for only about 2 per cent of England's total of about £166,000.[94]

Within England and Wales changes in market demand had a very variable effect upon trade between the major centres of demand and the regions that had come to supply them in the course of the twelfth and thirteenth centuries. The revolt of Glyn Dŵr and its aftermath, discussed in Chapter 3, was accompanied by increasing local disorder that was prejudicial to regular trade. However, the high demand for meat characteristic of London and the midlands encouraged long-distance trade in cattle, especially from the Welsh Marches and the west midlands to London and the south-east, and stimulated the development of some annual fairs where exchanges with local buyers took place.[95] Barley production became more commercialized as producers and merchants responded to the increased demand for barley malt over long distances; from Norfolk it was shipped along the coast.[96] The rising demand for import goods, a response to higher standards of living, ensured that many imported goods and good-quality manufactures travelled long distances over the roadways of Britain.[97] The best-recorded routes for imported goods are those leading out of fifteenth-century Southampton, which are documented in the city's brokerage books.[98] For more locally produced goods, especially bulky products of low unit value, the amount of traffic often declined. The grain trade, for example, must have been much reduced to judge from declining arable acreages and the declining number of active local markets. The market for agricultural equipment was similarly affected, and so probably was the market for low-grade local manufactures of textiles and leatherware. All these changes served to enhance the importance of middlemen in internal trade relative to the more direct exchange of products between producer and consumer.

NOTES

1. Above (Ch. 10).
2. J. Day, *The Medieval Market Economy* (Oxford, 1987), 1–54; P. Spufford, *Money and its Use in Medieval Europe* (Cambridge, 1988), 339–62; J. Hatcher, 'The Great Slump of the Mid-Fifteenth Century', in R. Britnell and J. Hatcher (eds.), *Progress and Problems in Medieval England: Essays in Honour of Edward Miller* (Cambridge, 1996), 237–72.
3. A. R. Bridbury, *Medieval English Clothmaking: An Economic Survey* (1982), 119; E. M. Carus-Wilson and O. Coleman, *England's Export Trade, 1275–1547* (Oxford, 1963), 54–7. The years cited here and in following sentences ended at Michaelmas: i.e. '1390' means Michaelmas 1389–Michaelmas 1390.
4. Bridbury, *Medieval English Clothmaking*, 119–20; Carus-Wilson and Coleman, *England's Export Trade*, 60–5.
5. A. Grant, *Independence and Nationhood: Scotland, 1306–1469* (1984), 237.
6. Bridbury, *Medieval English Clothmaking*, 121; Spufford, *Money and its Use*, 360.

7. R. H. Britnell, 'The Economic Context', in A. J. Pollard (ed.), *The Wars of the Roses* (Basingstoke, 1995), 57.

8. W. Childs, *Anglo-Castilian Trade in the Later Middle Ages* (Manchester, 1978), 87–95.

9. J. H. Munro, 'Industrial Transformation in the North-West European Textile Trades, c.1290–c.1340: Economic Progress or Economic Crisis', in B. M. S. Campbell (ed.), *Before the Black Death: Studies in the 'Crisis' of the Early Fourteenth Century* (Manchester, 1991), 120–30.

10. *The Libelle of Englyshe Polycye: A Poem on the Use of Sea-Power, 1436*, ed. G. Warner (Oxford, 1926), lines 1100–3, p. 55.

11. J. H. Munro, 'The "New Institutional Economics" and the Changing Fortunes of Fairs in Medieval and Early Modern Europe: The Textile Trades, Warfare, and Transaction Costs', *Vierteljahrschrift für Sozial- und Wirtschaftsgeschichte*, 88, (2001), 1–47.

12. W. Childs, 'Ireland's Trade with England in the Later Middle Ages', *Irish Economic and Social History*, 9 (1982), 7–12.

13. D. Ditchburn, 'Piracy and War at Sea in Late Medieval Scotland', in T. C. Smout (ed.), *Scotland and the Sea* (Edinburgh, 1992), 35–6, 52.

14. W. Childs, 'The *George* of Beverley and Olav Olavesson: Trading Conditions in the North Sea in 1464', *Northern History*, 31 (1995), 108–22.

15. J. Kermode, *Medieval Merchants: York, Beverley and Hull in the Later Middle Ages* (Cambridge, 1998), 215–21.

16. J. H. Munro, 'The "Industrial Crisis" of the English Textile Towns, c.1290–c.1330', in M. C. Prestwich, R. H. Britnell, and R. F. Frame (eds.), *Thirteenth Century England VII* (Woodbridge, 1999), 135–40; id., 'Industrial Transformation', 110–48.

17. D. Burwash, *English Merchant Shipping, 1460–1540* (Toronto, 1947), 52.

18. A. Hanham, *The Celys and their World: An English Merchant Family of the Fifteenth Century* (Cambridge, 1985), 362, 379–81.

19. Burwash, *English Merchant Shipping*, 82–6.

20. E. M. Carus-Wilson, 'The Overseas Trade of Bristol', in E. Power and M. M. Postan (eds.), *Studies in English Trade in the Fifteenth Century* (1933), 240.

21. M. K. James, *Studies in the Medieval Wine Trade*, ed. E. M. Veale (Oxford, 1971), 145–6, 151–3.

22. Carus-Wilson and Coleman, *England's Export Trade*, 43–4; E. W. Moore, *The Fairs of Medieval England: An Introductory Study* (Toronto, 1985), 43, 54–5, 57–8, 204–17.

23. P. Nightingale, *A Medieval Mercantile Community: The Grocers' Company and the Politics and Trade of London, 1000–1485* (New Haven, 1995), 368–9, 484; A. Everitt, 'The Marketing of Agricultural Produce', in J. Thirsk (ed.), *The Agrarian History of England and Wales*, iv: *1500–1640* (Cambridge, 1967), 535–6.

24. J. Stowe, *A Survey of London*, ed. C. L. Kingsford, corrected edn., 2 vols. (Oxford, 1971), i. 288; ii. 337.

25. Hanham, *Celys and their World*, 209–12.

26. D. Ditchburn, *Scotland and Europe: The Medieval Kingdom and its Contacts with Christendom, 1214–1560* (East Linton, 2001), 169–74.

27. Munro, 'New Institutional Economics', 29–30.

28. See below (Ch. 12).

29. P. Nightingale, 'Monetary Contraction and Mercantile Trade in Later Medieval England', *Economic History Review*, 2nd ser. 43 (1990), 560–75; ead., 'England and the European Depression of the Mid-Fifteenth Century', *Journal of European Economic History*, 26 (1997), 634–5, 638–43; P. Spufford, *Money and its Use in Medieval Europe* (Cambridge, 1988), 340–8.

30. E. T. Jones, 'River Navigation in Medieval England', *Journal of Historical Geography*, 26 (2000), 60–75; J. Langdon, 'Inland Water Transport in Medieval England—The View from the Mills: A Response to Jones', *Journal of Historical Geography*, 26 (2000), 75–82.

31. R. B. Peberdy, 'Navigation on the River Thames between London and Oxford in the Late Middle Ages: A Reconsideration', *Oxoniensia*, 61 (1996), 311–40.

32. The value of wool exported is estimated as 34,493 sacks (896,898 stones) of wool at an average price of 4s. 8d. a stone. An estimate for the late thirteenth-century exports suggests £5,000 for the value of hides and £150,000–180,000 for the value of wool: Carus-Wilson and Coleman, *England's Export Trade*, 1. Tin exports were worth perhaps £4,000–5,000: J. Hatcher, *English Tin Production and Trade before 1550* (Oxford, 1973), 90.

33. J. L. Bolton, *The Medieval English Economy, 1150–1500* (1980), 293, 307.

34. T. H. Lloyd, *The Movement of Wool Prices in England*, Economic History Review Supplement 6 (1973), 48–9.

35. Bolton, *Medieval English Economy*, 307.

36. Ditchburn, 'Piracy', 33; Grant, *Independence and Nationhood*, 79, 236–7.

37. W. Childs and T. O'Neill, 'Overseas Trade', in A. Cosgrove (ed.), *A New History of Ireland*, ii: *Medieval Ireland, 1169–1534* (Oxford, 1987), 515; A. F. O'Brien, 'The Royal Boroughs, the Seaport Towns and Royal Revenue in Ireland', *Journal of the Royal Society of Antiquaries of Ireland*, 118 (1988), 14–25.

38. J. G. Hurst, 'Medieval Pottery Imported into Ireland', in G. Mac Niocaill and P. F. Wallace (eds.), *Keimelia: Studies in Medieval Archaeology and History in Memory of Tom Delaney* (Galway, 1988), 238; A. F. O'Brien, 'Commercial Relations between Aquitaine and Ireland c.1000 to c.1550', in J.-M. Picard (ed.), *Aquitaine and Ireland in the Middle Ages* (Dublin, 1995), 56.

39. R. H. Britnell, 'The English Economy and the Government, 1450–1550', in J. L. Watts (ed.), *The End of the Middle Ages? England in the Fifteenth and Sixteenth Centuries* (Stroud, 1998), 94.

40. M. A. Lyons, 'Maritime Relations between Ireland and France, c.1480–c.1630', *Irish Economic and Social History*, 27 (2000), 3–5.

41. Carus-Wilson and Coleman, *England's Export Trade*, 40–1, 72–3.

42. Grant, *Independence and Nationhood*, 236; below, Table 20.3.

43. D. L. Farmer, 'Prices and Wages, 1350–1500', in E. Miller (ed.), *The Agrarian History of England and Wales*, iii: *1348–1500* (Cambridge, 1991), 462–3, 512; E. Gemmill and N. Mayhew, *Changing Values in Medieval Scotland: A Study of Prices, Money, and Weights and Measures* (Cambridge, 1995), 290; R. Nicholson, *Scotland: The Late Middle Ages* (Edinburgh, 1974), 286.

44. J. H. Munro, 'The Symbiosis of Towns and Textiles: Urban Institutions and the Changing Fortunes of Cloth Manufacturing in the Low Countries and England, 1270–1570', *The Journal of Early Modern History: Contacts, Comparisons, Contrasts*, 3 (1999), 25, 30, 37–8.

45. Ibid. 40–5.

46. T. H. Lloyd, *The English Wool Trade in the Middle Ages* (Cambridge, 1977), 145, 154; Carus-Wilson and Coleman, *England's Export Trade*, 194–6. For details of tax increases to 1377, see W. M. Ormrod, *The Reign of Edward III: Crown and Political Society in England, 1327–1377* (New Haven, 1990), 206.

47. Gemmill and Mayhew, *Changing Values*, 290; Nicholson, *Scotland: The Late Middle Ages*, 165.

48. I owe this information to Martin Rorke, who kindly made available to me his unpublished conclusions.

49. J. H. Munro, 'Industrial Protectionism in Medieval Flanders: Urban or National?', in H. A. Miskimin, D. Herlihy, and A. L. Udovitch (eds.), *The Medieval City* (New Haven, 1977), 254–5.

50. J. H. Munro, 'The Origins of the English "New Draperies": The Resurrection of an Old Flemish Industry, 1270–1570', in N. B. Harte (ed.), *The New Draperies in the Low Countries and England, 1300–1800* (Oxford, 1997), 47, 67.

51. Ditchburn, *Scotland and Europe*, 172–3; Munro, 'Origins', 67.

52. M. Rorke, 'Scottish and English Export Trends, 1275–1600', in *The Economic History Society, Annual Conference 7–9 April, 2000, Programme Including New Researchers' Papers and Abstracts of the Other Academic Papers* (Glasgow, 2000), 86–7.

53. Munro, 'Industrial Transformation', 134–6; id., 'Symbiosis of Towns and Textiles', 38–40.

54. Bridbury, *Medieval English Clothmaking*, 116, 118–22.

55. I. R. Jack, 'The Cloth Industry in Medieval Ruthin', *Transactions of Denbighshire Historical Society*, 12 (1963), 10–25.

56. Childs and O'Neill, 'Overseas Trade', 502.

57. Carus-Wilson, 'Overseas Trade of Bristol', 187–8.

58. Ditchburn, *Scotland and Europe*, 176–81; Grant, *Independence and Nationhood*, 80; Rorke, 'Scottish and English Export Trends', 88.

59. P. G. B. McNeill and H. L. MacQueen (eds.), *Atlas of Scottish History to 1707* (Edinburgh, 1996), 241; Bridbury, *Medieval English Clothmaking*, 116.

60. Grant, *Independence and Nationhood*, 236–7; McNeill and MacQueen (eds.), *Atlas*, 241.

61. Childs and O'Neill, 'Overseas Trade', 503–6.

62. McNeill and MacQueen (eds.), *Atlas*, 241.

63. Hatcher, *English Tin Production*, 90–6, 116–17, 126–7.

64. James, *Studies*, 59, 68–9; Childs and O'Neill, 'Overseas Trade', 507–8; Ditchburn, *Scotland and Europe*, 157.

65. H. S. Cobb, 'Textile Imports in the Fifteenth Century: The Evidence of the Customs Accounts', *Costume*, 29 (1995), 1–11.

66. Childs, *Anglo-Castilian Trade*, 112; ead., 'England's Iron Trade in the Fifteenth Century', *Economic History Review*, 2nd ser. 34 (1981), 26–33, 38, 45; Childs and O'Neill, 'Overseas Trade', 508–9; Ditchburn, *Scotland and Europe*, 188–9.

67. W. Childs, *The Trade and Shipping of Hull 1300–1500* (Beverley, 1990), 14–15.

68. A. R. Bridbury, *England and the Salt Trade in the Later Middle Ages* (Oxford, 1955), 116–19; Childs and O'Neill, 'Overseas Trade', 508; Ditchburn, *Scotland and Europe*, 184–7.

69. R. H. Britnell, *Growth and Decline in Colchester, 1300–1525* (Cambridge, 1986), 68–71, 277–8.

70. Childs, *Trade and Shipping of Hull*, 40–1; S. H. Rigby, *Medieval Grimsby: Growth and Decline* (Hull, 1993), 133–5.

71. D. Ditchburn, 'Port Towns: Scotland, 1300–1540', in D. M. Palliser (ed.), *The Cambridge Urban History of Britain*, i (Cambridge, 2000), 499–501; A. Stevenson, 'Trade with the South', 1070–1513, in M. Lynch, M. Spearman, and G. Stell (eds.), *The Scottish Medieval Town* (Edinburgh, 1988), 188; McNeill and MacQueen (eds.), *Atlas of Scottish History*, 239.

72. W. Childs, 'Irish Merchants and Seamen in Late Medieval England', *Irish Historical Studies*, 32 (2000), 23–5.

73. C. Barron, 'London, 1300–1540', in Palliser (ed.), *Cambridge Urban History of Britain*, i. 415, 418, 421, 423, 425; P. Nightingale, 'The Growth of London in the Medieval English Economy', in Britnell and Hatcher (eds.), *Progress and Problems*, 104–5.

74. E. M. Carus-Wilson, *Medieval Merchant Venturers*, 2nd edn. (1967), 143–82; *The York Mercers and Merchant Adventurers, 1356–1917*, ed. M. Sellers, Surtees Society, 129 (1918), 75–80.

75. Lloyd, *English Wool Trade*, 102, 232; E. Power, *The Wool Trade in English Medieval History* (1941), 98–9.

76. Bolton, *Medieval English Economy*, 296.

77. Carus-Wilson and Coleman, *England's Overseas Trade*, 80–2.

78. Bolton, *Medieval English Economy*, 307; Bridbury, *Medieval English Clothmaking*, 120–2; Carus-Wilson and Coleman, *England's Overseas Trade*, 80–2.

79. *The Cabot Voyages and Bristol Discovery under Henry VII*, ed. J. A. Williamson, Hakluyt Society, 2nd ser. 120 (1962 for 1961), 19–32, 116–44; W. Childs, 'The Commercial Shipping of South-Western England in the Later Fifteenth Century', *Mariner's Mirror*, 83 (1997), 272–92; M. Kowaleski, 'Port Towns: England and Wales, 1300–1540', in Palliser (ed.), *Cambridge Urban History of Britain*, i, 489.

80. M. D. O'Sullivan, *Old Galway: The History of a Norman Colony in Ireland* (Cambridge, 1942), 26–7, 38–9.

81. Ditchburn, 'Port Towns: Scotland', 503–4.

82. Ditchburn, *Scotland and Europe*, 159–6, 176, 178, 186; M. Lynch, 'Staple Ports', in id. (ed.), *The Oxford Companion to Scottish History* (Oxford, 2000), 590–1; S. G. E. Lythe, 'Economic Life', in J. M. Brown (ed.), *Scottish Society in the Fifteenth Century* (1977), 77–81; McNeill and MacQueen (eds.), *Atlas*, 261.

83. J. Donnelly, 'An Open Port: The Berwick Export Trade, 1311–1373', *Scottish Historical Review*, 78 (1999), 151–2; Stevenson, 'Trade with the South', 188, 190; Ditchburn, 'Piracy', 47.

84. Ditchburn, *Scotland and Europe*, 138–96.

85. Childs, *Trade and Shipping of Hull*, 23; J. F. Wade, 'The Overseas Trade of Newcastle upon Tyne in the Late Middle Ages', *Northern History*, 30 (1994), 37.

86. Gemmill and Mayhew, *Changing Values*, 144–5, 161–3.

87. J. A. Galloway and I. Murray, 'Scottish Migration to England, 1400–1560', *Scottish Geographical Magazine*, 112 (1996), 29–38; J. A. F. Thomson, 'Scots in England in the Fifteenth Century', *Scottish Historical Review*, 79 (2000), 1–16.

88. Gemmill and Mayhew, *Changing Values*, 19.

89. Childs, 'Ireland's Trade', 5–33.

90. C. A. Empey, 'The Manor of Carrick-on Suir in the Middle Ages', *Journal of the Butler Society*, 2 (1982), 208.

91. J. L. Bolton, 'Irish Migration to England in the Late Middle Ages: The Evidence of 1394 and 1440', *Irish Historical Studies*, 32 (2000), 1–21; Childs, 'Irish Merchants', 33–43.

92. R. A. Griffiths, 'Carmarthen', in id. (ed.), *Boroughs of Medieval Wales* (Cardiff, 1978), 155; id., *Conquerors and Conquered in Medieval Wales* (Stroud, 1994), 301.

93. G. Mac Niocaill, 'Socio-Economic Problems of the Late Medieval Irish Town', *Historical Studies*, 13 (1981), 19–20.

94. Childs, 'Ireland's Trade', 5–33.

95. M. Kowaleski, *Local Markets and Regional Trade in Medieval Exeter* (Cambridge, 1995), 293–300; A. Watkins, *Small Towns in the Forest of Arden in the Fifteenth Century* (Stratford upon Avon, 1998), 17.

96. J. A. Galloway, 'London's Grain Supply: Changes in Production, Distribution and Consumption during the Fourteenth Century', *Franco-British Studies*, 20 (1995), 23–34; id., 'Driven by Drink: Ale Consumption and the Agrarian Economy of the London Region, c.1300–1400', in M. Carlin and J. L. Rosenthal (eds.), *Food and Eating in Medieval Europe* (1998), 96–100; Britnell, *Growth and Decline*, 246–7.

97. R. H. Britnell, 'Urban Demand in the English Economy, 1300–1600', in J. A. Galloway (ed.), *Trade, Urban Hinterlands and Market Integration c.1300–1600* (2000), 9–19.

98. C. Platt, *Medieval Southampton: The Port and Trading Community, A.D. 1000–1600* (1973), 157–63.

FURTHER READING

Barron, C., 'London, 1300–1540', in D. M. Palliser (ed.), *The Cambridge Urban History of Britain*, i (Cambridge, 2000).

Blanchard, I., 'Northern Wools and Netherlands Markets at the Close of the Middle Ages', in G. G. Simpson (ed.), *Scotland and the Low Countries, 1124–1994* (East Linton, 1996).

Bolton, J. L., 'Irish Migration to England in the Late Middle Ages: The Evidence of 1394 and 1440', *Irish Historical Studies*, 32 (2000).

—— *The Medieval English Economy, 1150–1500* (1980).

Bridbury, A. R., *England and the Salt Trade in the Later Middle Ages* (Oxford, 1955).

—— *Medieval English Clothmaking: An Economic Survey* (1982).

Britnell, R. H., *The Growth and Decline of Colchester, 1300–1525* (Cambridge, 1986).

Carus-Wilson, E. M., *Medieval Merchant Venturers*, 2nd edn. (1967).

—— 'The Medieval Trade of the Ports of the Wash', *Medieval Archaeology*, 6, 7 (1962–3).

—— 'The Oversea Trade of Late Medieval Coventry', in *Economies et sociétés au Moyen Age: Mélanges offerts à Edouard Perroy* (Paris, 1973).

—— and Coleman, O., *England's Export Trade, 1275–1547* (Oxford, 1963).

Challis, C. E., *The Tudor Coinage* (Manchester, 1978).

—— (ed.), *A New History of the Royal Mint* (Cambridge, 1992).

Childs, W., *Anglo-Castilian Trade in the Later Middle Ages* (Manchester, 1978).

—— 'Anglo-Portuguese Trade in the Fifteenth Century', *Transactions of the Royal Historical Society*, 6th ser. 2 (1992).

—— 'England's Iron Trade in the Fifteenth Century', *Economic History Review*, 2nd ser. 34 (1981).

—— 'The English Trade in Cloth in the Fourteenth Century', in R. H. Britnell and J. Hatcher (eds.), *Progress and Problems in Medieval England: Essays in Honour of Edward Miller* (Cambridge, 1996).

—— 'The *George* of Beverley and Olav Olavesson: Trading Conditions in the North Sea in 1464', *Northern History*, 31 (1995).

—— 'Ireland's Trade with England in the Later Middle Ages', *Irish Economic and Social History*, 9 (1982).

—— 'Irish Merchants and Seamen in Late Medieval England', *Irish Historical Studies*, 32 (2000).

—— *The Trade and Shipping of Hull 1300–1500* (Beverley, 1990).

—— and O'Neill, T., 'Overseas Trade', in A. Cosgrove (ed.), *A New History of Ireland*, ii: *Medieval Ireland, 1169–1534* (Oxford, 1987).

Cobb, H. S., 'Textile Imports in the Fifteenth Century: The Evidence of the Customs Accounts', *Costume*, 29 (1995).

Day, J., *The Medieval Market Economy* (Oxford, 1987).

Ditchburn, D., 'Piracy and War at Sea in Late Medieval Scotland', in T. C. Smout (ed.), *Scotland and the Sea* (Edinburgh, 1992).

—— 'Port Towns: Scotland, 1300–1540', in D. M. Palliser (ed.), *The Cambridge Urban History of Britain*, i (Cambridge, 2000).

—— *Scotland and Europe: The Medieval Kingdom and its Contacts with Christendom, 1214–1560* (East Linton, 2001).

—— 'Trade with Northern Europe, 1297–1540', in M. Lynch, M. Spearman, and G. Stell (eds.), *The Scottish Medieval Town* (Edinburgh, 1988).

Fryde, E. B., *Studies in Medieval Trade and Finance* (London, 1983).

Fudge, D., *Cargoes, Embargoes, and Emissaries: The Commercial and Political Interaction of England and the German Hanse, 1450–1510* (Toronto, 1995).

Grant, A., *Independence and Nationhood: Scotland, 1306–1469* (1984).

Hanham, A., *The Celys and their World: An English Merchant Family of the Fifteenth Century* (Cambridge, 1985).

Hatcher, J., *English Tin Production and Trade before 1550* (Oxford, 1973).

James, M. K., *Studies in the Medieval Wine Trade*, ed. E. M. Veale (Oxford, 1971).

Kermode, J., *Medieval Merchants: York, Beverley and Hull in the Later Middle Ages* (Cambridge, 1998).

—— 'The Trade of Late Medieval Chester, 1500–1550', in R. Britnell and J. Hatcher (eds.), *Progress and Problems in Medieval England: Essays in Honour of Edward Miller* (Cambridge, 1996).

Kingsford, C. L., 'West Country Piracy: The School of English Seamen', in id., *Prejudice and Promise in XVth Century England* (Oxford, 1925).

Kowaleski, M., 'The Expansion of South-Western Fisheries in Late Medieval England', *Economic History Review*, 53 (2000).

—— 'Port Towns: England and Wales, 1300–1540', in D. M. Palliser (ed.), *The Cambridge Urban History of Britain*, i (Cambridge, 2000).

Lloyd, T. H., *Alien Merchants in England in the High Middle Ages* (Brighton, 1982).

—— *England and the German Hanse, 1157–1611* (Cambridge, 1991).

—— *The English Wool Trade in the Middle Ages* (Cambridge, 1977).

—— *The Movement of Wool Prices in England*, Economic History Review Supplement 6 (1973).

Lythe, S. G. E., 'Economic Life', in J. M. Brown (ed.), *Scottish Society in the Fifteenth Century* (1977).

McNeill, P. G. B., and MacQueen, H. L. (eds.), *Atlas of Scottish History to 1707* (Edinburgh, 1996).

Mayhew, N. (ed.), *Edwardian Monetary Affairs (1279–1344)* (Oxford, 1977).

—— 'Scotland: Economy and Society', in S. H. Rigby (ed.), *A Companion to Britain in the Later Middle Ages* (Oxford, 2003).

Metcalf, D. M., *Coinage in Medieval Scotland (1100–1600)* (Oxford, 1977).

Munro, J. H., 'Industrial Transformation in the North-West European Textile Trades, c.1290–c.1340: Economic Progress or Economic Crisis', in B. M. S. Campbell (ed.), *Before the Black Death: Studies in the 'Crisis' of the Early Fourteenth Century* (Manchester, 1991).

—— 'The "New Institutional Economics" and the Changing Fortunes of Fairs in Medieval and Early Modern Europe: The Textile Trades, Warfare, and Transaction Costs', *Vierteljahrschrift für Sozial- und Wirtschaftsgeschichte*, 88 (2001).

—— 'The Origins of the English "New Draperies": The Resurrection of an Old Flemish Industry, 1270–1570', in N. B. Harte, *The New Draperies in the Low Countries and England, 1300–1800* (Oxford, 1997).

—— 'The Symbiosis of Towns and Textiles: Urban Institutions and the Changing Fortunes of Cloth Manufacturing in the Low Countries and England, 1270–1570', *The Journal of Early Modern History: Contacts, Comparisons, Contrasts*, 3 (1999).

—— *Wool, Cloth and Gold: The Struggle for Bullion in Anglo-Burgundian Trade, 1340–1478* (Toronto, 1972).

Nicholas, D. M., 'The English Trade at Bruges in the Last Years of Edward III', *Journal of Medieval History*, 5 (1979).

Nightingale, P., *A Medieval Mercantile Community: The Grocers' Company and the Politics and Trade of London, 1000–1485* (New Haven, 1995).

—— 'Monetary Contraction and Mercantile Trade in Later Medieval England', *Economic History Review*, 2nd ser. 43 (1990).

O'Sullivan, M. D., *Old Galway: The History of a Norman Colony in Ireland* (Cambridge, 1942).

Power, E., and Postan, M. M. (eds.), *Studies in English Trade in the Fifteenth Century* (1933).

Ruddock, A. A., *Italian Merchants and Shipping in Southampton, 1270–1600* (Southampton, 1951).

Sherborne, *The Port of Bristol in the Middle Ages*, 3rd edn. (Bristol, 1987).

—— *William Canynges, 1402–1474* (Bristol, 1985).

Spufford, P., *Power and Profit: The Merchant in Medieval Europe* (2002).

—— *Money and its Use in Medieval Europe* (Cambridge, 1988).

Stevenson, A., 'Medieval Scottish Associations with Bruges', in T. Brotherstone and D. Ditchburn (eds.), *Freedom and Authority, Scotland c.1050–c.1650: Historical and Historiographical Essays Presented to Grant G. Simpson* (East Linton, 2000).

—— 'Trade with the South, 1070–1513', in M. Lynch, M. Spearman, and G. Stell (eds.), *The Scottish Medieval Town* (Edinburgh, 1988).

Stewart, I. H., *The Scottish Coinage*, rev. edn. (1967).

Sutton, A. F., 'The Early Linen and Worsted Industry of Norfolk and the Evolution of the London Mercers' Company', *Norfolk Archaeology*, 40 (1989).

—— 'Some Aspects of the Linen Trade c.1130s to 1500, and the Part Played by the Mercers of London', *Textile History*, 30 (1999).

—— 'William Shore, Merchant of London and Derby', *Derbyshire Archaeological Journal*, 106 (1986).

Threlfall-Holmes, M., 'Late Medieval Iron Production and Trade in the North-East', *Archaeologia Aeliana*, 5th ser. 27 (1999).

Van der Wee, H., *The Growth of the Antwerp Market*, 3 vols. (The Hague, 1963).

Van Uytven, R., 'Cloth in Medieval Literature of Western Europe', in N. B. Harte and K. G. Ponting, *Cloth and Clothing in Medieval Europe: Essays in Memory of E. M. Carus-Wilson* (1983).

Veale, E. M., *The English Fur Trade in the Later Middle Ages* (Oxford, 1966).

Wade, J. F., 'The Overseas Trade of Newcastle upon Tyne in the Late Middle Ages', *Northern History*, 30 (1994).

....

CHAPTER 17

Towns, Industry, and Local Trade

Though urban historians have long tried to establish some consensus of opinion relating to urban fortunes through the period 1300–1525, the task has proved more difficult than for the preceding 450 years. Securing agreement about the period between the ninth and the thirteenth centuries is facilitated by circumstances generally favourable to urban growth—increasing international communications, increasing population and internal trade, and expanding money supply. After 1300 such ease of generalization over time and space is no longer feasible. There was no sustained growth of internal or external trade, but neither was there any other pattern of development common to all towns. They varied markedly in the extent of their dependence on long-distance or local trade, and these differences affected their capacity for enterprise and growth. In the volatile international markets of the fourteenth and fifteenth centuries, commercial success in one generation could be undermined by competition from elsewhere during the next. All that historians have been able to agree on—and it may stand as at least a temporary conclusion to the debate—is that towns found it more difficult to increase their trade after the late thirteenth century than before, that some towns succeeded better than others at various times, and that in these circumstances urban fortunes differed greatly.

The basic urban structure of Britain had been created between the tenth century and the mid-thirteenth. After 1300 some communities were raised to borough or burgh status for the first time, formally or informally, without necessarily much alteration in the economic realities that sustained them. This was especially the case in Scotland, where there were numerous creations of 'burghs of barony', the equivalent of English seigniorial boroughs. Thirty-nine have been counted in the late fifteenth century, but since they cluster in the recession years of the 1450s and 1460s it is unlikely that their elevation represents expanding trade. Besides these 'burghs of barony', Rothesay and Falkland were made Scottish royal burghs in 1401 and 1458 respectively.[1] The Yorkshire townships of Seamer (in 1382) and

Middleham (in 1389) were provided with market charters by their lords, respectively Henry Percy and Ralph Neville, and both remained as small market towns in the sixteenth century.[2] Some new market towns emerged on favoured sites, much as in past centuries, though they were more unusual; such was Buntingford (Hertfordshire) on the main road know as Ermine Street, that acquired its market charter from Edward III in 1360, and grew at the expense of its neighbour, Standon.[3] More generally, though, except in the case of the smallest market towns, some of which lost their function,[4] the changes of the fourteenth and fifteenth centuries affected the demographic and economic ranking of towns rather than their existence. Even in Ireland, despite the vigour of Gaelic revival in the fourteenth century, most of the principal towns of the mid-thirteenth century still operated as marketing centres for inland trade in the fifteenth and sixteenth centuries, and, so far from being despised outside the colonial context, they were recontextualized by Gaelic and Anglo-Irish lords and subjected to native Irish law.[5]

Just as the total population of Britain and Ireland declined between 1300 and 1530,[6] so did the total urban population, though it may not have declined to the same extent. Had England's towns all kept to the same size as in 1300, they would have contained around half the total population of the kingdom in the later fifteenth century. Nobody has ever proposed that this was the case, so there is little scope for disagreement about 'urban decline' in this narrow demographic and aggregated sense. Declining numbers are empirically demonstrable in the history of many individual towns, and in a tendency for the smallest towns of the thirteenth century to revert to purely rural life. Some uncertainty surrounds population in the largest city of all, London, though even the most optimistic of estimates implies that it was no larger in 1525 than in 1300.[7] In a number of older English towns falling numbers between 1300 and 1500 were obvious to the eye; contemporary writers described the decline in the number of occupied houses. Scottish evidence tends to be anecdotal rather than reliably quantitative,[8] yet some towns yield accounts of urban decline similar to those in England; Inverkeithing in 1537 was 'decayed and fallen in poverty'. In Ireland the population of even the best-established boroughs, like Dublin, diminished.[9]

In their demographic history, however, as in all other respects, towns differed greatly. A comparison of 108 English urban populations between 1377 and 1524, two years in which the available data is exceptionally comprehensive, shows a very varied picture, with some towns in all regions showing major growth and others major decline (Figure 17.1). By 1377 most towns already had fewer inhabitants than in 1300 because of repeated epidemics, but 1377 is a convenient base year for comparison because of the poll tax statistics collected that year. The estimated combined net loss of their population over the period 1377–1524 was 8.1 per cent, but 58 of these towns had actually increased in size. The biggest losses came from

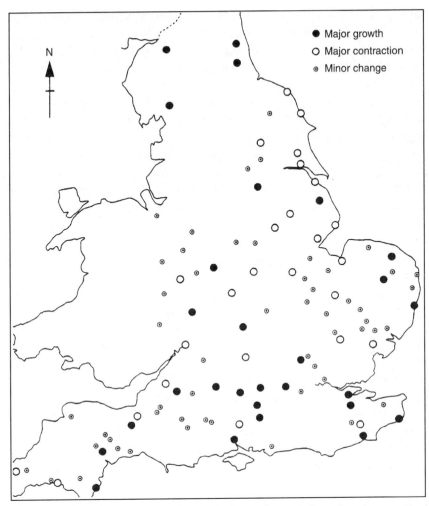

Fig. 17.1. English towns, 1377–1525: rates of population change. Debate about later medieval towns, largely conducted on English evidence, has concerned a wide range of issues, notably population, wealth, standards of living, volumes of trade, borough revenue. This map concerns only population estimates, but demonstrates the inadvisability of making a common generalization about all towns. Note, though, that this comparison between 1377 and 1525 does not take into account population losses in the major plague epidemics of 1348–9 and 1361–2, and relates to the period of greater stability thereafter.

Source: A. Dyer, ' "Urban Decline" in England, 1377–1525', in T. R. Slater (ed.), *Towns in Decline* (Aldershot, 2000), 283.

larger towns; a mere seven of the towns in question (York, Bristol, Lynn, Boston, Coventry, Winchester, and Lincoln) account for over half the total recorded losses.[10] It is noteworthy, in view of the discussion in the previous chapter, that three of these seven were major ports. A comparison between 1300 and 1524, if it were possible, would doubtless show a greater total loss of urban population.

Population is not everything in this debate, since towns deserve to be ranked according to the incomes they earned as well as the people they housed. In this respect it is more difficult to use the information at our disposal to make statistical comparisons. The only national income estimates that have been made (heroically) for England across this period relate to the years 1300, 1470, and 1526. They suggest that both in 1300 and 1470 urban incomes contributed about 18 per cent of the total, implying little change. To increase their total income in real terms townsmen would have had to increase their share of total output to over 21 per cent by 1526.[11] This is not impossible, and within the margin of error of the estimates, so in this respect the concept of urban decay is questionable, but there is currently no basis upon which to take the argument any further. There can be no doubt that average urban incomes had risen considerably during this period, a point that we shall examine further towards the end of this chapter, but we should expect urban trade and incomes, like urban populations, to vary widely. There can be little doubt that the trade and income of some towns, like Boston, contracted, just as in others, like Colchester, it increased. Different towns had different fortunes. Similar variability of fortune is in evidence in other parts of Britain and Ireland. At a time when Ireland's urban population was in decline, Galway expanded to become one of the leading Irish ports.[12]

The evidence of urban growth in some English towns across the period 1300–1530 cannot be matched with correspondingly strong evidence from Scotland or Ireland. Edinburgh seems to have grown during these years, though the chronology of such a development cannot be recovered; it is said to have had 400 houses in the 1380s, and may have had a population of 12,500 in 1560.[13] However, the growth of Edinburgh's trade probably made it more difficult for other Scottish burghs to maintain their former levels of population and activity.[14] And since the growth of export industry, notably woollen cloths, was a principal source of urban growth in England, it is unlikely that Scottish burghs, generally lacking this advantage, could have supplied many comparable examples. Urban growth in Scotland would have depended upon a growth of the home market which we have little reason to warrant. Probably the changes of the fourteenth and fifteenth century were more beneficial for England, and especially southern and eastern England, than for lands to the north and west, given the greater opportunities for commerce, investment, and accumulation south of the river Trent, and the resulting greater stimulus to urban livelihoods.[15] The growing textile industries were chiefly in this region, despite the outlying centres in Yorkshire and Westmorland. Expanding cloth manufacture, one of the chief foundations of urban prosperity, was more a distinctly English phenomenon than a more broadly based British one. Unless our observations are severely distorted, the level of urbanization was better maintained in the southern and eastern parts of Britain than in the parts furthest from the European continent, so that by 1530 the contrasts between different parts of Britain and Ireland were probably sharper than they had been in 1300.

Changing Fortunes

Even the most successful urban economies of the fourteenth and fifteenth centuries had their ups and downs. Some towns experienced difficulties before 1348. Every town, so far as we know, was affected by the Black Death of 1348–9, and by repeated epidemics after that.[16] Commercial circumstances were often volatile, as we saw in Chapter 16. Indeed, nowhere enjoyed sustained good fortune throughout the period 1300–1530. Colchester was undoubtedly one of the most fortunate towns in this period—it improved its ranking amongst English towns, in terms of taxable wealth, from fifty-third in 1334 to thirteenth in 1525—yet it is unlikely to have experienced economic growth for more than about a quarter of this period.[17] Some towns grew at the expense of others, as Edinburgh grew at the expense of smaller centres, perhaps even Aberdeen.[18] A pattern superimposed on all the varieties of urban experience is bound to fit loosely, and to be subject to revision. It is nevertheless clear from what we already know that among English towns, those whose manufactures performed well during the later fourteenth century were not the same as those performing well from the later fifteenth. Fifteenth-century recessions, and particularly the mid-fifteenth-century slump, seem to divide two different eras of urban development. It is also evident that though the running before 1400 was mostly made by well-established towns with local industrial traditions, the urban growth of the late fifteenth and early sixteenth centuries was chiefly in smaller market towns. The principal exception to this generalization is Exeter, an older town that doubled its population between 1377 and 1525, and whose trade grew vigorously during the years *c.*1425–45 and *c.*1475–1502.[19]

Two principal phases of development in England correspond to periods when overseas trade in cloth was particularly profitable, the first from about 1355 to 1402, and the second from about 1470 to 1520. In both cases the chief stimulus to increasing trade was the export of cloth. With the growth of English cloth exports the importance of mercantile organization increased, in part because merchants coordinated manufacturing production. Merchants bought wool and arranged for it to be spun and dyed, for the dyed yarn to be woven, and then for the woven cloth to be fulled and finished. These processes were often coordinated, too, by fullers and dyers, who characteristically had more capital than other artisans in the cloth industry. Many weavers were more independent than this putting-out system allowed for; they bought their own yarn, worked on their own account, and sold their work when they had finished it. For such men, too, the proximity of merchants was important because they offered a ready outlet for the cloth. A weaver weaving in one of the bigger cloth towns could be sure of the attentions of a number of merchants engaged in the buying up and exporting of standardized cloths. These aspects of industrial organization, in the late fourteenth century, favoured the growth of manufacturing in towns rather than industry scattered through the countryside. Since these surges in cloth exports were chiefly a phenomenon affecting England, it is unlikely that a similar chronology could be relevant to Scotland or Ireland. The Scottish boom in wool and hides during the 1370s and 1380s would have benefited rural producers and a few ports rather than inland towns.

The expansion of English clothmaking in the later fourteenth century, and in some cases into the early fifteenth, most conspicuously benefited older towns, some of which already had some reputation for their textiles. The industry of York began to grow from the early fourteenth century, both to serve the home market and for markets in Gascony, Prussia, and Flanders. It produced broadcloths, many of which were exported through Hull.[20] Norwich, which had suffered badly, and perhaps exceptionally badly, from the Black Death, enjoyed some recovery in the later fourteenth century, partly, at least, on the strength of its manufacture of worsted cloth, which in this period was exported chiefly through Yarmouth.[21] Coventry specialized in the manufacture of blue woollen cloths, many of which were exported through the ports of the Wash.[22] Salisbury played the leading role in the fourteenth-century development of clothmaking in Wiltshire, specializing in rayed cloth manufactured to narrower specifications than standard English broadcloth and exported through Southampton.[23] Colchester owed its export success to a middle-grade russet cloth, of a brown or grey colour, that was sold to markets as far away as the eastern Baltic, Bordeaux, and the towns of Tuscany, often through the ports of Ipswich and Colchester itself.[24] Numerous smaller towns were simultaneously developed as textile centres; at Leeds two new rents were recorded for constructing and enlarging dye vats in 1357, and between 1361 and 1374 the number of fulling mills there increased from one to two.[25] Hadleigh and Lavenham in Suffolk similarly grew as clothmaking centres. Both of these specialized in the manufacture of straits, that is, narrow cloths, which had a vigorous sale both at home and abroad. Besides some trade through Ipswich they sent manufactures to be exported through the port of London.[26] The Welsh textiles industry also expanded in this period, especially in the northern lordships of Bromfield and Yale, Chirk, Denbigh, and Dyffryn Clwyd.[27] As these comments imply, increasing exports of textiles in this period embraced a range of very different textile traditions and employed a variety of provincial as well as metropolitan mercantile networks.

This source of urban prosperity was most conspicuous in those outstandingly fortunate towns whose merchants launched them into continental markets, and was far from being universally accessible. We know less about other sources of growth, though they evidently existed. Some towns did well for unknown reasons. The farm of the borough of Brecon rose from £86 13s. 4d. in 1340, and £120 in 1370, to a peak of £180 in 1399, an increase of 108 per cent, but we do not know why.[28] Some port towns benefited from expanding exports, or hoped to benefit. Arbroath was planning to provide itself with a harbour in 1394, and Edinburgh took steps to expand the harbour at Leith in 1398.[29] The majority of towns, however, being dependent upon sales in their immediate environs, found the decades after the Black Death a difficult time, and even the ports of the south and east coast did not all benefit from the growth of cloth exports. Though they experienced some recovery between the 1350s and the 1370s, it was mild in comparison with the export-induced boom of the leading cloth towns. Irish towns seem universally to have shrunk in the later fourteenth century; some, like Carlow, suffered net emigration on top of losses from epidemics.[30] Welsh overseas trade seems not to have been growing at this time, so that external trade was a source of urban prosperity only to the extent that some towns gained at the expense of others. At Aberystwyth, where the borough rent had reached £22 in 1316–17 it fell to only £6 in 1352–3 and after some recovery it was still only £10 in 1413–14.[31] Many Welsh towns were adversely affected by the rebellion of Owain Glyn Dŵr between 1400 and 1408, just as northern English and southern Scottish boroughs were troubled by repeated Anglo-Scottish conflicts.

Even amongst the fortunate few, the growth to be derived from expanding exports was not sustained. Salisbury's cloth production was apparently at its zenith about 1400, and though it was still of considerable size in 1421 it was already in decline.[32] Colchester's industry was at its peak either around 1410–15 or, in a new cycle of growth, around 1443–4, but it dropped away after that.[33] York's prosperity fell away after 1440, landing the city in serious commercial decline by the 1460s and 1470s.[34] Coventry's expansion may have ended by the early 1440s, to judge from vacant building plots recorded in 1442, and it too was never to recover its former dynamism.[35] Opportunities for expanding the manufacture of textiles were nowhere very favourable during the depth of the recession from 1445 to 1465, but some gains were made by small centres of production where growth could be achieved by rather minor investments. The court rolls of Bisley, near Stroud (Gloucestershire) show dynamic development between 1447 and 1459, in the trough of the great slump.[36]

In the new cycle of expansion that began during the 1470s smaller centres, some barely more than villages, won out. Industrial growth was widely scattered, as before, though predominantly in southern England. The most extensive growth region was in the south-west, where Crediton, Tiverton, and Totnes revived as flourishing clothmaking townships exporting through Exeter.[37] Other major southern areas of manufacture were the Stroud Valley in Gloucestershire (centring on Stroud, Minchinhampton, and Nailsworth), western Wiltshire (centring on Westbury, Trowbridge, Malmesbury, and Bradford on Avon), the Kennet Valley (centred on Newbury), and southern Suffolk (centring on Lavenham). In the north of England the Yorkshire townships of Wakefield, Halifax, Leeds, and Bradford were taking employment away from York, and there was further expansion of textile making across the Pennines around Kendal. This phase of expansion extended, too, into some of the Welsh boroughs, as at Oswestry and Ruthin, where there were five fulling mills by 1460.[38] This transformation of the primary locus of the cloth industry used to be thought of as the growth of 'rural industry', though it has more recently been used to illustrate the growth of 'small towns'. The ambiguities of classification highlight something of the emptiness of the debate about urban fortunes, as well as the impossibility of generalizing about all towns as if they had common histories. The concept of 'rural industry' is not an empty one however; a number of developments of the late fifteenth and early sixteenth centuries, such as the development of the Weardale iron industry,[39] were essentially rural phenomena, and so make little impact on urban history except to the extent that they contributed to the profits of town-dwelling merchants.

This proliferation of provincial centres of manufacturing corresponds to a restructuring of mercantile networks, responding to London's role as the primary focus of England's overseas trade. London's rising share of trade in the home market created a critical mass of credit and business networking that made it more difficult for provincial merchants to compete. Increasingly provincial merchants were orienting their business to London, either through regular connections with the city, or by migrating there.[40] This, as we have seen, was the period when an increasing proportion of English cloth was being traded through the port of London. By 1500 London demand for barley and saffron was a significant factor in the trading patterns of the Cambridge region, where there were few local stimuli to increased production.[41] Mercantile networks in provincial England were often undermined, especially because of the inadequacy of their sources of credit,[42] though the extent to which they survived and expanded deserves more research. The south-western ports were more successful than those on the east coast in retaining a dynamism independent of London, partly because of their proximity to Gascony and Spain, and partly because of their lucrative fishing industry. Apart from London, Newcastle alone on the east coast seems to have been able to attract trade away from other ports.[43]

As we have seen, a similar concentration of trade took place in Scotland as Edinburgh became a more important focus of overseas trade than previously, particularly during the fifteenth century.[44] As in the case of London, this may have been the consequence of the superior ability of well-connected merchants to ride out recessions in the context of long-term commercial contraction. Other analogies with London's case are harder to find. Already in 1434/5 Edinburgh exported 59.2 per cent of all Scotland's cloth, and that proportion subsequently increased.[45] However, throughout the fifteenth century the cloth trade through Edinburgh was a very minor matter in comparison with the export of wool or wool fells.[46] Scotland's textile industries perhaps retained a localized character like that of the industry throughout Britain in the thirteenth century, and it is probably true that Scotland's mercantile networks in the manufacturing sector of the economy were weak.[47] Because of the subordinate role of manufactures in Scottish exports, the concentration of trade through Edinburgh was not accompanied by a restructuring of urban enterprise to the same extent as in England.

Not all entrepreneurial opportunities depended upon overseas trade, though foreign markets were the most likely to generate both vigorous booms and catastrophic slumps. The effect of declining population on urban economies was rendered complex by the associated rising standards of living through much of the century after the Black Death, which stimulated the domestic demand for higher qualities of food and clothing, and maybe to some extent of household furnishing.[48] The changing pattern of demand created opportunities for mercantile enterprise that were more successfully taken in some places than others, partly because people and money were more heavily concentrated in some regions and presented a larger market. No doubt some of the textiles of the leading cloth towns entered into the home market, replacing more locally produced fabrics of inferior quality. Buyers also purchased personal goods—buckles, ribbons, rings, beads, knives—of merchantable quality and suitable for some measure of specialization between manufacturing centres. In York and elsewhere the number of pewterers grew, even through the middle decades of the fifteenth century.[49] Cap making was an expanding trade in some towns in the later fifteenth century.[50] Pottery, too, was transformed by the shift out of coarse local wares into better qualities fetched over longer distances.[51] These initiatives, too, depended upon new merchant networks connecting the successful centres of supply to local markets, fairs, and other retail outlets.

It is difficult to identify such specialized centres of manufacture in Scotland, whose internal market was too restricted to encourage entrepreneurship along these lines. Most urban trades, though often demonstrating a high degree of competence, were supplying goods to regional markets. Fourteenth-century urban potteries served local markets, as at Elgin, Inverness, Aberdeen, Perth, Linlithgow, and doubtless elsewhere.[52] The chronicler Jean Froissart, who was used to a court environment of considerable elegance, exaggerated when he said of Scotland that 'it is almost impossible to get iron to make horseshoes, or leather for harness. Everything,' he said, 'comes ready made from Flanders, and failing that there is nothing.' Nevertheless, the first part of this comment was literally true of much of the highlands, as it was still in the mid-eighteenth century, and the weakness of mercantile networks probably hampered the development of regional specialization to supply the home market. Perhaps a larger proportion of more specialized manufactured goods required in Scotland was imported.[53]

In many towns it would be difficult to pinpoint any activity that was not largely geared to supplying local customers, and these towns were unlikely to experience much growth, even if they recovered gradually from the recession of the mid-fifteenth century. The home market grew significantly more slowly between 1470 and 1530 than it had done in the later fourteenth century.[54] The economic development of towns depending on local trade inevitably lacks the excitement of those that were more entrepreneurially driven. Such was the market town of Northallerton in Yorkshire, which, despite falling population, survived as a centre of local supply and local administration.[55] Battered survivors are in evidence all over Britain and Ireland. Since some of the towns most heavily dependent upon an immediate rural hinterland were those in the west and the north of Britain, it is not surprising that contracted towns are in evidence there. In 1487–8 Aberystwyth was still marked by vacant burgage plots whose abandonment represented a loss of £8 8s. 6d. of rent income.[56]

Regulation

The complex body of commercial regulations that had been introduced during the twelfth and thirteenth centuries continued to be enforced after 1300, augmented both throughout Britain by both government initiatives and urban by-laws, though the increasing weight of regulations was very much heavier in England than in Scotland.[57] There were now new concerns at work, resulting from the changed conditions of the times. Rising labour costs, and the greater difficulties faced by employers in retaining and disciplining workers, were a frequent source of legislation. Increased competition, both within Britain and between British and continental interests, gave further encouragement to the introduction of new controls. The changing structure of production that resulted from higher standards of living led to the regulation of activities that had not previously been sufficiently prominent to cause problems. Some cultural changes, too, affected the standards of behaviour expected of townsmen and prompted measures to enforce new criteria of public decency. The voluminous English urban regulations of these centuries offer a rich and, as yet, inadequately researched area of study. More restrictive policies were not peculiar to Britain, however, since similar problems confronted urban economies in many parts of Europe.[58]

After the Black Death the regulation of labour, in particular, became a major concern of the employing classes, which included wealthier urban artisans and wealthier peasants as well as merchants and the greater rural proprietors. In fact the shock of rising wages after 1349 affected the incomes of small producers more than those of larger ones, since the latter depended more on commercial advantage or rents, and less on the margin between commodity prices and production costs. Legislation to restrict wage increases was promulgated in England even while the plague was still raging, in the form of the Ordinance of Labourers of 18 June 1349, which pegged wages and the prices of manufactured goods at the levels of 1346; servants, labourers, or craftsmen who refused to work on these terms could be imprisoned until they consented to do so. This emergency measure was later complemented by the Statute of Labourers of 1351. Even though the principal application of this legislation was in rural occupations, it was also applied to urban activities.[59] The statute was enforced in Wales as well as in England. Dyddgu ferch Iorwerth ab Adda Ddu was fined at Beaumaris in 1351 for earning more than she should have done.[60] Not all English legislation was put into operation in Ireland, but in this case the administration acted promptly. The mayor and bailiffs of Dublin were instructed to enforce the Ordinance of Labourers as early as August 1349, and English labour legislation was made mandatory through Ireland by a Great Council in ordinances of 1351. Such legislation was later reinforced amongst the numerous provisions of the Statute of Kilkenny in 1366.[61] The government of Scotland at the time of the Black Death was weakened by the fact that the king of Scots was a prisoner in England, having been captured at the battle of Nevilles Cross in 1346. This perhaps explains why there was no Scottish Statute of Labourers in 1350. However, the Scottish merchant guilds, and the individual craft guilds that first appear in the fifteenth century, exercised some control over employment and wage rates which was momentarily recognized by the royal legislation of James I in 1426, which required the aldermen and council of each town to assess fair prices for craft goods and to set wages for workmen. The following year the Scottish royal council required prices to be vetted by a warden chosen annually for every craft in every burgh.[62] In England, too, from the later fourteenth century many secondary features of labour organization were controlled by urban regulation, often mediated by the ordinances of craft guilds.[63] The effectiveness of such measures has proved difficult to evaluate, but given the implausibility of the idea that medieval governments really had the power to block market forces, and given that it was in the interests of many employers to pay higher wages to secure the labour they wanted, it is unlikely that the law was anything more than a drag on the predictable course of events. To judge from the rural evidence, the laws affected the form in which workers were remunerated more than the level of remuneration.[64]

The multiplication of English craft guilds, though it took a very different course in different towns, was another feature of the distinctive forms of economic regulation in the fourteenth and fifteenth centuries. Though they were occasionally tempted to protect their own interests at the expense of consumers or other crafts, occupational guilds were usually tightly constrained by town councils, who vetted their rules and supervised their operations.[65] Some of the regulations of English crafts represented higher standards of consumer protection, such as the elimination of restrictive practices or the standardization of quality. A Colchester by-law of 1424–5 required tile makers to make their tiles to a standard size. Town authorities could insist on the appointment of 'searchers' who would go from workshop to workshop checking the quality of work. Some imply higher standards of public cleanliness, such as numerous ordinances relating to the activities of butchers and fishmongers. Others, especially in export industries, were designed to protect the competitiveness of manufactured goods, such as regulations relating to apprenticeship in the textile industry and the quality of woollen cloth. The appointment of searchers was a standard device in this context too. A by-law of Coventry in 1518 provided that the cloth industry of the town should be monitored by two weavers and two fullers examining the work of fellow weavers and fullers in this way, under the supervision of six drapers. In all these respects the level of formal regulation, and the machinery for enforcing rules and regulations, was higher throughout urban society in 1530 than it had been in 1300.[66]

In Scotland, by contrast, craft and trade regulations were primarily a matter for attention by the courts of merchant guilds, which also adjudicated disputes between guild members. Little attempt was made to distinguish merchants from artisans; all were predominantly independent traders. The guild was, in effect, a branch of burgh government to protect the burgh's trading rights and enforce regulations. The guild at Dunfermline, for example, punished forestallers, enforced regulations restricting the purchase and sale of wool, hides, and skins, controlled the quality of hides to be tanned, policed Sunday trading, and enforced the assize of ale. The Perth guild enforced the assize of bread, regulated weights and measures, and, again, controlled Sunday trading.[67] The reasons for the stronger survival of the single merchant guild in Scotland than in England have not been adequately explored. They must relate in part to the institutionalized monopolies that were part of the Scottish burgh system, but they probably also relate to a lesser mercantile dependence in Scotland on interregional and international trade. Even in Scotland, however, pressure on mercantile profit caused a heightened conflict of interests between merchants and craftsmen within merchant guilds.[68]

Welfare and Inequality

Loss of population, especially when accompanied by a loss of trade, carried troublesome implications for the ruling elites of some self-governing bodies, and these difficulties deserve some sympathy. Vocal complaints of 'urban decay' inevitably came from members of these elites, and they relate not to standards of living (which, as we have suggested, were generally high) but to the civic income that borough treasurers needed to meet their obligations to the crown or some other landlord. The sources of income available to urban authorities were very varied, but often they depended directly on the level of trade, either in the form of tolls, stall rents, or port dues. At Hull in 1464–5 about 44 per cent of the revenue collected by the chamberlains was from revenues directly dependent on the level of trade, including £40 from the customs revenues of the port, leased from the king, £10 10s. 0d. from river tolls, £4 13s. 4d. from tolls in the fish market, £5 17s. 4d. from various sources of income at 'the wool house', and £10 10s. from the revenues of a ferry.[69] Another source of income, varying considerably from town to town, was rents of houses, mills, land, and other property that had come into the possession of the borough as landlord, either because they were wasteland or because they had been donated to the borough treasury. Some responsibilities of local officials, such as the maintenance of roads, bridges, and chantries of deceased townsmen had been funded by donations of property both in the town streets and in the surrounding fields. These sources of income were all likely to be adversely affected by declining population and trade, even in towns whose inhabitants remained individually relatively well off, and it was consequently a problem to pay a fixed obligation to the crown—the borough farm—and to meet the rising costs of maintenance on town walls, roads, and bridges that was a responsibility of local officers. Declining trade was also likely to lead to loss of court income. The alternative way of raising money through levies on townsmen, though available to urban authorities, was inevitably more politically charged, and in practice many towns of the fifteenth century had problems with their budgets. The same problem seems not to arise in Scotland, presumably because burgh obligations to the crown were more frequently reassessed.

Declining communal incomes did not usually reflect the characteristic fortunes of individual urban households. In towns as elsewhere, despite marked inequalities of status and income, the average standard of living rose during the later fourteenth century, and through the fifteenth it was high by historical standards. Wage increases were not confined to towns enjoying industrial growth. One of the best-known indexes of rising wages in England is from the city of Oxford, which was not a particularly prosperous town after the Black Death. In the later fifteenth century building workers could buy about twice as much with their wages as they could around 1300, though that level was undermined by rising prices from the second decade of the sixteenth century.[70] Urban workmen benefited even more from the upward movement of wages after the Black Death than their rural kinsmen. Many categories of self-employed artisan and tradesmen, too, were able to raise their prices to secure a higher reward for their labour. As new commercial opportunities opened up, less remunerative and demeaning categories of self-employment were abandoned. In Colchester, for example, the fining of 'common forestallers' was abandoned from 1412.[71]

These common forestallers had often been women, and their diminishing importance was perhaps one of the signs of better opportunities for female employment. There was no expansion of administrative, legal, or clerical roles, and the elaboration of craft institutions, with the associated multiplication of supervisory offices, meant more authority for men rather than women. Nevertheless, the scarcity of labour that followed depopulation, especially after 1349, brought new opportunities for women, both in the form of higher wages and easier access to employment. Not all these opportunities were particularly lucrative. One was household service, which was more a female activity in towns than in the countryside, as we can tell from the English poll tax returns of 1377. The openings here were numerous; the proportion of urban households keeping servants ranged from about 15 per cent at Hull to 30–40 per cent in Dartmouth, Northampton, and York.[72] The growth of urban textile industries also increased relatively low-paid employment in preparing yarn by combing, carding, and spinning, which were almost always female activities, usually depending on entrepreneurs who would supply wool and pay a fixed rate of pay. But there were opportunities for more independence of action in weaving, and this was probably an activity more accessible to women after 1349. In the York ulnage accounts of 1394–5, recording the tax levied on sales of cloth, 180 out of 460 names are those of women. Knitting caps, a craft of growing commercial importance in fifteenth-century towns, was also associated with women. In other industries, women quite commonly occur as employed servants, but in some instances they were free to act as craftswomen in their own right, especially if carrying on a business after the death of a husband. A York dyers' ordinance of the 1380s includes four women among the fifty-nine dyers listed, one of whom was Stephen Littster's wife, Alice.[73] Urban prosperity seems to have favoured prostitution as a possible female career, especially in Southwark, but the fact that many of the prostitutes were immigrants from Flanders implies that the new opportunities were not enough to make it attractive even to the poor.[74] In some towns, improvements in standards of living created expanding opportunities in the ale trade, and allowed women more scope in opening up part of their home for customers to drink in. Both in England and Scotland ale brewing remained a predominantly female activity, but it must have required considerable cooperation from husbands when it involved taking over the home as a public house. This development also implies an increase in specialization, which became pronounced during the fifteenth century.[75] Women also sometimes engaged in mercantile trade, either in association with a husband or after a husband's death. An Edinburgh couple, Margaret and Robert Hogg, were granted a joint safe-conduct for trading purposes in 1362, and in 1365 Margaret was described as a Scottish merchant.[76]

The inequalities of income in urban societies were everywhere apparent from contrasts of housing and dress. For many groups, though, higher standards of living during the fourteenth and fifteenth centuries encouraged changes in lifestyle towards more food and drink (especially meat and ale), better clothing of both cloth and leather, a wider range of leisure activities, and better accommodation.[77] In many towns—even in central London between 1350 and 1500—low land values encouraged the amalgamation of properties along urban streets; this permitted the construction of larger houses and inns, the creation of improved gardens, or the establishment of orchards.[78] Improvements were most marked in towns that were able to expand their trade and employment and whose merchant class increased in numbers. Fifteenth-century towns, even when they had shrunk in population, were likely to be pleasanter places to live in than their thirteenth-century predecessors, with less unemployment, less destitution, and less squalor.

Our knowledge of standards of living in towns in southern and midland England is significantly better than that for other parts of Britain and Ireland. Differences in the volume of record survival are accentuated to such an extent that the voluminous writing about English towns in this period has little parallel in Wales, Scotland, and Ireland. It would be surprising if the English trend towards higher standards of living was equally pronounced everywhere. In this context, evidence of the changing distribution of English taxable wealth is particularly suggestive, since it is more likely to relate to different increases in per capita wealth, and so indirectly in per capita incomes, than to any redistribution of population. Between 1334 and 1524 tax assessments increased much more in southern and eastern England—especially south of a line draw between Bristol and Great Yarmouth— than in the north and the west. Increases were particularly low in Yorkshire, the Welsh Marches, and the northern midlands. This suggests, as we might expect, that improvements in living standards were highest in regions well placed to benefit from commercial opportunities.[79]

NOTES

1. A. Grant, *Independence and Nationhood: Scotland, 1306–1469* (1984), 86; G. S. Pryde, *The Burghs of Scotland: A Critical List* (1965), 23, 25.
2. *Calendar of Charter Rolls*, Public Record Office, 6 vols. (1903–27), v: *1341–1417*, 280, 310.

3. M. Bailey, 'A Tale of Two Towns: Buntingford and Standon in the Later Middle Ages', *Journal of Medieval History*, 19 (1993), 351–71.

4. R. H. Britnell, *The Commercialisation of English Society, 1000–1500*, 2nd edn. (Manchester, 1996), 157–60; M. Mate, 'The Rise and Fall of Markets in Southeast England', *Canadian Journal of History*, 31 (1996), 67–74.

5. H. B. Clarke, 'Decolonization and the Dynamics of Urban Decline in Ireland', in T. R. Slater (ed.), *Towns in Decline AD 100–1600* (Aldershot, 2000), 174–5.

6. See above (Ch. 4).

7. An optimistic estimate would be over 60,000 in 1525: J. C. K. Cornwall, *Wealth and Society in Early Sixteenth Century England* (1988), 64. For equivalent optimistic estimates of the city's population *c.*1300, see above (Ch. 7).

8. N. J. Mayhew, 'Scotland: Economy and Society', in S. H. Rigby (ed.), *A Companion to Britain in the Later Middle Ages* (Oxford, 2003), 119.

9. D. Ditchburn and A. Macdonald, 'Medieval Scotland, 1100–1560', in R. A. Houston and W. W. J. Knox (eds.), *The New Penguin History of Scotland from the Earliest Times to the Present Day* (2002), 115; G. Mac Niocaill, 'Socio-Economic Problems of the Late Medieval Irish Town'. *Historical Studies*, 13 (1981), 18–19.

10. A. Dyer, ' "Urban Decline" in England, 1377–1525', in T. R. Slater (ed.), *Towns in Decline AD 100–1600* (Aldershot, 2000), 272–86.

11. N. J. Mayhew, 'Population, Money Supply and the Velocity of Circulation in England, 1300–1700, *Economic History Review*, 48 (1995), 244, 249. I have taken the urban share in 1300 from id., "Modelling Medieval Monetisation", in R. H. Britnell and B. M. Campbell (eds.), *A Commercialising Economy: England 1086 to c.1300* (Manchester, 1995), 58.

12. M. D. O'Sullivan, *Old Galway: The History of a Norman Colony in Ireland* (Cambridge, 1942), 27, 39.

13. E. Ewan, *Townlife in Fourteenth-Century Scotland* (Edinburgh, 1990), 5; M. Lynch, 'The Social and Economic Structure of the Larger Towns, 1450–1600', in M. Lynch, M. Spearman, and G. Stell (eds.), *The Scottish Medieval Town* (Edinburgh, 1988), 279.

14. E. P. Dennison and G. G. Simpson, 'Scotland', in D. M. Palliser (ed.), *The Cambridge Urban History of Britain*, i (Cambridge, 2000), 729–30; Grant, *Independence and Nationhood*, 85; Mayhew, 'Scotland: Economy and Society', 119.

15. B. M. S. Campbell, 'People and Land in the Middle Ages, 1066–1500', in R. A. Dodgshon and R. A. Butlin (eds.), *An Historical Geography of England and* Wales, 2nd edn. (1990), 72.

16. R. H. Britnell, 'The Black Death in English Towns', *Urban History*, 21 (1994), 195–210.

17. R. H. Britnell, *Growth and Decline in Colchester, 1300–1525* (Cambridge, 1986), 266; A. Dyer, 'Appendix: Ranking of English Medieval Towns', in Palliser (ed.), *Cambridge Urban History*, i. 756, 765.

18. Mayhew, 'Scotland: Economy and Society', 119.

19. Dyer, ' "Urban Decline" in England', 278; M. Kowaleski, *Local Markets and Regional Trade in Medieval Exeter* (Cambridge, 1995), 92; E. M. Carus-Wilson and O. Coleman, *England's Export Trade, 1275–1547* (Oxford, 1963), 144–5.

20. J. N. Bartlett, 'The Expansion and Decline of York in the Later Middle Ages', *Economic History Review*, 2nd ser. 12 (1959–60), 17, 22–6.

21. J. Campbell, 'Norwich', in M. D. Lobel (ed.), *The Atlas of Historic Towns*, ii (London, 1975), 16.
22. E. M. Carus-Wilson, 'The Oversea Trade of Late Medieval Coventry', in *Economies et sociétés au Moyen Age: mélanges offerts à Edouard Perroy* (Paris, 1973), 372.
23. J. L. Bolton, *The Medieval English Economy, 1150–1500* (1980), 251; A. R. Bridbury, *Medieval English Clothmaking: An Economic Survey* (1982), 66–71.
24. Britnell, *Growth and Decline*, 54–68.
25. *Documents Relating to the Manor and Borough of Leeds, 1066–1400*, ed. J. Le Patourel, Thoresby Society, 45 (1957), 45, 49, 52.
26. R. H. Britnell, 'The Woollen Textile Industry of Suffolk in the Later Middle Ages', in L. Visser-Fuchs (ed.), *Tant d'Emprises—So Many Undertakings: Essays in Honour of Anne Sutton, The Ricardian*, 23 (2003), 88–95.
27. R. I. Jack, 'The Cloth Industry in Medieval Ruthin', *Transactions of Denbighshire Historical Society*, 12 (1963), 10–25; id., 'The Cloth Industry in Medieval Wales', *Welsh History Review*, 10 (1980–1), 449, 459.
28. R. R. Davies, 'Brecon', in R. A. Griffiths (ed.), *Boroughs of Medieval Wales* (Cardiff, 1978), 64.
29. Ewan, *Townlife*, 6.
30. M. Kelly, *A History of the Black Death in Ireland* (Stroud, 2001), 99–100.
31. R. A. Griffiths 'Aberystwyth', in id. (ed.), *Boroughs of Medieval Wales* (Cardiff, 1978), 43.
32. Bolton, *Medieval English Economy*, 251; Bridbury, *Medieval English Clothmaking*, 67, 69.
33. Britnell, *Growth and Decline*, 181.
34. A. J. Pollard, *North-Eastern England during the Wars of the Roses: Lay Society, War, and Politics, 1450–1500* (Oxford, 1990), 71–4.
35. C. Dyer and T. R. Slater, 'The Midlands', in Palliser (ed.), *Cambridge Urban History*, i. 635.
36. E. M. Carus-Wilson, 'Evidences of Industrial Growth on some Fifteenth-Century Manors', in ead. (ed.), *Essays in Economic History*, 3 vols. (1954–62) ii. 155–6.
37. Kowaleski, *Local Markets*, 19–27.
38. R. H. Britnell, 'The Economy of British Towns, 1300–1540', in Palliser (ed.), *Cambridge Urban History*, i. 319; R. I. Jack, 'Ruthin', in Griffiths (ed.), *Boroughs of Medieval Wales*, 255.
39. M. Threlfall-Holmes, 'Late Medieval Iron Production and Trade in the North-East', *Archaeologia Aeliana*, 5th ser. 27 (1999), 109–22.
40. R. H. Britnell, 'The English Economy and the Government, 1450–1550', in J. L. Watts (ed.), *The End of the Middle Ages? England in the Fifteenth and Sixteenth Centuries* (Stroud, 1998), 95–7.
41. J. Lee, 'The Trade of Fifteenth-Century Cambridge and its Region', in M. Hicks (ed.), *Revolution and Consumption in Late Medieval England* (Woodbridge, 2001), 136–9.
42. J. Kermode, 'Money and Credit in the Fifteenth Century: Some Lessons from Yorkshire', *Business History Review*, 65 (1991), 475–501.
43. M. Kowaleski, 'Port Towns: England and Wales, 1300–1540', in Palliser (ed.), *Cambridge Urban History*, i. 486–7; M. Threlfall-Holmes, 'Durham Cathedral Priory's Consumption of Imported Goods: Wine and Spices, 1464–1520', in Hicks (ed.), *Revolution and Consumption*, 156–8.

44. See above (Ch. 16).

45. A. Stevenson, 'Trade with the South, 1070–1513', in M. Lynch, M. Spearman, and G. Stell (eds.), *The Scottish Medieval Town* (Edinburgh, 1988), 195.

46. P. G. B. McNeill and H. L. MacQueen (eds.), *Atlas of Scottish History to 1707* (Edinburgh, 1996), 246.

47. S. G. E. Lythe, 'Economic Life', in J. M. Brown (ed.), *Scottish Society in the Fifteenth Century* (1977), 74.

48. See below (Ch. 18).

49. H. Swanson, *Medieval Artisans: An Urban Class in Late Medieval England* (Oxford, 1989), 77; D. Keene, *Survey of Medieval Winchester*, 2 vols. (Oxford, 1985), i. 282.

50. Britnell, 'English Economy and the Government', 99.

51. G. G. Astill, 'Economic Change in Later Medieval England: An Archaeological Review', in T. H. Aston, P. R. Coss, C. Dyer, and J. Thirsk (eds.), *Social Relations and Ideas: Essays in Honour of R. H. Hilton* (Cambridge, 1983), 225–9.

52. Ewan, *Townlife*, 33–7; Lythe, 'Economic Life', 76.

53. D. Ditchburn, *Scotland and Europe: The Medieval Kingdom and its Contacts with Christendom, 1214–1560* (East Linton, 2001), 189–92; Lythe, 'Economic Life', 73–4.

54. Britnell, 'English Economy and Government', 97–100.

55. C. M. Newman, *Late Medieval Northallerton: A Small Market Town and its Hinterland, c.1470–1540* (Stamford, 1999), 15–16, 94–115, 150.

56. Griffiths 'Aberystwyth', 43.

57. Britnell, *Commercialisation*, 171–8; E. Gemmill and N. Mayhew, *Changing Values in Medieval Scotland: A Study of Prices, Money, and Weights and Measures* (Cambridge, 1995), 25–80; P. Symms, 'Market Regulation in the Early 16th-Century Burgh', *Proceedings of the Society of Antiquaries of Scotland*, 118 (1988), 277–87.

58. A. B. Hibbert, 'The Economic Policies of Towns', in M. M. Postan, E. E. Rich, and E. Miller (eds.), *The Cambridge Economic History of Europe*, iii: *Economic Organization and Policies in the Middle Ages* (Cambridge, 1963), 206–29.

59. *The Black Death*, ed. and trans. R. Horrox (Manchester, 1994), 297–9, 312–16.

60. A. D. Carr, *Medieval Anglesey* (Langeffni, 1982), 308.

61. Kelly, *History of the Black Death in Ireland*, 99; J. A. Watt, 'The Anglo-Irish Colony under Strain', in A. Cosgrove (ed.), *A New History of Ireland*, ii: *Medieval Ireland, 1169–1534* (Oxford, 1987), 382.

62. *The Ancient Laws and Customs of the Burghs of Scotland*, ed. C. Innes and R. Renwick, 2 vols. (Edinburgh, 1868, 1910), ii. 10, 13–14; R. Nicholson, *Scotland: The Later Middle Ages* (Edinburgh, 1974), 308.

63. Swanson, *Medieval Artisans*, 113–16.

64. J. Hatcher, 'England in the Aftermath of the Black Death', *Past and Present*, 144 (1994), 19–25.

65. Swanson, *Medieval Artisans*, 107–20.

66. Britnell, *Commercialisation*, 171–8; id., *Growth and Decline*, 240–5; Swanson, *Medieval Artisans*, 14–20, 111–13, 116–17.

67. *The Guild Book of Dunfermline, 1433–1597*, ed. E. P. D. Torrie (Edinburgh, 1986), 7, 9,

18–19, 26, 28, 35; *The Perth Guildry Book, 1452–1601*, ed. M. L. Stavert (Edinburgh, 1993), 4, 9, 34; Ewan, *Townlife*, 58–63.

68. Lythe, 'Economic Life', 71.

69. *Selected Rentals and Accounts of Medieval Hull, 1293–1528*, ed. R. Horrox, Yorkshire Archaeological Society Record Series, 141 (1983), 91–4.

70. H. P. Brown and S. V. Hopkins, *A Perspective of Wages and Prices* (1981), 19, 28–9.

71. Britnell, *Growth and Decline*, 132.

72. P. J. P. Goldberg, *Women, Work and Life Cycle in a Medieval Economy: Women in York and Yorkshire, c.1300–1520* (Oxford, 1992), 158–61.

73. M. Carlin, *Medieval Southwark* (1996), 175; Kowaleski, *Local Markets*, 153–4; Swanson, *Medieval Artisans*, 30–1, 35, 42–3, 51, 58, 80, 103.

74. Carlin, *Medieval Southwark*, 209–29.

75. Britnell, *Growth and Decline*, 88–91; J. M. Bennett, *Ale, Beer and Brewsters in England* (Oxford, 1996), 20–1, 45–9; Ewan, *Townlife*, 32; Kowaleski, *Local Markets*, 131–6; M. Mate, *Daughters, Wives and Widows after the Black Death: Women in Sussex, 1350–1535* (Woodbridge, 1998), 62–4.

76. Ewan, *Townlife*, 81.

77. C. Dyer, *Standards of Living in the Later Middle Ages: Social Change in England, c.1200–1520* (Cambridge, 1989), 195–6, 199–205.

78. D. Keene, *Cheapside before the Great Fire* (Swindon, 1985), 19–20; id., *Survey of Medieval Winchester*, i. 143–55.

79. B. M. S. Campbell, 'People and Land in the Middle Ages', in R. A. Dodgshon and R. A. Butlin (eds.), *An Historical Geography of England and Wales*, 2nd edn. (1990), 72; R. S. Scofield, 'The Geographical Distribution of Wealth in England, 1334–1649', *Economic History Review*, 2nd ser. 18 (1965), 503–9.

FURTHER READING

Astill, G. G., 'Economic Change in Later Medieval England: An Archaeological Review', in T. H. Aston, P. R. Coss, C. Dyer, and J. Thirsk (eds.), *Social Relations and Ideas: Essays in Honour of R. H. Hilton* (Cambridge, 1983).

Barron, C., 'Centres of Conspicuous Consumption: The Aristocratic Town-House in London, 1200–1550', *London Journal*, 20 (1995).

Bartlett, J. N., 'The Expansion and Decline of York in the Later Middle Ages', *Economic History Review*, 2nd ser. 12 (1959–60).

Bennett, J. M., *Ale, Beer and Brewsters in England* (Oxford, 1996).

Bolton, J. L., *The Medieval English Economy, 1150–1500* (1980).

Bridbury, A. R., *Medieval English Clothmaking: An Economic Survey* (1982).

Britnell, R. H., *The Commercialisation of English Society, 1000–1500*, 2nd edn. (Manchester, 1997).

—— 'The Black Death in English Towns', *Urban History*, 21 (1994).

—— 'England: Towns, Trade and Industry', in S. H. Rigby (ed.), *A Companion to Britain in the Later Middle Ages* (Oxford, 2003).

Britnell, R. H., *Growth and Decline in Colchester, 1300–1525* (Cambridge, 1986).

—— 'Urban Demand in the English Economy, 1300–1600', in J. A. Galloway (ed.), *Trade, Urban Hinterlands and Market Integration c.1300–1600* (2000).

—— (ed.), *Daily Life in the Late Middle Ages* (Stroud, 1998).

Carlin, M., *Medieval Southwark* (1996).

Carus-Wilson, E. M., *The Expansion of Exeter at the Close of the Middle Ages* (Exeter, 1963).

—— *Medieval Merchant Venturers*, 2nd edn. (1967).

Clarke, H. B., 'Decolonization and the Dynamics of Urban Decline in Ireland', in T. R. Slater (ed.), *Towns in Decline AD 100–1600* (Aldershot, 2000).

Cobb, H. S., 'Textile Imports of the Fifteenth Century: The Evidence of the Customs Accounts', *Costume*, 29 (1995).

Ditchburn, D., and Macdonald, A. J., 'Medieval Scotland, 1100–1560', in R. A. Houston and W. W. J. Knox (eds.), *The New Penguin History of Scotland from the Earliest Times to the Present Day* (2002).

Dobson, R. B., 'Urban Decline in Late Medieval England', *Transactions of the Royal Historical Society*, 5th ser., 26 (1973).

Dyer, A., *Decline and Growth in English Towns, 1400–1640* (1991).

—— ' "Urban Decline" in England, 1377–1525', in T. R. Slater (ed.), *Towns in Decline AD 100–1600* (Aldershot, 2000).

Dyer, C., 'The Hidden Trade of the Middle Ages: Evidence from the West Midlands of England', in *Journal of Historical Geography*, 18 (1992).

Ewan, E., *Townlife in Fourteenth-Century Scotland* (Edinburgh, 1990).

Galloway, J. A., 'Driven by Drink: Ale Consumption and the Agrarian Economy of the London Region, c.1300–1400', in M. Carlin and J. L. Rosenthal (eds.), *Food and Eating in Medieval Europe* (1998).

—— 'London's Grain Supply: Changes in Production, Distribution and Consumption during the Fourteenth Century', *Franco-British Studies*, 20 (1995).

—— 'Town and Country in England, 1300–1570', in S. R. Epstein (ed.), *Town and Country in Europe, 1300–1800* (Cambridge, 2001).

Gemmill, E., and Mayhew, N., *Changing Values in Medieval Scotland: A Study of Prices, Money, and Weights and Measures* (Cambridge, 1995).

Goldberg, P. J. P., *Women, Work and Life Cycle in a Medieval Economy: Women in York and Yorkshire, c.1300–1520* (Oxford, 1992).

Griffiths, R. A. (ed.), *Boroughs of Medieval Wales* (Cardiff, 1978).

Jack, R. I., 'The Cloth Industry in Medieval Ruthin', *Transactions of Denbighshire Historical Society*, 12 (1963).

—— 'The Cloth Industry in Medieval Wales', *Welsh History Review*, 10 (1980–1).

Keene, D., *Survey of Medieval Winchester*, 2 vols. (Oxford, 1985).

Kermode, J., *Medieval Merchants: York, Beverley and Hull in the Later Middle Ages* (Cambridge, 1998).

Kowaleski, M., *Local Markets and Regional Trade in Medieval Exeter* (Cambridge, 1995).

Laughton, J., and Dyer, C., 'Small Towns in the East and West Midlands in the Later Middle Ages: A Comparison', *Midland History*, 24 (1999).

Lee, J., 'Feeding the Colleges: Cambridge's Food and Fuel Supplies, 1450–1560', *Economic History Review*, 56 (2003).

—— 'The Trade of Fifteenth-Century Cambridge and its Region', in M. Hicks (ed.), *Revolution and Consumption in Late Medieval England* (Woodbridge, 2001).

Lynch, M., Spearman, M., and Stell, G. (eds.), *The Scottish Medieval Town* (Edinburgh, 1988).

Lythe, S. G. E., 'Economic Life', in J. M. Brown (ed.), *Scottish Society in the Fifteenth Century* (1977).

Mac Niocaill, G., 'Socio-Economic Problems of the Late Medieval Irish Town', *Historical Studies*, 13 (1981).

Mate, M. E., *Daughters, Wives and Widows after the Black Death: Women in Sussex, 1350–1535* (Woodbridge, 1998).

—— 'The Rise and Fall of Markets in Southeast England', *Canadian Journal of History*, 31 (1996).

Mayhew, N. J., 'Scotland: Economy and Society', in S. H. Rigby (ed.), *A Companion to Britain in the Later Middle Ages* (Oxford, 2003).

Murphy, M., 'The Fuel Supply of Medieval London', *Franco-British Studies*, 20 (1995).

Newman, C. M., *Late Medieval Northallerton: A Small Market Town and its Hinterland, c.1470–1540* (Stamford, 1999).

Palliser, D. M. (ed.), *The Cambridge Urban History of Britain*, i (Cambridge, 2000).

Phythian-Adams, C., *Desolation of a City: Coventry and the Urban Crisis of the Late Middle Ages* (Cambridge, 1979).

—— 'Urban Decay in Late Medieval England', in P. Abrams and E. A. Wrigley (eds.), *Towns in Societies: Essays in Economic History and Historical Sociology* (Cambridge, 1978).

Platt, C., *Medieval Southampton: The Port and Trading Community, A.D. 1000–1600* (1973).

Postles, D., 'An English Small Town in the Later Middle Ages: Loughborough', *Urban History*, 20 (1993).

Pratt, D., 'The Medieval Borough of Chirk', *Transactions of Denbighshire Historical Society*, 46 (1997).

Rigby, S. H., *English Society in the Later Middle Ages* (1995).

—— 'Lay Medieval Urban Prosperity: The Evidence of Lay Subsidies', *Economic History Review*, 2nd ser. 39 (1986).

—— *Medieval Grimsby: Growth and Decline* (Hull, 1993).

Rosser, G., *Medieval Westminster, 1200–1540* (Oxford, 1989).

Swanson, H., 'Craft Guilds in Late Medieval English Towns', *Past and Present*, 121 (1988).

—— *Medieval Artisans: An Urban Class in Late Medieval England* (Oxford, 1989).

—— *Medieval British Towns* (Basingstoke, 1999).

Symms, P., 'Market Regulation in the Early 16th-Century Burgh', *Proceedings of the Society of Antiquaries of Scotland*, 118 (1988).

Thrupp, S. L., *The Merchant Class of Medieval London* (Chicago, 1948).

Woodward, D., *Men at Work: Labourers and Building Craftsmen in the Towns of Northern England 1450–1750* (Cambridge, 1995).

....

CHAPTER 18

Rural Settlement and Society

Since, as we saw in Chapter 4, the population of Britain declined between 1300 and 1530, we should expect abundant tangible evidence from rural sources. If total numbers in England fell from 4.5–6 m. in 1300 to around 2 m. in 1524, and if at least four-fifths of the population lived in rural settlements of various kinds, then rural population fell by at least 2.0–3.2 m. in the course of the period, and the decline was probably even greater between 1348 and the nadir of fifteenth-century contraction around 1450. If, too, many of the problems of the thirteenth-century countryside in southern England had resulted from shortages of land, we should expect those problems to be alleviated as the relationship between population and the land altered to increase per capita resources. Since Wales, Scotland, and Ireland experienced similar demographic contraction we should expect parallel evidence in their documentary and archaeological evidence. We should nevertheless expect the effects of rising resources per capita to be less marked in regions that had suffered less from land hunger before 1348 and that benefited less from manufacturing development and urban demand thereafter.

The Contraction of Settlement

The association between declining population and deserted villages is one of the best-known features of the period 1300–1530, though by definition it relates more to areas of nucleated settlement than to those of dispersed settlement. This was a principal theme of government rhetoric relating to the commonwealth during the reign of Henry VIII, given literary expression in Thomas More's *Utopia*, where the fictitious Ralph Hythloday observes how sheep farming depopulated fields, houses, and towns.[1] The discovery and excavation of deserted villages has also been a principal concern of the archaeology of the period; excavation is much more rewarding in villages deserted at an early date than in those that have been continuously occupied and reconstructed until the present day. So far from being rare, as was supposed before the mid-twentieth century, there are now estimated to be around 3,000 deserted sites in England alone, though not all of these had been deserted by 1530.[2] English deserted villages are well charted. Many of them have identifiable surface features, and are marked on Ordnance Survey maps. They can be picked out in aerial photographs by the banks that mark their house plots and roadways, as at Burston in Buckinghamshire, which was depopulated and converted to pasture in 1488. Even without excavation some characteristics of their size and layout can be known.[3]

Excavations at Wharram Percy, in the Yorkshire Wolds, have exposed a deserted settlement whose site was clearly visible from aerial photographs, and whose ruined church still stands above ground level. Though there was earlier scattered occupation of the site, the village was established as a planned nucleated settlement, probably some time between the tenth and the twelfth centuries. It had about thirty households in the late fourteenth century, and sixteen in 1458, but had disappeared by the early sixteenth century.[4] Other major excavations have been those at Goltho in Lincolnshire, and Upton in Gloucestershire.[5] The village of Whatborough in Leicestershire is a famous case of desertion because a plan of 1586 marks 'The place where the towne of whate boroughe stoode'. Fifteen households (of one sokeman, three villeins, and eleven bordars) had been recorded there in Domesday Book, implying perhaps 70 inhabitants in 1086. There were still a dozen taxpayers there at the time of the Poll Tax of 1377, implying perhaps 20 inhabitants, but the village had disappeared by 1525. In 1586 the site was occupied by a single house in which a shepherd lived.[6] There are hundreds of less well-documented sites in Britain, very few of them excavated, and they constitute a subject of perennial interest for archaeologists and historians alike.

Similar remains characterize sites in Wales, Scotland, and Ireland, though the preponderance of scattered settlement means that deserted villages are a less significant part of archaeological research in these countries. Twenty-six villages and hamlets known to have existed in 1307 in the commote of Laugharne in Carmarthenshire have reduced to four survivors, the remainder being represented on the modern map only by individual farmhouses. It is surmised that their population was reduced by epidemic disease in 1349 and subsequently by warfare, the confiscation of rebels' properties at the time of Owain Glyn Dŵr's revolt, and by flight from the burdens of bond tenure.[7] Other villages likely to have disappeared through depopulation and the concentration of ownership in a single estate were Penrhyn (Caernarvonshire) and Clemenston (Glamorgan).[8] Rural Irish settlements were vulnerable because of their small size, and some in exposed districts were subject to raiding by Gaelic chieftains. There are also some known sites of deserted Irish rural boroughs, like Kilmaclenine (Co. Cork), or Glenogra (Co. Limerick). The desertion of Irish settlements has been linked to a certain amount of migration from Ireland to England during the fourteenth and early fifteenth centuries. However, even when lost settlements in Ireland are known to have existed, their location and identification pose exceptional difficulties. The normal pattern in the Gaelic areas was one of isolated households or tiny, scattered settlements made up of thatched huts constructed of wattle and clay that leave few archaeological traces. Because they left behind few durable material objects, their formation and abandonment are also seriously difficult to date.[9] Much of Scotland was essentially similar, and the archaeological interpretation of settlements like Lix (Perthshire), which produced no trace of settlement before 1700, is further complicated by the recurrent shifting of settlements to new sites even in normal circumstances.[10] It follows that in many parts of Britain and Ireland the absence of well-defined deserted villages is not good evidence for the stability of settlement patterns. Despite the poor archaeological evidence, there are numerous references to deserted settlements in the rentals of Scottish royal estates following the Black Death, as well as to the widespread abandonment of other tenanted properties and loss of royal dues.[11] Both in Scotland and Ireland it seems agreed that deserted villages become more conspicuous from the seventeenth century onwards rather than earlier.[12]

Areas of scattered settlement in England also suffered a reduction in the number of occupied sites. This is not unexpected in the case of isolated farms and hamlets in remote or upland regions like Dartmoor or the Pennines, or in the fenlands of Cambridgeshire and Norfolk, though even there the pattern of desertion is far from predictable.[13] Some isolated farms established on wasteland in the Palatinate of Durham during the twelfth and thirteenth centuries not only often survived but in some cases were elevated in status as manors during the fourteenth and fifteenth centuries. The farm called Edderacres, which still survives, was the 'manor of Edirdacres' in 1383. The thirteenth-century Pespool, called 'the manor of Pespole' in 1383, still survives. Flemingfield was an independent farm a century after its foundation and survives today. However, the losses were also numerous. The hamlet of Crook, established on the Durham waste in the thirteenth century, is now lost. The moorland farm called Boisfield, was already in 1383 absorbed into Pespool (at a rent reduced from £2 10s. 0d. at some earlier time to a mere 13s. 4d.) and is now lost.[14] Some such sites are known from archaeological evidence in Scotland, such as Homefarm at Wardhouse (Aberdeenshire).[15] Even where scattered farms survived, their occupation was sometimes discontinuous. In less isolated regions, too, scattered settlements were thinned out in the course of time. In midland England, Quarrendon (Buckinghamshire), depopulated in the later fifteenth century, has been reinterpreted as having a dispersed settlement pattern rather than a nucleated one.[16]

In these ways the total number of occupied sites, whether nucleated or not, was reduced during the course of this period, though, exceptionally, there were regions of Britain, and remote ones at that, where more peaceful conditions and the development of pasture farming encouraged an increased scattering of minor settlements in the fifteenth century. This was the case, for example, in the western highlands and islands of Scotland, in Morvern, and on Islay and North Uist.[17]

Deserted villages and scattered settlements are more important for the relatively undisturbed condition of their remains than as an accurate record of changing settlement patterns over time. Although it is common to attribute them to the effects of the Black Death, there are no certain examples of villages permanently exterminated in 1349; Tusmore and Tilgarsley in Oxfordshire are possible cases.[18] Such sudden desertion represents only an extreme case of a phenomenon which was characteristically slow and piecemeal, and in some cases started before 1348.[19] The desertion of the Yorkshire village of Eske has been described as 'a long slow death, rather than a single event'.[20] Some villages, like Grenstein in Norfolk, decayed over several decades, to disappear during the earlier fifteenth century. Roel in Gloucestershire, which had about thirty tenants in the thirteenth century, had poor soil, servile tenures, and few opportunities for earnings outside agriculture, and had been abandoned by 1466.[21] But by far the commonest consequence of declining population was for a town or village to shrink in 1348–9, if not earlier, and to go on shrinking without disappearing. Newton Ketton (Durham County) was reduced from sixteen tenements in the 1340s to two by 1396, probably corresponding to the two surviving farms there.[22] Empty houses and cottages gradually fell down, and became overgrown, or were deliberately removed to allow the reorganization of neighbouring properties. Some villages still preserve traces of this shrinkage, as at Ogle in Northumberland.[23] Many deserted villages were not in fact deserted till more recent times. Despite the poverty of Breckland soils, the desertion of villages there was often delayed until the seventeenth and eighteenth centuries.[24] The deserted villages of Laugharne shrank during the fourteenth and fifteenth centuries but survived in 1530, and were deserted only when some improving landlord delivered the final blow at a later date.[25]

In eastern Ireland, depopulation followed a combination of misfortunes early in the fourteenth century. Between 1315 and 1318 Edward Bruce, the brother of the king of Scots, invaded Ireland, probably with the intention of assuming the lordship of Ireland. The effects of his widespread devastation were made much worse by the famines of 1315–18, brought about by adverse weather conditions. Had strong government been restored, the effects of the invasion should have been short-lived, but the subsequent weakening of law and order was unfavourable to recovery. The Bruce invasion contributed to the desertion of Rinndown (Co. Roscommon) and the near extinction of Fore (Co. Westmeath). Further serious depopulation was caused by the Black Death.[26] Even so, some of the best-known Irish examples of desertion have to be dated to the seventeenth century, as at the boroughs of Bannow and Clonmines (Co. Wexford), Kilixby (Co. Meath), and Newtown Jerpoint (Co. Kilkenny).[27] These caveats imply that the distribution of deserted villages across the landscape gives only an imperfect guide to the changing distribution of rural population and settlement between 1300 and 1530.

The environmental circumstances that affected settlement history inevitably included the varying quality of life that different locations could offer. Soil quality was far from being the only consideration here, since some regions with poor soils permitted a rich and comfortable livelihood from livestock, trade, and industry. The Breckland of Suffolk and Norfolk is a well-documented example of a poor-soil region that nevertheless continued to support a varied and commercially responsive economy even through the recessions of the fifteenth century.[28] If people could comfortably adapt to change by developing cattle raising and shepherding within an existing rural framework there was no reason for them to abandon existing settlements. In general deserted villages were relatively infrequent in those upland, woodland, and marshy regions where pasture farming was already lucrative and strongly emphasized before the period of declining population.[29] They were more common in arable regions where many small villages were grouped together. Even without external attractions, small villages were more likely to be completely abandoned than large ones, but all the more so where larger settlements nearby had a wider range of opportunities for trade and recreation. Remoter settlements with poor soil were also particularly likely to shed population because of the greater difficulty of raising crops, higher transaction costs in marketing produce, coldness, wetness, windiness, dirtiness, or remoteness from parish churches and other central institutions. The settlements in such regions were in any case often small. Some of the known examples of Scottish settlements deserted between 1300 and 1600 are high up on the Lammermuir hills.[30] At a time when landlords in sheltered and well-populated areas of better soil were looking for tenants, many families could expect to improve their quality of life by migrating.[31] The impetus for change no doubt often came from the young, for whom an early move meant a lifetime of difference.

Some English settlements were deliberately destroyed by landlords wanting to create sheep-runs or parks. The involvement of landlords in cases of total depopulation is implicit in the comments of John Rous concerning Warwickshire. 'What shall be said of the modern destruction of villages which brings dearth to the commonwealth? The root of this evil is greed. The plague of avarice infects these times and it blinds men.'[32] Misleading though it was as a general hypothesis, this was the explanation for depopulation and enclosure adopted by Tudor propagandists. Such unattractive conduct was not beyond the most princely landlord. The village of East Lilling in Yorkshire was destroyed sometime between 1471 and 1485 to make a deer park for Richard III, whether before he made himself king or afterwards.[33] However, only a small part of the depopulation of villages resulted from deliberate destruction; it mostly derived from falling population. How to get rid of tenants was not usually an issue for landlords, at least before the late fifteenth century; the main problem was rather how to find them and keep them without having to make too many concessions.[34] After about 1470, when an expansion of sheep farming was one of the few means by which it was possible to increase agricultural incomes, there are indeed more cases of landlords who deliberately removed settlements, sometimes by the most oppressive methods.[35] A landlord who wanted to get rid of a community altogether could behave in high-handed ways wholly inappropriate to one who wanted to maintain the status quo. Even so, settlements destroyed by landlords were often already considerably shrunken, and sometimes they could enclose without causing depopulation because villages were already deserted.[36] Depopulation for the sake of cows or sheep was, predictably, much less an issue in the many parts of Britain where the economy had always been more pastoral. References to enclosed land in Ireland become increasingly common after 1300, but no sinister interpretation was placed upon it.[37] The commissions issued by the English government in May 1517 for collecting evidence of enclosure, withdrawal of land from use as arable, and depopulation were not extended to the four northernmost counties of England, nor to Wales or Ireland.[38]

Warfare, though its direct effects on settlement patterns were secondary, had a more detrimental effect on settlement patterns in this period of declining population than it had done when the search for land was more actively pursued. There had been many local wars and devastations in Britain between 1050 and 1300, and though assessments of their consequences vary, any impact was temporary. Even after the most severe cases of devastation caused by war, such as the local havoc created in England by William I's suppression of rebellion, or the conflict of rival armies in Stephen's reign, land was resettled, numbers were made up, and population grew above its former level within a generation or two. In twelfth-century Wales and Ireland, invasion had been rapidly followed by an influx of settlers and a surge of new settlement. From the early fourteenth century, however, the effects of war were more baneful, not necessarily because wars were more destructive, but because the pressure to make good afterwards was no longer so strong. The Anglo-Scottish wars of Edward I and his successors cannot be held to account for the evidence of depopulation and declining output around the Anglo-Scottish border in the fourteenth and fifteenth centuries.[39] They, and later conflicts, nevertheless had a greater impact than they would have done in an economy with more potential for growth. Heightened warfare similarly defines a turning point in the history of Anglo-Norman settlement of Ireland following the Bruce invasion of 1315. Warfare contributed to the abandonment even of Roscommon town from 1360.[40] The effects of destruction incidental to Glyn Dŵr's rebellion in Wales were also longer lived than those of thirteenth-century warfare. Many of the losses incurred during the rebellion in the lordship of Newport had still not been made good by 1434–5; the mills destroyed then had mostly remained out of action, and in Newport itself burgages had been ruined since 1403.[41]

Most of the outstanding achievements of twelfth- and thirteenth-century settlement history survived the following period of contraction. Large numbers of nucleated villages, market towns, and boroughs survived into the modern world, even if with some reduction in the number of their residents. Even though the population in 1530 was barely larger than it had been in 1050, its distribution and occupational structure was greatly changed. Many isolated farms had continuous histories through these centuries where the land was good and owners had pride of possession. This shows that declining population after 1300 was not a full-scale retreat from the gains of the preceding centuries, and that great care is needed in defining what was abandoned and what retained. There is, in fact, no single key to these changes, since the attractiveness of different locations at different times depended upon a range of considerations, of which the 'natural fertility of the soil' was only one.

Standards of Living

Rentals from the fifteenth century illustrate the extent to which great inequalities remained within rural settlements, not to mention the great divides that often separated ordinary countrymen from their landlords. East Anglia, which had been conspicuous for its number of smallholders in the thirteenth century, retained large numbers of peasants dependent either upon high productivity of the land or side-earnings from occupations away from their tenements.

However, greater availability of land had implications for the distribution of property, given the inability of landlords to maintain rents and services at the old levels.[42] The relative ease with which families could acquire land is indicated by a significant reduction not only of the number of cottagers and other landless people but also of their proportion of the total rural population. Around 1300, cottagers, labourers, and servants probably accounted for over half of all English households, but in 1524 the proportion of poorer families that constituted the wage-earning class was down to one-third.[43] In terms of absolute numbers, across Britain as a whole, this change was dramatic, since the total population had in the meantime fallen so steeply.[44] The decline can be illustrated from particular villages, like Catesby (Northamptonshire), where during the fifteenth century the number of cottagers declined much more steeply than the number of tenants with land enough to sustain them.[45] A comparative study of three Devon villages suggests that cottagers were most likely to survive where there was a wide range of employment in rural trades and industries (as at Sidbury). In specialized pastoral communities (like Ashwater) there was little scope for them, since workers were expected to live with their employers to take care of livestock. In arable areas, since it became easier after 1348 to acquire land, the number of landless households diminished, though larger tenant farmers might take the opportunity to acquire empty cottages as a means of attracting labourers to work for them (as at Stokenham).[46] Cottars, crofters, and 'grassmen' rarely appear in Scottish estate records of the period, and some who do had smallholdings that relieved their total dependence on paid employment. Their rarity in the records can partly be explained by their having often been subtenants, but they were probably fewer in number than they had been at the height of Scotland's thirteenth-century population growth.[47]

As this implies, the problems of rural poverty apparent from thirteenth-century records were greatly alleviated as population declined and land became more available. These causes had a doubly beneficial effect for poorer families, however, because they had simultaneous implications for levels of wages. The simultaneous retreat of many surviving cottagers on to the land, even if it did not wholly reduce their dependence on occasional wage earning, meant a further reduction in the availability of labour in addition to the effects of depopulation. A dramatic decline in the labour force, most marked during the fourteenth century but continuing into the fifteenth, need not have brought much benefit to the survivors if at the same time the demand for labour had declined sufficiently to offset the smaller number of those seeking work. In fact, however, demand for labour exerted a powerful upward pressure on wages.

Already in the immediate aftermath of the epidemic of 1348–9 labourers realized that they could bargain for wages higher than the old rate, and looked round for better conditions. This occasioned the English labour legislation of 1349 and 1351 that was examined in Chapter 17.[48] Besides attempting to fix wages, the ordinance of 1349 gave landlords first claim to the labour of their own tenants, so long as they did not take more than they needed. Stocks were to be set up in each village to punish workers who would not swear to keep the law, or who broke it; at Cuxham a new pair of stocks 'for rebel servants (*famuli*)' was promptly installed by the lord of the manor.[49] Justices of labourers were appointed throughout the country to levy fines for breach of the regulations, or to commit labourers to prison. Often these commissions were combined with commissions of the peace, as in 1350, until eventually in 1368 the enforcement of the statute was made a regular duty of a JP. This legislation was augmented through the later fourteenth century; its enforcement was as vigorous in the 1370s as in the 1350s.[50] From 1390 the justices were given statutory discretion to fix maximum wages locally.[51] Yet real wages rose despite the Statutes of Labourers and all attempts to enforce it. In part this was because of grave imperfections in the drafting of the statute, which took no account of variations in skill and conditions of work.[52] But the major reason for the statute's failure was that in competing to attract sufficient labour some landlords, especially bigger landlords, were willing to pay more than others. In these circumstances employers and labourers alike conspired to evade the law.[53] The statute's lasting significance was not in holding wages down, but in creating a means for coercing the unemployed. It was in many respects a forerunner of the Elizabethan Poor Law, and stands at the head of centuries of legislation to compel the idle poor to be useful.

From the 1370s wages increased while prices on average did not, though as always fluctuating from year to year (Figure 18.1). A wage index for England and Wales, based chiefly on records from southern England, suggests that agricultural wages during the ten years 1456–65, when measured by what they would buy, were 62 per cent above their level before the Black Death.[54] The increase is amply attested in southern English manorial accounts, where it has long been a topic for research. Some classic early studies concentrated on the estates of the bishopric of Winchester and Westminster Abbey, which have left large collections of estate records.[55] But increasing wages were not confined to the south and south-east of England. In north-eastern England an increase in cash stipends was sustained until at least the mid-fifteenth century. Demesne servants on the prior of Durham's manor of Pittington improved their wage by several stages between the 1360s and the 1440s, and from the 1390s they also occur more frequently as lessees of parcels of meadow, implying a diversification of their sources of income.[56] In Cornwall money wage rates of both craftsmen and labourers at least doubled by three main stages, in the 1350s, the 1380s, and the 1420s.[57] Increases in wage levels are also recorded in Wales and the Welsh marches,[58] and there is reason to suppose that Ireland was similarly affected.[59] The Scottish evidence of wage movements is too poor to substantiate the general hypothesis, though Scottish historians are willing to assume that rural wages rose as elsewhere.[60] However, the Scottish economy, like that of northern England, was doubtless less dependent on wage labour than the more urbanized and commercialized regions of southern England. In addition, Scotland's distinctive experience of inflation after 1367, the result of successive debasements of the currency, probably masked the political implications of rising wages, and may have operated to cancel them out. It was perhaps for these reasons that high wage costs did not become so much a cause of alarm in Scotland as in England during the later fourteenth century.

Money wages need to be distinguished from the real value of wages in terms of what money would buy. Money wages probably rose most in Scotland because of the severe depreciation of the currency during the fourteenth and fifteenth centuries, which caused an inflation of Scottish prices unparalleled in England. Real wage rates, by contrast, probably rose farthest in regions of high demand for labour

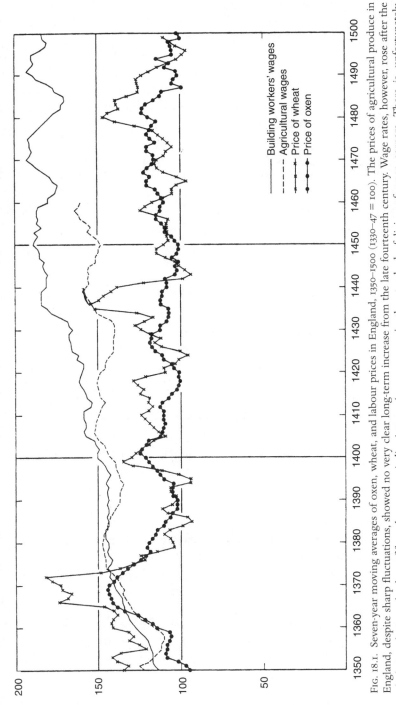

FIG. 18.1. Seven-year moving averages of oxen, wheat, and labour prices in England, 1350–1500 (1330–47 = 100). The prices of agricultural produce in England, despite sharp fluctuations, showed no very clear long-term increase from the late fourteenth century. Wage rates, however, rose after the Black Death into the later fifteenth century, indicating an improvement in the standard of living of wage earners. There is, unfortunately, no comparably coherent evidence for other parts of Britain and Ireland.

Source: D. L. Farmer, 'Prices and Wages, 1350–1500', in E. Miller (ed.), *The Agrarian History of England and Wales*, iii: *1348–1500* (Cambridge, 1991), 437.

where urban industry was expanding, such as the region round Colchester and Hadleigh, Salisbury or Coventry, though the data currently at our disposal are inadequate to test whether this was in fact the case. Differences of productivity between different groups of workers were signalled in their wages; differentials between the wages of men and women were maintained,[61] as were differentials between skilled and unskilled workers. However, scarcity of skilled labour led to some substitution of skilled for unskilled and some narrowing of the differentials.[62]

The legal status of women showed no significant improvement between 1300 and 1530 anywhere in rural Britain, and we suffer the same sorts of masking of evidence that affect the period before 1300. However, the richness of manorial records from the fourteenth century permits more intensive studies of gender roles and the opportunities available for women than the records of any earlier period.[63] The economic conditions affecting female employment changed more than the legal ones as labour became more expensive after the Black Death. As wage rates rose, women became increasingly significant as a reserve labour force. High mortality in the 1430s, for example, induces the servant in charge of Chalvington manor in Sussex to hire more women harvesters; eight women harvested for an average of 6.6 days each in 1441.[64] Women's wage rates were generally inferior to men's, presumably because they were reckoned not to be so product-ive.[65] For all that, the range of opportunities for female employment was to a limited extent widened in the century after 1349. Many country women moved into towns in the later fourteenth century to take advantage of the greater prosperity there; many were taken up as household servants, for example, in wealthier households.[66] The expansion of the commercial textile industry meanwhile created additional opportunities for some women who stayed in their villages, since urban clothmakers were likely to put out work in the countryside. Higher standards of living led to greater ale consumption, and another boost to women's employment opportunities, though brewing became more professional in the course of time, and by the early sixteenth century larger-scale and more regular brewing had squeezed out a good deal of more casual activity.[67] Whether the period 1350–1450, in particular, deserves too be labelled a 'golden age' for women has been a matter of some debate, but in any case it represented no permanent gain for female status. Much of what women did was still tied to the home and the family, differing little from what it had been before 1349, and women's employment was the first to suffer in periods of recession and rising male unemployment such as the 1450s.

Wage earners were perhaps the greatest beneficiaries from the changes of the fourteenth century, but other sections of the rural population also benefited from the greater availability of land. There remained many smallholders, especially in areas where peasant farming could be supplemented by income from nonagricultural employments. This was most conspicuously the case in East Anglia and central Essex, where even in the late fifteenth century it was not uncommon for a majority of tenants to hold less than 10 acres.[68] Even these poorer ranks of the peasantry, at least of those able-bodied, are likely to have improved their lot because of higher wage rates. However, the upper ranks did even better as a result of lower land values and an active land market. In the course of these changes economic divisions within the peasantry widened, especially from the 1390s.[69] In England a minority of countrymen was able to accumulate holdings appreciably larger than they needed to feed their families.[70]

A similar process of consolidation is in evidence in parts of northern Wales remote from major towns, even though Welsh custom meant that the way it came about was distinctive. It also probably depended less on commercial incentives. In Anglesey, for example, even though restraints on the alienation of free property were much tighter than under English common law, it was possible to break family rights of inheritance if land was repeatedly mortgaged over four generations, and by such means acquisitive families added parcels of arable, meadow, and pasture to create larger holdings. From this process emerged a class of yeomen farmers very much as in England. Some agglomerations of property raised formerly peasant families into the ranks of the gentry. Having been split up between heirs into separate *gwelyau* during periods of growing population after 1170, later, as population fell, the lands of Griffri and Carwed in Llysdulas were partly reassembled through the amalgamation of parcels. Existing gentry and burgess families, especially round the boroughs of north Wales, were also active in this land market. Perhaps the best illustration of this is the rental drawn up for a burgess of Conwy, Bartholomew Bolde, who acquired 600 acres of arable, 200 of meadow, and 1,000 of pasture by piecemeal accumulation in the commote of Arllechwedd Isaf between 1420 and 1453; his rental lists 165 properties.[71] Bond land in Wales also became available through the extinction or flight of the families that occupied them. The unfree status of such land may initially have deterred buyers from the Welsh upper classes, but it contributed to the accumulation of properties by lesser freemen, and eventually contributed to the wealth of the Welsh gentry. The Wynn family of Gwydir looked back to the accumulations of Maredudd ab Ieuan, who in the late fifteenth century had migrated from Eifionydd to Nanconwy in order to 'finde elbowe roome in that wast countrey amonge the bondmen'.[72]

The structure of tenures in Scotland in the period 1350–1500 is poorly illuminated by either documentary or archaeological sources. Even if their demographic history followed the same course as in England, which is not altogether certain, the implications for the distribution of land were not necessarily the same. It seems likely, however, that as elsewhere in Britain declining population increased the opportunities to accumulate land. In the thirteenth century husbandmen had characteristically occupied one or two oxgangs (each of about 13 acres), but in a rental of 1376–7, from the estates of Douglas of Dalkeith in Peebles, Dumfries, and Fife, each husbandman seems to have occupied at least four. This process of peasant accumulation by fortunate individuals continued on the estate into the fifteenth century, widening in the process the gap between the wealthiest and the poorest tenants. The fact that it was accompanied by declining rents indicates a pattern of change much like that in England.[73] The Scottish population may have been less struck by crisis mortality that the English, as some Scots historians have maintained, but if so the difference was a matter of degree; where they are observable the social effects followed much the same pattern as south of the border.

Ireland already had an elite of large peasant farmers in 1300,[74] so the course of change there was in this respect unlikely to be distinctive. The large freeholdings on the Irish estates of the Monmouthshire abbey of Llanthony Prima in 1408 were no new feature of colonial Ireland.[75] However, a rental of 1443 from Danesfort (Co. Kilkenny) lists forty-six tenants of whom only four had more than 10 acres. Some communities with numerous settled smallholders were evidently surviving in fifteenth-century Ireland.[76] The weakening of royal power and growing independence of Irish magnates (the Gaelic Revival) gave Ireland a distinctive course of rural change, in which political violence played a part. The region of Ireland subject to government from Dublin was reduced to the Pale, the four counties of Dublin, Kildare, Meath, and Louth. Local circumstances both of law enforcement and of political conflicts varied widely. A widespread response by magnates to the needs of local defence was the quartering of troops in the countryside, a revival and extension of the ancient Gaelic practice of *coinnmheadh*, known in Anglo-Irish society as 'coyne and livery'.[77] From 1390 references to nomadic bands of herdsmen, of both Gaelic and Anglo-Irish origin and known as 'creaghts' in Hiberno-English, become more numerous in northern Ireland. They were frequently aggressive—pasturing livestock on other people's land to the point of driving them away.[78] Under these various stresses the conversion of land to pasture farming was probably more marked than in southern England. The impact on settlement patterns was no doubt profound in some parts, but unfortunately there is little evidence by which to control imaginative reconstruction.[79]

The redistribution of land in much of Britain was associated with rising standards of welfare for a large proportion of the population. Quite apart from the measured increase in real wages, and the probability that larger tenancies meant higher standards of subsistence, there is the evidence of peasant housing, which represents the largest consumption item in peasant spending. Throughout much of southern England, especially in the south-east, there are surviving houses that testify to the high standards of construction available to upper ranks of peasant society. In Kent there are about 1,000 houses from the late fourteenth and fifteenth centuries, and in the Rape of Hastings alone as many as 110. More complicated rural house designs were devised as a result of the rising living standards of yeoman farmers, who were able to accumulate land and rents. One-storey buildings acquired an extra storey, slate roofs replaced thatch, stone hearths and chimneys were added, standards of carpentry improved. Where farms grew larger, the number of outbuildings also increased. Houses were built of different materials and to different designs, effectively broadening regional differences.[80]

Away from the south and the midlands of England such survivals are rarer, and where they are found they register fewer changes from earlier periods. Long-house design remained prevalent in areas of scattered settlement. There are very few surviving houses from northern England. Few Welsh examples are known, either; the common housing was too poor to have survived. In mountainous and remote parts of the country people lived in mere huts, and there were few houses that showed signs of increased rural prosperity.[81] In much of Scotland, rural housing was characteristically of wattle and turf on a timber frame, which had at least the advantage of being cheap and rapid to construct. In the western and northern highlands, where there were too few trees, more stone was used with mud or clay as a mortar.[82] Aeneas Sylvius, the future pope Pius II, who visited Scotland in 1435, observed rural housing that was mostly built of turf, with only an oxhide for a door in the poorest households.[83] In Ireland the poverty of the archaeological evidence implies that most housing was flimsy and impermanent, perhaps even seasonal, since some communities moved from winter to summer pastures and back again each year.[84] As these comments imply, the archaeological evidence for improved standards of living in rural society is much more convincing for southern, midland, and eastern England than for regions of Britain more remote from London.

NOTES

1. Thomas More, *Utopia*, ed. G. M. Logan, R. M. Adams, and C. H. Miller (Cambridge, 1995), 62–3.

2. M. W. Beresford and J. G. Hurst, *Wharram Percy: Deserted Medieval Village* (1990), 15.

3. M. W. Beresford and J. K. S. St Joseph, *Medieval England: An Aerial Survey*, 2nd edn. (Cambridge, 1979), 123.

4. Beresford and Hurst, *Wharram Percy*, 15, 79–84, 101.

5. C. Taylor, *Village and Farmstead* (1983), 122, 128.

6. Domesday Book, i, fo. 230ᵛ; M. W. Beresford, *History on the Ground*, new edn. (Gloucester, 1984), 119, 121–2, plate 9; T. Rowley and J. Wood, *Deserted Villages* (Princes Risborough, 1982), 58.

7. W. S. G. Thomas, 'Lost Villages in South-West Carmarthenshire', *Transactions of the Institute of British Geographers*, 47 (1969), 191–203.

8. L. A. S. Butler, 'The Study of Deserted Medieval Settlements in Wales (to 1968)', in M. W. Beresford and J. G. Hurst (eds.), *Deserted Medieval Villages: Studies* (1971), 255.

9. S. G. Ellis, *Tudor Ireland: Crown, Community and Conflict of Cultures, 1470–1603* (1985), 34–5; R. E. Glasscock, 'Moated Sites, and Deserted Boroughs and Villages: Two Neglected Aspects of Anglo-Norman Settlement in Ireland', in N. Stephens and R. E. Glasscock (eds.), *Irish Geographical Studies in Honour of E. Estyn Evans* (Belfast, 1970), 167–8, 171–2; R. E. Glasscock, 'The Study of Deserted Medieval Settlement in Ireland (to 1968)', in Beresford and Hurst (eds.), *Deserted Medieval Villages*, 288; K. Nicholls, *Gaelic and Gaelicised Ireland in the Middle Ages* (Dublin, 1972), 122–3; K. D. O'Conor, *The Archaeology of Medieval Rural Settlements in Ireland* (Dublin, 1998), 47–8.

10. R. A. Dodgshon, *Land and Society in Early Scotland* (Oxford, 1981), 172–3.

11. E. Gemmill and N. Mayhew, *Changing Values in Medieval Scotland: A Study of Prices, Money, and Weights and Measures* (Cambridge, 1995), 369–70; A. Grant, *Independence and Nationhood: Scotland, 1306–1469* (1984), 82; N. Mayhew, 'Scotland: Economy and Society', in S. H. Rigby (ed.), *A Companion to Britain in the Later Middle Ages* (Oxford, 2003), 111.

12. R. A. Dodgshon, 'Medieval Settlement and Colonisation', in M. L. Parry and T. R. Slater (eds.), *The Making of the Scottish Countryside* (1980), 62; T. B. Barry, ' "The People of the Country . . . Dwell Scattered": The Pattern of Rural Settlements in Ireland in the Later Middle Ages', in J. Bradley (ed.), *Settlement and Society in Medieval Ireland: Studies Presented to F. X. Martin, OSA* (Kilkenny, 1988), 353–5.

13. C. Taylor, *Village and Farmstead* (1983), 196–200.

14. *Bishop Hatfield's Survey*, ed. W. Greenwell, Surtees Society, 32 (1857), 127.

15. P. A. Yeoman, 'Medieval Rural Settlement: The Invisible Centuries', in W. S. Hanson and E. A. Slater (eds.), *Scottish Archaeology: New Perceptions* (Aberdeen, 1991), 121–4.

16. Beresford and St Joseph, *Medieval England*, 123–4; P. Everson, 'Peasants, Peers and Graziers: The Landscape of Quarrendon, Buckinghamshire, Interpreted', *Records of Buckinghamshire*, 41 (2001), 1–45.

17. Dodgshon, 'Medieval Settlement and Colonisation', 58–9.

18. Beresford, *History on the Ground*, 97, 99.

19. C. Dyer, *Everyday Life in Medieval England* (1994), 30–4.

20. B. English and K. Miller, 'The Deserted Village of Eske, East Yorkshire', *Landscape History*, 13 (1991), 5–32.

21. D. Aldred and C. Dyer, 'A Medieval Cotswold Village: Roel, Gloucestershire', *Transactions of the Bristol and Gloucestershire Archaeological Society*, 109 (1991), 139–70; Beresford and St Joseph, *Medieval England*, 144, 157–61.

22. R. Lomas, *North-East England in the Middle Ages* (Edinburgh, 1992), 161.

23. Beresford and St Joseph, *Medieval England*, 113–16.

24. M. Bailey, *A Marginal Economy? East Anglian Breckland in the Later Middle Ages* (Cambridge, 1989), 53–4.

25. Thomas, 'Lost Villages', 191–203.

26. T. B. Barry, *The Archaeology of Medieval Ireland* (1987), 173–4; R. Frame, 'The Bruces in Ireland, 1315–18', in id., *Ireland and Britain, 1170–1450* (1998), 78–9; J. Lydon, 'The Impact of

the Bruce Invasion, 1316–27', in A. Cosgrove (ed.), *A New History of Ireland*, ii: *Medieval Ireland, 1169–1534* (Oxford, 1987), 294–5.

27. Glasscock, 'Moated Sites and Deserted Boroughs', 169–70; O'Conor, *Archaeology of Medieval Rural Settlements*, 47–8.

28. Bailey, *Marginal Economy?*, 264, 318.

29. M. W. Beresford, *The Lost Villages of England* (1954), 229–32.

30. Dodgshon, 'Medieval Settlement and Colonisation', 62.

31. H. S. A. Fox, 'The People of the Wolds in English Settlement History', in M. Aston, D. Austin, and C. Dyer (eds.), *The Rural Settlements of Medieval England: Studies Dedicated to Maurice Beresford and John Hurst* (Oxford, 1989), 96–100.

32. Beresford, *Lost Villages*, 81.

33. V. G. Swan, D. A. Mackay, and B. E. A. Jones, 'East Lilling, North Yorkshire: The Deserted Medieval Village Reconsidered', *Yorkshire Archaeological Journal*, 62 (1990), 91–109.

34. Dyer, *Everyday Life*, 37–8.

35. E. B. Fryde, *Peasants and Landlords in Later Medieval England* (Stroud, 1996), 185–208.

36. Dyer, *Everyday Life*, 34–6; id., *Lords and Peasants in a Changing Society: The Estates of the Bishopric of Worcester, 680–1540* (Cambridge, 1980), 259.

37. K. Down, 'Colonial Society and Economy in the High Middle Ages', in Cosgrove (ed.), *New History of Ireland*, ii. 477.

38. *The Domesday of Enclosures, 1517–1518*, ed. I. S. Leadam, 2 vols. (1897), i. 81–6.

39. R. A. Lomas, 'The Impact of Border Warfare: The Scots and South Tweedside, c.1290–c.1520', *Scottish Historical Review*, 75 (1996), 143–67.

40. Barry, *Archaeology of Medieval Ireland*, 173.

41. *The Marcher Lordships of South Wales, 1415–1536: Select Documents*, ed. T. B. Pugh (Cardiff, 1963), 167–9, 171.

42. See above (Ch. 18).

43. J. C. K. Cornwall, *Wealth and Society in Early Sixteenth-Century England* (1988), 213–14.

44. Above (Ch. 4).

45. J. Laughton, 'Catesby in the Middle Ages: An Interdisciplinary Study', *Northamptonshire Past and Present*, 54 (2001), 7–32.

46. H. S. A. Fox, 'Servants, Cottagers and Tied Cottages during the Later Middle Ages: Towards a Regional Dimension', *Rural History*, 6 (1995), 125–54.

47. *Rental Book of the Cistercian Abbey of Cupar-Angus*, ed. C. Rogers, 2 vols., Grampian Club (1879–80), i. xxvii–xxviii; Grant, *Independence and Nationhood*, 67.

48. Above (Ch. 17).

49. *Manorial Records of Cuxham, Oxfordshire, c.1200–1359*, ed. P. D. A. Harvey (1976), 500.

50. J. L. Bolton, *The Medieval English Economy, 1150–1500* (1980), 213.

51. L. R. Poos, 'The Social Context of Statute of Labourers Enforcement', *Law and History Review*, 1 (1983), 29–30.

52. A. E. Levett, *Studies in Manorial History*, ed. H. M. Cam and others (Oxford, 1938), 291–2.

53. J. Hatcher, 'England in the Aftermath of the Black Death', *Past and Present*, 144 (1994), 19–25.

54. D. L. Farmer, 'Prices and Wages, 1350–1500', in E. Miller (ed.), *The Agrarian History of England and Wales*, iii: *1348–1500* (Cambridge, 1991), 523.

55. W. H. Beveridge, 'Wages in the Winchester Manors', *Economic History Review*, 7 (1936–7), 22–43; id., 'Westminster Wages in the Manorial Era', *Economic History Review*, 2nd ser. 8 (1955), 18–35.

56. B. Dodds, 'Workers on the Pittington Demesne in the Late Middle Ages', *Archaeologia Aeliana*, 5th ser. 28 (2000), 147–61.

57. J. Hatcher, *Rural Economy and Society in the Duchy of Cornwall, 1300–1500* (Cambridge, 1970), 144, 147, 156, 158, 290–1.

58. R. R. Davies, *Conquest, Coexistence and Change: Wales, 1063–1415* (Oxford, 1987), 426; W. Rees, *South Wales and the March, 1284–1415* (1924), 264–5.

59. M. Kelly, *The Black Death in Ireland* (Stroud, 2001), 86.

60. Grant, *Independence and Nationhood*, 77–8, 81.

61. S. Bardsley, 'Women's Work Reconsidered: Gender and Wage Differentiation in Late Medieval England', *Past and Present*, 165 (1999), 1–29; J. Hatcher, 'Women's Work Reconsidered: Gender and Wage Differentiation in Late Medieval England', *Past and Present*, 173 (2001), 191–8.

62. Beveridge, 'Wages in the Winchester Manors', 34–5, 42; M. M. Postan, *Essays on Medieval Agriculture and General Problems of the Medieval Economy* (Cambridge, 1973), 200–2.

63. See, in particular, J. M. Bennett, *Women in the Medieval English Countryside: Gender and Household in Brigstock before the Plague* (Oxford, 1987). A more student-friendly version of the findings of this research is J. M. Bennett, *A Medieval Life: Cecilia Pennifader of Brigstock, c.1295–1344* (Boston, 1999).

64. M. Mate, *Daughters, Wives and Widows after the Black Death: Women in Sussex, 1350–1535* (Woodbridge, 1998). 56.

65. Bardsley, 'Women's Work Reconsidered' 1–29; Hatcher, 'Women's Work Reconsidered' 191–8.

66. P. J. P. Goldberg, *Women, Work and Life Cycle in a Medieval Economy: Women in York and Yorkshire, c.1300–1520* (Oxford, 1992), 280–304.

67. J. M. Bennett, *Ale, Beer and Brewsters in England* (Oxford, 1996), 46–8; Mate, *Daughters*, 59–60.

68. R. H. Britnell, 'Tenant Farmers and Tenant Farming: Eastern England', in Miller (ed.), *Agrarian History of England and Wales*, iii. 614–17.

69. R. H. Hilton, *The Economic Development of some Leicestershire Estates in the 14th and 15th Centuries* (1947), 94–5, 129.

70. E. B. DeWindt, *Land and People in Holywell-cum-Needingworth: Structures of Tenure and Patterns of Social Organization in an East Midlands Village, 1252–1457* (Toronto, 1972), 107–61.

71. 'The Bolde Rental (Bangor ms. 1939)', ed. C. A. Gresham. *Transactions of the Caernarvonshire Historical Society*, 26 (1965), 31–49; G. R. J. Jones, 'Rural Settlement in Anglesey', in S. R. Eyre and G. R. J. Jones (eds.), *Geography as Human Ecology: Methodology by Example* (1966), 206–7.

72. T. J. Pierce, *Medieval Welsh Society: Selected Essays*, ed. J. B. Smith (Cardiff, 1972), 43–7; D. H. Owen, 'The Middle Ages', in id. (ed.), *Settlement and Society in Wales* (Cardiff, 1989), 211.

73. Grant, *Independence and Nationhood*, 78.

74. Above (Ch. 8).

75. *The Irish Cartularies of Llanthony Prima and Secunda*, ed. E. St. J. Brooks (Dublin, 1953), 178–93.

76. C. A. Empey, 'The Anglo-Norman Community in Tippera[r]y and Kilkenny in the Middle Ages: Change and Continuity', in G. Mac Niocaill and P. F. Wallace (eds.), *Keimelia: Studies in Medieval Archaeology and History in Memory of Tom Delaney* (Galway, 1988), 460.

77. A. Cosgrove, 'The Emergence of the Pale, 1399–1447', in id. (ed.), *New History of Ireland*, ii. 541–2.

78. K. Simms, 'Nomadry in Medieval Ireland', *Peritia*, 5 (1986), 380–2.

79. T. B. Barry, 'Late Medieval Ireland: The Debate on Social and Economic Transformation, 1350–1550', in B. J. Graham and L. J. Proudfoot, *An Historical Geography of Ireland* (1993), 117–19.

80. C. Dyer, *Standards of Living in the Later Middle Ages: Social Change in England, c.1200–1520* (Cambridge, 1989), 166–9; H. E. J. Le Patourel, 'Rural Building in England and Wales: England', in Miller (ed.), *Agrarian History of England and Wales*, iii. 843–65.

81. L. A. S. Butler, 'Rural Building in England and Wales: Wales', in Miller (ed.), *Agrarian History of England and Wales*, iii. 908–11.

82. H. Fairhurst and J. G. Dunbar, 'The Study of Deserted Medieval Settlements in Scotland (to 1968)', in Beresford and Hurst (eds.), *Deserted Medieval Villages*, 232, 242–3; Grant, *Independence and Nationhood*, 61.

83. *Early Travellers in Scotland*, ed. P. H. Brown (Edinburgh, 1891), 26–7.

84. Barry, *Archaeology of Medieval Ireland*, 195–7.

FURTHER READING

Aston, M., Austin, D. and Dyer, C. (eds.), *The Rural Settlements of Medieval England: Studies Dedicated to Maurice Beresford and John Hurst* (Oxford, 1989).

Bailey, M., *A Marginal Economy? East Anglian Breckland in the Later Middle Ages* (Cambridge, 1989).

—— 'Rural Society', in R. Horrox (ed.), *Fifteenth Century Attitudes: Perceptions of Society in Late Medieval England* (Cambridge, 1994).

Bardsley, S., 'Women's Work Reconsidered: Gender and Wage Differentiation in Late Medieval England', *Past and Present*, 165 (1999), 1–29.

Barry, T. B., *The Archaeology of Medieval Ireland* (1987).

—— 'Late Medieval Ireland: The Debate on Social and Economic Transformation, 1350–1550', in B. J. Graham and L. J. Proudfoot, *An Historical Geography of Ireland* (1993).

—— ' "The People of the Country . . . Dwell Scattered": The Pattern of Rural Settlements in Ireland in the Later Middle Ages', in J. Bradley (ed.), *Settlement and Society in Medieval Ireland: Studies Presented to F. X. Martin, OSA* (Kilkenny, 1988).

Bennett, J. M., *Ale, Beer and Brewsters in England* (Oxford, 1996).

—— *A Medieval Life: Cecilia Pennifader of Brigstock, c.1295–1344* (Boston, 1999).

—— *Women in the Medieval English Countryside: Gender and Household in Brigstock before the Plague* (Oxford, 1987).

Beresford, M. W., *The Lost Villages of England* (1954).

—— and Hurst, J. G., *Wharram Percy: Deserted Medieval Village* (1990).

—— (eds.), *Deserted Medieval Villages: Studies* (1971).

Carr, A. D., 'A Debatable Land: Arwystli in the Middle Ages', *Montgomeryshire Collections*, 80 (1992).

—— 'The Medieval Cantref of Rhos', *Transactions of Denbighshire Historical Society*, 41 (1992).

Davenport, F. G., *The Economic Development of a Norfolk Manor, 1086–1565* (Cambridge, 1906).

DeWindt, E. B., *Land and People in Holywell-cum-Needingworth: Structures of Tenure and Patterns of Social Organization in an East Midlands Village, 1252–1457* (Toronto, 1972).

Dodgshon, R. A., *Land and Society in Early Scotland* (Oxford, 1981).

—— 'Medieval Settlement and Colonisation', in M. L. Parry and T. R. Slater (eds.), *The Making of the Scottish Countryside* (1980).

Dyer, C., *Everyday Life in Medieval England* (1994).

—— 'Deserted Medieval Villages in the West Midlands', *Economic History Review*, 2nd ser. 35 (1982), and in id., *Everyday Life* (above).

—— *Lords and Peasants in a Changing Society: The Estates of the Bishopric of Worcester, 680–1540* (Cambridge, 1980).

—— *Standards of Living in the Later Middle Ages: Social Change in England, c.1200–1520* (Cambridge, 1989).

Fox, H. S. A., 'Servants, Cottagers and Tied Cottages during the Later Middle Ages: Towards a Regional Dimension', *Rural History*, 6 (1995).

Fryde, E. B., *Peasants and Landlords in Later Medieval England* (Stroud, 1996).

Glasscock, R. E., 'Moated Sites, and Deserted Boroughs and Villages: Two Neglected Aspects of Anglo-Norman Settlement in Ireland', in N. Stephens and R. E. Glasscock (eds.), *Irish Geographical Studies in Honour of E. Estyn Evans* (Belfast, 1970).

Goldberg, P. J. P., *Women, Work and Life Cycle in a Medieval Economy: Women in York and Yorkshire, c.1300–1520* (Oxford, 1992).

Grant, A., *Independence and Nationhood: Scotland, 1306–1469* (1984).

Hare, J., 'Regional Prosperity in Fifteenth-Century England: Some Evidence from Wessex', in M. Hicks (ed.), *Revolution and Consumption in Late Medieval England* (Woodbridge, 2001).

Hatcher, J., 'England in the Aftermath of the Black Death', *Past and Present*, 144 (1994).

—— *Rural Economy and Society in the Duchy of Cornwall, 1300–1500* (Cambridge, 1970).

—— 'Women's Work Reconsidered: Gender and Wage Differentiation in Late Medieval England', *Past and Present*, 173 (2001), 191–8.

Hilton, R. H., *The English Peasantry in the Later Middle Ages* (Oxford, 1975).

Lomas, R. A., 'The Impact of Border Warfare: The Scots and South Tweedside, c.1290–c.1520', *Scottish Historical Review*, 75 (1996).

—— *North-East England in the Middle Ages* (Edinburgh, 1992).

Mate, M. E., *Daughters, Wives and Widows after the Black Death: Women in Sussex, 1350–1535* (Woodbridge, 1998).

Miller E. (ed.), *The Agrarian History of England and Wales*, iii: 1348–1500 (Cambridge, 1991).

Nicholls, K., *Gaelic and Gaelicised Ireland in the Middle Ages* (Dublin, 1972).

O'Conor, K. D., *The Archaeology of Medieval Rural Settlements in Ireland* (Dublin, 1998).

Owen, D. H., 'The Middle Ages', in id. (ed.), *Settlement and Society in Wales* (Cardiff, 1989).

Penn, S. A. C., and Dyer, C., 'Wages and Earnings in Late Medieval England: Evidence from the Enforcement of the Labour Laws', *Economic History Review*, 2nd ser. 43 (1990).

Pierce, T. J., *Medieval Welsh Society: Selected Essays*, ed. J. B. Smith (Cardiff, 1972).

Poos, L. R., *A Rural Society after the Black Death: Essex 1350–1525* (Cambridge, 1991).

Postles, D., 'Brewing and the Peasant Economy: Some Manors in Late Medieval Devon', *Rural History*, 3 (1992).

Pratt, D., 'Fourteenth-Century Marford and Hoseley: A Maerdref in Transition', *Transactions of Denbighshire Archaeological Society*, 41 (1992).

Schofield, P. R., 'Extranei and the Market for Customary Land on a Westminster Manor in the Fifteenth Century', *Agricultural History Review*, 49 (2001).

—— *Peasant and Community in Medieval England, 1200–1500* (2003).

Simms, K., 'Nomadry in Medieval Ireland', *Peritia*, 5 (1986).

Smith, L. B., 'The Gage and the Land Market in Late Medieval Wales', *Economic History Review*, 2nd ser. 29 (1976).

Smith, R. M. (ed.), *Land, Kinship and Life-Cycle* (Cambridge, 1984).

Swanson, R. N., 'Clergy and Manorial Society in Late Medieval Staffordshire', *Staffordshire Studies*, 5 (1993).

Thomas, W. S. G., 'Lost Villages in South-West Carmarthenshire', *Transactions of the Institute of British Geographers*, 47 (1969).

Whittle, J., *The Development of Agrarian Capitalism: Land and Labour in Norfolk, 1440–1580* (Oxford, 2000).

—— 'Individualism and the Family-Land Bond: A Reassessment of Land Transfer Patterns among the English Peasantry, c.1270–1580', *Past and Present*, 160 (1998).

—— 'Inheritance, Marriage, Widowhood and Remarriage: A Comparative Perspective on Women and Land-Holding in North-East Norfolk, 1440–1580', *Continuity and Change*, 13 (1998).

—— and Yates, M., ' "Pays Réel or Pays Légal"? Contrasting Patterns of Land Tenure and Social Structure in Eastern Norfolk and Western Berkshire, 1450–1600', *Agricultural History Review*, 48 (2000).

Yeoman, P. A., 'Medieval Rural Settlement: The Invisible Centuries', in W. S. Hanson and E. A. Slater (eds.), *Scottish Archaeology: New Perceptions* (Aberdeen, 1991).

....

CHAPTER 19

Arable Husbandry

Of all areas of economic activity, arable husbandry was the one most severely disrupted by declining population during the fourteenth and fifteenth centuries, and the one about which there is least disagreement among historians. Grain production peaked around 1300, but in many areas of Britain the arable acreage contracted after about 1315, as bread consumption declined following a run of disastrous famines in the years 1315–18 and the dire effects of warfare in Scotland, northern England, and Ireland. By this period, too, imports of grain from the Baltic may have had an independent effect on grain prices in eastern England, contributing to the price depression of 1337–44.[1] This however was an effect of limited duration, soon swamped by the impact of the plunge in population and consumption levels that followed the Black Death of 1348–9.

The production of food did not decline directly in line with the fall in the number of consumers, since an easier relationship between population and resources, and higher real incomes, permitted improvements in the quantity and quality of everyday diets. In parts of England, such as Norfolk, where workers had been paid partly in inferior bread made of barley and rye, after the Black Death they received bread made of wheat. An increase in ale consumption, too, attested both by administrative records and by the reprimands of sermon writers, implies that more calories were being taken in this form, and increasingly from barley rather than oats. In spite of these improved possibilities, the total demand for grain declined partly because of the very magnitude of population loss and partly because people replaced grain in their diet with other sorts of food. Improvements in real incomes were expressed in a greater consumption of meat and fish than of cereals, and this change became more pronounced during the century after the Black Death, so that the relative contribution of cereals to total dietary intake declined during the later fourteenth century and even more in the fifteenth. Improvements in living standards also took the form of better clothing and shoes, requiring the supply of wool and hides.[2] This meant that increased real incomes did not benefit arable farming as much as they did pasture farming.

Widespread evidence for lower consumption of grain, despite rising standards of living, is to be found in the contraction of grain milling all over Britain. Not only did the number of mills decline, but the rents of those that survived frequently had to be lowered to secure a tenant.[3] References to ruinous mills are numerous not only in midland England, but around the moorlands of Cornwall.[4] This is imperfect evidence as an index of total cereals production, since in many of its uses grain did not need to be milled—notably if it was used for cattle feed, or for brewing—but it implies a considerable decline in bread making for human consumption. Contraction in milling activity must represent an absolute decline in the demand for grain at any given price level, rather than constraints on supply, given that real incomes had improved so markedly in many parts of Britain between 1350 and 1450.

Declining population and rising real wages affected not only the demand for grain but also the costs of supplying it. Arable farming was particularly exposed to scarcities of labour, since wages were a high proportion of the total costs of cultivation. The larger producers—landlords with demesne and some of the wealthier peasantry—were the most severely affected because of their dependence upon hired labour. Some manorial lords attempted to re-enforce labour services as a way of keeping costs down, but this possibility was chiefly relevant to large estates, and was in any case doomed to failure. In those parts of Britain where the repressive laws of 1349 and 1351 were in force some employers attempted to impose them. In practice, however, wage increases were inexorable, partly because landlords for whom arable farming remained profitable at the higher wage rates, or whose large incomes from rents made them less sensitive to labour costs, were willing to subvert their more vulnerable neighbours, and evade the spirit of the law, in the interests of attracting the labour they wanted.[5]

A severe reduction of demand for grain, accompanied by an increase in the costs of supply, had a predictable outcome. The resulting decline in cereals output was not as severe as the decline in population, but it was nevertheless one of the most striking features of agriculture after 1300. One reasoned modern estimate (inevitably tentative) suggests that the total cultivated area of England declined by about 31 per cent between 1300 and 1380 (from about 6.8 m. acres to 4.7 m.) as against a population decline of at least 44 per cent over these years.[6]

The Area of Cultivation and the Composition of Output

Evidence of a shrinking acreage of arable became increasingly visible as former ploughlands lying under pasture, often distinguished by distinctive ridge-and-furrow undulations of the land.[7] Some English contemporaries viewed this development with misgiving. John Rous, in his *Historia Regum Anglie*, reports that as early as 1459 he had attempted in parliament to persuade the government to take action to stem the tide, but that his bill had got nowhere. By the end of the century, however, the iniquities of landlords who converted arable to pasture were a commonplace of political rhetoric, since they were deemed to be the cause of depopulation that weakened England against her neighbours. In 1490 arable was protected by statute in the interests of the security of the realm, the maintenance of the Church and the sustaining of employment on the land. Further government measures followed in a royal ordinance of 1514–15, following a period of high grain prices, and a statute of 1515, which the government did its best to enforce by sending out commissions of investigation in 1517 and 1518. Throughout the 1520s those concerned with the state of the nation had no doubt that arable husbandry in England had seriously declined, and thought, indeed, that decline was continuing. This legislation may have assisted some groups of villagers to redress genuine grievances against tyrannical landlords, but its drafting was poorly geared even to that purpose, and rested on a misunderstanding. Most of the abandoned arable to be seen was the consequence of depopulation in the countryside, and not its cause.

Although the decline in arable acreages is usually demonstrated from the records of manorial demesnes, such evidence is flawed unless we can be sure that land withdrawn from growing crops for a manorial lord was not taken up and sown with grain by tenant farmers. In some instances this was undoubtedly the case, since smaller farmers could often cultivate land at lower cost than a large estate was able to do. Yet there are numerous instances where a reduction in demesne sowing is not accompanied by an increase in the leasing of demesne lands, and it is plausible to interpret these as evidence for a reduction in arable husbandry. At Bourchier Hall, on the edge of the Essex marshes, the average area sown fell from 253 acres in 1338–42 to 154 acres in 1401–6, and none of the abandoned land was leased to tenants.[8] An extreme example of reduced demesne farming was to be found in the large manor of Writtle (Essex), where the thirteenth-century demesne had contained about 1,290 acres of arable land, of which 860 were cultivated and 430 acres fallowed each year. By 1418 the area regularly cultivated had shrunk to 565 acres, of which 393¼ acres were sown, and there was probably a further decline to about 400 acres under cultivation (about 267 acres sown) by 1440.[9] Evidence of this sort is better for the later fourteenth century than for the fifteenth, since from the late fourteenth century it was increasingly normal for lords to lease their demesne lands; from that point onwards they had no need to record regular details of how much land was under crop.

The best evidence for the contraction of arable farming comes from tithe receipts, which relate to the output of whole parishes rather than just to that of particular estates within them. The great tithes, owned by parish rectors, in theory amounted to a tenth of the grain of lords and tenants alike. Good records relating to changing grain tithe receipts are surprisingly rare, considering the number of parishes in Britain, but where they exist they amply confirm the declining value of such tithes—which created a major problem for the funding of ecclesiastical establishments. Table 19.1 shows one example from the rectory of Feering (Essex), which belonged to Westminster Abbey and has an exceptionally fine set of accounts, though these do not carry far into the fifteenth century. They imply a steep fall in production following the Black Death, a period of recovery up to the 1370s and 1380s, and then a renewed decline at the end of the fourteenth century. Tithes, like demesne lands, could be leased out for cash sums, and in that case we have no exact record of how much grain was in fact received from the parish fields each year. However, on the understanding that the lease was a negotiated commercial deal, we can use what we know about prices to assess the way in which the output of cereals was changing over time. The evidence of tithe receipts from Durham Cathedral Priory, which possessed tithes in twelve large parishes between the rivers Tyne and Tees, shows that between 1350 and 1450 grain output never recovered the level of the 1340s, and that it reached a particularly low point in the mid-fifteenth century (Figure 19.1).[10]

As the Durham evidence suggests, arable was abandoned not only in the more commercialized parts of Britain, but in outlying and more pastoral regions as well. In the marches of Wales at Eardisley (Herefordshire), for example, part of the demesne lay uncultivated and untenanted in 1383.[11] A good deal of the resulting

TABLE 19.1. *Annual average tithe receipts at Feering Rectory, 1331–1403 (bushels)*

Years (number of years averaged in brackets)	Wheat	Rye and maslin	Legumes	Barley	Dredge	Oats
1331–47 (9)	419	6	73	—	—	178
1348–51 (4)	261	5	53	—	—	92
1352–5 (4)	297	12	107	—	—	135
1367–72 (6)	321	—	69	22	—	189
1382 (1)	454	3	235	153	—	174
1393–8 (4)	196	—	75	99	9	122
1399–1403 (5)	132	1	50	60	5	123

Note: Maslin is a mixture of wheat and rye, dredge a mixture of oats and barley.

Source: Westminster Abbey Muniments, 25659–25759; PRO, SC 6/841/6–10.

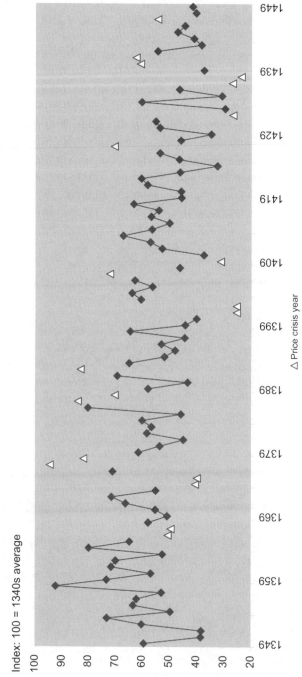

Fig. 19.1. An index of cereals output from Durham Priory parishes between Tyne and Wear, 1350–1450. The estimated output of crops from Durham Priory's numerous parishes shows a brief recovery after the Black Death followed by a contraction attributable largely to declining population in the region. Because the priory sold most of its tithe grain each year, estimates of its volume have to take into account fluctuations in cereal prices from year to year, which affected the value of each year's tithes as negotiated before the harvest. Price crisis years (here defined as the ten years of the highest prices and ten years of lowest prices) have been separated out because of the likelihood that in these years the negotiated value of tithes was less likely to be accurate.

Source: B. Dodds, 'Tithe and Agrarian Activity between the Tyne and Tees, 1350–1450' (unpublished Ph.D. thesis, Durham, 2002), 167.

waste was in situations most inhospitable for arable farming. On the estates of the bishop of Durham, the largest blocks were to be found on the edges of the Pennines. At Wolsingham in Weardale about 1383 the bishop's surveyors listed extensive wasteland, mostly south of the river, that had once paid in all £4 12s. 0d. in rent, including 50 acres called Pawfield, 40 acres called Horbe, 60 acres in a piece on Windy Hill, and 60 acres in another piece called Whitley.[12] It is not at all unlikely, for this reason, that the decline in arable acreages during the course of the fourteenth century was at least as severe in the western and northern parts of Britain and in Ireland as in the better-documented south and east of England. This is a difficult point to establish, for want of sufficiently coherent statistical data. It is impossible to be sure of the long-term significance of patchy evidence, especially when the abandonment of arable is said to have been caused by recent devastation in war. In the townships of the earl of Ormond's Irish manor of Carrick-on-Suir in 1415 large areas are described as waste—234 acres out of 314 at 'Leghwall', all 60 acres of 'Michelleston', all 120 acres at 'Menourston', all 60 acres at Carrick—but at 'Menourston this is attributed to the conflict between the earl and Katherine of Desmond, and at Carrick it is attributed to "the Geraldines" war'.[13] Such devastation was a one-off event as far as these particular places were concerned, but it was a frequent feature of the less settled politics of lands beyond the effect-ively centralized rule of the English and Scottish crowns. In the years 1442–6 royal bailiffs similarly reported reduced grain rents from Arran because the island had been devastated by raiders from Kintyre and Knapdale.[14] As these examples suggest, the costs of cereals production were particularly high in regions of political instability because of the higher risk that crops and buildings would be deliberately destroyed.

Farmers in regions where pasture predominated continued to provide grain for themselves, but even where peace prevailed there were fewer mouths requiring food. It is notorious that Ireland switched into more pastoral forms of life during the fourteenth century.[15] In parts of eastern Ireland acreages under crops were contracting to some extent even before the Black Death, as in northern England, and a growth of pastoralism was a very widespread phenomenon.[16] Evidence of agrarian change in Wales after the Black Death is founded more on rent movements than on details of agrarian production, but there too the widespread dilapidation of grain mills implies a decline in the consumption of grain products.[17] There is some evidence both of the contraction of arable farming on seigniorial demesnes and of the abandonment of tenant holdings.[18] Scottish evidence is even more indirect than that of Ireland and Wales, though the evidence of contraction may be reasonably assumed. It is known that settlement sites high on the Lammermuir Hills were abandoned during the period 1300–1600.[19]

TABLE 19.2. *Arable as a proportion of total land in private ownership*

	*c.*1350	*c.*1500
Warwickshire: Avon Valley	96	57
Warwickshire: Arden	71	34
Gloucestershire	83	46

Source: C. C. Dyer, 'The Occupation of the Land: The West Midlands', in E. Miller (ed.), *The Agrarian History of England and Wales*, iii: *1348–1500* (Cambridge, 1991), 78–9.

The reduction of arable acreages often resulted in a reclassification of land, so that the proportion of arable in estate surveys declined. Some examples of this may be seen in Table 19.2. In Devon and Cornwall the proportion of arable land is estimated to have declined from 66.5 per cent in 1295–1325 to 55.4 per cent in 1497–1509.[20] Such statistics are complicated by the fact that the decision to take land out of cultivation was not always clear-cut. One aspect of husbandry in the age of arable contraction was a more fuzzy distinction between arable and pasture, since some land was occasionally cultivated and then reverted to grass. Land classified as pasture in one estate survey can reappear as low-grade arable land in another, and both categorizations will be equally correct.[21] This explains why the proportion of arable land recorded in land surveys often declined less than might have been expected during the fourteenth and fifteenth centuries.

After a long period of contraction in the fourteenth century, sometimes continuing into the early fifteenth, the contraction of the arable acreage generally eased, though there were periods of depression when cereals husbandry declined even further. Cropping acreages were probably at their lowest in Britain and Ireland in the third quarter of the fifteenth century, but even afterwards there is only spasmodic indication of recovery beyond those fifteenth-century levels.[22] Most of the recorded enclosures or intakes of land from the waste in the period 1470–1530 were for the improvement of livestock husbandry. There is little evidence of expanding crop production in England during these decades. It was just then, in fact, that contemporaries became concerned about the reduction of arable acreages in favour of pasture. They would have had to be very blind to think in these terms had arable husbandry been profitable and expanding. Similar conclusions probably hold for the many pastoral regions. Successive nineteen-year leases of the grain tithes of Dunbarrow (Angus) by Arbroath Abbey suggest little

TABLE 19.3. *Four successive leases of the tithes of Dunbarrow (Angus)*

	Length of lease	Oatmeal	Barley
1 May 1483	19 years	2 chalders	8 bolls
11 May 1500	19 years	2 chalders 4 bolls	8 bolls
7 April 1510	19 years	2 chalders 4 bolls	8 bolls
10 January 1526	19 years	2 chalders 4 bolls	8 bolls

Note: 1 chalder = 16 bolls.

Source: *Liber S. Thome de Aberbrothoc*, ed. C. Innes and P. Chalmers, 2 parts, Bannatyne Club, 86 (1845–6), part 2, nos. 219, 405, 496, 612, pp. 192–3, 327–8, 393–4, 451–2.

sustained increase in output from the 1470s to the 1520s (Table 19.3). The money rents of some grain tithes (known in Scotland as garbal teinds) doubled during the course of the period,[23] but this can largely be explained by increases in the price of barley by 116 per cent and of oats by 66 per cent between the 1460s and the 1520s.[24]

Productivity

Having examined changes in the total arable acreage and in its value, it is opportune to turn to examining some of the accompanying changes in agricultural objectives, methods, and productivity.

As the demand for cereals declined during the fourteenth century, so did the pressures that had earlier made for long-distance trade in cereals and regional specialization. Farming became more mixed in type, with the surrender of arable land to pasture, and those regions of Britain that had been drawn into providing grain for distant markets were likely to depend more upon local demand. The range of different farming types narrowed.[25] As the character of farming became more mixed, so did the ratio of animals to arable acres, and the potential manure supply. In order to make any assessment of this change it is necessary to convert livestock figures into standard 'livestock units' according to the estimated value of their manure: horses are 1 unit each, bulls, oxen, and cows are 1.2 each, young cattle are 0.8, sheep and pigs are 0.1. On this foundation the evidence of manorial accounts can be used to assess the changing average number of livestock units per acre of demesne land over time, and these results are shown in overlapping fifty-year periods in Table 19.4. This evidence suggests that the potential amount of manure per acre increased by 64 per cent between the start of the fourteenth century and the middle of the fifteenth.

TABLE 19.4. *Livestock units per 100 cereal acres on English demesnes, 1300–1449*

	Units
1300–1349	47.9
1325–1374	55.8
1350–1399	62.8
1375–1424	69.9
1400–1449	78.6

Source: B. M. S. Campbell, 'Land, Labour, Livestock, and Productivity Trends in English Seignorial Agriculture, 1208–1450', in id. and M. Overton (eds.), *Land, Labour and Livestock: Historical Studies in European Agricultural Productivity* (Manchester, 1991), 153.

Not only did the potential amount of manure per acre increase after 1349, but also, as a result of increasing disposable incomes and the consequent changing patterns of demand, the balance of cropping changed away from cereals regarded as inferior. This was the result of regional rather than universal shifts, since the cropping of many regions was heavily circumscribed by what climate, terrain, and market conditions would permit. The arable husbandry of upland Wales and most of Scotland and Ireland remained dependent upon oats and barley.[26] Some rents and entry fines from the western Scottish isles of Arran and Bute were paid in barley or oats, but no other grain, throughout the fifteenth century.[27] The teinds (tithes) received between 1508 and 1512 by the bishop of Dunkeld at Dunkeld itself and at Clunie were all in barley and oats, though there were small amounts of wheat from his parishes elsewhere—at Perth, and at Cramond and Aberlady in the Lothians. But the volume of barley and wheat nowhere approached that of oats.[28] However, in much of England, and perhaps in Scotland and Wales, farmers were able to improve the average value of each acre under crops by shifting away from rye, oats, and mixed crops into higher proportions of more valuable crops. Table 19.5 shows this change as it can be assessed from a large body of evidence from Norfolk demesnes. The largest single change was an increase in the share of barley, which was a principal Norfolk crop. The growth of average ale consumption, and the preference for ale made with barley malt rather than oats malt, encouraged barley growing even to the point that on some demesnes the cultivation of barley increased absolutely. The other main change in land use was the retreat of rye and inferior bread grain, as a higher proportion of the population was

TABLE 19.5. *Cropping proportions in Norfolk*

	% of sown acreage	
	1250–1349	1350–1449
Wheat	16.3	15.2
Rye	11.3	6.0
Maslin (wheat + rye)	0.8	0.8
Barley	41.5	48.9
Oats	16.1	15.2
Dredge (barley + oats)	0.5	0.9
Peas and beans	13.5	13.2
Total	100.0	(100.0)

Source: B. M. S. Campbell and M. Overton, 'A New Perspective on Medieval and Early Modern Agriculture: Six Centuries of Norfolk Farming, c.1250–c.1850', *Past and Present*, 141 (1993), 54.

able to eat wheaten bread.[29] Both of these changes are recorded in parts of England other than Norfolk, though the leasing of demesne lands, and consequent disappearance of cropping details from manorial accounts, makes it increasingly difficult to establish information about cropping proportions the further one goes beyond the 1360s.

The striking regional differences in manuring practices and crop rotations that had been developed before 1300 were generally retained. Eastern Norfolk remained a region of intensive rotations, and eastern Essex one of less intensive ones.[30] Not surprisingly, though, methods of farming adapted in detail to the changed economic circumstances of the fourteenth and fifteenth centuries in different ways under different local pressures. In parts of the midlands, such as south-eastern Worcestershire, it was quite common for a two-field organization of arable husbandry to be converted into a four-field system.[31] It is difficult to interpret this as an intensification of cereals production, given what we know of the movement of output, so presumably it was designed rather to rationalize the relationship between arable and pasture either in response to changes in the size of the sown area or in response to changes in the composition of cropping. One common development was greater flexibility in the use of land, particularly in regions of heavy soils. We have already observed that the distinction between arable and pasture became more arbitrary after the mid-fourteenth century. This implies that pressure could be taken off current arable by ploughing up pastures from time to time. Some estates developed a more shifting system of cultivation in which the idea of an arable core was whittled away, or even disappeared, as decisions where to plough were taken year by year with little reference to any fixed scheme.[32] This development has been reported from contexts as diverse as the Essex marshes, the estates of the bishopric of Worcester in the west midlands, and the estates of Battle Abbey in Sussex.[33] It is also on record in Scotland in 1463 on the estates of Coupar Angus Abbey, which records a nine-year cycle of arable and pasture, with very favourable implications for crop yields.[34] Elsewhere, even in the English midlands, the adaptation to greater reserves of land took the form of an infield–outfield system, in which particular tracts of land were cultivated only occasionally.[35] This practice had been widespread in Devon and Cornwall even before 1300, and there are numerous instances later on. The usual method there, later called 'denshering' or 'devonshiring', was to burn off the turf that had grown over uncultivated land in preparation for cultivating it anew.[36]

Some such adjustment to greater reserves of unused arable may explain why in Scotland the cultivation of outfields begins to occur in records of this period. Infield–outfield husbandry there, as it developed from the fifteenth century, operated a twofold system in which intensive cropping rotations of oats and barley were concentrated on the infields, while a shifting cultivation of oats, interspersed with indefinitely long periods under grass, was practised on the outfields. The distinction between infield and outfield is not recorded before the late fifteenth century. The first reference to infield is from Arbroath in the 1470s. A deed of 1483 refers to the 'owtfeld' of the kirktown of Kirriemuir (Forfar).[37] Whatever the later justifications for this system, it seems impossible that it came into being as a result of the intensification of land use, if indeed its origins date from the fifteenth century, and the analogies with developments in England are probably more than coincidental.

The overall implications of change for methods of cultivation and for the productivity of arable farming can be assessed only with some difficulty. On the one hand the abandonment of less advantageous soils might have had a beneficial effect, since for each cultivated acre, on average, it would simultaneously raise the fertility of the soil and reduce the required labour inputs. The improved livestock ratios in parts of Britain that had previously been deficient in manure supplies might have worked in the same direction, since it meant that a declining arable acreage was benefiting from an expanding supply of manure. For both these reasons the productivity of arable farming might have been expected to improve. On the other hand, these advantages were offset by other considerations. Special reasons for dereliction and loss were apparent even before the Black Death in some localities. Coastal regions subject to inundation, already experiencing severe difficulties in the early fourteenth century,[38] were more under threat as the administrative and labour costs of maintaining drains and banks rose after 1349.[39] In regions subject to local warfare, the high cost of repairs made it less likely that they would be made. Even where these particular problems were absent, however, the higher cost of labour throughout the economy was bound to have long-term effects on how the land was cultivated.

Managers of manorial demesnes faced the particular difficulty of rising labour costs, which put pressure on profits and encouraged sacrifices of technological efficiency in the interests of economic efficiency. The final abandonment of labour services in the late fourteenth and fifteenth centuries probably had a beneficial effect on labour productivity,[40] but an adverse effect on the productivity of the soil. The high-wage regime encouraged landlords to concentrate their labour where it was most effective, which necessarily implied that many subordinate work routines were abandoned. As lords and estate officials struggled to cut the costs of arable farming, especially after 1375, they reduced the number of people they employed to the point that former tasks were neglected. Fallow ploughing in the spring and summer, which was known to benefit productivity when the fallows came to be cultivated, might be skimped or omitted altogether. Land was less frequently manured where this depended on heavy labour inputs, so reducing the advantage of larger flock ratios. At Lighthorne (Warwickshire) in the 1390s the full-time farm servants were required to take on weeding that had previously been the work of casual employees.[41] The same considerations led to a neglect of farm structures such as buildings and ditches, and so to a higher risk of damage or loss to crops.[42] Even economic efficiency was threatened by managerial problems. The increased difficulty of profit making, and more conflictual relations with employees and tenants, made it harder to recruit estate officers. Problems of this kind contributed to the decision of landlords to lease their demesnes, as they increasingly did from the later fourteenth century onwards. On the manor of Wisbech Barton there were twelve different reeves in the last twenty years of direct demesne farming between 1411 and 1430.[43] Even if the reeves had all been of high competence, such discontinuity would have undermined best practice in demesne management.

Although tenant farmers were not all constrained by the effects of having to pay higher wages, and not at all by the need to hire managers, the productivity of their farming is nevertheless likely to have been affected by changing circumstances. During the thirteenth century high productivity in peasant crop production was encouraged by the desire to feed large numbers of people from small farms. Even if output per head declined as more labour was put into tilling, sowing, weeding, and harvesting peasant holdings, it would often have been worth the while of larger families to increase the intensity of their methods of cultivation in order to grow more food. If that is a reasonable line of argument for the period of rising population, then the corollary is reasonable too; as family sizes shrank, and pressure on the land relaxed, families could provide their subsistence needs by less intensive techniques. Their enthusiasm for slogging on their own land would be tempered by the availability of employment at high wage rates elsewhere. So even if we assume that an hour's work on a peasant's own land was performed with better motivation and higher efficacy than an hour's hired work on a manorial demesne, it is likely that fewer hours per acre were worked. In the absence of peasant accounts there is little possibility of testing these suppositions. However, since the amount of leisure families enjoyed in the early sixteenth century was strongly related to their status and wealth, it is very doubtful whether the large and prosperous peasant families of the fifteenth and early sixteenth centuries were toiling as assiduously as their less affluent predecessors.[44] To the extent that they employed servants to work for them, the adverse effects of high wages upon the productivity of land would have been much the same as for manorial lords.

For these various reasons the productivity of land, insofar as it can be measured from the evidence of manorial accounts, showed none of the improvements that might have been predicted from the evidence of shrinking arable and expanding pasture. Yields per acre of land sown were lower in the fifteenth century than they had been at the peak of arable farming in the later thirteenth. This can be demonstrated even in Norfolk, whose agriculture remained one of the most advanced of the period (Table 19.6). A combined index of Norfolk crop yields per acre, weighted to take account of the price and acreage of each crop, implies a decline by 24 per cent between 1325–49 and 1425–49.[45] Of course, this decline, accompanied as it was by improving output per head and higher standards of nutrition, does not represent collective economic failure. Rather it illustrates one of the most important discoveries relating to agricultural practice between the thirteenth century and the sixteenth; farm managers were guided in their choice of techniques by considerations of profitability and family welfare, and not by the

TABLE 19.6. *Gross crop yields in Norfolk, 1325–1449 (bushels per acre)*

	Wheat	Rye	Barley	Oats
1325–49	15.6	10.5	17.2	15.0
1350–74	11.4	8.9	15.3	11.9
1375–99	12.9	10.1	17.3	14.0
1400–24	12.7	9.9	14.9	13.9
1425–49	10.7	12.0	15.4	14.5

Source: B. M. S. Campbell and M. Overton, 'A New Perspective on Medieval and Early Modern Agriculture: Six Centuries of Norfolk Farming, c.1250–c.1850', *Past and Present*, 141 (1993), 70.

most obvious technical measures such as output per acre or output per seed sown. They did not employ the most intensive techniques available when these would have involved unjustifiable expenditure and consequently less lower overall rewards.

Specialization and the Market

The development of large units of grain production during the late twelfth and thirteenth century had been encouraged by the growth of demand, and especially demand from the larger towns. Not only had individual demesnes often grown larger, but there had been better coordination of production across the demesnes of the larger estates. The higher costs of administering such enterprises, of local bailiffs, estate stewards, and auditors, had been justified by the high profitability of agriculture through a period of rising prices and cheap labour. The reduction of the pressure of demand for bread grain in the fourteenth and fifteenth centuries, accompanied by rising costs of labour and transport, reduced the profitability of large-scale grain production to the point that these administrative costs were no longer worth paying, and lords reverted to the leasing of their demesnes either as a whole or piecemeal. The course of change was not as predictable as this summary might suggest, though, since not all branches of the grain trade, and not all regions of Britain, were affected in the same way at the same time. Abstract analysis of the course of development needs to be closely monitored by such evidence as we are able to supply. Nevertheless, the leasing of demesnes was ultimately so widespread that it represented a major transformation of the locus of commercial decision making.

In some contexts even after the leasing of demesnes, which became almost universal between 1390 and 1450, estate officers retained a responsibility for marketing produce. This was particularly the case where grain producers were a long way from their potential customers. In these cases landlords sometimes assumed the role of middlemen, collecting part of their rents in grain and organizing their marketing at a distance. In this way the payment of rents in kind could be part and parcel of a commercialized economy. Many parts of Scotland were managed in this way in the fifteenth century, as in the eighteenth. The rents from the islands of Bute and Arran to the Scottish crown in 1496–7 comprised in all £203 16s. 9d. Scots in money, 51½ beef cattle (marts), 14 chalders, 7½ bolls of barley, and 1½ chalders of oatmeal. Cattle and grain here represent about 31 per cent of the total value of these rents.[46] In Gaelic Ireland, as in the past, some rents were similarly in grain. In the sixteenth century, and presumably earlier, it was normal for even quite substantial tenants to hold their land by a share-cropping scheme, by which they supplied the seed and ploughing apparatus but paid a quarter of the crop in rent.[47]

The collection of cereal rents for sale by landlords was by no means confined to relatively isolated parts of Britain. It was very common in Norfolk for landlords to levy rents in barley and to market them in bulk. In Brancaster and Deepdale after the Black Death the abbot of Ramsey adopted the policy of leasing for barley rents lands left vacant 'through the death of tenants'. He received a far greater value in grain for these tenements than he had previously received in cash. The barley received in this way rose from 25 quarters in 1352 to 68 quarters 3 bushels in 1369, when it accounted for about two-thirds of the total rent income by value. This grain was sold; the account of 1367–8 records 67 quarters of barley sold 'from the lease of vacant tenements'.[48] The Paston family, famous for their letters, depended on barley rents between the 1440s and the 1470s, usually selling the grain through merchants, though when they could not find a buyer locally they had to engage in active searches to find one.[49]

Most major landlords, including many in Norfolk, avoided such commercial responsibility by leasing their estates as a whole wherever possible, accepting rents in kind only when they needed them as a source of household supply. If seigniorial commercial enterprise did not disappear from many parts of Britain during the fifteenth century, that was largely the result of the continuing activity of relatively minor landlords. Even in the thirteenth century numerous smaller landlords of knightly or sub-knightly status had managed properties large enough to place them above the ranks of the ordinary villager. Many of them had the status of manorial lords, even if they had few tenants. Because rents were generally a minor part of their income, their money income depended heavily on being able to sell the produce of their estates.[50] Many such enterprises continued to be maintained through the fourteenth and fifteenth centuries. Some minor landlords, indeed, were willing to expand their activities by leasing demesne land from the large ecclesiastical and lay estates. About a third of all lessees of the archbishop of Canterbury's demesnes between 1502 and 1532 were gentlemen, and others were London merchants.[51] There were also enterprising farmers below the ranks of the gentry who nevertheless stood way above the ranks of peasant producers, like Roger Heritage of Burton Dassett (Warwickshire), who died in 1495. He derived most of his income from livestock, but nevertheless cultivated about 100 acres of arable each year and sold crops to the value of over £8.[52]

Even before the later fourteenth century, when English demesne farming was in full swing and peasant holdings rarely exceeded 40 acres, peasant enterprise had accounted for perhaps half of all the grain marketed. That share increased after 1349, and more spectacularly from the 1390s, as a result of the takeover of demesne leases by peasant tenants. For a century after the bishop of Winchester leased his demesne lands at Crawley (Hampshire) the tenants were 'reeves and bondmen'; gentlemen became involved only in the course of the sixteenth century.[53] This was a general pattern on Worcester bishopric estates, where peasant lessees predominated until the late fifteenth century to be replaced by lessees of higher social status from then on.[54] Elsewhere the movement of land into peasant hands was more difficult to reverse. At the earl of Norfolk's manor of Forncett (Norfolk), the arable was leased as a whole in 1373, but was subsequently split up. Leases there grew longer in the course of the fifteenth century, and by 1500 parcels of former demesne were being granted in perpetuity as heritable holdings.[55] Sometimes demesnes were leased to all the villagers, as at Sutton (Lincolnshire), where in 1367, at an assembly in the parish church, 1,000 acres of land with fisheries attached was leased 'to the whole homage . . . to divide among themselves according to the power and state of each of them' for the sum of £162 4s. 6d. This arrangement lasted over a hundred years, though the rent had been reduced by 21 per cent by 1422.[56] There seems to be no way of assessing the proportion of the land in the occupation of peasant producers in the fifteenth century, but it was well over two-thirds. In 1279 in the midland counties of England about 32 per cent of the land was in manorial demesnes and 68 per cent in the hands of villeins and free tenants.[57] After the leasing of the demesnes the proportion of the land in the hands of villeins and free tenants will have risen significantly above 68 per cent, since the evidence of small tenants in occupation of demesne land is more extensive than that of manorial lords taking over peasant holdings. Though the fifteenth century was the golden age of peasant enterprise, there is no need to visualize these peasant farmers as normally ruthless operators, even if some of them were. Peasant entrepreneurship was in fact least dynamic in predominantly arable areas, since profit opportunities there were rarely sufficient to shake producers out of a preference for greater leisure rather than acquisitiveness as a badge of status. They characteristically worked to achieve an income level appropriate to their status.[58] Nevertheless the shift in grain supply towards the wealthier peasantry, especially those farming tenements of between 20 and 100 acres, contrasts with the direction of change in the thirteenth century.

The implications of these changes for the proportion of total arable output that was marketed are inevitably obscure. Taking Britain as a whole, there seems little case for arguing that commercialization in this sector of the economy had made any very significant advance. Townsmen may have constituted a larger proportion of the population in much of England, but the difference cannot have been great. Some historians suppose the level of urbanization remained static across the fourteenth and fifteenth centuries. Because of the decline in the size of urban populations during the fourteenth century, however, the grain trade was a less attractive area for mercantile enterprise than it had been. The London bladers were never again as socially prominent as they had been in the early fourteenth century.[59] Meanwhile the proportion of food buyers in the countryside is likely to have declined with the reduction in the number of cottagers and wage dependants.

There is therefore no good reason for associating the growth of peasant enterprise in cereals production either with a new spirit of enterprise or with any increased orientation of arable husbandry to the market.

NOTES

1. N. Hybel, 'The Grain Trade in Northern Europe before 1350', *Economic History Review*, 55 (2002), 244–5.

2. C. Dyer, *Standards of Living in the Later Middle Ages: Social Change in England, c.1200–1520* (Cambridge, 1989), 158–60, 176–7.

3. R. Holt, *The Mills of Medieval England* (Oxford, 1988), 159–70.

4. H. S. A. Fox, 'The Occupation of the Land: Devon and Cornwall', in H. E. Hallam (ed.), *The Agrarian History of England and Wales*, ii: *1042–1350* (Cambridge, 1988), 161.

5. J. Hatcher, 'England in the Aftermath of the Black Death', *Past and Present*, 144 (1994), 21–4.

6. M. Overton and B. M. S. Campbell, 'Production et productivité dans l'agriculture anglaise, 1086–1871', *Histoire et mesure*, 11 (1996), 290.

7. e.g. C. Howell, *Land, Family and Inheritance in Transition: Kibworth Harcourt, 1280–1700* (Cambridge, 1983), 54.

8. R. H. Britnell, 'Agricultural Technology and the Margin of Cultivation in the Fourteenth Century', *Economic History Review*, 2nd ser. 30 (1977), 62–3.

9. K. C. Newton, *The Manor of Writtle* (Chichester, 1970), 69, 74–7.

10. B. Dodds, 'Tithe and Agrarian Output between the Tyne and the Tees, 1350–1450' (unpublished Ph.D. thesis, University of Durham, 2002), 168–212.

11. W. Rees, *South Wales and the March: A Social and Agrarian Study* (1924), 255–6.

12. *Bishop Hatfield's Survey*, ed. W. Greenwell, Surtees Society, 32 (1857), 67.

13. *The Red Book of Ormond*, ed. N. B. White (Dublin, 1932), 120–2.

14. *The Exchequer Rolls of Scotland*, ed. J. Stuart, G. Burnett, and others, 23 vols. (Edinburgh, 1878–1908), v. 167, 253.

15. K. Simms, 'Nomadry in Medieval Ireland', *Peritia*, 5 (1986), 379–91.

16. Above (Ch. 15).

17. A. D. Carr, *Medieval Anglesey* (Llangefni, 1982), 326–8.

18. D. H. Owen, 'The Occupation of the Land: Wales and the Marches', in Miller (ed.), *Agrarian History*, iii. 102–5.

19. A. Grant, *Independence and Nationhood, 1306–1469* (1984), 78; M. L. Parry, 'Secular Climate Change and Marginal Agriculture', *Transactions of the Institute of British Geographers*, 64 (1975), 1–14.

20. H. S. A. Fox, 'The Occupation of the Land: Devon and Cornwall', in Miller (ed.), *Agrarian History*, iii. 153.

21. R. H. Britnell, 'The Occupation of the Land: Eastern England', in Miller (ed.), *Agrarian History*, iii. 57–8.

22. R. H. Britnell, 'The English Economy and the Government, 1450–1550', in J. L. Watts (ed.), *The End of the Middle Ages? England in the Fifteenth and Sixteenth Centuries* (Stroud, 1998), 100.

23. *Liber S. Thome de Aberbrothoc*, ed. C. Innes and P. Chalmers, 2 parts, Bannatyne Club, 86 (1845–6), ii, nos. 187, 247, 613, 707, pp. 167, 213–14, 452, 487 (Inverness); nos. 218, 428, 443, 605, 711, pp. 192, 341–2, 352–3, 449, 488–9 (Banchory-Ternan); nos. 239, 377, 459, 587, 729, pp. 208, 306, 369, 443, 493–4 ('Garwock'); nos. 246, 519, 655, pp. 213, 408–9, 467 ('Abbirkerdor').

24. E. Gemmill and N. Mayhew, *Changing Values in Medieval Scotland: A Study of Prices, Money, and Weights and Measures* (Cambridge, 1995), 162, 189.

25. B. M. S. Campbell, 'Matching Supply to Demand: Crop Production and Disposal by English Demesnes in the Century of the Black Death', *Journal of Economic History*, 57 (1997), 827–58; B. M. S. Campbell, K. C. Bartley, and J. P. Power, 'Demesne-Farming Systems of Post-Black Death England: A Classification', *Agricultural History Review*, 44 (1996), 131–79.

26. K. W. Nicholls, 'Anglo-French Ireland and After', *Peritia*, 1 (1982), 398; G. Williams, *Recovery, Reorientation and Reformation: Wales, c.1415–1642* (Oxford, 1987), 62–3.

27. *Exchequer Rolls of Scotland*, ed. Stuart and others, v. 162–9; xi. 4–7.

28. *Rentale Dunkeldense*, ed. R. K. Hannay (Edinburgh, 1915), 75–264.

29. B. M. S. Campbell, *English Seigniorial Agriculture, 1250–1450* (Cambridge, 2000), 243–5.

30. R. H. Britnell, 'Farming Practice and Techniques: Eastern England', in Miller (ed.), *Agrarian History*, iii. 195–6, 200–3.

31. B. K. Roberts, 'Field Systems of the West Midlands', in A. R. H. Baker and R. A. Butlin (eds.), *Studies of Field Systems in the British Isles* (Cambridge, 1973), 200.

32. Britnell, 'Farming Practice', 196.

33. P. F. Brandon, 'Demesne Arable Farming in Coastal Sussex during the Later Middle Ages', *Agricultural History Review*, 19 (1971), 113–34; Britnell, 'Agricultural Technology', 53–66; C. Dyer, *Lords and Peasants in a Changing Society: The Estates of the Bishopric of Worcester, 680–1540* (Cambridge, 1980), 125; E. Searle, *Lordship and Community: Battle Abbey and its Banlieu, 1066–1538* (Toronto, 1974), 272–86.

34. S. G. E. Lythe, 'Economic Life', in J. M. Brown (ed.), *Scottish Society in the Fifteenth Century* (1977), 68.

35. E. King, 'The Occupation of the Land: The East Midlands', in Miller (ed.), *Agrarian History*, iii. 75.

36. H. S. A. Fox, 'Farming Practice and Techniques: Devon and Cornwall', in Miller (ed.), *Agrarian History*, iii. 309–10.

37. R. A. Dodgshon, *Land and Society in Early Scotland* (Oxford, 1981), 191.

38. M. Bailey, '*Per Impetum Maris*: Natural Disaster and Economic Decline in Eastern England, 1275–1350', in B. M. S. Campbell (ed.), *Before the Black Death: Studies in the 'Crisis' of the Early Fourteenth Century* (Manchester, 1991), 184–208.

39. P. F. Brandon, 'Agriculture and the Effects of Floods and Weather at Barnhorne, Sussex, during the Late Middle Ages', *Sussex Archaeological Collections*, 109 (1971), 78–93; H. C. Darby, *The Medieval Fenland* (Cambridge, 1940), 55–60, 147–68.

40. D. Stone, 'The Productivity of Hired and Customary Labour: Evidence from Wisbech Barton in the Fourteenth Century', *Economic History Review*, 50 (1997), 640–56.

41. C. Dyer, 'Farming Practice and Techniques: The West Midlands', in Miller (ed.), *Agrarian History*, iii. 231; Dyer, *Lords and Peasants*, 126–7.

42. D. V. Stern, *A Hertfordshire Demesne of Westminster Abbey: Profits, Productivity and Weather*, ed. C. Thornton (Hatfield, 1999), 142.

43. D. Stone, 'The Management of Resources on the Demesne Farm of Wisbech Barton, 1314–1430' (unpublished Ph.D. thesis, University of Cambridge, 1998), 203–4.

44. I. Blanchard, 'Social Structure and Social Organization in an English Village at the Close of the Middle Ages: Chewton 1526', in E. B. DeWindt, *The Salt of Common Life: Individuality and Choice in the Medieval Town, Countryside and Church. Essays Presented to J. Ambrose Raftis* (Kalamazoo, 1995), 324.

45. B. M. S. Campbell and M. Overton, 'A New Perspective on Medieval and Early Modern Agriculture: Six Centuries of Norfolk Farming, c.1250–c.1850', *Past and Present*, 141 (1993), 70.

46. *Exchequer Rolls of Scotland*, ed. Stuart and others, xi. 4–7. A chaldron was 16 bolls. Measures and prices here are taken from Gemmill and Mayhew, *Changing Values*, 170, 208, 241, 388–90.

47. K. Nicholls, *Gaelic and Gaelicised Ireland in the Middle Ages* (Dublin, 1972), 116.

48. The National Archives, Public Record Office, SC 6/931/5–10.

49. R. H. Britnell, 'The Pastons and their Norfolk', *Agricultural History Review*, 36 (1988), 134–9.

50. R. H. Britnell, 'Minor Landlords in England and Medieval Agrarian Capitalism', *Past and Present*, 89 (1980), 3–22.

51. F. R. H. Du Boulay, 'Who Were Farming the English Demesnes at the End of the Middle Ages?', *Economic History Review*, 2nd ser. 17 (1965), 450.

52. C. Dyer, 'Were there any Capitalists in Fifteenth-Century England', in J. Kermode (ed.), *Enterprise and Individuals in Fifteenth-Century England* (Stroud, 1991), 10–16.

53. N. S. B. Gras and E. C. Gras, *The Economic and Social History of an English Village (Crawley, Hampshire), A.D. 909–1928* (Cambridge, Mass., 1930), 99.

54. Dyer, *Lords and Peasants*, 211.

55. F. G. Davenport, *The Economic Development of a Norfolk Manor, 1086–1565* (Cambridge, 1906), 57.

56. W. O. Massingberd, 'Social and Economic History', in *Victoria County History of Lincolnshire*, ii (1906), 317.

57. E. A. Kosminsky, *Studies in the Agrarian History of England in the Thirteenth Century*, ed. R. H. Hilton, trans. R. Kisch (Oxford, 1956), 90–1.

58. Blanchard, 'Social Structure', 322–4; C. Dyer, *Warwickshire Farming, 1349–c.1520: Preparations for Agricultural Revolution* (Oxford, 1981), 32–4.

59. G. A. Williams, *Medieval London: From Commune to Capital*, 2nd edn. (1970), 163.

FURTHER READING

Bailey, M., *A Marginal Economy? East Anglian Breckland in the Later Middle Ages* (Cambridge, 1989).

Baker, A. R. H., and Butlin, R. A. (eds.), *Studies of Field Systems in the British Isles* (Cambridge, 1973).

Brandon, P. F., 'Agriculture and the Effects of Floods and Weather at Barnhorne, Sussex, during the Late Middle Ages', *Sussex Archaeological Collections*, 109 (1971), 69–93.

—— 'Cereal Yields on the Sussex Estates of Battle Abbey during the Later Middle Ages', *Economic History Review*, 2nd ser. 25 (1972).

—— 'Demesne Arable Farming in Coastal Sussex during the Later Middle Ages', *Agricultural History Review*, 19 (1971).

Britnell, R. H., 'Agricultural Technology and the Margin of Cultivation in the Fourteenth Century', *Economic History Review*, 2nd ser. 30 (1977).

—— *Growth and Decline in Colchester, 1300–1525* (Cambridge, 1986).

—— 'Minor Landlords in England and Medieval Agrarian Capitalism', *Past and Present*, 89 (1980).

—— 'The Pastons and their Norfolk', *Agricultural History Review*, 36 (1988).

—— 'Production for the Market on a Small Fourteenth-Century Estate', *Economic History Review*, 2nd ser. 19 (1966).

Campbell, B. M. S., *English Seigniorial Agriculture, 1250–1450* (Cambridge, 2000).

—— 'Land, Labour, Livestock, and Productivity Trends in English Seigniorial Agriculture, 1208–1450', in id. and Mark Overton (eds.), *Land, Labour and Livestock: Historical Studies in European Agricultural Productivity* (Manchester, 1991).

—— 'Matching Supply to Demand: Crop Production and Disposal by English Demesnes in the Century of the Black Death', *Journal of Economic History*, 57 (1997).

—— and Overton, M., 'A New Perspective on Medieval and Early Modern Agriculture: Six Centuries of Norfolk Farming, c.1250–c.1850', *Past and Present*, 141 (1993).

Dodgshon, R. A., *Land and Society in Early Scotland* (Oxford, 1981).

Du Boulay, F. R. H., 'Who Were Farming the English Demesnes at the End of the Middle Ages?', *Economic History Review*, 2nd ser. 17 (1965).

Dyer, C., 'Changes in Diet in the Late Middle Ages: The Case of Harvest Workers', *Agricultural History Review*, 36 (1988), repr. in id., *Everyday Life in Medieval England* (1994).

—— *Lords and Peasants in a Changing Society: The Estates of the Bishopric of Worcester 680–1540* (Cambridge, 1980).

—— *Warwickshire Farming, 1349–c.1520: Preparations for Agricultural Revolution* (Oxford, 1981).

Farmer, D. L., 'Crop Yields, Prices, and Wages in Medieval England,' *Studies in Medieval and Renaissance History*, new ser. 6 (1983).

—— 'Grain Yields on Westminster Abbey Manors, 1271–1410', *Canadian Journal of History*, 17 (1983).

—— 'Grain Yields on Winchester Manors in the Later Middle Ages', *Economic History Review*, 2nd ser. 30 (1977).

Finberg, H. P. R., *Tavistock Abbey: A Study in the Social and Economic History of Devon* (Cambridge, 1951).

Galloway, J. A., 'Driven by Drink? Ale Consumption and the Agrarian Economy of the London Region, c.1300–1400', in M. Carlin and J. T. Rosenthal (eds.), *Food and Eating in Medieval Europe* (1998).

Gemmill, E., and Mayhew, N., *Changing Values in Medieval Scotland: A Study of Prices, Money, and Weights and Measures* (Cambridge, 1995).

Grant, A., *Independence and Nationhood, 1306–1469* (1984).

Hatcher, J., *Rural Economy and Society in the Duchy of Cornwall, 1300–1500* (Cambridge, 1970).

Holt, R., *The Mills of Medieval England* (Oxford, 1988).

Hybel, N., 'The Grain Trade in Northern Europe before 1350', *Economic History Review*, 55 (2002).

Miller, E. (ed.)., *The Agrarian History of England and Wales*, iii: *1348–1500* (Cambridge, 1991).

Parry, M. L., 'Secular Climate Change and Marginal Agriculture', *Transactions of the Institute of British Geographers*, 64 (1975).

Raftis, J. A., *The Estates of Ramsey Abbey: A Study in Economic Growth and Organization* (Toronto, 1957).

Searle, E., *Lordship and Community: Battle Abbey and its Banlieu, 1066–1538* (Toronto, 1974).

Stern, D. V., *A Hertfordshire Demesne of Westminster Abbey: Profits, Productivity and Weather*, ed. C. Thornton (Hatfield, 1999).

Stone, D., 'Medieval Farm Management and Technological Mentalities: Hinderclay before the Black Death', *Economic History Review*, 54 (2001).

—— 'The Productivity of Hired and Customary Labour: Evidence from Wisbech Barton in the Fourteenth Century', *Economic History Review*, 50 (1997).

Thirsk, J. (ed.), *The Agrarian History of England and Wales*, iv: *1500–1640* (Cambridge, 1967).

Thornton, C., 'The Determinants of Land Productivity on the Bishop of Winchester's Demesne of Rimpton, 1208–1403', in B. M. S. Campbell and M. Overton (eds.), *Land, Labour and Livestock: Historical Studies in European Agricultural Productivity* (Manchester, 1991).

—— 'The Level of Arable Productivity on the Bishop of Winchester's Manor of Taunton, 1283–1348', in R. H. Britnell (ed.), *The Winchester Pipe Rolls and Medieval English Society* (Woodbridge, 2003).

Titow, J., 'Le Climat à travers les rôles de compatibilité de l'échêché de Winchester (1350–1450)', *Annales, économies, sociétés, civilisations*, 25 (1970).

—— 'Lost Rents, Vacant Holdings and the Contraction of Peasant Cultivation after the Black Death', *Agricultural History Review*, 42 (1994).

CHAPTER 20

Pastoral Husbandry

One of the main consequences of declining population for agriculture during the fourteenth and fifteenth centuries was a shift towards pastoral activity. Until the later thirteenth, although livestock husbandry had expanded, the most visible changes in the landscape in many parts of Britain had been the ploughing up of grass and heath, and the felling of woodlands to grow more crops. To this day there are many parts of Britain where thirteenth-century arable working is to be seen underlying the grass or heath to which it reverted in the context of declining crop production. There were various reasons for this later shift, which operated with different force in different locations. On the supply side, the increasing cost of wage labour after 1349 affected the pastoral sector significantly less than the arable sector because labour inputs constituted a lower fraction of the total costs of production. Spot checks from Bibury (Worcestershire) suggest that labour costs accounted there for about three-quarters of total variable costs in grain production (in 1371–2) but only about a third of the costs of producing wool (in 1383–4).[1] This was because many of the operations of shepherding or cattle raising required little labour. Some tasks such as washing and shearing sheep or dairying were often women's work,[2] and indeed one of the consequences of the development of pastoral activities was to place a greater degree of responsibility for household earnings into the hands of women. On peasant farms, where the activities required for cereals cultivation were predominantly assigned to men, many of those involved in the care of animals, and the sale of pastoral products, were associated with women. Milking cows, making butter and cheese, and marketing dairy produce were all characteristically women's work. So was the care of farmyard animals, and the sale of poultry and eggs.[3]

The demand for animal products, meanwhile, was stimulated more than the demand for cereal products by rising standards of living, which affected both the proportion of meat in the diet and the range and quality of clothing. The average amount of meat supplied to harvesters at Sedgeford (Norfolk) rose from 104 grams a day for each man in 1256 to 478 grams a day in 1424.[4] Evidence for high levels of meat consumption in Scottish towns suggests that this tendency was as characteristic of Scotland as of England.[5] In the later fourteenth century the most significant impact of rising levels of welfare was probably on sheep farming, but especially from the early fifteenth century there was also a surge in demands for beef and dairy produce, and a consequent expansion of cattle farming in many parts of Britain. Demand for pastoral products in much of Britain was influenced not only by rising incomes at home but also by the preferences of overseas buyers, to the extent that they substituted British wool, cloth, or hides for other available products. Even in the immediate aftermath of the Black Death, the growth of cloth exports, at a time when wool exports also remained high, was an invitation for estates to invest heavily in sheep. Finally we should also reckon with the longevity and variable usefulness of some farm animals that made them a viable store of wealth in peasant communities.

As these comments imply, the pastoral sector was subject to its own dynamic, and its development through the fourteenth and fifteenth centuries was not merely a response to the varying fortunes of cereals production. In most parts of Britain pasture farming expanded over former ploughlands. On the clay soils of the Nottinghamshire Wolds there was widespread conversion of arable to pasture between 1410 and 1440; at Stanton on the Wolds in 1475 there was a dispute about grazing rights on a field of 180 acres that had once been under the plough.[6] Throughout Wales there was an increase in former arable lands leased to grass.[7] But it was far from a foregone conclusion that abandoned arable land could be profitably used as pasture. Many abandoned fields disappear from the written record, and we can only speculate what became of them. In other instances abandoned land occurs as 'waste', either untenanted or let for a low rent. It was quite common in the later fourteenth and fifteenth centuries to see wasteland, marsh, and scrub that had once been under the plough. If the area of self-sown woodland did not everywhere increase during this period it was probably because even land of little value was sporadically used for grazing, temporary cropping, or some other purpose. Land of low value could be used for recreation as well as for agriculture. It was not uncommon for parkland to be expanded around the residences of landed families in some regions. Along the Hertfordshire border, for example, there was new emparkment at Oxhey (1360), Albury and Braughing (1366), Essendon (1406), Rickmansworth and Watford (1426), Stanstead Abbots (1443), and Sawbridgeworth and Thorley (1448).[8] Village sports may also have benefited from the greater availability of lightly used land. It is interesting, anyway, that early variants of football become better known from the fifteenth century; it is not obvious that this development should be explained in terms of rising standards of living, especially in the form of increased leisure. In Scotland the game of golf is also first heard of in the fifteenth century, probably for the same reason. In 1457 the Scottish parliament tried to promote military exercises by outlawing 'the fut ball ande the golf', instructing that barony courts should punish offenders.[9]

Arable land made particularly heavy demands on time and money if it was to be kept in good shape by draining, weeding, and manuring. As in the past, though, other sorts of land needed particular attention. The significance of woodland management was unevenly distributed between regions, and was greater for large estates than for small ones, but it nevertheless required both thought and investment if it was to be done properly. Woodland pasture accounted for about 10 per cent of the value of all demesne pasture.[10] It was especially used for pigs, though the value of individual woods varied from year to year according to the acorn harvest. Woodland was also a source for the timber needed by landlords for their own building, fencing, and so on. Some woodlands produced a regular income from sales of firewood, particularly in the vicinity of towns. Timber could also be a substantial asset to be reserved for when exceptional resources of cash were needed. When the Black Prince wanted extra cash in 1354 he put up for sale timber from Peckforton Park (Cheshire). A consortium of eleven buyers paid £533 6s. 8d. for all the wood except the great oaks, which were said to be worth a further £900.[11] The potential cash reserves on some estates were enormous. The big timber alone on the various East Anglian manors of the late earl of Pembroke during the winter and early spring of 1391–2 was estimated to cover 1,827 acres and valued at £9,431.[12] Not surprisingly there were well-established traditions of woodland conservation. The bishop of Ely's estate survey of 1356 noted a wood called Hayley Wood in Cambridgeshire containing an estimated 80 acres, from which 11 acres of underwood could be sold annually without causing destruction. The underwood of another wood called 'Litlelond' of 26 acres or so could be sold as a job lot every seven years. Another Cambridgeshire wood, Hardwick Wood, was said to have a five-year cycle of cutting. In practice, we know more about the details of woodmanship from surviving woodlands and woodland enclosures than from such documentary evidence. Some woods, like Hayley Wood (which survives) were kept simply as coppices, in which the trees were maintained to maximize the supply of timber. Others were kept as wood pastures or parkland, to combine timber production with grazing for animals, in which case the trees needed some protection, often by pollarding the trees.[13] In the course of the fourteenth and fifteenth centuries timber became relatively more important for landed incomes and the finer points of coppicing were more assiduously observed. Cycles of cutting became more regular, and fewer acres were cut each year.[14] The management of timber through coppicing was certainly practised in southern Wales and parts of southern Scotland; Dalkeith Oaks (Midlothian) are surviving testimony. Such policies were inevitably a direct response to the commercial value of woods, however, and were not pursued to anything like the same extent in parts of Britain where commercial incentives were insufficiently strong. The coppicing tradition in Ireland, for example, is less in evidence in this period, though it apparently survived until the seventeenth century.[15]

Pasture, too, was more than just unploughed land, and invited additional investment in periods when it was expanding. One of the features of the later fourteenth and fifteenth centuries that best attested the substitution of pasture for arable was enclosure, so much so that in early sixteenth-century English legislation enclosure became virtually synonymous with the decline of rural employment and population. Enclosure obviously implies some measurement of investment, of time if not of money, and is likeliest to have occurred in contexts where investment in livestock was a preferred option. Enclosures were no novelty of the fourteenth and fifteenth centuries. Some regions, like Essex, had been distinctive for large numbers of enclosed fields from time immemorial.[16] Enclosures had been widely created in the twelfth and thirteenth century in the course of piecemeal clearance of woodland, often on the edge of earlier systems of common fields, as around Stoneleigh in the Forest of Arden, near Coventry.[17] Other lands had been enclosed before 1300 in regions where pastoral husbandry was the preferred form of agrarian development, since enclosure facilitated the control of herds. The large, regular enclosures of the eastern part of the Irish central lowlands may derive from Anglo-Irish developments of the thirteenth century.[18] The distinctive feature of the later fourteenth and fifteenth centuries was the enclosure of former arable fields, particularly in order to make them more suitable for use as pasture. There is no shortage of references to such activity in English court rolls, since it was liable to cause resentment when one individual's enclosure blocked others off from their traditional rights of common pasture. Enclosure of this kind does not figure so prominently in the agrarian histories of Wales, Scotland, and Ireland, presumably because of generally more extensive systems of flock management, though there was some enclosure of wasteland in Wales to allow intensified grazing during the late fifteenth and early sixteenth centuries.[19]

The shift towards pasture farming that occurred during the fourteenth and fifteenth centuries was bound to cause friction, one way or another, in settlements that had evolved during earlier centuries to cope with a quite different composition of agricultural output. Growing numbers of animals in unenclosed landscapes were liable to be a nuisance to neighbours unless controlled by tethering or penning, and the growth of regulations relating to uncontrolled livestock is a recurrent feature of court records such as those of the bishop of Worcester's manor of Kempsey in the fifteenth century.[20] If in order to resolve such problems proprietors intended to enclose land, as a recognition of a final change in its use, they were well advised to negotiate with their neighbours through a manor court; this would characteristically imply recognizing that traditional common rights would be respected even after the land was enclosed. Such arrangements no doubt usually worked well enough, but with the best will in the world there were occasions when the separation off of open-field land to create this compromised 'severalty' led to disagreements. So both failure to enclose and enclosure generated their different sources of tension. Many of these conflicts were between fellow villagers. A by-law of 1477 was directed against the bishop of Worcester's tenants of Broomhall and Brookend for enclosing fields and preventing their neighbours from commoning animals there.[21] So although commonly analysed as a manifestation of class conflict between landlords and tenants, enclosure was not exclusively so. Because they had more land and more power, landlords were bound to be able to antagonize more people at once, and they were uniquely able to expropriate tenants and cause hardship.[22] However, the considerations that motivated them were also relevant to smaller occupants of the land.[23] The enclosures complained of at Kempsey in the late fifteenth century included those of villagers like Robert Parker, who had unilaterally enclosed his virgate tenement, and William Wyldon, who had enclosed a virgate and a half.[24]

Sheep

Though in the course of the fourteenth century shepherding often seemed the best option to estate owners and peasant farmers alike, its attractions were not sufficiently great to rescue the profitability of direct demesne management. In fact large-scale commercial sheep farming was more practised at the beginning of the fourteenth century and the early sixteenth than in the intervening period. As we have seen, the peak year for English exports of raw wool was 1304–5. On the assumption that a sack of wool contained 260 fleeces, the exports that year were contributed by over 12 m. sheep, and to judge from the Scottish customs figures of 1327–32 at least another 1.5 m. fleeces left Scotland.[25] The amount of wool going into British clothmaking industries was doubtless less, but even so the combined total represented very big business. It was in the early fourteenth century that some of the large estates were most actively involved in the management of large and complex sheep farms of the sort described in Chapter 12. Subsequently the largest flocks were reduced during the price recession of the 1330s and 1340s and probably never recovered their former level.

Demesne flocks, the big-business end of sheep farming, were expanded in the third quarter of the fourteenth century, though this was a transient phase. The leasing of demesne lands in the later fourteenth century was often accompanied by the leasing of demesne pastures, and the disappearance of sheep farming from the direct oversight of estate officers. The earl of Hereford maintained large sheep flocks across his estates, mostly on the Welsh hills at Brecon and Bronllys, and was able to sell on average 3,084 fleeces a year over the six years between 1367 and 1372, but by the end of the century these were split up and leased.[26] Large Scottish producers were similarly affected, to judge from evidence of reduced levels of exports by Melrose Abbey and the duke of Albany in the early fifteenth century.[27] Even where landlords were temporarily more optimistic about the future of wool, their hopes were rarely sustained through the fifteenth century. The duchy of Lancaster maintained sheep flocks in Berkshire, Wiltshire, and Dorset long after it had leased the arable component of its demesnes, but low prices of wool and the difficulty of making profits led to the abandonment of direct sheep farming from the 1440s.[28] This withdrawal from seigniorial sheep farming, which implied that estate officials were no longer answerable for sheep in their annual accounts, means that the statistical analysis of what happened in the fifteenth century is rarely possible in any documented context.

Declining profits in sheep farming were reflected in declining investment in the care bestowed on those sheep flocks that remained in lords' hands, and whose fortunes can consequently be charted from manorial accounts. On the estates of the bishopric of Winchester fleece weights varied from manor to manor, but over the estate as a whole they attained their highest levels (1.7 lb) at two peaks, first between 1315 and 1324, and then between 1350 and 1354. The latter was a period of rapid restocking on the estate as part of the readjustment after the Black Death. From then onward fleece weights declined, even during the 1360s and 1370s, commonly regarded as a period of 'high farming'. By the 1380s the average fleece weighed only 1.3 lb, and by the 1440s it had fallen to 1.0 lb. The manors of the Winchester estate all conformed to much the same pattern (Table 20.1).[29] Although attempts have been made to explain such changes by reference to natural environmental causes such as climatic change and epidemic disease amongst sheep, the close analysis of sheep management on fourteenth-century demesnes has demonstrated that though weather and disease might have temporary effects, long-term declining fleece weights were rather the result of decreased investment in sheep rearing, as an adjustment to changing determinants of profit. At Wisbech Barton, where the weight of fleeces declined by 20 per cent between 1327–48 and 1393–1428, from 2.35 lb to 1.88 lb, the decline can be attributed to poorer feeding, to exposure of sheep to health hazards by pasturing them on wet land, and to the abandonment of the practice of introducing new stock from outside rather than relying on inbreeding.[30]

The declining interest in large sheep flocks on the part of landlords did not imply the abandonment of sheep farming by others. Although the low prices that deterred the big estates were faced by small producers as well as large, the costs of lesser farmers were often low where there was abundant common pasture. Peasants

TABLE 20.1. *Index of fleece weights on the Winchester bishopric estate 1295–9 to 1450–4 (100% is the average weight for the period 1210–1454 – 1.35 lb)*

Years	Index %	Year	Index %
1295–9	87*	1375–9	94
1300–4	89	1380–4	95
1305–9	90	1385–9	91
1310–4	111	1390–4	98
1315–9	123	1395–9	87
1320–4	131*	1400–4	105
1325–9	113	1405–9	92*
1330–4	120	1410–4	86
1335–9	117	1415–9	93
1340–4	107	1420–4	93
1345–9	111	1425–9	98*
1350–4	126	1430–4	84
1355–9	110	1435–9	84*
1360–4	111	1440–4	79*
1365–9	114	1445–9	76*
1370–4	105*	1450–4	78

Note: The asterisked figures are calculated from the evidence of fewer than four out of the five years, and are consequently somewhat less reliable than the others.

Source: M. J. Stephenson, 'Wool Yields in the Medieval Economy', *Economic History Review*, 2nd ser. 41 (1988), 378.

probably also operated with lower profit margins than demesne farmers. Profitability was less closely monitored in a context where much of the labour input was unpaid, especially since much of the day-to-day shepherding could be allocated to younger members of families whose wage-earning potential was low. In peasant society, too, livestock was an indicator of status independently of the revenue it brought in. There are clear indications that some peasant flocks were growing in size in the fifteenth century, particularly in the quite widespread complaints of trespasses with larger numbers of sheep that were brought to local courts, and in complaints that commons were being overstocked.[31] The enclosure of fields to create sheep pastures, as we have seen, was commonly associated with small farmers, even if Tudor governments concentrated their attention on larger ones.

Unfortunately, however, we have very little clue about whether increases in peasant flocks compensated for the decline in demesne flocks.

Historians have inevitably speculated about what happened to long-term trends in total wool production in these circumstances. There was perhaps a simple diversion of sheep farming from landlords to tenants without any permanent decline in the total number of sheep, though this proposition remains unproved. It is relatively straightforward to take account of the increased amount of wool being exported in the form of cloth rather than wool; it is generally reckoned that a sack of wool could make 4½ cloths, and on that understanding the combined number of fleeces required for all export requirements can be calculated.[32] These figures imply that the volume of wool required to supply England's export markets in the 1450s and 1460s was less than half as much as in the early fourteenth century, and that even the strong growth of cloth exports at the end of the fifteenth century did not make up the shortfall (Table 20.2). In the second decade of the fifteenth century the wool going into exports was at least one-fifth less than in 1301–10 and 1351–60. Scottish wool exports declined steeply from 1375 without being compensated with increasing exports of cloth towards the end of the period. Consumption in the home market would have had to rise by at least 0.5 million lb in England and 1.5 million lb in Scotland between the 1320s and the 1520s simply to maintain the domestic flocks at the same level (Table 20.3).

Such a scenario is not impossible, despite the decline in population over this period, but it is unlikely. Wool production is more likely to have moved towards its former level in England than in Scotland, given the much greater difficulty in the north of absorbing losses from the decline of overseas trade into the home market. Even so, had English and Scottish consumers held the total sale of wool constant between the 1320s and the 1520s, overall per capita consumption of wool would have had to rise by about 146–220 per cent.[33] This would assume a high elasticity of demand for woollen products, since the increase is six to ten times higher than any conceivable increase in real incomes between the 1320s and the 1520s. Even the real wages of Oxford builders were only 22 per cent higher.[34]

Since the average weight of fleeces was declining—perhaps by as much as 30 per cent, from 1.4 to 1.0 lb during the hundred years following the 1320s—the number of sheep was perhaps maintained better than any contrast between the wool output of the 1320s and the 1520s suggests, but only on the assumption that fleece weights did not respond to the better investment opportunities following the mid-fifteenth-century recession. This would be a difficult assumption to justify. Around 1480 the normal weight of exported fleeces is said to have been 1.5 to 2.0 lb.[35] On the other hand, perhaps an increasing number of lambs were produced for consumption as meat, in which case the demand for wool is not the sole criterion for judging the

TABLE 20.2. *Export of wool (raw and manufactured) from England*

	Raw wool		Cloth		
	Tonnes	Woolsacks	Tonnes equivalent	Woolsack equivalent	Total tonnes
1301–10	5,695	34,876	n.a.	n.a.	5,695+
1311–20	5,066	31,024	n.a.	n.a.	5,066+
1321–30	4,172	25,549	n.a.	n.a.	4,172+
1331–40	4,882	29,897	n.a.	n.a.	4,882+
1341–50	3,634	22,255	n.a.	n.a.	3,634+
1351–60	5,391	33,014	236	1,445	5,627
1361–70	4,673	28,617	504	3,086	5,177
1371–80	3,837	23,498	537	3,289	4,374
1381–90	2,970	18,188	933	5,714	3,903
1391–1400	2,919	17,876	1,480	9,064	4,399
1401–10	2,298	14,073	1,163	7,122	3,461
1411–20	2,227	13,638	1,020	6,246	3,247
1421–30	2,261	13,846	1,532	9,382	3,793
1431–40	1,218	7,459	1,658	10,154	2,876
1441–50	1,552	9,504	1,816	11,121	3,368
1451–60	1,330	8,145	1,306	7,998	2,636
1461–70	1,360	8,329	1,229	7,526	2,589
1471–80	1,535	9,400	2,154	13,191	3,689
1481–90	1,462	8,953	1,877	11,495	3,339
1491–1500	1,345	8,237	2,291	14,030	3,636
1501–10	1,248	7,643	2,997	18,354	4,245
1511–20	1,260	7,716	3,211	19,664	4,471
1521–30	824	5,046	3,269	20,019	4,093

Source: A. R. Bridbury, *Medieval English Clothmaking: An Economic Survey* (1982), 116. A sack of wool is reckoned at 360 lb, implying 6.124 sacks per tonne. Cloths are converted to tonnes at the rate of 27.217 cloths per tonne and to woolsacks at 4.444 cloths per sack (81 lb of wool per cloth).

size of flocks. On this particular question, however, agnosticism is an acceptable position.

Of course, any comparison between the 1320s and the 1520s is artificial as a comment on long-term change given the turbulence of events in the wool trade during the intervening period. There can be no question of the home market

TABLE 20.3. *Export of wool (raw and manufactured) from Scotland*

	Raw wool		Cloth		
	Tonnes	Woolsack equivalents	Tonnes	Woolsack equivalents	Total tonnes
1327–32	858	5,254	n.a.	n.a.	858+
1361–70	853	5,224	n.a.	n.a.	853+
1371–80	881	5,395	n.a.	n.a.	881+
1381–90	599	3,668	n.a.	n.a.	599+
1391–1400	646	3,956	n.a.	n.a.	646+
1401–11	334	2,045	n.a.	n.a.	334+
1412–22	382	2,339	n.a.	n.a.	382+
1424–35	563	3,448	87	529	650
1445–9	452	2,768	n.a.	n.a.	452+
1450–9	219	1,341	n.a.	n.a.	219+
1460–9	344	2,107	43	261	387
1470–9	274	1,678	42	254	316
1480–9	200	1,225	31	185	231
1490–9	215	1,317	58	350	273
1500–9	236	1,445	51	350	287
1510–19	191	1170	38	261	229
1520–9	124	759	64	385	188

Source: P. G. B. McNeill and H. L. MacQueen (eds.), *Atlas of Scottish History to 1707* (Edinburgh, 1996), 241. A sack of wool is reckoned at 360 lb, implying 6.124 sacks per tonne, and ells of cloth are converted to tonnes at the rate of 881.84 ells per tonne (2.5 lb. of wool per ell).

normally making up for short-term contractions of overseas demand. The pattern of wage increases suggests that the transformation of the home market for wool was most achieved between 1349 and 1400, a period when the export trade in cloth also grew in a relatively well-sustained manner. Home demand may have continued to grow significantly into the early fifteenth century; the rising price of wool during the first decade is difficult to explain except in terms of the domestic market, given the contraction in wool and cloth exports below the level of the 1390s. However, it is unlikely that growth of the home market continued vigorously enough to compensate for the prolonged recession in raw wool exports between 1427 and 1439, nor in cloth exports between 1447 and 1465, nor for numerous other shorter periods of external shock affecting wool producers. From the 1430s, when the native cloth industry was beginning to rival the raw wool trade in its significance for wool producers, evidence of unemployment in the textiles trades coincides with periods of export crises, as in 1450 and 1522. To accommodate the decline in exports between the 1320s and the 1460s the home market would have had to absorb an additional 5.5 million lb of wool; per capita consumption would have had to be about 172–260 per cent higher in the 1460s than in the 1320s, even though real wages were no more than 75 per cent higher.[36] Peasant flocks can accordingly be expected to have gone through periods of contraction and disbandment comparable to those of demesne farmers at some periods of the fifteenth century, which helps to explain why landlords often found it difficult to lease pasture.

With the upturn in cloth exports in the last quarter of the fifteenth century, more large estates demonstrated an interest in investing in sheep, and there are again good examples of large flocks as a commercially attractive proposition. Because of changes in accounting practices, and the greater role of small enterprises, the growth of sheep farming after 1470 is not as well documented as that of some earlier periods, but the increase in exports from England between the 1460s and the 1520s must have represented the fleeces of at least 1.9 million sheep, and this was undoubtedly the most dynamic sector of the agrarian economy at the time. These were often the occasion for some of the more contentious instances of enclosure and depopulation by landlords. In 1475 Sir Roger I Townshend had 6,477 sheep in 10 flocks in west Norfolk, and raised the number to 11,627 in 14 flocks in 1490. His son and heir, Roger II, increased that number to a peak of 18,468 in 26 flocks in 1516, after which there was some contraction during the 1520s. The wool from these sheep was sold, often on credit, to a variety of buyers, and included supplies to the East Anglian cloth industry in Norwich, Hadleigh, and Lavenham. The expansion of the family's flock was a source of friction with neighbours over grazing rights, and in 1517 Roger II was reported to Wolsey's commissioners (probably misguidedly) for having converted arable to pasture at Helhoughton.[37] Scotland, too, benefited from the improvement in demand and expanded sheep runs even to the extent of deforesting large tracts of Ettrick Forest.[38] The second decade of the sixteenth century was the peak period of profitability, but for much of the time sheep were simply the best available opportunity rather than a major money-spinner.

Cows

If we knew the number of hides produced each year we should have good information about the changing extent of cattle raising. But the evidence of customs accounts relating to hides, usually dried and salted,[39] is considerably less helpful than that relating to wool, since both in England and Scotland the primary market for hides was at home, in the manufacture of leather and leather goods, rather than abroad. Leather working was to be found in towns right across Britain; it occurs in small market towns like Northallerton (Yorkshire), and Inverurie (Aberdeenshire) as well as being an important source of employment in major towns.[40] The customs evidence from Scotland is at least consistent with the growth of cattle rearing after the Black Death; exports peaked in the early 1380s at an annual average of 56,400 hides, a quantity 56 per cent higher than that implied in our earliest Scottish customs evidence from 1327 to 1332. From that high level they dropped steeply, and through the fifteenth century the number exported annually was usually below 25,000.[41] This, however, is more likely to correspond to a shift in overseas demand than to any increased costs of supply; it cannot be used to argue that Scottish cattle farming declined after the 1380s. English exports of hides were not only similarly stagnant through the fifteenth century but considerably lower than those of Scotland, rarely amounting to more than 2,000 a year in the fifteenth century, rising to over 20,000 in peak years of the early sixteenth (1510–11, 1512–13). This difference in scale cannot truly reflect the relative numbers of cattle in the two kingdoms.[42]

Although hides were in demand all over Britain, and exported from all parts, the economics of cattle rearing were determined principally by requirements of cattle for other reasons. Cattle rearing and dairy farming expanded in the fourteenth and fifteenth centuries for reasons that can be related much more closely to domestic demand than in the case of wool. One of these was as plough beasts, but this was a declining sector of pasture farming, given the steep reduction in the number of ploughed acres. The decline can only be imperfectly documented from manorial accounts, since in so many instances demesne arable husbandry was abandoned by 1400 or soon afterwards. At Crawley (Hampshire) where there are continuous records until 1449, the number of work horses declined from 6 (1300–71) to 4 (1407–49). The number of oxen was less predictable but declined from 30–5 (1300–07) to 17 (1420–49). This represents a halving in the number of plough teams from 4 to 2. The demesne acreage sown there had contracted from an average of 272 acres (1300–24) to 78 acres (1432–5).[43] A similar long view of contraction can be obtained for some Ramsey Abbey manors.[44] As the example of Crawley suggests, large composite plough teams remained through the fourteenth and fifteenth centuries—remained, indeed, very prevalent. The tendency for horses to replace oxen in the team had slowed down, even though it may have continued into the fifteenth century.[45] There is, of course, no reason to suppose that a contraction in the number of plough beasts was peculiar to the demesne estates. Amongst smaller producers, becoming more commercially minded in the course of the period, there is more evidence of willingness to innovate, with an increasing use of horses and a continuing preference for smaller plough teams.[46]

Meanwhile the role of cattle in the rural economy was transformed in many areas by an increasing demand for meat and dairy produce, which in turn reflected the higher standards of living achieved by most sectors of society following the Black Death. Pastoral products had always been a major constituent of the diet in Gaelic Ireland and parts of upland Britain, so the changes there are likely to have been less pronounced. In England, however, a richer and more varied diet depended on a growth of resources of land relative to people, which was brought about by declining population during the fourteenth and earlier fifteenth centuries. Rural workers came to expect more meat in their 'customary' allowances of food.[47] In towns the number of butchers in the fifteenth century was a good index of the improved standard of living there. In Colchester the number increased from 13 in 1359 to 21 in 1400.[48] Household accounts demonstrate the extent of meat eating among high-status groups. Outside the penitential seasons of Advent and Lent the monks of Westminster probably averaged nearly 2 lb of fresh meat a day around 1500, and on these days meat, milk, and cheese together made up about 22 per cent of the energy value of their rich diet.[49]

The switch into a greater consumption of dairy produce seems to have occurred quite rapidly after the Black Death. Dairy products were becoming increasingly prominent in rural diets from the 1360s onwards. Price movements suggest that dairy farming attracted more investment in the later fourteenth century. It became even more important for agrarian incomes in the first quarter of the fifteenth century, when expanding cattle and dairy farming was widespread in Britain, though not all regions received the same commercial stimuli from rising demand. In north-eastern England it is attested by rising rents for pasture in Arkengarthdale, Teesdale, and on Bowes Moor, where cattle raising was a principal source of income.[50] Between 1425 and 1438 the sacrist of Durham Priory developed a cattle farm at Sacriston.[51] At the other end of the kingdom, in the south-east of England, the 1420s were the peak of an expansion in pasture farming stimulated partly by war in France and the need to supply troops. The profitability of dairy farming in this region can also be shown to have benefited from high domestic demand, especially from the towns.[52] This was probably, too, a period of expanding cattle herds in the west midlands; specialized cattle farms had been created in the Forest of Arden by the 1430s and 1440s.[53]

Cattle, like sheep, did not offer endless opportunities for growth, and cannot be assumed to have helped farmers out of every tight corner. On the contrary, there were prolonged recessions in dairy farming as in every other branch of agriculture. Price history suggests that dairy and meat production was less battered by the mid-fifteenth-century recession than arable husbandry. In the west midlands there is even some evidence of new investment in cattle during the 1440s and 1450s, as for example by John Dey around Drakenage, and by John Brome of Baddesley Clinton.[54] But the expansive phase of dairying in south-eastern counties was over by the 1430s, and to judge from the declining demand for pasture did not recover during the 1440s and 1450s.[55] In northern England, where the cattle trade depended more on long-distance trade, dairy farming was also adversely affected by reduced demand in the second quarter of the fifteenth century.[56] Any recovery during the later fifteenth century, in England at least, was gradual, and heavily overshadowed within the pastoral sector by the successes of sheep farming during these years. It was normally supposed, in contemporary discussion, that sheep rather than cattle were the justification for enclosing arable land.

Pasture Farming and the Market

There was still a great deal of pasture farming, both in towns and rural settlements, that was chiefly intended for the sustenance of households. Pig keeping was often for household use rather than for sale. The lord of Wivenhoe had the right to levy ½d. every time one of his villeins in the village slaughtered a pig for household consumption, and the receipts of the manor between 1381 and 1413 show that on average they disposed of 32 pigs a year in this manner.[57]

Although growth in the pastoral sector was not sufficiently sustained, or independent of the rest of the economy, to prevent economic recessions, it nevertheless mitigated the effects of declining population on commercial agriculture, and in some periods provided good opportunities for investment and profit. The long-distance trade in pastoral products from all parts of Britain held up better through the period 1300–1530 than trade in grain. Quite apart from the sustained importance of wool and woollen cloths in overseas trade, the export of hides from various parts of Britain throughout the period, even if at a reduced level, ensured mercantile involvement with farming communities.[58] Trade in cattle and horses operated over long distances. In 1396 three plaintiffs jointly sued the Colchester butcher Richard Petrisburgh for a debt of £16 12s. 8d. for cows, steers, and other animals he had acquired on credit at Ely, 67 miles away, around the feast of St Andrew, 1394.[59] Exeter's supply of livestock stretched as far as Bodmin (Cornwall), 60 miles away.[60] Some supplying regions benefited at different times from changes in the distribution of manufacturing or trading activities. Although the great international fairs of the twelfth and earlier thirteenth century had long been in decline, and though livestock were not prominent in the trade of the major surviving fairs like Stourbridge and Westminster, some lesser fairs continued to specialize as nodes of internal exchanges in livestock and hides.[61] Thetford Priory between 1482 and 1530 bought livestock at distances up to 30 miles from various fairs, chiefly towards the end of the period—from Woolpit in 1520–1 and 1526–7, Wereham in 1519–20, Kenninghall in 1525–6, Wisbech in 1522–3, and Hoxne in 1526–7.[62]

Changes in long-distance internal trade in livestock and pastoral products are implied by the development of new specializations in dairy produce and meat production in areas like the west midlands, which supplied both local urban markets and towns further east. Demesne leasing, and the frequent reconstruction of agricultural operations into smaller units, perhaps favoured the development of local specialities, though this has probably more to do with the growth of London as a centre of consumption. There was as yet little standardized differentiation between local products; household accounts continued to record the purchase of butter and cheese as if they were homogeneous products. However, there are some indications of emerging discrimination in the fifteenth century. The Banbury cheese known to Shakespeare and his contemporaries is first recorded in 1430.[63] In 1481 William Cely dispatched to George Cely in Calais 'a[n] Essex cheese marked with my master's mark'.[64]

Higher standards of living also opened up new opportunities for pasture farming within the domestic market. Although sheep and cows were the most important divisions of livestock husbandry there were others, some of which responded well to higher living standards after 1349. Poultry and eggs were often consumed by those who produced them, and many others were paid by tenants to lords as part of their rent. Some, too, were paid to churchmen as churchscot, as on the estates of the bishop of Winchester.[65] However, they were also a feature of every urban market place, and a standard item in the consumption of households of all sizes. The construction of rabbit warrens and sale of rabbits expanded rapidly on the light soils of the East Anglian Brecklands during the 1380s and 1390s, apparently as a response to agrarian depression. Labour costs were low, and rabbits could be sold both for their meat and for their fur. The market for rabbits remained active during the fifteenth century, though the value of commercial warrens declined as a result of the escape of rabbits into the wild, as well as the growth of poaching.[66] The East Anglian Breckland illustrates well how it was possible even for an area of poor soils to avoid being marginalized, as population and cereals cultivation declined, by maintaining a strongly commercial agriculture with different branches of pasture farming as local specializations.[67]

NOTES

1. C. Dyer, *Lords and Peasants in a Changing Society: The Estates of the Bishopric of Worcester, 680–1540* (Cambridge, 1980), 132, 140.
2. P. J. P. Goldberg, *Women, Work, and Life Cycle in a Medieval Economy: Women in York and Yorkshire, c.1300–1520* (Oxford, 1992), 139–40.

3. J. M. Bennett, *Women in the Medieval English Countryside: Gender and Household in Bristock before the Plague* (New York, 1987), 116, 119.

4. C. Dyer, *Everyday Life in Medieval England* (1994), 81–92.

5. E. Ewan, *Town Life in Fourteenth-Century Scotland* (Edinburgh, 1990), 27, 37.

6. E. King, 'The Occupation of the Land: The East Midlands', in E. Miller (ed.), *The Agrarian History of England and Wales*, iii: *1348–1500* (Cambridge, 1991), 74–5.

7. R. R. Davies, *Conquest, Coexistence and Change: Wales, 1063–1415* (Oxford, 1987), 427.

8. P. D. A. Harvey, 'The Occupation of the Land: The Home Counties', in Miller (ed.), *Agrarian History*, iii. 118.

9. *The Acts of the Parliaments of Scotland*, ed. T. Thomson and C. Innes, 12 vols. (Edinburgh, 1814–75), ii. 48; M. Bailey, 'Rural Society', in R. Horrox (ed.). *Fifteenth Century Attitudes: Perceptions of Society in Late Medieval England* (Cambridge, 1994), 162–4.

10. B. M. S. Campbell, *English Seigniorial Agriculture, 1250–1450* (Cambridge, 2000), 85.

11. P. H. W. Booth, *The Financial Administration of the Lordship and County of Cheshire, 1272–1377*, Chetham Society, 3rd ser. 28 (1981), 131.

12. The National Archives, Public Record Office, DL 43 14/3, fos. 13d, 22d, 25r, 39r–47r.

13. O. Rackham, *Trees and Woodland in the British Landscape*, new edn. (1996), 59, 62, 64, 72, plate XL.

14. T. Gledhill, 'Medieval Woodland in North Yorkshire', in M. A. Atherden and R. A. Butlin (eds.), *Woodland in the Landscape: Past and Future Perspectives* (Leeds, c.1998), 114–15; Rackham, *Trees and Woodland*, 66.

15. F. H. A. Aalen, K. Wheland, and M. Stout (eds.), *Atlas of the Irish Rural Landscape* (Cork, 1997), 123; Rackham, *Trees and Woodland*, 86–9.

16. See above (Ch. 1).

17. R. H. Hilton, *Class Conflict and the Crisis of Feudalism* (1985), 38–9; id. *A Medieval Society: The West Midlands at the End of the Thirteenth Century*, rev. edn. (Cambridge, 1983), 21–2.

18. R. H. Buchanan, 'Field Systems of Ireland', in A. R. H. Baker and R. A. Butlin (eds.), *Studies of Field Systems in the British Isles* (Cambridge, 1973), 588–90.

19. D. Hooke, 'Place-Names and Vegetation History as a Key to Understanding Settlement in the Conwy Valley', in N. Edwards, *Landscape and Settlement in Medieval Wales* (Oxford, 1997), 90.

20. Dyer, *Lords and Peasants*, 330–1.

21. Ibid. 332.

22. See above (Ch. 18).

23. R. H. Tawney, *The Agrarian Problem in the Sixteenth Century* (1912), 154–5; R. Faith, 'Berkshire: Fourteenth and Fifteenth Centuries', in P. D. A. Harvey (ed.), *The Peasant Land Market in Medieval England* (Oxford, 1984), 168–70.

24. Dyer, *Lords and Peasants*, 333.

25. See above (Ch. 16). The number of fleeces per sack is estimated here on the evidence that a sack weighed 364 lb averdupois, and that around 1300 an average fleece weighed 1.4 lb: Campbell, *Seigniorial Agriculture*, 156; A. Hanham, *The Celys and their World: An English Merchant Family of the Fifteenth Century* (Cambridge, 1985), 115.

26. W. Rees, *South Wales and the March, 1284–1415* (1924), 257.

27. A. Grant, *Independence and Nationhood: Scotland, 1306–1469* (1984), 80.

28. T. H. Lloyd, *The Movement of Wool Prices in Medieval England*, Economic History Review Supplement, 6 (1973), 25–6.

29. M. J. Stephenson, 'Wool Yields in the Medieval Economy', *Economic History Review*, 2nd ser. 41 (1988), 376–81.

30. D. Stone, 'The Management of Resources on the Demesne Farm of Wisbech Barton, 1314–1430' (unpublished Ph.D. thesis, University of Cambridge, 1998), 248.

31. Lloyd, *Movement*, 27–8.

32. A full broadcloth required about 81 lb of wool: E. M. Carus-Wilson, *Medieval Merchant Venturers*, 2nd edn. (1967), 250.

33. This calculation holds for the assumption that the population of England and Scotland shrank from 6 to 2.5 million between the 1320s and the 1420s, that average consumption per capita in the 1320s was in the range 1–5 ells and that an average ell in 1300 contained 2.5–3 lb of wool.

34. H. P. Brown and S. V. Hopkins, *A Perspective of Wages and Prices* (1981), 28–9 (comparisons between ten-year averages, 1321–30, 1521–30).

35. Hanham, *Celys*, 112.

36. Brown and Hopkins, *Perspective*, 28–9 (comparisons between ten-year averages, 1321–30, 1461–70).

37. C. E. Moreton, *The Townshends and their World: Gentry, Law and Land in Norfolk, c.1450–1551* (Oxford, 1992), 172–5, 184–5, 225–6.

38. S. G. E. Lythe, 'Economic Life', in J. M. Brown (ed.), *Scottish Society in the Fifteenth Century* (1977), 70–1.

39. Ewan, *Town Life*, 30.

40. Ibid.; C. Newman, *Late Medieval Northallerton: A Small Market Town and its Hinterland, c.1470–1540* (Stamford, 1999), 94.

41. Grant, *Independence and Nationhood*, 236–7.

42. H. L. Gray, 'Tables of Enrolled Customs and Subsidy Accounts, 1399 to 1482: Introduction', in E. Power and M. M. Postan (eds.), *Studies in English Trade in the Fifteenth Century*, (1933) 323. Hide exports from 1509 are tabulated in G. Schanz, *Englische Handelspolitik gegen Ende des Mittelalters*, 2 vols. (Leipzig, 1881), ii. 109–17.

43. D. L. Farmer, 'Grain Yields on Winchester Manors in the Later Middle Ages', *Economic History Review*, 2nd ser. 30 (1977), 562; N. S. B. Gras and E. C. Gras, *The Economic and Social History of an English Village (Crawley, Hampshire), A.D. 909–1928* (Cambridge, Mass., 1930), 242, 377–87; J. Z. Titow, *Winchester Yields: A Study in Medieval Agricultural Productivity* (Cambridge, 1972), 137.

44. J. A. Raftis, *The Estates of Ramsey Abbey: A Study in Economic Growth and Organization* (Toronto, 1957), 129–36.

45. J. Langdon, *Horses, Oxen and Technological Innovation: The Use of Draught Animals in English Farming from 1066 to 1500* (Cambridge, 1986), 97–9.

46. Ibid. 212, 219–21, 241–4.

47. C. Dyer, *Standards of Living in the Later Middle Ages: Social Change in England, c.1200–1520* (Cambridge, 1989), 158.

48. R. H. Britnell, *Growth and Decline in Colchester, 1300–1525* (Cambridge, 1986), 131.

49. B. Harvey, *Living and Dying in England, 1100–1540: The Monastic Experience* (Oxford, 1993), 55.

50. A. J. Pollard, 'The North-Eastern Economy and the Agrarian Crisis of 1438–1440', *Northern History*, 25 (1989), 91–3; A. J. Pollard, *North-Eastern England during the Wars of the Roses: Lay Society, War and Politics, 1450–1500* (Oxford, 1990), 49–50.

51. R. A. Lomas, 'The Priory of Durham and its Demesnes in the Fourteenth and Fifteenth Centuries', *Economic History Review*, 2nd ser. 31 (1978), 350–1.

52. M. Mate, 'Pastoral Farming in South-East England in the Fifteenth Century', *Economic History Review*, 2nd ser. 40 (1987), 524–5; ead., 'The Occupation of the Land: Kent and Sussex', in E. Miller (ed.), *The Agrarian History of England and Wales*, iii: 1348–1500 (Cambridge, 1991), 120.

53. A. Watkins, 'Peasants in Arden', in R. H. Britnell (ed.), *Daily Life in the Late Middle Ages* (Stroud, 1998), 85.

54. C. Dyer, 'A Small Landowner in the Fifteenth Century', *Midland History*, 1 (1972), 6–8; A. Watkins, 'Cattle Grazing in the Forest of Arden in the Later Middle Ages', *Agricultural History Review*, 37 (1989), 18–19, 24.

55. Mate, 'Pastoral Farming', 531.

56. R. H. Britnell, 'The Economic Context', in A. J. Pollard (ed.), *The Wars of the Roses* (Basingstoke, 1995), 51; J. Hatcher, 'The Great Slump of the Mid-Fifteenth Century', in R. Britnell and J. Hatcher (eds.), *Progress and Problems in Medieval England: Essays in Honour of Edward Miller* (Cambridge, 1996), 253; J. McDonnell, 'Upland Pennine Hamlets', *Northern History*, 26 (1990), 27.

57. R. H. Britnell, *Growth and Decline in Colchester, 1300–1525* (Cambridge, 1986), 156–7.

58. Above (Ch. 16).

59. Essex Record Office, Colchester Borough Muniments, court roll 19, m. 25d.

60. M. Kowaleski, *Local Markets and Regional Trade in Medieval Exeter* (Cambridge, 1995), 294.

61. D. L. Farmer, 'Marketing the Produce of the Countryside, 1200–1500', in Miller (ed.), *Agrarian History*, iii. 384–5, 408; Kowaleski, *Local Markets*, 306.

62. *The Register of Thetford Priory*, ed. D. Dymond, 2 vols. (Oxford, 1995–6), i. 46–7; ii. 374, 388, 424, 480, 488, 499, 513.

63. P. D. A. Harvey, 'Banbury', 5, in M. D. Lobel, *Historic Towns*, i (1969).

64. *The Cely Letters, 1472–1488*, ed. A. Hanham, Early English Text Society, 273 (1975), no. 131, p. 118.

65. *The Pipe Roll of the Bishopric of Winchester, 1409–10*, ed. and trans. M. Page (Winchester, 1999), 68, 83–4, 96, etc.

66. M. Bailey, 'The Rabbit and the Medieval East Anglian Economy', *Agricultural History Review*, 36 (1988), 5, 10–15.

67. M. Bailey, *A Marginal Economy? East Anglian Breckland in the Later Middle Ages* (Cambridge, 1989), 264, 318.

FURTHER READING

Bailey, M., *A Marginal Economy? East Anglian Breckland in the Later Middle Ages* (Cambridge, 1989).

—— 'The Rabbit and the Medieval East Anglian Economy', *Agricultural History Review*, 36 (1988).

—— 'Sand into Gold: The Evolution of the Foldcourse System in West Suffolk', *Agricultural History Review*, 38 (1990).

Blanchard, I., 'Population Change, Enclosure and the Early Tudor Economy', *Economic History Review*, 2nd ser. 23 (1970).

Bolton, J. L., *The Medieval English Economy, 1150–1500* (1980).

Britnell, R. H., 'The Economic Context', in A. J. Pollard (ed.), *The Wars of the Roses* (Basingstoke, 1995).

Campbell, B. M. S., 'Commercial Dairy Production on Medieval English Demesnes: The Case of Norfolk', *Anthropozoologica*, 16 (1992).

—— *English Seigniorial Agriculture, 1250–1450* (Cambridge, 2000).

—— K. C. Bartley and J. P. Power, 'Demesne-Farming Systems of Post-Black Death England: A Classification', *Agricultural History Review*, 44 (1996).

Dyer, C., 'Deserted Medieval Villages in the West Midlands', *Economic History Review*, 2nd ser. 35 (1982).

—— *Lords and Peasants in a Changing Society: The Estates of the Bishopric of Worcester, 680–1540* (Cambridge, 1980).

—— 'Sheepcotes: Evidence for Medieval Sheep Farming', *Medieval Archaeology*, 39 (1995).

—— 'A Small Landowner in the Fifteenth Century', *Midland History*, 1 (1972).

—— *Warwickshire Farming 1349–c.1520: Preparation for Agricultural Revolution*, Dugdale Society Occasional Papers, 27 (1981).

Farmer, D. L., 'Prices and Wages, 1350–1500', in Miller (ed.), *Agrarian History*, iii.

Fox, H. S. A., 'The Chronology of Enclosure and Economic Development in Medieval Devon', *Economic History Review*, 2nd ser. 28 (1975).

Fryde, E. B., *Peasants and Lords in Later Medieval England* (Stroud, 1996).

Grant, A., *Independence and Nationhood: Scotland, 1306–1469* (1984).

Hanham, A., *The Celys and their World: An English Merchant Family of the Fifteenth Century* (Cambridge, 1985).

Harvey, B., *Living and Dying in England, 1100–1540: The Monastic Experience* (Oxford, 1993).

Hatcher, J., 'The Great Slump of the Mid-Fifteenth Century', in R. Britnell and J. Hatcher (eds.), *Progress and Problems in Medieval England: Essays in Honour of Edward Miller* (Cambridge, 1996).

Hilton, R. H., 'Old Enclosure in the West Midlands: A Hypothesis about their Late Medieval Development', in id. *Class Conflict and the Crisis of Feudalism: Essays in Medieval Social History* (1985).

—— 'A Study in the Pre-History of English Enclosure in the Fifteenth Century', in id., *The English Peasantry in the Later Middle Ages* (1975).

Langdon, J., *Horses, Oxen and Technological Innovation: The Use of Draught Animals in English Farming from 1066 to 1500* (Cambridge, 1986).

Lloyd, T. H., *The English Wool Trade in the Middle Ages* (Cambridge, 1977).

—— *The Movement of Wool Prices in Medieval England*, Economic History Review Supplement 6 (1973).

McDonnell, J., 'Upland Pennine Hamlets', *Northern History*, 26 (1990).

Mate, M., 'Pastoral Farming in South-East England in the Fifteenth Century', *Economic History Review*, 2nd ser. 40 (1987).

Miller, E. (ed.), *The Agrarian History of England and Wales*, iii: *1348–1500* (Cambridge, 1991).

Moreton, C. E., *The Townshends and their World: Gentry, Law and Land in Norfolk, c.1450–1551* (Oxford, 1992).

Munro, J. H., 'Wool-Price Schedules and the Qualities of English Wools in the Later Middle Ages, c.1270–1499', *Textile History*, 9 (1978), and in id., *Textiles, Towns and Trade: Essays in the Economic History of Late-Medieval England and the Low Countries* (Aldershot, 1994).

Overton, M., and Campbell, B. M. S., 'Norfolk Livestock Farming, 1250–1740: A Comparative Study of Manorial Accounts and Probate Inventories', *Journal of Historical Geography*, 18 (1992).

Page, M., 'The Technology of Medieval Sheep Farming: Some Evidence from Crawley, Hampshire, 1208–1349', *Agricultural History Review*, 51 (2003).

Pollard, A. J., *North-Eastern England during the Wars of the Roses: Lay Society, War and Politics, 1450–1500* (Oxford, 1990).

Power, E., *The Wool Trade in English Medieval History* (Oxford, 1941).

—— 'The Wool Trade in the Fifteenth Century', in ead. and M. M. Postan (eds.), *Studies in English Trade in the Fifteenth Century* (1933).

Ryder, M. L., 'The History of Sheep Breeds in Britain', *Agricultural History Review*, 12 (1964).

Simms, K., 'Nomadry in Medieval Ireland', *Peritia*, 5 (1986).

Stephenson, M. J., 'Wool Yields in the Medieval Economy', *Economic History Review*, 2nd ser. 41 (1988).

Stern, D. V., *A Hertfordshire Demesne of Westminster Abbey: Profits, Productivity and Weather* ed. C. Thornton (Hatfield, 2000).

Stone, D., 'The Productivity and Management of Sheep in Late Medieval England', *Agricultural History Review*, 51 (2003).

Trow-Smith, R., *A History of British Livestock Husbandry to 1700* (1957).

Ward, A., 'Transhumance and Settlement on the Welsh Uplands: A View from the Black Mountains', in N. Edwards (ed.), *Landscape and Settlement in Medieval Wales* (Oxford, 1997).

Watkins, A., 'Cattle Grazing in the Forest of Arden in the Later Middle Ages', *Agricultural History Review*, 37 (1989).

—— 'Peasants in Arden', in R. H. Britnell (ed.), *Daily Life in the Late Middle Ages* (Stroud, 1998).

....

CHAPTER 21

Lords and Tenants

Though relations between landlords and tenants after 1300 are very well documented for southern and midland England, it is far from safe to assume that inferences to be drawn from this region are going to help much in understanding the rest of Britain and Ireland. The institutions of English rural society were firmly embedded in customary expectations and, despite the Peasants Revolt in 1381, most fourteenth-century estate records display a remarkable resilience in the way established institutions of lordship survived repeated environmental disasters. The structures imposed elsewhere cannot be assumed to have had the same robustness. In Ireland, manorial institutions were being successfully challenged from without by the ambitions of native Irish lords beyond the authority of the English crown. The control exercised by Edward I's men in Dublin was already shaken by 1300, partly because they were starved of money to fund royal commitments elsewhere, and that weakness was soon to be fully exposed in Edward Bruce's invasion of Ireland from Scotland in 1315. The situation in north Wales in 1300 was different, since patterns of English lordship there were less challenged during the fourteenth century but so recently imposed that they had had no time to become customary. The situation in Scotland was different again, since the Scots were able to resist external aggression from England and retained their own traditions of custom and law. All parts of Britain and Ireland experienced declining population, but it cannot be assumed that its effects were predictable regardless of the institutional context in which it occurred.[1]

Estate Management

Structural change, in response to the changed circumstances of the fourteenth and fifteenth centuries, was most marked in the parts of Britain where agriculture had been heavily subject to commercial stimuli in the thirteenth century. These were the parts where direct demesne farming had become prevalent. It is true that through much of the fourteenth century, even after the disruptions caused by the Black Death, landlords in these regions were usually able to maintain their estate organization very much as it had been. They continued to trust their demesne farms to bailiffs who accounted directly to them. In England, traditional distinctions between freemen and serfs were maintained, and on some manors lords were even able to increase their income from manorial justice in order to compensate for the decline in other sources of revenue. They maintained traditional controls on the economic activities of their serfs; they often insisted that if a serf acquired freehold property he should convert it into a servile form of tenure.[2] The old servile dues payable for illegitimate children and for the marriage of serf girls off the manor continued to be levied. Landlords mostly defended the status quo with vigour, and this accounts in part for the form of discontent expressed in the Peasants' Revolt of 1381. However, it was from about the time of the Revolt that the established method of estate administration generally ceased to function, and lords had to adopt new expedients for the profitable use of their estates.

The result was a widespread resort to leasing and other expedients that reduced their direct responsibility for the year-to-year management of their properties. Unlike English lords of the twelfth century, who had leased whole manors, those of the fourteenth and fifteenth centuries commonly leased the demesne lands and retained the right to collect rents from the hereditary tenants and leaseholders of each manor. In practice this allowed a great deal of flexibility of management, since demesne lands could either be leased partially or as a whole, and they could be leased either to a number of tenants or to a single one. Lords could also retain control of any particular assets that they chose. The revenue of the earl of Kent in 1467–8 from his manor of Brampton (Huntingdonshire) comprised £27 16s. 0d. from the lease of the demesne lands and demesne mills, £43 15s. 11¾d. from the rents of the tenants of the manor and profits of the manor court, and £32 12s. 8d. from the sale of grass and pasturage. Estate officials, in this case, had apparently decided not to include pasture in with the lease of the demesne because they could negotiate a better deal by selling it from year to year.[3] This flexibility meant that on large estates there could be a wide variety of practice concerning the management of particular assets, but they commonly involved passing commercial risks and transaction costs away from estate officers.

The chronology of demesne leasing varied. It was not uncommon at any point after 1350, but became particularly widespread after grain prices started to fall in 1376. Few demesnes were still being cultivated directly by the mid-fifteenth century. The estates of the archbishopric of Canterbury and Durham Priory were being leased from about 1380,[4] and the trend to leasing gathered pace in the 1390s, as on the estates of the bishopric of Worcester, Westminster Abbey, and Canterbury Cathedral Priory.[5] The manors of Ramsey Abbey were systematically leased after

1400.[6] Not only did lords lease their former demesnes; they also granted leases of former tenant holdings that had fallen into their hands, and had in effect been added to their demesne lands, for want of a claimant. In the later fourteenth century such leases were sometimes regarded as temporary until the traditional tenure could be re-established. Sometimes, though, they were worth more at a commercial leasehold rent than they had been under customary tenure.[7]

This pattern of change relates mostly to English estates because of the exceptional extent of demesne land in England, though it is also relevant to some properties owned by English landlords elsewhere. In Wales the course of leasing seems indistinguishable from that in England. It was frequently resorted to in the later fourteenth century, and had become widespread by the early fifteenth century.[8] An extent of Chirk in 1332 itemizes 240 acres of demesne land, which may or may not have been leased at the time, but by 1391 what was left of it was divided between about sixteen Welsh tenants; some had been enclosed and added to a park.[9] As in England, leasing was generally a sign of diminishing confidence on the part of landlords. Adverse economic changes here too were compounded by the consequences of wartime destruction. Various manors of the lordship of Usk (Monmouthshire) had been managed directly in the earlier fourteenth century, but the demesne at Usk was leased by 1408, as were other demesne lands of the lordship, and there were numerous indications there of war damage.[10] In Ireland the end of direct demesne husbandry was hastened by internal conflict and lawlessness. Parcels of demesne land were increasingly leased from the early fourteenth century, and already by the time of the Black Death leasing was the norm on the estates of the earl of Kildare in Limerick and those of Lady Elizabeth de Burgh in Kilkenny, Tipperary, and Meath. The piecemeal leasing of the de Verdun family's demesnes was already advanced by 1316. By the fifteenth century demesnes were kept in hand only for their lord's own use, and not as commercial ventures.[11] Scottish landlords who had directly managed demesne lands up to the earlier fourteenth century were probably also relatively early in going over to demesne leases, partly because of the disruptive impact of warfare. Some demesnes of Coldingham Priory and Coupar Angus Abbey were being leased by the 1350s.[12] This change made less difference to Scotland than to England, however, since demesnes there occupied a smaller proportion of the land.

Status and Tenure

English lords generally tried to maintain the tenures of subordinate manorial tenures in their traditional forms, despite the demographic and commercial changes that made this difficult. Some circumstances favoured this endeavour in the third quarter of the fourteenth century. The number of previously landless or near landless families who wanted land and were prepared to pay the old rent for it was high; this was one of the reasons why labour became so scarce after the Black Death. Moreover, existing customary rents, just because they had usually been fixed far back in the past, were often not unfavourable to the tenant. Some highly regarded holdings were taken up on the old terms even when the new tenant had to pay an exceptionally high entry fine.[13] So English rents, at least, did not change as markedly as one might expect between the 1340s and the 1370s. In this period the reduction of total income from rent on the manors of Canterbury Cathedral Priory in Kent was sometimes as low as 3 per cent and rarely exceeded 15 per cent.[14] However, the use of force was an important element in the policy of many English estates during the generation after the Black Death, as landlords deployed and strained their legal rights to protect their incomes. The most striking example of this is from northern England. The bishop of Durham not only had large properties close together; he also exercised exceptional rights of jurisdiction by virtue of his palatine powers. Even before the Black Death the bishop's serfs were exceptionally servile; their hereditary rights over their holdings were less secure than in most of southern England. After the Black Death, when the problem was one of too few tenants to occupy the available lands, the bishop used his manorial courts to compel villagers to find tenants. Either the courts were required to name a tenant to take over vacant holdings, or alternatively empty lands became a charge on the whole body of tenants so that each one of them would face an increase in rent. In July 1354, for example, 90 acres were committed to the husbandmen of Shadforth and 75 acres to those of Cassop. The effect of this was to divide village communities within themselves in the search for potential tenants. If tenants were suspected of wanting to run away he compelled them to find pledges among their families and neighbours so that if they disappeared their pledges would lose large sums of money.[15]

In the long run the enforcement of landlords' wishes was largely unsuccessful in its aims, in Durham as elsewhere. An aggressive estate policy ran the inevitable danger of provoking retaliation when an occasion presented itself. The 1380s in the manor of Halesowen was a decade when tenant insubordination reached a peak. Sometimes the tenants cooperated to trespass on the abbey property, sometimes they engaged in individual acts of defiance. In 1383 a bond tenant called Thomas Harboury sneaked by night into the courtyard of Hales Abbey and released all the doves from the dovecotes, simply to spite the abbey.[16] It was difficult for most landlords to put much pressure on tenants who really wanted to move from their holdings. In the long run one of the main effects of landlords having used their powers to control serfs was to bring the laws and customs relating to serfdom to the forefront of men's minds as a source of grievance. The effect of landlords using their powers to impose new burdens was to encourage serfs to question the justice of the system under which they lived.

The three decades after the Black Death—the period of 'feudal reaction'—culminated in the most outspoken revolts against serfdom in the history of England. In 1381 the occasion for the Peasants' Revolt was the poll tax of 1380 and the way in which it was levied. But in the context of this revolt, whose causes were essentially political, all sorts of social questions were raised, and foremost amongst them was the status of serfs. At Mile End on 14 June, 'the commons complained to the king about their intolerable servitude and heavy oppressions which they neither could nor would sustain any longer'.[17] The prominence of serfdom as a source of discontent is also demonstrated by the events of the revolt in the provinces. The chief manifestation of unrest in East Anglia and Essex was the destruction of legal records, especially court rolls and other documents which recorded the details of local custom. In Essex there were bands of rebels travelling from village to village in search of court records which they proceeded to burn, and as a result there are many manors whose surviving court records start in 1382 or 1383; one of these is the royal manor of Havering.[18] From about this time serfdom in England was doomed, not because the rebels were successful in their aims but because families were able to escape from serfdom by moving away from the contexts in which they were servile. Declining prices, declining land values, and rising wage costs, all reduced the power of landlords to resist concessions to tenant interests.

The breakdown of earlier status distinctions of freedom and unfreedom was a very general feature of the fourteenth and fifteenth centuries, and some of the essential causes were everywhere present. It happened most rapidly in Scotland, where the stigma of serfdom was largely a personal one and where the identification of servile families with particular tenements was less pervasive than in England. Traditional tenurial forms in Scotland had perhaps been greatly diluted during the twelfth and thirteenth centuries through the need to attract settlers from England, and landlords had less to lose from their further decay. In any case, because of the different way the jurisdiction of royal courts had developed, Scottish law did not need to make the distinction between free and unfree that endeared the status quo to English landlords. Personal serfdom died out there during the fourteenth century, though many features of Scottish leases would in England have been considered servile. It remained usual for landlords to require rents in labour and in produce even under the terms of leasehold agreements. A lease drawn up by Coupar Angus Abbey in 1472 for part of the township of Balbrogie (Perthshire) required the tenant to pay annually 9 hens, 5 bolls of 'horse corn', 8 bolls of barley and meal, to dig 25 loads of peat, of which 12 loads were to be carried to the abbey, to cart lead, tiles or timber to the abbey once a year if required, as well as to pay a money rent of 5 marks.[19]

In England the disappearance of personal serfdom was more contested than in Scotland, and more prolonged, but the end result was the same. The bargaining power of peasant populations against their superior lords was enhanced by the difficulty lords faced in tenanting their estates, and the latter lacked the institutional means to maintain the status quo. Serfdom disappeared partly by serf families simply dying out, and partly by villeins buying their freedom, but there were also more dynamic forces at work. The surreptitious operation of market forces enabled rural families to threaten to abandon their land, and often to do so, in order to improve their lot after finding better opportunities elsewhere. The widespread flight from manors in the late fourteenth century, and the virtual disappearance of servile status in the fifteenth century, is at least partly explained by deliberate decisions to escape from servile status on the part of village families. This was not the only reason for migration, however, and on other occasions escape from servile status was more an indirect consequence of families moving from inherited land to renegotiate and improve their lot elsewhere.[20] Such migration is implied wherever serfs sought their lord's licence to leave their manor. Many Ramsey Abbey's tenants migrated from one of the abbey's manors to another; by implication they were not concerned to move to where their former status would be unknown.[21]

For all the institutional differences between Welsh and English rural society, the decline of serfdom there followed a closely comparable course. The distinction between free and unfree status was retained into the fourteenth century, and landlords generally resisted change, but the disappearance of villeinage was accelerated by the Black Death. The combination of economic contraction and warfare in the early fifteenth century made it impossible for lords to hold out long after 1400. By the middle of the fifteenth century bond status was rare in Wales and many formerly bond townships had become deserted. In parts of the Welsh March where labour services were not an issue, the distinction between free and unfree continued to matter into the early Tudor period. But in 1504–7 Henry VII freed the surviving bondmen in Caernarvonshire, Anglesey, and Merioneth and converted their lands to free tenure. Since the bondmen of this region were too few to constitute any sort of moving force, it is reasonably surmised that the pressure for this measure came from freeholders wanting to facilitate the acquisition and tenure of land that had up till then been tainted with servile status.[22]

As personal bondage gradually disappeared, lords were also constrained to modify the terms on which formerly servile holdings were held. As we have seen, this was partly the result of such tenures falling vacant and being added to the demesne, in which case lords would endeavour either to find a family willing to take them on the old terms or, increasingly probably after the 1350s, someone who would take them on lease. The terms of tenure for holdings that remained in occupation were renegotiated over the years, sometimes amicably, but sometimes after conflicts between lords and tenants. At Kibworth Harcourt (Leicestershire) there was repeated rebellion by the tenants from 1401 onwards against Merton College, Oxford, their landlord, culminating in the college's abandonment of tenure in villeinage (*in bondagio*) in 1427 and its replacement by a contractual tenure 'at the lord's will' (*ad voluntatem domini*), though still 'according to the custom of the manor'. The negotiated improvement in terms of tenure was demonstrably considered adequate compensation by the tenants both at Kibworth Harcourt and elsewhere.[23] In practice the lord's will was expected to be goodwill to the tenant, so that tenures would be hereditary so long as the tenant observed the contractual terms. A common feature of the renegotiated terms for customary tenures was the disappearance of aspects of tenure associated with servility, such as weekly labour services. In the decades after 1380, just at the time when demesnes were increasingly being leased, lords were having to abandon their claim to the plough-ing, hedging, ditching, and other tasks that villein tenants had been obliged to perform. Conditions were very different from those a hundred years earlier. In the late thirteenth century lords chose to take money instead of labour services because they could easily employ hired workers at low wages, and this allowed both more flexibility and higher labour productivity. In the late fourteenth century, by contrast, they were having to abandon labour services under duress at a time when wage labour was becoming increasingly more expensive and less tractable.

In Ireland depopulation and the rising value of labour similarly brought about a decrease in the number of betaghs from the late fourteenth century and their virtual disappearance by the early sixteenth.[24] In Scotland the remaining customary tenures were superseded by contractual ones. In a context where land was in plentiful supply there were considerable advantages to tenants in such leases because they permitted recontracting and mobility in search of a better deal. As in England, short leases were not necessarily ephemeral in practice. Scottish 'kindly' tenures acknowledged a tenant's moral right, if not a legal right, to continue in occupancy. In the Highlands such bonds of loyalty were often reinforced by real or fancied kinship ties. Despite certain similarities, the course of tenurial change differed from that in England in not being accompanied by the widespread abandonment of servile dues as incidents of tenure. In addition, because of the general switch to leasing, the smaller role of freehold, and the absence of an equivalent of copyhold, Scottish tenures were characteristically seen as more pre-carious than English ones. John Major's *History of Greater Britain* (1521) observes that the country people 'have no permanent holdings but hired only, or in lease for four or five years, at the pleasure of the lord of the soil'.[25] A further difference from England is that townships were often leased, or subleased, to groups of tenants rather than to individuals.[26]

As a result of both the leasing of demesnes and the abandonment of customary tenures, leasehold became very much more prevalent throughout British society than before. At the upper level of rural society this encouraged a conspicuous group of tenants producing far more than they needed for their households, and heavily engaged in marketing their surpluses. The wide variety of gentry, merchants, and yeomen who became responsible for the commercial management of the land were often, at least for part of their land, substantial leaseholders. The modern word 'farmer' derives directly from a medieval use of the Latin word *firmarius* to mean a leaseholder. The word *firma*, signifying 'lease', which is also behind the English word 'firm', meant 'unchanging'; the lessee's rent is 'firm' because it is fixed in advance for the duration of the lease. In Scotland a distinction was made between the 'fermour' or 'fermourar', who held land for a year only, and the 'tacksman' who held for a longer term.[27] The 'tack' was a Scottish and northern English word for a lease, related to modern English 'take', though the origins of this usage are obscure.[28] Major English and Scottish leaseholders differed because of some characteristic contrasts in the development of estate management. The English farmer characteristically leased only the demesne lands, and if he acquired other properties it would be to farm them himself, or perhaps to accommodate farmworkers. The Scottish tacksman, by contrast, often took over whole townships of subordinate leaseholders, and so came to be regarded more as an intermediate landlord than as someone directly engaged in production. In 1498, for example, James, duke of Ross, permitted Robert of Douglas of Loch Leven, who leased from him the lands of Muckhart and Bishopshire for a term of years, 'to set any steadings or tacks of the said lands but at his own free will and pleasure and till [to] his most honour and profit' during the term of his lease.[29]

As the Scottish distinction between farmer and tacksman implies, the terms of leases granted by landlords were varied. They varied even on the same estate at the same time, but there were perceptible shifts of practice in the course of the period. Optimistic landlords were inclined to grant only short leases in the hope that their bargaining power would improve; this had been characteristic of some thirteenth-century rents, and became increasingly the case through much of the fourteenth century. In 1376–8 Sir James Douglas of Dalkeith, whose lands were scattered widely through the southern Scottish counties, rented his demesne land to individual tacksmen, but normally rented townships to joint tenants for one or two years. The eighteen bovates of the township of West Linton (Peeblesshire), for example, were rented to nine tenants for two years for £10 13s. 4d. Scots, each tenant acting as guarantor for the others.[30] Leases of three to five years were common, though on the estates of Coupar Angus Abbey the norm was of five to seven years in the later fifteenth century.[31] In fifteenth-century England leases commonly became longer, as landlords came to value the security of having sitting tenants above the freedom to negotiate rents at frequent intervals. The assessionable manors of the duchy of Cornwall had a very straightforward leasing policy, since on each manor all leases were renewed at the same time every seven years, but even there tenures were lengthened by the introduction of 21-year leases from 1434.[32] The costs of administering a leasehold system were much higher when there were many minor peasant tenures of different lengths and different starting dates. On Ramsey Abbey's manor of Burwell (Cambridgeshire) in 1399 the leases of standard customary tenements (15, 20, and 24 acres) were variously for 1 year, 10 years, 14 years, 20 years, 24 years, 30 years, 40 years, and life. Of those let for 30 years, three were in their second year, one in the third year, two in the fifth year, one in the eighth year, one in the eleventh year, and one in the fourteenth year.[33] Landlords were the more willing to grant longer leases, in these circumstances, because they had the additional advantage of reducing administration costs. A policy of leasing did not necessarily imply that landlords lightly abandoned responsibility for the state of their property. Many fifteenth-century leases specify tight conditions for the upkeep of buildings and other assets.[34]

Many English leases of the later fifteenth century were so long as to be difficult to distinguish from freeholds, and some were converted—either deliberately or through administrative negligence—into fee farms (permanent leases) or even free-holdings. Table 21.1 demonstrates the progression of leasing norms at Forncett (Norfolk). The mode shifted from seven years (1376–1410) to ten years (1422–40), to twenty years (1451–60), to permanent fee farms (1461–1500). The effects of the mid-fifteenth-century recession in lowering landlords' expectations are here much in evidence. Something of the same effect was apparent in Scotland, where the equivalent of English fee farm was the feu ferm, which was heritable and held by a fixed due to the landlord. The Scottish parliament in 1457–8 encouraged the king to 'give example' to laity and clergy alike by creating new feu-ferm tenures.[35] Although this affected minor tenures only to a small extent, declining expectations were expressed in some increase in feuing rather than leasing.[36] Newbattle Abbey, for example, was granting feu farms of both rural properties and tenements in Edinburgh.[37]

The growth of leasehold, with some concomitant drift into fee farms and free-hold tenure, was not the only change affecting tenures in the period after the Black Death, though it was the dominant form of change in Wales and Scotland. A significantly large number of formerly customary tenures in England were con-verted not into leasehold but into tenures 'by copy', indicating that the tenant had been given a copy of the entry in the manor court roll that recorded his title and terms of tenure. One good reason for this was that these terms were often newly negotiated, so that it was less easy to know what the terms of tenure were simply on the evidence of past custom. Although the giving of a written record did not in itself constitute a new form of tenure in law, it amounted to a significant change from the former practice in which terms of tenure were entirely a matter of

TABLE 21.1. *The length of leases at Forncett in different time periods, 1376–1500*

Period	No of cases	Length of lease in years													Fee farms
		3	5	6	7	8	10	12	16/17	20	24/5	30/31	40	50	
1376–8	58	—	9	3	38	4	4	—	—	—	—	—	—	—	—
1401–10	33	1	4	—	22	—	6	—	—	—	—	—	—	—	—
1422–30	39	1	1	1	8	—	13	2	—	11	—	—	1	—	1
1431–40	74	—	1	1	9	1	44	3	—	10	—	—	—	—	5
1441–50	64	—	—	—	—	—	21	4	3	26	1	1	2	—	6
1451–60	44	—	1	—	—	—	1	4	—	20	2	1	5	1	9
1461–70	38	—	—	—	—	—	3	1	1	5	—	—	2	—	26
1471–80	31	—	—	1	—	—	1	—	—	4	1	1	1	—	23
1481–90	19	—	—	—	—	—	—	—	—	1	—	1	—	—	17
1491–1500	18	—	—	—	—	—	1	—	—	1	—	—	—	—	16

Source: F. G. Davenport, *The Economic Development of a Norfolk Manor, 1086–1565* (Cambridge, 1906), 77.

memory or of record in the lord's own archive. Sir Thomas Littleton's *Tenures*, written around 1465–75, which became a standard textbook on English land law, recognized tenure by copy as a form of tenure distinct from both tenure 'at will' and customary tenure—in effect a negotiated customary tenure. He described it more fully as tenure by copy 'at the will of the lord according to the custom of the manor', and opined that insofar as there was a customary element in the tenure the lord was obliged to respect it.[38] At varying speeds on different estates it replaced simple customary tenure. By 1500 it had become normal on some manors, such as Westminster Abbey's manor of Feering (Essex), to grant a copy whenever a customary tenure was taken up.[39] This change prepared the way for the redefinition of copyhold tenure as one effectively protected by the English royal courts. Before that time tenants had occasionally appealed to equity jurisdiction in the court of chancery upon the strength of their written evidence. But it was not until the later sixteenth century that English common law was prepared to defend a copyholder's title against his landlord.[40]

The decay of serfdom was but one of many signs that during the fourteenth and fifteenth centuries the relative power of lords and tenants shifted in favour of the latter. The change was, of course, only relative; lords were still in a strong position in 1530 to control aspects of rural society, both directly on their estates and through their wider political responsibilities locally and nationally. Yet, by the early sixteenth century, the extent to which the British agrarian society had come to accept and depend upon negotiated rents represented a permanent change away from earlier traditions in which ascribed social status was the prime determinant of economic power.

Rents and Revenues

Changes in the character of relations between lords and tenants were accompanied by changes in the rent burden the latter had to carry. The heightened willingness of lords to make concessions to tenants after about 1380 corresponded to a tendency for the value of land to decline, not surprisingly given the movement of agricultural prices. Rent movements can be charted for longer periods than direct evidence of land use, since increasingly landlords were depending on rents for their income after they had leased their demesnes and stopped recording details of agricultural practice. Yet there are severe difficulties even with this sort of evidence. It is rarely explicit just how land was being used by tenants, so that rents of arable and pasture land are not always distinguishable. More serious, though, is the persistence throughout England of many rents that were fixed by tradition. This meant that negotiations between lords and tenants over the terms of tenure often concerned incidents of tenure such as the level of the entry fine rather than basic rent.

Even contractual rents, such as those multiplying with the increasing role of short contracts, can be difficult to interpret. Increasingly in the fifteenth century, long leases meant that rent movements became unresponsive to all but the longest trends in prices and wages. In England fluctuations in the real rent of the land are likely to be found in the history of arrears of rent, and rents uncollected, rather than in the history of rent itself. Simultaneously, the increasing willingness of lords to allow tenants to accumulate holdings and hold them at a combined rent, and the willingness of some wealthier villagers to add parcel to parcel when they could secure a bargain, means that it is often impossible to follow through the rents for particular properties for long periods. Often at some stage in the fifteenth century, a property that had so far been separately leased with a clearly defined rent became combined with other lands at a new agreed rent for the lot. Since in many parts of Britain there is a simultaneous problem of converting traditional tenures (such as bovates and virgates) to standard acres, the problem of creating a reliable rent index of any quality is virtually insuperable. That is why, despite the vast amount of estate material from England in the fourteenth and fifteenth centuries, and despite the widespread resort of landlords to becoming rentiers, there is still no adequate general survey of rent movements.

The most satisfactory study of rents based on a large sample is from the duchy of Cornwall, where the evidence is exceptionally homogeneous. Although the records for some years are lost, the evidence constitutes an unusually full series of observations from the 1290s through to the 1470s, capable of being charted without complex ambiguities. On parts of the estate the development of the local textile industry, together with tin mining, encouraged arable farming in the later fourteenth century. At Climsland, Liskeard, and Helstone in Triggshire rents not only made a remarkable recovery from the Black Death between 1349 and 1378 but rose again during the first third of the fifteenth century. On manors without these locational advantages (Tybesta, Tewington) rents recovered wholly or in part up to the 1370s, but after that went into prolonged decline. This evidence from Cornwall demonstrates how important it is to allow for local influences on rent levels, and not to assume that a single story can do for the whole of Britain.[41]

The stimulus to arable farming and rents to be found at Climsland, Liskeard, and Helstone in Triggshire between 1348 and 1430 might be paralleled elsewhere in the vicinity of fortunate textile towns and other industrial centres, but it was none the less unusual. More commonly recovery, or partial recovery, during the years 1349–76 was followed by prolonged stagnation or decline as at Tybesta and Tewington. Table 21.2 shows the fragmentary evidence from what are nevertheless longish series of data from some Breckland manors, showing that although some signs of recovery after the Black Death are repeated in the three cases for which there is

TABLE 21.2. *Mean leasehold arable rent per acre on five Breckland manors, 1350–1490 (pence per acre)*

	Lakenheath	Fornham	Mildenhall	Risby	Methwold
1350–9	6.76	12.57	—	8.53	—
1360–9	7.31	13.64	—	9.61	—
1370–9	7.26	13.56	—	10.73	—
1380–9	6.28	—	21.41	8.63	—
1390–9	6.82	10.04	21.72	9.06	8.00
1400–9	—	9.47	19.01	8.16	8.00
1410–9	—	10.11	17.79	7.55	6.23
1420–9	5.88	10.13	17.74	—	6.23
1430–9	5.82	10.18	—	—	6.23
1440–9	5.56	9.39	14.77	—	6.58
1450–9	5.51	—	—	—	—
1460–9	5.57	8.76	13.95	—	—
1470–9	—	—	—	—	—
1480–9	5.63	—	—	—	—
1490–9	—	—	—	—	—
1500–9	—	—	13.61	—	—

Source: Mark Bailey, *A Marginal Economy? East Anglian Breckland in the Later Middle Ages* (Cambridge, 1989), 228–9, 268–9.

evidence there was no sustained improvement after the downturn in prices after the mid-1370s. Even at Fornham, where there was gentle recovery from the 1410s to the 1430s, the level of rents per acre remained below that of the 1360s and 1370s. Another series of leasehold rents per acre from Forncett in Norfolk shows a similar pattern to that of Mildenhall, with no recovery in the early fifteenth century, and with its lowest points in the 1450s and 1470s (Table 21.3).

There is evidence of declining rents in most parts of Britain from the later fourteenth century, even if it is often patchy. The chronology of change in Wales was similar to that in England, except that the drop in rents was generally more severe, especially in the fifteenth century, when economic problems were compounded by warfare and loss of administrative control. In some circumstances seigniorial revenues in Wales could still be raised up to the 1370s by the ruthless enforcement of lordship and the exploitation of native custom for maximum financial gain. The introduction of periodic new judicial sessions from the mid-fourteenth century brought an important additional source of income.[42] In the

Table 21.3. *Average annual rents for leased demesne arable at Forncett (Norfolk) (pence per acre, to the nearest farthing)*

Years	Pence	Years	Pence
1376–8	10¾	1451–60	6¼
1401–10	9	1461–70	7¾
1421–30	7¾	1471–80	6½
1431–40	8	1481–90	8
1441–50	7¾	1491–1500	7¼

Source: F.G. Davenport, *The Economic Development of a Norfolk Manor, 1086–1565* (Cambridge, 1906), 78.

lordship of Usk, as in some others, rents could be raised in the first quarter of the fourteenth century. Seigniorial income from the lordship of Chirk rose from about £300 to £500 between 1322 and 1379, partly from leasehold rents, partly by additional large sums extracted from tenants in exchange for charters of liberty.[43] In the lordship of Denbigh, though the manorial demesnes were already leased before the Black Death, rents were stable after that until 1397.[44] However, there is good evidence of declining rents in Anglesey even before the 1380s.[45] In parts of south Wales, too, rents were often either lower than they had been or uncollectable between 1350 and the 1370s.[46] After 1400, conditions became universally less favourable to landlords. Those English estates with a large component of Welsh or marcher lordships lost rent income at the time of Glyn Dŵr's rebellion. The revenues of the lordship of Denbigh were only two-thirds or less of their fourteenth-century levels in 1426. These estates suffered further severe shortfalls in the income they could collect in the 1440s and 1450s, when the collapse in the incomes of the Welsh marcher lordships was catastrophic, for reasons that remain unexplained. The revenues of the duke of Buckingham's lordships of Brecon, Hay, and Huntington, valued at a net £1,014 in 1448, had fallen to £515 by the years 1453–5. There was little recovery in the later fifteenth century.[47]

Scotland and Ireland both experienced earlier difficulties because of warfare in the early fourteenth century. For Ireland there is good evidence of disruption in the second decade of the fourteenth century, and good reason to doubt whether rents recovered their thirteenth-century levels. The Black Death had variable effects, but there is no evidence of the recovery of rents that characterized some English estates in the third quarter of the fourteenth century, probably because there were no reserves of landless families to take over unwanted tenancies. Many holdings remained permanently vacant.[48] There is little basis on which to discuss the long-term movement of Irish rents, but the evidence of the estates of the earldom of Kildare implies a more severe decline in rent levels than in most of England between 1300 and the mid-fifteenth century. Inquiries following the deaths of the second earl in 1328 and the third earl in 1331 show that the estates were valued at only half what they had been worth in the late thirteenth century, and their value had declined even further by the time of the fifth earl's death in 1432. The estate was probably at its lowest state in the 1450s, as the result of the devastation of some properties and the loss of others; from about £430 a year in 1328 and 1331 its value had declined to £250 a year or less in the early 1450s. The great growth of the income of the earls of Kildare in the later fifteenth century owed more to the recovery and new acquisition of property, and the capacity to defend what they had, than to any improvement in rent levels.[49] A serious loss of control caused losses of income on the Irish estates of the Gloucestershire abbey of Llanthony Secunda in 1381.[50] In a context where title to property had to be maintained by force, rentier incomes were inevitably governed by political considerations more than the market for agrarian produce, and even if an index of rent levels were to be had, it would be difficult to interpret.

Scottish evidence is somewhat better, even if the examples are isolated. Land values and rent reductions resulted from commercial or military disruption well before the Black Death. The Wars of Independence left much of Scotland unscathed, but had devastated many of the most productive parts of the kingdom.[51] Nor was this the end of losses caused by the threefold scourge of war, famine, and disease. The canons of Scone were recognized by King David II in 1343 as suffering from lower rents as a result of warfare.[52] Rents remained low, or declined further, after the Black Death. In 1359, for example, the value of Edmonston was said to have fallen to £10 13s. 4d. from its former £13 6s. 8d. in peacetime.[53] When the estates of Mary Douglas of Liddlesdale were surveyed in 1367 after her death it was reported that three estates valued together in the late thirteenth century at £71 13s. 4d. were now worth only £32, each of them having declined in value by at least 50 per cent.[54] The most convincing evidence of declining land values before 1367, largely one supposes a result of the Black Death, is the contrast between the value of lands and rents in Alexander III's reign (1249–86) and in 1366, when a new assessment was made for taxation purposes. They suggest that land values were less than half what they had been in current terms, despite the intervening devaluation of the Scottish coinage.[55] Rents often recovered for two generations after 1366, because of the effects of debasement of the currency; they may have increased by about 50 per cent between 1366 and 1424. However, they then levelled off, and until towards the end of the century lagged behind inflation.[56] There were more opportunities for rent increases in the earlier sixteenth century, to judge from a eulogy of Thomas Crystall, abbot of Kinloss from 1505 to 1535, who is said to have recovered by his vigilance what his predecessors had lost.[57]

The Land Market

In an age of declining population larger landholdings came together merely by the operation of laws of inheritance. When family size was characteristically growing before about 1300 inheritance had worked for the dismemberment of family properties, especially where—as with the gavelkind tenures of Kent, or the *gwelyau* of Wales—lands were customarily divided between male heirs. Even under the rule of primogeniture in English common law estates were regularly split when a landlord left two or more daughters and no legitimate son. After 1300, however, the number of heirs was more restricted because death rates were high and family size was smaller, so that the well-connected benefited more from the deaths of their kinsmen. Perhaps the most famous example, and one with major political implications, is that of Richard Plantagenet, the father of the two Yorkist kings of England, who in 1425 succeeded to the titles and properties of two uncles, Edward, duke of York, and Edmund, earl of March. But this inheritance effect was not confined to magnates. It could also operate in peasant society. As population declined, peasant holdings could become larger for reasons that had nothing to do with the operation of the land market. Yet such inheritance effects were of very secondary importance in the long run. Had they been the predominant cause of peasant accumulation, they would have been most apparent in the period when population declined most dramatically, that is between 1348 and 1400. In fact, however, the accumulation of holdings that created a peasant aristocracy is most apparent in the fifteenth century: at Coltishall (Norfolk) a contraction of population by as much as 80 per cent was not accompanied by an increase in the proportion of tenants holding more than 8 acres during the later fourteenth century.[58] Furthermore, when fifteenth-century peasant accumulations are analysed in detail they can normally be shown to be deliberate acquisitions rather than the chance results of inheritance.[59]

Although purchasing and leasing were essentially different operations in law, their social implications were not very different, especially given the propensity of fifteenth-century landlords to grant long leases. The distinguishing feature of these forms of accumulation is that they necessarily involved a definite wish to accumulate. Examples can be found from many different levels of wealth. Some lawyers, merchants, and gentlemen enlarged their properties, sometimes by buying into existing estates, but sometimes by acquiring land previously occupied by peasant farmers.[60] The same phenomenon is to be observed in Wales and its March from the late fourteenth century, where the land market adapted to a declining population and increase in the amount of land unclaimed by any heir.[61] In order to attract tenants to empty lands, landlords extended the operation of English law at the expense of Welsh law, which allowed families less control over the disposal of their property.[62] As we have seen, between 1420 and 1453 Bartholomew Bolde of Conway acquired hundreds of freehold properties from peasant farmers in the Conway Valley.[63] In village societies smaller accumulations were very common, and in England historians have adopted the term 'yeoman' to describe freeholders who built up holdings of 60 acres or more, often combining lands that had been occupied by several families in the thirteenth century.[64]

The land market was subordinate to family arrangements and political attachments in permitting accumulations of property amongst landowners in the uppermost ranks of society. Even they, however, stooped to acquire former peasant lands either through failures of inheritance or by purchase. The process was encouraged by the transformation of older tenures to leasehold, fee farm, or copyhold, since this increased their attractiveness to a wide range of potential buyers. In the short term many peasant accumulations were ephemeral, because families died out, or because properties were split between heiresses, or because fathers chose to distribute their accumulated properties between their children. At any given moment, however, the distribution of peasant holdings in the later fifteenth century was very unlike what it had been in the earlier fourteenth, and some of these accumulations were the basis for higher things, as in the case of the Paston family, which is first known as a family of Norfolk yeomen. Clement Paston, who died in 1419, is described as having 100–120 acres in Paston (Norfolk), much of which was customary. From that position the family rose within half a century to be one of the most prominent gentry families in the county.[65] The role of buying and selling needs bearing in mind, in discussing change in rural society during this period, since it transfers to the operations of trade in land much of the weight that might otherwise be attributed to the arbitrary exercise of power by landlords. Most estate records of the fifteenth century imply that landlords were in rather a weak position because of the difficulty of finding tenants, and the accumulation of large holdings amongst some of their tenants reduced their bargaining power yet further during the course of the period.[66]

NOTES

1. This point is particularly associated with the work of Robert Brenner and has inspired a good deal of recent research. For the foundations, see T. H. Aston and C. H. E. Philpin (eds.), *The Brenner Debate: Agrarian Class Structure and Economic Development in Pre-Industrial Europe* (Cambridge, 1985).

2. C. Dyer, 'The Social and Economic Background to the Rural Revolt of 1381', in R. H. Hilton and T. H. Aston (eds.), *The English Rising of 1381* (Cambridge, 1984), 28–9.

3. *The Grey of Ruthin Valor: The Valor of the English Lands of Edmund Grey, Earl of Kent, Drawn up from the Ministers' Accounts of 1467–8*, ed. R. I. Jack (Sydney, 1965), 125–6.

4. F. R. H. DuBoulay, *The Lordship of Canterbury* (1966), 220; R. A. Lomas, 'The Priory of Durham and its Demesnes in the Fourteenth and Fifteenth Centuries', *Economic History Review*, 2nd ser. 31 (1978), 345.

5. C. Dyer, *Lords and Peasants in a Changing Society: The Estates of the Bishopric of Worcester 680–1540* (Cambridge, 1980), 147; B. Harvey, *Westminster Abbey and its Estates in the Middle Ages* (Oxford, 1977), 268; M. Mate, 'Agrarian Economy after the Black Death: The Manors of Canterbury Cathedral Priory, 1348–91', *Economic History Review*, 2nd ser. 37 (1984), 354; R. A. L. Smith, *Canterbury Cathedral Priory: A Study in Monastic Administration* (Cambridge, 1943), 190–1.

6. J. A. Raftis, *The Estates of Ramsey Abbey: A Study in Economic Growth and Organization* (Toronto, 1957), 265–6

7. Above (Ch. 19); J. Titow, 'Lost Rents, Vacant Holdings and the Contraction of Peasant Cultivation after the Black Death', *Agricultural History Review*, 42 (1994), 103.

8. W. Rees, *South Wales and the March, 1284–1415* (1924), 243, 247, 251, 253–6.

9. *The Extent of Chirkland, 1391–1393*, ed. G. P. Jones (1933), 7–8, 90.

10. G. A. Holmes, *The Estates of the Higher Nobility in Fourteenth-Century England* (Cambridge, 1957), 102–7.

11. K. Down, 'Colonial Society and Economy in the High Middle Ages', in A. Cosgrove (ed.), *A New History of Ireland*, ii: *Medieval Ireland, 1169–1534* (Oxford, 1987), 461–2; M. S. Hagger, *The Fortunes of a Norman Family: The de Verduns in England, Ireland and Wales, 1066–1316* (Dublin, 2001), 147–50.

12. *The Correspondence, Inventories, Account Rolls and Law Proceedings of the Priory of Coldingham*, ed. J. Raine, Surtees Society, 12 (1841), appendix, xxii–xxxv; R. A. Dodgshon, *Land and Society in Early Scotland* (Oxford, 1981), 123.

13. Z. Razi, *Life, Marriage and Death in a Medieval Parish: Economy, Society and Demography in Halesowen, 1270–1400* (Cambridge, 1980), 111–12.

14. Dyer, 'Social and Economic Background', 30.

15. R. H. Britnell, 'Feudal Reaction after the Black Death in the Palatinate of Durham', *Past and Present*, 128 (1990), 28–47; R. Horrox, *The Black Death* (Manchester, 1994), 283–4, 326–31.

16. Z. Razi, 'The Struggles between the Abbots of Halesowen and their Tenants in the Thirteenth and Fourteenth Centuries', in T. H. Aston, P. R. Coss, C. Dyer, and J. Thirsk (eds.), *Social Relations and Ideas: Essays in Honour of R. H. Hilton* (Cambridge, 1983), 165.

17. R. B. Dobson (ed.), *The Peasants' Revolt of 1381*, 2nd edn. (1983), 183.

18. M. K. McIntosh, *Autonomy and Community: The Royal Manor of Havering, 1200–1500* (Cambridge, 1986), 82–4.

19. *Rental Book of the Cistercian Abbey of Cupar-Angus*, ed. C. Rogers, 2 vols., Grampian Club (1879–80), i, pp. xxvi–xxvii, 168.

20. E. B. Fryde, *Peasants and Landlords in Later Medieval England* (Stroud, 1996), 122–34; R. H. Hilton, *The Decline of Serfdom in England* (1969), 32–43; C. Howell, *Land, Family and Inheritance in Transition: Kibworth Harcourt, 1280–1700* (Cambridge, 1983), 42–53.

21. J. A. Raftis, *Tenure and Mobility: Studies in the Social History of the Medieval English Village* (Toronto, 1964), 170–2.

22. T. J. Pierce, *Medieval Welsh Society: Selected Essays*, ed. J. B. Smith (Cardiff, 1972), 48, 62, 322; R. R. Davies, *Lordship and Society in the March of Wales, 1282–1400* (Oxford, 1978), 390–1; G. Williams, *Recovery, Reorientation and Reformation: Wales, c.1415–1642* (Oxford, 1987), 104–5.

23. Howell, *Land, Family and Inheritance*, 50–3.

24. Down, 'Colonial Society', 459.

25. J. Major, *A History of Greater Britain as well England as Scotland*, ed. and trans. A. Constable (Edinburgh, 1892), 30–1.

26. Dodgshon, *Land and Society*, 97–8, 109–13.

27. A. McCulloch, *Galloway: A Land Apart* (Edinburgh, 2000), 240–1; R. Nicholson, *Scotland: The Later Middle Ages* (Edinburgh, 1974), 380.

28. For a northern English example, see S. H. Rigby, *Medieval Grimsby: Growth and Decline* (Hull, 1993), 81.

29. *Registrum Honoris de Morton*, ed. T. Thomson, A. Macdonald, and C. Innes, 2 vols., Bannatyne Club, 94 (1853), ii, no. 237, pp. 247–8.

30. *Registrum Honoris de Morton*, i, pp. xlvii–lxxvi (West Linton, li).

31. I. F. Grant, *The Social and Economic Development of Scotland before 1603* (Edinburgh, 1930), 254–5; S. G. E. Lythe, 'Economic Life', in J. M. Brown (ed.), *Scottish Society in the Fifteenth Century* (1977), 69.

32. J. Hatcher, *Rural Economy and Society in the Duchy of Cornwall, 1300–1500* (Cambridge, 1970), 52–8, 156–8.

33. The National Archives, Public Record Office, SC 6/765/10.

34. *Rental Book of the Cistercian Abbey of Cupar-Angus*, i, pp. xxviii–xxxi; Lythe, 'Economic Life', 69.

35. *The Acts of the Parliaments of Scotland*, ed. T. Thomson and C. Innes, 12 vols. (Edinburgh, 1814–75), ii. 49.

36. Nicholson, *Scotland*, 381.

37. *Registrum S. Marie de Neubotle*, ed. C. Innes, Bannatyne Club, 89 (1849), nos. 279–81, 284, 304–5, 309, pp. 236–8, 240–2, 275–6, 277–9, 282–4.

38. *Littleton's Tenures in English*, ed. E. Wambaugh (Washington, 1903), 33–5.

39. R. H. Britnell: 'Tenant Farmers and Farming: Eastern England', in E. Miller (ed.), *The Agrarian History of England and Wales, iii: 1348–1500* (Cambridge, 1991), 621.

40. Fryde, *Peasants and Landlords*, 228, 230–3, 238–41.

41. Hatcher, *Rural Economy*, 261–6.

42. R. R. Davies, *Conquest, Coexistence and Change: Wales, 1063–1415* (Oxford, 1987), 401–3.

43. Holmes, *Estates*, 103, 105; L. B. Smith, 'Seignorial Income in the Fourteenth Century: The Arundels in Chirk', *Bulletin of the Board of Celtic Studies*, 28 (1979), 443–57.

44. Holmes, *Estates*, 97.

45. A. D. Carr, *Medieval Anglesey* (Llangefni, 1982), 309–12.

46. Rees, *South Wales and the March*, 247–8, 251–2.

47. *The Marcher Lordships of South Wales, 1415–1536: Select Documents*, ed. T. B. Pugh (Cardiff, 1963), 164–83; Carr, *Medieval Anglesey*, 326–30; Holmes, *Estates*, 101, 104, 106; T. B. Pugh, 'The Estates, Finances and Regal Ambitions of Richard Plantagenet (1411–1460), Duke of York', in M. Hicks (ed.), *Revolution and Consumption in Late Medieval England* (Woodbridge, 2001), 74–5; C. Rawcliffe, *The Staffords, Earls of Stafford and Dukes of Buckingham, 1394–1521* (Cambridge, 1978), 105, 107, 113–14, 131–2; Rees, *South Wales and the March*, 274–80.

48. M. Kelly, *A History of the Black Death in Ireland* (Stroud, 2001), 80–3, 86–7, 89–90.

49. S. G. Ellis, *Tudor Frontiers and Noble Power: The Making of the British State* (Oxford, 1995), 110–25.

50. *The Irish Cartularies of Llanthony Prima and Secunda*, ed. E. St. J. Brooks (Dublin, 1953), 289–311.

51. Nicholson, *Scotland*, 106–7.

52. *Liber Ecclesie de Scon*, ed. C. Innes, Bannatyne Club, 78 (1843), no. 161, pp. 119–20.

53. *Registrum de Dunfermelyn*, ed. C. Innes, Bannatyne Club, 74 (1842), no. 388, pp. 267–8.

54. *Registrum Honoris de Morton*, ii, no. 83, p. 64.

55. A. Grant, *Independence and Nationhood; Scotland 1306–1469* (1984), 77; Nicholson, *Scotland*, 175.

56. E. Gemmill and N. Mayhew, *Changing Values in Medieval Scotland: A Study of Prices, Money, and Weights and Measures* (Cambridge, 1995), 377–8; Nicholson, *Scotland*, 455.

57. *Records of the Monastery of Kinloss*, ed. J. Stuart (Edinburgh, 1872), 36–7.

58. B. M. S. Campbell, 'Population Pressure, Inheritance and the Land Market in a Fourteenth-Century Peasant Community', in R. M. Smith (ed.), *Land, Kinship and Life-Cycle* (Cambridge, 1984), 98–9, 103.

59. e.g. F. G. Davenport, *The Economic Development of a Norfolk Manor, 1086–1565* (Cambridge, 1906), 86–7; J. Whittle, *The Development of Agrarian Capitalism: Land and Labour in Norfolk, 1440–1580* (Oxford, 2000), 164–73.

60. M. Mate, 'The East Sussex Land Market and Agrarian Class Structure in the Late Middle Ages', *Past and Present*, 139 (1993), 58–9, 62–3.

61. Davies, *Lordship and Society*, 429–31.

62. A. D. M. Barrell and R. R. Davies, 'Land, Lineage and Revolt in North-East Wales, 1243–1441: A Case Study', *Cambrian Medieval Celtic Studies*, 29 (1995), 27–51.

63. T. J. Pierce, 'The *Gafael* in Bangor Manuscript 1939', in id., *Medieval Welsh Society*, 196.

64. Above (Ch. 19).

65. *Paston Letters and Papers of the Fifteenth Century*, ed. N. Davis, 2 vols. (Oxford, 1971, 1976), i, pp. xl–xlii.

66. Mate, 'East Sussex Land Market', 52–5, 62–3, 65.

FURTHER READING

Arvanigian, M., 'Free Rents in the Palatinate of Durham and the Crisis of the Late 1430s', *Archaeologia Aeliana*, 5th ser. 24 (1996).

Aston, T. H., and Philpin, C. H. E. (eds.), *The Brenner Debate: Agrarian Class Structure and Economic Development in Pre-Industrial Europe* (Cambridge, 1985).

Barrell, A. D. M., and Davies, R. R., 'Land, Lineage and Revolt in North-East Wales, 1243–1441: A Case Study', *Cambrian Medieval Celtic Studies*, 29 (1995).

Bean, J. M. W., *The Estates of the Percy Family, 1416–1537* (1958).

Britnell, R. H., 'Feudal Reaction after the Black Death in the Palatinate of Durham', *Past and Present*, 128 (1990).

Davenport, F. G., *The Economic Development of a Norfolk Manor, 1086–1565* (Cambridge, 1906).

Davies, R. R., *Lordship and Society in the March of Wales, 1282–1400* (Oxford, 1978).

Dobson, R. B. (ed.), *The Peasants' Revolt of 1381*, 2nd edn. (1983).

Dodgshon, R. A., *Land and Society in Early Scotland* (Oxford, 1981).

DuBoulay, R. H., *The Lordship of Canterbury* (1966).

Dyer, C., *Everyday Life in Medieval England* (1994).

—— *Lords and Peasants in a Changing Society: The Estates of the Bishopric of Worcester 680–1540* (Cambridge, 1980).

—— 'A Redistribution of Incomes in Fifteenth-Century England?', *Past and Present*, 39 (1968), and in R. H. Hilton (ed.), *Peasants. Knights and Heretics: Studies in Medieval English Social History* (Cambridge, 1976).

Fryde, E. B., *Peasants and Landlords in Later Medieval England* (Stroud, 1996).

Harvey, B., *Westminster Abbey and its Estates in the Middle Ages* (Oxford, 1977).

Harvey, P. D. A. (ed.), *The Peasant Land Market in Medieval England* (Oxford, 1984).

Hatcher, J., *Rural Economy and Society in the Duchy of Cornwall, 1300–1500* (Cambridge, 1970).

Hilton, R. H., *Class Conflict and the Crisis of Feudalism* (1985).

—— *The Decline of Serfdom in England* (1969).

—— *The Economic Development of some Leicestershire Estates in the 14th and 15th Centuries* (1947).

—— *The English Peasantry in the Later Middle Ages* (Oxford, 1975).

—— and Aston, T. H., *The English Rising of 1381* (Cambridge, 1984).

Howell, C., *Land, Family and Inheritance in Transition: Kibworth Harcourt, 1280–1700* (Cambridge, 1983).

Lomas, R. A., 'The Priory of Durham and its Demesnes in the Fourteenth and Fifteenth Centuries', *Economic History Review*, 2nd ser. 31 (1978).

McIntosh, M. K., *Autonomy and Community: The Royal Manor of Havering, 1200–1500* (Cambridge, 1986).

Maitland, F. W., 'The History of a Cambridgeshire Manor' in id., *Collected Papers*, 3 vols. (Cambridge, 1911), ii.

Mate, M., 'Agrarian Economy after the Black Death: The Manors of Canterbury Cathedral Priory, 1348–91', *Economic History Review*, 2nd ser. 37 (1984).

—— 'The East Sussex Land Market and Agrarian Class Structure in the Late Middle Ages', *Past and Present*, 139 (1993).

Miller, E. (ed.), *The Agrarian History of England and Wales*, iii: *1348–1500* (Cambridge, 1991).

Mullan, J., 'The Transfer of Customary Land on the Estate of the Bishopric of Winchester between the Black Death and the Plague of 1361', in R. H. Britnell (ed.), *The Winchester Pipe Rolls and Medieval English Society* (Woodbridge, 2003).

Parker, C. 'Paterfamilias and *Parentela*: The Le Poer Lineage in Fourteenth-Century Waterford', *Proceedings of the Royal Irish Academy*, 95, C2 (1995).

Poos, L. R., *A Rural Society after the Black Death: Essex, 1350–1525* (Cambridge, 1991).

Raftis, J. A., *The Estates of Ramsey Abbey: A Study in Economic Growth and Organization* (Toronto, 1957).

—— *Tenure and Mobility: Studies in the Social History of the Medieval English Village* (Toronto, 1964).

Razi, Z., *Life, Marriage and Death in a Medieval Parish: Economy, Society and Demography in Halesowen, 1270–1400* (Cambridge, 1980).

—— 'The Struggles between the Abbots of Halesowen and their Tenants in the Thirteenth and Fourteenth Centuries', in T. H. Aston, P. R. Coss, C. Dyer, and J. Thirsk (eds.), *Social Relations and Ideas: Essays in Honour of R. H. Hilton* (Cambridge, 1983).

—— and R. M. Smith (eds.), *Medieval Society and the Manor Court* (Oxford, 1996).

Rees, W., *South Wales and the March, 1284–1415* (1924).

Reeves, A. C., *Newport Lordship, 1317–1536* (Ann Arbor, 1979).

Rigby, S. H., *English Society in the Later Middle Ages: Class, Status and Gender* (1995).

Schofield, P. R., '*Extranei* and the Market for Customary Land on a Westminster Abbey Manor in the Fifteenth Century', *Agricultural History Review*, 49 (2001).

—— 'Tenurial Developments and the Availability of Customary Land in a Later Medieval Community', *Economic History Review*, 49 (1996).

Smith, L. B., 'Seignorial Income in the Fourteenth Century: The Arundels in Chirk', *Bulletin of the Board of Celtic Studies*, 28 (1979).

Tawney, R. H., *The Agrarian Problem in the Sixteenth Century* (1912).

Titow, J. Z., 'Lost Rents, Vacant Holdings and the Contraction of Peasant Cultivation after the Black Death', *Agricultural History Review*, 42 (1994).

Whittle, J., *The Development of Agrarian Capitalism: Land and Labour in Norfolk, 1440–1580* (Oxford, 2000).

CHAPTER 22

....

Government

During the period 1050–1300 the impact of central governments on the economy had increased through the extension of its range. The power of English kings had reached northwards into northern England (finally checked only by the Scottish wars of independence) and westwards into Wales and Ireland. By the time of Alexander III's death in 1286 Scottish kingship stretched westwards and northwards to embrace almost the whole of modern Scotland. Only Orkney and Shetland remained as fiefs of Norway. Between 1300 and 1530 there were significant differences in the capacity of the two monarchies to retain these earlier extensions to their authority. The range of the English crown's authority contracted, both because the government revenues required to maintain its former extended rule were no longer available, and because the more peripheral parts of Britain and Ireland could no longer produce surpluses sufficiently large to justify heavy expenditure. After Edward I's death, English kings turned their faces eastwards to pursue glory, if at all, in France. The western and northern boundaries of their territories interested them only insofar as they might be vulnerable to invasion. Even as late as 1521 Henry VIII was unprepared to finance anything more than a holding operation in Ireland, and was impervious to the duke of Surrey's requests for funds to engage in something more ambitious.[1] As a result much of Ireland became and remained largely an area of powerful local chiefdoms independent of the English crown. English authority in Wales was less seriously diminished, but it was severely shaken in the early fifteenth century. After a long period when English lordship had been tightening its grip on Welsh resources in the fourteenth century, the rebellion of Owain Glyn Dŵr between 1400 and 1408 was an attempt to establish an independent Welsh Wales. The threat was sufficiently severe to justify government resources being used to regain control. Though this was eventually achieved, after years of serious devastation, the Lancastrian kings did not use this as an opportunity to extend the power of English central government over Wales and its lordships, and in that respect the fourteenth and fifteenth centuries were a period of marking time. Only in 1536 did Henry VIII's government under Thomas Cromwell take the next major step in the administrative assimilation of Wales to English institutions.

A reversal similar to that in Ireland affected the kings of Scots in the west of their kingdom during this period, but it was less long-lasting, and ended in positive gains to Scottish royal authority. The decline of their authority in the west during the fourteenth century is best illustrated through the rise of the lordship of Islay under John MacDonald and his son Donald, whose descent from the twelfth-century warlord Somerled gave them impeccable credentials as leaders of Gaeldom. They used the title 'Lord of the Isles', which John's father Angus Og MacDonald had already adopted by 1336, and under John the title acquired increasing significance as he extended his empire over the inner and outer Hebrides, as well as over large stretches of the mainland both north and south of the Great Glen. By 1400 the influence of the Macdonalds predominated over much of the Highlands. Unlike Gaelic Ireland, however, Gaelic Scotland met with effective resistance from the Scottish crown. The independence of the MacDonald lords was eventually curbed by means of royal alliances with their aristocratic rivals. In 1493 James IV felt strong enough to confiscate the lordship of the Isles, and the clan was weakened by internal conflicts.[2] Meanwhile, Orkney and Shetland had been given to James III in 1468–9 and annexed to the Scottish crown in 1472. These were major achievements, though royal success did not imply the integration of the west into the rest of the Scottish kingdom. Some Gaelic lordships were to retain characteristics of independent chiefdoms into the eighteenth century.[3]

Besides changes in the extent of effective kingship there were developments of its scope. Both English and the Scottish monarchies frequently intervened in the economy, either through legislation or minting policy, in attempts to redress those problems of which they were aware. Although it is perhaps too early to be thinking in terms of government economic policies, there were undoubtedly numerous ad hoc economic measures, and it is possible to identify some underlying ideas that motivated them. One, already fully formed before 1300, was the concept of just measures and fair prices, which it was the duty of kings and their agents to ensure through local policing. Another, driven by class interest, was the importance of just wages, labour discipline, and the prevention of unjustifiable begging or idleness. Finally, from the late fourteenth century, lawmakers shared the view that 'shortage of money' was a misfortune to be prevented or corrected by measures to prevent the outflow of bullion and encourage its inflow. Underlying all these ideas was suspicion of private interest, the sin of Avarice, which was conceived as necessarily hostile to the general interest. From the mid-fifteenth century, English writers on political matters increasingly spoke of the 'commonwealth' or 'commonweal', the common well-being, as an identifiable interest that could be damaged by private greed. Governments in this period were considerably more sceptical of private interest than modern ones, though in practice they intervened in the market much less.

On the other hand, these centuries saw no sustained reduction in the willingness of the English crown, in particular, to wage war for reasons that had nothing to do with the common well-being and more to do with dynastic claims and interests. There were some periods when kings showed signs of valuing the advantages of peace, as under Richard II and again (from 1438) by Henry VI, until this became the normal preference in the later fifteenth century. Peace was at this time forced on kings who, like England's Henry VI, lacked the means to pursue any alternative. But the period 1300–1530 was one of the most belligerent in English history. It opened with destructive attempts to establish Edward I's overlordship of Scotland from 1296 until his death in 1307, and war with France between 1294 and 1303 to recover Gascony, following its confiscation by Philip IV of France. The English claims to France were raised by Edward III as high as a claim to the throne, through his mother, and this—though with variations—was the pretext for repeated warfare and endemic piracy after 1338.[4] As we have seen, the greater incidence of war from the 1290s was a cause of increasing transaction costs and economic recession during the early fourteenth century.[5]

In terms of the weight of the impact of governments on the regions under their jurisdiction, in some ways the fourteenth and fifteenth centuries anticipated the complicated relationship between economic and military concerns that was to be a feature of the sixteenth and seventeenth. Unfortunately, though, there are few easy generalizations to be made about the effects on the domestic economy of either peacetime concerns or warfare. Many government measures, like the English labour legislation of the fourteenth century, would not be condoned by any modern economist, and the best one can say of them is that they did not work very well. The effects of warfare, on the other hand, were not always detrimental; wars were far from continuous and affected commerce in different ways at different times. It is consequently not possible to define intervention for economic ends as beneficial for economic performance and warfare as detrimental. Warfare was necessarily costly, and at times raised tax levels to the point that levels of demand in the domestic economy were temporarily depressed, but for much of the time taxes were remarkably light throughout Britain.

Government and Transaction Costs

The first phase of increased English belligerence originated in Edward I's challenge to the independence of the Scottish kingdom. The principal Scottish port, Berwick, was sacked in 1296, and Scottish overseas trade was seriously damaged. However, warfare in this period was not without an impact on English merchants. England's normal export of wool to Flanders was disturbed by conflict with Flanders in 1291–2, which was followed by war with France from 1294 to 1303; Flanders at this time was a county subordinate to France. The precise effects of the war, which was complicated by conflict between France and Flanders, are difficult to gauge because of the absence of adequate customs accounts for the 1290s, when the customs at many ports were leased, but there were numerous political interventions in normal trading patterns, and the costs of trade were further increased by the incidence of piracy in the North Sea. In 1296 a system of convoys, for which merchants had to pay, was needed to protect ships crossing to Zeeland.[6] The restoration of peace between England and France, and then between France and Flanders, was the occasion for a major commercial boom, that carried English wool exports to their highest recorded level before modern times in 1304–5.

A new phase of war with France began in 1337, when Edward III of England laid claim to the French throne. This so-called Hundred Years War was in fact a series of wars of different character, lasting off and on for well over a hundred years, notably in the years 1338–40, 1345–7, 1355–60, 1369–74, 1415–20, 1422–53, 1475, 1492, 1512–13, and 1522–3. Conflicts with the Hanseatic League of a more overtly commercial origin, marked by reprisals and counter-reprisals in which merchants were arrested and their goods detained, were another recurrent source of commercial disruption, notably in the years 1385–8, 1405–8, 1431–7, 1449–50, 1468–74.[7] Many of the crises that punctuated the history of British overseas trade in the fourteenth and fifteenth centuries were the direct result of these confrontations. Recessions in both English and Scottish customs receipts between the late 1420s and early 1460s are at least partly attributable to the impact of warfare and piracy. The reopening of war with France in 1449, for example, contributed directly to the severity of the mid-fifteenth-century recession throughout Britain.[8] Fluctuations were subject to too many determinants to be explained solely in terms of the alternation of war and peace, but the rising costs of trade resulting from war and piracy, together with political adaptations to the requirements of military activity, undoubtedly affected the level and organization of trade.

War was detrimental to England's trade with France, which contracted, with intermittent periods of recovery, well into the fifteenth century. The wine trade with Bordeaux was directly hit by Edward III's wars with France between 1338 and 1360, and again after the reopening of war in 1369.[9] Ships had to be protected by convoys, and by adding armed men to their crews. Freight charges from Bordeaux to England increased from about 8s. a ton around 1300 to 12s. 0d. or 13s. 4d. a ton around 1350, and in periods of exceptional danger, as in 1372, they rose to as much as £1 2s. 0d. a ton. These changes cannot be explained by any comparable increase in labour costs. Quantities of wine imported fell, and the price of wine doubled between the early 1330s and the 1350s from £3 a tun to about £6. The volume of wine imports to England in the fifteenth century, characteristically about 10,000 tuns a year, was only half what it had been before the beginning of the Hundred Years War.[10] The import of salt from Bourgneuf Bay in southern Brittany was also burdened with the need to defend ships against pirates.[11]

Secondary effects of warfare upon trade derived from the ways in which military activity was financed. The English wool trade suffered in the late 1330s and 1340s from Edward III's determination to make it pay for the war, both by raising export duties and by monopolizing exports in the hands of royal agents. Average annual exports declined from about 31,500 sacks a year between 1329/30 and 1335/6 to 21,200 between 1337/8 and 1342/3.[12] Increased rates of customs duty were a major cause of the slow contraction of the English wool trade during the hundred years after 1354, though, as we have seen, because of the boom following the Black Death those effects were delayed until the 1360s.[13]

A common means by which European kings and princes raised cash for military and other purposes was to debase the coinage; this policy was pursued, for example, by Duke Philip of Burgundy in 1386–8, when he minted debased coins, and in 1388–9 when he minted debased gold. On the assumption that it was good to attract bullion into their kingdoms, rulers could also present debasement as a policy in the public interest. Debasement encouraged merchants to take bullion to a mint for coinage because they received back more money (at face value) than they would have done before the debasement had occurred. This policy was particularly successful if a mint could produce counterfeit versions of popularly accepted foreign coins. So long as prices did not instantly adjust to take account of the fact that there was less silver or gold in the coinage than before, the debasement would profit the merchant. The Scottish crown under David II adopted this policy in October 1367, 'on account of the scarcity of money in our realm at present', a scarcity greatly exacerbated by the need to pay David II's ransom. This had the effect, after 200 years when Scotland respected the sterling standard, of moving Scottish coins away from parity with English coins of the same denomination. A Scottish penny now had only 93 per cent of the silver contained in an English one. By 1470 the Scots penny contained only 3½ grains of silver and was mostly made of copper. Subsequent debasements reduced the intrinsic value of the Scottish penny further; the quality of silver was so low that in 1482 high prices were blamed on 'black coin'. Some pennies minted by the bishop of St Andrews in the mid-fifteenth century and some Irish half-farthings of about 1460 were perhaps pure copper currencies.[14] A Scottish penny had only 22 per cent of the silver in an English penny by 1526 (Figure 22.1). Further complexities in the relationship

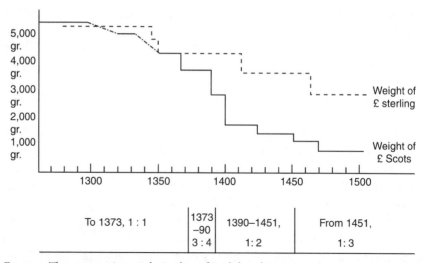

FIG. 22.1. The comparative weight in silver of English and Scots pounds (240 pence in grains), 1260–1500. After having pegged closely together for the century before 1367, the debasement of the Scottish currency proceeded more rapidly than that of the English currency to the point that by the later fifteenth century the silver content of an English penny was worth about three times that of one from a Scottish mint. 1000 grains are equal to 64.8 grammes.

Source: A. Grant, Independence and Nationhood: Scotland, 1306–1469 (1984), 240.

between the English and Scottish currencies were introduced by independent variations in the fineness and weight of the silver currency of higher denominations, the groat, and in that of the gold currencies that England innovated in 1344 and Scotland in about 1357. The divergence in minting policies of the English and Scots reduced the facility with which currency could cross the Anglo-Scottish border, and so complicated Anglo-Scottish trade.[15] English coins, which had dominated the Scottish currency in the early fourteenth century, became decreasingly prominent, though some remained in circulation through the fifteenth century at a suitably elevated rate of exchange with their Scottish equivalent. The English, for their part, not only ruled out the circulation of Scottish coins in England but severely undervalued their bullion content. In the 1390s a Scottish penny was valued in the English mint as worth only half an English penny, even though the true ratio, measured by silver content, was more like 64 per cent.[16]

Debasement was not unknown as a policy of the English crown. In 1335 Edward III debased the silver coinage for the first time since 1279, and four subsequent debasements occurred in 1344, 1345, 1346, and 1351. Even Edward's new gold coinage was reduced in weight in 1346 and again in 1351, a wartime policy which nevertheless met with opposition in parliament. In 1351 debasement of the currency received some of the blame for rising prices after the catastrophe of the

Black Death. In 1352 the king accepted in parliament the Statute of Purveyors, which included the promise that the current coin of the realm should not be altered in weight or in its metal content. There was no further debasement of the currency in the period up to 1530 except in 1411 and 1464–5. On the former occasion the debasement, which was authorized in parliament, was a defensive measure against Flemish counterfeits of English coins which were coming into the country and undermining the quality of the currency. On the second occasion the debasement was imposed by a royal ordinance in August 1464 without consulting parliament, and probably had a fiscal motive, though it was justified as a response to 'scarcity of money'; the king argued that because bullion was underpriced in the English mints merchants were taking bullion to be minted elsewhere.[17]

Throughout the period between 1351 and 1500, therefore, the English crown was exceptionally hampered in its ability to attract money to the mint. Meanwhile, the aggressive minting policies of continental rulers, especially Flanders, had a direct effect upon the amount of currency minted in England, and on the minting profits which accrued to the crown. Munro describes the period 1384–1415 as the period of the War of the Gold Nobles. Particularly between 1389 and 1397 Duke Philip's policies aimed to curtail minting in England. Hardly any silver was minted by Richard II between 1391 and 1397.[18] The aggressive nature of monetary policy arose from the fact that clearly if one mint gained another lost. The chief consequence of this form of international rivalry was England's dependence on alternative policies to achieve the same effect as debasement through currency controls. Instead of debasing the currency to attract silver and gold into the country, the crown occasionally required merchants to import foreign bullion and present it at the mint for recoinage.

A more important consideration relating to the coinage, quite independent of the royal concern for mint revenues, was a widespread anxiety amongst northern European governments concerning the money supplies of their respective territories, chiefly because they associated the recurrent economic recessions of the age with 'scarcity of money'. Debate within an English parliamentary committee of 1381, appointed to discuss the shortage of money in England, drew from the officers of the English mint the first known formulation of a bullionist balance of trade theory. Richard Leicester recommended that each merchant importing merchandise into England should export commodities of equal value, and that no bullion should be exported. Richard Aylesbury agreed, arguing that if overseas trade was properly managed 'money will remain in England and a great amount of money will come from overseas'.[19] Complaints that money was scarce mounted after 1385; prices were falling, demand for foodstuffs was slackening.[20] Because fourteenth- and fifteenth-century governments analysed problems of recession in monetary terms, they responded with bullionist measures to maintain and augment the volume of currency in circulation. These policies could create international rivalries that were largely the result of such economic considerations.

In practice, governments had operated on bullionist assumptions long before 1381. One recurrent response to these problems was the requirement that merchants should bring money to the mint in direct accordance with the value of goods they exported, as in English regulations of 1340, 1341, and 1343. This policy had ceased to be enforced by 1348, but new regulations of a similar kind were not long in being reintroduced. In 1363 Edward set up a mint at Calais for the purpose.[21] Further measures to compel merchants to supply English mints were introduced in 1379, in 1391, in Richard II's Bullion Ordinance of 1397, and again in an ordinance of Henry IV's in 1402. In 1381 the alarm was such that exports of coin out of the country were prohibited. Scotland, too, suffering even more acutely from the same problems, restricted the export of bullion in 1385 and subsequently. Another tack was to encourage exports. In 1390 came the first of many English 'employment' Acts of Parliament, requiring merchants to spend at least half of what they earned at home in selling their imports in buying up English goods for export.[22]

There were many later attempts to manipulate trade to prevent the outflow of bullion and encourage its inflow. Of particular importance for fifteenth-century England were policies designed to draw bullion from Burgundy in payment for English wool. In 1422 the Calais mint was reopened after nineteen years in abeyance and the export of English coin was prohibited. Then in 1429 Richard II's ordinance of 1397 was renewed, in more draconian form, in the Calais Staple Partition and Bullion Ordinances. Merchants were required to sell wool in Calais for nothing but gold or silver, of which one-third was to be exchanged for English coin at the Calais mint. These laws, renewed in 1433, remained in force until 1442. A similar but less severe set of rules was in force between 1463 and 1473. Such economic aggression inevitably met with retaliation, and its effects on the wool trade were adverse. Insistence on sales of wool for cash rather than on credit nevertheless persisted till 1478, when this bullionist policy was finally renounced in the negotiations which prepared for rapprochement between England and Burgundy at that time.[23]

Scotland fought against her fifteenth-century currency problems with essentially the same bullionist arsenal. Legislation of 1436 prohibited exports of gold, silver, and jewellery, and required merchants to bring three ounces of silver to the royal mint for every sack of wool, or its equivalent in other commodities that they exported. A 40 per cent tax on bullion exports was imposed by the Scottish parliament in 1424. From 1436 a series of laws required merchants to import bullion in proportion to the value of their exports, and from 1449 the export of coin was restricted. Bullionist legislation came particularly thick and fast between 1465 and 1468, following a detailed discussion of monetary problems by the Scottish lords at

Berwick in 1465. Exports of coin were totally banned in 1466 except for extremely limited 'expenses', and past measures to attract an inflow of bullion were reaffirmed in 1467, 1468, 1473, and later. The Act of 1473 mentions special searchers appointed to prevent illegal bullion exports, and they remained a feature of Scottish policy in 1526.[24] Scotland, too, took measures to inhibit imports and encourage exports. Consumption of silk was restricted in 1471, and imports of English cloth were prohibited in 1473 (repeating an earlier measure of the mid-fifteenth century).[25]

In this respect, as in others, the late fourteenth and early fifteenth centuries saw the formulation of restrictive policies which were to be of relevance for a very long time. The bullionist theories relating to trade formulated in the later fourteenth and fifteenth centuries were the foundation of mercantilist thinking in the sixteenth and seventeenth. They were not the principal reason for the increased difficulties of trading between the 1340s and the 1470s; rather they were a response to the effects of enhanced international competition, commercial recessions, and declining monetary circulation, which added to the costs and risks of trade. They nevertheless represent a strong contrast to the relatively less regulated trade of the period of international commercial expansion during the twelfth and thirteenth centuries.

English government intervention in the home market was also in some respects more far-reaching in the fourteenth and fifteenth centuries than earlier. In particular, the regulation of manufactures was often a necessary part of building up custom in distant markets, equivalent to quality controls now more commonly internal to the operations of manufacturing firms. Richard I's assize of cloth of 1196, which had standardized the width of English cloth at two yards, was repeatedly modified during the fourteenth century. The Statute of Northampton of 1328 revised the older assize of cloth to standardize length as well as width, though the regulations needed numerous later modifications.[26] Government remained generally alert to the cloth industry's interests, but its responsibility was in part delegated to urban communities, who in turn passed it to craft guilds and their wardens. This was the preferred policy of the Scottish crown, which was less interventionist in the affairs of the textile industry and left industrial regulation to the burgh guilds. The smaller importance of exports for the development of Scottish textile manufacture is probably the chief explanation for this difference between the two kingdoms.

Other aspects of government intervention in trade are less commendable, especially when they were designed to control prices and wages. These interventions can be regarded as responses to what the legislating classes saw as major problems of the age—rising prices and wage costs, poor labour discipline. The English Ordinance of Labourers (1349) and Statute of Labourers (1351) were over-ambitious attempts to curb the negotiating power of all sorts of manual workers following severe depopulation in 1348–9.[27] The price controls introduced under these laws as a check on profit levels supplemented the older rules against fore-stalling, which in England came to be regarded as statutory from about the 1290s.[28] Similar price controls were enforced in Scotland, and as in England the offence they were designed to check became more loosely defined and their scope was broad-ened by local courts to include a wider range of commodities.[29] To the extent that the new powers given to local authorities and justices of the peace succeeded in restraining wage increases they presumably held down manufacturing costs, but it is difficult to attribute to them any significant economic virtue; had they succeeded, they would also have encouraged the misallocation of labour and reduced the size of the home market. In addition to their other defects, all these regulations relating to prices and wages increased the arbitrariness of the law. By the time local juries had interpreted statutes to suit themselves, there was plenty of scope for rough justice.

Governments and the Distribution of Income

A characteristic of the thirteenth century, over parts of Britain subject to the English crown, had been the development of direct taxes on the personal wealth of the king's subjects.[30] Taxes on the laity were voted in parliament, and taxes on the clergy in the clerical convocations of Canterbury and York. These direct taxes were more important in England's royal finance than Scotland's, and were accepted as a frequent, though unpredictable, necessity. Clerical taxes in England were levied on the basis of an assessment made in 1291–2.[31] Lay taxes were separately assessed on each occasion until 1334, but from then on the assessments for a 'fifteenth and tenth' on each tax community were fixed, so that a known sum was due from each village or borough, making up a total of about £37,500 from the kingdom as a whole. Wales and the palatinates of Durham and Chester, whose inhabitants were exploited in other ways, were not liable to pay them.[32] From 1334, once the assessed value of each settlement was fixed, the structure of assessments became increasingly unrelated to the real distribution of wealth. The basis of individual tax assessment now shifted; because assessors were obliged to raise a definite sum, they could not leave the distribution of individual assessments to chance, and the contributions of individual taxpayers tended to become more fixed. The tax base, meanwhile, was widened to include most householders, so that a larger number of taxpayers paid a smaller average sum.[33] Another change, over a century later, derived from the economic recessions of the mid-fifteenth century and political problems of the crown. First of all the government thought it advisable in 1433 and again in 1446 to lower a number of tax assessments in the light of widespread complaints of poverty, reducing the yield of a 'fifteenth and tenth' to about £31,000.[34] From the 1450s, economic discontent, and the end of war with France in 1453, coupled with mistrust of the government, made parliament more unwilling than in the past to make tax grants.[35] English direct taxation under the Yorkist kings was conspicuously low (Figures 22.2 and 22.3). One reason why Sir John Fortescue was so impressed by the powers of the English parliament in comparison with its French equivalent at the time he was writing his treatise *On the Governance of England* in the early 1470s, was that the power of the English crown to tax was more constrained than in earlier generations.

In Ireland as in England the basis upon which direct taxes were levied changed in the course of the fourteenth and fifteenth centuries, but it changed differently and even more profoundly. These taxes required the authorization of the Irish parliament, whose authority over the whole of Ireland dwindled in the course of the Gaelic revival. Assessments came to be based on possession of arable land, like the geld of Anglo-Saxon England. Between 1369 and 1371 this tax could raise as much as £1,500, but from that high point the yield declined to at most £400 by 1420 and to no more than £325 by the early 1470s. One reason for this decline was that, with the exception of Waterford and Wexford, subsidies could no longer be levied outside the region known as the Pale—the four medieval counties of Dublin, Louth, Meath, and Kildare. The sums raised were no longer large enough by the 1470s to support the Irish administration, which consequently had to be bolstered with subventions from England. Under the Lancastrians these amounted to about £2,000 a year.[36]

The Scottish parliament authorized a similar direct tax on property in the years 1358, 1359, and 1360 as a means to pay off the heavy ransom demanded by the English crown for the return of King David II from imprisonment in England. Unlike the English 'fifteenths and tenths', this tax was levied on the assessed value of rents as well as movable goods, crops, and livestock. But such direct taxation never became as frequent in Scotland as in England, chiefly because the Scots were both poorer and less belligerent than the English. Some heavy taxes were associated with extreme financial emergencies such as the need to make peace with England in 1328, and to ransom kings—David II in 1357, James II in 1424—from captivity in England. On other occasions the Scottish parliament was even more successful than the English in resisting such taxes. Only 22 direct levies were raised between 1306 and 1469, and most of these raised only about £2,000. James IV (1473–1513) stepped up the regularity of direct taxes between 1488 and 1497, but the hostility he encountered drove him to look for funds from other quarters. In the absence of a regular system of direct taxation the kings of Scotland were obliged to make shift from their own resources, and by ad hoc expedients, much as the English crown had done under the Angevin kings.[37]

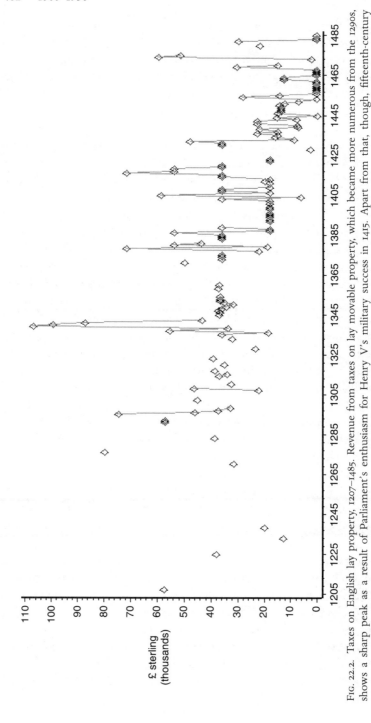

Fig. 22.2. Taxes on English lay property, 1207–1485. Revenue from taxes on lay movable property, which became more numerous from the 1290s, shows a sharp peak as a result of Parliament's enthusiasm for Henry V's military success in 1415. Apart from that, though, fifteenth-century governments found it difficult to achieve the level of taxation characteristic of the earlier fourteenth century.

Source: W. M. Ormrod, 'England in the Middle Ages', in R. Bonney (ed.), *The Rise of the Fiscal State in Europe, c.1200–1815* (Oxford, 1999), 30.

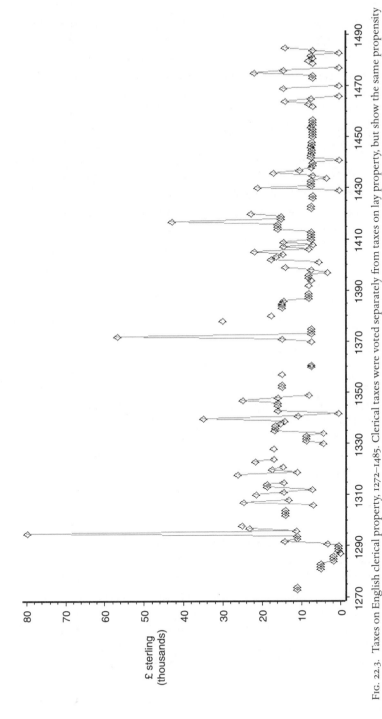

Fig. 22.3. Taxes on English clerical property, 1272–1485. Clerical taxes were voted separately from taxes on lay property, but show the same propensity to decrease in amount, especially from the late fourteenth century.

Source: W. M. Ormrod, 'England in the Middle Ages', in R. Bonney (ed.), *The Rise of the Fiscal State in Europe, c.1200–1815* (Oxford, 1999), 31.

By the 1470s, subjects of the English and Scottish crowns were very little subject to direct taxes. Meanwhile, however, both crowns had become dependent on indirect taxes on trade. Rates of English customs duties were jacked up at the start of the Hundred Years War, as we have seen, and the crown revenue from overseas trade leapt upwards at this period. In Scotland export duties were quadrupled in 1368 in order to pay off David II's ransom, and as in England they remained less politically contentious than grants of direct taxes. Yet in both kingdoms the total level of customs income was closely tied to the amount of wool exported, and this was in turn adversely affected in the long run by the high level of export duties imposed upon it. The English crown, more than the Scottish, benefited from an increased export of woollen cloth, but the duties levied on this were nowhere near enough to compensate for the decline in the wool trade. Whereas England's wools had a distinct enough status in international trade to bear a high export tax, her cloths did not; they had to compete in international markets with numerous rivals. Both governments suffered from the contraction of customs revenue during the fifteenth century, with a particularly severe dip in the mid-fifteenth-century slump. In both kingdoms customs revenues fell by a third of their former level in money of account between the early 1370s and the 1480s—from around £10,000 to £3,300 in Scotland, and from about £72,000 to £21,000 in England (Figure 22.4)[38]—though this represents a more severe decline in Scotland because of the effects of debasement after 1367. Irish customs revenues collapsed in the later thirteenth and earlier fourteenth century, from about £1,400 in the 1270s to £360 by 1344, and unlike the customs revenues of England and Scotland there was no mid-fourteenth-century upward hike. In 1420 and 1443 the Irish customs raised less than £200 a year, though a subsequent trade revival brought that sum to £300 a year or more by the 1480s.[39]

As a result of the contraction of the principal forms of direct and indirect taxation, the total burden of taxation declined more sharply than the population throughout Britain during most of the fifteenth century, and it is consequently impossible to attribute the economic doldrums of the mid and later part of the century to the effects of high taxation. Both England and Scotland, in effect, had seen taxation decline in importance relative to royal income of a more personal character. This had gone farthest in Scotland, where about 1486 customs dues and direct taxes accounted for only about a fifth of James III's income, and crown lands for over two-thirds.[40] Partly because of the difficulty of raising income by taxes, kings of the later fifteenth century developed a greater interest than their predecessors in developing and enlarging their estates, and even in exploiting old-fashioned rights of lordship. The Yorkist kings of England, Edward IV (1461–70, 1471–83) and Richard III (1483–5), and their Tudor successor Henry VII (1485–1509) augmented the revenues from the royal estates and their feudal dues, ensuring that the revenues were accounted for in their own household rather than through the

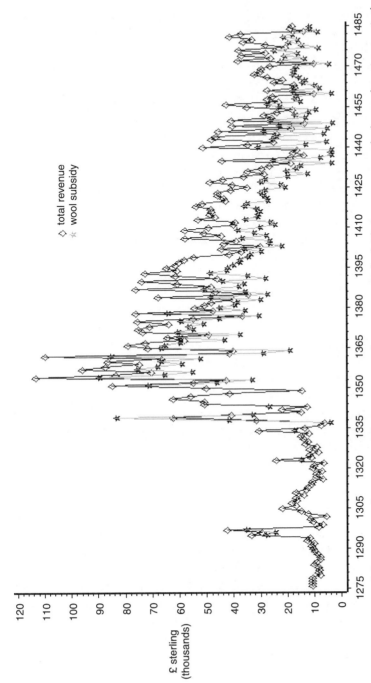

FIG. 22.4. Taxes on English overseas trade, 1276–1485. The gross revenue from customs and subsidies on overseas trade shows a huge increase in the mid-fourteenth century, chiefly as a result of the taxes on wool exports imposed to finance warfare with France. Falling revenue from overseas trade thereafter demonstrates the extent to which the king's income suffered from the decline of England's wool trade.

Source: W. M. Ormrod, 'England in the Middle Ages', in R. Bonney (ed.), *The Rise of the Fiscal State in Europe, c.1200–1815* (Oxford, 1999), 33.

more remote operations of the exchequer.[41] Comparable policies were pursued, at an earlier date and with even greater necessity by Scottish kings, whose tax base was so conspicuously weak. James I (1406–37) created two central financial offices; a treasurer was to receive the rents from crown lands and burghs, and a comptroller was to receive feudal dues, the profits of justice and taxes. From 1431 he gained a reputation for avarice (like Henry VII of England seventy years later) because of his rigour in raising money. The growing importance of crown lands as a source of revenue for the King of Scots is indicated by the creation of a new system of local bailies or receivers (*ballivi ad extra*) to manage and account for individual properties.[42] These policies were vigorously continued under their successors. James IV, like his English contemporaries Edward IV, Richard III, and Henry VII raised royal income by tight administration of crown lands and the exploitation of royal dues. He raised royal income threefold in real terms by these means; his treasurer's annual receipts rose from £4,500 Scots in 1496–7 to £28,000 by 1512.[43] Such policies represented a sustained Scottish shift away from 'tax state' to those of a 'domain state' under pressure of political and economic change; in other words kings were becoming more dependent upon their own royal resources rather than their ability to tax.[44] These policies were more significant for political relations between kings and their principal subjects than for the distribution of incomes and levels of welfare, but they serve well to illustrate the extent to which taxation became a problematic issue during the fourteenth and fifteenth centuries.

There was, however, a major difference between the English and Scottish crowns in that in England the cultivation of 'domain' revenues was accompanied by the early stages of a revival in tax revenues from about 1470, both from direct and indirect sources. That was much less the case in Scotland, where direct taxation remained subordinate. Nor did the revival in Scottish customs receipts after the trough of the 1450s run, as in England, into a sustained expansion of trade; there was no sustained upwards trend in average annual customs receipts between the 1460s and the 1510s, and even the higher levels of the 1520s did not represent more than a temporary achievement.[45] Between 1470 and 1530 the financial systems of the two kingdoms drew increasingly apart. The Scottish kings remained obliged to build up their finances on domain revenues and other windfalls, such as those arising from the exploitation of ecclesiastical revenues and the dowries that James V obtained by his marriages to the unfortunate French Princess Madeleine (who died soon after her arrival in Scotland) and Mary of Guise, the mother of Mary Queen of Scots; their combined dowries amounted to £168,750.[46] By Henry VIII's reign, by contrast, the English monarchy was moving strongly back towards a heavier reliance on taxation—to the forms of a 'tax state' rather than a 'domain state'.

The return to heavier taxation in England, chiefly to fund wars abroad, was not achieved quickly, nor without considerable opposition. However, when they felt they had a good enough case to argue, kings were able to call on the tradition of parliamentary taxes on movables, which had never finally been abandoned. Sometimes, as in 1472 and 1489, they were allowed to experiment with new forms of levy that imposed a liability for tax more in line with the real distribution of income. In 1497 and 1504 they worked with the old county assessments for fifteenths and tenths, but reallocated the burdens on individual villages and towns. Finally they achieved the creation of a new form of assessed subsidy, based on the assessed capacity of taxpayers to pay without reference to traditional tax liabilities, though this did not replace the older form of assessments entirely. Henry VIII was allowed this development in response to the wartime demands of the years 1513–15. In 1523, again under pressure of wartime commitments, he won parliamentary consent to another heavy subsidy over four years, based on a similar assessment. As a result of these episodic successes, royal income from direct lay taxation increased from an annual average of about £12,200 between 1450 and 1472, to about £12,650 between 1473 and 1513, and £21,775 between 1514 and 1529.[47] There was an echo of this increased dependence on taxes in the parts of Ireland subject to the English crown, where taxation became heavier from the 1470s, though on the same basis as before. Higher taxes were made necessary by the withdrawal of financial subventions from England during the reign of Edward IV, who passed the burden of finding funds on to the resident governor. In 1477 the Irish parliament authorized a level of taxation without precedent during the fifteenth century, and from that time the normal levy of a subsidy was higher than before. In the early sixteenth century subsidies were levied more frequently in Ireland than in England, though they raised only £500 a year or so.[48] Meanwhile, Wales remained outside this development, since it was not subject to English taxation bills until the Subsidy Act of 1543.[49]

English indirect taxes also increased from the 1470s onwards, as a result of reviving trade, though this was chiefly the result of growing trade through London and Southampton. By the first two decades of the sixteenth century the customs revenue of the English crown had risen to about £40,000 a year, though it averaged only £35,305 between 1521 and 1529.[50] This increase up to that point owed something to the framework of international relations created by English foreign policy, though the active expansion of trade with the Low Countries was the work of merchants and the government had little direct part to play. Away from southern England, other parts of Britain did not experience the same commercial revival, and so could not benefit government revenues to the same extent. There was no comparable trade expansion on the west coast or in the Irish Sea. Irish customs revenues showed no sustained increase between 1485 and 1530.[51]

This rising level of English taxation was therefore the result both of political revival that enabled kings to command more authority, and more of the resources of their subjects, and of a narrowly based trade revival from the 1470s. The extent to which higher tax rates also implied a significant increase in average personal incomes is a problem, given our current evidence. From 1513 English parliaments showed a grudging willingness to grant higher taxation than in the past, given appropriate wartime circumstances, but under the early Tudors taxpayers had a high propensity to resist novelties, in effect rejecting parliamentary authority. In the absence of better information about the movement of national income in this period, it is reasonable to suppose that increased taxation was in part at the expense of standards of private consumption and investment. Higher taxes, in other words, could jeopardize those high standards of living that Fortescue had seen as one of the advantages of low taxation in the 1470s. The relevance of this last observation is largely restricted, however, to England in the 1520s.[52] For most of the period it is difficult to argue that government taxation policies had any adverse affect on economic development or social welfare. It is noteworthy, though, how little the low-tax regimes of fifteenth-century Britain positively benefited economic growth during that century.

NOTES

1. D. B. Quinn, 'The Hegemony of the Earls of Kildare, 1494–1520', in A. Cosgrove (ed.), *A New History of Ireland, ii: Medieval Ireland, 1169–1534* (Oxford, 1987), 666–7.
2. M. Lynch (ed.), *The Oxford Companion to Scottish History* (Oxford, 2001), 295, 347–8.
3. R. A. Dodgshon, *From Chiefs to Landlords: Social and Economic Change in the Western Highlands and Islands, c.1493–1820* (Edinburgh, 1998).
4. Above (Ch. 16).
5. Above (Ch. 4).
6. T. H. Lloyd, *The English Wool Trade in the Middle Ages* (Cambridge, 1977), 74–101.
7. M. M. Postan, 'The Economic and Political Relations of England and the Hanse from 1400 to 1475', in E. Power and M. M. Postan, *Studies in English Trade in the Fifteenth Century* (1933), 91–153.
8. R. H. Britnell, 'The Economic Context', in A. J. Pollard (ed.), *The Wars of the Roses* (Basingstoke, 1995), 44–6; A. Stevenson, 'Trade with the South, 1070–1513', in M. Lynch, M. Spearman, and G. Stell (eds.), *The Scottish Medieval Town* (Edinburgh, 1988), 197–8.
9. M. K. James, *Studies in the Medieval Wine Trade*, ed. E. M. Veale (Oxford, 1971), 15, 26.
10. J. L. Bolton, *The Medieval English Economy, 1150–1500* (1980), 290; James, *Studies in the Medieval Wine Trade*, 24–8, 32–7, 41–3, 55–9.
11. A. R. Bridbury, *England and the Salt Trade in the Later Middle Ages* (Oxford, 1955), 76–7.
12. E. M. Carus-Wilson and O. Coleman, *England's Export Trade, 1275–1547* (Oxford, 1963), 44–6.
13. Above (Ch. 16).

14. G. C. Brooke, *English Coins*, 3rd edn. (1950), 122, 171, 184; C. E. Challis (ed.), *A New History of the Royal Mint* (Cambridge, 1992), 712; A Grant, *Independence and Nationhood: Scotland 1306–1469* (1984), 80, 240; J. E. L. Murray, 'The Black Money of James III', in D. M. Metcalf, *Coinage in Medieval Scotland (1100–1600)* (Oxford, 1977), 116; P. Spufford, *Money and its Use in Medieval Europe* (Cambridge, 1988), 362.

15. Above (Ch. 16).

16. E. Gemmill and N. Mayhew, *Changing Values in Medieval Scotland: A Study of Prices, Money, and Weights and Measures* (Cambridge, 1995), 116–42.

17. J. Munro, *Wool, Cloth and Gold: The Struggle for Bullion in Anglo-Burgundian Trade, 1340–1478* (Toronto, 1972), 26–7, 47–50, 161.

18. C. E. Challis, 'Appendix 1. Mint Output, 1220–1985', in id. (ed.), *New History*, 682; Munro, *Wool, Cloth and Gold*, 53.

19. *Rotuli Parliamentorum; ut et Petitiones et Placita in Parliamento*, 6 vols. (1783), i. 126–7; C. D. Liddy, 'The Estate of Merchants in the Parliament of 1381', *Historical Research*, 74 (2001), 331–45; Lloyd, 'Overseas Trade', 117; Munro, *Wool, Cloth and Gold*, 44.

20. Lloyd, *English Wool Trade*, 242–6; Munro, *Wool, Cloth and Gold*, 60–1.

21. T. H. Lloyd, 'Overseas Trade and the English Money Supply in the Fourteenth Century', in N. J. Mayhew (ed.), *Edwardian Monetary Affairs (1279–1344)*, British Archaeological Reports, 36 (Oxford, 1977), 109–10, 115; Munro, *Wool, Cloth and Gold*, 36–40.

22. Lloyd, 'Overseas Trade', 117; Munro, *Wool, Cloth and Gold*, 45–6, 54–6, 60–1; R. Nicholson, *Scotland: The Later Middle Ages* (Edinburgh, 1974), 268.

23. N. J. Mayhew, 'From Regional to Central Minting, 1158–1464', in Challis (ed.), *New History*, 151; Munro, *Wool, Cloth and Gold*, 73, 84–6, 99, 124, 159–60, 176–7.

24. *The Acts of the Parliaments of Scotland*, ed. T. Thomson and C. Innes, 12 vols. (Edinburgh, 1814–75), ii. 5, 23, 37, 86, 90, 92, 105, 106, 306.

25. Nicholson, *Scotland*, 307, 432–3.

26. A. R. Bridbury, *Medieval English Clothmaking: An Economic Survey* (1982), 54–5.

27. See above (Ch. 17, 18).

28. R. H. Britnell, 'Forestall, Forestalling and the Statute of Forestallers', *English Historical Review*, 202 (1987), 101.

29. R. H. Britnell, *Growth and Decline in Colchester, 1300–1525* (Cambridge, 1986), 236–8; Gemmill and Mayhew, *Changing Values*, 66–7.

30. Above (Ch. 12).

31. Detail assessments are available on the internet at 'The Taxatio Database', **www.taxatio.man.ac.uk/index.aspx.**

32. *The Lay Subsidy of 1334*, ed. R. E. Glasscock (1975), xvi; R. R. Davies, *Conquest, Co-existence and Change: Wales, 1063–1415* (Oxford, 1987), 402; W. M. Ormrod, 'England in the Middle Ages', in R. Bonney (ed.), *The Rise of the Fiscal State in Europe, c.1200–1815* (Oxford, 1999), 43.

33. C. Dyer, 'Taxation and Communities in Late Medieval England', in R. Britnell and J. Hatcher (eds.), *Progress and Problems in Medieval England: Essays in Honour of Edward Miller* (Cambridge, 1996), 173–4.

34. M. Jurkowski, C. L. Smith, and D. Crook, *Lay Taxes in England and Wales, 1188–1688* (Kew, 1998), 89–90, 98–9.

35. Britnell, 'Economic Context', 60–2.

36. S. G. Ellis, *Reform and Revival: English Government in Ireland 1470–1534* (Woodbridge, 1986), 67–8; id., *Tudor Ireland: Crown, Community and the Conflict of Cultures 1470–1603* (1985), 20, 60.

37. Grant, *Independence and Nationhood*, 162–3; N. Macdougall, *James IV* (Edinburgh, 1989), 147–50; Nicholson, *Scotland*, 164, 175–6, 188, 217, 283–4, 304, 317, 453–4, 567.

38. Nicholson, *Scotland*, 177, 187–8, 454. Details of English receipts are currently available on the internet from the European State Finance data base at **www.le.ac.uk/hi/bon/ESFDB/index.html.**

39. Ellis, *Reform and Revival*, 72.

40. Nicholson, *Scotland*, 454.

41. B. P. Wolffe, *The Royal Demesne in English History: The Crown Estate in the Governance of the Realm from the Conquest to 1509* (1971), 143–225.

42. M. Brown, *James I* (Edinburgh, 1994), 149; Nicholson, *Scotland*, 313, 380; Scottish Record Office, *Guide to the National Archives of Scotland* (Edinburgh, 1996), 35.

43. Nicholson, *Scotland*, 566–72; N. Macdougall, 'James IV', in Lynch (ed.), *Oxford Companion to Scottish History*, 352; id., *James IV*, 157–65.

44. For this distinction, see Ormrod, 'England', 21.

45. P. G. B. McNeill and H. L. MacQueen (eds.), *Atlas of Scottish History to 1707* (Edinburgh, 1996), 240.

46. N. Macdougall, 'James V', in Lynch (ed.), *Oxford Companion to Scottish History*, 354.

47. R. H. Britnell, *The Closing of the Middle Ages? England, 1471–1529* (Oxford, 1997), 114–16; id., 'Economic Context', 60–1.

48. Ellis, *Reform and Revival*, 49–50, 68–9.

49. G. Williams, *Recovery, Reorientation and Reformation: Wales, c.1415–1642* (Oxford, 1987), 267.

50. R. Hoyle, 'War and Public Finance', in D. MacCulloch, (ed.), *The Reign of Henry VIII: Politics, Policy and Piety* (1995), 77.

51. Ellis, *Reform and Revival*, 72–3.

52. R. H. Britnell, 'The English Economy and the Government, 1450–1550', in J. L. Watts (ed.), *The End of the Middle Ages? England in the Fifteenth and Sixteenth Centuries* (Stroud, 1998), 101–4.

FURTHER READING

Archer, R. (ed.), *Crown, Government and People in the Fifteenth Century* (Stroud, 1995).

Bernard, G. W., *War, Taxation and Rebellion in Tudor England: Henry VIII, Wolsey and the Amicable Grant* (Brighton, 1986).

Boardman, S., *The Early Stewart Kings: Robert II and Robert III, 1371–1406* (East Linton, 1996).

Britnell, R. H., *The Closing of the Middle Ages? England, 1471–1529* (Oxford, 1997).

—— 'The Economic Context', in A. J. Pollard (ed.), *The Wars of the Roses* (Basingstoke, 1995).

—— 'The English Economy and the Government, 1450–1550', in J. L. Watts (ed.), *The End of the Middle Ages? England in the Fifteenth and Sixteenth Centuries* (Stroud, 1998).

Brown, M., *James I* (Edinburgh, 1994).

Challis, C. E. (ed.), *A New History of the Royal Mint* (Cambridge, 1992).

Childs, W., 'Finance and Trade under Edward II', in J. Taylor and W. Childs (eds.), *Politics and Crisis in Fourteenth-Century England* (Gloucester, 1990).

Cosgrove, A. (ed.), *A New History of Ireland*, ii: *Medieval Ireland, 1169–1534* (Oxford, 1987).

Davies, R. R., *Conquest, Coexistence and Change: Wales, 1063–1415* (Oxford, 1987).

Dyer, C., 'Taxation and Communities in Late Medieval England', in R. H. Britnell and J. Hatcher (eds.), *Progress and Problems in Medieval England: Essays in Honour of Edward Miller* (Cambridge, 1996).

Ellis, S. G., *Reform and Revival: English Government in Ireland 1470–1534* (Woodbridge, 1986).

—— *Tudor Ireland: Crown, Community and the Conflict of Cultures, 1470–1603* (Harlow, 1985).

Frame, R., *The Political Development of the Brtish Isles, 1100–1400* (Oxford, 1990).

Grant, A., *Independence and Nationhood: Scotland 1306–1469* (1984).

—— *Henry VII: The Importance of his Reign in English History* (1985).

Gunn, S. J., *Early Tudor Government, 1485–1558* (1995).

Harriss, G. L., *King, Parliament and Public Finance in Medieval England to 1369* (Oxford, 1975).

—— (ed.), *Henry V: The Practice of Kingship* (Oxford, 1985).

Harvey, I. M. W., 'Was there Popular Politics in Fifteenth-Century England?', in R. H. Britnell and A. J. Pollard (eds.), *The McFarlane Legacy: Studies in Late Medieval Politics and Society* (Stroud, 1995).

Hilton, R. H., and Aston, T. H., *The English Rising of 1381* (Cambridge, 1984).

Hoyle, R., 'War and Public Finance', in D. MacCulloch (ed.), *The Reign of Henry VIII: Politics, Policy and Piety* (1995).

Jurkowski, M., Smith, C. L., and Crook, D., *Lay Taxes in England and Wales, 1188–1688* (Kew, 1998).

Lander, J. R., *The Limitations of English Monarchy in the Later Middle Ages* (Toronto, 1989).

Macdougall, N., *James III: A Political Study* (Edinburgh, 1992).

—— *James IV* (Edinburgh, 1989).

McGladdery, C., *James II* (Edinburgh, 1990).

Metcalf, D. M., *Coinage in Medieval Scotland (1100–1600)* (Oxford, 1977).

Munro, J., *Wool, Cloth and Gold: The Struggle for Bullion in Anglo-Burgundian Trade, 1340–1478* (Toronto, 1972).

Nicholson, R., *Scotland: The Later Middle Ages* (Edinburgh, 1974).

Ormrod, W. M., *The Reign of Edward III: Crown and Political Society in England* (New Haven, 1990).

—— 'England in the Middle Ages', in R. Bonney (ed.), *The Rise of the Fiscal State in Europe, c.1200–1815* (Oxford, 1999).

—— 'The Politics of Pestilence: Government in England after the Black Death', in id. and P. Lindley (eds.), *The Black Death in England* (Stamford, 1996).

Palmer, R. C., *English Law in the Age of the Black Death 1348–1381* (Chapel Hill, NC, 1993).

Pollard, A. J., *North-Eastern England during the Wars of the Roses: Lay Society, War, and Politics 1450–1500* (Oxford, 1990).

Rigby, S. H., *A Companion to Britain in the Later Middle Ages* (Oxford, 2003).

Ross, C., *Edward IV* (1984).

Schofield, R., 'Taxation and the Political Limits of the Tudor State', in C. Cross, D. M. Loades, and J. J. Scarisbrick (eds.), *Law and Government under the Tudors* (Cambridge, 1988).

Walker, D., *Medieval Wales* (Cambridge, 1990).

Willard, J. F., *Parliamentary Taxes on Personal Property, 1290 to 1334: A Study in Medieval English Financial Administration* (Cambridge, Mass., 1934).

Williams, G., *Recovery, Reorientation and Reformation: Wales, c.1415–1642* (Oxford, 1987).

Wolffe, B. P., *The Crown Lands, 1461–1536* (1970).

—— *The Royal Demesne in English History: The Crown Estate in the Governance of the Realm from the Conquest to 1509* (1971).

CHAPTER 23

Procedural Routines and the Uses of Literacy

The history of records and record keeping between 1050 and 1300 is one of dramatic growth, as so often with the origins and early development of new techniques. The following two centuries, by contrast, have less novelty to offer. By 1300 the use of writing as an aid to communication and administrative control was so thoroughly embedded in the way government and legal institutions worked that it would have taken greater catastrophes than those of the fourteenth century to undermine it, and historians using records of the fourteenth and fifteenth centuries have generally been more impressed at the degree of continuity with the past than by change, except in regions of severe political instability like parts of Ireland.[1] Bureaucratic conservatism can make it look superficially as if nothing had altered, even if closer analysis of what is recorded demonstrates that that was not the case. Nevertheless, changes in the way institutions worked, changes in the costs of producing records, and other social and cultural developments, inevitably had some impact on the form of administrative recording, and as before there are pronounced regional differences in what has come down to us.

Continuity and Change

Continuity of practice is worth dwelling on, for a moment, because it has important implications for the robustness of economic, legal, and political institutions. By 1300 the power structures within which records were preserved had a strikingly long history with little serious disruption. Properties and offices had changed hands, but methods of operation had been adapted gradually to solve emerging problems or adapt to new opportunities, and the fundamental institutions of government and lordship were able to absorb major shocks without crumbling. It is true that conditions turned less favourable to landlords in the course of the fourteenth century, and that their capacity to increase their revenues was undermined by falling demand for agricultural prices and rising labour costs. Yet the major institutions of government and society were able to absorb these changes with only superficial alterations in their mode of operation until the very end of the century, and they were then transformed by a process of rational deliberation aimed at reducing risk and uncertainty rather than by collapse. In Ireland the development of traditions of manorial record keeping that had taken root by the early fourteenth century was severely hampered by the difficulties of managing large estates in times of trouble, but even there regular accounts were drawn up for the Clare estates in Counties Kilkenny, Tipperary, Dublin, and Meath through the 1350s.[2]

During the thirteenth century vernacular languages had become a normal vehicle for informal records throughout France, the Low Counties, Germany, Italy, and Castile. Though kings, churchmen, and notaries might retain Latin as the normal language for legal instruments, by 1300 thousands of routine conveyances and other deeds, especially between laymen, were written in languages that their recipients could understand.[3] Britain moved slowly in the same direction. Vernacular Scots gained ground for many administrative and business documents from the 1380s, and had become the norm for all but the most formal documents by the early sixteenth century; even many legal instruments were written in Scots, though Latin was used for notaries' records and for letters under the king's great seal.[4] Churchmen were more likely to use Latin for routine administrative purposes, such as the bishopric of Dunkeld accounts of 1505–17.[5] England was perhaps even slower to move. English was used increasingly from the later fourteenth century for non-traditional or less formal records as in many ordinances, wills, and letters between laymen, but even in the early sixteenth century charters and routine accounts and court records were commonly composed in Latin. English clerks also used law French, which the legal profession retained as a ritualized argot, mostly in written form, long after they ceased being able to speak French as a living language. Once the technical terms of English law had been defined, fixed, and taught in Latin and French, it would have taken a very positive determination on the part of the profession to write technical documents in English, and this they lacked for reasons that any sociologist could explain.[6] Theologians wrote in Latin for much the same reasons, though with more positive advantages, insofar as theology was a genuinely international academic discipline.

Just as clerks retained Latin and French as languages of record, so they maintained and developed professional habits of conveyancing, legal recording, and accounting that derived from earlier traditions. Few of these procedures have been studied with the care they deserve, and numerous developments are still to be identified and explained. But the underlying continuity is unmistakable. The operations of royal central offices were rule bound, and much the same could be said for some of the traditions of seigniorial jurisdiction and estate administration, particularly in England. English economic historians have good cause to complain about the traditionalism with which some fifteenth-century accountants carried forward from year to year rents that no one was paying and debts that would never be paid.[7] The only significant portion of a long account is often the tailpiece in which the clerk records sums of money the auditors allowed to be written off as uncollectable. Another frustrating bureaucratic habit was to draw up enrolled accounts or legal records for preservation but then fail to protect the more informative working documents upon which the formal record was based.[8]

This last observation relates closely to the retention of the use of parchment rolls in many traditional contexts in which judicial and financial administrations in Italy, Spain, and France had adopted ledgers or registers in book form, often made of paper.[9] British administrations followed in this direction in the fourteenth and fifteenth centuries for certain types of record. In England the king's wardrobe had begun to use registers under Edward I, and some subsidiary royal household accounts and other materials were kept in book form.[10] By the later fifteenth century clerks of the signet were keeping registers of memoranda and documents they had issued.[11] In Scotland the record of documents issued under the great seal was transferred to book form during the fifteenth century—the earliest extant registers are from 1424—and so were other Scottish legal and parliamentary records. Private administrations also abandoned the rolls format in some instances. The bishops of Durham kept transcripts of their hallmoot records in parchment ledgers from the mid-fourteenth century. The great series of Winchester pipe rolls was also converted to a series of registers, though only in 1454.[12] The expenditure accounts of Thetford Priory were kept in register form from 1482.[13] However, very many administrative records continued to be compiled as rolls. Rolls take up less shelf space than ledgers because they can be piled up, and so are easier to store. Parchment is more likely than paper to survive careless custody. Parchment rolls were also preferable for short records compiled in the shires for transmission to London or Edinburgh, such as the accounts of local collectors. We should, no doubt, be grateful for the number of records preserved as parchment rolls that would otherwise have been thrown out to make room for more if they had been more bulky, or rotted with poor archival practice had they been made of paper. But the advantage of longevity was more than offset, for bureaucratic purposes, by the greater difficulty of handling parchment rolls, which could grow to a preposterous weight and bulk in a large administration. Royal records are undoubtedly the worst, from this point of view, especially when membranes of parchment were sewn end to end in 'chancery fashion'. The central Irish administration employed practices derived from Westminster, and its forms of record keeping were essentially similar.[14]

Having discussed aspects of the conservatism of British administrations, it remains to comment on some of the ways in which clerks adapted to changing circumstances in the long period 1300–1530. One of these, perhaps predictably, was a response to rising costs. Record keeping, like all forms of labour, became more expensive during the fourteenth century, and this affected the way in which clerks were expected to operate. In this context it is not difficult to see rationality at work in the form of labour-saving devices, few of which are to a historian's advantage. One of these was a greater propensity to routinize clerical operations through the multiplication of set formulae. Both in England and Scotland this is apparent in the form of legal instruments, which up to 1300 constitute a major source of information for some aspects of both urban and rural institutions, and for topography. By the fourteenth century conveyances by written deed were normal even among peasant freeholders in all parts of England and had become familiar in Wales and Scotland. From north Wales, the *Survey of Denbigh* of 1334 records numerous tenants whose title to their property was secured by a charter or, more specifically, 'by a charter from the lord'.[15] The standardization of formulae, which we have already seen as a feature of thirteenth-century development, became universal by the mid-fourteenth century, so that whole classes of legal instruments—charters of conveyance, leases, mortgages, recognizances of debt— are rarely worth printing in full. Conveyancers had become adept at drafting records in such a way that the experienced eye could skim through to the variable clauses, knowing where to find them, taking most of the verbiage for granted. Even complicated family settlements, which took longer to work out, were drawn up with little departure from stock expressions. In Scotland a wide variety of legal formulae in the later fourteenth century had been rationalized by 1500 to the point that the terminology of lowland tenures, at least, 'would have been familiar to an eighteenth-century family lawyer'.[16]

Even some of the archives that survive in greatest profusion become in the course of time less informative about economic and social change than they had been when first invented. Besides devices to save clerical labour, there are other reasons for this, especially the abandonment of former controls and alteration in institutional practices. One example of the abandonment of controls affects evidence of English tax assessments, which, as we have seen, became fixed for each township or borough.[17] From 1334 onwards records of so-called 'fifteenth and tenths' have no independent value as economic information, since any assessments they record were increasingly unrealistic as indicators of comparative wealth between different places. Another example of the abandonment of former controls is landlords' leasing of manorial demesnes. Though in England manorial accounts continued to be produced all through the fifteenth century they were character- istically much shorter records than they had been, usually recording no more than rents owed by tenants and by the lessee of the demesne farm. The absence of detailed information about agricultural practice is a severe loss for economic and social historians. Not only does the change deprive us of details about how much was produced on demesne farms, and how demesne managers responded to crises. It also removes one of the most important sources of information about wages and prices. Some English estates continued to be managed directly until the 1450s, and they supply a narrow thread of information of high quality up to that time, but accounts with such information from after the 1450s are exceedingly rare.[18] Those of the late fifteenth and early sixteenth centuries are often badly disorganized, and difficult to interpret, since the former art of agricultural accounting had by that time been lost.[19]

Though the products of the major clerical establishments become less rewarding in the course of the period, in other respects innovation in administrative practices, or some other feature of social change, introduced new forms of record keeping without earlier precedent, and some of these are unambiguously of the greatest interest and importance. Some new sources became available spasmodically in the course of time as a result of experimentation by the government in ways of raising income. The accounts of the English tax called ulnage, levied on sales of cloth, even though they need to be used with caution, are a unique source of information for the development of the fourteenth- and fifteenth-century textile industry.[20] The English poll tax lists of 1377, 1379, and 1381 are a unique source of demographic information.[21] Richard II's interest in the doings of guilds and fraternities generated a bulk of informative returns.[22] Other important government initiatives are associated with Cardinal Wolsey, who innovated several inquiries in the 1520s in an attempt to assess England's resources of manpower and taxable wealth; his musters inquiry of 1522 and new taxation assessments of 1524 are the basis for the most satisfactory estimates of English population since 1377.[23] Developments of this kind generally represent the government responding to economic and social change— such as the growth of the cloth industry, the multiplication of religious fraternities, the threat of depopulation. Even if the resulting evidence is tantalizingly imperfect it often allows us to assess developments whose magnitude would otherwise be hidden.

Amongst private records, the most interesting development was the writing, and occasionally the preserving, of informal private correspondence in English or Scots. Although we have correspondence from earlier centuries it is almost all of a very formal political, judicial, or administrative character, written in Latin or French. It seem likely that the vernacular letters of the fifteenth century represent a new cultural phenomenon, though not one it is easy to explain. It may relate to a growth of literacy amongst the laity, but against this it can be objected that many of the letters were written by professional clerks, and that there is no reason to suppose that comparable levels of literacy were not achieved in many families before the fifteenth century. It may relate more to the freer development of written English and Scots during the fourteenth and fifteenth centuries. Although surviving letter collections are not numerous, they enable us to examine many aspects of social and economic activity from a more human angle than accounts and court proceedings allow. The Paston family's letters, including hundreds of original letters to and from family members, are rich in information about a Norfolk family's income and estates, as well as aspects of its purchases.[24] The Stonor family's collection is a less extensive but comparably rich collection from an Oxfordshire family.[25] The Armburgh papers, discovered only recently, survive as a roll comprising copies of documents from the period c.1417–53, mostly relating to a dispute about properties in Hertfordshire, Essex, and Warwickshire.[26] The Plumpton family letters and papers, mostly from the period 1460–90, survive as copies transcribed in the seventeenth century.[27] The Cely family's letters, from the late fifteenth century, are of considerable interest in understanding how a merchant family lived and operated in exporting wool from southern England through the staple at Calais.[28] These collections imply that letter writing was a well-recognized practice amongst English gentry families during the fifteenth century. They attract particular attention because they are in English and mostly relate to secular matters, but many monasteries also kept copies of their letters in register form, mostly in Latin, such as the letter books of the prior of Durham Cathedral Priory.

Although, as we have seen, established routines did not always convert from roll form to ledger form, ledgers and registers become more numerous in the fourteenth and fifteenth centuries in some new contexts. Registers had long been used for cartularies, which continued to be compiled through the fourteenth and fifteenth centuries in most parts of Britain and Ireland,[29] and monastic archives contained increasing numbers of registers of various kinds for more ephemeral material.[30] Registers also continued to be used by bishops for the recording of letters, mandates, and appointments to office.[31] They were increasingly used after 1300 for new but analogous purposes, and especially for informal or semi-formal memoranda, or for copies or abstracts of documents useful for management. Some important urban records are in this form. The London Letter Books, running from Edward I's reign to that of James II, are the largest and most complete set of such registers, and their contents are very miscellaneous.[32] The very different York House Books record York council minutes from 1461 onwards.[33] The origins of the great Coventry Leet Book are known, since it records an ordinance made in 1421 by the Coventry council 'that all good ordinance of the leets be sought up and written in a register, that they may be of record for evermore, by oversight of the recorder, for worship and honesty of this city'. The leet was the principal court for policing purposes.[34] These are all major and exceptional examples of urban registers, but numerous British towns have one or two such volumes. Aberdeen's first surviving court book (containing extraneous material) covers the years 1398–1407, and the first separate guild book starts in 1441. Dunfermline's guild court records were kept in a paper register from at least 1433, and the surviving Perth Guildry Book starts in 1452. There are Ayr burgh court records on separate folios (not on parchment rolls) from 1428 to 1478.[35] Urban registers also survive from late fifteenth-century Ireland, the Liber Antiquissimus of Waterford and Liber A of Galway.[36] The binding of such books was often colour-coded for easy identification, as in the Red Parchment Book of Colchester or the Black Book of Winchester.[37] Similar volumes were also kept for family archives, like the important Red Book of Ormond that contains some of the best fourteenth-century Irish estate surveys,[38] or the Red Book of Kildare, begun in 1503.[39]

Another form of register, unique to the Scottish legal system, was the notary's register, known in Scotland as a protocol book. During the fourteenth century, but more particularly in the fifteenth, the Scots adopted a system characteristic of Mediterranean Europe in which formal records of transactions and contracts were drawn up and authorized by professional public notaries. Public notaries are on record in Scotland from the 1280s, but they became a dominant part of the process of attesting transactions and contracts from about 1400. The earliest had credentials from internationally recognized authorities—the pope or the emperor (or, indeed, both)—but from 1469 the Scottish crown assumed the power to appoint notaries and to delegate this power of appointment to Scottish bishops. Insofar as notaries drew up titles to property—the major part of their business—their activities were about equivalent to the idiosyncratic English system of registering title to freehold property as 'final concords' in the king's courts.[40] They were expected to register a copy of each document they drew up, so that their books, where they survive, are important documents of social history. The earliest surviving notaries' books, those of James Darow and John Kerd, date from 1469 and 1471 respectively.[41]

Survival

Though the keeping of records was taken for granted as a professional activity in so many areas of everyday administration, there are serious gaps in the available record. Often it is hard to say whether these gaps are there because records were never made, or because they have been lost. The survival of records from this date is still very imperfect. It is no good asking in whose material interests it was to preserve administrative records, since it would be difficult to explain the survival of any records from this period in purely utilitarian terms. Many non-European societies created large archives but felt no necessity to keep them. Preserving records seems to be more a matter of habit in some institutions in some cultures, as if the institutions themselves acquired some venerable status by association with accumulated clutter. But even with this allowance, not all institutions were sufficiently continuous to pass on their records from generation to generation. Bishoprics and abbeys were perhaps the most highly favoured and, despite the unprecedented hazards of the Reformation, a large proportion of what survives comes from such archives. By far the largest deposit with a continuous history was the English royal archive in Westminster, which accumulated not only large amounts of material compiled in the course of royal government and legal administration but also an enormous volume of material from other sources collected when estates escheated to the crown, or in the course of litigation in the king's courts. After Edward I's failure to subjugate Scotland, the restoration of a Scottish monarchy under Robert I (1306–29) permitted a new start in the accumulation of archives; the Scottish public records preserve administrative material from the 1320s, though many records have been lost through subsequent accidents. There were losses in 1660 when 85 hogsheads of Scottish records were lost at sea while being transferred back to Edinburgh following the restoration of Charles II.[42] There was once another large government archive in Dublin, but it was almost wholly destroyed by fire when the Irish Public Record Office burned down in June 1922, a casualty of civil war.[43]

The survival of material from lay estates was less reliable than from ecclesiastical estates, because of the discontinuities of family history. Lands pass from family to family, are split up and reconstituted in different ways, and the records are often passed with them from hand to hand. The absence of any fixed abode, or of any pious association with past family members, made their survival much less secure than that of episcopal or monastic documents. Some fine collections have survived in families with an exceptionally continuous line of succession, like the Berkeley family of Berkeley (Gloucestershire) and the Percy family, earls of Northumberland. Other important collections, such as that for the honour of Clare, which relate to estates in Wales and Ireland as well as in England, survived in the royal archive. The archive of the Butler earls of Ormond is the most important such collection from a lay estate in Ireland. For most family archives, however, the chances of survival as an intact collection were slim. The archives of secular lords were repeatedly dispersed and reconstituted with the passage of property from hand to hand, and in some instances they were doubtless deliberately destroyed as useless. The scarcity of estate accounts from ordinary lay estates is one of the recurrent laments of specialists in agrarian history. However, some records were retained as evidence of title to property and other rights, so that the total volume of surviving material from parts of England is impressive. There are very many good series of manorial court rolls, especially from the more southerly English counties.[44] Vast numbers of lay charters also survive, often outside their original context, having been passed on with individual properties century by century, and though their usefulness for economic history is in general lower than that of administrative records they can make an invaluable contribution to the study of social and political relationships even in the absence of other material.[45]

The records of merchants were even more ephemeral than those of landlords. Most of them concerned not landed estate and property rights but commercial transactions carrying few implications for the future. Once debts had been paid and balances struck there could be little further use for accounts and memorandum books. The circumstances of merchant family life were more unfavourable to the preservation of records than those of landed families. Merchants' houses were smaller, not appropriate for the accumulation of archives in the first place, let alone the archives of previous occupants or past generations. Their private records were therefore invariably destroyed sooner or later. Nothing survives of them outside the records of other administrations, and that is thin enough. It would be possible, by studying certain types of litigation in public courts, to establish some of the types of record that merchants normally kept—they inevitably included current bonds and other contracts, and the larger merchants kept memorandum books with some form of running accounts. A rare example is the ledger of William Maghfeld, a London merchant, dating from the 1390s, preserved amongst the miscellanea of the King's Remembrancer in the Exchequer. It is an informal document in which he noted memoranda from day to day, writing down both his debts and his expenses. This record is preserved in the public records because Maghfeld ran into debt for customs dues owed to Richard II, so when he died in 1397 his goods and chattels were forfeited to the king.[46] The Cely letters, accounts, and memoranda, numbering about 450 items all told, the largest English mercantile archive from the fifteenth century, survive because of a dispute in Chancery in 1489 between two family members, which resulted in the papers being required by the court as evidence.[47] The ledger of Andrew Halyburton, which records in his own hand the business of a prominent Scottish merchant operating in the Netherlands between 1492 and 1503, is a precious survival of major importance for the study of late fifteenth-century Scottish trade. The document survives in the General Register House, Edinburgh, only because for some reason it was taken up into the Scottish royal archive.[48]

These various considerations help us to appreciate the extent to which the records that survive are a biased sample of what once existed. Commercial documentation is outstandingly under-represented, and there is relatively poor survival of administrative material from lay estates, and especially the very large number of small ones. There is a greater abundance of monastic and episcopal records because of the greater continuity of the institutions they represent. There are extensive records of the royal administration for lands subject to the English and Scottish crowns, and these absorbed documents from other sources as a result of lands escheating to the crown, or being administered during wardships and vacancies. Title deeds and other forms of legal instrument, as always since the thirteenth century, survive in abundance, whether as originals, copies, or both.

Regional Differences

In the earlier fourteenth century the records of English royal administration, which had been growing ever more elaborate since the early twelfth century, were still being created in full flood, with a remarkable capacity to illustrate the private affairs of the king's subjects as well as those of his own household and administration. They remained extensive throughout the fourteenth and fifteenth centuries. The earlier extension of English rule into Ireland and Wales meant that the English government was also collecting taxes, administering justice, and collecting information in those areas. Although the Dublin Irish archive is lost, some of the material it contained may be recovered from English royal administrative records.[49]

The first surviving original account from the royal Scottish archive dates from 1325–6, and the first enrolled sheriffs' and bailiffs' account from 1327. The long series of royal accounts from that date permit the almost continuous analysis of Scotland's overseas trade from then onwards, as well as supplying a remarkable series of accounts from receivers on royal estates, with unprecedented information about relatively remote parts of Britain. However, the volume of material is considerably smaller than that available for England because of the less complex financial and legal structures of Scottish administration. The number of judicial records is particularly small because of the decentralized nature of the Scots' legal system. And although the judicial business of the Scottish parliament began to be recorded in the fourteenth century, surviving records date only from 1466 in the acts of the lords auditors, and in those of the lords of council from 1478.[50]

A profusion of English manorial accounts and court rolls survive from the fourteenth century; up to its final quarter it remains a golden age for agricultural historians interested in precisely how demesnes were stocked and cultivated, how farming was managed, and how productive its different sections were. Not surprisingly, forms of record keeping familiar in England continued to be used on the private estates of English families in Wales and Ireland, so that the fourteenth century is in these countries, too, a period of archival riches. The surviving estate accounts, for example, include important series from the lordships of Usk and Denbigh, which survive in the English Public Records Office, and another from the lordship of Chirk preserved in Chirk Castle.[51] There is a major court roll series from 1294 onwards from the lordship of Ruthin or Dyffryn Clwyd and a less complete one from the lordship of Clun.[52] There are also a few estate accounts from Ireland, though the best series ends with the death of Roger Bigod in 1306. Amongst the most celebrated economic records of north Wales and Ireland from this period are the great estate surveys, the most important of which are listed in Table 23.1. Surviving Scottish estate records of the fourteenth and fifteenth centuries are fewer

TABLE 23.1. *The principal surviving estate surveys from Wales and Ireland, 1300–1530*

Estate	Date
Wales	
Bishopric of Bangor	1306
Lordship of Bromfield and Yale	1315
Lordship of Dyffryn-Clwyd	1324
Bishopric of St David's	1326
Lordship of Denbigh	1334
Principality of Wales (Caernarvonshire, Anglesey)	1353–4
Lordship of Chirkland	1391–3
Bartholomew Bolde's estate	c.1450
Lordship of Dyffryn-Clwyd	1465
Ireland	
Earldom of Ormond	1300–11
Archbishopric of Dublin	1326
Manor of Lisronagh	1333
Bishopric of Cloyne	c.1364–5
Abbey of Llanthony Secunda	1381
Abbey of Llanthony Prima	1408

Sources: The First Extent of Bromfield and Yale, A.D. 1315, ed. T. P. Ellis, Cymmrodorion Record Ser. 11 (London, 1924); 'The lordship of Dyffryn Clwyd in 1324', ed. R. Ian Jack, *Transactions of Denbighshire Historical* Society, 17 (1968), 7–53; *The Black Book of St. David's*, ed. J. W. Willis-Bund, Cymmrodorion Record Series, 5 (London, 1902); *Survey of the Honour of Denbigh, 1334*, ed. Paul Vinogradoff and Frank Morgan, British Academy, Records of the Social and Economic History of England and Wales, 1 (London, 1914); *Registrum vulgariter nuncupatum 'The Record of Caernarvon'*, ed. Henry Ellis, Record Commission (London, 1838); *The Extent of Chirkland, 1391–1393*, ed. G.P. Jones (Liverpool, 1933); 'The Bolde rental (Bangor ms. 1939)', ed. C. A. Gresham, *Transactions of the Caernarvonshire Historical Society*, 26 (1965), 31–49; 'The Lordship of Dyffryn-Clwyd in 1465', *Transactions of Denbighshire Historical* Society, 15 (1966), 15–54; *The Red Book of Ormond*, ed. Newport B. White (Dublin, 1932); *Liber Niger Alani 1172–1534: The Calendar of Archbishop Alen's Register*, ed. Charles McNeill (Dublin, 1950); 'Rental of the Manor of Lisronagh, 1333, and notes on "Betagh" Tenure in Medieval Ireland', *Proceedings of the Royal Irish Academy*, 43, Section C (1935–7), 41–76; *The Pipe Roll of Cloyne (rotulus pipae Clonensis)*, ed. Paul MacCotter and Kenneth Nicholls (Midleton, 1996); *The Irish Cartularies of Llanthony Prima and Secunda*, ed. Eric St John Brooks (Dublin, 1953), no. 165, pp. 178–93, and no. 98, pp. 289–311.

and farther between, though they were compiled on larger estates at least. An incomplete rental of 1376–7 and another from 1424 survive from the Douglas of Dalkeith estates in Peebles, Dumfries, and Fife.[53] A rental from the Cistercian abbey of Coupar Angus records leases of land and other property from 1443.[54] These records are of a type already known in the thirteenth century, but the surviving examples exceed their antecedents both in size and quality of information and consequently in their value for the study of medieval rural society.

The same contrasts may be observed in borough records, which begin to be quite abundant in fourteenth-century England. Most of the urban records from Wales survive from seigniorial boroughs as part of an estate archive, such as the rich series relating to Newport, but there are others. Caernarvon, for example, has thirty-nine borough court rolls from the years 1391–1402.[55] Scottish urban muniments, though more patchy than the English ones, contain some riches from this period. The most outstanding are those from Aberdeen, whose council registers record sessions of the burgh courts from 1398 onwards, together with a wide range of council business relating to economic and social regulation.[56] As we have seen, however, there are significant urban records from other towns, notably Ayr, Dunfermline, and Perth. The pattern of development was comparable to that in English boroughs, notably a growing inclination to record legal proceedings and keep financial accounts. In Ayr the latter development can be dated to 1429.[57]

However, the geographical and cultural pattern of record keeping in the fourteenth and fifteenth centuries does not appear to have expanded appreciably beyond its limits in 1300, and there are extensive regions of Britain and Ireland which, if not pre-archival, were governed in ways that made administrative records unnecessary. The archives of Scottish royal government contain a good deal of economic information from royal estates, even as far from Edinburgh as the inner Hebrides.[58] However in general there are few records relating to Scottish rural society and seigniorial incomes; most of the archives that survive from Scottish landlords are in the form of charters. Irish lords, too, were largely unconcerned to multiply records in this period. Throughout the fourteenth and fifteenth centuries it remains impossible to study the societies and economies of these regions in any detail.

It is also noteworthy that within the regions from which records survive, and which can be regarded as well documented, the broad regional pattern of archive creation remains differentiated very much as it had been in the thirteenth century. Southern, eastern, and midland England remain, with few exceptions, the best-documented parts of Britain. Some important northern archival sources that were beginning to be important in the late thirteenth century become much more reliable for the fourteenth and fifteenth, such as the obedientiary accounts and estate records of Durham Cathedral Priory, the city records of York, and the Wakefield court rolls. There are other important northern English series beginning in this period, such as the Durham episcopal estate archive from the 1380s, and the Percy family estate archive, which is sparse before the 1430s. Nevertheless, with the exception of the Palatinate of Durham, northern England remains less well documented than England south of the Trent. Lowland Scotland has no surviving estate archive of any size from this period, whether religious or secular and even urban records are generally few and far between before the 1430s. Coldingham Priory is a significant exception, since the surviving records are from the time when it was administered from Durham.[59] Records of local jurisdiction anywhere in Scotland, whether from burghs or baronies, are very rare before the early sixteenth century.[60] Archive keeping in Wales has the mark of something imposed from outside; the principal records for the study of Welsh society were compiled for the English crown and for large marcher lordships.[61] There is little evidence of a demand for estate documentation amongst local landowners comparable to that experienced in East Anglia or Essex.

In some respects there was even a contraction of archival coverage from the late fourteenth century, especially in Ireland and Wales. In part this was the effect of changes in estate organization equivalent to those that impoverished English estate archives in the same period. With the leasing of manors there was no longer the call for detailed estate surveys and accounts like those of the thirteenth and early fourteenth centuries. The Hatfield Survey of the estates of the bishopric of Durham, from about 1383, is a relatively late example of the genre, and it is interesting that the attempt to renew this record around 1418–21 was abandoned.[62] In some regions, as in those from which Anglo-Norman lordship retreated in Ireland, poorer documentation was also in part the effect of loss of control by the owners of large estates. There are some good Welsh administrative records from the fifteenth century, like the financial records of the lordship of Newport, the exceptional run of manorial records from Porthcaseg (1262–1527), Cawrse (1455–1544) and Over Gorther (1367–1524), or the bailiffs' accounts from Dinas Powys (1373–1456),[63] but lords of lands in Wales were no longer able to wring money out of the local inhabitants to the extent they had been able to in the century before, and the quality of recorded information is poorer. Across the whole of Britain and Ireland, the period 1280–1380 is almost everywhere better documented than the period 1380–1530. Although the loss of detail is doubtless to the historian's disadvantage when considering the later period, whose changes often seem shadowy compared to those of the great age of estate documentation, its implications for contemporary society were surely benign. There is no intrinsic merit in forms of documentation whose primary purpose is to increase the power and wealth of kings and landlords.

NOTES

1. For an outstanding monastic example of such continuity, see Barbara Harvey, *The Obedientiaries of Westminster Abbey and their Financial Records, c.1275–1540* (Woodbridge, 2002).

2. P. Connolly, *Medieval Record Sources* (Dublin, 2002), 52.

3. R. H. Britnell, 'Pragmatic Literacy in Latin Christendom', in id. (ed.), *Pragmatic Literacy East and West, 1200–1330* (Woodbridge, 1997), 18–23.

4. G. W. S. Barrow, 'The Pattern of Non-Literary Manuscript Production and Survival in Scotland, 1200–1330', in Britnell (ed.), *Pragmatic Literacy*, 138–9.

5. *Rentale Dunkeldense, Being the Accounts of the Bishopric (A.D. 1505–1517)*, ed. R. K. Hannay (Edinburgh, 1915).

6. J. H. Baker, *Manual of Law French*, 2nd edn. (Aldershot, 1990), 1–4.

7. P. D. A. Harvey, *Manorial Records*, rev. edn. (1999), 36–7.

8. R. H. Britnell, 'Colchester Courts and Court Records, 1310–1525', *Essex Archaeology and History*, 17 (1986), 138–9.

9. Britnell, 'Pragmatic Literacy in Latin Christendom', 17–18.

10. M. Prestwich, 'English Government Records', in Britnell (ed.), *Pragmatic Literacy*, 96.

11. *British Library Harleian Manuscript 433*, ed. R. Horrox and P. W. Hammond, 4 vols. (1979–83).

12. M. Page, *The Medieval Bishops of Winchester: Estate, Archive and Administration* (Winchester, 2002), 12.

13. *The Register of Thetford Priory*, ed. D. Dymond, 2 vols. (Oxford, 1995–6).

14. Connolly, *Medieval Record Sources*, 23–6.

15. *Survey of the Honour of Denbigh, 1334*, ed. P. Vinogradoff and F. Morgan, (1914), 10, 12, 13, 16, 37, 43, etc.

16. S. G. E. Lythe, 'Economic Life', in J. M. Brown (ed.), *Scottish Society in the Fifteenth Century* (1977), 67.

17. Above (Ch. 22).

18. An exceptionally late series is discussed in R. A. Lomas, 'A Northern Farm at the End of the Middle Ages: Elvethall Manor, Durham, 1443/4–1513/14', *Northern History*, 18 (1982), 26–53.

19. e.g. British Library, Add. Roll 66051, of 1483–4, discussed in L. R. Poos, *A Rural Society after the Black Death: Essex 1350–1525* (Cambridge, 1991), 212–20.

20. E. M. Carus-Wilson, 'The Aulnage Accounts: A Criticism', reprinted in ead., *Medieval Merchant Venturers*, 2nd edn. (1967), 279–91. For a more positive evaluation, see A. R. Bridbury, *Economic Growth: England in the Later Middle Ages* (1962), 33–5.

21. *The Poll Taxes of 1377, 1379 and 1381*, 2 vols. so far (Oxford, 1998, 2001).

22. *English Gilds: The Original Ordinances of More than One Hundred Early English Gilds*, ed. T. Smith and L. T. Smith, Early English Text Society, original ser. 40 (1870), xxiv–xxvi, 1–123.

23. B. M. S. Campbell, 'The Population of Early Tudor England: A Re-evaluation of the 1522 Muster Returns and 1524 and 1525 Lay Subsidies'. *Journal of Historical Geography*, 7 (1981), 145–54; J. Cornwall, 'English Population in the Early Sixteenth Century', *Economic History Review*, 2nd ser. 37 (1961–2), 7–28.

24. *Paston Letters and Papers of the Fifteenth Century*, ed. Norman Davis, 2 vols. (Oxford, 1971, 1976); R. H. Britnell, 'The Pastons and their Norfolk', *Agricultural History Review*, 36 (1988), 32–44.

25. *Kingsford's Stonor Letters and Papers, 1290–1453*, ed. C. Carpenter (Cambridge, 1996).

26. *The Armburgh Papers: The Brockhole Inheritance in Warwickshire, Hertfordshire and Essex, c.1417–c.1453*, ed. C. Carpenter (Woodbridge, 1998).

27. *The Plumpton Letters and Papers*, ed. J. Kirby, Camden 5th ser. 8 (1996).

28. *The Cely Letters, 1472–1488*, ed. A. Hanham, Early English Text Society, 273 (1975).

29. Above (Ch. 13); G. R. C. Davies, *Medieval Cartularies of Great Britain: A Short Catalogue* (1958); Connolly, *Medieval Record Sources*, 47–8.

30. e.g. J. D. Martin, *The Cartularies and Registers of Peterborough Abbey*, Northamptonshire Record Society, 28 (1978).

31. D. M. Smith, *Guide to Bishops' Registers of England and Wales* (1981); Connolly, *Medieval Record Sources*, 42–3.

32. *Calendar of Letter-Books Preserved among the Archives of the Corporation of the City of London, 1275–1498*, ed. R. R. Sharpe, 11 vols. (1899–1912).

33. *York House Books, 1461–1490*, ed. L. C. Attreed, 2 vols. (Stroud, 1991).

34. *The Coventry Leet Book or Mayor's Register*, ed. M. D. Harris, 4 parts, Early English Text Society, 134, 135, 138, 146 (1907–13), i, ix.

35. *Early Records of the Burgh of Aberdeen, 1317, 1398–1407*, ed. W. C. Dickinson, Scottish History Society, 3rd ser. 49 (1957), cx, cxvi, cxviii–cxix; *The Gild Court Book of Dunfermline, 1433–1597*, ed. E. P. D. Torrie, Scottish Record Society, new ser. 12 (1986), xi; *The Perth Guildry Book, 1452–1601*, ed. M. L. Stavert, Scottish Record Society, new ser. 19 (1993), i; W. C. Dickinson, 'The Acts of the Parliament at Perth, 6 March 1429/30', *Scottish Historical Review*, 29 (1950), 1.

36. Connolly, *Medieval Record Sources*, 33.

37. *The Red Book of Colchester*, ed. W. G. Benham (Colchester, 1902); *The Black Book of Winchester*, ed. W. H. B. Bird (Winchester, 1925).

38. *The Red Parchment Book of Ormond*, ed. N. B. White (Dublin, 1932).

39. Connolly, *Medieval Record Sources*, 51.

40. Barrow, 'Non-Literary Manuscript Production', 137–8; B. Webster, *Scotland from the Eleventh Century to 1603* (Ithaca, NY, 1975), 212–13.

41. D. M. Walker, *A Legal History of Scotland*, 2 vols. (Edinburgh, 1988–90), ii. 271–7; *Protocol Book of James Young, 1485–1515*, ed. G. Donaldson, Scottish Record Society, old ser. 74 (1952), vi.

42. Webster, *Scotland*, 125–6; Scottish Record Office, *Guide to the National Archives of Scotland* (Edinburgh, 1996), x–xi.

43. Connolly, *Medieval Record Sources*, 9–10.

44. J. Cripps, R. H. Hilton, and J. Williamson, 'Appendix: A Survey of Medieval Manorial Court Rolls in England', in Z. Razi and R. M. Smith (eds.), *Medieval Society and the Manor Court* (Oxford, 1996), 569–637.

45. e.g. A. Grant, 'Acts of Lordship: The Records of Archibald, Fourth Earl of Douglas', in T. Brotherstone and D. Ditchburn (eds.), *Freedom and Authority: Scotland c.1050–c.1650:*

Historical and Historiographical Essays Presented to Grant G. Simpson (East Linton, 2000), 235–74.

46. It is discussed in M. K. James, *Studies in the Medieval Wine Trade*, ed. E. M. Veale (Oxford, 1971), 196–217.

47. *The Cely Letters, 1472–1488*, ed. A. Hanham, Early English Text Society 273 (1975), viii.

48. *Ledger of Andrew Halyburton, Conservator of the Privileges of the Scottish Nation in the Netherlands, 1492–1503*, ed. C. Innes (Edinburgh, 1867).

49. e.g. *Irish Exchequer Payments, 1270–1446*, ed. P. Connolly (Dublin, 1998).

50. Webster, *Scotland*, 159–60.

51. G. A. Holmes, *The Estates of the Higher Nobility in Fourteenth-Century England* (Cambridge, 1957), 93–107, 158–63; L. B. Smith, 'Seignorial Income in the Fourteenth Century: The Arundels in Chirk', *Bulletin of the Board of Celtic Studies*, 28 (1979), 443–57.

52. A. D. M. Barrell, R. R. Davies, O. J. Padel, and L. B. Smith, 'The Dyffryn Clwyd Court Roll Project, 1340–1352 and 1389–1399: A Methodology and some Preliminary Findings', in Razi and Smith (eds.), *Medieval Society and the Manor Court*, 266.

53. *Registrum Honoris de Morton*, ed. T. Thomson, A. Macdonald, and C. Innes, 2 vols., Bannatyne Club, 94 (1853), i, pp. xlvii–lxxvi. I owe my knowledge of the later of these rentals to Sandy Grant.

54. *Rental Book of the Cistercian Abbey of Cupar-Angus*, ed. C. Rogers, 2 vols., Grampian Club (1879–80).

55. A. C. Reeves, *Newport Lordship, 1317–1536* (Ann Arbor, 1979), 112–49; *Caernarvon Court Rolls, 1361–1402*, ed. G. P. Jones and H. Owen, Caernarvon Historical Society Record Ser. 1 (1951).

56. E. Gemmill and N. Mayhew, *Changing Values in Medieval Scotland: A Study of Prices, Money, and Weights and Measures* (Cambridge, 1995), 25, 27.

57. G. S. Pryde, 'Development of the Burgh', in A. I. Dunlop, *The Royal Burgh of Ayr* (Edinburgh, 1953), 27–8.

58. *The Exchequer Rolls of Scotland*, ed. J. Stuart, G. Burnett, and others, 23 vols. (Edinburgh, 1878–1908).

59. *The Correspondence, Inventories, Account Rolls and Law Proceedings of the Priory of Coldingham*, ed. J. Raine, Surtees Society, 1 (1841).

60. Webster, *Scotland*, 212.

61. M. Richards, 'Some Unpublished Source-Material for the History of the Lordships of Denbighshire', *Transactions of Denbighshire Historical Society*, 14 (1965), 197–208.

62. R. H. Britnell, 'The Langley Survey of the Durham Bishopric Estates, 1418–21', *Archaeologia Aeliana*, 5th ser. 16 (1988), 213–21.

63. *The Marcher Lordships of South Wales, 1415–1536*, ed. T. B. Pugh (Cardiff, 1963), 145–236; R. I. Jack, *Medieval Wales* (1972), 109, 115–16.

FURTHER READING

Barron, C. M., 'The Education and Training of Girls in Fifteenth-Century London', in D. E. S. Dunn (ed.), *Courts, Counties and the Capital in the Later Middle Ages* (Stroud, 1996).

Booth, P. H. W., *The Financial Administration of the Lordship and County of Chester, 1272–1377*, Chetham Society, 3rd ser. 28 (1981).

Britnell, R. H., 'Colchester Courts and Court Records, 1310–1525', *Essex Archaeology and History*, 17 (1986).

—— 'The Langley Survey of the Durham Bishopric Estates, 1418–21', *Archaeologia Aeliana*, 5th ser. 16 (1988).

—— 'Minor Landlords in England and Medieval Agrarian Capitalism', *Past and Present*, 89 (1980).

—— *The Winchester Pipe Rolls and Medieval English Society* (Woodbridge, 2003).

Carus-Wilson, E. M., 'The Aulnage Accounts: A Criticism', *Economic History Review*, 2 (1929), repr. in ead., *Medieval Merchant Venturers*, 2nd edn. (1967).

Chaplais, P., *English Royal Documents, King John–Henry VI, 1199–1461* (Oxford, 1971).

Connolly, P., *Medieval Record Sources* (Dublin, 2002).

Chrimes, S. B., *An Introduction to the Administrative History of Medieval England* (Oxford, 1959).

Grant, A., 'Acts of Lordship: The Records of Archibald, Fourth Earl of Douglas', in T. Brotherstone and D. Ditchburn (eds.), *Freedom and Authority: Scotland c.1050–c.1650: Historical and Historiographical Essays Presented to Grant G. Simpson* (East Linton, 2000).

Hanham, A., *The Celys and their World: An English Merchant Family of the Fifteenth Century* (Cambridge, 1985).

Harvey, B., *The Obedientiaries of Westminster Abbey and their Financial Records, c.1275–1540* (Woodbridge, 2002).

Harvey, P. D. A. *Manorial Records*, rev. edn. (1999).

Jack, R. I., *Medieval Wales* (1972).

James, M. K., 'Gilbert Maghfeld: A London Merchant of the Fourteenth Century', in ead., *Studies in the Medieval Wine Trade*, ed. E. M. Veale (Oxford, 1971).

Lomas, R. A., 'A Northern Farm at the End of the Middle Ages: Elvethall Manor, Durham, 1443/4–1513/14', *Northern History*, 18 (1982).

Razi, Z., and Smith, R. M. (eds.), *Medieval Society and the Manor Court* (Oxford, 1996).

Webster, B., *Scotland from the Eleventh Century to 1603* (Ithaca, NY, 1975).

Primary Sources for British Economic and Social History in Modern English

Account Roll of the Priory of the Holy Trinity, Dublin, 1337–1346, ed. J. Mills, 2nd edn. (Dublin, 1996).

The Bailiffs' Minute Book of Dunwich, 1404–1430, ed. M. Bailey Suffolk Records Society, 34 (1992).

The Black Death, ed. R. Horrox (Manchester, 1994).

'The Bolde Rental (Bangor Ms. 1939)', ed. C. A. Gresham, *Transactions of the Caernarvonshire Historical Society*, 26 (1965).

Bolton Priory Rentals and Ministers's Accounts, 1473–1539, ed. I. Kershaw, Yorkshire Archaeological Society Record Ser. 132 (1970).

A Calendar of the Cartularies of John Pyel and Adam Fraunceys, ed. S. J. O'Connor, Camden 5th ser. 2 (1993).

Calendar of Ormond Deeds, ed. Edmund Curtis, 6 vols. (1932–43).

The Court Rolls of Walsham le Willows, 1303–50, ed. R. Lock, Suffolk Records Society, 41 (1998).

The Court Rolls of Walsham le Willows, 1351–99, ed. R. Lock, Suffolk Records Society, 45 (2002).

Documents Relating to the Manor and Borough of Leeds, 1066–1400, ed. J. Le Patourel, Thoresby Society, 45 (1957 for 1956).

The English Manor, c.1200–c.1500, ed. M. Bailey (Manchester, 2002).

The Havener's Accounts of the Earldom and Duchy of Cornwall, 1287–1356, ed. M. Kowaleski, Devon and Cornwall Record Society, new ser. 44 (2001).

Irish Exchequer Payments, 1270–1446, ed. P. Connolly (Dublin, 1998).

The Lay Subsidy of 1334, ed. R. E. Glasscock (1975).

Local Customs Accounts of the Port of Exeter, 1266–1321, ed. M. Kowaleski, Devon and Cornwall Record Society, new ser. 6 (1993).

London Bridge Accounts, 1381–1538, ed. V. Harding and L. Wright, London Record Society Publications, 31 (1995 for 1994).

Newstead Priory Cartulary, 1344 and Other Archives, ed. D. Gray and trans. V. W. Walker (Nottingham, 1940).

The Overseas Trade of London: Exchequer Customs Accounts, 1480–1, ed. H. S. Cobb, London Record Society Publications, 27 (1990).

The Pipe Roll of the Bishopric of Winchester, 1301–2, ed. M. Page, Hampshire Record Ser. 14 (1996).

The Pipe Roll of the Bishopric of Winchester, 1409–1410, ed. M. Page, Hampshire Record Ser. 16 1999).

Protocol Book of James Foular, 1500–1534, ed. W. Macleod, M. Wood, and J. Durkan, Scottish Record Society, 64, 72, 75, and new ser. 10 (1930–85).

Protocol Book of James Young, 1485–1515, ed. G. Donaldson, Scottish Record Society, 74 (1952).

Rental Book of the Cistercian Abbey of Cupar-Angus, ed. C. Rogers, 2 vols., Grampian Club (1879–80).

'A Rental of the Manor of East Malling, A.D. 1410', ed. C. L. S. Williams, in *A Kentish Miscellany*, ed. F. Hull, Kent Archaeological Society, Kent Records, 21 (1979).

Select Cases in Manorial Courts, ed. L. R. Poos and L. Bonfield, Selden Society, 114 (1998).

Selected Rentals and Accounts of Medieval Hull, 1293–1528, ed. R. Horrox, Yorkshire Archaeological Record Ser., 141 (1983).

The Southampton Terrier of 1454, ed. L. A. Burgess, P. D. A. Harvey, and A. D. Saunders (1976).

Thaxted in the Fourteenth Century: An Account of the Manor and Borough with Translated Texts, ed. K. C. Newton (Chelmsford, 1960).

....

CHAPTER 24

Stability and Crisis

Contrasts between the periods 1050–1300 and 1300–1520 are inclined to be exaggerated because of the superior information available for the later period, which enables fluctuations of all sorts to be identified with greater clarity. Yet there were real differences between the two periods, if only because the crises of 1300–1530 had such a deleterious effect upon the long-term development of population and arable farming. No single cause can account for the reduction in numbers in all parts of Britain and Ireland during the fourteenth and fifteenth centuries, even if epidemic disease outstrips all others in severity and the permanence of its impact.[1] There were interludes of economic and demographic recovery, but recurrent crises repeatedly subverted earlier gains. The biggest disasters were the famines of 1315–18 and, even more catastrophically, the Black Death of 1348–9; their impact and scale warrant a more extended treatment than other crises of the period. Nevertheless, some discussion of the lesser economic fluctuations of the period 1350–1500 is merited in order to counteract the idea that late medieval economic performance was downhill all the way, or alternatively that nothing was happening during this long period.

The principal catastrophe of the earlier fourteenth century was the famine of the years 1315–16, 1316–17, and, to a less acute degree, of 1317–18. The food shortages experienced during these years have no parallel in British history. They were not confined to the more populous parts of Britain, though the evidence for other parts is less good. In north Wales exceptional measures were needed to provision the castles and towns of Conway, Caernarvon, and Beaumaris.[2] Famine is also recorded by Irish annalists, together with the extreme climatic conditions that had caused it.[3] Hardships were first alleviated by a better harvest in 1317, but prices remained higher than they had been before 1315, so in effect the famine lasted through 1317–18 as well. The problems of these years were compounded by an exceptionally high mortality among sheep. The amount of wool produced was inevitably affected; comparing the ten years before and after 1315 the amount of

wool exported from English ports fell by nearly one-third. Even after 1318, however, the run of bad luck continued. There was a widespread epidemic among cattle
between 1319 and 1321, the worst between 1200 and 1500; recovery inevitably took
several years.[4] There were poor harvests again in 1320 and 1321 so that food was in
short supply and the prices of cereals were again raised. This combination of
misfortunes was extraordinary. To some extent the problems were linked through
poor weather conditions and inadequate feed for animals, but there was also, it
would seem, an element of exceptionally bad luck.

Problems caused by bad weather were severely exacerbated in parts of Britain
and Ireland by the local effects of war. After the Battle of Bannockburn the whole
of northern England lay open to the Scottish invasion, and raids became numerous
partly because of the severity of conditions in Scotland. Plunder was one of the
main objects of these raiding parties, and the inhabitants of undefended towns and
villages could do little other than buy them off or flee. Because the Scots met so
little opposition they penetrated as far as Lancaster and Preston on the west coast
and Holderness on the east coast, taking prisoners, seizing coinage, plate, and
treasure, driving away horses but also commandeering grain and meat supplies to
make up deficiencies back home[5]. Meanwhile, in eastern Ireland, too, the adverse
effects of poor harvests and famine were compounded between June 1315 and
October 1318 by the invasion from Scotland of Edward Bruce, with the intention of
taking Ireland from the English. The raiders were able to pass from Ulster deep into
the regions of Anglo-Norman supremacy, as far south and west as Cashel (Co.
Tipperary) and Castleconnell (Co. Limerick). Property was burned, livestock destroyed, and lands laid waste. The destruction was sufficiently severe to set back
some parts for over a generation. A large area of Dublin was pulled down and
burned in the course of attempts to ward off Scottish attacks. In Louth, where
destruction was particularly severe, the Scots burned Dundalk and numerous
smaller townships.[6] The Irish economy contracted severely as a result.[7]

Even in southern England the high mortality of 1315–18 had a significant effect
on population and prosperity. Some villages from Essex have left a good indication
of the changing size of their populations in this period because each male resident
over the age of 12 owed a penny a year to the lord of the manor. At Great Waltham
and High Easter together the number of males in this category fell by 15 per
cent between 1306 and 1318 and by a further 10 per cent between 1318 and 1320
(Figure 4.3). The evidence of some of the bishop of Winchester's manors in southern and south-western England shows an unprecedented level of hardship and
mortality.[8]

The bad harvests of 1316–18 were followed by recovery in some parts of
England, notably the south-west.[9] They had little impact on the estates of the
Duchy of Cornwall; Cornish agriculture benefited from supplying grain to other

regions. Rents there rose in the 1320s and 1330s, and the output of Cornish tin increased to unprecedented levels.[10] Even where there was no exceptional growth there was sometimes recovery. At Halesowen the population started to increase again in the late 1320s following the famines, and by 1348 had regained the level attained at the beginning of the century.[11] In the West Riding of Yorkshire, in Gloucestershire, in the Weald, new clearances from forest land were made between the 1320s and 1340s.[12] In some places there were more tenants in the 1330s and 1340s than in Edward I's reign.[13]

However, there are other parts of Britain where recovery from the crises of 1315–18 was either incomplete or wholly absent. In northern England and Ireland the high mortality of the years 1315–22 began a long-term reduction of settlement. The income of Durham Priory from its estates and its tithe receipts plummeted in these years suffered long-term reduction. In Cumbria, similarly, the population and agricultural output never regained their earlier levels. In Ireland famine and war brought a decisive turn for the worse in both the agriculture and trade of the most commercially advanced regions.[14] The fact that these regions were not particularly densely populated undermines the idea that population decline in the fourteenth century was uniquely a consequence of earlier overpopulation. However, population and output similarly failed to recover in more crowded parts of southern England, as at High Easter and Great Waltham.[15] Taking Britain and Ireland all together, it is unlikely that population and arable husbandry had recovered by the eve of the Black Death to their level in 1300. In this qualified sense it is legitimate to argue that their populations had already started to decline before the Black Death and that the famines of 1315–18 were a turning point, though presumably numbers would have recovered their former level if the Black Death had not supervened.

Recovery from the famines of 1315–18 was hampered by war. England's drain of cash to Scotland in protection money under Edward II was offset in 1328–31 by burdensome Scottish reparation payments of £20,000 to England under the terms of peace.[16] But the monetary effects of war with France in 1337 were more serious for both England and Scotland. In modern societies, because the monetary system is not tied to precious metals, governments have characteristically increased the money supply in wartime, causing inflation. By contrast, from the outbreak of the Hundred Years War silver flowed abroad to pay Edward III's expenses on the Continent, draining coinage from both England and, less directly, from Scotland. The currency in circulation in England may have halved during these years. The consequent low level of prices caused severe depression in agriculture because wages, transport charges, and other costs were much more traditionally fixed than the prices of agricultural produce and did not decline in the same proportion as the prices of grain and wool. The problems of English agriculture were exacerbated by the ways in which the war was financed. Taxes levied in England annually in the late 1330s were a significant burden, and increased poverty, especially in rural communities. The wool trade was severely disrupted by Edward III's experiments in taxation on wool exports and the accompanying monopolization of the wool trade by licensed groups of merchants. These expedients had the disadvantage of depressing the price of wool even more seriously than deflation itself had done. On top of this, villagers were often subjected to compulsory sales of produce to the king's agents for the purpose of supplying troops or the king's household. These impositions, as we have seen, had the fatal drawback that the sellers had to wait for their money, and it was often a long and costly business getting back what they were owed.[17] Compared with these sources of economic recession the development of the textiles industry in these years was a minor matter, and had little power to affect the overall picture of recession.[18]

In the midst of warfare came the Black Death, with little warning and even less remedy. 'Black Death' was not an expression used by contemporaries, or indeed by anyone until it was introduced in the nineteenth century to describe the appalling epidemic that swept Britain in 1348–9. Geoffrey the Baker supplies a description of the disease as it appeared to him in England. He says that victims were 'tormented by boils which broke out suddenly in various parts of the body, and were so hard and dry that when they were lanced hardly any liquid flowed out. Many of these people escaped, by lancing the boils or by long suffering. Other victims had little black pustules scattered over the skin of the whole body. Of these people very few, indeed hardly any, recovered life and health.' Like all other observers, Baker was impressed with the virulence of the disease. He commented that, finally, London and all England 'were so violently attacked that scarcely a tenth of either sex survived'.[19] There is some debate about just what the disease was. Though conventionally identified as bubonic plague, it was more virulent than any modern form of the disease, and prevailed in a wider variety of environments. Its transmission in Britain did not depend on rats and fleas, the classic carriers of plague in the modern world.[20]

Though Baker's estimate of mortality from the Black Death is exaggerated, the reality was grim enough. In England about 27 per cent of the king's tenants in chief died, but this group had a better chance of escaping the plague than any other because their housing was detached. Ecclesiastical records suggest that among beneficed clergy and the inhabitants of larger monasteries the death rate from plague was between 40 and 45 per cent. For much of the country the proportion was at least as high as that, even in lightly populated areas like the palatinate of Durham. Mortality rates reached about 42 per cent of tenants on fifteen manors of the bishop of Worcester, 50 per cent on Winchester bishopric manors, 50 per cent on the extensive estates of Durham Priory, 55 per cent on twenty-two manors of Glastonbury Abbey, and 56 per cent on three manors of Crowland Abbey.[21] Some estates supply more precise demographic statistics. At Halesowen in Worcestershire about 43 per cent of the male population over the age of 12 died.[22] A particularly reliable sample of 977 labourers on the Glastonbury estates implies that 57 per cent died between 1348 and 1350.[23] Few urban populations can be analysed with any accuracy. Henry Knighton implies it was very severe in Bristol. He also mentions a high mortality in Leicester. In Rochester 50 per cent of the tenants of Canterbury Cathedral Priory seem to have died between 1348 and 1350.[24]

The evidence from Wales is remarkable, given the more scattered nature of settlement there. Plague was ravaging the lordship of Abergavenny by March 1349, almost wiping out some villages and hamlets. It had travelled to west Wales soon afterwards; at Llanllwch, near Carmarthen, it killed eleven out of twelve of the tenants who paid money rents. In the north it reached the lordship of Ruthin in early June with devastating effect, and also swept through the lordship of Denbigh. In 1351 the burgesses of Rhuddlan were allowed a reduction of £13 6s. 8d. for the following two years from their annual payment of £40 to the king's chamberlain of Chester 'on account of the fewness of the people because of the pestilence'. The epidemic was even more serious in the principality of north Wales than in the more accessible south. Large numbers of tenements escheated in Anglesey and in all the commotes of Cardigan because of the deaths of tenants with no known heirs.[25] A mortality rate of 68 per cent is recorded from the commote of Nantconwy in Caernarvonshire.[26] Given the frequency of maritime contacts between Ireland, Britain, and France by this time, it is not surprising that Ireland did not escape. According to a Franciscan writer at Kilkenny, who himself died in the epidemic, the disease reached the east coast of Ireland at Howth or Dalkey and rapidly spread to Dublin and Drogheda in early August 1348. It then spread inland, reaching Kilkenny by Christmas. At Youghal the mortality rate is estimated at 45 per cent. Although it is sometimes supposed that mortality was lower in the west of Ireland, the plague is reliably reported to have reached the counties of Limerick, Clare, and Roscommon.[27] The Black Death reached Scotland in 1349 by way of England. Mortality there may have been less than further south, though the evidence is woefully thin. The Scottish chronicler John Fordun supposed that a third of the human race had died of pestilence.[28] It is not known how far the epidemic penetrated the Highlands. In short, the epidemic attacked Wales, Ireland, and northern Britain seemingly with hardly much less virulence than is recorded in the most thickly populated parts of the Mediterranean, until it began to subside late in 1349.

Contemporaries living through the plague were in no doubt that its implications for landlords, employers, and wage earners were immediate and striking. The fact that labour costs shot up as a result of labour shortages was so obvious that English legislation to restrain wages was introduced during the epidemic. Henry Knighton commented on the abandonment of property after the plague. 'After the pestilence,' he wrote, 'many buildings both great and small in all cities, boroughs and townships fell into ruins for lack of inhabitants, and in the same way many villages and hamlets were depopulated, and there were no houses left in them, all who had lived therein being dead.' As a result of the change in economic circumstances after the plague, he says, 'the magnates of the realm, and also lesser lords who had tenants, remitted the payment of rents lest their tenants should quit for want of labour, and the high cost of living'.[29] Similarly, those tenants who owed labour services had to have them remitted to induce them to stay on the land. Knighton's picture oversimplifies reality and ignores some aspects of life which were more favourable to landlords. But he correctly identified the underlying effects of depopulation in 1348–9—an increase in the value of labour and a decrease in the value of property.

The immediate economic effects of the Black Death were less devastating than a loss of nearly half the population might suggest. Many previously landless families unexpectedly acquired holdings by inheritance, or by licence from a landlord, so that much of the land was re-tenanted during the 1350s, depleting yet further the number of men and women available for wage earning. The cash inherited from deceased relatives seems to have prompted a brief spending spree amongst survivors, particularly to the advantage of the clothing industries. A number of regions, too, benefited from the continuing success of the woollen textile industry in meeting foreign competition; during the 1350s and 1360s English cloth began to make inroads into markets abroad, particularly in south-western France and the Baltic. Scotland, though without the equivalent of England's rising cloth exports, nevertheless benefited from an upswing in overseas trade in wool during the 1360s and 1370s.[30] More secure livelihoods for tenants, higher levels of employment and higher average incomes amongst labourers, whether in cash or in kind, helped to maintain a higher per capita demand for basic manufactures and agricultural produce in this much reduced sector of the population. Although the cultivation of bread grains declined along with the decline in the number of mouths, there was some compensating increase in the demand for ale and wool. Many families of the 1370s must have been aware of enjoying a lifestyle significantly more comfortable than that of previous generations. Recovery after 1349 was not confined to cloth-making regions. Scotland experienced a period of tentative recovery, based partly on expanding wool exports, though landlords' incomes remained more severely reduced than those of southern English lords.[31] In Caernarvonshire, a due levied on villeins called *staurum* was reimposed in 1362 after twelve years in abeyance.[32] But the strength of that recovery was regionally very varied. In north-eastern England, to judge from the tithe evidence of Durham Priory, it was halted by the early

1360s.[33] Elsewhere it lasted a generation. Even a recurrence of plague in 1361–2, which was particularly serious for children born since 1349, and which in Scotland was said to be as serious as the Black Death,[34] did not arrest the course of economic restructuring in southern England. Yet at the peak of this revival, to judge from the poll tax lists of 1377, England's population was only about 2.2–3 million, perhaps half its level around 1300.

That recovery was not maintained beyond a single generation. Real wage rates rose further during the late fourteenth century, simply because prices fell while wage rates remained steady. Where in the 1350s employers had been able to compensate for high wages by the combined benefit of high prices and new commercial opportunities, in the late 1370s they had neither of these advantages, and the squeeze on their incomes had its effect in falling production, the abandonment of land, and sometimes the splitting up of demesnes amongst leaseholders. Many landlords delayed making any fundamental adjustment to their operations till the 1390s, following severe epidemics in 1389–91 and a decline in raw wool prices and exports. For the moment the performance of the English cloth industry was firmly against this downward trend as a result of soaring cloth exports to the end of the century, partly perhaps the favourable result of falling wool prices on manufacturing costs. But the cloth industry was not large enough to counteract the effects of depressed prices in the rural economy, with the result that English landlords for the first time began in droves to abandon direct farming in the interests of more stable incomes from leasehold rents. In Scotland, as we have seen, the late fourteenth century was a period of declining exports, and the Scots shared fully in the recession experienced south of the border, but since demesnes were less important to their incomes the institutional impact was less apparent.[35]

The reasons for the late fourteenth-century slump are not wholly understood, especially for the 1380s. It is unlikely, though, that it can be explained entirely in terms internal to British history, since it corresponds to a widespread downturn in activity across Europe, closely related to a reduction in expenditure and monetary crises. Reduced incomes among England's overseas customers affected exports of English wool, which were lower in the 1380s than they had been for over a hundred years. Cloth exports continued to rise, but even they fell after 1402 to a trough in the 1410s.[36] Scottish wool exports contracted all through this period from their highest recorded point of about 7,360 sacks a year in 1370–4 to 1,840 sacks in 1400–5. This was the most dismal period of debasement of the Scottish currency, which presumably had a severe effect on creditors and those with fixed elements in their income.[37] Yet there were also internal shocks affecting economic performance. The impact of epidemics on the recession of the late fourteenth century is hard to evaluate for want of a clear record of changes in population levels. We have numerous records of individual epidemics, without any clear information about their seriousness or their cumulative effect, though contemporaries were well aware of the early 1390s as a period of exceptionally high mortality. In Ireland, following the major epidemics of 1349 and 1361 there are reports of recurrent outbreaks of plague in 1384, 1392–3, 1398–9, 1401, 1404, 1408, 1414, and 1419.[38] In Scotland epidemics are reported for 1361–2, 1379–80, 1392, 1401–3, 1430–2, 1439, and 1455.[39]

The rebellion of Owain Glyn Dŵr between 1400 and its collapse in 1406 added an additional source of economic recession in Wales and the Marches, chiefly because Glyn Dŵr adopted the policy of systematically devastating areas from which the English might draw resources.[40] In 1401–2 the local officers of the earl of Stafford's lordship of Newport had paid £534 5s. 5d. to the central receiver of the lordship, but after a raid in 1403 it was recorded as worth nothing, and the lord received no income till after the collapse of the rebellion. Even in 1408 the lordship could be leased for only £100.[41] Recovery cannot have been helped by the heavy fine inflicted upon those rebels who submitted; a record from Anglesey in 1406 records fines of £537 7s. 0d. imposed on 2,096 (or 2,068) rebels.[42]

Following the prolonged recession of 1375–1410 there was a patchy recovery for about twenty-five years; its vigour and duration varied very greatly from region to region. This revival was led in agriculture by an expansion of cattle raising for meat and for dairy produce that is recorded in many parts of England. Some rents recovered or even—as in the case of some Duchy of Cornwall manors—rose to unprecedented levels.[43] In northern England, as we have seen, rents of some moorland pastures were raised.[44] There was also a strong revival of English cloth exports which passed the level of the 1390s and was better sustained, bringing greater prosperity to those parts able to benefit. The number of cloths more than doubled within thirty years. This was the last period of successful adaptation for some major textile towns, like Colchester, that were already coming under competition from new and smaller centres of production.[45] Scottish wool exports, too, recovered hesitantly from their low point in the first decade of the century to an annual average of 3,760 sacks in 1424–9 and 3,020 in 1430–4. Some striking improvements in assessed land values are recorded in Scotland by the 1420s, implying in some cases a doubling since 1366.[46]

The recovery of this period, having already levelled out in many places in the later 1420s, was reversed in the later 1430s by a sequence of events similar, as it happened, to that of 1376–1415—a prolonged agricultural downturn followed by a recession in manufacturing for export. In the north-east rents fell following an epidemic in 1438–40. Between 1435 and 1450 the earl of Northumberland's income from the Northumberland manors of his barony of Alnwick fell by a quarter.[47] The income from the bishop of Durham's estates suffered a severe permanent reduction at this time, and between 1436 and 1446 Durham Priory's financial affairs ran into chaos. Lord FitzHugh's manors around Middleham in the North Riding of

Yorkshire suffered reductions of income varying between 11 and 20 per cent.[48] Rents in Derbyshire, outside the High Peak region, were declining during the 1430s and 1440s, despite some opportunities for developing pasture farming.[49] The sharp drop in Scotland's wool exports from 3,020 sacks a year in 1430–4 to 1,580 in the early 1440s suggests that some Scottish farmers, at least, were sharing experiences similar to those of northern England.[50] The northern depression bottomed out during the 1440s and a measure of recovery was achieved during the 1450s.[51]

Up to the late 1440s agrarian recession in southern England was partly offset by the continuing expansion of cloth exports, which brought high employment to some cloth towns and also prevented a severe drop in pasture rents. But this was not to last. The sluggish performance of the agrarian economy during the 1440s led into the severest recession of the late Middle Ages, the mid-fifteenth-century slump, in which both agricultural and industrial sectors of the economy were involved.[52] The sources of the crisis were complex. One root was a reduction of domestic expenditure, resulting from increased hoarding as a consequence of political uncertainty. Another was the impact of crises in foreign trade, when sales abroad were adversely affected by war, trade embargoes, or contracting demand in foreign markets. When cloth exports contracted after 1447, the agrarian recession rapidly deepened. In the High Peak area of Derbyshire, which had so far experienced few falling rents, recession began to bite at this point, especially because of the declining profitability of sheep farming.[53] The effects of disrupted overseas trade affected the whole country, but they were felt most in regions where employment depended on exports. In Wiltshire falling rents and accumulating arrears were more characteristic of the 1450s and early 1460s than any other decades of the fifteenth century; up to that point in the textile regions of the county rents had been static or rising. Having benefited from local industrial development for several decades, Winchester College's tenants of Durrington, near Salisbury, ran into arrears of rent during the 1450s, and in 1461 the warden and fellows were obliged to lower their rents by 20 per cent.[54]

The economic history of the long period from about 1470 to 1525 has been very differently described by different historians. As we saw in Chapter 16, it was a period of rapid expansion in English cloth exports, and to that extent comparable with the later fourteenth century, though these developments have no parallel in the development of Scottish wool exports, for which the period is one of prolonged stagnation, the 1520s being a decade of particularly low activity.[55] The export of English minerals, particularly tin and lead, similarly increased. These growing exporting sectors were nevertheless too small to generate growth throughout the economy, and have tended to attract more attention than they deserve in characterizations of the period as a whole. The amount of new employment they created amounted to only a few per cent of the labour force in 1530, and their contribution to national income at that date was probably no more than about 4 per cent. Although these industries do not give a complete picture of the export sector, it would be hazardous to build an interpretation of the English economy as a whole, let alone the economy of all Britain, on the strength of evidence from overseas trade.[56]

In the domestic economy, as in the history of population, evidence of growth of output or rising rents is localized even towards the end of the period when prices had started to rise. No very positive optimistic interpretation of English economic performance is warranted, even though there are signs of slow recovery from the trough of the 1450s and early 1460s. The level of rent for arable land remained stagnant, and the signs of new commercial enterprise are few and far between. The most significant forms of new development, directly responding to the successes of the textile exports, were in cloth manufacture, sheep farming, and wool production. Rents for natural pasture were more likely to rise than other rents, and there was some commercially induced substitution of pasture for arable land, accompanied by enclosure, though this was nothing new.[57] In northern England local iron from Weardale, supplied by local agents, increasingly supplanted imported Spanish iron in the purchases of Durham Priory after the mid-1480s.[58] There iron industry was also growing in the Sussex Weald.[59] The coal industry was also probably expanding in various parts of Britain, as on the Durham coalfield. Exports of coal through Newcastle grew slowly from the 1490s.[60] In Scotland there was some expansion of salt making, associated with a temporary surge of exports to a peak of 256 chalders a year during the 1480s.[61] Even so, the potential of these industries for creating new employment was much less than that of woollen textiles. Although early sixteenth-century judgements that the English economy was suffering from declining employment and population are definitely unsafe, the evidence would not have warranted contemporary observers believing that they were living through a period of rapid growth.[62]

Evidence of population during this period suggests that there can have been little overall growth until its very end, which was probably all to the good, protecting the higher standards of living achieved for a large proportion of the wage-earning, farming, and mercantile population during the preceding hundred years. Some historians have argued that Scottish and Irish population levels recovered more rapidly than those in England, though the evidence in their favour is not over-whelming.[63] The more convincing evidence of population growth is associated with industry and trade rather than with agriculture. Parts of London were growing vigorously, and so were numerous smaller towns where the textile industry was prospering. Yet in England, outside this narrow, largely export-driven sector, the indications of growth are far from universal. Where there is statistical evidence, as in some Essex manors, or on the Aquila honour in Sussex, the figures show no inclination to increase, and we know of some depressed places, like Coventry and Shrewsbury, where they declined. Some local population increases represent migration in search of employment from these towns that were manifestly failing.[64] The later fifteenth century was a particularly unhealthy period, to judge from the high levels of mortality registered independently in the Benedictine monasteries of Canterbury, Westminster, and Durham, which experienced severe epidemics after 1450 and show a particularly low expectation of life for monks who entered the abbey between 1445 and 1470; at Canterbury tuberculosis, sweating sickness, and plague were the principal killers.[65]

In short, there was no very well-defined divide between slow recovery from the major economic recessions of the fifteenth century and a subsequent period of more rapid development. Towards 1530 population growth perhaps accelerated, since there is good reason to suppose that population growth had become more widespread during the 1520s. The reasons for this are as yet obscure, however, and the problems arising from this observation can best be examined by turning to a concluding account of the state of Britain in the early sixteenth century.

NOTES

1. For a discussion of these general issues, see above (Ch. 4).
2. A. D. Carr, *Medieval Anglesey* (Llangefni, 1982), 300–1.
3. J. Lydon, 'The Impact of the Bruce Invasion, 1315–27', in A. Cosgrove (ed.), *A New History of Ireland*, ii: *Medieval Ireland, 1169–1534* (Oxford, 1987), 285.
4. I. Kershaw, 'The Great Famine and Agrarian Crisis in England, 1315–1322', in R. H. Hilton (ed.), *Peasants, Knights and Heretics: Studies in Medieval English Social History* (Cambridge, 1976), 105, 108–10.
5. G. W. S. Barrow, *Robert Bruce and the Community of the Realm of Scotland* (Edinburgh, 1976), 333, 336–8; I. Kershaw, *Bolton Priory: The Economy of a Northern Monastery, 1286–1325* (1973), 16–17.
6. Lydon, 'Bruce Invasion', 275–302; B. Smith, *Colonisation and Conquest in Medieval Ireland: The English in Louth, 1170–1330* (Cambridge, 1999), 105–9.
7. M. Kelly, *A History of the Black Death in Ireland* (Stroud, 2001), 74–8.
8. M. M. Postan and J. Z. Titow, 'Heriots and Prices on Winchester Manors', repr. in M. M. Postan, *Essays on Medieval Agriculture and General Problems of the Medieval Economy* (Cambridge, 1973), 169; Kershaw, 'Great Famine', 93.
9. B. F. Harvey, 'The Population Trend in England between 1300 and 1348', *Transactions of the Royal Historical Society*, 5th ser. 16 (1966), 23–42.
10. J. Hatcher, *Rural Economy and Society in the Duchy of Cornwall, 1300–1500* (Cambridge, 1970), 82–5, 92–3.
11. Z. Razi, *Life, Marriage and Death in a Medieval Parish: Economy, Society and Demography in Halesowen, 1270–1400* (Cambridge, 1980), 94.
12. Kershaw, 'Great Famine', 125.

13. J. L. Bolton, *The Medieval English Economy, 1150–1500* (1980), 191.

14. C. A. Empey, 'The Manor of Carrick-on Suir in the Middle Ages', *Journal of the Butler Society*, 2 (1982), 208; H. Jäger, 'Land Use in Medieval Ireland: A Review of the Documentary Evidence', *Irish Economic and Social History*, 10 (1983), 56, 64–5.

15. Above (Ch. 4).

16. A. Grant, *Independence and Nationhood: Scotland, 1306–1469* (1984), 162–3.

17. M. Prestwich, 'Currency and the Economy of Early Fourteenth-Century England', in N. J. Mayhew (ed.), *Edwardian Monetary Affairs (1279–1344)*, British Archaeological Reports 36 (Oxford, 1977), 46–52.

18. E. M. Carus-Wilson, *Medieval Merchant Venturers*, 2nd edn. (1967), 239–45.

19. R. Horrox, *The Black Death* (Manchester, 1994), 81.

20. S. K. Cohn, *The Black Death Transformed: Disease and Culture in Early Renaissance Europe* (2002), 41–54.

21. C. Dyer, *Lords and Peasants in a Changing Society: The Estates of the Bishopric of Worcester, 680–1540* (Cambridge, 1980), 239; R. A. Lomas, 'The Black Death in County Durham', *Journal of Medieval History*, 15 (1989), 127–40; Razi, *Life, Marriage and Death*, 99–100.

22. Razi, *Life, Marriage and Death*, 103.

23. M. Ecclestone, 'Mortality and Rural Landless Men before the Black Death: The Glastonbury Head-Tax Lists', *Local Population Studies*, 63 (1999), 6–29.

24. A. F. Butcher, 'English Urban Society and the Revolt of 1381', in R. H. Hilton and T. H. Aston, *The English Rising of 1381* (Cambridge, 1984), 93–5.

25. *Flintshire Ministers' Accounts, 1328–1353*, ed. D. L. Evans, Flintshire Historical Society Record Ser. 2 (1929), 41–2; W. Rees, 'The Black Death in Wales', repr. in R. W. Southern (ed.), *Essays in Medieval History: Selected from the Transactions of the Royal Historical Society on the Occasion of its Centenary* (1968), 179–99; id., *South Wales and the March, 1284–1415* (1924), 241–6.

26. Carr, *Medieval Anglesey*, 307–8.

27. K. Down, 'Colonial Society and Economy in the High Middle Ages', in Cosgrove (ed.), *New History of Ireland*, ii. 449; A. Gwynn, 'The Black Death in Ireland', *Studies: An Irish Quarterly Review*, 24 (1935), 25–8, 33; Kelly, *History of the Black Death*, 34–7, 98.

28. *Johannis de Fordun Chronica Gentis Scotorum*, ed. W. F. Skene (Edinburgh, 1871), 368–9.

29. *Knighton's Chronicle, 1337–1396*, ed. G. H. Martin (Oxford, 1995), 104–5.

30. P. G. B. McNeill and H. L. MacQueen (eds.), *Atlas of Scottish History to 1707* (Edinburgh, 1996), 240–1.

31. E. Gemmill and N. Mayhew, *Changing Values in Medieval Scotland: A Study of Prices, Money, and Weights and Measures* (Cambridge, 1995), 18, 371; Grant, *Independence and Nationhood*, 79.

32. T. J. Pierce, *Medieval Welsh Society: Selected Essays*, ed. J. B. Smith (Cardiff, 1972), 43.

33. B. Dodds, 'Durham Priory Tithes and the Black Death between Tyne and Tees', *Northern History*, 39 (2002), 20–1.

34. *Johannis de Fordun Chronica*, 380–1.

35. Grant, *Independence and Nationhood*, 79–80.

36. E. M. Carus-Wilson and O. Coleman, *England's Export Trade, 1275–1547* (Oxford, 1963), 122, 138,

37. Grant, *Independence and Nationhood*, 80, 236, 240.

38. G. Mac Niocaill, *Irish Population before Petty: Problems and Possibilities* (Dublin, 1981), 11.

39. Grant, *Independence and Nationhood*, 74.

40. R. R. Davies, *Conquest, Coexistence and Change: Wales, 1063–1415* (Oxford, 1987), 456.

41. *The Marcher Lordships of South Wales, 1415–1536*, ed. T. B. Pugh (Cardiff, 1963), 151–3.

42. 'The Anglesey Submission of 1406', ed. G. Roberts, *Bulletin of the Board of Celtic Studies*, 15 (1952–4), 39–61.

43. Hatcher, *Rural Economy*, 262 (Climsland), 263 (Liskeard), 264 (Helstone-in-Triggshire)

44. A. J. Pollard, 'The North-Eastern Economy and the Agrarian Crisis of 1438–1440', *Northern History*, 25 (1989), 91–3; id., *North-Eastern England during the Wars of the Roses: Lay Society, War and Politics, 1450–1500* (Oxford, 1990), 49–50.

45. R. H. Britnell, *Growth and Decline in Colchester, 1300–1525* (Cambridge, 1986), 163–8.

46. Grant, *Independence and Nationhood*, 81, 236–7.

47. J. M. W. Bean, *The Estates of the Percy Family, 1416–1537* (1958), 29–30.

48. R. B. Dobson, *Durham Priory, 1400–1450* (Cambridge, 1973), 269–70; Pollard, 'North-Eastern Economy', 94–7; id., *North-Eastern England*, 50–2.

49. I. S. W. Blanchard, 'Economic Change in Derbyshire in the Late Middle Ages' (unpublished Ph.D. thesis, University of London, 1967), 89, 94, 97–9, 214–15.

50. Grant, *Independence and Nationhood*, 237.

51. R. H. Britnell, 'The Economic Context', in A. J. Pollard (ed.), *The Wars of the Roses* (Basingstoke, 1995), 52.

52. J. Hatcher, 'The Great Slump of the Mid-Fifteenth Century', in R. H. Britnell and J. Hatcher (eds.), *Progress and Problems in Medieval England: Essays in Honour of Edward Miller* (Cambridge, 1996), 237–72.

53. Blanchard, 'Economic Change', 94–7, 212–17, 220.

54. J. N. Hare, 'Durrington: A Chalkland Village in the Later Middle Ages', *Wiltshire Archaeological Magazine*, 74–5 (1981), 141.

55. Above (Ch. 16); McNeill and MacQueen (eds.), *Atlas of Scottish History*, 241.

56. R. H. Britnell, 'The English Economy and the Government, 1450–1550', in J. L. Watts (ed.), *The End of the Middle Ages? England in the Fifteenth and Sixteenth Centuries* (Stroud, 1998), 90–4.

57. Above (Ch. 22).

58. M. Threlfall-Holmes, 'Late Medieval Iron Production and Trade in the North-East', *Archaeologia Aeliana*, 5th ser. 27 (1999), 111–12.

59. H. R. Schubert, *History of the British Iron and Steel Industry from c.450 B.C. to A.D. 1775* (1957), 147–8, 157–67.

60. J. F. Wade, 'The Overseas Trade of Newcastle upon Tyne in the Late Middle Ages', *Northern History*, 30 (1994), 33, 39–40; J. Hatcher, *The History of the British Coal Industry*, i: *Before 1700* (Oxford, 1993), 77, 487.

61. R. Nicholson, *Scotland: The Later Middle Ages* (Edinburgh, 1974), 439; McNeill and MacQueen (eds.), *Atlas*, 241.

62. Britnell, 'English Economy', 89–116.

63. Grant, *Independence and Nationhood*, 74–5; Kelly, *History of the Black Death*, 107–8.

64. Britnell, 'English Economy', 110–11. To references there, add M. Yates, 'Change and Continuities in Rural Society from the Later Middle Ages to the Sixteenth Century: The Contribution of West Berkshire', *Economic History Review*, 52 (1999).

65. B. F. Harvey, *Living and Dying in England, 1100–1540: The Monastic Experience* (Oxford, 1993), 127–8; J. Hatcher, 'Mortality in the Fifteenth Century: Some New Evidence', *Economic History Review*, 2nd ser. 39 (1986), 28–9. I owe the information about Durham to John Hatcher.

FURTHER READING

Allen, M., 'The Volume of the English Currency, 1158–1470', *Economic History Review*, 54 (2001).

Bailey, M., Demographic Decline in Late Medieval England: Some Thoughts on Recent Research', *Economic History Review*, 49 (1996).

Blanchard, I., 'Population Change, Enclosure and the Early Tudor Economy', *Economic History Review*, 2nd ser. 23 (1970).

Britnell, R. H., 'The Black Death in English Towns', *Urban History*, 21 (1994).

—— 'The Economic Context', in A. J. Pollard (ed.), *The Wars of the Roses* (Basingstoke, 1995).

—— 'The English Economy and the Government, 1450–1550', in J. L. Watts (ed.), *The End of the Middle Ages? England in the Fifteenth and Sixteenth Centuries* (Stroud, 1998).

—— *Growth and Decline in Colchester, 1300–1530* (Cambridge, 1986).

—— 'The Pastons and their Norfolk', *Agricultural History Review*, 36 (1988).

Campbell, B. M. S. (ed.), *Before the Black Death: Studies in the 'Crisis' of the Early Fourteenth Century* (Manchester, 1991).

Carr, A. D., 'The Black Death in Caernarvonshire', *Transactions of Caernarvonshire Historical Society*, 61 (2000).

Cohn, S. K., *The Black Death Transformed: Disease and Culture in Early Renaissance Europe* (2002).

Day, J., *The Medieval Market Economy* (Oxford, 1987).

Dobson, R. B., *Durham Priory, 1400–1450* (Cambridge, 1973).

Dodds, B., 'Durham Priory Tithes and the Black Death between Tyne and Tees', *Northern History*, 39 (2002).

Dyer, C., *Lords and Peasants in a Changing Society: The Estates of the Bishopric of Worcester, 680–1540* (Cambridge, 1980).

Ecclestone, M., 'Mortality and Rural Landless Men before the Black Death: The Glastonbury Head-Tax Lists', *Local Population Studies*, 63 (1999).

Gemmill, E., and Mayhew, N., *Changing Values in Medieval Scotland: A Study of Prices, Money, and Weights and Measures* (Cambridge, 1995).

Goldberg, P. J. P., *Women, Work, and Life Cycle in a Medieval Economy: Women in York and Yorkshire, c.1300–1520* (Oxford, 1992).

Grant, A., *Independence and Nationhood: Scotland 1306–1469* (1984).

Hare, J., 'Growth and Recession in the Fifteenth-Century Economy: The Wiltshire Textile Industry and the Countryside', *Economic History Review*, 52 (1999).

Harvey, B. F., 'The Population Trend in England between 1300 and 1348', *Transactions of the Royal Historical Society*, 5th ser. 16 (1966).

—— *Living and Dying in England, 1100–1540: The Monastic Experience* (Oxford, 1993).

Hatcher, J., *English Tin Production and Trade before 1550* (Oxford, 1973).

—— 'The Great Slump of the Mid-Fifteenth Century', in R. H. Britnell and J. Hatcher (eds.), *Progress and Problems in Medieval England: Essays in Honour of Edward Miller* (Cambridge, 1996).

—— 'Mortality in the Fifteenth Century: Some New Evidence', *Economic History Review*, 2nd ser. 39 (1986).

—— *Plague Population and the English Economy, 1348–1530* (1977).

—— *Rural Economy and Society in the Duchy of Cornwall, 1300–1500* (Cambridge, 1970).

Horrox, R., *The Black Death* (Manchester, 1994).

Jordan, W. C., *The Great Famine: Northern Europe in the Early Fourteenth Century* (Princeton, 1996).

Kelly, M., *A History of the Black Death in Ireland* (Stroud, 2001).

Kershaw, I., 'The Great Famine and Agrarian Crisis in England, 1315–1322', *Past and Present*, 59 (1973), 3–50, repr. in R. H. Hilton (ed.), *Peasants, Knights and Heretics: Studies in Medieval English Social History* (Cambridge, 1976).

Lock, R., 'The Black Death in Walsham-le-Willows', *Proceedings of the Suffolk Institute of Archaeology and History*, 37 (1992).

Lomas, R. A., 'The Black Death in County Durham', *Journal of Medieval History*, 15 (1989).

—— 'The Impact of Border Warfare: The Scots and South Tweedside, c.1290–c.1520', *Scottish Historical Review*, 75 (1996).

Mate, M., 'Agrarian Economy after the Black Death: The Manors of Canterbury Cathedral Priory, 1348–91', *Economic History Review*, 2nd ser. 37 (1984).

Mayhew, N. J., 'Numismatic Evidence and Falling Prices in the Fourteenth Century', *Economic History Review*, 2nd ser. 27 (1974).

Nightingale, P., 'England and the European Depression of the Mid-Fifteenth Century', *Journal of European Economic History* (1997).

Pollard, A. J., 'The North-Eastern Economy and the Agrarian Crisis of 1438–1440', *Northern History*, 25 (1989).

—— *North-Eastern England during the Wars of the Roses: Lay Society, War and Politics, 1450–1500* (Oxford, 1990).

Poos, L. R., 'The Rural Population of Essex in the Later Middle Ages', *Economic History Review*, 2nd ser. 38 (1985).

—— *A Rural Society after the Black Death: Essex 1350–1525* (Cambridge, 1991).

Postan, M. M., and Titow, J. Z., 'Heriots and Prices on Winchester Manors', *Economic History Review*, 2nd ser. 11 (1959) repr. in M. M. Postan, *Essays on Medieval Agriculture and General Problems of the Medieval Economy* (Cambridge, 1973).

Postles, D., 'Demographic Change in Kibworth Harcourt in the Later Middle Ages', *Local Population Studies*, 48 (1992).

Prestwich, M., 'Currency and the Economy of Early Fourteenth-Century England', in N. J. Mayhew (ed.), *Edwardian Monetary Affairs (1279–1344)*, British Archaeological Reports 36 (Oxford, 1977).

Razi, Z., *Life, Marriage and Death in a Medieval Parish: Economy, Society and Demography in Halesowen, 1270–1400* (Cambridge, 1980).

Rees, W., 'The Black Death in Wales', *Transactions of the Royal Historical Society*, 4th ser. 3 (1920), repr. in R. W. Southern (ed.), *Essays in Medieval History: Selected from the Transactions of the Royal Historical Society on the Occasion of its Centenary* (1968).

Sussman, N., 'The Late Medieval Bullion Famine Reconsidered', *Journal of Economic History* (1998).

Yates, M., 'Change and Continuities in Rural Society from the Later Middle Ages to the Sixteenth Century: The Contribution of West Berkshire', *Economic History Review*, 52 (1999).

Conclusion

....

CHAPTER 25

Britain and Ireland in the Early Sixteenth Century

In the early sixteenth century, as we saw in Chapter 4, the population of Britain and Ireland was still much lower than it had been at its peak around 1300. There is no reason to suppose that England's population was any higher in the years 1522–4 than it had been in the later eleventh century; the available estimates, of 1.8–2.3 million, are well within the margin of error for the precarious estimates derived from Domesday Book. There is less basis for assessing how far the populations of Wales, Scotland, and Ireland diverged from their eleventh-century levels. Wales is estimated to have had about 250,000 inhabitants, and Scotland probably had at most 700,000 (many fewer, if the estimate of 250,000 for the fifteenth century is to be believed),[1] implying a total of perhaps only 2.75–3.25 million for Britain as a whole. Ireland's population was perhaps less than a million.[2] These are unlikely to be much above eleventh-century levels. Nevertheless, any impression of long-term changelessness implied by such population estimates is misleading. The societies and economies of Britain and Ireland in the early fifteenth century were different in many ways from their condition 450 years earlier. Most of the more fundamental changes had occurred in the twelfth and thirteenth centuries, but declining population during the fourteenth and fifteenth centuries had brought its own package of institutional and structural responses. A retrospective view of the state of affairs in the years 1500–30 can profitably begin by examining similarities with the eleventh century that separate the sixteenth-century economy from that of our own day, and secondly move on to discussing some of the changes that had taken place during the period discussed in this book. Finally, we shall examine some of the ways in which Britain and Ireland compared with other parts of western Europe at the end of this period.

Continuities

Still, at the end of our period, the vast majority of people of Britain lived in the countryside. Whereas over 90 per cent of the population is now urban, the proportion in the 1520s was about the reverse, with under 20 per cent of the population in towns of any size. This had obvious implications for occupational structure and trading patterns. There were close and regular contacts between townsmen and countrymen, the former supplying manufactured and imported goods to the villagers in exchange for food and raw materials. A large part of total output, especially of foodstuffs, was sold locally to neighbours, to known contacts by prior agreement, or in nearby markets. This meant that dietary patterns were still localized. John Major, a Scot, writing a description of Britain published in 1521, observed that bread made from oats was a staple throughout much of the island, specifically Wales, northern England, and Scotland, and commented that this suited him well because he preferred oaten bread to bread made with barley and wheat.[3]

London was very exceptional in the range over which it drew provisions and the region it supplied. A medium-sized town like Cambridge, of about 3,500 people, drew most of its grain from within only a 10-mile radius (Figure 25.1).[4] The supply region of a town like Northallerton, with a population of perhaps about 700, was even smaller.[5] Many small Scottish burghs were 'so small as to be inconspicuous in the setting of dispersed rural settlement'.[6] However, even this local pattern of reciprocal exchange was not everywhere established. In parts of Britain and Ireland towards the north and west, town life remained little developed without other sources of demand having presented themselves, and in these regions the economic differences between the sixteenth and the eleventh century are impossible to specify; commodities could be traded only through the medium of landlord enterprise, since the costs were too high for individual peasant producers. There was consequently still in 1530 little cash in circulation in parts of western and northern Scotland or western Ireland.

As at all periods since the mid-eleventh century, the wealth of Britain remained concentrated in the most urbanized zone south and east of a line drawn from the Severn to the Tyne estuaries. A comparison between the English evidence from Domesday Book in 1086 and the tax assessments of the 1520s shows a similar distribution of wealth per square mile at both dates, the chief contrast being the development of the south-western counties of Devon and Cornwall.[7] No comparable analysis can be made of Scottish wealth, but there was a long-term tendency for wealth to concentrate in the eastern counties, in Berwickshire and the Lothians, the shires of Clackmannan, Kinross, and Fife, and north of the Tay from east Perthshire as far north as Kincardineshire. The main Scottish trade routes were all eastward. It would be surprising if this focus had shifted greatly between

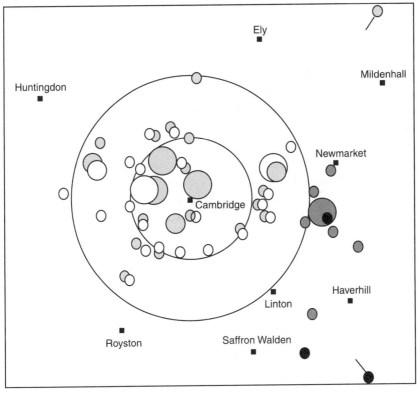

FIG. 25.1. Suppliers of King's Hall, Cambridge, 1450–1500. The purchases of grain and fuel by King's Hall, Cambridge (later part of Trinity College), show its reliance on local suppliers. Few purchases of wheat or barley were made over 10 miles away. The distribution of woodland imposed a less concentric pattern of supply, but most fuel came from within 15 miles.

Source: J. S. Lee, 'The Trade of Fifteenth-Century Cambridge and its Region', in M. Hicks (ed.), *Revolution and Consumption in Late Medieval England* (Woodbridge, 2001), 133.

the eleventh century and the sixteenth; a westward shift of wealth to Clydeside depended upon the later growth of Atlantic trade routes.[8]

The long-term geographical constraints on commercial development in western and northern Britain discussed in Chapter 1 remained fully operative in the early sixteenth century. The main outlets for English exports were on the east coast, especially through London, and through Exeter on the south coast. Bristol and Chester were the only ports of much significance on the west coast. Scotland had no major west-coast port; the trade of Irvine, Ayr of Kirkudbright, was of minor importance in comparison with principal ports of the east coast, Leith, Aberdeen, and Dundee.[9] Trade with Ireland having shrunk since the thirteenth century, what remained was not sufficient to provide much stimulus to western British trade, even though there were interesting new developments in Irish overseas enterprise. Dublin and Waterford traded principally with British ports, but the southern Irish ports looked chiefly to Spain and France. The range of trade in the Irish Sea had changed little for centuries; fish, hides, and woolfells were prominent amongst exports from Ireland, commonly in exchange for re-exports such as wine.[10] England's own exports still depended heavily on the kingdom's wool production and metals, as it had done since records begin, but with the difference that the trade in raw wool had dwindled to below 5,000 sacks a year by the 1530s. The growing importance of the English export of cloth, rather than raw wool, that had taken place since the mid-fourteenth century, was becoming ever more marked between 1500 and 1530.[11]

In the early 1520s even the most commercially developed parts of Britain remained less monetized and closer to production for subsistence than today. The availability of money depended on the circulation of coined silver and gold, and the amount in circulation in England in 1526 was only about £0.70 a head. Though credit was commonly given, especially in commercial transaction, it depended heavily on personal relationships, and there was no banking system. This restricted the extent to which households could advance their welfare by trade. The ideal of maximum household self-sufficiency was of necessity imposed on regions like western Scotland, but it was everywhere still common for people to make and repair their own equipment and household goods, where they could, rather than buying them or employing specialist craftsmen. John Fitzherbert, in his *Book of Husbandry*, was particular in advising young farmers to make their own wooden equipment in order to save money.[12] Many obligations, too, were settled in goods. Tithes, which were universal, were paid in produce, often direct from the field. In many parts of Britain and Ireland grain rents survived, as they still did in the eighteenth century. In the western Highlands chiefs maintained 'girnal' houses for storing produce they received in this way. The commonest produce rents were in grain, oatmeal, beer, cheese, butter, poultry, eggs, sheep and cattle.[13] The accounts of the bishopric of Dunkeld between 1505 and 1517 record numerous rents in capons, grain, and hay, and not all of these were anciently established; the rent of Nether Fordie in Tibbermore, near Perth, was converted from a money rent of £8 Scots to a produce rent of twenty-four capons, four trusses of hay, and four bolls of oats in 1508, shortly after the bishop acquired the property.[14] From Ireland, the Kildare rental begun in 1518 contains numerous examples of tithes, lands, and mills let for produce rents, such as grain, oxen, cows, eels, and honey, to a much greater extent than would normally be found in a contemporary English rental. Irish chiefs characteristically received oxen, oats, and butter as the main components in the tribute they drew from the townships they controlled, as well as labour services for ploughing and reaping their lands.[15] Produce rents were by no means unknown in England. Durham Priory received many of its rents in the form of grain, fish, and other commodities 'bought' from its own tenants.[16]

Despite technological advances on innumerable fronts, the essential features of early sixteenth-century technology had changed little since the eleventh century. It is difficult to say how far agricultural knowledge had progressed, since we know very little about farming methods before the mid-thirteenth century, and our information about early sixteenth-century methods is also weak in the absence of detailed farm accounts. Not all the cropping techniques developed during the period of high land values in the late thirteenth and early fourteenth century had remained in use in the subsequent period of lower agrarian investment. The principal widespread change in farming methods was perhaps in the use of horses for traction, particularly amongst the peasantry, though its importance probably related at least as much to reducing transaction costs as to any improvement in productivity.[17] The use of water power and sail power, the chief alternatives to human or animal muscle power, was already well developed long before 1050, though there had been substantial progress in the design of mills and ships, and in the application of water power to new processes.[18] The fourteenth-century development of clock mechanisms and guns, although portentous for the future, had no significant impact on industrial productivity before 1530. Historians who brand the whole period between the eleventh and the eighteenth century as one of traditional technology have a point, even if they exaggerate both the extent to which productivity stagnated during these centuries and the rapidity with which it increased during the industrial revolution.

The organization of enterprise, too, remained characteristically of a pre-industrial, pre-capitalist kind, based on individual households and other small units. Households of all sizes were units of authority, and many too were units of cooperation and production. The largest and most complex organizational units of any kind at this period were the great households of the king, the higher nobility and the upper clergy. There was no manufacturing workshop or factory equivalent in size to Cardinal Wolsey's household in the 1520s, which had about 500 members, or the comparably large households of the fifth earl of Northumberland and the third duke of Buckingham.[19] Although, of course, not manufacturing enterprises, these households were important administrative centres for large estates. Even substantial gentry households were larger than most productive enterprises, and required more managerial ability. Lower down the social scale the characteristic manufacturing unit was an artisan and his household (wife, older children, servants, and apprentices). The peasant household was similarly the most common unit of agricultural life. Not all families were able to subsist entirely from their own land, but there were several alternatives to working for others. One was to depend upon common rights to maintain livestock as a supplementary source of income, though the extent of these rights varied from place to place.[20] Another option, instead or in addition to common grazing, was to engage in part-time manufacturing, though this latter option too was regionally variable, as well as being subject to the vagaries of changing market demand. In Cornwall there was tin mining, in Devon fishing and woollen textiles, in the Forest of Dean and the Sussex Weald ironworking, in Norfolk both woollen and worsted manufacture, and so on.[21] The household was a focus for a variety of different money-making activities, some gender specific, rather than a specialized unit of agriculture, industry, or trade.

Agrarian communities were almost everywhere strongly differentiated by income, but the extent to which they depended upon a class of wage earners varied greatly. Because of the break-up of demesne farms since the later fourteenth century, the rural economy was more peasant based and less dependent upon landless labour in the 1520s than in the 1290s—not surprisingly, since the high cost of labour had been the chief reason for the abandonment of direct demesne management. Many smallholders were able to cultivate their own land without drawing on labour outside the family, especially in regions of more pastoral husbandry where one person could guard a herd of cows or sheep. There were few landless labourers in the more pastoral parts of Britain—in upland Wales, the northern English counties, and Scotland. In Wales hired labourers were more numerous in the lowlands where farms were larger than they were in the hills.[22] East Anglia was one of the regions most devoted to growing cereals commercially, and here wage earners made up a sizeable share of the population. In Norfolk about 36 per cent of taxpayers were wage earners in 1524–5, a proportion that remained much the same all through the sixteenth century.[23] Where arable farms were larger, even many peasants could not operate without wage labour, which is why wage rates remained a matter of considerable concern in many rural communities.

The importance of industry and commerce in the political thinking of the 1520s was significantly lower than it has been in Britain and Ireland since the eighteenth century, despite imperfect policies designed to prevent the outflow of money or to restrain increases in prices and wages. English government propaganda made much use of the 'commonwealth' ideal, but simultaneously operated with a dynastic mentality of a very ancient kind. Amongst the forces that checked economic expansion was the aggressive military policy that kings liked to pursue from time to time. Henry VIII had ambitions to achieve glory in France like his forerunners Edward III and Henry V, and he periodically indulged them. From the time of the war of 1513, English levels of taxation rose, chiefly through the development of the assessed subsidy. As a proportion of total English national output, taxation was light by modern standards—perhaps about 1.7 per cent between 1522 and 1527.[24] However, in terms of its impact upon this imperfectly monetized economy, the level of taxes is best considered in relation not to national income but to money in circulation. If the circulation in 1526 was only £1.4 million, this implies that about a fifteenth of the stock was diverted to government spending in that year. Periods of high military activity, such as 1512–13, 1522–4, and 1528, disrupted exports, and so caused setbacks in the economy's dynamic sectors. They also reduced domestic spending. The poet John Skelton in 1522 criticized high taxes on the grounds that they led to falling investment, reduced employment, and impoverished townsmen. He made particular reference to the problems it brought to Thomas Spring of Lavenham, one of the wealthiest clothiers of the day.[25] The growth trends that our sources hint at from the later 1520s, together with the associated inflation, would have been more pronounced at an earlier date if it had not been for Henry VIII's fits of bellicosity. The proportion of resources that went into arms and armies in England, Wales, and lowland Scotland, was nevertheless probably as nothing compared to the burden of military activity in the lordships beyond the scope of central governments. The form of government in Gaelic Ireland and Scotland was still that of the chieftainship outside the direct control of the nascent nation states of England and Scotland, and their organization was correspondingly governed by the exigencies of frequent conflicts for territory and prestige.[26]

Another source of disruption to growth arose from natural disasters in the form of failed harvests and epidemics. The economy was still heavily influenced from year to year by the state of the weather, just as in the eleventh and twelfth centuries. Though international trade had grown sufficiently to alleviate such crises, it was not able to iron them out. Wheat prices were exceptionally high—over 40 per cent above the later fifteenth-century average—in 1502, 1512, 1519–21, and 1527–30. There were particular problems if royal foreign policy interfered with the normal pattern of the grain trade. By far the most severe shortage of the years 1500–30 occurred in 1527, as a result of excessive rain during the preceding winter months but exacerbated by wartime trade disruption. Londoners blamed the government for having supported France against the Empire, so cutting off supplies of grain from northern Germany.[27] Epidemics, too, were a recurrent source of disruption and loss. There was a severe plague outbreak in 1499–1500 and again in 1513. In

1508 there was an epidemic of sweating sickness, and there was another serious epidemic of the same disease in the summer of 1528, in which several men close to Henry VIII died and the king himself was so afraid that for a while he moved from place to place almost daily.[28] Many serious outbreaks of disease were quite localized, and so do not conform to any chronology of national epidemics. There were serious mortality crises on the estates of the bishop of Worcester in the years 1522–6.[29]

Economic and Social Change, 1050–1530

In spite of these similarities between the eleventh and the sixteenth-century economies, a great deal had changed, even if the changes were not great enough to bring about a capitalist economy, primarily founded on wage labour, or to achieve sustained modern economic growth, on the basis of ongoing technological and institutional development. Historians who have commented disparagingly about the technical progress in medieval society have generally overlooked the much more important infrastructural institutional changes that lowered transaction costs and raised incentives, transforming the context in which just about every productive occupation was carried out. The organizational structures of commerce and of financial and legal administration changed and developed beyond all recognition between 1050 and 1530. At one time the teaching of history over this period was dominated by discussion of constitutional and administrative history, especially the history of parliaments, and of the legal and financial departments of royal governments. Even economic history was principally concerned with institutional developments relating to manorial and urban custom and administration, markets, fairs, commercial law, guilds, property rights, instruments of credit, and other formal aspects of the social relations of production. This emphasis was to some extent myopic, but it was far from misguided. The importance of these developing institutions, with the accompanying vast increase in the amount of written documentation, can hardly be exaggerated. Even the history of the English, Scottish, and Irish parliaments, though conventionally taught as topics in constitutional history, was of immense significance for economic development, since it demonstrably controlled the forms of taxation and limited the rapacity of kings, as well as regulating aspects of property rights and labour contracts. If, as with most historians, we are to class British society both in 1050 and 1530 as 'medieval' or 'feudal', it must be with the caveat that, notwithstanding the apparent restrictions on population growth between these years there was radical institutional change in every aspect of economic activity, so that by 1530 Britain had most of the institutions it needed for development through the sixteenth and seventeenth centuries. These changes were not recent in 1530; they can be traced through a long, frequently disrupted, and far from predictable history of evolution throughout the preceding five centuries.

Institutional change had contributed above all to facilitating commercial development, brought about by innumerable responses to economic pressures and opportunities over the years. One measure of this is the increase in the amount of money in circulation related to population size. Even though this was still small in 1530 by modern standards, the change since 1050 was great enough to have raised per capita currency in circulation by thirty or forty times; the amount of English currency in circulation had increased from about £37,500 in William I's England to £1.4 m. in 1526. Unfortunately there seems to be no basis for comparing Scottish currency in circulation with that of England. Between 1484 and 1486 Scottish minting of silver is estimated to have been 13 per cent of England's, a low proportion that reflects Scotland's greater problems in establishing export markets. Nevertheless, Scotland's economy remained significantly more monetized than in the eleventh century.[30] As this implies, currency was almost everywhere more available than in 1050 for everyday transactions.

Although there were archaic survivals in many places, through much of England and through the more populous parts of Scotland and Ireland the produce and labour rents that had figured prominently in twelfth-century rentals had mostly been replaced by cash payments. Even from the western Scottish islands the crown expected some cash rents alongside renders of grain.[31] The majority of rents within the Irish Pale were in cash, and money was evidently circulating to some extent in Gaelic Ireland, since the earl of Kildare was able to levy tribute from some Irish chieftaincies in the form of a levy of 4*d*. on every cow, or in some instances a fixed money payment.[32] Even where produce rents survived, their destination and use had often changed with time, and they did not necessarily indicate an economy unaffected by trade in agrarian produce. Often they were sold by the landlord who received them, and so contributed to market supply—a characteristic of Norfolk estates in one of the most commercialized regions of Britain. The reasons behind the substitution of cash for goods and labour were complex. Up to about 1300 money rents had been a landlord's preferred option because of the flexibility they allowed in the handling of estate revenues, but in the fourteenth and fifteenth centuries the pressure for commutation had probably come more from tenants. However it had come about, where money rents prevailed farmers had to sell produce to pay rents, as well as to buy necessaries such as clothing, fish, tar, nails, locks and hinges, metal tools, plough irons, horse harness, and horseshoes—all this before there was any talk of luxuries.[33]

Even though Britain and Ireland in 1530 were lightly urbanized by modern standards, the expansion of domestic and foreign trade since 1050 had permitted changes of long-term importance. Though overall densities of settlement were little different from their eleventh-century level, towns were more numerous, more widely spread, and contained a larger proportion of the total population. There were now about ten British towns with more than 6,000 inhabitants. London, which was both England's major port and close to the centre of government in Westminster, was about five times larger than any other British city. Norwich, with about 10,000 came second, and Bristol, Exeter, Salisbury, York, Canterbury, Newcastle upon Tyne, Coventry, and Colchester were the other eight. Outside this zone, even Edinburgh and Dublin probably had fewer than 10,000 inhabitants, for all their importance as commercial and political centres.[34] Many of these larger towns showed signs of recent contraction, but they nevertheless retained extensive links in at least some aspect of their trade. London, Bristol, Exeter, and Newcastle were major ports, as were Leith (the port of Edinburgh) and Dublin; Norwich, York, Salisbury, Colchester, and Coventry were all major cloth towns, even if reduced from their former pre-eminence by competition from elsewhere. The majority of the inhabitants in all larger towns depended on earning money in some way in order to buy food, and perhaps about a third of their populations engaged at least part of the time in supplying food and drink to the rest in the form of bread, ale, fish, and meat.

The changing role of London deserves particular emphasis, since its history makes a valuable bridge between British economic development before 1530 and its subsequent course in modern times. The city had grown to be several times larger than its Norman predecessor, and in the intervening period had become increasingly prominent as a centre of both political and economic power. Increasingly after 1300 it had assumed a metropolitan role in domestic commercial enterprise, and by 1530 it had begun to experience the exceptionally rapid rise in population that was to carry it to its exceptional heights in the early modern period. Westminster evidence suggests that recovery there was from about 1470, and the same seems to be true of some of London's suburbs, though rents in Cheapside showed no tendency to increase until the middle of the sixteenth century. Southwark's population and property values rose from 1460, especially after 1500. According to a commonly accepted estimate, London's population grew from about 50,000 in 1500 to 63,000 in 1535, implying a growth rate significantly higher than that of England as a whole.[35] Feeding this number required supplies from an exceptionally wide area. The city's growth was partly based on commercial success. A rising proportion of English cloth exports was shipped from the Thames—79 per cent in 1524–8.[36] Not all London's expansion was the result of growing exports, however, since much of it is attributable to the growth of inland trade and of government employment.

The Merchant Adventurers who dominated London's export trade were a powerful group; they traded as individuals, but the company chartered ships, organized their loading, and negotiated details of sailing from the port of London and the freight rates to be charged. They demonstrate how the growth of commerce had been accompanied by the development of a self-confident native merchant class with institutions and traditions of which there is hardly a trace in the eleventh century. This, incidentally, is one of the many reasons for doubting whether overseas trade can have contributed very much to the aggregate income of any part of Britain in the eleventh century, despite some remarkably high but unsafe estimates.[37] The merchant classes of early Tudor Britain were restricted in the range of their enterprise, but they were widely spread and politically influential.

Mercantile activity had come to involve more than merely buying and selling; from the thirteenth century onwards it had also, in different contexts, included forms of industrial organization. In England the late fifteenth and early sixteenth centuries knew a distinctive group of entrepreneurs in the expanding areas of textile industry who coordinated the various stages of production, and to that extent reduced the autonomy of the workmen they employed. By the 1520s most clothmaking regions yield examples of such clothiers whose enterprise absorbed a significant proportion of local trade. At Lavenham Thomas Spring, who died in 1523 leaving a fortune of £3,200, was famous for his importance as an employer in the textile industry, and the withdrawal of his capital from the industry after his death may have been more significant than high taxation in causing local unemployment and disaffection in 1525. There were many big names in the Wiltshire industry. One was Thomas Horton (died 1530), whose attractive manor house still stands at Westwood. At Tiverton in Devon the principal operator of the early sixteenth century was John Greenway (died 1529), whose ornate chantry chapel, decorated with scenes from the life of Christ and a frieze of merchant ships, is to be seen in the south aisle of the parish church. Collompton's leading cloth merchant was John Lane (died 1529), whose chantry chapel has angels clutching teasel-frames and cloth-shears. In Newbury, John Winchcombe (died 1519) was long remembered as an innovator who had put his workers together in a single workshop, and he has accordingly been celebrated as a pioneer of factory production. By this time the cloth industry was clearly very different in structure even from that of the early and mid-fifteenth century, when clothworkers had operated much more independently of merchant capital even though they had depended on merchants to create outlets for their cloth. Some insight into both the workings of the trade between Suffolk and London and the importance of capitalist clothiers is to be found in a petition to Cardinal Wolsey written from prison on 19 May 1528 by Humfrey Monmouth, a London draper and cloth exporter, who argued that his imprisonment was detrimental to the commonwealth, both because of the amount of employment he provided, and because of his contribution to the king's income from customs duties.[38]

A change of outstanding importance, whose roots were complex but partly resulted from economic development, concerned the construction of social rank. In 1086 not only were there slaves throughout Britain, but the majority of the population was regarded as in some sense unfree and subject to hereditary obligations and disabilities. In England that situation had permitted the development of new legal theories relating to villeinage or serfdom during the twelfth and thirteenth centuries. Closely related distinctions had been imposed or remodelled in conquered territories in Wales and Ireland. By 1530, although all parts of Britain and Ireland retained highly differentiated structures of social rank, the distinction between free and unfree had lost most of its earlier force. This was not simply the result of commercial growth, however. Indeed, though the growth of settlements, urban populations, and monetized relationships had increased the proportion of free tenants and the prominence of money rents, English landlords had showed little inclination before the late fourteenth century to abandon their right to servile dues and labour services. In Scotland this 'great, peaceful, silent revolution', as Cosmo Innes called it, happened earlier than in England, but it would be difficult to argue that this was because Scotland was more commercially advanced.[39] The decline of English serfdom, as of Irish betaghry, owed much more to the weakened position of landlords during the fourteenth and fifteenth centuries, when tenants were in a much stronger position than before to resist their landlords and to remould rural institutions. In England it was also to owe much to the development of legal systems, which offered a chance for copyhold tenants to implead their landlords in the king's court of chancery, and so went a long way to removing one of the legal disabilities that had been characteristic of thirteenth-century villeinage. For all their faults, the legal systems of England and Scotland were a shield against the worst excesses of arbitrary power on the parts of landlords. The most despotic landlords were those beyond the reach of royal jurisdiction in western Ireland or highland Scotland.[40] The insecurity of Irish lordships in the fifteenth century, and the consequent militarization of Irish society, had had there the effect, running counter to tendencies elsewhere, that lords maintained private armies that they billetted on their tenants.[41]

Britain, Ireland, and Europe in 1530

The comparative history of European economies is an undeveloped subject, more for want of motivation amongst historians than because of any intrinsic difficulties. Any observations about the differences to be observed around 1530 must be tentative, since this is notoriously a topic where superficial impressions can mislead. There are three observations worth making because of their wide-reaching significance for the role of British governments in the early sixteenth century and for the general shape of British economic history between 1300 and 1700.

The first of these observations concerns the size of the English and Scottish kingdoms and the resources of their respective governments. In the twelfth century the Angevin empire had been one of Europe's pre-eminent power blocs. Not only was the government of England exceptionally unified, at least in normal circumstances, with exceptionally lucrative systems of taxation, but it had attached to it some of the wealthiest parts of France; Henry II could draw revenues from Normandy, Anjou, and Aquitaine. The situation in 1530 was very different. England remained an exceptionally unified kingdom, but the king's leading subjects had used that unity to impose checks upon the royal power to tax. The English monarchy had been humbled, as the French saw it, by the power of parliament. Sir John Fortescue's satisfaction with the constrained authority of the English crown, as compared with that of France, represented a characteristically English viewpoint. In the meantime, state building in Europe by the French and Spanish monarchies and the Holy Roman Empire had created new powers that put England, as well as Scotland, in the shade. With its population of only 1.8–2.3 million in the 1520s, England was no match for the kingdom of France, with about 16.4 million inhabitants in 1500, or Spain with about 6.8 million.[42] It is not surprising that the English government in these circumstances was concerned with the size of the English population, and feared depopulation. Nor could the incomes of the English or Scottish crowns compare with their main continental allies and rivals. The incomes of Francis I of France and the Emperor Charles V, king of Spain, in the 1520s were equivalent to about £800,000 and £1,100,000, as against Henry VIII's normal income of £80,000–90,000, which might be stretched to £150,000–170,000 in wartime through exceptional and much-resented levels of taxation.[43] England had been marginalized in international affairs partly through the failure of the crown to retain territories in France, partly because of rival political developments elsewhere in Europe.

These political developments were accompanied by a certain loss of ground that resulted in part from the very delayed recovery of the British population from the demographic recession of the fifteenth centuries. The English population perhaps grew even more slowly than the Scottish and Irish in the later fifteenth and early sixteenth centuries.[44] There are indications of earlier recovery elsewhere in Europe; it was already under way in some regions in the 1460s, and widespread by the 1520s. Despite pronounced regional variations in the rate of recovery, the population of Provence increased vigorously between 1471 and 1540.[45] In northern France population grew and towns expanded between 1450 and 1500, though growth slowed down thereafter.[46] The commercial activity of Venice brought about a particularly early recovery there; according to one estimate population rose from about 65,000–70,000 in the 1360s to 110,000 in 1509 and 131,000 in 1540. In Italy generally there was widespread increase in numbers between the mid-fifteenth and mid-sixteenth centuries, and in some parts, as around Florence, the turning point can be identified as early as 1460.[47] Sicily experienced growth at the rate of 1.4 per cent a year between 1460 and 1501, partly as a result of immigration.[48] Portugal's population is estimated to have increased from about 806,400 in 1422 to 1,000,000 in 1492 and 1,349,033 in 1527.[49] In north-west Europe, too, there were regions recovering and developing much more rapidly than most of Britain. The city of Antwerp, as its trade increased, grew through the fifteenth century to reach almost 7,000 hearths in 1500 and almost 9,000 in 1526.[50] There was early and spectacular recovery in rural parts of the Low Countries, such as inland Flanders, where recovery began as early as the 1380s. The population of West Friesland experienced a surge in the century after the Black Death unlike anything in British history, so that by 1477 the population was perhaps a third higher than in 1335, and even though there was a dip in the last quarter of the fifteenth century, numbers doubled during the sixteenth.[51] These examples suggest that, from being a comparatively rapidly growing economy in the twelfth and thirteenth centuries, when the opportunities for growth were generally highest in north-western Europe, Britain and Ireland had become slow developers in the fifteenth and early sixteenth centuries. These discrepancies are not easily accounted for; they are not to be explained by royal rapacity, since England's tax burden was particularly low, at least before the 1520s, but they relate to areas of historical debate where causation is notoriously difficult to establish.

A final point of contrast concerns the development of international trade. Partly no doubt because of failure of government initiative and support, partly because of slow domestic growth, the British were relatively slow in developing new commercial initiatives in the fifteenth and early sixteenth centuries. London merchants, for all their growing importance in the internal economy of England, were conservative in their ambitions, concentrating principally on short routes across the Channel and the North Sea to Middelburg or Antwerp. By the early sixteenth century great explorers were already beginning to open up access to the world westward of Ireland. But British and Irish merchants made only a minor and transitory contribution to this enterprise; interest there was confined to Bristol and the south-west. John Cabot had made two voyages across the Atlantic from Bristol in 1497 and 1498. In 1502 Henry VII chartered a group of pioneers to America shortly known as the Company Adventurers to the New Found Land, based in Bristol.[52] As yet the capacity of the Atlantic economy to stimulate English enterprise and raise the profile of western ports lay in the future. Numerous references to America in early sixteenth-century texts show clearly that people knew something of the excitement associated with new discovery. Its power to stimulate the imagination is nowhere better shown than in Sir Thomas More's account of the island of Utopia. However, by this time such literary activity was about the limit of any ongoing commitment to knowledge of the New World. From about 1505 for several generations, British interest was more intellectual than commercial.

International contrasts such as these are often mistakenly taken as surrogate indications of economic welfare, as if there was some inevitable link between mercantile and urban development and modern economic growth. In fact, most of Britain was not regarded as poor in the early sixteenth century. On the contrary, visitors were often impressed, as they always had been, by the island's wealth of resources and the high standards of living they found there. One of the most interesting documents in this respect is the description of Britain made about 1500 by a visitor from Venice, one of Europe's most illustrious commercial cities. He observed that 'the riches of England are greater than those of any other country of Europe, as I have been told by the oldest and most experienced merchants, and also as I myself can vouch, from what I have seen'. He observed from personal experience that 'everyone who makes a tour in the island will soon become aware of this great wealth, . . . for there is no small innkeeper, however poor and humble he may be, who does not serve his table with silver dishes and drinking cups'. He regarded the wealth of the English Church as phenomenal.[53] The point is similar to that made thirty years or so earlier by Sir John Fortescue, who thought the English standard of living was higher than in France, and described his fellow-countrymen as wealthy and well provided.[54] According to the available estimates, the average real income of the English in 1526 was over twice what it had been in 1300 and 1086.[55] Perhaps at this point families were benefiting from the relatively low rate of population growth over the previous century. Don Pedro de Ayala, the Spanish ambassador to the court of James IV of Scotland, supposed in 1498 that the Scots were poorer than the English, but he was informed that the kingdom had greatly advanced in prosperity during the previous ten years.[56]

The changes that had taken place between 1050 and 1530, although they had left England and Scotland as relatively minor military powers, had nevertheless substantially kept pace with appropriate organizational and technological change elsewhere in Europe and prepared the ground for further institutional and technological development in the sixteenth and seventeenth centuries. There is no single key to explaining those earlier changes. The environment, the culture, and the forms of government from which the story began in Chapters 1–3 will explain many of the constraints and opportunities that had affected them. In addition, we can take for granted, in varying measure, tendencies for couples to breed, workers to innovate, property owners to invest, landlords and governments to exploit, tenants to resist, all of which explain various parts of social and economic change. The history of economies and societies is no more amenable than the history of biological species to simple predictive models over large periods of time. As in that case, though, historical analysis can both identify surprisingly radical changes and go a long way towards explaining them. The changes between 1050 and 1530 bridge two quite strongly contrasted societies, the latter being very much better endowed with knowledge and institutional infrastructure than the former, as a result of adaptations by governments, lords, townsmen, and peasants to varied and changing circumstances.

NOTES

1. R. E. Tyson, 'Population Patterns, to 1770', in M. Lynch (ed.), *The Oxford Companion to Scottish History* (Oxford, 2001), 488; G. Williams, *Recovery, Reorientation and Reformation: Wales, c.1415–1642* (Oxford, 1987), 90.

2. S. G. Ellis, *Tudor Ireland: Crown, Community and Conflict of Cultures, 1470–1603* (1985), 40.

3. John Major, *A History of Greater Britain as well England as Scotland*, ed. and trans. A. Constable (Edinburgh, 1892), 8.

4. J. Lee, 'The Trade of Fifteenth-Century Cambridge and its Region', in M. Hicks (ed.), *Revolution and Consumption in Late Medieval England* (Woodbridge, 2001), 132–3.

5. C. Newman, *Late Medieval Northallerton: A Small Market Town and its Hinterland, c.1470–1540* (Stamford, 1999), 15, 100–115.

6. G. Donaldson, *Scotland: James V to James VII* (Edinburgh, 1965), 10.

7. H. C. Darby, *Domesday England* (Cambridge, 1977), 228; H. C. Darby (ed.), *A New Historical Geography of England before 1600* (Cambridge, 1976), 196.

8. I. F. Grant, *The Social and Economic Development of Scotland before 1603* (Edinburgh, 1930), 355; P. G. B. McNeill and H. L. MacQueen (eds.), *Atlas of Scottish History to 1707* (Edinburgh, 1996), 298–305.

9. McNeill and MacQueen (eds.), *Atlas*, 250.

10. Ellis, *Tudor Ireland*, 38. Trade in the late fifteenth century is analysed in detail in W. Childs, 'Ireland's Trade with England in the Later Middle Ages', *Irish Economic and Social History*, 9 (1982), 5–33.

11. E. M. Carus-Wilson and O. Coleman, *England's Export Trade, 1275–1547* (Oxford, 1963), 123, 141.

12. *The Book of Husbandry by Master Fitzherbert*, ed. W. W. Skeat (London, 1882), 15.

13. R. A. Dodgshon, *From Chiefs to Landlords* (Edinburgh, 1998), 60–70; id., 'West Highland Chiefdoms, 1500–1745: A Study in Redistributive Exchange', in R. Mitchison and P. Roebuck (eds.), *Economy and Society in Scotland and Ireland, 1500–1939* (Edinburgh, 1988), 29; Grant, *Social and Economic Development*, 298.

14. *Rentale Dunkeldense*, trans. and ed. R. K. Hannay, Scottish History Society, 2nd series, 10 (1915), 48–51.

15. *Crown Surveys of Lands, 1540–1, with the Kildare Rental Begun in 1518*, ed. G. Mac Niocaill (Dublin, 1992), 232–357; Ellis, *Tudor Ireland*, 41.

16. R. A. Lomas, 'A Priory and its Tenants', in R. H. Britnell (ed.), *Daily Life in the Middle Ages* (Stroud, 1998), 118–20.

17. J. Langdon, *Horses, Oxen and Technological Innovation: The Use of Draught Animals in English Farming from 1066 to 1500* (Cambridge, 1986), 265–73.

18. See above (Chs. 4, 6, 16).

19. K. Mertes, *The English Noble Household, 1250–1600* (Oxford, 1988), 208, 210, 215.

20. R. H. Tawney, *The Agrarian Problem in the Sixteenth Century* (1912), 239–42.

21. J. Cornwall, *Wealth and Society in Early Sixteenth Century England* (1988), 80–1; J. Whittle, *The Development of Agrarian Capitalism: Land and Labour in Norfolk, 1440–1580* (Oxford, 2000), 247–52.

22. Williams, *Recovery, Reorientation and Reformation*, 105.

23. Whittle, *Development of Agrarian Capitalism*, 228, 237.

24. R. H. Britnell, 'The English Economy and the Government, 1450–1550', in J. L. Watts (ed.), *The End of the Middle Ages? England in the Fifteenth and Sixteenth Centuries* (Stroud, 1998), 101–2.

25. J. Skelton, 'Why come ye nat to courte', in id., *The Complete Poems*, ed. J. Scattergood (Harmondsworth, 1983), 302.

26. Dodgshon, *From Chiefs to Landlords*, 87–90; Ellis, *Tudor Ireland*, 41–5.

27. P. Bowden, 'Statistical Appendix', in J. Thirsk (ed.), *The Agrarian History of England and Wales*, iv: *1500–1640* (Cambridge, 1967), 817; E. Hall, *The Union of the Two Noble and Illustre Famelies of Lancastre and Yorke* (1809), 721, 736; D. Dymond, 'The Famine of 1527 in Essex', *Local Population Studies*, 26 (1981), 29.

28. Hall, *Union*, 750; W. G. Hoskins, *The Age of Plunder: The England of Henry VIII, 1500–1547* (1976), 8.

29. C. Dyer, *Lords and Peasants in a Changing Society: The Estates of the Bishopric of Worcester, 680–1540* (Cambridge, 1980), 223–4.

30. E. Gemmill and N. Mayhew, *Changing Values in Medieval Scotland: A Study of Prices, Money, and Weights and Measures* (Cambridge, 1995), 141.

31. Dodgshon, 'West Highland Chiefdoms', 28–9.

32. *Crown Surveys of Lands*, 264–77.

33. C. Dyer, *Standards of Living in the Later Middle Ages: Social Change in England, c.1200–1520* (Cambridge, 1989), 115–16, 169–72.

34. Grant, *Social and Economic Development*, 351; G. Mac Niocaill, 'Socio-Economic Problems of the Late Medieval Irish Town', *History Studies*, 13 (1981), 18–19.

35. M. Carlin, *Medieval Southwark* (1996), 133–5; S. Rappaport, *Worlds within Worlds: Structures of Life in Sixteenth-Century London* (Cambridge, 1989), 50; G. Rosser, *Medieval Westminster, 1200–1540* (Oxford, 1989), 86–92, 177.

36. Carus-Wilson and Coleman, *England's Overseas Trade*, 116.

37. G. D. Snooks, 'The Dynamic Role of the Market in the Anglo-Norman Economy and Beyond, 1086–1300', in R. H. Britnell and B. M. S. Campbell (eds.), *A Commercialising Economy: England 1086 to c.1300* (Manchester, 1995), 37–8.

38. R. H. Britnell, 'The Woollen Textile Industry of Suffolk in the Later Middle Ages', *The Ricardian*, 13 (2003), 94–5.

39. Grant, *Social and Economic Development*, 91–2.

40. K. W. Nicholls, 'Gaelic Landownership in Tipperary in the Light of Surviving Irish Deeds', in W. Nolan (ed.), *Tipperary: History and Society: Interdisciplinary Essays on the History of an Irish County* (Dublin, 1985), 103.

41. C. A. Empey, 'The Sacred and the Secular: The Augustinian Priory of Kells in Ossary, 1193–1541', *Irish Historical Studies*, 24 (1984), 143–4.

42. J. de Vries, *European Urbanization, 1500–1800* (1984), 36.

43. R. H. Britnell, *The Closing of the Middle Ages? England, 1471–1529* (Oxford, 1997), 45–6; R. Hoyle, 'War and Public Finance', in D. MacCulloch (ed.), *The Reign of Henry VIII: Politics, Policy and Piety* (1995), 77, 89.

44. Above (Ch. 24).

45. E. Baratier, *La Démographie provençale du XIIIe au XVIe siècle* (Paris, 1961), 88–94.

46. G. Bois, *The Crisis of Feudalism: Economy and Society in Eastern Normandy, c.1300–1550* (Cambridge, 1984), 67–73.

47. D. Herlihy and C. Klapisch-Zuber, *Tuscans and their Families: A Study of the Florentine Catasto of 1427* (New Haven, 1985), 73–8; J. C. Russell, *Late Ancient and Medieval Population*, Transactions of the American Philosophical Society, new ser. 48.3 (1958), 126–8.

48. S. R. Epstein, *An Island for Itself: Economic Development and Social Change in Medieval Sicily* (Cambridge, 1992), 72–3.

49. Russell, *Late Ancient and Medieval Population*, 118.

50. N. J. G. Pounds, *An Historical Geography of Europe, 1500–1840* (Cambridge, 1979), 129.

51. B. J. P. van Bavel, 'People and Land: Rural Population Developments and Property Structures in the Low Countries, c.1300–c.1600', *Continuity and Change*, 17 (2002), 13–14.

52. *The Cabot Voyages and Bristol Discovery under Henry VII*, ed. J. A. Williamson, Hakluyt Society, 2nd ser., 120 (1962), 60, 101, 132–4

53. *English Historical Documents*, v: *1485–1558*, ed. C. H. Williams (1971), 197–8.

54. J. Fortescue, *The Governance of England*, ed. C. Plummer (1885), 114–15.

55. N. Mayhew, 'Modelling Medieval Monetisation', in Britnell and Campbell (eds.), *Commercialising Economy*, 72; id., 'Population, Money Supply, and the Velocity of Circulation in England, 1300–1700', *Economic History Review*, 48 (1995), 244.

56. *Early Travellers in Scotland*, ed. P. H. Brown (Edinburgh, 1891), 48.

FURTHER READING

Bernard, G. W., *War, Taxation and Rebellion in Tudor England: Henry VIII, Wolsey and the Amicable Grant* (Brighton, 1986).

Blanchard, I., 'Population Change, Enclosure and the Early Tudor Economy', *Economic History Review*, 2nd ser. 23 (1970).

—— 'Social Structure and Social Organization in an English Village at the Close of the Middle Ages: Chewton 1526', in E. B. DeWindt (ed.), *The Salt of Common Life: Individuality and Choice in the Medieval Town, Countryside and Church. Essays Presented to J. Ambrose Raftis* (Kalamazoo, 1995).

Britnell, R. H., *The Closing of The Middle Ages? England, 1471–1529* (Oxford, 1997).

—— 'The English Economy and the Government, 1450–1550', in J. L. Watts (ed.), *The End of the Middle Ages? England in the Fifteenth and Sixteenth Centuries* (Stroud, 1998).

Campbell, B. M. S., 'The Population of Early Tudor England: A Re-evaluation of the 1522 Muster Returns and 1524 and 1525 Lay Subsidies', *Journal of Historical Geography*, 7 (1981).

Carlin, M., *Medieval Southwark* (1996).

Carus-Wilson, E. M., *The Expansion of Exeter at the Close of the Middle Ages* (Exeter, 1963).

Challis, C. E. (ed.), *A New History of the Royal Mint* (Cambridge, 1992).

Cornwall, J., 'English Population in the Early Sixteenth Century', *Economic History Review*, 2nd ser. 37 (1961–2).

—— *Wealth and Society in Early Sixteenth Century England* (1988).

Ditchburn, *Scotland and Europe: The Medieval Kingdom and its Contacts with Christendom, 1214–1560* (East Linton, 2000).

Dolley, M., 'Coinage to 1534: The Sign of the Times', in A. Cosgrove (ed.), *A New History of Ireland*, ii: *Medieval Ireland, 1169–1534* (Oxford, 1987).

Dyer, C., *Lords and Peasants in a Changing Society: The Estates of the Bishopric of Worcester, 680–1540* (Cambridge, 1980).

—— *Standards of Living in the Later Middle Ages: Social Change in England, c.1200–1520* (Cambridge, 1989).

Dymond, D., and Betterton, A., *Lavenham: Industrial Town* (Lavenham, 1989).

Ellis, S. G., *Reform and Revival: English Government in Ireland, 1470–1534* (Woodbridge, 1986).

—— *Tudor Frontiers and Noble Power: The Making of the British State* (Oxford, 1995).

—— *Tudor Ireland: Crown, Community and Conflict of Cultures, 1470–1603* (1985).

Gemmill, E., and Mayhew, N., *Changing Values in Medieval Scotland: A Study of Prices, Money, and Weights and Measures* (Cambridge, 1995).

Goring, J. J., 'The General Proscription of 1522', *English Historical Review*, 341 (1971).

Grant, I. F., *The Social and Economic Development of Scotland before 1603* (Edinburgh, 1930).

Harvey, B., *Living and Dying in England, 1100–1540: The Monastic Experience* (Oxford, 1993).

Hoskins, W. G., *The Age of Plunder: The England of Henry VIII, 1500–1547* (1976).

Hoyle, R., 'War and Public Finance', in D. MacCulloch (ed.), *The Reign of Henry VIII: Politics, Policy and Piety* (1995).

Kermode, J., 'The Trade of Late Medieval Chester, 1500–1550', in R. Britnell and J. Hatcher (eds.), *Progress and Problems in Medieval England: Essays on Honour of Edward Miller* (Cambridge, 1996).

Moreton, C. E., *The Townshends and their World: Gentry, Law and Land in Norfolk, c.1450–1551* (Oxford, 1992).

Newman, C., 'Employment on the Priory of Durham Estates, 1494–1519: The Priory as an Employer', *Northern History*, 36 (2000).

—— 'Work and Wages at Durham Priory, 1494–1519', *Continuity and Change*, 16 (2001).

—— *Late Medieval Northallerton: A Small Market Town and its Hinterland, c.1470–1540* (Stamford, 1999).

Palliser, D. M., *The Cambridge Urban History of Britain*, i: *600–1540* (Cambridge, 2000).

Phythian-Adams, C., *Desolation of a City: Coventry and the Urban Crisis of the Late Middle Ages* (Cambridge, 1979).

Rappaport, S., *Worlds within Worlds: Structures of Life in Sixteenth-Century London* (Cambridge, 1989).

Rosser, G., *Medieval Westminster, 1200–1540* (Oxford, 1989).

Schofield, R. S., 'The Geographical Distribution of Wealth in England, 1334–1649', *Economic History Review*, 2nd ser. 18 (1965).

Sheail, J., 'The Distribution of Taxable Population and Wealth in England during the Early Sixteenth Century', *Transactions of the Institute of British Geographers*, 55 (1972).

Thirsk, J. (ed.), *The Agrarian History of England and Wales*, iv: *1500–1640* (Cambridge, 1967).

Threlfall-Holmes, M., 'Durham Cathedral Priory's Consumption of Imported Goods: Wines and Spices, 1464–1520', in M. Hicks (ed.), *Revolution and Consumption in Late Medieval England* (Woodbridge, 2001).

Whittle, J., *The Development of Agrarian Capitalism: Land and Labour in Norfolk, 1440–1580* (Oxford, 2000).

Williams, G., *Recovery, Reorientation and Reformation: Wales, c.1415–1642* (Oxford, 1987).

Woodward, D., *Men at Work: Labourers and Building Craftsmen in the Towns of Northern England, 1450–1750* (Cambridge, 1995).

Wrightson, K., *Earthly Necessities: Economic Lives in Early Modern Britain* (New Haven, 2000).

Yates, M., 'Change and Continuities in Rural Society from the Later Middle Ages to the Sixteenth Century: The Contribution of West Berkshire', *Economic History Review*, 52 (1999).

GLOSSARY

arable land used for growing crops, some of which would be rested as *fallow in any given year.

assart a parcel of land cleared of trees, usually for cultivation.

barony (1) an English lordship held from the crown in return for contributing a stipulated number of knights to the king's army and other obligations. The properties attached to a barony were usually scattered *manors, but it had a head manor (often, in the twelfth century, with some sort of castle) and a number of dependent knights *fees. Barons might hold a court for feudal dependants, but this jurisdiction was undermined from the later twelfth century by the growth of royal jurisdiction. (2) A Scottish feudal lordship, usually corresponding to a territorial area and based often on a multiple estate. Its jurisdiction was less challenged than that of English baronies by royal courts, and so became much more central to the Scottish system of local justice.

betagh a native Irish tenant, defined after the English conquest as an unfree tenant roughly equivalent to an English *villein. The status of betaghs before the English conquest is disputed. Betaghs character-istically formed distinctive communities and were jointly responsible for the rents and services issuing from them.

Black Death the most severe epidemic of the last 1,000 years. It ravaged Britain, together with much of the rest of the world, in 1348–50. The nature of the disease is disputed, though it is now generally agreed that it was not the same as bubonic plague.

boll a Scottish measure of volume. It was variable, but roughly equivalent to a sixteenth of a *chalder or to two English *bushels.

bond a written and legally binding obligation to perform some action. See also *husbandman for a quite different meaning.

bordar a customary smallholder, occurring frequently in *Domesday Book. Though the term was employed loosely, the bordar often had no more than four or five acres, and was sometimes indistinguishable from the *cottar.

borough (1) a settlement with plots held by *burgage tenure, usually to accommodate craftsmen and traders; (2) a settlement with liberties affecting tenures, trade, and local administration granted either by the king or some other lord.

bovate (or **oxgang**) a standardized peasant tenure in northern England and Scotland, equivalent to an eighth of a *ploughland and commonly of 12–15 acres. Bovates could be either compact units or dispersed within the fields of a township.

burgage a plot in a *borough or *burgh, usually without more than about half an acre of attached land and held for a money rent.

burgh the Scottish equivalent of a *borough.

bushel a measure of volume used in England for grain, and equivalent to one eighth of a *quarter. A bushel was equivalent to 8 gallons (i.e. about 36 litres), though the precise amount of grain depended on how the measure was used—for example, whether it was heaped or not.

cain (1) a royal due payable in kind from royal estates all over Scotland, except the Lothians. It was also (unlike *conveth) due to the king from earldoms and other lordships, unless it was replaced by other forms of service. (2) A tax on shipping in Scottish ports instituted by David I.

cartulary a register in which a property owner recorded the texts of his *charters, often written out in full. For many estates cartularies survive even though the original charters are lost.

chalder a measure of volume in northern England and Scotland equivalent to four English *quarters.

charter a document, usually on a small piece of parchment, usually written in Latin, created as evidence of the conveyance of property or other rights, or the recognition of such rights and renunciation of legal claims. Charters

were never signed; they were ratified by the seals of those principally involved.

coign (or **coyne**) a seigniorial due equivalent to *conveth in Scotland, but often discharged through the billeting of troops in rural settlements.

common field a field over which all villagers had the right to pasture animals in years when it lay fallow. The **common field system** was one in which the land of a township was divided between large fields (usually two to four) cropped in rotation in such a way that each field in turn was fallowed and subject to common rights for one year.

commons land (usually moor, heath, rough pasture) over which villagers had the right to pasture animals, usually every year.

commote the principle unit of local administration under native Welsh rulers.

conveth a seigniorial revenue in kind in Scotland, equivalent to *coign in Ireland. Later medieval Scots records often translate this as 'waiting'. The name signifies an annual debt of hospitality to be paid to a lord by his dependants, but the obligation was collected in various forms, often as a fixed payment in agricultural produce.

cottar a rural tenant holding only a small house ('cot') and either no land or only a few acres. Such tenants would not be able to support themselves from their own land, and would depend either on hired employment, or on income from some trade and manufacturing, or on both.

crannock a measure of grain used in Wales and Ireland. It was not effectively standardized, and varied in different contexts and for different cereals. For purposes of tax assessment in 1292–3 the Welsh crannock was required to contain four English *bushels (half a *quarter), but there was considerable variation around this. The Irish crannock when used for the measurement of wheat was about the equivalent of an English **quarter**, but for the measurement of oats it could be twice that.

custumal a record listing the names of manorial tenants with the rents and customs owed by them individually and collectively.

davoch (or **davach**) an agricultural unit used in some regions of predominantly Gaelic settlement north of the Forth–Clyde line. Its size was variable and is now difficult to define, but it was probably somewhat larger in acreage than the southern Scottish *ploughgate.

dawnbwyd the food rent owed by the unfree tenants of a Welsh *commote.

demesne the part of a *manor that a landlord could dispose of *either* by managing it directly through representatives or servants *or* by renting it to a tenant at a negotiated rent. Demesne *arable was sometimes dispersed among the lands of tenants, sometimes separate from them.

Domesday Book a survey of England ordered by William I at Christmas 1085, and mostly compiled during the following year. The information was compiled, county by county, into two volumes, the one Little Domesday Book for Essex, Suffolk, and Norfolk, and the Great Domesday Book for the other thirty counties surveyed. Within each county, properties (usually designated manors) are listed according to their owners. For each unit of property the survey records its assessment for geld, the number of ploughs, the number and rank of its subtenants, its woodland, meadow, and pasture, its mills and fishponds, and its 'value'. Little Domesday Book has additional information about livestock. Some comparative information was required both for 1086 and for 1066.

ell a measure of length, approximately 1.14 metres.

eyre a French word derived from the Latin *iter* (a journey). It was used as a name for courts held in the English provinces by royal justices ('justices in eyre') who travelled out from Westminster for the purpose.

fair an annual trading event, lasting usually only a few days, but sometimes a fortnight or more. The great fair of St Giles at Winchester was authorized in 1155 to run for as long as sixteen days. There was usually a wider range of goods on sale at a fair than at a weekly *market.

fallow arable land lying uncultivated for a year or more and allowed to grow weeds and grass to restore its fertility and to supplement pasture resources.

famulus a retained servant, as opposed to one casually employed. Farm servants of this kind, often retained a year at a time to work on *demesne land, replaced slaves on many estates after the eleventh century. Their forms of remuneration varied, but were often largely in grain, at least until the fifteenth century. Some were retained in return for small landholdings or for rent rebates.

fee (or **feu** or **fief**, from the Latin 'feudum') a property held in accordance with feudal custom by some sort of service. A knight's fee was a property held in return for the performance of knight's service or its recognized monetary equivalent. Many knights fees belonged to a *barony, but there were also such fees on the estates of bishops and some major abbeys.

feet of fines a written agreement of a settlement of a property dispute in the English royal courts. The fine was a tripartite document, each part containing an identical record of the agreement. The parties to the dispute each took a copy, and the third (the 'foot') was retained by the court. Because of its high status as a title to property, many fines were the result of collusive actions rather than of real disputes. Most feet of fines are known from the surviving files in the English public records.

feudalism (or **feudal system**) there are various logically independent meanings to these terms, of which the principle ones are covered under the following definitions. (1) A system of land law in which some lands were held from superior lords, whether for life or by inheritance, in exchange for personal services rather than for a commercial rent. The service in question, often a military obligation, was frequently in practice commuted for money payments and those payments became standardized in the course of the twelfth and thirteenth centuries. In England from the reign of William I the king was superior lord of lords, so that no land in the kingdom was without a lord. (2) A political system in which power was widely diffused so that members of the lay and ecclesiastical nobility had independent powers of jurisdiction, taxation, and military coordination that would not be tolerated in a modern state. Degree of aristocratic autonomy varied widely both between different political structures and within them. (3) A weakly commercialized economy in which developments in the agricultural sector governed changes in the urban economy, towns and trade were poorly developed, units of production were small, and predominantly in the hands of small farmers or artisans, innovation and accumulation of capital was little in evidence, and economic relationships were hereditary rather than contractual. (4) An agrarian system characterized by the existence of *villeinage.

fifteenth and tenth an English system of taxation based up to 1334 on the assessed value of movable goods surplus to basic subsistence. From 1334 it was raised on fixed assessments from each *township and *borough. Boroughs before 1334 paid a higher rate of their assessed value than ordinary townships did (but not always a tenth). Once the assessments were fixed the distinction between a borough rate and an ordinary rate was purely notional.

forest an area of countryside (not all of which would be wooded) subject to special laws for the protection of game in the interests of the crown. These laws regulated hunting, but those living and working in forest areas had restrictions on their use of trees and their keeping of dogs.

fraternity a society committed to some pious observation (usually honouring a particular church festival and a particular saint) and committed in some degree to the welfare of its members.

furlong a subdivision of a larger field, comprising a number of *selions running parallel to each other. Furlongs differed greatly in total size, depending (amongst other things) on the lie of the land and the reasons for their original formation.

geld a tax levied on land by English kings between 991 and 1162, the basic unit of taxation being the *ploughland or *hide. The amount levied on each ploughland (and fractions of a hide) varied.

guild (or **gild**) (1) an association of urban traders to enforce trading regulations in a *borough (or *burgh), commonly known as a 'merchant gild', or, more quaintly, as a 'gild merchant'; (2) an association of craftsmen to enforce trading regulations relating to their craft or crafts, subject to the supervision of a borough council or merchant guild, commonly known as a 'craft guild' (or simply 'a craft') or a 'mistery'; (3) a *fraternity.

gwestfa food rents owed by the freemen of a *commote.

halmote the characteristic form of seigniorial jurisdiction over tenants in northern England. They were no doubt equivalent to *manor courts, on the smallest estates. On large estates, however, halmotes were characteristically— so far as our evidence stretches—held at a few central points on the estate to which tenants from other townships had to travel.

hide a *ploughland, originally defined as the 'land for one family', though hides rarely survived intact as individual tenures by the later eleventh century.

hundred a territorial unit of royal administration, being a subdivision of a *shire. Hundreds had courts for local policing and for private litigation. The administration and profits of many hundreds were delegated to private landlords, lay and ecclesiastical, and attached to *manors of their estate.

Hundred Rolls the record of a survey of English *manors and their tenants compiled under Edward I in 1274–5. It is the most detailed survey since *Domesday Book and in some respects more detailed, especially with regard to rural tenancies and rents, but not all of the returns survive.

husbandland the landholding of a *husbandman or *bond.

husbandman (or **bond**) the characteristic customary tenant in northern England, and probably in much of Scotland too before the fourteenth century. The northern English bond characteristically held two *bovates in exchange for a variety of obligations including light labour services. In English law the husbandman was equated with the *villein.

inquisition post mortem a survey conducted following the death of one of the English king's *tenants-in-chief to establish what he or she owned, to identify the heir, and to define the king's rights.

knight's fee a *fee held in return for knight's service.

maerdref the chief township of a Welsh *commote, usually with *arable land belonging to the lord of the commote.

manor (1) a house or hall where a property was administered, rents collected, and where the lord and his family, or their servants, could be accommodated; (2) an assemblage of lands lying close together, and usually attached to a particular house or hall, though not necessarily in a single block. These lands might correspond to the territory of a single *township but many townships contained the lands of more than one manor, and some large manors contained more than one *township. The lands of a manor were commonly divided between *demesne and lands over which tenants had hereditary rights. Manors held *manor courts with varying degrees of authority over their tenants. The definition of lordships as manors is characteristic chiefly of southern and midland England, though the word was stretched to accommodate forms of lordship under English influence elsewhere.

manor court a private law court held on behalf of the lord of a *manor for his tenants. Characteristically separate courts were held for each manor, though their frequency and volume of business varied greatly. The jurisdiction of a manor court covered (*a*) minor private jurisdiction between tenants in matters of debt, breach of contract, assault, (*b*) transfers of land between tenants and other matters relating to tenures on the manor, (*c*) the punishment of offences against the lord of the manor or against agreed by-laws, (*d*) (sometimes) minor policing jurisdiction on behalf of the crown relating to minor breaches of the peace, obstruction of highways, and trading offences.

market (1) a place in the centre of a town or *township set aside for trade, but with numerous other public functions (Latin *forum*); (2) a formally regulated meeting of buyers and sellers, usually once a week in smaller townships, in a particular market place on a particular day (or days) of the week and at set times (Latin *mercatum*). The right to organize and profit from such a market was—at least from after 1066 in England, and not long afterwards in Scotland—regarded as a franchise from the crown to which the entitlement was either by ancient right or by explicit royal grant.

meadow grassland on which the grass was allowed to grow to be mown as hay, which was kept over winter as fodder (cf. *pasture).

merchet in England, a payment due to a manorial lord when the daughter of one of his *villeins married.

multiple estate a territorial unit of lordship comprising scattered settlements, whether townships, hamlets, or isolated farms, all in a territorial block and owing services at a central hall. Some parts of the estate were *demesne land producing grain or pastoral produce for the use of the lord of the estate.

multure the grain owed to a miller to pay for the work of milling it for flour, otherwise known as mill toll; this was usually a fixed proportion of the amount of grain taken to the mill.

neif (from the Latin 'nativus' meaning 'native') a customary tenant, usually regarded as 'bound to the soil', that is, obliged to remain on a particular piece of land. The term is often used as an equivalent of *villein. In northern England, and probably Scotland, neifs constituted a subset of the *husbandmen and *cottars whose freedom was particularly circumscribed.

notary a legal clerk authorized by higher authority (lay or ecclesiastical) to make an official record of contracts and property transactions, of which he was obliged to keep an official copy in a *register. Notaries were of minor importance in English legal recording, but became very important in the authenticating of transaction in Scotland during the fifteenth century.

open field a large tract of land subdivided by *furlongs without hedges as divisions, also sometimes known as a 'subdivided field'. In central England open fields were usually *common fields and in such cases the **open-field system** is equivalent to 'common-field system'.

outfield land outside a regular system of crop rotation, cultivated erratically and returned to pasture when not under crops.

oxgang *a bovate.

parish a territorial unit attached to a church to which tithes were due and to which the inhabitants of the parish (parishioners) owed religious obligations.

pasture grassland on which animals were allowed to graze (cf. *meadow).

penny (plural **pence**) the principle unit of minted currency in Britain and Ireland before the mid-fourteenth century.

ploughgate the Scots equivalent of *plough-land, equivalent to eight 'oxgates'.

ploughland notionally the amount of land a single plough team could cultivate. Often it was assumed to be equivalent to 120 acres, but in practice ploughlands were often smaller. Ploughlands were often divided into tenancies of four *virgates or eight *bovates. Up to the later twelfth century the ploughland was used in England as a taxable unit for the assessment of *geld.

poll tax a royal tax levied as a (fixed or graded) obligation of individual adults rather than an assessed charge on property. The only significant poll taxes were those of 1377, 1378, and 1380, the last of which triggered the English Peasants' Revolt of 1381.

pound (abbreviated to l. or lib., from which is derived the symbol £) (1) a unit of weight, usually equivalent to 16 ounces; (2) a monetary unit of account equivalent to 240 *pence and 20 *shillings, so called because originally 240 pence were struck from a pound (by weight) of silver.

quarter a measure of volume, used especially for grain in England. Originally it was perceived as a quarter of a *chalder, but the latter measure survived principally in northern England and Scotland. A quarter was equivalent to eight *bushels.

rector the person or institution entitled to receive the great *tithes of a parish. An individual rector could be a cleric or layman; an institutional rector was commonly a religious house, but could also be a college. Where the rector was not serving the parish church he (or it) was obliged to provide a *vicar to be paid out of the proceeds of the parish income.

register a record kept in book form rather than as a *roll.

roll a record kept on one or more unbound parchment membranes, either sewn end to end or stitched together at the head of each membrane.

runrig a field system having intermixed peasant strips.

sack a measure of wool, usually reckoned as weighing 364 lb.

selion a strip of ploughland, usually 200–300 metres long. In *open fields selions were grouped parallel to each other in *furlongs.

severalty land held by a single owner and not subject to common rights. This usually implied some sort of enclosure.

sheiling a summer pasture, usually in the hills, and usually with temporary accommodation for those attending the herds or flocks pastured there.

shilling (abbreviated to *s.*) a monetary unit of account equivalent to twelve pence and one twentieth of a *pound.

shire (1) a territorial unit of royal local administration. English shires were units of jurisdiction (in the county court), of tax collection, of military recruitment, and from the thirteenth century of parliamentary representation; (2) a territorial unit of lordship, equivalent to a *multiple estate.

soke (1) the right of seigniorial jurisdiction, sometimes expressed in the archaic legal formula 'sake and soke'; (2) occasionally, a territorial unit, equivalent to a private *hundred, over which a particular lord exercised hundredal jurisdiction.

sterling the English coinage.

tallage a payment (often of arbitrary amount) exacted by right of lordship, sometimes annually. The best-known examples are (1) payments exacted by the lord of a *manor from his tenants, (2) payments exacted by English kings from each royal *borough, (3) payments exacted by English kings from Jewish communities. Traces of tallages in Scotland are few.

teinds the Scottish equivalent of *tithes.

tenant-in-chief a tenant of freehold land from the King without any intermediary lord.

thegn a freeman of high status in Anglo-Saxon England; many thegns held a *manor.

tithes the principle form of income of each parish church, which took the form of a (notional) tenth of parishioners' incomes. In practice this was commonly equivalent to a tenth of the grain harvest (the 'great tithes' or 'garbal teinds' owed to the parish *rector) and a tenth of pastoral and garden output ('small tithes', generally owed to a *vicar, if the rector was not personally serving the parish church). The practice of tithing was subject to considerable local variation.

township (or **vill**) an Anglo-Scottish translation of the Latin term *villa*. A settlement with a recognized territory of fields, pastures, woods, or meadows, often with definite bounds. A township was sometimes equivalent to a *parish, but this was not universal, and such an equivalence was very uncommon in northern England and Scotland where many townships were tiny hamlets. In northern England and Scotland the township was often also a unit of lordship, equivalent to a *manor, but this was less common in southern and midland England. The term is used in this book to mean a settlement of unspecified size (hamlet, village, or town).

vicar a paid deputy. The term is usually used of priests employed by a *rector to serve a *parish.

vill a *township.

villein an English tenant holding land from a manorial lord by customary tenure and with customary personal obligations. Unless it was replaced by a cash equivalent, the villein owed labour services on his lord's *demesne, including week work (i.e. a certain number of days each week). The most characteristic personal obligation was a payment due when a villein's daughter married, called *merchet. From the twelfth century villeins were distinguished from free tenants by the inability to defend their tenure in the royal courts.

virgate a standardized peasant holding, often dispersed within the fields of a *township, on which rents and services were levied for the lord of the manor. It was equivalent to a quarter of a *hide. In size it compared roughly to two *bovates (oxgangs). As that implies, its size varied; often it was of about 30 acres, but could range between about 20 and 40.

wapentake an administrative subdivision of the shire, equivalent to *hundred.

yardland a *virgate.

yield per acre the average amount of grain harvested per acre of land. So if 4 quarters of grain are harvested from 4 acres the average yield per acre is 1 quarter.

yield per seed the ratio of the amount of grain harvested to the seed sown. So if 1 quarter of wheat is sown and 4 quarters are harvested the yield per seed is 4.0 (traditionally expressed as 'fourfold').

INDEX

Places are located by reference to county divisions as they were before 1974. References marked with an asterisk are those that supply a definition of the term in question.